Studies in Sanskrit Grammars

Proceedings of Vyākaraṇa Section of the 14th World Sanskrit Conference

Studies in Sanskrit Grammars

Edited by

George Cardona

Ashok Aklujkar

Hideyo Ogawa

D.K. Printworld (P) Ltd.

Publishers of Indian Traditions

Cataloging in Publication Data –DK
[Courtesy: D.K. Agencies (P) Ltd. <docinfo@dkagencies.com>]

World Sanskrit Conference (14th : 2009 : Kyoto, Japan).
Vyākaraṇa Section.
Studies in Sanskrit grammars : proceedings of the Vyākaraṇa Section of the 14th World Sanskrit Conference / edited by George Cardona, Ashok Aklujkar, Hideyo Ogawa.
p. cm.
ISBN 13: 9788124606087

1. Sanskrit language – Grammar – Congresses. 2. Pāṇini Aṣṭādhyāyī – Congresses. I. Cardona, George, 1936- II. Aklujkar, Ashok. III. Ogawa, Hideyo, 1954- IV. Title.

DDC 491.25 23

First published in India, 2012
ISBN 13: 978-81-246-0608-7 ISBN 10: 81-246-0608-0

Published and printed by:
D.K. Printworld (P) Ltd.
Regd. Office: 'Vedaśrī', F-395, Sudarshan Park
(Metro Station: Ramesh Nagar)
New Delhi – 110 015-11
Phones: (011) 2545 3975; 2546 6019; Fax: (011) 2546 5926
E-mail: indology@dkprintworld.com
Website: www.dkprintworld.com

Contents

Preface

The articles in this volume stem from sixteen of the papers presented at the vyākaraṇa section of the fourteenth World Sanskrit Conference held in Kyoto, Japan, September 1st–5th 2009. As could be expected, most of the articles concern Pāṇini in one way or another, but there is also considerable variety in the particular areas studied.

There are, to begin with, articles considering technical aspects of Pāṇini's system. Two authors consider decision procedures with which Pāṇini operates to ensure that sūtras of his Aṣṭādhyāyī apply to account for desired results. Peter Scharf deals with relations such as those which obtain between general rules (*utsarga*) and related exceptions (*apavāda*) and internally conditioned (*antaraṅga*) and externally conditioned (*bahiraṅga*) operations. George Cardona argues that, though they are stated under the heading (*adhikāra*) A 8.2.1: *pūrvatrāsiddham*, some rules of the tripādī are not suspended (*asiddha*) with respect to preceding rules and that this is known by inference. Kalindi Shukla considers heading rules (*adhikārasūtra*) in general, from a historical viewpoint, arguing that the source of this type of sūtras is to be found in pre-Pāṇinian prātiśākhya treatises.

Also dealing with technical aspects of grammar, Amba Kulkarni and Akshar Bharati consider what the notion of 'subject' corresponds to in the Pāṇinian system.

Boris Zakharyin deals with Pāṇinian sūtras that introduce the augment *sUṬ* to bases such as *kṛ* used with certain preverbs, as in *saṁ-skartum* 'to adorn, purify, form a group', both formally and in connection with the Proto-Indo-European source of the augmented base *skṛ*.

Several authors concentrate on post-Pāṇinian works. One, Shri Krishan Sharma, describes a very recent work, the Śabdajyotsnā of Pt. Bhiksharama (1887–1975), which is doubtless modelled on such post-Pāṇinian grammars as the Jainendravyākaraṇa. Other studies pertain more directly to Pāṇini. Malhar Kulkarni considers issues pertinent to editing the texts which incorporate groups of items (*gaṇa*) referred to in Pāṇinian sūtras stating operations relative to such sets, as incorporated in the Kāśikāvṛtti (7th c. AD). Maria Piera Candotti takes up the question of how groups of examples illustrating the application of rules relate to the composition of later recasts of the Aṣṭādhyāyī that organize sūtras in conformity with the procedure (*prakriyā*) involved in deriving forms of various classes. Jan E. M. Houben considers the suffix *Śe*, which Pāṇini introduces as a replacement for certain nominal endings in Vedic usage, as this is dealt with in the Prakriyāsarvasva of Melputtūr Nārāyaṇa Bhaṭṭa (Nārāyaṇabhaṭṭa, 16th–17th c. AD).

Two contributions concern Bhartṛhari (4th–5th c. AD). Hideyo Ogawa studies discussions in this author's Mahābhāṣyadīpikā and autocommentary on his Vākyapadīya that deal with the interpretations of the rule *ig yaṇaḥ samprasāraṇam* (Aṣṭādhyāyī 1.1.45), concentrating on Bhartṛhari's views concerning utterances and their meanings. Jaehyung Yi takes up the phrase *eke pracakṣate* 'some say' used in the Vākyapadīya, in order to determine whom Bhartṛhari referred to by *eke* 'some'.

Two papers have to do more narrowly with terminology. R. K. Sharma discusses the term *vibhakti* as used in the Aṣṭādhyāyī. Ashok N. Aklujkar deals at considerable length with the term *pratyaṅga* as used in Patañjali's (2nd c. BC) Mahābhāṣya and elsewhere.

Ranging farther afield, we have a pilot study by Émilie Aussant on how models of Sanskrit grammar—primarily the Pāṇinian model—could be used in describing other languages. The author takes up Pāṇinian features in the Līlātilakam (14th c. AD), which describes the mediaeval literary language of Kerala. Also related to Kerala, we have a study by Carmela Mastrangelo concerning the Sidharubam seu Grammatica Samscrdamica of the Carmelite priest Paulinus a Sanco Bartolomeo, who spent over a decade (1776–89) in this part of South India. Finally, Biliana Müller considers whether formal hand gestures used in Indian dance can possibly come within the range of what is called *vyākaraṇa.*

The subject matter covered by contributors to this volume is wide ranging and we trust these studies will contribute substantively to the appreciation of Indian grammatical thought.

The editors intended this volume to be published prior to the fifteenth World Sanskrit Conference, to be held in Delhi in January of 2012. The great majority of authors, moreover, were most cooperative in submitting their scripts and proofs and reacting promptly to editorial comments, for which we are grateful. I personally wish also to acknowledge the devotion and hard work of Hideyo Ogawa, who took on the burden of setting the texts and distributing comments and proofs to authors.

George Cardona

6 January 2011

Acknowledgments

Professor Akihiko Akamatsu of the University of Kyoto worked very hard and efficiently for the organization of the 14th World Sanskrit Conference at his university. The effort he and his team of capable, well-informed and cheerful helpers, including both faculty and students, invested did result in a successful and smooth running of the conference. The participation of Professor Masaaki Hattori, the doyen of Japanese Indologists, Professor Yasuke Ikari, a regional director of the International Association of Sanskrit Studies, Professor Muneo Tokunaga, the chairman of the Conference, and Professors Masato Fujii and Yuko Yokochi. who constituted the Conference Secretariat along with Professor Akamatsu, also contributed to the success, grace and pleasant atmosphere of the week-long event.

Later, in the matter of helping with the publication of this volume containing select papers read in the Vyākaraṇa section, Akamatsu continued with his usual constructive collegiality and facilitated the financial assistance that a scholarly publication like the present one needs. The editors are grateful to him and the International Association of Sanskrit Studies for the indirect but invaluable contribution which led to the realization of the following collection of historical, textual, and critical essays.

After the initial arrangements were in place, Mr. Susheel K. Mittal of DK Printworld moved expeditiously and agreed to publish the volume at an early date. We the editors wish to thank him for his professionalism as well as accommodative spirit.

The contributors to this volume have been patient and generous in their interactions with the editors. They have shown awareness of the other commitments the editors were trying to meet during the period of editing, and they have taken the differences of views and suggestions for improvement with an open mind as one expects in the case of true scholars. Without their cooperation, the project would not have proceeded as well as it did.

In my personal capacity as one of the editors, I would particularly like to put on record my appreciation of the especially significant role played by Professor Hideyo Ogawa in the management of the editing process and in ensuring that the volume attains a respectable and consistent scholarly form. He was the one who converted the varying computer inputs sent to him into one uniform input. He did the demanding initial proof reading of each article. His eye was always alert in the area of making sure that the volume did not deviate from the style sheet we had adopted. He was the one who communicated with the authors in most instances and kept track of the several proofs that were exchanged. While discharging these responsibilities, he had to carry out his usual teaching and administrative responsibilities at the University of Hiroshima. In the final stage of editing, he even had to attend to the needs of families affected by the earthquake and tsunami in Japan. Along with Professor George Cardona (see Preface), I consider myself fortunate and honored to have collaborated with Professor Ogawa in bringing the present collection of Vyākaraṇa essays to completion.

Ashok Aklujkar

Contributors

ASHOK AKLUJKAR	University of British Columbia ashok.aklujkar@ubc.ca
ÉMILIE AUSSANT	CNRS UMR 7597 HTL Univ Paris Diderot, Sorbonne Paris Cité F-75013, Paris, France eaussant@linguist.jussieu.fr
MARIA PIERA CANDOTTI	Université de Lausanne and EPHE, Paris mariapiera.candotti@gmail.com
GEORGE CARDONA	University of Pennsylvania cardonagj@verizon.net
JAN E. M. HOUBEN	École Pratique des Hautes Études, Section des Sciences Historiques et Philologiques, Paris jemhouben@gmail.com
AMBA KULKARNI	Department of Sanskrit Studies, University of Hyderabad ambapradeep@gmail.com
MALHAR KULKARNI	Indian Institute of Technology Bombay, Mumbai malharku@gmail.com
CARMELA MASTRANGELO	Sapienza Università di Roma sgueps@katamail.com
BILIANA MÜLLER	Department of Slavonic and Finnno-Ugrian Studies, University of Delhi biliana@arcor.de
HIDEYO OGAWA	Department of Indian Philosophy, Hiroshima University vrddhi@nifty.com hogawa@hiroshima-u.ac.jp
PETER M. SCHARF	Director, The Sanskrit Library, Brown University http://sanskritlibrary.org/ scharf@brown.edu
RAM KARAN SHARMA	Ex-president, International Association of Sanskrit Studies ramkaransharma@yahoo.com
SHRI KRISHAN SHARMA	Institute of Sanskrit and Indological Studies, Kurukshetra University sksisis@yahoo.com

KALINDI SHUKLA	Department of Sanskrit, S. V. Arts College, Ahmedabad kalindis1@gmail.com
JAEHYUNG YI	Department of Indian Philosophy, Hiroshima University dignaga2000@yahoo.co.jp
BORIS A. ZAKHARYIN	Moscow State University lvik@orc.ru

The word *pratyaṅga* in Patañjali's Vyākaraṇa-mahābhāṣya*

Ashok Aklujkar

N.B.: In the present essay, relatively long sections discussing textual evidence unavoidably come between sections expressing parts of my interpretation and argumentation. For this reason, some readers may find it convenient to read §§3.1–2, §§3.6–8, §4.1 and §§4.13–14 first, without reading the sections in between. Secondly, in addition to its main theme, the essay seeks, out of necessity, to explore the issues involved in the understanding of Mahābhāṣya 6.4.110 (§§2.13–14), Mīmāṁsā-sūtra 6.6.15 (§4.5), Bhāgavata-purāṇa 3.1.23 (§4.10),

*I am beholden to Professors Hideyo Ogawa, Albrecht Wezler and George Cardona for catching my oversights and helping me in improving the quality of this paper. I am grateful to Prof. Paolo Magnone for assistance in the completion of the Skanda-purāṇa quotation in §4.7, to Dr. Adheesh Sathaye for providing the full text of the Caṇḍa-kauśika passage in §5.9 and to Professors Abhijit Ghosh and Mandakranta Bose for the information from Bengali given in note 54b. When the first draft of this paper was presented at Kyoto, Prof. Ghosh confirmed my guess that *pratyaṅga* generally occurred only in the form *aṅga-pratyaṅga* in modern Bengali. Prof. Bose provided a precise Bengali dictionary reference for *pratyaṅga* when I was preparing the present version. As mentioned in note 70a, special thanks are also due to Dr. Vinayaka P. Bhatta. In the final stage, Mr. Bidur Bhattarai, a graduate student at Philipps Universität, Marburg, helped me in tracing a few passages to the publications which had remained inaccessible to me in Vancouver. My thanks to him, too.

In my statements as well as the statements I cite, I italicize only those non-English (primarily Sanskrit) words which are mentioned (as distinct from used). The titles of book-length texts, volumes, journals, etc. are italicized only in the bibliography at the end and, in the main text, only when the title is not Sanskrit.

Following a practice that has now become well-known, I print the *it* markers employed by Pāṇini (= P) in uppercase letters when they appear as words in English sentences.

The abbreviations employed are explained in the "References and abbreviations" section below. I have used them also in the passages I quote from other scholars, just as I have made the transliteration in the quoted passages consistent with mine. See Aklujkar 2008a: 41 for clarification regarding transliteration.

Mānava-dharma-śāstra or Manu-smṛti 8.208 (§4.11), Anargha-rāghava 3.7 (§5.9), Chāndogya-brāhmaṇa 2.2.2–3 = Kāṭhaka-saṁhitā 38.4.51–52 = Vājasaneyi-mādhyandina-saṁhitā 20.10 (§5.10a–c, e–f), Wackernagel 1905: II.1.257–258 and Pāṇini 2.4.84 (§5.10d). Some readers may wish to note the discussions of these text pieces, as well as the discussion of the meaning of *śarīra* (§2.10), independently of the discussion of the main theme expressed in the title above.

Background

§1.1 I became interested in the issue I am going to discuss because of my interest in determining if the epithets understood by certain traditional Sanskrit authors as applicable to or as standing for Patañjali (= "Pat" hereafter) could actually have been his epithets. These epithets are *gonardīya* and *goṇikā-putra*. In an article published in *Linguistic Traditions of Kashmir* (2008), I have argued that *gonardīya,* in the form *gonandīya,* was almost certainly the epithet of Pat, the Mahābhāṣya (= MB) author, and *goṇikā-putra* as well could have been the same. We cannot be equally certain in the case of the latter, because there is only one attestation of the word in the MB and that one attestation could have come about either from a marginal note in an early manuscript (= ms) or could have been preceded by a text portion lost to us. In the case of *gonardīya/gonandīya,* on the other hand, we have four passages enabling us to make a more informed and certain determination.

§1.2 Another contextualizing statement I should make is that I do not always have to get into the intricacies of Pāṇini's (= P) derivation process in order to determine the meaning of *pratyaṅga* (= *ptg*) presupposed by Pat. How the word is used in the MB and how it has been understood by the commentators of Pat can be discussed, in most instances, independently of how the word forms concerned are arrived at through the Pāṇinian procedure. Therefore, even if I offer translations of the four occurrence passages, my reader need not involve himself or herself with whether the derived form should be this or that or with what the details of the derivation process should be. Focusing on the forms of *ptg* and how the commentators gloss those forms should suffice. Moreover, readers having some familiarity with śāstra Sanskrit can justifiably be presupposed in an essay like the present one. Therefore, I will not translate those passages in the case of which the import can be gathered from the comments I make and the differences of translation are not likely to affect the intended point.

§1.3 Franz Kielhorn explored the issue of *gonardīya* being another way of referring to Pat in an 1886 article. He naturally had to study the occurrence of the epithet in MB 1.1.29. In this occurrence, he came across the word *ptg* and, on p. 83, informed his readers as follows: "... the word *pratyaṅga* (for *antar-aṅga*) ... in this technical sense is found only in a kārikā on P. 6.4.110, and in the Bhāṣya on P. 6.3.138, where Pat repeats a statement of *other* grammarians (Vol. III p. 177, *ihānya ācāryāś cau pratyaṅgasya pratiṣedham āhuḥ*)." Kielhorn's intention was to prove that Pat was referring to Gonardīya as someone other than himself and that all the views attributed to Gonardīya were reported views, not views originating with Pat himself. What I need to note at this stage is only that Kielhorn missed a fourth occurrence of *ptg*, namely the one in MB on P 1.1.57. Such an oversight was natural, given the absence of indices and electronic edns of the MB in his time. At best, Kielhorn could have had only a self-prepared 'working' word-index of the MB or select notes on certain MB passages that seemed problematic or worthy of further exploration to him.

On the following pages, I will first take up for consideration MB 1.1.29, 1.1.57, 6.3.138 and 6.4.110 in the indicated order, that is, in the order in which the *ptg* passages occur in Pat's text. On each passage I will offer observations that are pertinent from the point of view of the focus of this essay. I will state what the passages suggest collectively in §3.1.

MB occurrences studied in detail

§2.1 Occurrence passage 1: **MB on P 1.1.29** (*na bahu-vrīhau*), Kielhorn edn p. I.91:

> *gonardīya* [→ °*dīyas tv* / *gonandīyas tv*] *āha. 'akac-svarau tu kartavyau pratyaṅgaṁ* [→ °*tyaṅge*] *mukta-saṁśayau /' tvakat-pitṛko makat-pitṛka ity eva bhavitavyam iti.*[1]

Kielhorn (1886: 82) translates the passage as follows:

> "Gonardīya says that (the words termed *sarva-nāman*) ought without any doubt to take *ak(a)C* and to receive the accent (due to them as *sarva-nāmāni*, even in a bahu-vrīhi compound) because (both *ak(a)C* and that accent present themselves before the composition takes place and) are (therefore in regard to it) antar-aṅga; that accordingly one ought (not) to say (*tvatka-pitṛka*, *matka-pitṛka*, but) *tvakat-pitṛka*, *makat-pitṛka*, (and that P's rule 1.1.29 is superfluous and may be dispensed with)."

[1] For the background of the passage, for its explanation imperfectly preserved in Bhartṛ-hari's Mahābhāṣya-ṭīkā and for the first reading change suggested above, see Aklujkar 2008: 113–121, 130–134, 142–143, 163–171.

Subrahmanya Sastri in his *Lectures on Patañjali's Mahābhāṣya* (1951: 197) avoids a precise translation (he does this in many other cases as well) and summarizes the part that concerns this essay with: "Gonardīya says that undoubtedly the svara and *ak(a)C* due to *sarva-nāman* should be had. Hence in his opinion the forms should be *tvakat-pitr̥kaḥ* and *makat-pitr̥kaḥ*." It will be noticed that Subrahmanya Sastri has dodged the issue of how *ptg* should be understood.

Among the direct and indirect commentators of the MB accessible to us we find more or less the same story as far as MB 1.1.29 is concerned.[2] They remain silent as to how the word on which we are focusing should be understood.[3] Surprisingly, no commentator, except Śiva-rāmendra-sarasvatī (p. II.175), paraphrases *ptg* at its first occurrence.[4] Śiva-rāmendra's gloss is:

> ***pratyaṅgam*** *iti. yathārtha-vīpsāyām avyayī-bhāvaḥ. aṅga-śabdo 'tra viṣaya-paraḥ. prativiṣayaṁ, sarvasmin sva-viṣaya iti yāvat.*

Probably taking his cue from this, Nāgeśa, the sub-commentator of Kaiyaṭa, writes:

> *eṣā smr̥tir* [that is, *akac-svarau tu kartavyau pratyaṅgaṁ mukta-saṁśayau*] *aviśeṣāt sarva-prakaraṇa-viṣayā.*

However, no explicit explanation of *ptg* is available in Nāgeśa's Uddyota. He merely seems to have substituted *prakaraṇa* for Śiva-rāmendra's *viṣaya*.

§2.2 The immediate gain for us in noting the earlier explanations of MB 1.1.29 is, thus, of a negative kind. At least in the occurrence in which Kielhorn took *ptg* to mean 'antar-aṅga', the traditional commentators offer him no explicit support. But, as we will see in §2.11 and §2.15, Kielhorn is not without their support.

Secondly, only one commentator, namely Śiva-rāmendra-sarasvatī, openly acknowledges *pratyaṅgam* as the reading. Nāgeśa, too, probably had the

[2]See Aklujkar 2008: 117–121 for the texts of these commentators and pp. 108–109 for the dates of Kaiyaṭa's commentators (= Pat's sub-commentators).

[3]In Bhartr̥-hari's case, the silence may be a perceived silence, caused by loss of text, not a real silence; cf. Aklujkar 2008: 117 fn 38.

[4]Why Kaiyaṭa should not consider it necessary to explain *ptg* at its first occurrence is difficult to determine. Possibilities such as he committed an oversight or insertion of additional notes was cumbersome in the age of mss cannot be ruled out. There is at least one other case in his comm of being silent at an earlier occurrence of a word and offering an explanation at a later occasion. The case concerns the particle *nanu*. Kaiyaṭa explains the particle's kāku or rhetorical use under MB 5.2.39 and 5.2.94, but not under MB 1.1.72 (p. I.188 after Vt 28b) etc., in which, too, the same explanation would have helped a reader of the MB.

same reading before him, given his use of *sarva-prakaraṇa-viṣayā*, which indicates a vīpsā understanding,[5] which, in turn, presupposes an avyayī-bhāva (= avy). But Bhartṛ-hari and Kaiyaṭa could have had a different case form of the word in their MB mss. If Kaiyaṭa's commentators consulted any MB mss at this point, they are silent about what they found in those mss.

Apart from the non-confirmation of *ptg* ending in *am* in the writings of the earliest accessible commentators and possible evidence of discomfort with *pratyaṅgam* in the writings of the later commentators,[6] we have reasons—reasons of a positive kind—to implement my second suggestion for a reading change. As will be seen below, Pat uses *ptg* as a substantive in the other passages, three out of four, in which he employs the word. In his usage there is also the suggestion that the noun is a technical or nearly technical term (see occurrence passages 3 and 4 below). It is, therefore, very unlikely that he would use the same word as an adverb in his discussion of P 1.1.29, where, too, the context is technical.

Kielhorn (1886: 82, fn. 2) informs us that his Kashmir ms had the reading *pratyaṅgau*. This ms generally had distinctive and superior readings. If for this reason and because the reading comes across as a *lectio difficilior* we decide to check if it fits, the only grammatical way of accommodating it would be to take it as a bahu-vrīhi adjective of *akac-svarau* in some such sense as '*pratigate aṅge anayoḥ/yayoḥ*'. The word *ptg*, being neuter in occurrence passage 3 below and in almost all of the uses in other works collected in §§5.4–9 (exceptions for specific reasons in §3.7g, §4.4), will not otherwise yield the masculine nominative dual *pratyaṅgau* that the syntax of the sentence would need. Also, a sense like '*pratigate aṅge anayoḥ/yayoḥ*' will not go well with *akac-svarau*. The aṅgas or bases in which the insertion of *ak(a)C* or the introduction of udātta accent on the first syllable takes place cannot be said to move in the reverse (*pratigata*) direction. There is also the possibility that the *-au* in the Kashmir ms reading is due to the influence of the immediately preceding °*svarau*.

Although, thus, we cannot replace *pratyaṅgaṁ* with *pratyaṅgau*, the latter reading suggests that a top mark other than the anusvāra could have

---

[5]In *prati-* avy compounds, the set is known from the word that follows *prati*. vīpsā (= *viśeṣeṇa āptum icchā*) is that phenomenon in which the action or state expressed in a sentence applies individually and fully to all items in a set.

[6]Note that Śiva-rāmendra-sarasvatī, Nāgeśa et al do not explain how *ptg* as an avy fits the rest of the sentence syntactically. They also do not explain how the word can yield a meaning like 'sarva-prakaraṇa-viṣayā' (one can understand how it could mean 'sarvāṅga-viṣayā', but *aṅga* is not *prakaraṇa*, unless the context makes it clear that the word is being applied to a body of discourse or literature). See also §2.5 and note 13 in which the problem felt by the commentators with *ptg* (and *pratiśarīra*) in the second occurrence passage is pointed out in a different way.

been a part of the original reading. Now, corruption of an e-mātrā into an anusvāra or the change of an anusvāra, through ink smearing, into an e-mātrā are not rare in Nāgarī mss on which Kielhorn and other MB editors have so far exclusively relied ("almost exclusively" in the case of Kielhorn). Therefore, the anusvāra in *pratyaṅgaṁ* currently found in the MB edns could have come from an e-mātrā, and we should be willing to emend *akac-svarau tu kartavyau pratyaṅgaṁ mukta-saṁśayau* to °*vyau pratyaṅge mu*°. This gives us a smooth syntax and a contextually suitable translation:

> "But G says that, in the pratyaṅga (of *mat* + *pitṛ* + *ka* or *tvat* + *pitṛ* + *ka*, that is, in *mat* or *tvat*),[7] one should effect *ak(a)C* and the accent (proper to a sarva-nāman stem) without (bearing in mind) any doubt. (The derived forms) should be none other than *tvakat-pitṛka* (and) *makat-pitṛka* (not *tvatka-pitṛka* and *matka-pitṛka* as presupposed by the questioner)."

§2.3 Occurrence passage 2: **MB on P 1.1.57** (*acaḥ parasmin pūrva-vidhau*), Kielhorn edn p. I.145:

> *sā cāpy eṣā* [= the paribhāṣā *asiddhaṁ bahir-aṅga-lakṣaṇam antar-aṅga-lakṣaṇe*] *lokataḥ siddhā. katham? pratyaṅga-vartī loko lakṣyate. tad yathā. puruṣo 'yaṁ prātar utthāya, yāny asya pratiśarīraṁ*[8] *kāryāṇi tāni tāvat karoti, tataḥ suhṛdāṁ, tataḥ saṁbandhinām.*
>
> Tr.: "We get this (metarule, namely *asiddhaṁ bahir-aṅga-lakṣaṇam antar-aṅga-lakṣaṇe*[9]) from the human world (that is, by arriving at or utilizing a generalization regarding how society operates; that generalization serves as an analogy to the

[7]Since the forms endorsed immediately after the citation are *makat-pitṛka* and *tvakat-pitṛka*, whatever *ptg* denotes in Pat's understanding must be at the point indicated by "@" in the following string: *m@at* + *pitṛ* + *ka*, *tv@at* + *pitṛ* + *ka*. The sūtra *avyaya-sarva-nāmnām akac prāk ṭeḥ* (P 5.3.71) also requires that *ak(a)C* be inserted before *ṭi*, that is, before the *at* in *mat* and *tvat*.

[8]Kielhorn's original edn of 1880 and the revised edn of 1962 prepared by Abhyankar read this word as two words, *prati śarīraṁ*, and turn the avy compound into a karma-pravacanīya phrase. As can be seen in §2.6, this is in keeping with what Īśvarānanda, Annaṁ-bhaṭṭa and Nāgeśa say, but, as I point out in §§2.9–10, the splitting is not justified and the 'one word' view is preferable. The Nirnaya Sagara Press edn (fifth enlarged and revised release of 1951 with Bhārgava Bhikājī Jośī as the editor, p. 474) reads *pratiśarīraṁ* as one word, but the comm of Nāgeśa included in the edn speaks in favor of separating *prati* and *śarīraṁ*.

[9]Tr.: "A grammatical operation possible through a rule pertaining to the external is to be thought of as not existing with respect to a grammatical operation possible through a rule pertaining to the internal."

> rule, establishing that the rule is just an extension of the kind of thinking that is found in the ways of the world). How so? The human world comes across as existing in/on pratyaṅga (that is, as concerned with pratyaṅga). To wit: a man, having gotten up in the morning, first does those actions which are for each śarīra, then he does those actions which are for cordially connected persons (and) then he does those actions which are for (merely) connected persons."

Pat's intent or main point is clear: To give priority to internal grammatical operations is a matter of commonsense. When that priority is given, the external operations are suspended—one pretends that they do not exist or have not taken place. The principle involved is similar to what men and women in the world display. They first attend to what is near to them, then to what is slightly distant and then to what is more distant (here "near" and "distant" are not to be understood only in a spatial or physical sense; metaphorical nearness or distance is also intended). They presuppose segmentation and a specific sequence within the (consciously or subconsciously) presupposed segmentation. They first take care of their own or 'selfish' needs, then of the needs of those who are psychologically near to them and then of the needs of those who are connected with them because of happenstance and socially expected roles.

§2.4 Smart readers (such as yourself) must have noticed that in the translation and explication given above I have not translated *ptg* and *śarīra*, and offered translations of *suhr̥d* and *saṁbandhin* that are unusual. How we translate the last three, particularly the last two, is not of crucial importance to how the following exploration proceeds. Our conclusion will logically remain unaffected even if a difference in translation comes about; *suhr̥d* is most commonly translated with 'friend' and, in a context like the present one, it is not unusual to translate *saṁbandhin* with 'relative, kinsman'. If we adopt these otherwise justified translations, a question may arise as to how friends could be nearer than relations—why the 'blood is thicker' principle is set aside. Therefore, we should entertain the possibility that Pat had a specific section of friends and a specific section of relatives in mind or that the senses of *suhr̥d* and *saṁbandhin* he had in mind were not as general as 'friend' and 'relative'. To judge from the literal meaning of *suhr̥d*, 'one of good heart', a rendering like 'those who are favorably inclined, those who are like-minded, those who share one's own interests' will enable us to bypass the problem that mere 'friend' is likely to raise. Similarly, the very generality of the meaning of s*aṁbandhin* in the company of a word meaning 'one of good heart' will tell us that the saṁbandhins meant here do not include those who are primarily endearing—with whom one is 'friendly' or particularly close. One does not always have close or cordial connections with one's own relatives or business associates and hence one is not always nearer to them than to one's friends (cf. the frequently made remarks to the effect: 'one can choose one's friends but not one's relatives').

§2.5 Given the closeness in the meanings of *aṅga* and *śarīra* (the former more commonly means 'limb, body part' and less commonly 'body'; the latter commonly means 'body'), an interpreter of the passage would be tempted to equate *ptg* with *pratiśarīra*. He/she might even get away with the claim that Pat himself has provided us with a gloss on *ptg*. The traditional Sanskrit commentators, however, were generally very perceptive. They seem to have realized that *aṅga* in *ptg* should apply to all three constituents: 'doing things for oneself', 'doing things for those whom one particularly likes' and 'doing things for those to whom one is obligated'. Taking *ptg* as co-extensive with *pratiśarīra* will leave the latter two parts of Pat's statement beyond the range of *ptg*. Realizing this, most of Pat's direct and indirect commentators do not propose or presuppose an equation of *ptg* with *pratiśarīra*. The only exception I could so far find is Śiva-rāmendra-sarasvatī (p. III.59). Normally perceptive, especially in his criticism of Kaiyaṭa, he writes the following in his rejection of Kaiyaṭa: *sākṣād bhagavataivāṅga-śabdasya śarīra-paratayā vyākhyātatvena ...* "because the revered one (= Pat) himself has explained the word *aṅga* as standing for *śarīra*."

§2.6 On the passage as a whole, the commentators have the following remarks to offer:

(a) Kaiyaṭa NSP edn p. I.474: ***pratyaṅga-vartīti.*** *pratyāsanna-vācī pratyaṅga-śabdaḥ. aṅga-śabdena pratyāsattir lakṣyate, aṅgānāṁ pratyāsannatvāt. aṅgam aṅgaṁ prati pratyaṅgam ity avyayī-bhāvaḥ.* ***pratiśarīram*** *iti. śarīrasya bhogāyatanatvāt.* ***tataḥ suhṛdām*** *iti. sauhārdasyāsatti-hetutvāt.* ***tataḥ saṁbandhinām*** *iti. avaśya-kartavyatvāt.*

Tr: "***pratyaṅga-vartī.*** Here the word *ptg* means 'near'; the word *aṅga* ('limb') conveys nearness as its secondary meaning; (it can do so) because the limbs (of anybody or anything) are (normally) near each other. The word *ptg* is an avy compound, with *aṅgam aṅgaṁ prati* 'applying to each limb' (as its dissolution). (The Bhāṣyakāra puts) ***pratiśarīram*** (in the first place), because a body is the basis of worldly experience. (The Bhāṣyakāra then uses) ***tataḥ suhṛdām***, because friendship (or having good hearts, kind thoughts, for each other) is a cause of coming near to each other. (As for the subsequent phrase) ***tataḥ saṁbandhinām***, the reason (for its last placing) is that what one does for one's relatives is a matter of obligation."[10]

Kaiyaṭa's commentators, presented below in accordance with their relative chronology (Aklujkar 2008: 108–109), explain him as follows:

> Rāma-candra-sarasvatī p. III.55: *nanv aṅgasyāṅgi-sāpekṣatvāt "pratyaṅga-vartī lokaḥ" ity-atra loka-śabdena yady aṅgy abhidhīyate tatas tasya pratyaṅga-vartitvam anupapannaṁ, na hi śarīrādy aṅgī hastādiṣv aṅgeṣu pratyekaṁ parisamāpya samavaitīty-ata āha* ***pratyāsanneti****. nanv aṅgam aṅgaṁ prati pratyaṅgam iti vyutpādyamānasya yaugikatvān na rūḍhyā pratyāsanna-vācitvaṁ saṁbhavatīty-ata āha* ***aṅga-śabdenety-****ādinā. vibhor ātmanaḥ sva-śarīram iva suhṛdo pratyāsannā evety-ata āha* ***śarīrasyeti****.* ***bhogaḥ*** *sukha-duḥkha-sākṣātkāraḥ.*

> Īśvarānanda, p. III.56: [Regarding the MB] *"pratyaṅga-vartī" ity-atrāṅga-śabdenāvayavābhidhānāt loka-śabdenāvayavy abhidhīyata iti na mantavyam, avayavino vyāsajya-vṛttitvena pratyavayava-vṛttitvābhāvāt, prakṛtānupayoga-prasaṅgāc cety abhipretyāha* [regarding Kaiyaṭa's Pradīpa] ***pratyāsanneti****.* ***pratyāsannatvāt*** *aṅginaṁ pratīti śeṣaḥ. bhāṣye* ***śarīraṁ pratīty*** *anvayaḥ. sva-śarīram iti cārthaḥ. pratyāsattiś ca tena, na saṁyuktatvāt, vibhor ātmanas tasya sarvatrāviśeṣāt, kiṁtv anyathety āha* ***śarīrasyeti****.* ***bhogaḥ*** *sukha-duḥkha-sākṣātkāraḥ.*

> Annaṁ-bhaṭṭa p. III.57: *nanv aṅga-śabdasyāvayava-vācitvāl loka-śabdo 'vayavi-paraḥ. na cāvayavī pratyavayava-paryāpta-vṛttiḥ, vyāsajya-vṛttitvāt. prakṛtānupayogaś ca. ata āha* ***pratyāsanneti****. lakṣaṇā-bījam āha* ***aṅgānām*** *iti.* ***bhogeti****. tathā cetarāpekṣayā pratyāsannatvam ity arthaḥ. bhāṣye* ***pratiśarīraṁ*** *śarīraṁ prati.*

> Nāgeśa p. I.475: *nanu pratyavayava-vartī loka-rūpo 'vayavī lakṣyata iti nārthaḥ, prakṛtānupayogād, ity-ata āha* ***pratyāsanneti****.* ***aṅgānām*** *iti. aṅginaṁ pratīti śeṣaḥ.* ***aṅgam***

[10](a) Kaiyaṭa is unlikely to have thought it necessary to explain the meanings of such simple words as *pratiśarīram, tataḥ suhṛdām* and *tataḥ saṁbandhinām* to his readers, whose knowledge of Sanskrit was advanced enough to study a work like the MB. What he explains, then, is the implication or presumed purpose in Pat's employment of the words. This is borne out also by the ablative-ending expressions that follow the cited words.

(b) The essence of Kaiyaṭa's statement is not different from that of my statement in §§2.4–5 and §2.7: 'Do not go by the common meanings of the words. See if a special sense can be read in them.' Only my way of going beyond the common meanings (§3.3, §3.8, §§4.1–13) is different; it is diachronic or historical.

aṅgam iti. *pratyāsanna-pratyāsanna-vartī [tat-]tat-kāryābhiniviṣṭo loko dṛśyata iti bhāvaḥ. pratyāsannatvaṁ ca prathamopasthitatva-rūpam. bhāṣye* ***śarīraṁ pratīty*** *anvayaḥ. pratiyoge dvitīyā* [cf. P 1.4.90 and 2.3.8].

(b) Śiva-rāmendra-sarasvatī p. III.59: ***pratyaṅgavartīti.*** *aṅga-śabdena śarīra-lakṣakeṇa lakṣaṇa-vācinaḥ prati-śabdasya "lakṣaṇenābhi-pratī ābhimukhye"* [P 2.1.14] *ity-anenāvyayī-bhāvaḥ. tasminn upapade "supy ajātau ṇinis tācchilye"* [P 3.2.78] *iti vṛter ṇiniḥ. aṅgaṁ prati vartanaṁ nāma śaucācamana-danta-dhāvana-snānādy-anuṣṭhānam. tad abhipretyoktaṁ* ***prati-śarīraṁ yānīti.*** *etena "pratyāsanna-vācī pratyaṅga-śabdaḥ. aṅga-śabdena pratyāsattir lakṣyate, aṅgānāṁ pratyāsannatvāt. aṅgam aṅgaṁ prati pratyaṅgam ity avayayī-bhāvaḥ" iti kaiyaṭo nirastaḥ. sākṣād bhagavataivāṅga-śabdasya śarīra-paratayā vyākhyātatvena tad-virodhena tasya pratyāsatti-lakṣakatvena vyākhyāne aucitya-māna-prayojanānām abhāvāt.*

§2.7 It will be noticed that, in their explanations of why Kaiyaṭa glosses *ptg* with *pratyāsanna*, the sub-commentators in §2.6a have given an explanation that is *structurally* similar to what I have observed in §2.5. If the human world is taken as an avayavin or whole, its three avayavas or parts mentioned in Pat's sentence *puruṣo 'yaṁ ... saṁbandhinām* will not add up to what *ptg* literally conveys. This discrepancy presented itself to Kaiyaṭa because initially he took *ptg* as 'each limb/part' and connected it with *-vartin* adverbially. His way to get out of the difficulty was to attach a secondary meaning 'pratyāsatti' to *aṅga* and the adjectival meaning 'pratyāsanna' to the composite. Kaiyaṭa's commentators explain this move well. However, neither Kaiyaṭa nor they give instances in which *aṅga* can definitely and exclusively be said to convey 'pratyāsatti'.

The comment on Kaiyaṭa's explanation offered by Śiva-rāmendra-sarasvatī also ultimately ends up only in indicating that the latter had a dislike for the former that he could not, even as a monk (note *-sarasvatī* at the end of his name), shake off. The problem with his own equation of *ptg* with *pratiśarīra* has already been pointed out in §2.5 above.

I recognize the need to interpret *ptg* in such a way as would lead to a parallelism with the tripartite situation in *puruṣo 'yaṁ ... saṁbandhinām.* However, I do not see a need to stick to 'each' as the sense of *prati.* To avoid the difficulties it creates for Kaiyaṭa, Śiva-rāmendra-sarasvatī and the commentators of the former, one must, in my view, be open to accepting a different kind of compound in *ptg* (the one I will argue for in §3.8).

§2.8 Kaiyaṭa's interpretive activity moves from forming an idea about the meaning of *ptg* that the passage needs to how the needed meaning can be attached to *ptg* grammatically and in keeping with the common semantic processes; it does not move from the etymological (yaugika) or established conventional (rūḍha) meaning of *ptg* to the interpretation of the passage. He rightly determines that Pat is talking about relative nearness and that the nearness in the analogy must be sentiment-based and hence metaphorical, not physical. However, his manner of making *ptg* mean 'pratyāsanna' or 'near' is forced (compare §3.6).

One can deduce that a part must be near to a whole, because it is a part of the whole. But how would the deduced nearness combine with *prati* 'each'? The concept that is contextually needed is not 'existing (*-vartin*) in each nearness' but 'following a scale of nearnesses, moving from what is very near to near and thence to what is relatively distant'.

If we allow Kaiyaṭa's initial avy move, *pratyaṅga-vartin* could convey distributive occupation in fullness ('existing on each individual item in the presumed set collectively') or recurrent/successive occupation in fullness ('existing on each individual item in the presumed set fully but one by one'). But how would the composite word convey the 'gradation' or 'relativity' aspect the context suggests as needed in the process of occupation? 'First X, then Y' is the pattern implicit in *asiddhaṁ bahir-aṅga-lakṣaṇam antar-aṅga-lakṣaṇe*; the same pattern is explicit in the analogy *yāny asya pratiśarīraṁ kāryāṇi tāni tāvat karoti, tataḥ suhr̥dāṁ, tataḥ saṁbandhinām*. In either statement, the pattern is not 'Occupy fully or distributively each member of the set to which X, Y, and Z belong'. (In the domain of grammar, the dārṣṭāntika, 'occupation' should be understood as 'application'.)

The point made just now suggests that the format of the analogy statement requires that *ptg* be a substantive taking more than one activity under its wings, not an adverb or avy compound meaning 'in the case of each part, applying to every item'. The dissolution or vigraha-vākya of *pratyaṅga-vartin* should be '*pratyaṅge/pratyaṅgeṣu vartate iti*', not '*pratyaṅgaṁ vartate iti*'. This deduction is confirmed by the other composites formed with *-vartin*; e.g. *cakra-vartin, nikaṭa-vartin, samīpa-vartin, madhya-vartin, dūra-vartin* etc. In all of these, *-vartin* appears after a substantive or an adjective that has acquired the value of a substantive.

There is also another problem in allowing the initial avy move: attaching derivates such as *-vartin* to *pratyaṅga(m)* leads to an element of redundancy. In the resultant composites, the first member already covers 'existence in/on each aṅga' because of the vīpsā meaning element (note 5) it contains. The addition of *-vartin* would express the 'existence' element again. If the addition is to be made purposive, *ptg* must be understood in some such sense as 'the state/phase of being applicable to each limb/part' or 'one which is an individual/discrete limb/part',[11] that is, the adverbial meaning must be changed into a substantive meaning, and the avy must be thought of as replaced by a noun.[12]

§2.9 Given the preceding unraveling of the issue, it should not come as a surprise that three of Kaiyaṭa's commentators, Īśvarānanda, Annaṁ-bhaṭṭa and Nāgeśa, propose that *pratiśarīram* be understood as *śarīraṁ prati.*[13] Pat, as far as I can check, never puts his karma-pravacanīya *prati* in the first place. If he had in mind the sense 'regarding/concerning the body' that Īśvarānanda et al specify, he would have used *śarīraṁ prati.*[14]

[11]The latter development in the meaning of *ptg* actually takes place at a later time as the passages in §5.9 establish. The oddity (from our point of view) is that the authors concerned write as if 'each, all' is also a part of the meaning of the word—as if *prati* has done "double duty," first to lead us to the notion of individual items and then to re-assert itself to express vīpsā with respect to all those items. Meaning delivery, however, cannot be made to go back to an earlier stage (just as it cannot be halting; cf. Mammaṭa, Kāvya-prakāśa 2.16: *na ca śabdaḥ skhalad-gatiḥ*). The story is different when a certain meaning comes to be associated with a particular word through convention (rūḍhi).

[12](a) That such a meaning will not fit the context of Pat's use in MB 1.1.57 is another problem. His intention is clearly not to say that a person engages with every part of what can be done during the course of a day but to say that a person deals with his/her obligations according to a certain scale of priorities.

(b) Śiva-rāmendra-sarasvatī is justified in objecting to the gloss of *aṅga* as 'pratyāsanna', but his reason is different from mine, and his starting point, equivalence of *ptg* and *pratiśarīra*, is flawed (see §2.5). Another problem with his comment in the case of *ptg* is that he does not offer a constant explanation of the word. Under MB 1.1.29, he derives it as an avy by appealing to the vīpsā meaning under the *yathārtha* part of P 2.1.6 (*avyayaṁ vibhakti-...*) and under MB 1.1.57 by appealing to P 2.1.14 (*lakṣaṇenābhi-pratī ābhimukhye*). He does not inform us as to how the difference can be justified. As in the case of Kaiyaṭa and his commentators, how Śiva-rāmendra syntactically reconciles the avys with the other words of the sentences involved is not clear. His comment on the remaining two occurrence passages is not available.

[13]Since Śiva-rāmendra points out the equivalence of *ptg* and *pratiśarīra*, he must have read the latter as one word. This is supported by his use of *avyayī-bhāva* in reference to *ptg*. How Kaiyaṭa and Kaiyaṭa's earliest accessible commentator Rāma-candra-sarasvatī understood the word grammatically is not explicit. They have not given the literal sense of *pratiśarīram* through a gloss.

[14]This is also the most common and anciently corroborated word order in the use of *prati* as a karma-pravacanīya; cf. P 1.4.37: *krudha-druherṣyāsūyārthānāṁ yaṁ prati kopaḥ* and Kāli-dāsa, Abhijñāna-śakuntalā, several stage directions such as *sakhyau prati.*

The specified explanation of *pratiśarīram* comes almost immediately after Kaiyaṭa's dissolution of *pratyaṅga(m)* as an avy (*aṅgam aṅgaṁ prati*).[15] The commentators, other than Śiva-rāmendra, had sensed the difficulty in treating *ptg* and *pratiśarīra* as synonyms (§2.6, §2.8). One part of overcoming the difficulty was to take *ptg* in the sense 'pratipratyāsanna', that is, as expressive of different degrees of nearness. However, 'each' as the sense of *prati* still did not apply well to *pratiśarīram*. It is clearly not the case that the generalized person or ordinary man in the analogy does his/her duty with respect to each body. Therefore, what looked like identically formed words, namely *ptg* and *pratiśarīra*, had to be given different grammatical analyses—an avy dissolution for the former and a karma-pravacanīya phrasing for the latter. If Śiva-rāmendra lost in one way, Īśvarānanda, Annaṁ-bhaṭṭa and Nāgeśa had to lose in another and split *pratiśarīram* in a way that did not agree with Pat's usage.[16]

§2.10 What Kaiyaṭa's commentators should have tried as a solution to the problem is to ascertain if *śarīra* could have had a different sense in Pat's usage from that of *aṅga* and from the one with which they were familiar ('body, whole body, entire outside of an animate form'). One can understand their difficulty in doing so, given the absence of etymological or historically oriented dictionaries, indexed studies etc. in their time, but, just as they tried to attach a secondary meaning to *aṅga* on the strength of the context, they could have proposed some such meaning as 'not the whole body or body in an unqualified sense, but those parts of the body to which a man attends or is likely to attend after getting up in the morning' (cf. *prātar utthāya* employed by Pat immediately before the *pratiśarīram* clause). Parts that need regular cleaning and/or care would almost immediately have come to mind as intended by *śarīra* in Pat's sentence. In fact, Śiva-rāmendra has the wording *śaucācamana-danta-dhāvana-snānādy-anuṣṭhānam*, but he em-

[15]How Kaiyaṭa could take *ptg* in *pratyaṅga-vartī* as *aṅgam aṅgam prati* but not offer a dissolution of *pratiśarīram* (i.e., only state why it is where we find it in Pat's statement) is not explained by Īśvarānanda, Annaṁ-bhaṭṭa or Nāgeśa.

[16]Interestingly, Jinendra-buddhi, in his Nyāsa or Vivaraṇa-pañjikā on Kāśikā 1.4.2, writes a passage that is very similar to the one in the MB in its reasoning and structure but avoids the *prati* words: *antar-aṅga-bahir-aṅgayor antar-aṅgaṁ balavad iti. lokata eva dr̥ṣṭatvāt. loko hi prātar utthāyāntar-aṅgāṇi mukha-prakṣālanādīni kāryāṇi karoti, paścād bahir-aṅgāṇi rāja-gr̥ha-gamanādīni kāryāṇi kartum ārabhate. śāstre 'py evaṁ veditavyam.*

In his Paribhāṣendu-śekhara, paribhāṣā 50 (p. 96 of Abhyankar's edn), Nāgeśa also avoids the problem essentially by rewriting Pat's sentences as *idam antar-aṅgatvaṁ loka-nyāya-siddham iti manuṣyo 'yaṁ prātar utthāya śarīra-kāryāṇi karoti, tataḥ suhr̥dāṁ, tataḥ sambandhinām.*

ploys it with reference to *ptg*, not *pratiśarīra*.[17] Since he makes no difference between what the two words convey, he can be understood as taking *śarīra* as referring to only certain body parts. This way was not open to Kaiyaṭa and his commentators. But even the singular number in *puruṣo 'yam* could have led them to the conclusion that Pat was unlikely to have meant a whole body when he used *pratiśarīram*. There would need to be at least two bodies for a proper use of *prati* meaning 'each'. Normally, a single person does not have them. So, they could have deduced that *śarīra* here must mean 'a body part' or 'a collectivity of certain body parts', not just 'body', but they do not offer any such guess.

The guess is at least not contradicted by the other occurrences of *śarīra* in the MB:

> (a) Pat 1.3.67 (*ṇer aṇau* ...) Vt 9 p. I.292 and 3.1.87 (*karmavat karmaṇā tulya-kriyaḥ*) Vt. 10 p. II.68: *dvāv ātmānāv antar-ātmā śarīrātmā ca. antar-ātmā tat karma karoti yena śarīrātmā sukha-duḥkhe anubhavati. śarīrātmā tat karma karoti yenāntar-ātmā sukha-duḥkhe anubhavatīti.*
>
> (b) Pat 5.1.9 (*ātman-viśva-jana-bhogottara-padāt khaḥ*) Vt 3 p. II.340: *athavā bhoga-śabdaḥ śarīra-vācy api dṛśyate. tad yathā "ahir iva bhogaiḥ paryeti bāhum"* [source unknown] *iti. ahir iva śarīrair iti gamyate. evaṁ pitṛ-śarīrāya hitaḥ pitṛ-bhogīṇa iti.*
>
> (c) Pat 5.3.47 (*yāpye pāśap*) p. II.411: *atha vaiyākaraṇaḥ śarīreṇa kṛśo vyākaraṇena ca śobhanaḥ, kartavyo vaiyākaraṇapāśa iti. na kartavyaḥ. ...*
>
> (d) Pat 6.4.24 (*an-id-itāṁ hala upadhāyāḥ kṅiti*) Vt 1 (*an-id-itāṁ na-lope laṅgi-kampyor upatāpa-śarīra-vikārayoḥ upasaṁkhyānam*) p. III.194: *an-id-itām na-lope laṅgi-kampyor upatāpa-śarīra-vikārayor upasaṁkhyānaṁ kartavyam. vilagitaḥ, vikapitaḥ. upatāpa-śarīra-vikārayor iti kim-artham? vilaṅgitaḥ, vikampitaḥ.*
>
> (e) P. 8.1.8 (*vākyāder āmantritasya* ...) Vt 1 p. III.367: *nanu ca bho akupitā api dṛśyante dārakān bhartsayamānāḥ. antatas te tām śarīrākṛtiṁ kurvanti yā kupitasya bhavati.*

In (a), not *śarīra* but *śarīrātman* has been used for what can act in relation to the antar-ātman. One can read in this a suggestion that those parts of

[17]Although, in later Sanskrit, words such as *śarīra*, *kāya*, *deha* and *tanu* are used as if they are perfect synonyms, they must have had distinct meanings at the time of their coming into currency. A natural language rarely has perfect synonyms, especially between words that originate in itself—are not borrowed from other languages.

(what we nowadays normally call) *śarīra* which can perform some action form a unit (ātman) and that the primary meaning of *śarīra* for Pat is 'a body part which can act or become a means for action', 'those karmendriyas which involve movement and the frame that supports movement', not the entire physical body.

This surmise is supported in its 'movement' element by the words in (b) and (e). To go around someone's arm, a moving body part is needed. To convey the message that one is angry when one may not really be angry, actions such as raising of the hand to slap are frequently done. Immediately after the expression of this social observation, the MB has the verse "*sāmr̥taiḥ pāṇibhir ghnanti guravo, na viṣokṣitaiḥ / lāḍanāśrayiṇo doṣās.tāḍanāśrayiṇo guṇāḥ //*"

In (c) and (d), on the other hand, the movement-supporting body frame as well as the body parts capable of moving may be meant. If *vikapita* refers to tremors or involuntary movement (as in Parkinson's disease), it is more likely to be applicable to parts that can move.[18]

Pat might also have meant those body parts which are particularly or observably vulnerable to decay and stand in need of repeated or regular care. This would be in accordance with the most likely etymology of *śarīra* from root *śr̥* 'to cover' or *śr̥̄* 'to tear, split, dissipate' or 'to hurt, injure'.[19]

[18]It need not be supposed that the commentators of Pat had nowhere sensed the possibility of *śarīra* having a more specific meaning in Pat's own language. In his comment on P 1.3.67, Nāgeśa, while explaining the śarīrātman's experience of pleasure and pain (caused in his view by accumulated merit and demerit, dharmādharma), gives prominence to 'pādādi-sauṣṭhavādi', that is, to properties of specific parts associated with movement. In the context of the cause of the antar-ātman's experience of pleasure and pain, he writes *śarīrātmanaḥ karma ceṣṭādi-rūpaṁ sukha-duḥkha-janakam*, mentioning ceṣṭā, which involves physical movement. Similarly, in explaining the citation made by Pat under 5.1.9, *ahir iva bhogaiḥ paryeti bāhum* "It/he/she surrounds the arm with bhogas like a snake," Kaiyaṭa writes: *samudāye vr̥tto bhoga-śabda eka-deśeṣu phaṇeṣu prayujyate*, which would suggest that *śarīra*, which appears as a synonym of *bhoga* in Pat's sentence under discussion, would also, in Kaiyaṭa's view, stand for a part at least in certain contexts. These intimations are, however, not pursued to explain passages like Pat 1.1.57 more justifiably.

[19]Cf. Mayrhofer 1976: III.307, 1996: II.618; Śabda-kalpa-druma p. V.30, following the Uṇ-ādi-sūtra, *śīryate rogādinā yat.* Vācaspatya p. VI.5087: *pratikṣaṇaṁ kṣīyamāṇe.*

The basic meaning of *śarīra* that Mayrhofer and others have given is 'skeleton, the frame that bones form, solid parts of the body'. Questions such as the following need to be asked: "Did the basic meaning have further meaning elements associated with it—elements such as perishability or capability for movement?" "What did P precisely mean by *śarīra* in sūtra 4.3.55 (*śarīrāvayavād yat*)?" "What concept of śarīra is borne out by the items included in the Śārīra-sthāna books of

In either case, thinking about a more specific meaning of *śarīra* would have provided a better solution to the problem the commentators faced.

§2.11 Occurrence passage 3: **MB on P 6.3.138** (*cau*), Kielhorn edn p. III.177:

> *ihānya ācāryāś cau pratyaṅgasya pratiṣedham āhuḥ. tad ihāpi sādhyam. naiṣa doṣaḥ. etaj jñāpayati na cau pratyaṅgaṁ bhavatīti, yad ayaṁ cau dīrghatvaṁ śāsti.*
>
> Tr.: "In this matter, other teachers speak of prohibition of pratyaṅga when *cu* (= *acu* derived from the root *añc* in its Dhātu-pāṭha form *añcU*) follows.[20] That is to be brought about here too. This is not (i.e., this would not amount to) a blemish (on our part). (Ācārya Pāṇini) indicates that there is no pratyaṅga (i.e., a pratyaṅga-based grammatical operation) when *cu* follows in that he teaches lengthening when *cu* follows."

Here, *ptg* is clearly used as a noun by Pat. The genitive *pratyaṅgasya* and the nominative *pratyaṅgaṁ* (the verb *bhavati* needs a subject) will not otherwise fit.

Secondly, *ptg* must primarily refer to something inside a stem and secondarily, on the strength of *bhavati* in *na cau pratyaṅgaṁ bhavati*, to the operation that the inside item would usually undergo. The operation would be ekādeśa, replacement of two sounds by one sound, in the case of *pra* + *añc* etc. and *yaṆ*-ādeśa, replacement of two sounds by one sound in the case of *dadhi* + *añc*, *madhu* + *añc* etc. The sūtra blocks the ekādeśa and *yaṆ*-ādeśa possibilities in the case of (a) *a* + *a* and (b) *i* and *u*, respectively, and brings about the usual sandhi in the case of the former and a lengthening in the case of the latter.

---

early Āyur-veda texts?" In short, a comprehensive and detailed study of the early occurrences of *śarīra* from the point of view of some of the possibilities suggested here is needed. My immediate need is to establish that *ptg* and *pratiśarīra* are not synonymous in the context concerned. That need is met by the discussion in this section.

[20]This unusual specification of what *cau* stands for would not be known to us without the help of texts like the Kāśikā, which remarks: *cāv ity añcatir lupta-nakāro gr̥hyate.* The purpose is to derive the long form of the middle vowel (a) in *dadhīcaḥ*, *dadhīcā* and *dadhīce* from the base *dadhyañc* and (b) in *madhūcaḥ*, *madhūcā* and *madhūce* from the base *madhvañc*. The words *pūrvasya* and *dīrghaḥ* recur from P 6.3.111. The process is *dadhyañc* + accusative plural or ablative/genitive singular suffix *as* → *dadhīc* + *as*. Similarly, before the same case suffixes, *madhvañc* → *madhūc* + *as*. The Kāśikā clarifies: *antar-aṅgo 'pi hi yaṇ-ādeśo dīrgha-vidhāna-sāmarthyān na pravartate.*

§2.12 The relevant parts of the traditional commentaries on occurrence passage 3 are:

> Kaiyaṭa (NSP edn p. V.265): *prācā, dadhīcety-ādāv antar-aṅgatvād ekādeśa-yaṇ-ādeśayoḥ kṛtayor anaj-antatvād dīrgho na prāpnotīty [→ °tīty ata?]*[21] *āha* ***ihānya*** *iti.*
>
> Nārāyaṇa p. IX.265: *bhāṣye 'ntar-aṅgasya kāryasya pratiṣedhoktiṁ codayitvā jñāpakena tat-siddhir uktā. kim-arthaṁ tad ity āśaṅkyāha* ***prāceti****. "cau pratyaṅgasya" ity-atra bhāṣye pratyaṅga-śabdenāntar-aṅgaṁ bodhyam. tathā cāyam arthaḥ "cau"-sūtraṁ prati yad antar-aṅgaṁ tasya pratiṣedho vaktavyaḥ [iti].*
>
> Annaṁ-bhaṭṭa (p. IX: 264–265: ***prāceti****. pra ac ā [**dadhi** ac ā] iti sthite, "acaḥ"* [P 6.4.138] *ity akāra-lopasyāṅga-saṁjñā-sāpekṣatvena bahir-aṅgatvād varṇa-mātrāpekṣatayā**ntar-aṅgayoḥ** savarṇa-dīrgha-**yaṇ-ādeśayoḥ kṛtayoḥ** paścād akāra-lope dīrgha-bhāvino 'ntyasyābhāvād **dīrgho na** syāt. ekādeśasyāpi parādi-grahaṇena lopāt pra-śabdasyāpy anackatvam. antar-aṅgatvād eva ca "vārṇād āṅgaṁ balīyaḥ"* [MB 3.2.3 p. II.96][22] *iti na pravartate. evaṁ ca cau dīrgha-vidhāna-sāmarthyāt pūrvam akāra-lopo bahir-aṅgo 'pi bhavatīti vijñāyata ity arthaḥ.* ***ity āha*** *ity ata āha.*
>
> Nāgeśa (p. NSP edn V.265): *bhāṣye pratyaṅga-śabdo 'ntar-aṅga-vācī. evaṁ ca "cau"-sūtraṁ prati yad antar-aṅgaṁ tasya pratiṣedho vaktavya ity arthaḥ.* ***ity āheti*** *ity ata āhety arthaḥ.*

Kaiyaṭa does not gloss *pratyaṅgasya* or *pratyaṅgam*, but his commentators Nārāyaṇa and Nāgeśa do so, respectively, with *pratyaṅga-śabdenāntar-aṅgaṁ bodhyam* and *bhāṣye pratyaṅga-śabdo 'ntar-aṅga-vācī*. Annaṁ-bhaṭṭa,

[21] Annaṁ-bhaṭṭa and Nāgeśa indicate that the meaning would have been clearer if Kaiyaṭa had used *ity ataḥ* instead of only *iti*.

[22] The sentence *vārṇād āṅgaṁ balīyaḥ* is found in three or four pre-Annaṁ-bhaṭṭa Pāṇinian paribhāṣā texts: the Paribhāṣā-pāṭha (no. 49) and Laghu-paribhāṣā-vṛtti (no. 74) of Puruṣottama-deva (12th century A.D.) and the Bṛhat-paribhāṣā-vṛtti of Sīra-deva (no. 66). It is also found in some mss of the Paribhāṣā-pāṭha ascribed to Vyāḍi (no. 39), but not in the Paribhāṣā-sūcana or Paribhāṣā-vṛtti ascribed to the same scholar. As Nīla-kaṇṭha Dīkṣita/Vājapeyin, author of the Paribhāṣā-vṛtti, lived at about the same time (first half of the 17th century) as Annaṁ-bhaṭṭa—as the time gap between the two is very small, we cannot assert that Annaṁ-bhaṭṭa was aware of the acceptance of the MB sentence as a paribhāṣā in Nīla-kaṇṭha's work (no. 60). Later paribhāṣā authors, Hari-bhāskara (no. 68), Nāgeśa (no. 55) and Śeṣādri-nātha (no. 47), include the MB sentence as a paribhāṣā in their works (cf. Abhyankar 1967: 488–489), but they could obviously not have been Annaṁ-bhaṭṭa's source.

too, clearly presumes the same understanding of the term. Kaiyaṭa's use of *antar-aṅgatvāt* in the statement of the problem the bhāṣya is supposed to address indicates that his commentators have read him correctly. Thus, two occurrences removed from where Kielhorn read it, we have a corroboration of the sense 'antar-aṅga' that he attached to *ptg*.

Nārāyaṇa and Nāgeśa seem to try to soften the subjecthood and the nominative case of *pratyaṅgam*. In their gloss *"cau"-sūtraṁ prati yad antar-aṅgaṁ tasya pratiṣedho vaktavyaḥ*, they take *pratyaṅgam* as two words, supply *sūtram* to enable the karma-pravacanīya *prati* to form a phrase, and write as if *sūtram* is to be compounded with *cau*.[23] When one compares this with the Kāśikā explication of the sūtra (*cau parataḥ pūrva-padasya dīrgho bhavati*), in which *cau* is naturally taken to be a reference to a derivational element and not to the sūtra text, the arbitrary nature of the construing Nārāyaṇa and Nāgeśa imposed on Pat's sentence becomes evident. The construing also forces the interpreters to take the partial form *aṅga* as standing for *antar-aṅga*, given as the synonym of the full form *ptg*.

§**2.13** Occurrence passage 4: **MB on P 6.4.110** (*ata ut sārvadhātuke*),[24] Kielhorn p. III.216–217: Here I reproduce a longer extract than is necessary for our immediate purpose, because Kielhorn's reasoning rests to some extent on the occurrence of *ptg* in a śloka-vt, and the śloka-vt is spread over several lines. As the following compromise between a translation and an elucidation will indicate, Pat touches upon several complex aspects of the derivational process in a colloquial style, making it difficult at several places to identify the sūtras and derivation string items he has in mind. Furthermore, where the Vt content is reproduced in a prose gloss, I am required to offer a single translation combining the details in both. I am also forced by the nature of the passage to number the parts of Pat's discussion with letters of the alphabet and give extracts from traditional commentators in §2.15 in the order of those letters.

[23]In the common practice, the expression would have been *cāv-iti-sūtraṁ prati*. Use of the abbreviated forms of sūtras, especially of the more frequently needed and hence better-known sūtras is, however, found.

[24]The derivation stages can briefly be specified as follows in the case of the intended examples: *kr̥* + *u* (class sign; P 3.1.79) + *tas* (a sārvadhātuka marked by *ṅ*; P 1.2.4 *sārvadhātukam apit*) → *kar* (P 7.3.84 *sārvadhātukārdhadhātukayoḥ*) + *u* + *tas* → *kur* (P 6.4.110) + *u* + *tas* → *kurutas/kurutaḥ*. Similarly *kr̥* + *u* + *anti* → *kar* (P 7.3.84) + *u* + *anti* → *kur* (P 6.4.110) + *u* + *anti* → *kurv* + *anti* (P 6.1.77).

(a) *tad eva tarhi prayojanaṁ "śnasor*[25] *al-lopa"* [P 6.4.111] *iti.*

"Then the purpose (behind using *sārvadhātuke* in P. 6.4.110) is (to allow recurrence of that the word in) *"śnasor aL-lopaḥ* (the next sūtra).""

(b) *nanu coktaṁ 'śnaḥ sārvadhātuka eva, aster apy ārdhadhātuke bhū-bhāvena bhavitavyam' iti.*

"But was this not pointed out (only a few lines earlier) that *Śna* takes place only when a sārvadhātuka suffix follows (and) also that *as* becomes *bhū* (according to P 2.4.52) when an ārdhadhātuka suffix follows? (Therefore, nothing is gained by making *sārvadhātuke* recur in *śnasor al-lopaḥ*)."

(c) [śloka-vt part:] *"anuprayoge tu bhuvāsty-abādhanaṁ smaranti kartur vacanān manīṣiṇaḥ /"*[26] [Paraphrase:] *anuprayoge tu bhuvāster abādhanam iṣyate. īhāmāsa, īhāmāsatuḥ, īhāmāsur iti.*

"The wise have passed down the following (view): If the context is one in which an item is uttered after another item, *bhū* does not block *as*. Their reason for adopting this view is the statement of the author (of the Aṣṭādhyāyī, namely the sūtra *kr̥ñ cānuprayujyate liṭi* (P 3.1.40), in which *kr̥ñ* stands for itself as well as *bhū* and *as*, and thus allows *as* to appear after the suffix *ām*, leading to forms) *īhām-āsa*, *īhām-āsatuḥ* and *īhām-āsuḥ*."[27]

[In most of the following sentences, the object language forms or derivation string items to which they are intended to refer are not specified. From the mention of (i) anaCkatva 'vowellessness,' (ii) dvir-vacana 'doubling' and (iii) abhyāsa 'the first of what results from doubling' and from the examples *cakratuḥ* and

---

[25] That the original reading of this sūtra must have been *śnāsor*, that is, with a long vowel form in the first syllable, has been pointed out in Aklujkar 1983: 2–3.

[26] Śobhita-miśra in his edn of the Kāśikā (p. 135, under P 2.4.52) gives the following text as the first half of the verse cited here: *bhv-asau vihāyābhyadhitaiṣa kr̥ñ-padaṁ gr̥hītu-kāmas [→ grahī°] tritayaṁ tad eva hi /*. He does not specify the source.

[27] For the argument involved here, see Kāśikā on *ām-pratyayavat kr̥ño 'nuprayogasya*, P 1.3.63: *kathaṁ punar asyānuprayogaḥ* [→ *anayor anu°*; the question should be about two roots, *as* and *bhū*] *yāvatā "kr̥ñ cānuprayujyate liṭi"* (P 3.1.40) *ity ucyate? kr̥ñ iti pratyāhāra-grahaṇaṁ tatra vijñāyate. kva saṁniviṣṭānāṁ pratyāhāraḥ? "abhūta-tad-bhāve kr̥-bhv-asti-yoge saṁpadya-kartari cviḥ"* (P 5.4.50) *iti kr̥-śabdād ārabhya yāvat "kr̥ño dvitīya-tr̥tīya-śamba-bījāt kr̥ṣau"* (P 5.4.58) *iti ñakāram.* Also, Kāśikā 3.1.40: *kr̥ñ iti pratyāhāreṇa kr̥-bhv-astayo gr̥hyante. tat-sāmarthyād aster bhū-bhāvaḥ* [according to P 2.4.52] *na bhavati.*

ninyatuḥ given by Nārāyaṇa and Nāgeśa (§2.15), it seems that Pat is continuing with the domain of perfect tense verbal forms, to which *āsa*, *āsatuḥ* and *āsuḥ* figuring in *īhāmāsa*, *īhāmāsatuḥ* and *īhāmāsu* cited above belong.[28] I have, therefore, taken most of the initial sentences as concerned with the perfect forms of root *as*. The mention of that root in the following sūtra, *śnasor [= śnāsor] al-lopaḥ*, I have understood as supporting this surmise and indicating a continuation of Pat's engagement with that sūtra. This has helped me in providing denotata to *atra* and *lopaḥ* in the first sentence, which is otherwise unusually non-specific. Fortunately, the listed difficulties do not come in the way of knowing how the commentators interpreted *ptg*.]

(d) *kiṁ ca syād yady atra lopaḥ syāt?*

"What would happen if a lopa were to take place in this (*āsa*, *āsatuḥ*, *āsuḥ*—a lopa by P 6.4.111 not containing the *sārva-dhātuke* limitation and thereby becoming applicable to perfect tense forms, which are termed *ārdhadhātuka* by P 3.4.115)?"[29]

(e) [śloka-vt part:] *"lope dvir-vacanāsiddhiḥ"* [Paraphrase:] *lope kr̥te 'nackatvād dvir-vacanaṁ na syāt.*

"If the lopa were effected, there would be no doubling, because there would be no vowel (left in the base *as* when it is reduced to *s*)."[30]

(f) *sthānivad-bhāvād bhaviṣyati.*

"(The doubling) will take place because of sthānivad-bhāva (the provision for attaching the properties of an item subjected to substitution to an item which comes as a substitute)."[31]

[28]If Kaiyaṭa is right in mentioning the undesired outcome as *satuḥ* and *suḥ* in the passage reproduced in §2.15i, the derivation under consideration could initially be that of the verbal root *as* in the perfect tense. How the consideration then moves away from the perfect tense forms to that of roots like *kr̥* in other tenses and moods is not clear. Pat himself cites only *kuru* as a derivate toward the end of the discussion, which is in keeping with the concern of P 6.4.110 with the change of *a* to *u*.

[29]From the response in the next sentence we can infer that the lopa spoken of here must be that of a vowel, but we do not come to know where this vowel is. It must be in an item (or an item part) that can undergo doubling.

[30]P 6.1.1 *ekāco dve prathamasya* needs the presence of a vowel for doubling. P 6.1.8 *liṭi dhātor anabhyāsasya* prescribes doubling in the derivation of perfect forms.

[31]A lopa, which is distinct in its function from the deletions marked with *luk*, *Ślu* or *lup*, is thought of as an ādeśa 'substitute' and hence is eligible, according

(g) [śloka-vt part:] *"sthānivad iti cet kr̥te bhaved dvitve."* [Paraphrase:] *kr̥te dvitve lopaḥ prāpnoti.*

"If recourse is taken to sthānivad-bhāva and doubling is effected, the lopa will (again) present itself (that is, the sequence '*a as*' will not be immune to the application of P 6.4.111)."[32]

(h) *astu tarhi parasya lopaḥ. abhyāsasya yo 'kāras tasya dīrghatvaṁ bhaviṣyati.*[33]

"Let, then, there be a lopa of the subsequent one. (After that) there will be a lengthening of *a* in the first syllable (as P 7.4.70 *ata ādeḥ* teaches; *a as* → *a s* → *ās*, which is adequate for the derivation of the perfect forms *āsa*, *āsatuḥ* and *āsuḥ*)."

(i) [śloka-vt part:] *"naivaṁ sidhyati, kasmāt, pratyaṅgatvād, bhaved dhi para-rūpam /"* [Paraphrase:] *naivaṁ sidhyati. kasmāt? pratyaṅgatvāt para-rūpaṁ prāpnoti.*

"(The goal) is not achieved this way. Why? Because (the item on which the operation is to take place) is a pratyaṅga. So, only the following (sound) would remain—the preceding sound would be subsumed into the following sound (*a as* → *as*)."

(j) [śloka-vt part:] *"tasmiṁś ca kr̥te lopaḥ."* [Paraphrase:] *para-rūpe ca kr̥te lopaḥ prāpnoti.*

"And when the form of the following (sound alone) is allowed to remain, lopa presents itself (*as* → *s*) as an undesirable outcome."

---

to P 1.1.56, to inherit the properties of the item in the place of which it occurs.

[32](a) From the next course of action, *parasya lopaḥ*, that is suggested, we can infer that the lopa proposed at this point pertains to a preceding item. There is a difficulty with this understanding as the statements of the commentators reproduced in §2.15g show. Particularly noteworthy is the comment by Annaṁbhaṭṭa.

(b) In such contexts, *prāpnoti* has a negative shade of meaning, similar to that of *prasaṅga*. It indicates that the form arrived at will be an undesirable or unintended consequence.

[33]This is the way the sentences are printed in the edns. Not making a separate paragraph of the second sentence indicates that the editors considered that sentence to be a logical extension of the first sentence—to be a sentence pointing out the benefit of para-lopa. Kaiyaṭa and his commentators do not provide any guidance on the matter.

(k) [śloka-vt part:] *"dīrghatvaṁ bādhakaṁ bhavet tatra."* [Paraphrase:] *"ata ādeḥ"* [P 7.4.70] *iti dīrghatvaṁ bādhakaṁ bhaviṣyati.*

"The lengthening taught by *ata ādeḥ* will block (the lopa; *as* will become *ās*, which is adequate for the derivation of the perfect forms *āsa*, *āsatuḥ* and *āsuḥ*)."

(l) *idaṁ tarhi prayojanaṁ sārvadhātuke bhūta-pūrva-mātre 'pi yathā syāt. kurv iti*

"Let this then be the purpose (to be served by the sūtra 6.4.110): Even when a suffix that substituted a sārvadhātuka follows, (the desired operation, the change of *a* to *u*) should take place (as would be the case in the form) *kuru.*"[34]

§2.14 As Kielhorn stated, the fourth occurrence is found in a verse (with śāstric content, a kārikā). In the passage in §2.13, if we put *naivaṁ sidhyati, kasmāt, pratyaṅgatvād bhaved dhi para-rūpam* together with *tasmiṁś ca kr̥te lopaḥ* and *dīrghatvaṁ bādhakaṁ bhavet tatra*, we get a complete verse in āryā meter. From the fact that it has been paraphrased it would be fair to propose that it has been quoted. Thus, the fourth occurrence resembles the first occurrence in being metrical and being a quotation.

As I have pointed out in Aklujkar 2008: 140–141, the MB can justifiably be said to contain Pat's own metrical compositions (not always full verses) at several places. This may be especially true where the context is one of specifying the desired forms or the desired course of action—when the statements concerned are iṣṭis.

Even if the present verse were to be regarded as someone else's statement, it would not follow that all MB statements containing *ptg* come from an author other than Pat and that *ptg* is an older technical term merely inherited by Pat, absent from his own usage. As shown in Aklujkar 2008: 130–134, the first *ptg* statement, the one under P 1.1.29, coming from Gonardīya/Gonandīya, can be regarded as Pat's statement on good grounds. In the case of occurrence 2, found in the discussion of P 1.1.57 (overlooked by Kielhorn), there is no reason even to raise the possibility that the statement containing *pratyaṅga-vartī* comes from anyone other than the MB author Pat. Further, in the case of the occurrence under 6.3.138, paraphrasing or

[34] *kr̥* + *u* (P 3.1.79) → *hi* (imperative second person singular suffix, sārvadhātuka by P 3.4.113 and 1.1.56) → *kar* (P 7.3.84) + *u* + *hi* → *kar* + *u* + (replacement of *hi* by luk/deletion; P 6.4.106) → *kur* (P 6.4.110) + *u* + (luk) → *kuru.* The deletion coming in the place of *hi* gets the erstwhile (bhūta-pūrva) designation, namely sārvadhātuka, in this understanding and becomes eligible for the '*a* → *u*' change taught in P 6.4.110.

summarizing, rather than exact quotation, seems likely. Thus, only one out of the four occurrence passages, namely MB 6.4.110, can be said to contain signs *possibly* indicating that Pat borrowed the *ptg* statements from an earlier author, and even in the case of that one passage, the signs would be there only if we rule out the possibility that Pat restated in prose the contents of the verse parts of his own iṣṭis.

§2.15 Like the second and third occurrences, the fourth occurrence confirms the status of *ptg* as a noun. An abstraction suffix like *-tva* cannot be added to a non-noun. Even in usages such as *nīlatva* etc., the adjectives *nīla*, etc. acquire the role of words denoting reified entities as can be seen from their translations such as 'the condition of being a nīla (color, property, thing)' or 'that which is common to all instances of nīla (color)'. Even if *ptg* were an avy for Pat, it would not take an abstraction suffix unless it is reduced to the bahu-vrīhi underlying it as can be seen from a possible translation like 'the *state* of being one which is associated or concerned with each limb or part'. Bahu-vrīhis are adjectives by nature. They frequently acquire the value of nouns.

§2.16 The fourth occurrence, like the third (and indirectly the second), confirms that Kielhorn had followed traditional scholars when he explained *ptg* as meaning 'antar-aṅga'. The explanations of these scholars, related to the letter-numbered MB sentences in §2.13, read thus:

[(c)] Annaṁ-bhaṭṭa p. IX.356: *bhāṣye* ***kartuḥ*** *sūtrakārasya.*

[(f)] Annaṁ-bhaṭṭa p. IX.356: *bhāṣye* ***sthānivad-bhāvāt*** *"dvir-vacane 'ci"* [P 1.1.59] *ity-anena.*

(g) Kaiyaṭa (p. V.342); ***kr̥te dvitve lopaḥ prāpnotīti.*** *nanu ca niyata-kālatvāt*[35] *sthānivad-bhāvasya, kr̥te dvir-vacane, lakṣaṇa-pravr̥ttim antareṇa, svata evādeśa-rūpam avatiṣṭhata iti lopasya kathaṁ prāptiḥ? ucyate. punaḥ pravr̥ttir lakṣaṇasyeti sthānivad-bhāva-prakaraṇe pratipāditam.*

Tr.: "The sthānivad-bhāva is confined to a specific time. After the doubling is effected, without (any) sūtra being activated, the form of the substitute (= short *u* in P 6.4.110?) will automatically present itself. How has Pat then spoken of the occurrence of lopa? Answer: It has been stated in the sthānivad-bhāva section that the relevant sūtra again proceeds forth—again becomes applicable."

[35] Cf. Kāśikā 1.1.59: *dvir-vacana-nimitte 'ci aj-ādeśaḥ sthānivad bhavati, dvir-vacana eva kartavye. rūpātideśaś cāyaṁ niyata-kālaḥ. tena kr̥te dvir-vacane punar ādeśa-rūpam evāvatiṣṭhate. āl-lopopadhā-lopa-yaṇ-ay-av-āy-āv-ādeśāḥ prayojanam.*

Nārāyaṇa p. IX.357: ***nanu ca niyata-kālatvād*** *iti. "dvir-vacana eva kartavye" ity avadhāraṇān niyata-kālatvaṁ sthānivad-bhāvasyoktaṁ rūpātideśaś ca. tatra, kr̥te dvir-vacane, ādeśasya rūpam eva cakratuḥ ity-ādau bhavatīti punar lopo na kartavya ity arthaḥ.* ***punaḥ pravr̥ttir*** *iti. ata eva ninyatuḥ ity-ādau pūrvaṁ pravr̥tto 'pīyaṅ dvir-vacana-kāle 'pahr̥ta iti punaḥ pravr̥ttau prāptāyām anekāctvād yaṇā bādhyate. evaṁ cakratuḥ ity-ādau punar yaṇ-lakṣaṇa-pravr̥ttiḥ.*

Annaṁ-bhaṭṭa p. IX.356: ***nanv*** *iti. dvir-vacane sthānivad-bhāvaḥ, kr̥te tu dvir-vacane punaḥ sthānivattvābhāvāt sthāny-abhāve kathaṁ tasya lopa ity arthaḥ.* ***ucyate punaḥ pravr̥ttir iti.*** *yady apy etat tasmin prakaraṇe bhāṣya-pradīpayor na dr̥śyate, "dvir-vacane 'ci"* [P 1.1.59] *ity-asya punaḥ pravr̥ttau prayojanaṁ ca nāsti, na ca nimitāpekṣayā pūrvatva-pakṣe "acaḥ parasmin ..."* [P 1.1.57] *ity-anena sthānivad-bhāvaḥ, tasya rūpātideśatvābhāvena lopa-vidhāv anupayogāt, tathāpy etad-bhāṣya-vārttika-saṁgataye punaḥ pravr̥tty-abhyupagama ity atra tātparyam.*

Nāgeśa p. V.342–343: ***niyata-kālatvād*** *iti. "dvir-vacana eva kartavye" ity avadhāraṇān niyata-kālatvaṁ sthānivattvasyoktam. tatra, kr̥te dvitva, ādeśa-rūpam eva cakratur ity-ādau bhavatīti punar lopāprāptir ity arthaḥ. rūpātideśa āha* ***punaḥ pravr̥ttir*** *iti. ata eva ninyatur ity-ādau pūrvaṁ pravr̥tto 'pīyaṅ dvir-vacana-kāle 'pahr̥ta iti punaḥ pravr̥ttau prāptāyām anekāctvād yaṇā bādhyata ity arthaḥ.*

Tr. of Nāgeśa (and effectively of Nārāyana, since Nāgeśa's wording is almost identical with Nārāyaṇa's): "***niyata-kālatvād*** *iti.* sthānivad-bhāva has been said to be confined to a certain time because of the delimiting (in the interpretation of P 1.1.59 as) *dvir-vacana eva kartavye* [cf. Kāśikā 1.1.59]. In that case, after the doubling is effected, only the form of the substitute takes place in the derivates such as *cakratuḥ*. There will then be no occasion for the lopa to re-appear. ***punaḥ pravr̥ttir*** *iti* ("the relevant sūtra again proceeds forth"): For this very reason, in the derivation of *ninyatuḥ*, (the following happens): the *iyaṅ*, although it becomes applicable first, is removed at the time of doubling. When its re-introduction becomes imminent, it is blocked by the *yaṆ*-ādeśa on account of the presence of more than one vowel."

(h) Kaiyaṭa p. V.342: ***astu tarhīti.*** *"anantya-vikāre 'ntya-sadeśasye"ti vacanāt* [= paribhāṣā 52 in Vyāḍi, with different numbers in other paribhāṣā works]. *athavā kṅity anantarasyākārasya lopaḥ. tatra "yena nāvyavadhānam"* [= paribhāṣā 39 in Vyāḍi, with different numbers in other paribhāṣā works] *ity eka-varṇa-vyavahitasya lopaḥ.* ***dīrghatvam*** *iti. "ata ādeḥ" ity-anena.*
Tr.: "***astu tarhīti*** (conveys this:) because of the (paribhāṣā) statement *anantya-vikāre 'ntya-sadeśasya.* Alternatively, when an item marked with Ṅ follows (as P 6.4.110 is with the recurrence of *KṄiti* from 6.4.98 provides), there will be a lopa of the *a* immediately before it. When that lopa has taken place, there will be the lopa of what is intervened by only one phoneme. (This latter lopa will take place) according to the metarule *yena nāvyavadhānam tena vyavahite 'pi vacana-prāmāṇyāt* ("If a certain item never fails to intervene, then even if it intervenes, the relevant operation takes place"), because the statement (of that operation) has (to have) its validity."

Nārāyaṇa p. IX.357: *nanu "parasyaiva lopa" iti niyamaḥ kathaṁ labhyata ity-atrāha* ***anantyeti. ṅity-anantarasyeti.*** *"kṅiti"* [imported into 6.4.110 from P 6.4.98] *ity-anenākāro viśeṣyate, na tv aṅgam iti bhāvaḥ.*

Annaṁ-bhaṭṭa p. IX.356: *nanu parasyeti kathaṁ, pūrvasyāpi lopa-saṁbhavāt, ata āha* ***anantyeti.*** *nanv iyaṁ paribhāṣā prayojanābhāvān nāśrīyata ity uktam, ata āha* ***athaveti.*** *akāra-lope savarṇa-dīrghāsaṁbhavād āha* ***ata āder*** *iti.*

Nāgeśa p. V.343: *parasyaiva lopaḥ iti niyamaḥ katham? ata āha* ***anantyeti. athaveti.*** *ādyasyottareṇāvyavadhānād iti bhāvaḥ. anarthakatvāc cety api bodhyam.*

Tr.: "Why is there the restriction that a deletion only of the subsequent takes place? (The sentence beginning with) ***anantya*** (answers this question). (As for the sentence beginning with) ***athavā*** (its) purport is (that the deletion will take place) because the first (sound) is not intervened by the later (sound) One should understand the following also at this point: 'and because there is no meaning associated (with the first sound/sounds)."

(i) Kaiyaṭa p. V.343: ***pratyaṅgatvād*** *iti. varṇāśrayatvāt para-rūpam antar-aṅgam. tatra [= tasmin] kṛte, al-lope ca , 'satuḥ' 'suḥ' iti prāpnoti.*
Tr.: "Because it rests on a phoneme, (the reduction to) the form of the latter is (an operation that takes place) inside. After it and the deletion of the phoneme take place, the resulting forms would be (the undesirable) *satuḥ* (and) *suḥ.*"

Nārāyaṇa p. IX.357: ***pratyaṅgatvād*** *ity-asyāntar-aṅgatvād ity artharṁ darśayati* ***varṇāśrayatvād*** *iti.*

Annaṁ-bhaṭṭa p. IX.356: *antar-aṅgatvāt pūrvaṁ para-rūpe, paścād al-lope 'niṣṭa-prasaṅgam āha* ***satur*** *iti.*

Nāgeśa p. V.343: ***pratyaṅgatvād*** *ity-asyāntar-aṅgatvād ity artha ity āha* ***varṇāśrayatvād*** *iti. "vārṇād āṅgam"* [see note 22] *ity anāśrityedam.*

(k) Kaiyaṭa p. V.343: *dīrghatvam iti. "yena nāprāpti"-nyāyena para-rūpaṁ bādhitvā dīrghatvaṁ bhaviṣyatīty arthaḥ.*

Tr.: "(As for the Bhāṣyakāra's way of blocking the undesirable result through) dīrghatva: the lengthening supersedes reduction to the form of the latter phoneme on the basis of the maxim *yena nāprāpte yo vidhir ārabhyate sa tasya bādhako bhavati* 'A rule X which is composed when (another rule) Y cannot fail to apply, blocks that Y'."

Nārāyaṇa p. IX.357: *kathaṁ punar antar-aṅgaṁ para-rūpaṁ bahir-aṅgo dīrgho bādhetety-atrāha* ***yena nāprāptī****ti.*

Annaṁ-bhaṭṭa p. IX.356: *dīrghatvaṁ lopasya bādhakam iti śaṅkāṁ nirāha* ***yene****ti.*

Nāgeśa p. V.343: *antar-aṅgasya kathaṁ bahir-aṅgaṁ bādhakam ata āha* ***yena ne****ti.*

(l) Kaiyaṭa p. V.343: ***kurv*** *iti. atra "na lumatāṅgasya"* [P 1.1.63] *iti pratyaya-lakṣaṇa-pratiṣedhād utvaṁ na syād iti bhūta-pūrva-gaty-arthāt sārvadhātuka-grahaṇād bhavati.*

Nārāyaṇa p. IX.357: *nanu pratyaya-lakṣaṇena saṁprati heḥ paratva-saṁbhave bhūta-pūrva-gatyāśrayaṇam ayuktam ity-ata āha* ***atre****ti.*

Annaṁ-bhaṭṭa p. IX.356: *nanu her luky api pratyaya-lakṣaṇeno-tvaṁ syāt, at āha* ***atra na lumate****ti.*

Nāgeśa p. V.343: *nanu pratyaya-lakṣaṇena heḥ paratva-saṁbhave bhūta-pūrva-gatyāśrayaṇam ayuktam ity-ata āha* ***atra ne****ti. na ca "sārvadhātuke"* [P 6.4.110] *ity-asyābhāva ukārāntā-ṅgāvayava-karoter "ata ut"* [P 6.4.110] *ity-arthena tṛjvat-sūtre* [P 7.1.95] *"yuvor anākau"* [P 7.1.1] *ity-ādau ca vakṣyamāṇa-bhāṣya-rītyāṅga-saṁjñāyā pratyaya-lakṣaṇenāṅgīkāreṇa kurv ity-atra siddho lopaḥ:, hiluka ābhīyāsiddhatvāc ceti vācyam. "idaṁ tarhī"ty-ādi "kurv" ity-anta-bhāṣyasyaika-deśy-uktitvāt. sārva-dhātuka-grahaṇaṁ tu spaṣṭārtham eveti dik.*

An interesting difference emerges in (l), the last section. Kaiyaṭa explains why Pat takes recourse to bhūta-pūrva-gati, 'appeal to the erstwhile nature (of the suffix)'. Nāgeśa adds a further clarification to this but ultimately parts company with Kaiyaṭa and other commentators. He tells us that Pat's entire discussion presented in §2.12 should be viewed as an eka-deśy-ukti, 'statement of a person who has found only a partial and/or non-final solution to the issue'. While this pronouncement does not affect what we have noted about *ptg* in the fourth occurrence passage, it confirms our feeling about the strain involved in following Pat's argument.

Summation of what we find in the occurrences of *ptg* in and out of the MB

§3.1 Our detailed and comprehensive study of the MB passages in which *ptg* is used enables us to come to the following conclusions:

(a) While the possibility that some uses of *ptg* come from a pre-Pat author, particularly a śloka-vt author, cannot be ruled out, the probability is that all of them come from Pat. This, however, does not mean that the word cannot be older than Pat. His use of it without feeling any need to explain it and the occurrences discussed §§4.4–6 and in §5.4–10 below leave no doubt that the word is older than Pat's time.

(b) Nor should the word be thought of as taken over by Pat only from the Vt authors as Kielhorn's comment may suggest. There is ample evidence in the passages discussed below that makes it likely that Pat came to know the word from a number of sources; *ptg* is unlikely to have been a rare or obsolete word in his time.

(c) The commentators do not assign one meaning to *ptg* in what they might have taken as Vt contexts and another meaning when the word occurs in non-Vt sentences. We cannot proceed on the assumption that *ptg* occurs in a technical sense only in the Vts and infer therefrom, as Kielhorn was inclined to do, that Gonardīya/Gonandīya, as the author of *akac-svarau tu kartavyau pratyaṅgaṁ mukta-saṁśayau*, must be different from the MB author Pat.

(d) The traditional commentators are uncertain or inconsistent about the grammatical features of *ptg*. Sometimes they take it as an avy, which has no case variation. At other times, they seem to think of it (or seem to have been forced to think of it) as a noun capable of occurring in various case forms.

At its first occurrence, all of them, except Śiva-rāmendra-sarasvatī, are silent about the meaning of *ptg*. In the second, third and fourth, the meaning specified or presumed is 'antar-aṅga', except by Śiva-rāmendra, whose commentary is unavailable in the case of the third and fourth occurrence passages.

On the relatively rare occasions in which they mention the word as an avy, they generally do not specify the Pāṇinian sūtra which supports the avy derivation. Only Śiva-rāmendra is explicit on the matter, but he gives two different derivations in two occurrences not far apart from each other (§2.1, §2.6b).

The nominal role does not get any explicit recognition from the commentators. One can only infer it from their equating of *ptg* with *antar-aṅga*.

Nor do they spell out how the literal meaning of *ptg* culminates in 'antar-aṅga'. There is no bridging in their works of the grammatical analysis of *ptg* and the rendering as 'antar-aṅga'. In at least one instance (§2.11), one feels that they make a desperate attempt to deny *ptg* the status of a noun.

They also do not squarely face the issue of the semantic gap I have pointed out in starting the derivation process with *prati* in the sense of 'each' (§§2.7–10, §2.15).

Thus, the impression one forms is that the commentators did not know really or fully what Pat really meant by *ptg*. Particularly, they did not know how the contextually workable meaning of the word ('something other than the regular aṅga' or 'something inside') could be reconciled with what they took to be its etymological meaning.

(e) Pat provides evidence only of *ptg* as a noun. The avy *pratyaṅgam* could, of course, have been possible in his time (note in particular the Mīmāṁsā-sūtra and Vaikhānasa-gṛhya-sūtra occurrences that I have cited in §5.3), but it does not occur in his work.[36]

(f) Kielhorn was not expressing a new view about the meaning of *ptg*. His confident mention of 'antar-aṅga' as the meaning was based on the commentaries, if not on what he learned from his helpers, śāstrins and paṇḍitas, in Poona/Pune.

(g) At least in the present state of our knowledge, all the MB commentators supporting Kielhorn's view belong to the period beginning with the tenth century A.D.[37] Kaiyaṭa himself does not gloss *ptg* with *antar-aṅga*, but his use of *antar-aṅgatvāt* while explaining occurrence passage 3 and his attempt to explain *ptg* with *pratyāsanna* 'near' or *pratipratyāsatti* 'in the case of each (progressively declining) nearness' under occurrence passage 2

[36]Thus, the placing of a MB occurrence by Monier-Williams (1899: 663–664) in the avy part of his entry on *ptg* is an error. The following explanations he gives are also less than exact "for one's own person, Pat. (cf. *-vartin*); ... (in gram.) in each base, P 1.1.29, Pat. ... *-vartin* mfn. occupying one's self with one's own person, Pat." Similar is the case of Böhtlingk 1883: 151: under *pratyaṅgam* as adverb: "4) *bei jedem grammatischen Thema.*"

[37]On the basis of what I have read about the relative chronology of Kaiyaṭa, Helā-rāja and Hara-datta, I tend to think of Kaiyaṭa as living around 940 A.D.

indicate that he attributed at least the ordinary language sense of *antar-aṅga* to *ptg*[38] and that his commentators have read him correctly. Besides, since we find Jinendra-buddhi, who cannot be dated later than the early 8th A.D. (Steinkellner 2005: xlii), substituting *ptg* with *antar-aṅga* (note 16), we can deduce that the meaning Kielhorn adopted was known at least a century earlier than Kaiyaṭa.

(h) There is a suggestion in the four passages that Pat is familiar with the ordinary as well as technical senses of *ptg*. In the *pratyaṅga-vartī* of the second passage, the meaning of the word can only be non-technical. In the first, third and fourth passages, the use gives every indication of being technical. Therefore, *ptg* must be an object language term (cf. Purāṇic and Epic occurrences in §§5.5–8) that assumed a technical role in the tradition of the Pāṇinīyas.

(i) But the use of *ptg* is unlikely to be identical with the use of *antar-aṅga* precisely because Pat, who is conversant with *antar-aṅga*, has opted for *ptg* only in certain passages. The simultaneous presence of the two words in the contexts of occurrence passages 1[39] and 2 also indicates that their meanings, while relatable to each other, must be distinct.[40]

---

[38]Regarding the technical senses of *antar-aṅga*, we learn the following from Abhyankar-&-Shukla 1977: 28: "The antar-aṅgatva is taken in a variety of ways by Grammarians [= the Pāṇinīyas]: (1) having causes of application within or before those of another, . . . (2) having causes of application occurring before those of another in the wording [= constitution?] of the form, (3) having a smaller number of causes, (4) occurring earlier in the order of several operations which take place in arriving at the complete form of a word, (5) not having saṁjñā (technical term) as a cause of its application, (6) not depending on two words or padas, (7) depending upon a cause or causes of a general nature (sāmānyāpekṣa) as opposed to one which depends on causes of a specific nature (viśeṣāpekṣa)."

The variety of ways in which antar-aṅgatva is taken by the Pāṇinīyas is so great that some operlapping of the different understandings recorded by Abhyankar-Shukla is bound to occur in practice. Besides, the sophistication developed in the tradition in the area of arriving at the same result in different ways is of such a high order that it should not surprise us if a well-trained Pāṇinīya demonstrates that an instance of *ptg* as 'antar-aṅga' in one understanding is also an instance of *ptg* as antar-aṅga in some other understanding.

[39]The sentences *kathaṁ punar icchatāpi bhavatā bahir-aṅgeṇa pratiṣedhenāntar-aṅgo vidhiḥ śakyo bādhitum? antar-aṅgān api vidhīn bahir-aṅgo vidhir bādhate . . .* occur a little before the *ptg* sentence in MB 1.1.29.

[40](a) There is also a difference in the way the two terms occur in the MB. While *antar-aṅga* is found employed as a bahu-vrīhi taking on the gender of the noun with which it is associated in a sentence, there is no sign of gender variation or adjectival meaning in the employment of *ptg*. Cf. for example, MB on Pratyāhāra-sūtra 3–4 p. I.26.13–14 (*bahir-aṅgā vr̥ddhiḥ. antar-aṅgaṁ ṇatvam*); 1.1.5 p. I.54.11–12 (*bahir-aṅge guṇa-vr̥ddhī antar-aṅgaḥ pratiṣedhaḥ*), p. I.55.3

(j) While commenting on occurrence passages 3 and 4, Ananṁ-bhaṭṭa and Nāgeśa find it necessary to specify that the metarule *vārṇād āṅgaṁ balīyaḥ* does not apply. In the commentaries on the remaining two occurrence passages, the word *varṇa* or a derivative of it is not employed, but, in one, the operation, namely the insertion of *ak(a)C* and introduction of a particular accent, takes place with a varṇa (the *a* in *mat*) as the basis. In the technical sense of *ptg*, thus, there seems to be an element of being inside a larger unit or being at a deeper level of derivation. This element is found also in the non-technical use in passage 2. The pratyaṅgas expressed by *śarīra-kārya*, *suhṛt-kārya* and *saṁbandhi-kārya* are all inside the world or loka. The situation is not inamenable to at least the non-technical, etymological or literal sense of *antar-aṅga*. However, as noted in (i), there must also be at least some difference between what the two terms convey in technical contexts. To speak in approximate terms, it seems that while *antar-aṅga* is assumed to be operative on the plane of morphology, the plane of operation for *ptg* is presumed to be that of phones and phonemes.

§3.2 The cumulative message of the observations in §3.1 is this: How the commentators and Kielhorn took *ptg* is not to be rejected—at least not wholly or in an unqualified way, but our pursuit for the precise meaning intended by Pat or for a different original meaning is to be continued. For a proper continuation, we should note (a) the various meanings of *prati*, (b) the compound words formed with a prefix other than *prati* as the first member and *aṅga* as the second member, and (c) the meanings of *ptg* recorded in the dictionaries on which we usually rely. The compilers of these dictionaries must have given thought to some of the issues with which we had or may have to deal. Further, some insights may emerge from the items to

(*bahir-aṅgo guṇaḥ. antar-aṅgaḥ pratiṣedhaḥ*); 1.1.39 p. I.97.18; (*bahir-aṅgaṁ hrasvatvam. antar-aṅgas tuk*), 1.3.60 p. I.286.15 (*antar-aṅgas tarhi lādeśaḥ*). It is true that in occurrence passage 3, *pratyaṅgam* is found used in the sense 'pratyaṅga operation or application' and this sense is similar to that of *antar-aṅga* in passages such as MB 1.1.3 p. I.49 lines 15, 17. 18, 21 in which we find *antar-aṅgaṁ bhavati, antar-aṅgaṁ syāt* and *antar-aṅgam asti*. However, there are no actual instances of gender and number variation of *ptg* in the MB.

(b) In the case of *antar-aṅgaṁ bhavati* etc., we can understand *kāryam* and take the sentences as having meanings such as 'that grammatical operation whose aṅga is inside takes place'. This will be in conformity with the bahu-vrīhi use of *antar-aṅga*. However, noticing the parallel with *pratyaṅgaṁ bhavati*, we could also hold that antar-aṅga stands for both 'the aṅga which is inside' and 'the antar-aṅga-pertaining operation'—that what we have on our hands is a case of development of secondary meaning and the similarity with the other uses of *antar-aṅga* is deceptive. This alternative may have a role to play in the efforts to determine the meaning(s) of the antar-aṅga paribhāṣā intended by Pat.

which *ptg* is applied and what the contexts contain. Finally, if the meaning we determine serves to explain some oddities that earlier research unearthed or 'pushed under the rug', we will have confirmation of having followed the right path.

§3.3 The relatively extensive statements on the meanings of *prati* that I have come across are presented below:[41]

> Anonymous. Laghūpasarga-vṛtti:[42] *sādṛśyādāna-rug.ghiṁsā-tad-yoge vyāpti-vāraṇe / nivṛtti-pratibimbābhimukhye syād vyatyaye prati //*
>
> "(The prefix) *prati* conveys 'similarity', 'acceptance', 'discomfort, affliction', 'killing, destruction', 'applying oneself to that (= thing specified by the associated word; cf. *udyoga* in the other list)', 'dispersal over each group item', 'warding off', 'retreat', 'reflection', 'facing', 'exchange, bartering'."
>
> Candra-gomin? Viṁśaty-upasarga-vṛtti (p. 38 of the edn by Dragomir Dimitrov): *sādṛśyādāna-hiṁsodyoga-vinimaya-pratinidhi-nivṛtti-vyādhy-ābhimukhya-vyāpti-vāraṇeṣu. prati ity ayam upasarga eteṣv artheṣu vartate.*
>
> "The upasarga *prati* conveys these meanings: 'similarity', 'acceptance', 'killing, destruction', 'effort', 'exchange, bartering', 'substitution', 'retreat', 'pain, discomfort', 'facing', 'dispersal', and 'warding off'."

[41](a) I have followed the probable chronological order of my sources. Since almost all the German glosses have found their equivalents in the cited English dictionary, I have not translated them separately. I have dropped the intervening examples and occurrence references, so as to bring the meanings and their various articulations into the foreground and to keep the full range of possibilities in view.

(b) Discussion about the cognates of *prati* can be found in Mayrhofer 1963: p. II.358. He seems to regard "zu, zu—hin, gegen, wieder, auf / towards, against, again, upon ..." as the basic meaning of *prati*. In 1996: 176, however, the sequence of meanings given is "gegen, entgegen, nach - hin, zur Zeit von, um."

(c) Regarding the formation of the stem *prati*, we learn the following from Burrow (1955: 176): "There are occasional neuter ĭ-stems which have come to be used as adverbs : *sáci* 'with'. *práti* 'against' (*pr-ati, ti*-stem)."

[42]This work is edited by V. Krishnamacharya in the Adyar Library Bulletin 25: 81–90 in 1962. It could be later than the Viṁśaty-upasarga-vṛtti in the tradition of Cāndra grammar cited next. The extent of similarity of wording in the two works makes it quite likely that they come from a common source.

Tilaka. Nipātāvyayopasarga-vṛtti, p. 48: *prati[ḥ?] sthāne vinimaye niṣedhe pratipālane / nivṛtty-aṅgīkṛti-jñāna-pratīpotsāha-niṣkraye // yatna-pratijñā-saṁkṣepa-vaiparītye bhṛśe dṛśi / sādṛśya-bhraṁśa-dig-yoga-vyāpti-saṁbhāvanā-ruji // ... lakṣaṇādau karma-pravacanīyaḥ.*

"(Prefixed to verbs or nouns) *prati* conveys the senses) 'standing, staying in one place', 'exchange, giving something in return', 'rejection, non-admission', 'waiting, remaining in a state of expectation', 'returning', 'acceptance', 'experiencing, becoming aware', 'opposition, acting in reverse direction', 'encouraging', 'discharging', 'making preparation against, defence', 'promise', 'abbreviation, contraction', 'reversal, turning in the other direction', 'bhṛśa = present oneself to → accumulation, enrichment?', 'citing, appearing', 'similarity, being substitutable', 'scattering, becoming dispersed', 'creating likelihood', and 'pain, discomfort'.[43] In senses such as 'pointing out', it acts as a karma-pravacanīya."[44]

Böhtlingk-&-Roth. 1855–1875: vol 4 (1862–1865): 943–944: "praep. ... 1) *gegen, nach, zu* (auf die Frage *wohin, nach welcher Richtung hin, zu wem*). ... am Anf[ang] eines adv. comp. P. 2.1.14. ... P. 6.2.33, Sch.[45] - 2) *gegen* so v.a. *vor* (schützen) ... 3) *gegen, gegenüber von* ... 4) *gegen* (in der Vergleichung) P. 1.4.92 ... 5) *gegen* so v.a. *in der Richtung von, in der Gegend von, an, bei; zur Zeit von, um* ... 6) *auf den Antheil von, für, zu Gunsten von* ... P. 1.4.90. ... 7) *für, zum Ersatz von* P. 1.4.92. ... 8) *in Beziehung auf, in Betreff von* ... P. 1.4.90. ... 9) *nach, gemäss, zu Folge*, franz[ösich] selon ... 10) *bei, in*, mit dem Nebenbegriff *der stetigen Wiederholung* (vīpsā) P. 1.4.90 ... Gewöhnlich wird *prati* in dieser Bed[eutung] mit der Ergänzung zu einem adv. comp. verbunden Sch. zu P 2.1.6.

[43] This impressive list based on a wide consideration of usage and showing the author's ability to separate various shades of meaning can be reduced to fewer basic meanings as Wackernagel's listing below shows.

[44] In addition to lakṣaṇa, 'pointing out', the author illustrates itthaṁbhūtākhyāna 'narration in a matter of fact tone, reporting', bhāga 'division, share', vīpsā 'applying individually', pratinidhi 'capability to take someone's or something's place', pratidāna 'bartering'.

[45] The sūtra referred to, P 6.2.33, primarily informs about the accent (prakṛti-svara). It conveys the omission of the denotatum of the subsequent member of a compound like *pratipūrvāhṇam* secondarily. Also, along with *prati*, it pertains to *pari*, *upa* and *apa* as first members of the avys such as *paritrigartam*, *upapūrvāhṇam* and *apatrigartam*.

> ... 11) am Ende eines adv. comp. so v.a. *ein wenig* (mātrārthe) P. 2.1.9."

> Böhtlingk 1879–1889. Vol 4 (1883): 137: "1) Adv. in Verbindung mit Verben und in Comp. mit Substantives *gegen, entgegen, zurück, wieder, rĕ-*. Vor Substantives auch so v. a. *jeder.* 2) Praep. ... *gegen, nach,* ... *gegenüber von, angesichts, vor* ... *in der Gegend von,* ... am Anfange eines adv. Comp."[46]

> Monier-Williams 1899: 661: "towards, near to; against, in opposition to; back, again, in return; down upon, upon, on; before nouns it expresses also likeness or comparison ... or it forms Avyayī-bhāvas of different kinds ... or as a prep. with usually preceding acc., in the sense of towards, against, to, upon, in the direction of ... opposite, before, in the presence of ... in comparison, on a par with, in proportion to ... in compar[ison] with ... in the vicinity of, near, beside, at, on ... at the time of, about, through, for ... or used distributively to express at every, in or on every, severally ... in favour of, for ... on account of, with regard to, concerning ... conformably or according to ... as, for (after a verb meaning 'to regard, consider' ... or as prep. with abl. in return or as compensation for, instead or in the place of ..."[47]

> Wackernagel 1905: II.1.260: "1) gegenüberliegend ... 2) gegnerisch 3) erwidernd ... 4) zurück ... 5) ebenbürtig, als Ersatz eintretend, sekundär, ... 6) distributiv."

At first sight, it may seem that one and the same morpheme or lexeme has been assigned two contradictory meanings: (a) 'in opposition to' and (b) 'likeness'. However, it is not difficult to explain how both (a) and (b) could have come about from the same source. All upasargas, except *dus* and *su* in Pāṇini's list,[48] presume a view or perspective of the speaker. How

---

[46] I have referred to this dictionary, which is an abbreviated and occasionally updated version of Böhtlingk-&-Roth 1855–1875, only because some of the German equivalents it gives are different. It does not give any radically different meanings under *prati*.

[47] Since the extensive coverage in Apte 1979: 1067 does not add anything significantly different to the preceding, I have not reproduced it here.

[48] A case can also be made for the inclusion of *ku, antar, bahis, śrat, marut* and maybe a few others in the upasarga class (see Kāśikā on 1.4.59; some inclusions justified in terms of meaning; some, as in the case of *marut*, in terms of derivational convenience). But the inclusion will not affect the predominance of movement-based use. Even in the case of *dus* and *su*, if the original meaning is taken to be adverbial ('badly, with difficulty' and 'well, smoothly, comfortably'), presumption

the speaker views the space around him/her (horizontally, vertically, unidimensionally, circularly etc.) underlies their use. The basic spatial notion associated with *prati* is 'on the other side, against, opposite'. It implies occupation of a place on the other side of a reference point presumed by the speaker. Now, the speaker can feel otherness because of difference as well as similarity. His/her viewing of the item can be for maintaining distinction or for comparing. Thus, *prati* can end up in expressing opposition (in a mild or strong way) or in conveying resemblance (to varying degree). In this way, *prati* can perform the roles of both "counter-" and "counterpart."

Most of the meanings in the lists above can be seen as natural developments of the meaning 'one (a person, thing or concept, thought etc.) on the other side' as the sequence in Wackernagel's listing of meanings would suggest. Such an entity can then be seen as (a) facing, (b) in concern/engagement with or (c) doing an action that the subject perceives as returning or moving to a point or state previously occupied. The other more specific meanings can be derived from one of these meanings without much stretching, except the meaning 'each, every, all' that *prati* conveys. Wackernagel (1905: II.1.257) seems to have formed a similar impression. He remarks, "Eine eigentümliche Entwicklung zeigt *práti*, indem es kl[assisch] neben den älteren Bedeutungen ... auch distributive Funktion erlangt hat."

One could propose a semantic development from upasarga *prati* 'on the other side', through karma-pravacanīya *prati* 'toward, concerning', to avy-forming *prati* 'each'.[49] However, I have not come across any statement of this or similar semantic development and I doubt that the statement will be convincing. The first part seems plausible. To argue for the latter part, one will probably have to assume a movement from such expressions as *vr̥kṣaṁ vr̥kṣaṁ prati* (*siñcati*, mentioned in Böhtlingk's dictionary, an instance—a doubtful instance—of karma-pravacanīya phrasing) to expressions like *prativr̥kṣaṁ*, that is, one will have to assume that syntactic compounding has taken place. However, the assumption involves a transfer of *prati* from a subsequent position to an initial position. Change of positions is not noticed in syntactic compounds (e.g. *itihāsa* resulting from *iti ha āsa* or *adya-śva* implicit in *adyaśvīna*). Theoretically one has the option of assuming that the base expression was *prati vr̥kṣaṁ vr̥kṣam*. But initial placing of karma-pravacanīya *prati*, if at all it occurs, is very rare in Sanskrit prose.

---

that a movement-expressive root meaning 'to fair, to pass through' originally accompanied them will give them the usage feature ('association with movement') that the other upasargas have.

[49]To simplify my presentation, I will leave out "every" from the third meaning and use only "each" in the remainder of this essay. It should also be understood that in some contexts, "all" serves better to convey the meaning of *prati*.

The observation made in the preceding paragraph needs to be borne in mind, along with the semantic jump pointed out in §2.5 and §2.8, when we study *ptg* with the assumption that it is used as an adverb in the MB (in the form *pratyaṅgam*, explicit or implicit). It is possible that the avy-forming *prati* meaning 'each' is historically a different stem from the upasarga *prati* and the karma-pravacanīya *prati* (there is no difficulty in treating the latter two as originally the same stem, especially given the separability of upasargas in Vedic Sanskrit). It is worth noting in this context that P does not say that the karma-pravacanīya *prati* is the same as the *prati* in the prādi class that acquires the upasarga designation or the *prati* that goes into the formation of an avy.[50] The nature of his presentation is 'three homophonous stems play three different roles'.

§3.4 Besides *ptg*, the following words have the 'prefix + *aṅga*' structure: *anvaṅgam* (indeclinable) 'after a member or part', *apāṅga* (neuter noun) 'corner or side of the eye', *upāṅga* (neuter noun) 'member of something', 'a minor limb', 'ancillary literature', 'supplement' and *vyaṅga* (bahu-vrīhi adjective, rarely a neuter noun, 'lacking a limb or member, crippled, deficient', 'bodily deficiency or disfigurement'. The prefixes in these, except for *vi*, have been specifically recognized as capable of karma-pravacanīya use in P 1.4.83–97. Only *anvaṅgam* is found as an adverb, but that, too, rarely. Its sense, unlike that of *prati* in *pratyaṅgam* (as illustrated in §5.3), does not differ significantly from that of the corresponding upasarga. Retention of or closeness to the upasarga sense is also the feature of *apāṅga*, *upāṅga*, and *vyaṅga*. Consequently, they are only superficially useful in tracing the semantic history of *ptg*.

Rarely, *upāṅga* has been used where, given the Āyur-veda uses listed in §5.4–5, we would expect to find *ptg*. This is the case with Bhāva-miśra's Bhāva-prakāśa pūrva-khaṇḍa garbha-prakaraṇa verses 70–100 (quoted under *śarīra* in Vācaspatya p. VI.5087). Closer attention to the passage, however, reveals that Bhāva-miśra is more likely to have consciously deviated from the 'aṅga : pratyaṅga' account of other authors. While the items he lists overlap with those in the 'aṅga : pratyaṅga' lists, he speaks of eight aṅgas instead of six[51] and attributes individual upāṅgas to each of the aṅgas specifically. Such an attribution of pratyaṅgas is not found in the other works of the genre. There the pratyaṅgas as a whole belong

[50]There has been some debate in the Sanskrit tradition regarding whether karma-pravacanīya should be admitted as a fifth word category beyond nāman, ākhyāta, upasarga and nipāta. See Vākyapadīya 2.199–204 and the Vṛtti thereto.

[51]The 'eight limbs' tradition is found also in Jain Prakrit literature (cf. Ratnacandra 1923: p. I.18). Whether all the particulars are the same as in Bhāvamiśra's account needs is yet to be determined.

to the body as a whole, and there is no necessary confinement of them to particular aṅga items. Therefore, it is more likely that it is Bhāva-miśra's awareness of the different orientation of his scheme that keeps him from using the term *ptg* in the context concerned than that he is using a different term to capture an old classification, thereby making *upāṅga* a synonym of *ptg*.

This surmise is partly confirmed by the awareness of pratyaṅgas that Bhāva-miśra shows in lines such as Bhāva-prakāśa, Madhya-khaṇḍa, chapter 71, verse 146 (edn K.R. Srikantha Murthy): *aṅga-pratyaṅga-deśe tu rujā yatrāsya (= bālasya) jāyate.* The probability of his making the 'upāṅga : pratyaṅga' distinction is strengthened also by the following passages found outside his work in which *upāṅga* and *pratyaṅga* are juxtaposed: Vāmana-purāṇa 80.31 (= 54.31 of the critical edn): *aṅgopāṅgāni, devarṣe, pūjayitvā jagad-guroḥ / surūpāṇy abhijāyante pratyaṅgāṅgāni caiva hi //*[52] and (text name not known at present) I.298.8: *aṅgair upāṅgaiḥ pratyaṅgair gati-mātrānugāmibhiḥ /* and V.109.16: *pratyaṅgopāṅgayor aṅge snaigdhyam ārogyam ārjavam /.*

§3.5 The dictionaries accessible to me give the following meanings for *ptg* (see note 41):

> Böhtlingk-&-Roth 1862–1865: IV.997: "1) *Nebenglied ... Am menschlichen Leibe sind Rumpf, Kopf, Arme und Beine die sechs Glieder* (aṅga); *die Nebenglieder sind Stirn, Nase, Kinn, Ohren, Finger u.s.w.* ...—2) *Abtheilung, Theil* ...—3) *Waffe.* [Under *pratyaṅgam* as a separate entry:]) 1) *auf —, an jedem Theile des Körpers* ... 2) *für jeden Theil* (z.B. einer Opferhandlung) ...3) *bei jedem Thema* Pat. zu P. 1.1.29."
>
> Böhtlingk Vol 4 (1883): 151: "n. 1) Nebenglied des Körpers: Stirn, Nase, Kinn, Ohren, Finger u. s. w. ...—2) Abtheilung, Theil. —3) Waffe ... m. ein best. Tact [Moving to *pratyaṅgam*:] Adv. 1) *auf —, an jedem Theile des Körpers.* —2) *für die eigene Person.* —3) *für jeden Theil (einer Opferhandlung).* —4) *bei jedem grammatischen Thema.* °*pratyaṅgatva* n. Zugehörigkeit zu Comm. zu TS Prāt.' ...*pratyaṅga-vartin* adj. *mit der eigenen Person sich beschäftigend.*"
>
> Monier-Williams 1899: 663–664: "a minor or secondary member of the body (as the forehead, nose, chin, fingers, ears &c; the 6 Aṅgas or chief members being the trunk, head, arms and legs), ...a division, section, part, ...a subdivision (of a science &c.); a

[52]For the general idea in *aṅgopāṅgāni pratyaṅgāṅgāni ca surūpāṇy abhijāyante*, see Manu 2.147 and Medhātithi's comment quoted in §5.5 below.

> weapon . . . ; a kind of measure [of a musical beat]; N. of a prince. (i[n the] b[eginning of a] c[ompound]. or *am*, ind.) on every part or member of the body, on the limbs severally, . . . for one's own person, Pat. (cf. *-vartin*; for every part or subdivision (of a sacrifice &c.), M[a]n[u]; (in gram) in each base, Pāṇ[ini]. 1.1.29, Pat.; *-tva*, n. the belonging to, T[aittirīya] Prāt[iśākhya; see note 64a]; *-dakṣiṇā*, f. a fee for each part (of a sacrifice), M[a]n[u].; *-vartin*, mfn. occupying one's self with one's own person, Pat."

As I have stated or indicated in earlier sections such as §2.5, some of the meanings given here call for modification or rejection. Similar will be the message of sections like §4.10 that are to follow. What is to be noted in the above extracts is the division of meanings generally in keeping with the prefix, post-position and adverb division as in the upasarga, karma-pravacanīya and avy division of the Pāṇinīyas and the separate treatment given to the avys.

§3.6 As observed in §3.1g–j, it is possible to accommodate the meaning 'antar-aṅga' in the MB occurrences of *ptg* (but we should not stop there). An entity included in something else is naturally thought of as smaller, minor or secondary or as a part, section or product of dividing. However, we should pause before we take any of these meanings as directly resulting from the *prati* of *ptg*. There is nothing in the basic meaning of the upasarga *prati* that would *naturally* lead to 'internal', 'smaller', 'minor' or 'secondary' as a meaning element. Nor is there anything in the common karma-pravacanīya meaning, 'toward, concerning' that would so lead (even if we were to imagine, against almost all attested usage, that this karma-pravacanīya *prati* commonly occurs before the word expressive of the object of concern or regard, and that a syntactic compound has come about from the phrase *pratyaṅgam*). If the *prati* that is seen in the formation of the avys is held to be identical with the upasarga and/or karma-pravacanīya *prati*, it may be considered reasonable to move from the sense 'each' to the sense 'internal', 'smaller' or 'secondary' if the following member is a word meaning 'limb, part'. It may be thought that a 'limb' allowing the application of 'each' will naturally imply that the whole has other limbs, and that, since the limbs must be inside the whole, they must be smaller than the whole. However, the examples in §5.4 do not suggest that the body parts or constituents covered by *ptg* were so called because they were viewed as stationed in a particular aṅga (or as smaller than the aṅga(s) or as secondary in the sense 'less prominent' or 'less important').

What the examples naturally indicate is that there were two ways of classifying the body. The aṅga way covered the more obvious reality (and hence was simpler and is more likely to have been older). It brought under one umbrella those parts of the body which almost any man would consider undeniable constituents of the human physical frame or skeleton (*piṇḍa*): (1) head, (2) middle part or torso area, extending from neck to waist, (3–4) two arms and (5–6) two thighs.[53] The second way involved such considerations as how the body functions and how its proper functioning can be maintained. It included studies of the inside of the body and led to the formation of a group that presumed the existence of the first group (aṅgas) but did not have an item by item correspondence with it. The group included eyes, nostrils, ears, lips, breasts, heart, navel, palms, fingers, generative organs etc.—in all 56 items, inclusive of the srotas, 'inner conduits or currents', kalās, dhātus etc., that is, even some elements not having a stable shape or configuration. If the items it contained were all smaller than the aṅga items or were found in one or more of the aṅga items, that was due to the sheer fact that they were, like the aṅgas, located on the body. Being in a one-to-one relationship, being inside or being smaller (and therefore being minor or secondary) was not what *prati* originally signified. If any of these meaning elements came about, they came about later. In the initial use of the class name—which had to be a physiological or anatomical use, given the primary meaning of *aṅga*—the role of *prati* was to convey that the set being presented was a differently motivated analysis of the human body—an analysis 'on the other side of the aṅga analysis', a parallel and complementary analysis, not a continuous and increasingly deeper analysis. Böhtlingk-&-Roth's "Nebenglied" was thus an insightful rendering of *ptg*.

§3.7 The data presented in the Appendix (= §§5.1–10), establish the following as facts:

(a) *ptg* is an old word that has been used in a variety of genres over most stages of Sanskrit language and literature—almost continuously since the period of the composition of the late Brāhmaṇas and Yāska's Nirukta, if not earlier from the period of the composition of the relatively late Saṁhitās such as the Vājasaneyi and Kāṭhaka (see §5.9). *ptg* is present in Pāli and Prakrit as *paccaṅga* and *paccaṁga*, respectively (Rhys Davids and Stede 1925: 8, Ratna-candra 1923: I.18). It continues to be used in modern Indian languages, although mostly in Sanskritic discussions and probably

[53](a) This is clearly dependent on a deeper three-fold division, with the neck and waist serving as boundaries, and special recognition given to the extendable and more prominently movable parts, namely the arms (inclusive of hands, palms, elbows, fingers etc.) and thighs (inclusive of legs, feet, toes, heels etc.)

(b) As pointed out in §3.4, a minority tradition of eight parts also seems to have existed. Whether it existed only to provide a basis for the upāṅga account needs to be investigated.

only as the second member of the compound *aṅga-pratyaṅga*.[54]

(b) Most uses of *ptg*, understandably, occur with *aṅga* present in the background, explicitly or implicitly, in its literal or metaphorical sense. Since the primary meaning of *aṅga* relates itself to physical body, the occurrences of *ptg* in the context formed by words such as *aṅga, śarīra* etc. should be taken as indicative of its older or original meaning. In other words, the usage in the texts of Āyur-veda and Nāṭya-śāstra should be taken as representing the oldest accessible stage in the semantic history of *ptg*, although the metaphorical use in Yāska's Nirukta may be older than the uses in Caraka's Saṁhitā and Bharata's Nāṭya-śāstra.

(c) From human body, the literal usage moves to animal bodies. However, when we move away from the field of anatomy, *aṅga* 'limb' loses its usual literal meaning and, in effect, becomes a synonym of 'part, constituent, section, product of division'. Thus, the elements of any system, system unit or structure can be spoken of as pratyaṅgas. Thus, we get the following as denotata of the word: (in literature) 'division of a text', (in architecture) 'part of a building', (in music) 'member of a set of musical instruments', 'a particular tāla or beat cycle', (in relatively abstract domains) 'a factor or constituent involved in a particular kind of scholarship, art, expertise or skill'. Cf. §§5.6–7.

(d) The trs and dictionary explanations of *ptg* as 'minor limb, secondary member', 'internal part, inside element' or 'division, subdivision, section' are not always inapplicable, but they are not to be understood as originally or primarily intended meanings. Cf. §3.6.

(e) The word always had the potential to mean something small, subtle or minor (in size if not in importance) because of the items it covered and the lists of such items that were available in the commonly studied texts. Because of this potential, we get a few uses in which we can suspect that the word has been used to cover all parts. The user could have used an expression like *sarvāṅga* in such contexts. However, he/she is found preferring *ptg*. His/her subconscious mind probably worked thus: "small part(s)

[54](a) By "Sanskritic discussions" I mean the discussions in which subjects or themes inherited from the Sanskrit culture or texts (such as medicine, dramaturgy) are discussed. Most of the listings of *ptg* in such dictionaries as the ones mentioned in (b) below are probably based on occurrences in relatively learned exchanges.

(b) Cf. Molesworth 1857: 538 and *Samsad Bengali English Dictionary* 1985: 594 for the Marathi and Bengali explanations of *ptg*, respectively.

(c) If the Sinhalese use of *ptg* in the form *pasănga* that is recorded by Turner (1966: 487) covers the modern phase of Sinhalese, then at least one exception must be said to exist to my statement above.

(d) The compound *aṅga-pratyaṅga* has an impressive degree of antiquity as can be seen from the occurrences marked with "&" in §5.5.

→ inclusive of even small part(s) → inclusive of every part → thoroughly, comprehensively." Cf. §5.8.

(f) The same meaning transformation is seen more frequently and prominently in the longer compound *aṅga-pratyaṅga* (§5.5). Initially, this dvandva compound probably meant 'easily observable parts of the body frame (largely corresponding to physiological parts) *and* parts coming from a second list of inner parts (largely corresponding to anatomical constituents)'. Later, it came to mean 'large and small parts' or 'major and minor parts'. Through frequent usage, this led to 'all parts of the body, regardless of their size and role' as the meaning of the expression.[55]

(g) The status of *ptg* as a substantive is beyond doubt. The word is mostly treated as a neuter noun (which is consistent with the neuter gender of its second member), but a few attestations of its use as a masculine noun exist (see §4.4 and some of the Samarāṅgaṇa-sūtradhāra passages in §5.7, if they have not come down to us in a corrupt form). In either case, its forms should not be confused with the avy *pratyaṅgam* (see §2.8, §2.15). Despite the inconvenient semantic gap or jump involved, *ptg* has become an avy-based noun meaning 'each limb, all limbs' (§5.9). But this has happened only in later Sanskrit, that is, after about the seventh century A.D. (assuming the present dating of the relevant texts does not change). At about the same time the 'pratyaṅga = antar-aṅga' understanding finds articulation in the Pāṇinian tradition.

§3.8 The conclusions drawn and the method followed in §§3.1–7 suggest that the explanations of *ptg* offered by Pat's commentators were a result of (a) working under the influence of *prati* avys, (b) making semantic extensions on the basis of the lists of aṅgas and pratyaṅgas that were available in well-known texts dealing with human and other animate bodies, (c) guessing by studying the contexts carefully and (d) having no access to an older meaning of the word. Since the preceding sections and §5.4–10 already contain the evidence and arguments favoring (a)–(c), I will now only deal with (d). What could have been the older meaning? Do we have signs of its having been lost or its having been nearly lost, so that the MB commentators' lack of awareness becomes probable? Does the older and so far unearthed meaning enable us to make a consistent sense of the relevant MB passages?

[55]Molesworth (1857: 6) explains *aṅga-pratyaṅga* as "The body and its members, the whole body." In my view, 'every part of the body, including each little part' would bring out the sense better.

External evidence for ptg as 'like aṅga'

§4.1 The very literal or etymological meaning of *ptg* can be either ('that which stands on a side other than the one on which aṅga stands', 'that which can come to the position of aṅga but has not done so' →) 'that which is opposed to aṅga' or 'that which is like an aṅga but not quite an aṅga'.

The meaning 'that which is opposed to aṅga' does not agree with the uses of *ptg* collected in this essay. There is no suggestion in any of them that *ptg* was the opposite or contrary of *aṅga*, but there is ample suggestion that *ptg* denoted apposite or agreeing entities on the other side.

The model present in the formation of *ptg*, then, should be thought of as coming from the following group of nouns, some of which may be older than *ptg* and some later: *pratikarkaśa* 'equally hard or rough'; *pratikr̥ti* 'replica, image, copy'; *pratigraha* 'acceptance', *pratinidhi* 'replacement, substitute'; *pratiṣṭhāna* (as a town name) 'station, stable place (of a ruler)'; compare *pratyadhiṣṭhāna*, *pratirājadhānī*), *pratyadhidevatā* 'tutelary deity'; *pratyamitra* 'enemy'; *pratyanantara* 'immediate'; *pratyandhakāra* 'shadow, darkness'; *pratyanta* 'end, border'; *pratyarka* 'second/mock sun, parhelion'; *pratyāśā* 'hope, aspiration'. (The preceding is not an exhaustive list; many more examples can be found in Böhtlingk-&-Roth, Apte, Monier-Williams and Wackernagel).

Some of these examples may be disputable or explicable in more than one way (recall that *pratibimba* can be 'bimba (orb) on the other side' or 'a thing similar to bimba'). Still, there will be enough of them left to prove that a class of *prati* words of the described kind exists. This class has been recognized through words such as *sādr̥śya* for several hundred years (§3.3). It is characterized by the fact that its members have a meaning that is very similar to the meaning of the word without *prati* or have a meaning of the type 'resembling X', 'virtually the same as X', 'counterpart in the second-order set' etc., in which X stands for the denotatum of the part after *prati*. (Contrast: *praty-anīka* 'army on the other side, enemy army', *praty-anumāna* 'opposite inference, contrary conclusion' etc.).

In some cases, the originally existing distinctive meaning can be quite plausibly posited; e.g. *pratyadhidevatā* 'tutelary deity' could come from 'next presiding deity, a deity that comes as a replacement for one of the great gods'; *pratyamitra* 'enemy' from 'one close to the recognized enemy, collaborator of an enemy'.

The distinctive meanings could have been gradually lost. Historical explanations other than the ones I have thought of can, of course, be offered, but that does not mean that a meaning transformation did not take place or that the attested meaning similar to the meaning of the word without *prati* did not exist. The crucial consideration is that, unless an original distinctive meaning is presumed, there would be no explanation of why a *prati*-prefixed word came into being when a *prati*-less word was already there to express the same idea. Living languages generally do not have perfect synonymy. If they have it, it is quite limited and arises out of historical and cultural causes. Therefore, the synonymy that is attested can be very old, but it cannot be the very first stage in the semantics of words like *pratikarkaśa* and *pratikṛti*.

'Non-conflict with or dependence on the denotatum of the compound member following *prati*' or 'being complementary to something thought to be already existing' is an element that is noticed in the primary-level employment of *ptg* as pointed out in §3.6. Even when Yāska uses *ptg* metaphorically to speak of the individual Vedic gods as parts of the Great ātman in the passage cited in §4.6 below, the commentators Durga and Skanda-&-Maheśvara tell us, respectively, *na cāṅgāny anapekṣya pratyaṅgāni bhavanti* and *aṅgāny apekṣya pratyaṅgam.* Another metaphorical use of *ptg* in texts of architecture such as the Samarāṅgaṇa-sūtradhāra (§5.7), likewise, leads the specialists to understand the word as 'moulding', an object that complements the pillar bases etc.[56]

[56](a) Cf. Acharya (1927: 368) explains *ptg* as 'a minor limb' and 'a moulding of the entablature'. Of this, 'minor limb' seems to be in deference to the general Sanskrit-English dictionaries of Acharya's time. These dictionaries, as shown in this essay, would have been more justified in using "nearby / deeper / subtler limb" instead of "minor."

(b) Sudarshan Kumar Sharma (2007), whose translation of the Samarāṅgaṇa-sūtradhāra is full of problems, translates *ptg* sometimes with 'quarter position of the roof' and sometimes with 'each limb'. The sources he refers to under 57.19 and on p. 151 for the former meaning are anything but clear. He shows no awareness of the meaning given by Acharya, his well-known predecessor in the study of Indian architecture.

(c) In architecture, other similarly expressive words are: *pratipaṭṭa* 'a moulding of the entablature', *pratimukha* 'a moulding of the base', *prativaktra* 'a moulding of the band', and *prativājana* 'a moulding of the cavetti' (cf. Acharya 1934: 365). Meister-&-Dhaky (1983 vol 1.1: 292; 1986 vol 1.2: 241) add *pratibhadra* 'wall projection between bhadra and karṇa parts, flanking bhadra', 'subdivision in plan and elevation adjoining the bhadra', *pratikaṇṭha* 'kaṇṭha with prati moulding above', and *pratikarṇa* 'wall projection flanking karṇa'. The same two scholars explain *prativājana* as 'oversailing rectilinear fillet'.

(d) Probably *pratiśraya* 'a shelter-house for travelers' also had at its root a sense like 'a dwelling which complements the regular dwelling'.

(e) Acharya (1934: 366) and Meister-Dhaky (1983 vol 1.1: 292 and 1986: vol 1.2: 241) would be correct in thinking of *prati* as a separable noun meaning 'moulding' or 'plank-moulding' if the word is used by itself. It may, however, be the case that they have misread the grammatical relation or nature of *prati*, although they determined its meaning correctly.

§4.2 As for the evidence that directly pertains to my particular concern in this essay, I will proceed in two steps. I will first cite passages in which a meaning that is in keeping with §4.1 is rather easy to see. Then I will take up passages in which the commentators come across as perplexed or inaccurate but can be helped by pointing out a meaning along the lines in §4.1. The very fact that the freshly suggested meaning gives us a contextually suitable and straightforward interpretation will mean that that meaning is correct. In both steps, I will take up for discussion the relevant passages in the Roman alphabetical order of the titles of texts from which they come.

Bhaviṣya-purāṇa 1.52.12–20, Brahmāṇḍa-purāṇa 1.22.66–70, Matsya-purāṇa 125.42–44ab and Vāyu-purāṇa 1.51.59–66: These passages can be thought of as constituting one passage. The similarity of content and wording in them is such that one has no alternative to concluding that they come from a common source. (This common source may be the earliest Purāṇa among them or a source that has so far not come to our attention.) For this reason, I will quote the complete text from only one Purāṇa, and only the lines containing *ptg* from the remaining.

> Brahmāṇḍa-purāṇa 1.22.66–70: *athaitāni tu sūryasya pratyaṅgāni rathasya ha // saṁvatsarasyāvayavaiḥ kalpitasya yathā-kramam / ahas tu nābhiḥ saurasya eka-cakrasya vai smr̥taḥ // arāḥ pañcārtavāṁs [→ pañcartavas = pañca r̥tavas?] tasya nemiḥ ṣaḍ r̥tavaḥ smr̥tāḥ / ratha-nīḍaḥ smr̥to hy eṣa cāyane kūbarāv ubhau // muhūrtā bandhurās tasya ramyāś cāsya kalāḥ smr̥tāḥ / tasya kāṣṭhā smr̥tā ghoṇā akṣa-daṇḍaḥ kṣaṇas tu vai // nimeṣaś cānukarṣo 'sya hīṣā cāsya lavāḥ smr̥tāḥ / rātrir varūtho dharmo 'sya dhvaja ūrdhva samucchritaḥ //*
>
> Bhaviṣya-purāṇa, Brāhma-parvan, adhyāya 52, verses 15–20: *athaitāni tu sūryasya pratyaṅgāni rathasya tu // saṁvatsarasyāvyavaiḥ kalpitāni yathā-kramam //*
>
> Matsya-purāṇa 125.42–44ab: *athāṅgāni tu sūryasya pratyaṅgāni rathasya ca /*
>
> Vāyu-purāṇa 1.51.59–66 (= prakriyā-pāda, adhyāya 51, verses 59–66): *athemāni tu sūryasya pratyaṅgāni rathasya tu /*[57]

The verses spell out the parallelism between the chariot of the Sun and the year. They constitute an extended metaphor, based on the notion that the Sun god crosses the expanse of the sky in a chariot. Several parts of the chariot have been identified with abstract entities mostly based on divisions of time. It is these abstract entities that have been collectively referred to

[57] *kampitāni* for *kalpitāni* in the Anandashrama Sanskrit Series edn is obviously an error.

as pratyaṅgas. Therefore, *ptg* must have the sense 'corresponding things on the other side (namely, the side of the upamāna)'.

§4.3

> Brahmāṇḍa-purāṇa 1.32.44–60: *pratyaṅgāni ca vakṣyāmi dharmasyeha tu lakṣaṇam //* After describing what constitutes satya, tapas etc.: *pratyaṅgānāṁ tu dharmasya tv ity etal lakṣaṇaṁ smṛtam //*
>
> Matsya-purāṇa 145.40: *pratyaṅgāni pravakṣyāmi dharmasyeha tu lakṣaṇam //* Conclusion in 145.55: *pratyaṅgāni tu dharmasya cety-etal lakṣaṇaṃ smṛtam /*
>
> Vāyu-purāṇa 1.59.39: *pratyaṅgāni tu vakṣyāmi dharmasyeha tu lakṣaṇam.* Then satya, tapas etc. are described. Conclusion in 1.59.55: *pratyaṅgānāṁ tu dharmasya ity etal lakṣaṇaṁ smṛtam /*

The rhetorical device or trope used here is the same as the one mentioned in §4.2. Again, we have a passage shared by the same Purāṇas. Dharma is personified. What it is said to have are called pratyaṅgas consisting, again, of abstract entities: truth, practice of austerities etc. In other words, the constituents of religio-spiritual practice are spoken of as entities similar to the aṅgas of a person. The metaphor is there, without any insistence on having a one-to-one correspondence.

§4.4

> Mahābhārata 1.1.178: *mahā-purāṇaḥ saṁbhāvyaḥ pratyaṅgaḥ parahā śrutiḥ.*

This piece of textual evidence is not as explicit or direct as the pieces I have mentioned above or below. However, it is not so roundabout either as not to deserve a mention. It contains a list of the descendants of Raivata Manu. Why would a descendant in a royal family be named *ptg*? The idea could have been that this son looked like or was expected to be a replica of his father or an earlier ancestor (cf. Kālidāsa, Raghu-vaṁśa 5.34–37: *pravartito dīpa iva pradīpāt*; compare usages such as "chip of the old block" and "Like father, like son"). Probably, the person who chose the name had to do nothing more than change the neuter gender to the masculine gender so that it would fit a male. The similitude-based understanding must have been already there.

§4.5

> Mīmāṁsā-sūtra 6.6.15: *pāṇeḥ pratyaṅga-bhāvād* (→ °*ga-bhūtatvād*, Śabara's reading) *asaṁbandhaḥ pratīyeta.*

The context is formed by the question, "What is the meaning of *rāja-purohitau* in *etena rāja-purohitau sāyujya-kāmau yajeyātām* specified in the case of the kulāya sacrificial worship? Does the word mean 'two priests of the king' or 'the king and the priest'?" The pūrva-pakṣa argues that the former should be the meaning. In *añjalinā juhoti* only one person's palms are taken as forming the añjali 'folded or cupped palms'. The singular number indicated in the form *añjalinā* is taken seriously. The same way the dual in *rāja-purohitau* should be honored.

Against this, the uttara-pakṣin points out that strict conformity with grammar is justified in the context in which the sentence *añjalinā juhoti* occurs. One cannot have an añjali without bringing the two palms of a single individual together. However, when in the kulāya context the scripture prescribes the participation of both the king and his priest in the act of offering, it is not necessary that the two should form a single añjali. The Mīmāṁsā-sūtra quoted above points out the difference caused by the consideration 'one cannot have an añjali without bringing the two palms of a single individual together'. Therefore, what *pratyaṅga-bhūta* in that text should convey is this: 'The left hand has already taken a supportive role with respect to the right hand; there would be no añjali that the Vedic sentence mentions if the two hands are not involved jointly'.

Bhāṣyakāra Śabara's comment makes this intent of the discussion clear, but the editors of the edns accessible to me do not seem to have paid adequate attention to what his wording should be. They print the relevant sentences as *añjaliṁ pratyaṅga-bhūto dakṣiṇasya pāṇeḥ savyaḥ pāṇiḥ. tena vinā añjalir eva na bhavati. na hi dvābhyāṁ dakṣiṇābhyām añjaliḥ iti ucyate.* Here, if we read *pratyaṅga-bhūto* as two words (*praty* and *aṅga-bhūto*), we will have correct grammar with respect to the accusative *añjalim*, but our move will clash with the phrase *pāṇeḥ pratyaṅga-bhāvāt* (/°*-ṅga-bhūtatvāt*) in Jaimini's sūtra. There, the genitive *pāṇeḥ* will not go well with *prati*. If, for this reason, we abandon the thought of splitting *pratyaṅga*° in Śabara's phrase *añjaliṁ pratyaṅga-bhūtaḥ*, the word *añjalim* in that phrase will remain dangling. What the editors should have noticed is that another *prati* is necessary to make the bhāṣya statement grammatically unproblematic without creating a clash with the sūtra wording: *añjaliṁ [prati] pratyaṅga-bhūto dakṣiṇasya pāṇeḥ savyaḥ pāṇiḥ* "In regard to folded palms (that is, as far as the detail 'folded palms' is concerned), the left palm has (already) become a pratyaṅga of the right palm." The first, uncompounded, *prati* could easily have been lost due to haplography in the mss, the press copy of the edn or the compositor's work. Restoring it not only gives us a smoother construction but also tells us that the meaning of *ptg* intended by Jaimini and Śabara at Mīmāṁsā-sūtra 6.6.15 must have been something like 'contributing, co-participant, complementary', not 'opposing, contrary'.[58]

§4.6

> Nirukta 7.3 (= 7.4 in the edn with Skanda-&-Maheśvara's comm): *māhābhāgyād devatāyā eka ātmā bahudhā stūyata, ekasyātmano 'nye devāḥ pratyaṅgāni bhavanti.*

Sarup translates these sentences as follows: "On account of the supereminence of the deity, a single soul is praised in various ways. Other gods are the individual limbs of a single soul." While essentially correct, this translation can be made more useful to a contemporary reader by using "self/Self" in the place of "soul." More importantly, something like 'representations', 'likenesses' or 'intimations' will be better as a translation of *pratyaṅgāni*. Laudations are more likely to be spoken of as directed toward an entity that can resemble or remind of the Great Divine Self and are less likely to be spoken of as having parts of that Self as their objects. The oneness of the pratyaṅgas (and therefore of the aṅgas)[59] with the Great Divine Self that is stated in the commentaries of Durga and Skanda-&-Maheśvara points in the same direction. Both commentators play down the potential in *ptg* to mean 'a part' or 'a smaller part':

> Durga: ***māhābhāgyād ekasya devatātma****naḥ prakṛti-bhedena vāprakṛti-bhedena veti. cetanācetana-vikaraṇa-dharmitvād ātmānaṁ vikurvato 'sya anye* ***devāḥ pratyaṅgāni bhavanti****. agnīndra-sūryāṇāṁ parasparāpekṣam anyatvam, ananyatvam tv ekena devatātmanā mahatā saha, yathā ghaṭādīnāṁ mṛdā. na*

[58]Another way of solving the textual problem would be to accept the reading *añjalau* in the place of *añjaliṁ*. The Bibliotheca Indica edn notes this reading. Swami Kevalānanda ((p. I.187) accepts it in his Mīmāṁsā-koṣa. If in a critical edn of the Śābara-bhāṣya this reading turns out to be objectively strong, we would have no need for the emendation mentioned above. It would not affect the suggested sense of *ptg* ('contributory toward (the entity called) folded palms'). However, there is a possibility that *añjalau* itself could have come into existence as a reading because the problem I have pointed out with regard to the current reading in the edns was felt.

[59]Cf. the passage from Durga cited immediately below. He realizes that a mention of pratyaṅga without aṅga would be rather odd. Therefore, he supplies the link that may have been presumed by Yāska. The (major devas) Agni, Indra, Sūrya who figure in yāgas are the aṅgas of the supreme reality, the Great ātman, while (the other devas such as) Jātavedas, Vāyu and Bhaga or (extraordinary) birds, horses etc. that are aspects of the (major devas) function as pratyaṅgas.

> *hy aṅginam aṅgāny atiricyante bhedenāgrahaṇāt. na cāṅgāny anapekṣya pratyaṅgāni bhavanti. na hy adhiṣṭhānam anapekṣya pratyadhiṣṭhānaṁ nāma bhavati. tasmād agnīndra-sūryā ekasya devatātmano 'ṅgāni, jāta-vedo-vāyu-bhaga-prabhṛtīni śakuny-aśva-prabhṛtayaś ca pratyaṅgāni. sa eṣa mahān ātmā agnīndra-sūryādy-aṅga-pratyaṅga-bhāvena vyūham anubhavann eko 'pi san* ***bahudhā stūyate.***

Here, particularly useful for our present concern is the remark: *na cāṅgāny anapekṣya pratyaṅgāni bhavanti. na hy adhiṣṭhānam anapekṣya pratyadhiṣṭhānaṁ nāma bhavati.* Clearly Durga sees *pratyaṅga* as implying aṅga and the '*aṅga* : *pratyaṅga*' distinction as paralleling the '*adhiṣṭhāna* : *pratyadhiṣṭhāna*' distinction. The second word in the second pair has rightly been noted in our dictionaries as agreeing in meaning with the first word of the pair; that is, no significant difference has been seen between *adhiṣṭhāna* and *pratyadhiṣṭhāna*. The role of *ptg*, therefore, should also not be that of an antonym.

> Skanda-&-Maheśvara: *etasmād eva ca kāraṇād mahābhāga-lakṣaṇād [māhābhāgya-la° ?]* ***ekasya devtātmano 'nye devāḥ pratyaṅgāni bhavanti****. aṅgāny eva* ***pratyaṅgāni****. athavā aṅgāny apekṣya pratyaṅgam. hastādīny aṅgam. aṅgulyādīni pratyaṅgam. anena vāṅga-pratyaṅga-bhāvā... riktāni*[60] */ evam* ***eka****smād* ***devatātm****ano 'nye devā avyatiriktā ity abhiprāyaḥ. ... na ca kevala-devatātmana [→ °valaṁ de°] eva* ***māhābhāgyād anye devāḥ pratyaṅgāni bhavanti****. kiṁ tarhi? [****api ca sattvānāṁ prakṛti-bhūmabhir ṛṣayaḥ stuvantīty āhuḥ****] api ca sattvānām anye devāḥ pratyaṅgāni bhavanti. yat-prakṛter devatātma-bhūtāyā ye bhūmānas tair bhūmabhir mahattvair ity arthaḥ. ṛṣayo mantrāḥ "dyaus te pṛṣṭham"* [Maitrāyaṇi-saṁhitā 2.72.2] *ity-ādayaḥ.*[61]

---

[60]Sarup's ms. C reads °*na cāṅga-pratyaṅgābhā... riktāni evam ...* He suggests that we should read the sentence as *anena cāṅga-pratyaṅga-bhāvātmanā yathā hastādīny aṅgulyādīni cāvyatiriktāni.* He seems right about reading *ca* as the second word instead of *vā* and *bhāva-* as the end of the third word. In the rest, however, he has proceeded only by asking what the context requires and has not wondered if the words chosen fit Skanda-&-Maheśvara's style or why they are likely to be lost (if there is any reason such as haplography that would make their loss probable).

[61]Sarup should have printed the text in the following way: *kiṁ tarhi ...* ***api ca sattvānāṁ*** *... yat-****prakṛt****er devatātma-bhūtāyā ye bhūmānas tair* ***bhūmabhir*** *mahattvair ity arthaḥ.* ***ṛṣayo*** *mantrāḥ* [the rest as in his edn]. The sentence *anye devāḥ pratyaṅgāni bhavanti* is an instance of redundant writing. It was not

As can be seen, the text of Skanda-&-Maheśvara's comm is not as well-preserved as Durga's. Nor is it as specific as Durga's in identifying what is aṅga and what is pratyaṅga in the Devatā context. Yet it is clear in asserting avyatiriktatva 'non-separation'.

§4.7

> Skanda-purāṇa 7.1.11.88–89ab: *tataḥ pitr̥-gr̥haṁ gantuṁ kr̥ta-buddhir yaśasvinī / chāyāmayīm ātma-tanuṁ pratyaṅgam iva nirmitām // saṁmukhaṁ prekṣya tāṁ devīṁ svāṁ chāyāṁ vākyam abravīt //*

Tagare's tr of the six-quarter verse is: "After deciding to go to her father's house, the lady of great renown looked at her own reflection (Chāyā), which appeared to be made similar to her in every limb. Seeing that divine being in front of her, her own Chāyā, she spoke these words." Here, the translation of *pratyaṅgam iva nirmitām* with "which appeared to be made similar to her in every limb" either turns an utprekṣā (the trope 'fancy') into an upamā (the trope simile) or makes *iva* do 'double duty' as 'appeared' and 'similar'. Further, the translation requires that the noun *ātma-tanum* be understood as a tame adjective meaning 'similar to her' and does not do justice to the fact that the phrase *pratyaṅgam iva nirmitām* constitutes a pāda by itself. Taking *ptg* as a noun meaning 'a duplicate body, close likeness' would remove these blemishes and enable us to translate the verse in a manner closer to the original: "Then the renowned (Saṁjñā), who had made up her mind to go (back) to her father's/parents' house, after seeing her own body in front—a body consisting of reflection/shadow,[62] created like a replica[63]—said this to that divine/lustrous reflection/shadow of herself."

---

necessary to add the whole Nirukta sentence *api . . . āhuḥ* in brackets. Remnants of it are already there in the mss of Skanda-&-Maheśvara's commentary.

[62]A reflection is more likely to show the closeness of the original and the new creation. However, since there is no mention in the preceding verses of Saṁjñā's looking into a reflecting substance and she is spoken of as being in the company of the Sun, the translation of *chāyā* as 'shadow' should not be ruled out.

[63]Grammatically, the phrase can also be translated as 'as if created/crafted in every limb'. This would preserve the utprekṣā trope, but will not give us an expression that makes a significant or particularly appropriate addition to the meaning of *chāyāmayīm ātma-tanum*.

§4.8

> Tri-bhāṣya-ratna comm on Taittirīya Prātiśākhya 1.34 (Whitney edn p. 29): *"anusvāraḥ svara-bhaktiś ca"* [Taittirīya Prātiśākhya 21.6] *iti svara-pratyaṅgatva-vidhānād anusvārasya vyañjanatvam.*[64]
>
> "Since the sūtra "*anusvāraḥ svara-bhaktiś ca*" lays down that the anusvāra is a pratyaṅga of vowels, the (original) character of the anusvāra must be that of a consonant."

Unless *ptg* had the sense of amenability, this remark of the author of the Tri-bhāṣya-ratna comm would not make sense. The argument contained in the remark is: 'If the anusvāra were a vowel to begin with in the view of the Sūtrakāra, he would not qualify it as a pratyaṅga of the (preceding) vowel. That he does so indicates that the anusvāra by itself is not a vowel—that it is a consonant, that it has the properties of a consonant.' If *ptg* did not mean 'the similar other', the commentator's argument would not work.

§4.9

> Tri-bhāṣya-ratna comm on Taittirīya Prātiśākhya 21.1: *vyañjanaṁ kevalam avasthātuṁ na śaknoti, kiṁ tu sāpekṣam. svaras tu nirapekṣaḥ. sāpekṣa-nirapekṣayor nirapekṣaṁ eva viśiṣṭam ācakṣate prekṣāvantaḥ. viśiṣṭa-pratyaṅgatvam aviśiṣṭasyaiva.*
>
> Tr.: "A consonant cannot remain in existence by itself; it can so remain only in dependence (that is, only when it is followed by a

[64](a) For this occurrence of *pratyaṅgatva*, Monier-Williams (p. 663) gives the reference as Taittirīya Prātiśākhya 1.34 and includes it in his second group, the one in which he is concerned with *ptg* as an avy. Actually, the reference should be to the commentary on the Taittirīya Prātiśākhya, and *ptg* should be treated as a noun; *-tva* cannot be added when *prati aṅga* is taken as an avy-forming combination. If it is added, a meaning like 'the state of being each limb/part' can be assigned to the word, but that meaning will not fit the context as the part 'the belonging to (each base)' in Monier-Williams's own rendering °§3.9) suggests. There will also be redundancy in 'state' and 'being'.

(b) The Tri-bhāṣya-ratna author's discussion under the sūtra 21.6 which it quotes (Whitney edn p. 382) mentions that an anusvāra becomes an aṅga of the preceding vowel, whereas a svara-bhakti can be found as an aṅga of the preceding as well as of the following. To substantiate the latter situation, he refers to an instance outside the Taittirīya Saṁhitā. To accommodate that rare instance, he suggests that sūtra 21.6 should be split as *anusvāraḥ* and *svara-bhaktiś ca*. However he does not actually split it. He comments on it the way it is. The discussion is a very good instance of how observant the commentators were of variations within the Vedic texts and how they tried to provide sanction for the variation without tampering with a received sūtra text.

> vowel). A vowel, on the other hand, has no (similar) dependence. The observant ones declare that, between a dependent one and an independent one, only the independent one has excellence. Only the one without excellence can become a pratyaṅga of that which has excellence."[65]

The variations seen in the mss of the Taittirīya Prātiśākhya comm Tri-bhāṣya-ratna indicate uncertainty about *ptg* as a single nominal stem (see Whitney edn p. 29 fn 3 to the text in fn 34; p. 376 fn 9 to the text in continued fn 1); *svarapratyaṅga°* appears as *svaraṁ pratyaṅga°* and *viśiṣṭapratyaṅga°* appears as *viśiṣṭaṁ pratyaṅga°*, which can be accommodated only by splitting *pratyaṅga* as *praty aṅga°*. The Bibliotheca Indica edn of the Taittirīya Prātiśākhya, in fact, accepts these readings under 1.34 as well as 21.1 (I have discussed the former in §4.8).

The uncertainty must be due to inability to make a contextually proper sense of the word. Once the logic of the last remark in the Tri-bhāṣya-ratna is understood, *ptg* should not present a problem. That remark clearly implies or presupposes that two excellences cannot go together (something like 'We cannot paint a painted surface well until we remove the first paint'). That which has excellence can take only a non-excelling one as its pratyaṅga. The meaning of *ptg*, then, must be 'something that is compatible, something which goes well with the aṅga'.

§4.10 Cases in which a less problematic or totally unproblematic interpretation results after *ptg* is taken in the 'agreeing other' sense I am advocating are the following:

> Bhāgavata-purāṇa 3.1.23: *anyāni ceha dvija-deva-devaiḥ kr̥tāni nānāyatanāni viṣṇoḥ / pratyaṅga-mukhyāṅkita-mandirāṇi yad-darśanāt kr̥ṣṇam anusmaranti //*

Śrīdhara-svāmin, the most commonly studied commentator of the Bhāgavata, takes *ptg* as āyudha 'weapon'.[66] Following him, Böhtlingk-&-Roth

[65]Whitney's paraphrase, which is as close to the original as a translation would be, is essentially the same: "...a consonant is incapable of standing alone, and so is dependent, while a vowel is independent; ...between a dependent and an independent, the enlightened regard the independent as superior; and it belongs to the inferior to be adjunct to the superior."

[66]Sridhara, Bhāvārtha-dīpikā 3.1.23: ***dvija-devair*** *r̥ṣibhir* ***devaiś*** *ca* ***kr̥tāni,*** *aṅgam āṅgaṁ prati vartante iti* ***pratyaṅgāny*** *āyudhāni, teṣu* ***mukhyaṁ*** *cakraṁ, tenā****ṅkitāni*** *mūrdhanya-hema-kumbheṣu cihnitāni* ***mandirāṇi*** *yeṣu tāni nānā-vidhāni viṣṇor* ***āyatanāni*** *kṣetrāṇi tīrthāni cāsiṣeve. yeṣāṁ cakrāṅkita-mandiravatāṁ* ***darśanāc.*** *chrī-****kr̥ṣṇa-smara****ṇaṁ bhavati.*

and Monier-Williams gave 'Waffe' and 'weapon' as meanings of *ptg* in their dictionaries (cf. §3.5). In relatively recent times, we come across translations such as the following (N. Raghunathan 1976: 127): "And he [= Kṣattṛ, Vidura] made a pilgrimage to the many temples dedicated by the sages and the gods to Vishnu and marked by the sign of his principal weapon (the discus), which puts men in mind of Krishna."

However, there is no corroboration of this meaning in any of the other occurrences of *ptg*, and there is nothing in the Bhāgavata context that would warrant a sudden reference, specific or general, to what Viṣṇu carries on his body. While there is a tradition of personifying Viṣṇu's/Kṛṣṇa's weapons, there is no evidence that these weapons were referred to as *pratyaṅgas* or that there were temples carrying only their images, whether they be mukhya ('chief, principal') or undistinguished (cf. Gail 1980–1981). Even Śrīdhara-svāmin is required to add that the cakra, which he takes as the reference of *pratyaṅga-mukhya*, was carved on the golden jars placed on top of the temples.

A. C. Bhaktivedanta (1972: 23) probably realized one or more of these reasons and replaced "weapon" with "emblem" when he translated the verse as: "There were also many other temples of various forms of the Supreme Personality of Godhead Viṣṇu, established by great sages and demigods. These temples were marked with the chief emblems of the Lord, and they reminded one always of the original Personality of Godhead, Lord Kṛṣṇa."

However, it would be more justifiable, especially in view of the evidence we have collected, to take *pratyaṅga-mukhyāṅkita-mandirāṇi*, which is an adjective of *āyatanāni*, in the sense 'in which the buildings were marked with the likenesses of Viṣṇu (or of his incarnations)'. In §4.7 above, we have an attestation in Skanda-purāṇa of *ptg* in the sense of 'replication, image'. Furthermore, the occurrence of *ptg* in an old sense would agree with the frequently made observation that the Bhāgavata author has a far-reaching vocabulary and an extraordinary ability to compose in an archaic style.

§4.11

> Manu 8.208: *yasmin karmaṇi yās tu syur uktāḥ pratyaṅga-dakṣiṇāḥ / sa eva tā ādadīta bhajeran sarva eva vā //*

Patrick Olivelle translates this as follows: "At a ritual where sacrificial fees are specified for each component, the priest performing a given component should receive the specified fee or all should share the entire fee."

As Olivelle (2005: 316) states, most commentators seem to have missed the intent of this Manu verse:

Medhātithi: *tatra ca keṣucid ajarya-karmasu pratipadam anyā dakṣiṇāmnātā puruṣa-viśeṣa-saṁyogena "hiraṇmaye prakāśavad avayava"* [= source?] *ityādi. tāḥ pratyaṅga-dakṣiṇāḥ saṁpadyante. kim adhvaryoś cāturvidyāvādikavad dadāti-saṁbandhaḥ, sarveṣām ṛtvijāṁ dakṣiṇā, adhvaryus tu dvāra-mātram, uta **tāś** caiva sāmānyā [= **tāḥ** sarva-sā°?], anyeṣāṁ prakṛta evāṁśaḥ? saṁśayopanyāsārthaḥ ślokaḥ. **pratipadaṁ** puruṣa-viśeṣāśrayā **aṅgeṣu** dakṣiṇāḥ pratyaṅga-dakṣiṇāḥ. athavā vīpsāyāṁ pratyaṅga-śabdaḥ. aṅgam aṅgam āśritāḥ **pratyaṅgāḥ**. sa eṣa tā ādadīta. mukhya eva puruṣasya dadātinā saṁyoge uttara-kartṛtvāviśeṣād [→ ?] anye 'pi **bhajeraṁl** labheran, pradhāna-**dakṣiṇāyā*** [something like *aṁśam* 'part' missing?] *iva.*

Sarvajña-nārāyaṇa: ***pratyaṅga-dakṣiṇāḥ** pratisvaṁ karmaṇāṁ dakṣiṇāḥ. **sa eva vādadīta**, yam ṛtvijaṁ prati yathodyate. sarve **bhajeran** yatrartvig-viśeṣānuktiḥ.*

Kullūka: ***yasmin karmaṇy** ādhānādāv aṅgam aṅgaṁ prati yā **dakṣiṇā** yat-saṁbandhena śrutāḥ syuḥ, **sa eva tā ādadīta**, na tat-tad-bhāga-mātraṁ sarve vibhajya gṛhṇīrann iti saṁśayaḥ.*

Rāghavānanda: *dakṣiṇā-prasaṅgena tad-vibhāgam āha **yasminn** iti dvābhyām. ādhānādau **pratyaṅga-dakṣiṇāḥ** aṅgam aṅgaṁ prati yā bhinna-bhinna-kārikā [= °kālikā?] dakṣiṇā yat-saṁbandhena śrutā "hotram"* [source?] *ity-ādinā samākhyātaḥ, **sa evartvik tāḥ** sarvāḥ prāpnuyād uta sarve veti saṁśaye. **sa eveti** pūrva-pakṣe.*

Nandana: ***sa eva** tasya karmaṇaḥ.*[67]

Rāma-candra. ***yasmin karmaṇi yāḥ pratyaṅga**-karma-**dakṣiṇā uktāḥ syus tā dakṣiṇāḥ sa eva** puruṣa **ādadīta. sarva eva vā bhajeran vā** [→ eva vibha°? **bhajeran** vibhajeran?].*[68]

---

[67] Whether Nandana left the verse essentially uncommented or the ms of his comm that the editor used was incomplete cannot be determined.

[68] (a) If the *vā* at the end of the sentence is not to be redundant, the wording here should be either as shown above, with a change of *vā* to *vi*, or ***bhajeran** vibhajeran*, in which first a word is cited from the commentandum and then glossed. The cited word could have been lost later due to haplography.

(b) Rāma-candra offers no real comment except for the addition of *karma* after *pratyaṅga*.

Govinda-rāja: ***yasmin karmaṇi*** *ādhānāgnau aṅgam* ***aṅgaṁ*** *prati* ***yā dakṣiṇāś*** *ca uditāḥ [→ °ṇāś coditāḥ?]* ***syuḥ***, *yathā-rabdham [→ yathā "ratham] adhvaryum"* [cited from a Vedic text; cf. next Manu verse] *ity-ādau, pradhāna-dakṣiṇāś ca gāvo deyāḥ, ādinā kiyat [→?] uddeśena [→* ***ādadīteti*** *yad-uddeśena?] śrūyante* ***sa eva*** *śrutatvāt svī-kuryāt. atha parṣadvārikāvat [→ °ṣad-dvā°?* cp. *dvāra-mātram* in Medhātithi.*] pratigraha-mātrā-vyāparāt* ***sarva eva*** *uditaḥ iti [→ evādadīteti?] saṁdehe upanyāsaḥ. avaśyatvāt* [= because the Śruti says so and one cannot go against the Śruti?] *tādarthya-pakṣam āśritya nirṇayam āha* ***ratham*** *iti* [= next Manu verse: *rathaṁ hareta cādhvaryur, brahmādhāne ca vājinam / hotā vāpi hared aśvam, udgātā cāpy anaḥ kraye //*]

If the verse is to have a proper syntax, the *saḥ* in quarter 'c' should refer back to what *ptg* denotes, that is, it should be a reference to a person, not to a part of the sacrifice or rite (or to each component as in Olivelle's translation). In the context furnished by the remaining words and the verses nearby, this person should be one who is like the regular rite performers (hotṛ, adhvaryu etc.) but is not one of them. The compound *pratyaṅga-dakṣiṇāḥ* should then mean 'the sacrificial fees of a pratyaṅga', that is, 'the sacrificial fees associated with, meant for a pratyaṅga'. Consequently, the meaning of *ptg* would be 'an almost expected member, a co-opted member, a non-regular but necessary associate in a particular rite'. Given the complexity of the rites, the assistance of specialists must have been required from time to time. Ages and physical limitations of the senior performers may also have occasionally necessitated that they assign the performance of certain ritual actions to knowledgeable and able-bodied junior colleagues.

Apart from the syntactic argument, there is also the consideration that there would be no need of saying—nothing would be gained by saying, that a particular priest performing a particular part should get the fee mentioned for that part. If the fee is prescribed for a part, it will naturally follow that the performer of that part should get it. On the other hand, it would be devoid of justification and unfair to say that the fee of a part performer should be distributed among all performers. It would have been another matter if the statement had a wording to the effect that, *even though* the fees are mentioned for a part performer, all the performers should get them—that a group distribution should take place. But such is not the wording of Manu's statement.

In what I consider to be the proper interpretation, Manu knows the situations in which an additional person (probably a specialist of an uncommon sub-rite) takes part in the performance of a rite. If no fee is mentioned for his contribution to the rite, it will follow that he is not paid any fee or he gets whatever fee the yajamāna deems right. If, however, a fee is mentioned in the authoritative scripture, either he alone is paid that fee (and the statement in the scripture is honored in the best possible way, without resorting to any secondary meaning) or he gets it along with the other (regular) officiating priests (and a recognition is shown of the fact that they had not stopped contributing to the performance of the rite when the additional specialist or helper entered the performance scene).

§4.12 In both instances, the problems the commentators felt disappear (and no need to force a connection of Manu 8.208 with Manu 8.209 in a substantial way remains) when the understanding of *ptg* is changed. Thus, the proposal made in the context of Pat's MB is not only supported positively by several other *prati*-words and more than eight occurrences of *ptg* itself in relatively early works (or early parts of certain works) but also negatively by at least two passages in which it serves to remove the element of puzzlement, desperation or arbitrariness present in traditional commentaries. The question that now arises is whether the meaning I have proposed is likely to have remained unknown to Jinendra-buddhi (note 16) and the MB commentators like Kaiyaṭa.

I have already observed that it was natural to think first of *ptg* as the base of an avy compound. This must have been the case especially in the post-Murāri period (which, to speak in approximate terms, can be thought of as not beginning any later than the ninth century A.D.), in which the use of *ptg* as a noun meaning 'each limb' is attested (§5.9)[69] and in which the times of the MB commentators cited above fall. Further, the commonly known lists of pratyaṅgas (cf. §5.4) could easily have spread the impression that internal or smaller parts of the body, as distinct from deeper or subtler parts, were covered by *ptg*. This situation must have made it unlikely that the later Pāṇinīyas would even think of searching for an older meaning, even if the means available to us were available in them. The older meaning could, therefore, have easily remained unknown to specialists of the MB who lived closer to Kaiyaṭa's time.

The case of the specified likelihood is strengthened by the fact that the commentators of works other than the MB also had to try their best to figure out the meaning of *ptg* on the strength of context (approximately) in the post-Skanda-&-Maheśvara period (the seventh century A.D. at the latest). Further, the evidence in §§4.2–11 suggests that what I consider to be a better way of understanding *ptg* survived in diffused traditions of learning and in isolated texts composed in different parts of India. It could

[69]See §2.8 (last paragraph), §2.15 and notes 11 and 64a for the explanation of how use of *ptg* as a noun with an iterative meaning element involves a semantic gap and is problematic to that extent.

not have been easy for the MB specialists or the commentators of Manu and the Bhāgavata-purāṇa to tap into the passages that have guided me to the earlier and most probably original meaning of *ptg*.

§4.13 The development from (a) 'one on the other side' to (b) 'deeper/internal', 'subtler/minor/smaller' or 'dependent/subsidiary'—which development we cannot rule out in the case of *ptg* (§3.1g, §3.6, §3.7f–g)—is not merely a matter of the latter being logically implied by the former. If Y comes into thinking because X is presumed to exist—if Y is logically 'other' with respect to a presupposed or logically primary X, it is not necessarily viewed as physically included in or dependent on X. A conceptual dependence or relativity does not always lead to subsumption or secondary status. If that status is to come about in the case of *ptg* (as it evidently did), there must have been a conceptual element in its genesis or early usage—an element in addition to the presumption of priority of aṅga—that facilitated the inclusion of pratyaṅga items in aṅga items and thereby the development of the connotations 'small/minor' and 'secondary'. In other words, our starting point in the semantic reconstruction of *ptg* should not be that stage or group of words in which *prati* conveys 'contrary nature' or 'opposition', but the stage or group in which *prati* connotes similarity and comparability. Going, therefore, for *prati* as conveying 'resemblance, amenability to serve as a substitute', we can take *ptg* as originally having the sense 'one which is very much like an aṅga, one which is not in the usual list or conception of aṅgas but is standing by to serve as aṅga'.

If, on the background of the preceding evidence and its analysis, we interpret Pat's *ptg* as 'almost an aṅga, yet not quite the same thing as aṅga', or as 'one which can come in the place of aṅga, not the defined aṅga (P 1.4.13: *yasmāt pratyaya-vidhis tad-ādi pratyaye 'ṅgam*) but something close to it', we can interpret the MB passages in a uniform way without having to contend with the difficulties that an avy starting point creates. We can then also understand why the commentators who were not aware of the older sense of *ptg* and were forced to figure out the sense on the strength of the context thought of *antar-aṅga* as the gloss.

The reconstructed semantic history also helps in accounting for the suggestion of a technical meaning in MB 6.3.138 (a technical meaning existing by the side of the ordinary meaning in MB 1.1.57). Like *antar-aṅga*, the word refers to a specific kind of word part (MB 6.4.110 and the slightly emended MB 1.1.29), as well as the operation pertaining to that word part (MB 6.3.138). The statements of the learned commentators to the effect that the pratyaṅga operations take place at the varṇa level (§3.1j), whereas the aṅga operations take place at the morphemic level, also then begin to make sense.

§4.14 The incidental but significant gains of our study are:

(a) As far as the attestations in the MB are concerned, *ptg* is only a noun, not an avy.

(b) This noun should not be confused with the later noun *ptg* that means 'each limb' or 'all limbs'.

(c) The development of the later noun is a case of subtle aberration.

(d) The dictionaries and indices available at present contain some errors in their *ptg* listings.

(e) In particular, the compilers of the dictionaries and indices would have been justified if they had separated the entries of avy *pratyaṅga*(*m*) from *ptg* as a declinable noun. The former combines a distinctive sense or function of *prati* (cf. Wackernagel cited in §3.3) with *aṅga*.

(f) The compilers would also have been better off if they had consistently separated *prati* serving in avy formation and meaning 'each, every, all' from *prati* serving as an upasarga and meaning 'opposite, contrary' or 'like, similar, agreeing', as well as from *prati* serving as a karmapravacanīya and meaning 'in regard to' etc.

(g) There is a significant descriptive gain in Pāṇini's separate treatment of the three *prati*s and his separation of the avy-ending *-am* from the neuter accusative singular suffix *-am*.

APPENDIX

Non-MB occurrences of *pratyaṅga*
See also §2.1, §2.3, §2.11, §2.13, and §§4.2–11

§5.1 Sound leads and not-so-sound leads to the occurrences: The following collection of occurrences is based on (a) the relevant slips in the Scriptorium of the *Encyclopaedic Dictionary of Sanskrit on Historical Principles* at Deccan College, Pune,[70] (b) the specific and general references made in the extensive dictionaries, such as those of Böhtlingk-&-Roth, Monier-Williams and Apte, and the historical grammars of Sanskrit, such as that of Wackernagel, (c) the *Vaidika-padānukrama-kośa* of Vishvabandhu

[70](a) My thanks to Dr. Vinayaka P. Bhatta, Director of the EDSHP project, for the access he gave me to the relevant parts of this valuable resource. Without this acceess, certain questions that eventually resulted in improving my historical reconstruction would not have occurred to me. I hope the discussion in the present essay will be useful when the EDSHP project reaches the vocables starting with *pra*.

(b) As clarified in §1.2, I will generally not translate the passages collected below.

Shastri, (d) the *Digital Corpus of Sanskrit* at http://kjc-fs-cluster.kjc.uni-heidelberg.de/dcs/ and (e) my own reading and searches of select electronic texts.

While most of the guidance provided in the sources (a)–(d) was useful for my immediate purpose, some could not be used or could not be used beyond the part quoted on the slips or in the dictionary entries, because the texts mentioned or the specific edns thereof were not accessible to me. The former was the situation in the case of "Madana-ketu-carita 21 (a)" and "Rāghavīya 18.49," and the latter in the case of Aho-bala's "Saṁgīta-pārijāta 4–70." It is also possible, although not very likely, that the references specified were not accurate, and hence I was unable to verify and study them in their contexts.

The occurrences of *ptg*, in the case of which I had to remain contented with the text parts cited in my sources and could not verify the citation by conculting the original text are preceded by "#." Access to the contexts of such occurrences may change the number of attestations of this or that sense of *ptg*, but the change will not be so great as to affect the argument of this essay.

The unspecific references in older dictionaries have been made specific and updated with superior edns and e-texts wherever possible.

Under each meaning or role of *ptg*, the occurrences are arranged according to the Roman alphabetical order of the text titles.

§5.2 Turner (1966: 487) prints *pratyañc* 'facing towards' under the head-word *pratyaṅga*, conflating the root *añc* 'to go, move' or 'bend' with some other root such as *añj* 'to smear, annoint' or *aṅg* 'to move'. Compare Mayrhofer 1956: I.21 and 1992: I.48.

In the EDSHP scriptorium, two of the five slips titled "Dictionary of Inscriptional Sanskrit" actually contain *pratyañc*. The remaining three are:

(a) "Guntur Dt., 121 [volume] 12 p. 192 [line] 57": Motupalli Pillar Inscription of Gaṇa-pati-deva: *aśvaṁ yasyāśvamedhaṁ kvacid apaharato bhāti patyuḥ surāṇāṁ pratyaṅgaṁ yat kalamba-vraṇa-paṭalam ivākṣīṇam akṣāṁ sahasram.* This would come under §5.3.

(b) "EI [= Epigraphia Indica] XVI p. 295 l[ine] 160" with no specification of region: this contains an occurrence of *pratyaṅgama* [=?], not *ptg.*

(c) "Canjeevaram EI 13.197.10" with no specification of region but with *pratyaṁśena* as a note and 'one share' as the note's explanation. The EI vol has "Conjee°" as the spelling of the place name. The passage specified contains an occurrence of *pratyañc*, not *ptg.*[71]

[71]The details given here of the inapplicable passages and comments are primarily meant to caution future researchers. It should be borne in mind that the *ptg* part of the Scriptorium is in its preliminary stage. The EDSHP staff has not yet

See also §5.10 below.

§5.3 *ptg* as adverb:
In light of §3.3 (last two paragraphs), §3.7g and §4.14, this Appendix should be concerned only with the noun *ptg*. As such, I should set aside the occurrences of the adverb *pratyaṅgam*, which means 'in such a way as to include all limbs or parts', or 'with applicability of the specified action in its totality to each limb or part' and which, in the final analysis, can be said to contain occurrences of *aṅga*, not *ptg*. However, some of my sources have not separated these occurrences from the occurrences of *ptg* as a noun.[72] Hence I list below the occurrences of *pratyaṅgam* as an avy known to me so far:

- Avanti-sundarī-kathā-sāra 3.90: *so 'yaṁ dīrghāyur eṣāham evaṁ-bhūtāsmi vihvalā / tataḥ snigdhaṁ gr̥hītvainaṁ pratyaṅgaṁ pariṣasvaje //*
- Caṇḍa-kauśika 1.8 (subject sleep): *cittaṁ prasādayati, lāghavam ādadhāti, pratyaṅgam ujjvalayati pratibhā-viśeṣaṁ / doṣān udasyati karoti ca dhātu-sāmyam ānandam arpayati yoga-viśeṣa-gamyam //*
- Gīta-govinda 1.46: *viśveṣām anurañjanena janayann ānandam indīvara-śreṇī-śyāmala-komalair upanayann aṅgair anaṅgotsavam / svacchandaṁ vraja-sundarībhir abhitaḥ pratyaṅgam āliṅgitaḥ śr̥ṅgāraḥ sakhi mūrtimān iva madhau mugdho hariḥ krīḍati //*
- Gīta-govinda 11.10: *sā māṁ drakṣyati vakṣyati smara-kathāṁ pratyaṅgam āliṅganaiḥ prītiṁ yāsyati raṁsyate sakhi samāgatyeti cintākulaḥ / sa tvāṁ paśyati vepate pulakayaty ānandati svidyati pratyudgacchati mūrcchati sthira-tamaḥ-puñje nikuñje priyaḥ //* = Śārṅgadhara-paddhati 3499, except for a few variant readings.
- Hitopadeśa 1.90 (1.98 in some edns): *gharmārtaṁ na tathā suśītala-jalaiḥ snānaṁ na muktāvalī, na śrī-khaṇḍa-vilepanaṁ sukhayati pratyaṅgam apy arpitam / prītyai sajjana-bhāṣitaṁ prabhavati prāyo yathā cetasaḥ sad-yuktyā ca puraskr̥taṁ sukr̥tinām ākr̥ṣṭi-mantropamam //* Cited according to *Indische Sprüche* 886 referred to in Böhtlingk-&-Roth 1862–1865: IV.997.
- Kathā-sarit-sāgara 49.210: *ity ūcivān prasaṅgena pr̥ṣṭas tasmai śaśaṁsa saḥ / pratyaṅgaṁ tilakādīnāṁ phalaṁ strī-puṁsayoḥ pr̥thak //*
- Kaumudī-mitrānanda 6.1: *katham aparayā ... vipakṣa-kṣitipāla-karāla-karavāla-prahārair vijaya-varmaṇaḥ pratyaṅgaṁ vraṇena vaiśasam.*
- Liṅga-purāṇa, 1.88.55: *tatas tu garbha-saṁyuktaḥ pañcabhir vāyubhir vr̥taḥ / pituḥ śarīrāt pratyaṅgaṁ rūpam asyopajāyate //*

scrutinized the slips for their accuracy or comprehensiveness. I might also have made a mistake or two in typing the contents of the slips in the little time I had at my disposal.

[72] See §5.9 for a related point. See §5.2a for another instance of *ptg* as an adverb.

- Mīmāṁsā-sūtra 10.7.2: *pratyaṅgaṁ vā grahavad aṅgānāṁ pr̥thak-prakalpanatvāt.*[73]
- Mīmāṁsā-sūtra 11.4.48/49: *kaṇḍūyane pratyaṅgaṁ karma-bhedaḥ syāt.*[74]
- Pañca-tantra Mitra-bheda kathā 23: *anyathā sarveṣām api vadhaṁ vidhāya, carma vidārya, pratyaṅgaṁ prekṣya, dhanaṁ neṣyāmaḥ.*
- Pañca-tantra Kākolūkīya katha 10: *asti kasmiṁścin nagare devaśaktir nāma rājā / tasya ca putro jaṭhara-valmīkāśrayeṇoragena pratidinaṁ pratyaṅgaṁ kṣīyate.*
- Rāmāyaṇa 7.30.19: *so 'haṁ tāsāṁ* [= *prajānāṁ*, which were identical up to that point] *viśeṣārthaṁ striyam ekāṁ vinirmame / yad yat prajānāṁ pratyaṅgaṁ viśiṣṭaṃ tat tad uddhr̥tam //*
- Śārṅgadhara-paddhati 3283: *kṣobhaṁ dhatte yad api bahalaḥ snigdha-lāvaṇya-pūraḥ, pratyaṅgaṁ yat taṭam anusaranty ūrmayo vibhramāṇām / unmagnaṁ yat sphurati ca manāk kumbhayor dvandvam etat, tan manye 'syāḥ smara-gaja-yuvā gāhate hr̥t-taḍāgam //*
- Śārṅgadhara-paddhati 3499: *"sā māṁ drakṣyati, vakṣyati priya-kathāṁ pratyaṅgam āliṅganaiḥ, prītiṁ yāsyati, raṁsyate" sakhi-samāgatyeti cintākulaḥ / mārgaṁ paśyati, vepate, pulakayaty ānandati svidyati, pratyudgacchati, mūrchati priyatamaḥ kuñje nikuñja-priyaḥ //* Same as Gīta-govinda 11.10, except for a few variant readings.
- Sūkti-muktāvalī 52.8d: *tanvaṅgyā nava-yauvanena kimapi pratyaṅgam unmīlitam.*
- Vaikhānasa-gr̥hya-sūtra 1.2: ... *pratyaṅgam apaś ca spr̥ṣṭvā jaṅghayor vāme pāṇāv apy abhyukṣya sarvābhir murdhānaṁ spr̥śati.*

§5.4 Lists of aṅgas and pratyaṅgas, mostly from āyurvedic texts: It will be seen that the aṅgas are held to be six and to include the head, the antarādhi/waist, the two thighs/legs and the two arms. Because the lists are given in a metrical form, we sometimes have the name of a pratyaṅga item (e.g., *kara*) used for an aṅga item where the synonymity or near synonymity of names exists in non-technical Sanskrit, but the list is, on the whole, uniform in the names of individual aṅgas. Considerable uniformity exists

[73]In his commentary on the preceding (pūrva-pakṣa) sūtra Śabara articulates the issue being discussed with the words *kiṁ kr̥tsnaḥ paśur ekaṁ haviḥ, uta pratyaṅgaṁ havir-bhedaḥ.* From this, it is clear that in this instance *pratyaṅgam* is an avy; cf. Kevalānanda 1960: V.2486–2487.

[74]The *Vaidika-padānukrama-kośa* compilers have erred in these two instances in presenting *ptg* as if it were an indivisible noun (as distinct from a composition of *prati* and *aṅga*). Note the distinction I have made between the occurrences listed in this section and the occurrences in §5.9.

also in the list of pratyaṅgas. Occasionally, their total is also specified. They are said to be 56.

- Aṣṭāṅga-hṛdaya 2.3.1: *siro'ntarādhir dvau bāhū sakthinīti samāsataḥ / ṣaḍ-aṅgam aṅgaṁ. pratyaṅgaṁ tasyākṣi-hṛdayādikam.*
- Aṣṭāṅga-saṁgraha Śārīra-sthāna 5.2: *sakalam api śarīram aṅgam ity ucyate. tatra punaḥ ṣaḍ-aṅgaṁ śiro 'ntarādhir dvau bāhū sakthinī ca netra-nābhi-pāṇi-pādādīni tv asya pratyaṅgāni. tato mātṛ-hṛdayād āhāra-raso dhamanībhiḥ syandamāno 'parām upaiti.*
- Bhāva-prakāśa 3.73.22: *jaṅghoru-bāhu-grīvādiḥ pratyaṅgam iti kathyate //*
- Bhela-saṁhitā, Śārīra-sthāna, adhyāya 7, prose on p. 236 of Krishnamurthy's edn: *ṣaṭ-pañcāśat pratyaṅgāni.* A list follows.
- Caraka-saṁhitā: 4.7.11: *ṣaṭ-pañcāśat pratyaṅgāni, ṣaṭsv aṅgeṣūpanibaddhāni ...*
- Kāśyapa-saṁhitā, Śārīra-sthāna, adhyāya 4, verses 13–18 (pp. 76–77 of Satyapāla's edn): *... pratyaṅgāni nibodha me // akṣiṇī nāsike karṇau stanāv oṣṭhau kakundarau ... aṅgulīḥ //* The srotas are enumerated in three verses following this list.
- Nibandha-saṁgraha on Suśruta-saṁhitā 3.3.18: *śākhāś catasro mūrdhoraḥ-pṛṣṭhodarāṇy aṅgāni cibuka-nāsauṣṭha-śravaṇāṅguli-pārṣṇi-prabhṛtīni pratyaṅgāni.*
- #Nyāya-sudhā on Aṇu-vyākhyāna 2.2.11 (420b 12): *pratyaṅgāni hastādīni.*
- #Paryāya-ratna-mālā 71.1736: *pratyaṅgaṁ karṇa-nāsoṣṭha- liṅgāṅguli-karādikam /*
- Saṁgīta-ratnākara adhyāya 1, section 2, verse 75: *piṇḍasyāhuḥ ṣaḍ aṅgāni śiraḥ pādau karau tathā / madhyaṁ cety. atha vakṣyante pratyaṅgāny akhilāny api //* Lists of kalās, dhātus etc. follow almost to the end of the section in verse 167.
- Suśruta-saṁhitā 3.5.4: *ataḥ paraṁ pratyaṅgāni vakṣyante—mastakodara-pṛṣṭha-nābhi-lalāṭa-nāsā-cibuka-basti-grīvā ity etā ekaikāḥ, karṇa-netra-bhrū-śaṅkhāṁsa-gaṇḍa-kakṣa-stana-vṛṣaṇa-pārśva-sphig-jānu-bāhūru-prabhṛtayo dve dve, viṁśatir aṅgulayaḥ, srotāṁsi vakṣyamāṇāni. eṣa pratyaṅga-vibhāga uktaḥ.*

§5.5 In reference to human bodies:
On the background of the anatomical analysis as in §5.4, we get passages such as the following, which presuppose a division of limbs into aṅga and pratyaṅga (in some only the latter is present; in some, the former and the

latter are separated from each other; and in some, the compound *aṅga-pratyaṅga*, marked here by the ampersand sign at the beginning, occurs):[75]

- Aṣṭāṅga-hṛdaya-saṁgraha 13.29.2: *sarvāṅgaḥ sarva-gataṁ, pratyaṅgeṣu tad-āśrayaḥ.*
- &Agni-purāṇa 341.1 (according to the Ānandaśrama edn and the Chowkhamba's Kashi Sanskrit Series edn credited to Baladeva Upādhyāya; in other edns, the adhyāya number may be 340; context; information regarding nṛtya): *ceṣṭā-viśeṣam apy aṅga-pratyaṅge karma cānayoḥ / śarīrārambham icchanti. prāyaḥ pūrvo 'balāśrayaḥ //*
- &Aṣṭāṅga-saṁgraha Śārīra-sthāna 2.13: *caturthe 'ṅga-pratyaṅga-vibhāgaḥ pravyakto, garbhaś ca sthiro bhavati.*
- &Aṣṭāṅga-saṁgraha Śārīra-sthāna 2.17: *tato vyaktī-bhavad-aṅga-pratyaṅgasyāsya nābhyāṁ pratibaddhā nāḍī. nāḍyām aparā. tasyāṁ mātṛ-hṛdayam.*
- &Aṣṭāṅga-saṁgraha Sūtra-sthāna 28.4: *anilo hi doṣāṇāṁ netā sarva-śarīra-ceṣṭaika-kāraṇaṁ pañcātmatayāṅga-pratyaṅga-vyāpī ...*
- &Aṣṭāṅga-saṁgraha Sūtra-sthāna 34.38: *mṛdu-māṁsa-khaṇḍeṣv agni-kṣārāvacaraṇa-yogyām. pustamaya-puruṣāṅga-pratyaṅgeṣu bandhana-yogyām.*
- &Avanti-sundarī-kathā p. 192.16: *tenāpi nipuṇam aṅga-pratyaṅgāni calita* [text lost in the ms].
- Bhāva-prakāśa, Pūrva-khaṇḍa, Garbha-prakaraṇa 329: *aṅga-pratyaṅga-nirvṛttiḥ sva-bhāvād eva jāyate / saṁniveśaś ca gātrāṇāṁ, nātrāste kāraṇāntaram // aṅga-pratyaṅga-nirvṛttau ye bhavanty aguṇā guṇāḥ / te te garbhasya vijñeyā dharmādharma-nimittajāḥ //*
- &Bhāva-prakāśa, Madhya-khaṇḍa, chapter 71, verse 146 (edn K. R. Srikantha Murthy): *aṅga-pratyaṅga-deśe tu rujā yatrāsya (= bālasya) jāyate.*
- Bhela-saṁhitā, Indriya-sthāna, adhyāya 1, verse 12, p. 248 of Krishnamurthy's edn: *sthūla-sthūlāṅgulī pāṇī nakhā yasyāpi lohitāḥ / kalyāṇa-deśa-pratyaṅgaḥ pañcāśad-varṣa eva ca //*
- &Brahmāṇḍa-purāṇa 1,13.121: *aṅga-pratyaṅga-saṁyogāt kālātmā prapitāmahaḥ / ṛk-sāma-yajuṣāṁ yoniḥ pañcānāṁ patir īśvaraḥ //*
- &Brahmāṇḍa-purāṇa 1,13.137: *īśvaraḥ sarva-bhūtānāṁ praṇavo yo 'tha paṭhyate / ātmāveśena bhūtānām aṅga-pratyaṅga- saṁbhavaḥ //*

[75] *aṅga-paccaṅga* occurs in Pāli in the sense 'by-limb' or 'small limb' according to Rhys Davids and Stede (1921: 6, 383). The passages they list in the relevant entries should be checked to ascertain if 'all limbs, each and every limb' will be more likely as a meaning in the contexts concerned.

- Buddha-carita 3.5: *pratyaṅga-hīnān vikalendriyāṁś ca jīrṇāturādīn kṛpaṇāṁś ca dikṣu /*
- Caraka-saṁhitā: 4.5.12 (context: expectations from a disciple): ... *supta-sthita-gata-prekṣitāhāra-vihāra-pratyaṅga-ceṣṭādikeṣv ārambheṣu smṛti-pūrvikā pravṛttiḥ,* ...
- Gaṇa-kārikā ṭīkā 1.7.2: ... *āpāda-tala-mastakaṃ yāvat prabhūtena bhasmanāṅgaṃ pratyaṅgaṃ ca prayatnātiśayena nighṛṣya nighṛṣya, snānam ācared. ity-evaṃ madhyāhnāparāhṇa-saṃdhyayor apīti.*
- &Kullūka-bhaṭṭa on Manu 2.147: ... *yad* ***yonau*** *mātṛ-kukṣāv* ***abhijāyate*** *'ṅga-pratyaṅgāni labhate.* The same words in Medhātithi on Manu 2.147.
- &#Lakṣmī-tantra 4.22a: *aṅga-pratyaṅga-buddhyādir naiṣāṁ bhūta-mayaḥ smṛtaḥ.*
- &Mahābhārata 3.214.18: (specification 3, 14317 according to Böht-lingk-&-Roth 1862–1865: IV.997): *aṅga-pratyaṅga-saṁbhūtaś catu-rthyām abhavad guhaḥ /*
- &Medhātithi on Manu 2.147: ... *yad* ***yonau*** *mātṛ-kukṣāv* ***abhijāyate*** *'ṅga-pratyaṅgāni labhate.* The same words in Kullūka on Manu 2.147.
- &Nāṭya-śāstra,[76] adhyāya 7, prose part after kārikā 7: *yathā hi samāna-lakṣaṇās tulya-pāṇi-pādodara-śarīrāḥ samānāṅga-pratyaṅgā api puruṣāḥ kula-śīla-vidyā-karma-śilpa-vicakṣaṇatvād rājatvam āpnu-vanti* ... If the reading °*māna-pratyayā api* adopted in P. Kumar's edn (p. I.279) turns out to be objectively strong in a critical edn, this occurrence must be eliminated from the present collection.
- &Nāṭya-śāstra 18.169: (→ 24.178 in P. Kumar edn p. II.843): *aṅga-pratyaṅga-līlābhir vāk-ceṣṭā-hasitekṣaṇaiḥ [/ °tekṣitaiḥ] / nāsty anyaḥ sadṛśas te(ne)ty etat syād guṇa-kīrtanam //*
- &Nāṭya-śāstra 35.05 P. Kumar edn p. III.1448: (context: the actor to be chosen to play the role of a god): *aṅga-pratyaṅga-saṁyuktam ahīnāṅgaṁ vayonvitam / na sthūlaṁ na kṛśaṁ caiva na dīrghaṁ na ca mantharam /*
- &Nāṭya-śāstra 35.10 (while describing the actors to be given the roles of princes and kings): *svaṅga-pratyaṅga-saṁyuktā na dīrghā na ca mantharāḥ / na sthūlā na kṛśāś caiva sva-bhāvena vyavasthitāḥ //*

[76] As is well known to the specialists, some of the adhyāya and verse numbers are unsettled in the Nāṭya-śāstra text. Also, reading differences are quite frequent. I have, therefore, given the numbers found in my sources, as well as the numbers and pages of Pushpendra Kumār's edn. He generally refers to the placing and numbering found in the earlier edns and occasionally reproduces the variant readings. In two passages included in this Appendix, there will be no occurrence of *ptg* if his readings turn out to be objectively strong.

The reading of quarter 'b' is °*ktā dīrghāś ca mada-mantharāḥ* in P. Kumar edn, p. III.1448.

- &Padma-purāṇa (in the speech of god of love) 2.53.16c: *aṅgeṣv evaṁ pratyaṅgeṣu sarvatra nivasāmy aham /*
- Rāmāyaṇa 2.68.5: *utpapātāśu saṃhṛṣṭaḥ sarva-pratyaṅga-bhūṣaṇaḥ /*
- &Rāmāyaṇa critical edn. 2.68.14: *aṅga-pratyaṅgajaḥ putro hṛdayāc cāpi jāyate / tasmāt priyataro mātuḥ priyatvān na tu bāndhavaḥ //* According to Böhtlingk-&-Roth 1862–1865: IV.997, this is Rāmāyaṇa "2, 74, 11 (76, 16 Gorr.)."
- #Rasārṇava 1.36: *sūto 'yaṁ mat-samo, devi, mama pratyaṅga-sambhavaḥ.*[77]
- &Śākta-vijñāna 1.20: *ekaikaṁ bhramayaty aṅgam aṅga-pratyaṅga-sandhiṣu /*
- &Sāma-rahasyopaniṣad, p. 234:12: *kvacin nānā-puṣpair aṅga-pratyaṅgeṣu parasparaṁ śṛṅgāraṁ kurvanti. kvacit puṣpa-mālābhir aṅga-pratyaṅgaiḥ śṛṅgāra-rasaṁ kurvanti;*
- &Sāma-rahasyopaniṣad, pp. 259:23–260.1: *tad vṛndā-vaneśvarī-rūpam aṅga-pratyaṅgaṁ rasikānandena saha yo dhyāyati sa eva krīḍāyāṁ mano-bhāvāpanno bhavati.*
- &Saṅgha-bheda-vastu 1.22: *bhavati gautama sa samayo yad ayaṃ lokaḥ saṃvartate. saṃvartamāne loke yad-bhūyasā sattvā ābhāsvare deva-nikāye upapadyante te tatra bhavanti rūpiṇo manomayāḥ avikalā ahīnendriyāḥ sarvāṅga-pratyaṅgopetāḥ śubhā varṇa-sthāyinaḥ svayam-prabhā vihāyasaṁgamāḥ prīti-bhakṣāḥ prīty-āhārāḥ dīrghāyuṣo dīrgham adhvānaṃ tiṣṭhanti /*
- &Saṅgha-bheda-vastu 1.26: *te iha bhavanti rūpiṇo manomayā avikalā ahīnendriyāḥ sarvāṅga-pratyaṅgopetāḥ śubhā varṇa-sthāyinaḥ svayam-prabhā vihāyasaṃgamāḥ prīti-bhakṣāḥ prīty-āhārā dīrghāyuṣo dīrgham adhvānaṃ tiṣṭhanti //*
- &Sārāvali (of Kalyāṇa-varman, a jyotiṣa text) 40.72: *aṅga-pratyaṅgā-nāṁ chedaṁ vidadhāti ṣaṣṭha-śatru-daśā /*
- &Skanda-purāṇa, Revā-khaṇḍa 159.43: *śarīrāvayavair yukto hy aṅga-pratyaṅga-saṁyutaḥ /*
- &Skanda-purāṇa, Revā-khaṇḍa 26.103: *tasyā janmāni ṣaṭ-triṁśad aṅga-pratyaṅga-sandhiṣu /*
- *Skanda-purāṇa, Revā-khaṇḍa 33.9: *aṅga-pratyaṅga-saṁpannā ya-smāl lokeṣu viśrutā /*

[77]The Sarva-darśana-saṁgraha 3.3 is said to quote the line with *supto 'yaṁ* as the beginning. The Rasārṇava mentioned here is different from Siṁha-bhūpāla's Rasārṇava-sudhākara.

- &Śrī-vṛṣabha on Trikāṇḍī or Vākyapadīya 1.52 (p. 110 of Subramania Iyer's edn): *yathā mayūrādīnām aṇḍeṣu rasa utpatsyamānāṅga-pratyaṅga-candrakādīnāṁ rūpopasaṁhāreṇa ....*
- &Suśruta-saṁhitā 1.1.38: *evam etat puruṣo vyādhir auṣadhaṁ kriyā kāla iti catuṣṭayaṁ samāsena vyākhyātam / tatra puruṣa-grahaṇāt tat-saṁbhava-dravya-samūho bhūtādir uktas tad-aṅga-pratyaṅga-vikalpāś ca tvaṅ-māṁsāsthi-sirā-snāyu-prabhṛtayaḥ.*
- &Suśruta-saṁhitā 1.35.12: *atha punar āyuṣo vijñānārthām aṅga-pratyaṅga-pramāṇa-sārān upadekṣyāmaḥ. tatrāṅgāny antarādhi-sakthi-bāhu-śirāṁsi. tad-avayavāḥ pratyaṅgānīti.*
- &Suśruta-saṁhitā 1.35.17: *viśeṣato 'ṅga-pratyaṅga-pramāṇād atha sārataḥ / parīkṣyāyuḥ sunipuṇo bhiṣak sidhyati karmasu //*
- &Suśruta-saṁhitā 1.9.4: *... pustamaya-puruṣāṅga-pratyaṅga-viśeṣeṣu bandhana-yogyāṁ ...*
- &Suśruta-saṁhitā 3.3.18: *tatra prathame māsi kalalaṁ jāyate; dvitīye śītoṣmānilair abhiprapacyamānānāṁ mahā-bhūtānāṁ saṁghāto ghanaḥ saṁjāyate. yadi piṇḍaḥ pumān, strī cet peśī, napuṁsakaṁ ced arbudam iti; tṛtīye hasta-pāda-śirasāṁ pañca piṇḍakā nirvartante [→ °vartyante?] 'ṅga-pratyaṅga-vibhāgaś ca sūkṣmo bhavati; caturthe sarvāṅga-pratyaṅga-vibhāgaḥ pravyakto bhavati.*
- &Suśruta-saṁhitā 3.3.30: *pañcame manaḥ pratibuddhataraṁ bhavati, ṣaṣṭhe buddhiḥ, saptame sarvāṅga-pratyaṅga-vibhāgaḥ pravyakta-taraḥ ...*
- &Suśruta-saṁhitā 3.3.31: *mātus tu khalu rasavahāyāṁ nāḍyāṁ garbha-nābhi-nāḍī pratibaddhā. sāsya mātur āhāra-rasa-vīryam abhi-vahati. tenopasnehenāsyābhivṛddhir bhavati. *asaṁjātāṅga-pratyaṅga-pravibhāgam ā niṣekāt*[78] ** ...*
- &Suśruta-saṁhitā 3.3.32: *sarvāṇy aṅga-pratyaṅgāni yugapat saṁ-bhavantīty āha dhanvantariḥ.*[79]
- &Suśruta-saṁhitā 3.3.36 *aṅga-pratyaṅga-nirvṛttiḥ sva-bhāvād eva jāyate / aṅga-pratyaṅga-nirvṛttau ye bhavanti guṇāguṇāḥ / te te garbhasya vijñeyā dharmādharma-nimittajāḥ //*[80]

[78]It seems that this sūtra has a variant reading: *asaṁjātāṅga-pratyaṅga-vibhāgaṁ tu garbhe niṣekāt prabhṛti.*

[79]&Nibandha-saṁgraha comm on Suśruta-saṁhitā 3.3.32: *nanv aṅga-pratyaṅga-pravyaktī-bhāve garbha-nābhi-nāḍī mātur āhāra-rasa-vīryam abhiva-hati, aṅga-pratyaṅga-pravyaktī-bhāvāt tu pūrvaṃ kathaṃ garbha-puṣṭiḥ syād, ity āha* ***asaṃjātāṅga-pratyaṅga-vibhāgam*** *ity-ādi //*

[80]&Nibandha-saṁgraha commentary on Suśruta-saṁhitā 3.3.36: *sva-bhāvam īśvaram ity-ādi-ślokena yā sva-bhāvād aṅga-pratyaṅga-nirvṛttiḥ sūcitā tāṃ pratipādya tan-nirvṛttau prāktana-ślokābhihita-guṇāguṇopapattiṃ dharmādharma-hetutayā nirdiśann āha* ***aṅga-pratyaṅge****ty-ādi.*

- &Suśruta-saṁhitā 3.5.49: *tasmāt samasta-gātram aviṣopahatam adīrgha-vyādhi-pīḍitam avarṣaśatikaṁ niḥsṛṣṭāntra-purīṣaṁ puruṣam avahanty āmāpagāyāṁ nibaddhaṁ pañjarasthaṁ *muñja-valkala-kuśa-śaṇādīnām anyatamenāveṣṭitāṅga-pratyaṅgam aprakāśe deśe kothayet, samyak-prakuthitaṁ coddhṛtya tato dehaṁ sapta-rātrād uśīra-bāla-veṇu-valkala-kūrcānām anyatamena śanaiḥ śanair avagharṣayaṁs tvag-ādīn sarvān eva bāhyābhyantarān aṅga-pratyaṅga-viśeṣān yathoktān lakṣayec cakṣuṣā.*
- &Suśruta-saṁhitā 3.10.34: *aṅga-pratyaṅga-deśe tu rujā yatrāsya jāyate / muhur muhuḥ spṛśati taṁ spṛśyamāne ca roditi //*
- Suśruta-saṁhitā 4.3.22cd: ***pratyaṅga**-bhagnasya vidhir ata ūrdhvaṁ pravakṣyate.*[81]
- Tāpasa-vatsarāja 1.16: *phullendīvara-kānanāni nayane, pāṇī sarojākarās, tanvīyaṁ jaghana-sthaloru-pulinā romāvalī nimnagā / pratyaṅgeṣu navaiva saṁprati śaral-lakṣmīr iyaṁ dṛśyate, tac cihnair adhunā prasādhana-vidhau baddho vṛthaivādaraḥ //*
- &Tattva-bindu 9.3bc: (p. 9 of V.A. Ramaswami Sastri's edn): *sa khalv ayam eko vākyātmā vākyārtha-dhī-hetur anubhavād vā vyavasthāpyate, artha-dhī-bhedād vā anyathā 'nupapadyamānāt. anubhavo 'pi ca vākyātmānam ekam avayavinam aneka-varṇa-pada-vyāsaṅginam, aṅga-pratyaṅga-vartinam iva deva-dattam, anubhavet, pratyastamita-varṇa-pada-vibhāgaṁ vā.*[82]
- Triṣaṣṭi-śalākā-puruṣa-caritra 1.2.926: *asādhu-sādhane sādhu-pālane kṛta-karmaṇaḥ / pratyaṅgāni svakānīva, mantriṇo vidadhe vibhuḥ //*
- &Vāmana-purāṇa 80.31c [= critical edn 54.31]: *aṅgopāṅgāni, devarṣe, pūjayitvā jagad-guroḥ / surūpāṇy abhijāyante pratyaṅgāṅgāni caiva hi //*[83]

[81]The subsequent verses describe how the injuries of certain limbs should be treated.

[82]Ṛṣi-putra Parameśvara's Tattva-vibhāvanā commentary on this: ***aṅgāni** kara-caraṇādīni, **pratyaṅgāni** kūrparādīni, **varṇa-pada-vyāsaṅginam** ity **aṅga-prtyaṅga-vartinam ivety** anayoḥ pratyaṅgopameyatā varṇānām, aṅgopameyatā padānām iti draṣṭavyam /*

[83]Daśavaikālika-sūtra 8.58 and Uttarādhyayana-sūtra 16.428 have *aṁga-paccaṁga-saṁṭhāṇa*, in which *aṁga* and *paccaṁga* have the same sense as in the Sanskrit Āyurvedic texts; cf. Ratna-candra 1923: I.18. 3. 392.

§5.6 In reference to animal bodies:
From the human body, the '*aṅga* : *pratyaṅga*' distinction is extended to animal bodies as can be seen from the following passages:[84]

- Hasty-āyur-veda[85] 2.71 p. 336.8–9 (context: explanation of aṁsa-saṅga, a malady): *urontar-maṇi-vikṣobhāvaśeṣotsaṅga-guhā-bhāga-pratyaṅgānām aṁsa-deśānām uddharaṇaṁ gamana-praveśanaṁ ca syād ity uraḥ-saṅga-lakṣaṇam. pratyaṅga-sāṁkarya-mukha-śiraḥ-śiro-dharāṇāṁ kṛcchrād udvahanam ity aṁsa-saṅgaḥ.*
- Hasty-āyur-veda 3.15 p. 477.9 (context: the parts in which the wounds and nāḍīs are treatable): *tatra danta-veṣṭāsthi-saṁdhi-kakṣānugatā nakha-nayana-marma-tala-proha-viṣkāpaskarāṣṭhīvya-pali(ta)-hasta-nakhāntara-pratyaṅga-pratīkāśa-kukṣy-aṅguli- . . .*
- Hasty-āyur-veda 3.20 p. 501.10,18 (context: names of marmans): *tatra gudāṇḍa-kośe hṛdaya-meḍhra-madhyodara-kara-pratyaṅgaṁ sapratīkāsa-pratīmāna-guha-stana-proha-saṁdāna-bhāga-. . . aṣṭhīvya-guha-bhoga-pratyaṅga-saguhāntara-bāhu-grīvā-vibhāgāpaskare . . .*
- &Hasty-āyur-veda 3.29 p. 525.4: *iha khalu śarīraṁ mūlam. tan-mūlāny aṅga-pratyaṅgāni loka-prasiddhāni. pañca-daśa pradeśāḥ pratyaṅgānīty-anarthāntaram.*
- Hasty-āyur-veda 3.5 p. 386.4 (context: signs of a burning knot formed on an elephant's body): *tadāṅgaṁ pratyaṅgaṁ vāvamṛśyodvijate.*
- Mānava-śrauta-sūtra, kalpa 5, adhyāya 2 khaṇḍa 9.4: *dvi-paśu-prabhṛti-pratyaṅgānāṁ bahu-vacanāni.*[86]
- #Mātaṅga-līlā 6.5: *atisthūlā . . . ye gajāḥ / teṣām aṅgāny ameyāni pratyaṅgāni ca pārthiva //*
- Yaśas-tilaka-campū pt. 1 p. 298 line 2 of the Nirnaya Sagara Press edns of 1901 and 1916 (context: description of an extraordinary elephant): *. . . dvādaśasv api kṣetreṣu śubha-samudāya-pratyaṅga-phalam . . .*[87]

---

[84]We do not know if precise and well-established or closed lists of secondary limbs existed even in the case of animals, but fairly constant lists seem to have existed.

[85]In the specification of the cited passages, the first number stands for sthāna (= 'book' in this context) and the second for adhyāya. These two are followed by page and line specification of the Ānandāśrama Sanskrit Series edn. The two sthānas in which the word occurs are Kṣudra-roga-sthāna (= 2) and Śalya-sthāna (= 3).

[86]Tr. Gelder 1961: 174: "For the limbs of two or more animals the plural (is used instead of the dual)." The examples that follow contain references to forelegs, forefeet, shoulders, buttocks, thighs and knee-caps.

[87](a) The commentator Śruta-deva-sūri explains: ***dvādaśasv api kṣetreṣu***

§5.7 Secondary, extended or metaphorical use:
The '*aṅga* : *pratyaṅga*' way of describing or theorizing about the body leads to lākṣaṇika or metaphorical uses of *ptg* as the use of "body" or its equivalents does in many other languages.

- &Nāṭya-śāstra 8.13 (→ 12 in P. Kumar edn p. I.316): *śiro hasta-kaṭī-vakṣaḥ-pārśva-pāda-samanvitaḥ / aṅga-pratyaṅga-saṁyuktaḥ ṣaḍ-aṅgo nāṭya-saṁgrahaḥ //*[88]
- Nāṭya-śāstra 21.117 (→ 113 in P. Kumar edn p. II.733): *vṛtti-pratyaṅga-saṁpannaṁ patākārtha-pratikriyam / [/ vṛtti-vṛtty-aṅga-sampannaṁ padārtha-prakṛti-kṣamam] pañcāvasthā-samutpannaṁ pañcabhiḥ sandhibhir yutam //*
- Nāṭya-śāstra 26.90 (→ 95 in P. Kumar edn p. II.908): *pratyaṅga-hīnaṁ yad vākyaṁ [/ yat kāvyaṁ] vikṛtaṁ ca prayujyate / na lakṣaṇa-kṛte [/ °kṛtas] tatra kāryas tv abhinayo budhaiḥ //*
- &Nāṭya-śāstra 33.13–16: (→ 14.14–17 in P. Kumar edn pp. 1349–1350): *ātodya-samavāye tu yāni yojyāni vādakaiḥ / aṅga-pratyaṅga-yogena gadato me nibodhata //13// vipañcī caiva citrā ca dāravīṣv aṅga-saṁjñite / kacchapī-ghoṣakādīni pratyaṅgāni tathaiva ca //14// mṛdaṅgā darduraś caiva paṇavāś cāṅga-saṁjñitāḥ [/ °ṇaveṣv aṅga-saṁjñite] / jhallarī-paṭahādīni pratyaṅgāni tathaiva ca //15// aṅga-lakṣaṇa-saṁyukto vijñeyo vaṁśa eva hi / śākhatuṇḍikinī caiva pratyaṅge parikīrtite//16//* [variants found: *śaṅkhas* for *śākha*, *tuṇḍa* for *tuṇḍi*, and *tu ḍakkinī* for *tuṇḍikinī*.]
- Nīti-prakāśikā[89] 7.7cd (context: foot-soldiers meant to accompany army units): *padātayaḥ sahasraṁ tu pratyaṅgeṣv anuyāyinaḥ /*
- #Nityotsava 99.12: *pratyaṅga-mantra.*[90]

---

dvādaśa-rāja-maṇḍalīṣu dvādaśa-kāyeṣu ***śubha-samudāya-pratyaṅga-phalam*** *kalyāṇa-samūha-śarīra-phalaṁ vijñāpayati. kāni tāni dvādaśa-kṣetrāṇi dvādaśa-śarīrāṇi? hasta-radana-mukha-śiro-nayana-karṇa-grīvā-gātroro-jaghana-meḍhra-kāya-lakṣaṇāni.*

(b) Here, the meaning of *ptg* is very similar to the one we find in the Hastyāyur-veda. It stands for specific body parts of an elephant.

[88] This is a displaced verse. It must have originally occurred in some other chapter of the Nāṭya-śāstra. The eighth chapter, its present location, is devoted to gestures of the aṅgas, the major limbs. In the preceding śloka or anuṣṭubh verse of that chapter, a division according to aṅga and upāṅga is mentioned. The āryā which follows gives a list of the aṅgas and the upāṅgas. The current 8.13/12 introducing a different 'aṅga : pratyaṅga' division, and that too in a metaphorical sense, does not fit in the middle.

[89] Some have thought of this text or its parts as a modern work passed off as an old work.

[90] The meaning could be 'mantra to be recited while touching individual limbs

- Samarāṅgaṇa-sūtradhāra[91] 57.19: *dvi-padaḥ karṇa-kandaś ca praty-aṅgaṁ padikaṁ smṛtam / nirgataṁ cārdha-bhāgena catur-dikṣu vyava-sthitam //*
- Samarāṅgaṇa-sūtradhāra 57.54: *praviṣṭaṁ ca padenaikaṁ tad evātra jalāntaram / padena karṇe koṇaḥ syāt pratyaṅge pada-vistṛte //*
- Samarāṅgaṇa-sūtradhāra 57.82: *vibhajya daśadhā kuryāl latāḥ pañcāti-sundarīḥ / hema-kūṭasya karṇeṣu pratyaṅge nara-kinnarāḥ //*[92]
- Samarāṅgaṇa-sūtradhāra 57 p. II.59 of Sastri's edn, p. II.477 of Sharma's edn: *pratya(ṅgas tu va?ṅgeṣu ca)*[93] *kūṭāni sārdhāṁśocchrā-yavanti ca / dvitīyaḥ siṁha-karṇaḥ syāt siṁha-karṇasya mastake //*
- Samarāṅgaṇa-sūtradhāra 57 p. II.65 of Sastri's edn, p. II.487 of Sharma's edn: *dvi-padaṁ kārayet karṇaṁ bhāgārdham udakāntaram / pratyaṅgaṁ sārdha-bhāge (sā? syāt) śālā caiva catuṣpadā //*
- Samarāṅgaṇa-sūtradhāra 57 p. II.76 of Sastri's edn, p. II.505 of Sharma's edn: *tri-bhāgam asya pratyaṅgaṁ pada-dvitaya-nirgamam / vedi-candrāvalokābhyāṁ pratyaṅge karma kalpayet //*
- Samarāṅgaṇa-sūtradhāra 57 p. II.80 of Sastri's edn, p. II.511 of Sharma's edn: *++bhāgāyatā kārya sā bhavehi (?) vicakṣaṇaiḥ / śālā(karṇa-padādvatu?) pratyaṅgaṁ bhāga-mānataḥ //*

(which action is a common part of worship, especially non-Śrauta worship in India)' or 'a mantra in which the word *ptg* occurs'.

[91] The preserved text of this work is more uncertain than that of most other Sanskrit works said to be textually unsettled. As far as I can determine, the edns by Pushpendra Kumar and Sudarshan Kumar Sharma are based on the work of the pioneer editor T. Ganapati Sastri. There has been no discovery of new mss or a fresh consultation of the unique ms utilized by Shastri. I do not at present have access to the edn and translation by Pushpendra Kumar. The one by Sharma frequently does not try even to create a syntactically satisfactory English sentence from the word trs that are offered. In the listing I have presented in the following lines, some verses may contain *ptg* in the sense 'each limb'. See note 56b for Sharma's translations of *ptg*.

[92] (a) The following occurrences, before the adhyāya number changes, are associated with adhyāya 57 but have not been assigned numbers either by Ganapati Sastri or Sudarshan Kumar Sharma. Hence I put page numbers where I would have normally given verse numbers.

(b) Sharma prints the specified verses in an appendix and characterizes them as an interpolation. He does not explain how either action is justified. Ganapati Sastri (p. 55) seems to have refrained from numbering the verses only because the ms he was using lacked two leaves that probably contained about 50 verses subsequent to 57.211ab.

[93] The parenthetical conjectures and emendations in this collection of Samarāṅgaṇa-sūtradhāra passages come from Ganapati Sastri. Some of them are due to the illegibility of the ms.

- Samarāṅgaṇa-sūtradhāra 57 p. II.82 of Sastri's edn, p. II.516 of Sharma's edn: *pratyaṅgāni padaṁ sārdhaṁ ++++jalāntaram / dvi-padaṁ karṇa-mānaṁ ca kāryaṁ koṣa-catuṣṭaya (yaṁ? ye) //*
- Samarāṅgaṇa-sūtradhāra 57 p. II.83 of Sastri's edn, p. II.517 of Sharma's edn: *madhye latāyāḥ karṇasya velakaḥ ṣaḍ-vidhaḥ kramaḥ / pratyaṅge tilakā kūṭāḥ pañcālārdhā dvi-pakṣakaḥ (?) //*
- Samarāṅgaṇa-sūtradhāra 57 p. II.94 of Sastri's edn, p. II.535 of Sharma's edn, three slightly separated verses: *valabhīḥ kārayet tad-vad (dvi? dig)-bhāgeṣu caturṣv api / pratyaṅgaṁ dvi-padaṁ karṇa-śālā-valabhikāntare // ... vijñe(ye? yaṁ) tac ca dig-bhadre sūtra-mārgānusārataḥ / jalāntarāṇi kurvīta pratyaṅge pārśvayor api // ... candrikā-kalaśotsedhaṁ pādenaikena kalpayet / pratyaṅge tilakās try-aṁśā ghaṇṭā-kalaśa-saṁyutāḥ //*
- Samarāṅgaṇa-sūtradhāra 57 p. II.106 of Sastri's edn, p. II.556 of Sharma's edn: *rathakaṁ tri-padaṁ kuryāt pratyaṅgāt sārdhabhāgikāt / dvi-padaṁ karṇam asyāhur vidikṣu catasṛṣv api //*
- Samarāṅgaṇa-sūtradhāra 57 p. II.107 of Sastri's edn, p. II.557 of Sharma's edn: *ṣaḍ-bhāga-vistṛtaṁ skandhaṁ bhājayed daśabhiḥ padaiḥ / yathā mūle tathā skandhe 'py aṅga-pratyaṅga-kalpanā // ... anumātra-guṇaṁ*[94] *sūtraṁ tri-bhāgena samanvitam / bhramayet (koṇa-rekhā syāt pratyaṅgestatrapañcakān?)*[95]
- Samarāṅgaṇa-sūtradhāra 57 p. II.112 of Sastri's edn, p. II.566 of Sharma's edn: *bhāgaṁ bhāgaṁ bhavet karṇe bhāgārdhaṁ bhadra-nirgamaḥ / pratyaṅgaṁ dvi-padaṁ kuryād vāri-margeṇa saṁyutam //*
- Samarāṅgaṇa-sūtradhāra 57 p. II.114 of Sastri's edn, p. II.568 of Sharma's edn: *ekaikasyāḥ padārdhena prakṣepaḥ syāt paras-param / koṇe kūṭāni kurvīta pratyaṅge ti (kā?la)kāni ca //*
- Samarāṅgaṇa-sūtradhāra 64.35: *dvi-bhāgikaḥ pratirathaḥ śālā syāt pañca-bhāgikā / śālā-pratyaṅgayor antar-bhāgārdhenodakāntaram //*
- Samarāṅgaṇa-sūtradhāra 64.5: *koṇo dvi-bhāga-vistāraḥ. pratyaṅgau bhāgikau smṛtau /*
- Saṁgīta-makaranda 2–2–5: name of a tāla: *pratyaṅgo ma-gaṇaḥ laghu-dvayam.*
- Saṁgīta-ratnākara 5.241ab (context: a list of 120 deśī 'regional' tālas): *raṅgaḥ śrī-raṅga-caccaryau pratyaṅgo yati-lagnakaḥ* ... In verse 266 of the same adhyāya, the tāla is defined as *pratyaṅgo ma-gaṇo lau dvau.*

[94] Sharma translates as if *aṇu-mātra* 'atom' is the reading.

[95] On what basis, Ganapati Sastri has added the matter in parentheses is not known to me. The case form of *ptg* in quarter 'd' is not clear. Perhaps we should read *pratyaṅgais tatra pañcakān.*

- Saṁgīta-ratnākara 6.113 (about the vīṇā called matta-kokilā which has other vīṇās as its pratyaṅgas): *mukhyeyaṁ sarva-vīṇānāṁ tri-sthānaiḥ saptabhiḥ svaraiḥ / saṁpannatvād. tad-anyās tu tasyāḥ pratyaṅgam īritāḥ.*
- Saṁgīta-ratnākara 7.39 (context: limbs used to dance): *pratyaṅgāni punar grīvā bāhū pṛṣṭhaṁ tathodaram / ūru-jaṅghe ṣaḍ ...*
- Suśruta-saṁhitā 1.1.7–8 (context: branches of Āyur-veda): *tad yathā śalyaṁ śālākyaṁ kāya-cikitsā bhūta-vidyā kaumārabhṛtyaṁ agada-tantraṁ rasāyana-tantraṁ vājī-karaṇa-tantram iti / athāsya praty-aṅga-lakṣaṇa-samāsaḥ.* A definition of śalya follows and is followed by the definitions of other branches.
- Tattva-saṁgraha 3146 (context: question asked by an objector to the omniscience of the Buddha and others like him): *na ca vedopavedāṅga-pratyaṅgādy-artha-bodhanam / buddhāder dṛśyate vākyaṁ [→ vākye?]. sa sarvajñaḥ kathaṁ mudhā //*[96]

The passages discussed in §§4.2–11 in particular contain more examples of metaphorical use.

§5.8 *ptg* as 'all limbs':

In some passages one gets the feeling that the dividing line between *aṅga* and *ptg* is blurred and the latter word is used to mean 'all limbs, every part'. The probable thinking resulting in this usage is spelled out in §3.7e–f:

- Bhaviṣya-purāṇa Uttara-parvan, adhyāya 74, verse 43 in the Venkateswar Steam Press edn; context: Māgha-dvādaśī-vrata): *tatodakasya*[97] *dhārās tāḥ pratyaṅgeṣu samanvitāḥ / śirasā dhārayet tūṣṇīṁ tad-gatenāntar-ātmanā*[98] *//*
- Brahmāṇḍa-purāṇa 3.24.74: *atha devy-ājñayā daṇḍa-nāthā pratyaṅga-rakṣiṇī / tiras-karaṇikā devī samuttasthau raṇājire //*
- Kathā-sarit-sāgara 4.54: *atiṣṭhan mardayantyas tat-pratyaṅgaṁ yāvad asya tāḥ / tāvad dvitīye prahare sa purodhā upāgamat //*
- Vākyapadīya-vṛtti 1.1: *na cāsyordhvam adhas tiryag vā mūrtātma-parivarta-pratyaṅgānāṁ kvacit kaścid vyavacchedo 'bhyupagamyate.*[99]

---

[96] Kamala-śīla in his commentary on this: *aṅgāni vedānāṁ ṣaṭ, śikṣā, kalpo, vyākaraṇaṁ, chando, niruktaṁ, jyotiṣam iti. pratyaṅgāni tad-avayavā dhātv-ādayaḥ.*

[97] One should allow here either a double sandhi of *tataḥ udakasya* or the existence of *daka* as a synonym of *udaka*. Either move can be supported by evidence from the Purāṇas.

[98] *tad* stands here for *viṣṇu*.

[99] Śrī-vṛṣabha explains *ptg* as *avayava*.

§5.9 Occurrences of *ptg* as a noun having the same meaning as the adverb *ptg*:

- Anargha-rāghava 3.7: *tadātva-pronmīlan-mradima-ramaṇīyāt kaṭhinatāṁ nicitya pratyaṅgād iva taruṇa-bhāvena ghaṭitau / stanau saṁbibhrāṇāḥ kṣaṇa-vinaya-vaiyātya-masṛṇa-smaronmeṣāḥ keṣāṁ upari na rasānāṁ yuvatayaḥ //*
Tr.: "Youth fashions (the breasts of young women) as if by collecting hardness bit by bit from every limb that is pretty on account of the freshly expanding softness. Which rasa do the young women bearing (such) breasts (and) smoothly casting the God of Love through modesty at one moment and daringly at another not transcend!"

In this verse illustrating Murāri's ability to capture an experience by combining the sensations received by various senses, *pratyaṅgāt* can best be understood as 'from every part of the body'. The commentator Ruci-pati (NSP edn p. 114) rightly glosses *pratyaṅgāt* with *sarvāvayavāt*, probably meaning 'from every limb that can be qualified with *tadātva-pronmīlan-mradima-ramaṇīya*'. Viṣṇu-bhaṭṭa (edn by Harinarayana Bhat) does not comment on *pratyaṅgāt*, but his restatements of the main propositions in the verse with *yauvane 'py aṅgāni yathocitaṁ puṣṭāni ca mṛdūni ca bhavanti* and *aṅga-kāṭhinyam eva stanatvena pariṇatam* suggest that he understood the word in the same way as Ruci-pati. To take the word as an ablative-ending avy is also possible because of the qualification *apañcamyāḥ* in P 2.4.83. However, neither commentator invokes that sūtra, which fact could suggest that they were used to seeing *ptg* as a noun meaning 'each limb, a collectivity of all limbs'.

- Caṇḍa-kauśika 2.17 *ko 'yaṁ tapo-vana-viruddham anātmanīnaṁ krūro nṛśaṁsam anutiṣṭhati karma ghoram / tasyaiṣa bāṇa-parilūna-śiro-dharasya pratyaṅgam ujjvala-śikhe dahane juhomi //*

As the object of *juhomi*, the verb, *ptg* must be a noun contextually meaning 'each limb, each body part'.

- Caṇḍa-kauśika, stage direction for Śaibyā after verse 5.7: *sasparśaṁ sutasya pratyaṅgam ālokya*
Tr.: "having looked at every limb of the (dead) son as she touches (the body)."
- Kīcaka-vadha of Nīti-varman 2.14: *viśeṣayantī pratyaṅgair aśokān nava-pallavān / pade pade 'śru-prabhavān uṣṇoṣṇān nava-pallavān //*
Tr.: "That (Draupadī) each of whose limbs excelled the Aśoka trees with new leaves (i.e., very tender Aśoka trees) (shed), at every step, very hot drops of tears."

The commentator Janārdana-sena glosses *pratyaṅgaiḥ* with *pratyavayavaiḥ*.

- Prabodha-candrodaya 5.5: *viṣṇor āyatanāny apāsya, saritāṁ kūlāny, araṇya-sthalīḥ puṇyāḥ, puṇyakṛtāṁ manāṁsi ca, bhavān mlecchān vrajeḥ sānugaḥ / no cet, santu kṛpāṇa-dārita-bhavat-pratyaṅga-dhārā-kṣarad-rakta-sphīta-vidīrṇa-vaktra-viśarat-pheṭkāriṇaḥ pheravāḥ.*

Here, 'each limb' makes sense as can be seen from the following translation by Matthew T. Kapstein (2009: 193): "You [= Mahāmoha] and your rabble must quit Viṣṇu's shrines, merit-makers' minds, riverbanks and holy forest groves, and depart to barbarous abodes. If not, let jackals barking, with their snouts wide-open, gaping, lap up streams of blood flowing from your every limb cut by my blade."

- Śārṅgadhara-paddhati 1095 (anyokti): *aye vārāṁ rāśe kuliśa-kara-kopa-pratibhayād ayaṁ pakṣa-premṇā giri-parivṛdhas tvām upagataḥ / tvad-antar-vāstavyād yadi punar ayaṁ vāḍava-śikhī pradīptaḥ pratyaṅgaṁ glapayati tataḥ ko 'sya śaraṇam //*
- Subhāṣita-ratna-kośa 15.17: *vāraṁ vāram anekadhā, sakhi, mayā cūta-drumāṇāṁ vane pītaḥ karṇa-darī-praṇāla-valitaḥ puṁskokilānāṁ dhvaniḥ / tasminn adya punaḥ śruti-praṇayini pratyaṅgam utkampitaṁ, tāpaś cetasi, netrayos taralimā, kasmād akasmān mama //*

§5.10a One particularly complex case:

Kāṭhaka-saṁhitā of the Kṛṣṇa Yajur-veda (sthānaka 38, anuvāka 4, mantras 51-52), Vājasaneyi-mādhyandina-saṁhitā of the Śukla Yajur-Veda (20.10) and Chāndogya-brāhmaṇa (its Mantra-brāhmaṇa part) 2.2.2–3 have an almost identical passage.[100] I became acquainted with it first in an edn of the last-named text by Devendra-nātha Pāṇḍeya. It ran thus:

> *pratikṣatre pratitiṣṭhāmi rāṣṭre, pratyaśveṣu pratitiṣṭhāmi goṣu / pratiprāṇe pratitiṣṭhāmi puṣṭau, pratyaṅgeṣu pratitiṣṭhāmy ātmani // pratidyāvā-pṛthivyoḥ pratitiṣṭhāmi yajñe /*

Note here particularly how the initial words of sentences appear. In his Hindi translation, however, Pāṇḍeya treats *prati* as if it were both, a compounded avy-forming morpheme as well as a separate word that goes also with the non-initial *rāṣṭre, goṣu,* and *aṅgeṣu*, and, despite the intervening words, forms expressions yielding meanings similar to those of the avys. As

[100]The Saṁhitās read *ātman* in the place of *ātmani* (appearance of the stem form where a locative singular is expected is an occasional feature of Vedic Sanskrit) and *puṣṭe* in the place of *puṣṭau*. These are inconsequential differences in the present context.

my mention of only some non-initial or sentence-end locatives may indicate, Pāṇḍeya is not consistent. He translates *pratyaśveṣu* without any recognition of *prati* and does not connect *prati* with *puṣṭau, ātmani* (translated as if the word was *aṅga*), *dyāvā-pṛthivī* and *yajñe.*

In Durgamohan Bhattacharyya's edn, which became available to me later and which Pāṇḍeya evidently follows (without acknowledgment and without reproducing its footnotes beyond the first page), the *prati* in each sentence is separated from the following word, except where the application of usual sandhi rules requires it to be joined to the following word (that is, only in pādas 2 and 4, we find the printing *pratyaśveṣu* and *pratyaṅgeṣu*). This description applies also to the printing of the passage in the Vājasaneyi- and Kāṭhaka-saṁhitās (but not to an edn of the Mādhyandina-saṁhitā published as no. 84 of the Śrī Gokula-dāsa Saṁskṛta Grantha-mālā, Vārāṇasī, Dillī: Chaukhambhā Orientalia, 1991).[101] The only difference is that, in separating *prati*, Bhattacharyya goes even to the extent of printing *pratitiṣṭhāmi* as *prati ti*°.

In an electronic recast of the Chāndogya-brāhmaṇa mantra text alone prepared on the basis of the 1901 and 1911 edns by Heinrich Stönner (first prapāṭhaka only with extracts from comms) and Hans Jörgensen (second prapāṭhaka only with Sāyaṇa's comm), respectively, the relevant word splitting is the same as in Bhattacharyya's edn, except that *pratitiṣṭhāmi* is not split as *prati ti*°.[102]

Since all the five sentences form a symmetry (although only the first four are in the triṣṭubh meter and are considered a ṛk, whereas the fifth is not in the same meter and is considered a yajus), the editors' intention, one assumes, must be to view all sentence-initial *prati*s either as separate words or as first members of compound expressions. Even where *prati* is joined to the following word in printing because of sandhi, they can be expected to have viewed it as separable if they separated it elsewhere.[103] Thus,

[101] At this point, Bhattacharyya also refers to "Āpastamba-mantra-pāṭha 2.18.3 dra; Hiraṇya-keśi-gṛhya-sūtra 2.17.4; Gobhila-gṛhya-sūtra 3.9.11; Khādira-gṛhya-sūtra 3.3.19 dra." The significance of his "dra" is not clear to me (probably it is a short form of *draṣṭavya*, signaling to the reader that he/she should look up the text place specified). I do not have access to the Āpastamba-mantra-pāṭha. The Gṛhya-sūtras quote only a small part of the passage we are discussing, only to enable their readers to identify the passage.

[102] (a) I leave out Jörgensen's edn in the following remarks, since it is not available to me and since he might not have seen Guṇa-viṣṇu's comm. (b) Bhattacharyya (1958: xix) mentions two earlier edns published by Satyavrata Sāmaśramī in 1872 and 1890. I cannot determine at present how the text was printed in them.

[103] As a feature indirectly supporting this deduction, we should note the following: The author of the passage employs an identical sentence construction in all five sentences. He has made no attempt syntactically to join the two locatives

we have a consistent difference in the editorial understanding of Pāṇḍeya, on the one hand, and Bhattacharyya (and possibly the earlier editors of the Chandogya-brāhmaṇa) and the Yajur-veda-saṁhitā editors (except for one), on the other. Pāṇḍeya thought of the five sentences as containing five avys (although this understanding is not reflected fully in his inexact and sub-standard translation), whereas the other editors were at least not committing themselves to any exclusivist understanding of the syntax.

§5.10b Since *prati* is not needed as an upasarga of the verb (it already has its own *prati*), it is possible that the other editors thought of *prati* as a karma-pravacanīya, as the normal practice is to treat the avys as single words and the karma-pravacanīyas as self-standing words.[104] However, it is also possible that *prati* was in their view a separable upasarga (as is frequently the case with upasargas in Vedic Sanskrit). This second possibility, in fact, receives support from the accentuation found in the Vājasaneyi-mādhyandina-saṁhitā preservation of the passage; *prati* has its own accent in this preservation, indicating that *prati* and each of the other words relat-

that flank *pratitiṣṭhāmi*. Conjunctions such as *ca* and *vā* are absent throughout. (As we shall see below, it is the commentators and translators who add *tathā* and *evam*, in effect functioning as *ca*, to each sentence.) Further, the author's engagement with sentence symmetry is deeper and more serious than it may initially appear. Not only does he place the locatives in each sentence only at the beginning and the end and make only the first locative of each sentence follow *prati*, he alternates the grammatical numbers in the first locatives from the singular to the plural (the last sentence not being a part of the triṣṭubh verse, can have the dual, perhaps even as a well-needed pattern-breaker). The first sentence speaks of a kingdom or a unit of government; the second of domesticated animals that have crucial importance in ancient societies in terms of survival, transportation etc.; the third of nourishment; the fourth of physical and mental well-being; and the fifth of maintenance of the cycle of creation—all in keeping with a scale of concerns and values we see in a number of Vedic texts. It is, therefore, unlikely that the author would be inconsistent in the *prati* words or phrases with regard to the grammatical category involved. He could have engaged in mere word play and tried only to maintain phonetic similarity in the initial parts of *pratikṣetre*, *pratyaśveśu*, *pratiprāṇe*, *pratyaṅgeṣu*, and *pratidyāvā-pṛthivyoḥ* without worrying about making all of them only compounds, only karma-pravacanīya phrases or only preverbs serving as reminders of the full verb form. However, the consistency in other respects that I have pointed out suggests that a hypothesis which would simultaneously assert the existence of (a) surface level similarity and (b) syntactic and semantic dissimilarity should not be entertained.

[104]Compare Bhattacharyya's statement on p. xxii: "I have generally adopted in the texts of the Ch[āndogya]. Br[āhmaṇa], the readings explained by Guṇ[a-viṣṇu], even where those readings seemed not preferable. But I have always pointed out the better readings in my notes on the texts concerned."

able to it simply co-occur; no composition of *prati* with the word following it takes place. The passage then becomes a series consisting of the following sentences: *kṣatre pratitiṣṭhāmi, rāṣṭre pratiti°, aśveṣu pratiti°, goṣu pratiti°, aṅgeṣu pratiti°, ātman/ātmani* (see note 100) *pratiti°, prāṇeṣu pratiti°, puṣṭe/puṣṭau* (see note 100) *pratiti°, dyāvā-pṛthivyoḥ pratiti°*, and *yajñe pratiti°*. Whether *prati* should be printed joined to *tiṣṭhāmi* in these sentences then becomes a matter of convention, and the passage cannot be said to contain an instance of *pratyaṅga*, only of *aṅga* (see §§5.2–3).

Before we accept the conclusion in the last clause of the preceding paragraph (as I eventually will), some further discussion is necessary (a) to be certain that that conclusion provides the best way to understand the passage and (b) to clear the research field of some possible but ultimately problematic alternatives. The first step toward this goal will be to ascertain if the traditional commentaries can offer any guidance.

As we carry out this ascertainment, we should keep in mind that, in the case of the mss on which the edns of the commentaries are based, the consideration whether the words are written separately is inapplicable. The tradition commonly followed in the mss is to write all the words of a sentence without any spaces in between. Also, in orally preserved literature such as the Vedic texts, the visual or script aspect is largely inconsequential. How the text is/was recited carries greater evidentiary weight. Therefore, when we read what the traditional commentators mentioned below have written about the passage under consideration, we cannot immediately make a hermeneutic deduction like the one we have made above about the modern editors. The word spacing in the explanations reproduced below is, therefore, not to be taken as absolutely settled.

§5.10c Guṇa-viṣṇu (not later than the 12th–13th century A.D.), the earliest available commentator of the Chāndogya-brāhmaṇa, comments on the passage as follows (p. 127 of Bhattacharyya's edn; pp. 122–123 of Pāṇḍeya's edn):[105]

> ***prati kṣatra*** *iti. triṣṭub asya chandaḥ.* ***prati dyāvā-pṛthivyor*** *ity-ādi yajuḥ. jape viniyogaḥ. agnir devatā. yajamāna idaṁ prārthayate. he agne,* ***pratikṣatre*** *kṣatraṁ kṣatraṁ [→ kṣatre kṣatre?]*[106] ***pratitiṣṭhāmi.*** *liṅ-arthe leṭ [→ laṭ?]*[107] ***rāṣṭre***

[105]The use of boldface type for the words cited from the commentandum is my addition.

[106]The phrase *kṣatraṁ kṣatraṁ*, even if it were to be taken as an instance of dittography and were to be reduced to *kṣatram*, would not fit syntactically. Erasure of an *e* stroke to such an extent that it becomes indistinguishable from an anusvāra is found in mss. Note also Sāyaṇa's explanation below with *kṣatre*.

[107]The form actually found in the verse, *pratitiṣṭhāmi*, is a laṭ, 'present tense',

> *rājye* [delete the preceding two words][108] *pratiṣṭhito 'haṁ*[109] *bhaveyam. pratiṣṭhā tapo-brahma-varcasādibhir guṇair mama bhavatv ity arthaḥ. tathā* ***rāṣṭre*** *deśe. [tathā?]* ***pratyaśveṣu prati*** *samantād vājiṣu. tathā* ***goṣu****. tathā* ***pratiprāṇe*** *dīrghāyuṣi. tathā* ***puṣṭau*** *bale. tathā* ***pratyaṅgeṣu*** *pāṇi-pādādiṣu dṛḍhatvena. tathā* ***ātmani*** *kṣetrajñe sva-rūpa-parijñānena. tathā* ***prati dyāvā-pṛthivyoḥ*** *sarva-bhūtānāṁ dhāraṇāvakāśa-dātṛtvena. tathā* ***yajñe*** *agni.ṣṭomādau karma-rūpe phala-rūpe ca.* ***pratitiṣṭhāmīty*** *uktārtham.*[110]

As can easily be seen from the readings I have queried, the comment has not come down to us in its original or author-finalized form (if indeed there ever was a final form distinct from the author's initial draft form). Beyond the textual problems, which are mostly manageable and only one of which has a bearing on the issue at hand, there is, however, also the question of Guṇa-viṣṇu's consistency and/or certainty. If his *kṣatraṁ kṣatraṁ* gives the impression of assumption of an avy, *prati samantāt* seems more likely under a karma-pravacanīya understanding. The third *prati* word, *pratiprāṇe* or *prati prāṇe*, receives only a direct gloss, *dīrghāyuṣi*, from him. In its case, one could somehow connect *āyus* with *prāṇa* but not *dīrgha* with any usual meaning of *prati*. Yet we do not get any guidance from Guṇa-viṣṇu enabling us to start with *prati* and arrive at *dīrgha*. As for *pratyaṅgeṣu*, it is not absolutely clear if he took it as a compound word or as *praty aṅgeṣu*. The *pāṇi* part of his paraphrase usually figures in the pratyaṅga lists (cf. §5.4), but, if *pāda* is a substitute for *sakthi*, the paraphrase could indicate that he presupposed a reference to the aṅgas (again, see §5.4). The addition of the explanatory *dṛḍhatvena* supports the latter understanding (as do the glosses in the other comms mentioned below); pratyaṅgas cannot be said to have an

form. If the emendation of *leṭ* to *laṭ* is accepted, one need not provide a reference to P 3.4.7, *liṅ-arthe leṭ*, as Bhattacharyya and Pāṇḍeya have.

[108]The word *rāṣṭre* is explained a little later in the cited paragraph. What the immediate context needs is an explanation of *pratitiṣṭhāmi*. Also, the expected *tathā* does not occur before the first *rāṣṭre*. After this first *rāṣṭre* was wrongly written here, someone could have added *rājye* as its gloss. Another possibility is that, later in the paragraph, the original wording was *rāṣṭre rajye deśe [vā tathā / vā... tathā]*.

[109]Pāṇḍeya drops *ahaṁ* from Bhattacharyya's text, an inconsequential difference.

[110]The editors print *prati kṣatra* (← *kṣatre*) once and *pratikṣatre* the next time. They print the third relevant word only as *pratiprāṇe*. In the remaining two cases, *pratyaśveṣu* and *pratyaṅgeṣu*, they cannot help the fact that sandhi robs them of the possibility of indicating their understanding of Guṇa-viṣṇu's understanding of the grammatical categories concerned (using a virāma sign under *y* would have gone against their normal orthographic practice).

association with dr̥ḍhatva 'firmness, strength', but the aṅgas can be. With *prati dyāvā-pr̥thivyoḥ*, however, we come back to the situation of non-clarity that we witness in the case of *pratiprāṇe*. Guṇa-viṣṇu articulates only the common concepts 'holding, supporting' associated with *pr̥thivī* 'earth' and 'providing space, making room' associated with *dyo/dyau* 'sky, space'.

In any case, if the reading *kṣatraṁ kṣatram* is emendable to *kṣatre kṣatre*, it will be justifiable to hold that the possibility of an avy understanding had occurred several centuries before Devendra-nātha Pāṇḍeya's time. This raises three questions: (a) Can avys ending in a locative be accommodated in the passage? (b) Must the conjectured emendation be accepted? (c) Is there any way in which the oddities of Guṇa-viṣṇu's explanation pointed out above can be so understood that they no longer remain oddities?

§5.10d Before I answer question (a), I might be asked why I am speaking only of the avy possibility and ruling out the '*prati* as a karma-pravacanīya' possibility. A karma-pravacanīya *prati* going with a locative is technically possible under P 2.3.9 (*yasmād adhikaṁ yasya ceśvara-vacanaṁ tatra saptamī*), but the commentators of P 2.3.9 do not cite any examples with *prati*. Nor is there any passage in the passages I have studied in this essay that would furnish an example for P 2.3.9. Furthermore, it would be difficult to argue that the resulting sense[111] would be probable in a Vedic passage, even if one were to assume that a *prati* example fitting P 2.3.9 existed once.

On the other hand, P 2.4.84 (*tr̥tīyā-saptamyor bahulam*) allows a composition in which *prati* acts as an avy-forming morpheme and which has a locative suffix at the end. Wackernagel 1905: II.1.257-258 contains examples attesting to the existence of such a composition when it cites the following as examples of avys not ending in *-am*:[112]

- Bhāgavata-purāṇa 12.6.59: *bāṣkaliḥ pratiśākhābhyo vālakhilyākhya-saṁhitām / cakre. vālāyanir bhajyaḥ kāsāraś caiva tāṁ dadhuḥ //*

[111]For example: "I establish myself in a governance domain that is higher than the essence of the protector-administrator class. I establish myself in cattle that are superior to horses. I establish myself in a sustenance that surpasses vital breath. I establish myself in the Self that is higher than the physical limbs. I establish myself in a sacrificial worship that transcends heaven and earth."

[112]Since I could not find a specification of the edns used by Wackernagel, I had to use the edns I could access. Secondly, wherever it was possible, I have cited complete lines where Wackernagel cited only the relevant forms, so that why the avy characterization of the cited forms fits may be known easily. In a few cases, Wackernagel has added a word or two to indicate how the meaning elements involved in the other words of the sentence lead an author to opt for a case other than the accusative or a number other than the singular. His observations are worthy of serious consideration, but they need not detain us here.

- Brahma-vaivarta-purāṇa 2.1.90: *tena maṅgala-caṇḍī sā paṇḍitaiḥ parikīrtitā / pratimaṅgala-vāreṣu prativilveṣu* (or *pratibilveṣu* or *prativiśveṣu*) *pūjitā //*
- Catur-varga-cintā-maṇi, khaṇḍa 1, adhyāya 5, Bibliotheca Indica edn p. 257: *anena vidhinā yas tu go-sahasraprado bhavet... pratimanvantare* [see the Hema-candra citation below] *tiṣṭhed... tāsāṁ [= gavāṁ] śr̥ṅgāṇi hemnātha pratiśr̥ṅgeṇa bandhayet /... kaṇṭha-deśataḥ / pratiniṣkeṇa kartavyaṁ...*
- Hema-candra 1.187.13 *pratimanvantare.*[113] Cf. the Catur-varga-cintā-maṇi citation above.
- Hitopadeśa 4, śloka 122 (according to some edns 131): *paricchinnaṁ phalaṁ yatra pratiskandhena dīyate / skandhopaneyaṁ taṁ prāhuḥ sandhiṁ sandhi-vicakṣaṇāḥ //*
- Muṇḍaka Upaniṣad 3.2.7: *gatāḥ kalāḥ pañca-daśa pratiṣṭhā devāś ca sarve pratidevatāsu / karmāṇi vijñānamayaś ca ātmā pare 'vyaye sarva ekī-bhavanti //* Nr̥siṁha-[uttara]-tāpanīyopaniṣad [khaṇḍa] 2 [page line?] 7: *mātrā mātrāḥ pratimātrāḥ kuryāt.*
- Nr̥siṁha-[uttara]-tāpanīyopaniṣad [khaṇḍa] 3 [page line?] 6: *bhavati ca sarveṣu pādeṣu catur-ātmā sthūla-sūkṣma-bīja-sākṣibhir pratimātrāḥ kr̥tvotānujñātr-anujñā-vikalpa-rūpaṁ cintayan ...*
- Pāraskara-gr̥hya Sūtra 1.3.1-2: *ṣaḍ arghyā bhavanty ācārya r̥tvig vaivāhyo* [→ °*vāhyau*, to bring the number to the expected six] *rājā priyaḥ snātaka iti. pratisaṁvatsarān arhayeyuḥ.*

Therefore, the locative case endings of the post-*prati* words of the five Chandogya-brāhmaṇa sentences need not come in the way of their acceptance as avys.[114] Yet it seems preferable to conclude that Guṇa-viṣṇu's original wording was not *kṣatre kṣatre.* Taking the second *kṣatraṁ* in *kṣatraṁ*

[113]I could not determine which work of Hema-candra Wackernagel had in mind and if he was referring to the books and chapters of the original work or to the volume, page and line numbers of the edn used. His translation of *pratimanvantare* is, as one would expect, 'in jeder Manuperiode'.

[114]It might be thought that Wackernagel's collection of avys that do not end in *-am* , while supporting P 2.4.84, proves the inadequacy of the sūtra, since it contains uses in cases other than the instrumental and locative stipulated by P through *tr̥tīyā-saptamyoḥ.* However, it is precisely these other case uses in Wackernagel's collection that deserve reconsideration. Are they really avys? The contexts of *pratiśākhābhyaḥ* (ablative), *pratimātrāḥ* (accusative) and *pratisaṁvatsarān* (accusative) suggest that the words could be understood, respectively, as (a) 'resembling Veda-śākhās → not really one of the regular, recognized or well-known, branches (of the Veda)', (b) 'corresponding elements, next-order elements, those elements which arise from the basic elements' and (c) 'for the duration of approximately a year, roughly for a year'. Historians of Vedic religion have de-

kṣatraṁ as a case of dittography and emending only one *kṣatraṁ* to *kṣatre* will be at least as defensible an emendation as the emendation of *kṣatraṁ kṣatraṁ* to *kṣatre kṣatre*—in fact, it will be a more defensible emendation, because Guṇa-viṣṇu does not render any of the other words possibly beginning with *prati* as avys and *kṣatre* is found employed by Sāyaṇa in the corresponding place in his commentary (reproduced below). Thus, while *pratikṣatre* is admissible as a locative-ending avy, it should not be viewed as a reading in Chāndogya-brāhmaṇa 2.2.2–3 as known to Guṇa-viṣṇu, and the emendation which can serve as the basis of that reading should be set aside in favor of the emendation *kṣatre*.

§5.10e Sāyaṇa (14th century A.D.) offers the following explanation:[115]

> *homānantaraṁ* ***prati kṣatra*** *iti japet. tathā ca sūtraṁ "nyañcau pāṇī kṛtvā prati kṣatra iti japed"* [Khādira-gṛhya-sūtra 3.3.19] *iti.* ***prati kṣatra*** *iti. triṣṭub asya chandaḥ. agni-liṅgābhāve 'pi tat-saṁnidhau prārthyamānatvād agnir devatā. he agne tvad-anugrahād ahaṁ* ***kṣatre****, kṣatāt trāyata iti kṣatraṁ balaṁ, tasmin,* ***pratitiṣṭhāmīti*** *saṁbandhaḥ. evam uttareṣv api prati-śabdeṣu yojyam. tathā* ***rāṣṭre*** *rājye* ***pratitiṣṭhāmi*** *pratiṣṭhito bhavāmi. tath****āśveṣu goṣu*** *ca pratitiṣṭhāmi. asmākaṁ gavo 'śvāś cāvicalitā bhavantv ity arthaḥ. kiṁ ca,* ***prāṇe*** *madīye*

tected hints to the effect that the Vālakhilyas were somewhat on the outside of mainstream Vedic society. The Veda they followed could have been viewed as 'not quite the original, uncontaminated or unchanged authentic one'. Similarly, in the case of *pratisaṁvatsarān* occurring in Pāraskara-gṛhya Sūtra 1.3.1–2 the intention is unlikely to have been to stipulate that the persons named should be honored each year. Relatively few of them would have been easily accessible every year. Nor could have they been constrained to remain accessible for exactly a year. Therefore, the intention must have been to teach that, for about a year, one should be particularly attentive to the possibilities of honoring them and use all opportunities that come up. Thus it seems more defensible to me to take *pratiśṛṅgeṇa, pratiskandhena, pratimaṅgala-vāreṣu, prativilveṣu, pratimanvantare* and *pratidevatāsu* as avys exemplifying P 2.4.84 and *pratimātrāḥ, pratisaṁvatsarān* and *pratiśākhābhyaḥ* as tat-puruṣa nouns of the type exemplified in §4.1 and to conclude that the qualification *tṛtīyā-saptamyoḥ* in P 2.4.84 is justified and adequate. The word *bahulam* of that sūtra might have been intended to cover variation in grammatical number.

[115] I do not need to decide whether this Sāyaṇa is the same as the Sāyaṇa who commented on the Ṛg-veda etc. I am quite willing to accept the possibility that all the comms of Vedic texts going under Sāyaṇa's name were productions of committees of specialists supervised, to a greater or smaller extent, by a learned administrator named Sāyaṇa.

prāṇa-vāyau pratitiṣṭhāmi.[116] *prāṇo 'pi māṁ mā muñcatv ity arthaḥ. tathā* ***puṣṭau*** *śarīra-poṣe pratitiṣṭhāmi. evam* ***aṅgeṣu*** *cakṣur-ādy-avayaveṣu*[117] *pratitiṣṭhāmi. madīyāny aṅgāni pratiṣṭhitāni santv ity arthaḥ. evam* ***ātmany*** *api. jīvātmāhaṁ paramātmani* ***pratitiṣṭhāmi*** *sva-rūpa-niṣṭho bhavāmīty arthaḥ. athav**ātmā** buddhiḥ. sthira-buddhir bhavāmīty arthaḥ.* ***prati dyāvā-pṛthivyor*** *iti ukte viniyoga-devate. yajur-mantro 'yam. ato na.cchandaḥ. he agne,* ***dyāvā-pṛthivyor*** *madhye* ***pratitiṣṭhāmi.*** *divi pṛthivyāṁ ca ye bhogāḥ santi te mayi sthirā bhavantv ity arthaḥ. evaṁ* ***yajñe*** *'gniṣṭomādau* ***pratitiṣṭhāmi*** *sthiro bhavāmīty arthaḥ.*

What is remarkable here is that there is no reflection of *prati* in Sāyaṇa's glosses of *pratikṣatre, pratyaśveṣu, pratiprāṇe, pratyaṅgeṣu* and *pratidyāvā-pṛthivyoḥ* (or the counterparts of these words resulting from a space imagined after *prati*). That he had a *prati* at the beginnings of sentences is something we know only from what precedes the gloss on *kṣatre* and the sentence *evam uttareṣv api prati-śabdeṣu yojyam.*

The very first interpretation of this sentence that would occur to a reader—primarily because of the point at which the sentence occurs—would be that "Just as I, namely Sāyaṇa, have connected *[prati]kṣatre* and *pratitiṣṭhāmi*, you, readers of my comm, should connect the later *prati*-words, that is, the words *pratyaśveṣu* (or *praty aśveṣu*) etc." One wonders, however, if this needs to be told in the case of short sentences of three (or four) words and when Sāyaṇa himself explicitly connects the locative forms with *pratitiṣṭhāmi.* If a general statement about the intended syntax is to be made because the verb already has its own *prati,* one expects to be informed about why and how the verb would take another *prati* or *prati* word.

This means that we should take Sāyaṇa's sentence *evam uttareṣv api prati-śabdeṣu yojyam* in some other sense such as: "Just as I, namely Sāyaṇa, have connected *prati* in *prati kṣatre* with *tiṣṭhāmi*, you, readers of my comm, should connect the later self-standing *prati* words with *tiṣṭhāmi.*" Such an interpretation will also explain why there is an absence of avy dissolutions in Sāyaṇa's commentary.

If, with this experience, we look back at Guṇa-viṣṇu, we can say that there is a fundamental agreement between Sāyaṇa and him regarding the part that concerns us most directly in the present context. Neither scholar

[116]The two sentences from *asmākaṁ* to *pratitiṣṭhāmi* are missing in Pāṇḍeya's reproduction of Bhaṭṭācāryya's text, a haplography caused by the occurrence of *pratitiṣṭhāmi* in the preceding sentence (and one more piece of evidence indicating the sub-standard nature of Pāṇḍeya's book).

[117]This gloss, unlike Guṇa-viṣṇu's *pāṇi-pādādiṣu*, seems to presuppose ptg as the background notion (cf. §5.4). However, Sāyaṇa uses only *aṅgeṣu* before his gloss.

feels the need to give prominence to *prati* and to account for its repeated presence in specific ways. Neither cites any authority for the way he treats *prati*. This feature of their explanations suggests that they took *prati* in its most common or well-known role, namely in the role of an upasarga.

§5.10f If we look at the commentators of the Vājasaneyi-saṁhitā (I am not aware of any comm on the Kāṭhaka-saṁhitā), we find essentially the same situation. Uvaṭa, in his bhāṣya, takes *pratitiṣṭhāmi* with all the locatives and supplies *ca* for each of them except for three. He does not explain what the pāda-initial *prati* conveys (or why he does not use *ca* in some cases):

> *kr̥ṣṇājine 'varohati* ***prati-kṣatram*** *iti yajuṣā. pratitiṣṭhāmi kṣatre, pratitiṣṭhāmi rāṣṭre, pratitiṣṭhāmi ca aśveṣu, pratitiṣṭhāmi goṣu, pratitiṣṭhāmi ca aṅgeṣu, pratitiṣṭhāmi ca ātmani, pratitiṣṭhāmi ca prāṇeṣu, pratitiṣṭhāmi ca puṣṭe, pratitiṣṭhāmi ca dyāvā-pr̥thivyoḥ, pratitiṣṭhāmi ca yajñe.*

Essentially, the same stance is taken by Mahīdhara in his Veda-dīpa comm, although he does not actually repeat *prati*:[118]

> *"kr̥ṣṇājine 'varohati prati-kṣatra iti"* [Kā 19.4.23][119] *āsandīto yajamānaḥ kr̥ṣṇājine 'vatarati. viśva-deva-devatyaṁ yajuḥ atiśakvarī. ahaṁ* ***kṣatre pratitiṣṭhāmi*** *kṣatriya-jātau pratiṣṭhā-yukto bhavāmi.* ***rāṣṭre*** *deśe,* ***aśveṣu, goṣu, aṅgeṣu*** *kara-pādādy-avayaveṣu* ***ātman*** *ātmani citte, prāṇeṣu pañcasu,* ***puṣṭe*** *puṣṭau samr̥ddhau,* ***dyāvā-pr̥thivyoḥ*** *svargeha-lokayoḥ,* ***yajñe*** *jyotiṣṭomādau ca pratitiṣṭhāmi. kriyā-padāvr̥ttiḥ phalātiśaya-dyotanārthā. kṣatriya-deśayoḥ pratiṣṭhā vaśī-karaṇam. gośva-pratiṣṭhā tat-prāptiḥ. prāṇāṅga-pratiṣṭhā nīrogatvam. ātma-pratiṣṭhā nirādhitvam. puṣṭa-pratiṣṭhā dhana-samr̥ddhiḥ. dyāvā-pr̥thivyoḥ pratiṣṭhābhaya-loka-kīrtiḥ. yajñe pratiṣṭhā yajña-karaṇam. vaśya-viśvaḥ paśumān, nirādhi-vyādhiḥ śrīmān yajña-kartā ca bhaveyam iti bhāvaḥ.*

Thus, the explanations of Guṇa-viṣṇu, Sāyaṇa, Uvaṭa and Mahīdhara are essentially in agreement. All of them conform to the attested accen-

[118]The distinctive addition in Mahīdhara's work consists in the following points: (a) The verb repetition is for the sake of connoting phalātiśaya '(increasing) enrichment of the outcome'. (b) What pratiṣṭhā boils down to in the case of each object in the locative case is different and can be spelt out. (c) The sequence of sentences is significant. Sāyaṇa and Guṇa-viṣṇu also make point (b) to a smaller extent. Compare note 103 above.

[119]I suppose this is the editor's specification of where the passage occurs in the Kāṇva recension.

tuation.[120] The following translation by Griffith (1899: 321), which can be improved in the rendition of individual words, is also syntactically justified: "I take my stand on princely power and Kingship, on cows am I dependent, and on horses. On members I depend, and on the body, on vital breath dependent and on welfare, on heaven and earth and sacrifice dependent."[121] Our conclusion then should be that the Kāṭhaka-saṁhitā, Vājasaneyi-saṁhitā and Chāndogya-brāhmaṇa do not contain an occurrence of *ptg* as a compound at the places specified in the first paragraph of §5.10a (they contain only an occurrence of *aṅga* joined in sandhi to *prati*), although the printing in Devendra-nāthā Pāṇḍeya's edn and in one edn of the Mādhyandina-saṁhitā (specified in the third paragraph of §5.10a) may lead a reader to attribute a *ptg* occurrence to these texts.[122]

[120]Wackernagel thinks that the uses he has collected come from Late Classical Sanskrit; cf. "Weiterhin wird spätklassisch das distributive *prati*-Kompositum mit einer Kasusendung versehen, zur genauern Angabe der Beziehung, worin der in Wiederholung gedachte Begriff zum Satzganzen steht." I consider it possible that the *consistent* use of the accusative singular suffix (or of the suffix *-am* in P 2.4.93) was not the original stage but a later development and that the deviating forms cited by Wackernagel come from older literature (they might have survived as fossils in later literature). The affinity of some of them with expressions in Avestan pointed out by Wackernagel himself makes it more likely that such indeed is the case.

[121]Mainly, the verbs "take stand on" and "depend" (along with "dependent") should be replaced by "place myself firmly " or "establish myself." If the context for the mantra given by Guṇa-viṣṇu, Sāyaṇa, Uvaṭa and Mahīdhara is correct, as it probably is, we can also use "I wish to establish" or "May I establish" in the place of "I establish" throughout this passage.

[122]Taking *prati* as an upasarga indicating or co-signifying 'similar, counterpart or complementary", we can translate the passage concerned along the following lines: "I establish myself in a governance domain that is virtually the essence of the protector-administrator class. I establish myself in cattle that are horse-like (animals in their strength). I establish myself in sustenance that is no less than vital breath. I establish myself in the inner being that is deeper or subtler body parts (i.e., the senses of cognition and faculties of movement, whatever requires consciousness). I establish myself in a sacrificial worship that is a replication of heaven and earth." This translation treats all *prati* words uniformly. It does not need addition of *ca* or *tathā*. The contents it conveys are not at odds with what the Vedic texts convey. Yet I would not recommend its acceptance anymore than of any avy-based translation. The attestations of *pratikṣatra, pratyaśva, pratiprāṇa* and *pratidyāva-pṛthivī* in the senses I have attached to them are lacking. The last one sounds particularly unlikely. It may be set aside as coming after the triṣṭubh verse, but then the appeal I have made to similarity of formation (note 103) will be weakened.

References and abbreviations

(I have generally not specified publication details of the edns and trs of Sanskrit texts mentioned in the main essay and the Appendix. Inclusion of these details would have made the article too long. Besides, all of them can now be easily gathered by accessing the electronic catalogues of various libraries. The only exception made is that of the edns of the MB and its comms and sub-comms, as they have a direct bearing on the central concern of the essay.)

Abhyankar, K. V.

1967 *Paribhāṣā-saṁgraha.* Postgraduate and Research Department Series, no. 7. Poona: Bhandarkar Oriental Research Institute.

1977 *A Dictionary of Sanskrit Grammar.* Revised in collaboration with J.M. Shukla. Gaekwad's Oriental Series 134. First edn 1961. Baroda: Oriental Institute.

Acharya, Prasanna Kumar

1927 *A Dictionary of Hindu Architecture* or *An Encyclopaedia of Hindu Architecture.* Reprint, London: Oxford University Press, 1946. Māna-sāra Series 7 [= 2nd rev. ed. of Māna-sāra Series 1]. Reprint, Bhopal: J.K. Pub. House, 1978. Reprint, Delhi: Oriental Books [= Oriental Books Reprint Corp.?], 1979. Reprint, New Delhi: Munshiram Manoharlal Publishers, 1993. Reprint, New Dehli: Cosmo, 1994. Vols 2. [Preface date; actual publication probably in 1934. Although this reprint carries the title *Encyclopaedia of Hindu Architecture*, it really seems to be a reprint of the first edn published under the title *A Dictionary of Hindu Architecture*, since the number of total pages in its two vols is specified as "XX, 861."]

Aklujkar, Ashok

1983 Pāṇini's Aṣṭādhyāyī as a case in textual criticism. In *Proceedings of the International Seminar on Studies in the Aṣṭādhyāyī of Pāṇini*, edited by S. D. Joshi and S. D. Laddu, 1–10. Poona: Centre of Advanced Study in Sanskrit, University of Poona.

2008a Patañjali's Mahābhāṣya as a key to happy Kashmir. In *Linguistic Traditions of Kashmir*, edited by Mrinal Kaul and Ashok Aklujkar, 41–87. New Delhi: D.K. Printworld.

2008b Gonardīya, Goṇikā-putra, Patañjali and Gonandīya. In *Linguistic Traditions of Kashmir*, edited by Mrinal Kaul and Ashok Aklujkar, 88–172. New Delhi: D.K. Printworld.

2008c Patañjali: a Kashmirian. In *Linguistic Traditions of Kashmir*, edited by Mrinal Kaul and Ashok Aklujkar, 173–205. New Delhi: D.K. Printworld.

Annaṁ-bhaṭṭa: see Narasimhacharya.

Apte, Vaman Shivram
1890 *The Practical Sanskrit-English Dictionary.* A revised and enlarged edn in three parts by P.K. Gode and C. G. Karve. Poona: Prasad Prakashan, 1957–59. Parts II and III of the enlarged edn reprinted in 1979. Three parts published in one volume in a photographically reduced size: Kyoto: Rinsen Book Company; Delhi: Motilal Banarsidass.

avy = avyayī-bhāva.

Böhtlingk, Otto von
1879–1889 *Sanskrit Wörterbuch in Kürzerer Fassung.* Vol. 1: 1879, vol. 2: 1881, vol. 3: 1882, vol. 4: 1883, vol. 5: 1884, vol. 6: 1886, vol. 7: 1889. Reprint, Graz: Akademische Druck-u. Verlagsanstalt, 1959. Reprint (called "first Indian edn"), 1990–91: Delhi: Motilal Banarsidass, 1990–91. See the following entry for vol. 8.

Böhtlingk, Otto von, and Rudolph Roth
1855–1875 *Sanskrit-Wörterbuch.* St. Petersburg: Kaiserliche Akademie. 7 vols. Vol. 1: 1852–1855 Vocale, vol. 2: 1856–1858 *ka-cha*, vol. 3: 1859–1861 *ja-dha*, vol. 4: 1862–1865 *na-pha*, vol. 5: 1865–1868 *ba-ma*, vol. 6: 1868–1871 *ya-va*, vol. 7: 1872–1875 *śa-ha*. Reprint, Osnabrück: O. Zeller, 1966, 1983. Reprint (called "first Indian edn"), Delhi: Motilal Banarsidass, 1990–1991. 8 vols (vol. 8: *Nachträge zum Sanskrit-Wörterbuch in Kürzerer Fassung von Otto Böhtlingk*, edited by Richard Schmidt, 1924–28.)

Burrow, Thomas
1955 *The Sanskrit Language.* Series: Great languages. London: Faber, 1973. 2nd impression, 1965.

EDSHP = *An Encyclopaedic Dictionary of Sanskrit on Historical Principles*, being prepared at Deccan College, Pune.

Gail, Adalbert J.
1980–81 Āyudha-puruṣa[:] die anthropomorphen Waffen Viṣṇus in Literatur und Kunst. *Indologica Taurinensia* 8–9: 181–186.

Gelder, Jeanette Maria van
1961 *The Mānava-śrauta-sūtra belonging to the Maitrāyaṇīya Saṁhitā.* New Delhi: International Academy of Indian Culture.

Īśvarānanda: see Narasimhacharya.

Kaiyaṭa: see Patañjali and Narasimhacharya.

Kevalānanda-sarasvatī
1952–1966 *Mīmāṁsā-koṣa.* 7 vols. Prājña Pāṭha-śālā Maṇḍala Grantha Mālā. Wai: Prājña Pāṭha-śālā.

Kielhorn, Franz
1886 Notes on the Mahābhāṣya. *Indian Antiquary* 15: 80–84. Reprint: *Kleine Schriften* 1969: 202–206.

Mayrhofer, Manfred

1956–1976 *Kurzgefasstes etymologisches Wörterbuch des Altindischen.* Vol. I (a -th): 1956, vol. II (d-m): 1963, vol. III (y-h): 1976. Heidelberg: Carl Winter Universitätsverlag.

1986–1997 *Etymologisches Wörterbuch des Altindoarischen.* Part 1: Ältere Sprache; vol. I (a-dh): 1992, vol. II (na-ha): 1996. Part 2: Jüngere Sprache: 1997. Heidelberg: Carl Winter Universitätsverlag.

MB = Mahābhāṣya, Vyākaraṇa-mahābhāṣya. See Patañjali.

Meister, Michael W., Madhusudan A. Dhaky, and George Michell

1983–2001 *Encyclopaedia of Indian Temple Architecture.* New Delhi: American Institute of Indian Studies and Oxford University Press; Philadelphia: University of Pennsylvania Press. For vol. 2 pt. 2: Princeton, N.J.: Princeton University Press. Vol. I: South India. Pt. 1: Lower Drāviḍa-deśa, 200 B.C.–A.D. 1324. Pt. 2: Upper Drāviḍa-deśa, Early Phase, B.C. 550–1075. Pt. 3: Upper Drāviḍa-deśa, Later phase, A.D. 973–1326. In association with Indira Gandhi National Centre for the Arts, New Delhi. Pt. 4-A: Drāviḍa-deśa, Later Phase, *c.* A.D. 1289–1798. Edited by George Michell. Coordinated by U. S. Moorti. Vol. 2 North India. Pt. 1: Foundations of North Indian Style *c.* 250 B.C.–A.D. 1100. Pt. 2: Period of Early Maturity, *c.* A.D. 700–900.

Molesworth, J. T.

1857 *A Dictionary of Marathi and English.* 2nd edn., revised and enlarged. Bombay: Printed for Govt. at the Bombay Education Society's Press. Reprint, Poona: Shubhada-Saraswat, 1975, 1991.

Monier-Williams, Monier

1872, 1888 *A Sanskrit-English Dictionary ....* Revised ed., 1889/1899. Oxford: Clarendon Press. Reprinted many times.

Nāgeśa: see Patañjali.

Narasimhacharya, M.S.

1973 *Mahābhāśya-Pradīpa-vyākhyānāni.* 10 vols. Vol. 1: 1973, vol. 2: 1975, vol. 3: 1976, vol. 4: 1977, vol. 5: 1978, vol. 6: 1979, vol. 7: 1980, vol. 8: 1981, vol. 9: 1982, vol. 10: 1983. Publications de l'Institut Français d'Indologie, no. 51. Pondichéry: Institute Français d'Indologie Pondichéry.

Nārāyaṇa: see Narasimhacharya.

NSP = Nirnaya Sagara/Sagar Press.

P = Pāṇini.

Pat = Patañjali.

Patañjali. *Vyākaraṇa-mahābhāṣya.* (a) Franz Kielhorn. 3 vols. 1st ed., 1880–1885. Third revised edition by K.V. Abhyankar. Poona/Pune: Bhandarkar Oriental Research Institute, 1962–1972. (b) *with the Commentaries Pradīpa, Uddyota and Chāyā.* 5 vols (incomplete edn). Vol. 1 (adhyāya 1, pāda 1 or Navāhnikī), edited by Shivadatta D [= Dādhimatha] Kuddāla [= Kudāla], 1917; fifth edn edited by Bhārgava-śāstrī Bhikājī Jośī, 1951; vol. 2 (adhyāya 1, pāda 2 to adhyāya 2), edited by Shivadatta D. Kuddāla, 1912; vol. 3 (adhyāya 3), edited by Raghunātha Śarmā and Shivadatta D. Kuddāla, 1937; vol. 4 (adhyāyas 4–5), edited by Bhārgava-śāstrī Bhikājī Jośī, 1942; vol. 5 (adhyāya 6), edited by Bhārgava-śāstrī Bhikājī Jośī, 1945. Bombay/Mumbai: Nirnaya Sagara Press. (c) *with the commentaries Pradīpa by Kaiyaṭa and Uddyota by Nāgeśa-bhaṭṭa.* Delhi: Motilal Banarsidass. 1967. 3 vols.

ptg = *pratyaṅga*, mostly only where the word is mentioned (as distinct from used) but not in passages quoted from Sanskrit texts, where the full form is allowed to stand.

Rāma-candra-sarasvatī: see Narasimhacharya.

Ratna-candra, Muni
1923 *Sacitra Ardha-māgadhī Koṣa: An Illustrated Ardha-magadhi Dictionary.* 5 vols. Reprint, Delhi: Motilal Banarsidass, 1988.

Rhys Davids, William Thomas, and William Stede
1921 *The Pali Text Society's Pali-English Dictionary.* London: Pali Text Society. Reprint, Oxford: Pali Text Society, 1995.

Śiva-rāmendra-sarasvatī: see Narasimhacharya.

Steinkellner, Ernst, Helmut Krasser, and Horst Lasic
2005 *Pramāṇa-samuccaya-ṭīkā Viśālāmalavatī of Jinendra-buddhi.* Series: Sanskrit Texts from the Tibetan Autonomous Region, no. 1/II. Beijing-Vienna: China Tibetology Research Center, Austrian Academy of Sciences.

Tārānātha Tarka-vācaspati Bhaṭṭācārya
1873–84 *Vācaspatyam / Vāchaspatyam.* 1873–1884. 6 vols. Chowkhamba Sanskrit Series, no. 94. Reprint, 1962. Varanasi: Chowkhamba Sanskrit Series Office.

Turner, Ralph Lilley, and Dorothy Rivers (Goulty) Turner
1971 *A Comparative Dictionary of the Indo-Aryan Languages: Phonetic Analysis.* London, New York: Oxford University Press.

Vt = Vārttika.

Pāṇinian Features of the Oldest Known Malayāḷam Description*

ÉMILIE AUSSANT

Introduction

The work presented here represents one of the first steps in a research program called "Grammaire sanskrite étendue/Extended Sanskrit Grammar" led by Jean-Luc Chevillard (CNRS, Paris), Vincenzo Vergiani (Cambridge University) and me. The aim is to study the way in which descriptive models elaborated for Sanskrit (the *Aṣṭādhyāyī* of Pāṇini, as well as works of other grammatical schools) have been used to describe other languages, as for instance Tamil, Telugu, Malayāḷam, etc.

The oldest known grammatical observations from Kerala are found in a poetical treatise of the 14th century: the *Līlātilakam*. This text, composed of Sanskrit *sūtras*, describes—among other things—morphological and phonological characteristics of Maṇipravāḷam,[1] the mediaeval literary language of Kerala, which is defined as a mixture of the Keraḷabhāṣā and Sanskrit (hence the name *Maṇipravāḷam*: *maṇi* 'rubies' [Malayāḷam] and *pravāḷam* 'coral' [Sanskrit]).[2] The grammatical section of the *Līlātilakam*,

*I warmly thank Jean-Luc Chevillard for his useful comments and suggestions.

[1]The term *maṇipravāḷam*—or rather *maṇippiravāḷam*—is defined in *kārikai* 182 of the *Vīracōḻiyam* (a grammar of Tamil of the 11th century):

> *iṭaiyē vaṭa eḻuttu eytil viraviyal* [...] *maṇippiravāḷam nal teyvac colliṉ* [...].
>
> "When Sanskrit letters are interspersed with Tamil, the style is known as a 'mixture' (*viraviyal*); when Sanskrit words are mixed with Tamil, the style is known as rubies and coral." [trans. Monius (2001: 119)]

[2]The very first *sūtra* reads: *bhāṣāsaṃskṛtayōgō maṇipravāḷaṃ* "*maṇipravāḷaṃ* [is] a mixture of *bhāṣā* and Sanskrit." Maṇipravāḷam compositions are mainly hymns to Gods, royal panegyrics and poems. By the time of the *Līlātilakam*, most of Maṇipravāḷam works were devoted to description and praise of heroines (this is, at least, what the examples quoted in the *Līlātilakam* tend to show).

because it reveals a Pāṇinian influence, merits special attention within the context of this research program.

1. Overview of the *Līlātilakam*

Nothing is known of the author of the *Līlātilakam*, nor of his life or the conditions under which he composed the treatise, except that he was a pandit versed in both the Sanskrit and Tamil traditions.[3] It was in 1916 that the first complete edition of the Sanskrit *sūtras* with Malayāḷam translation of the Sanskrit commentary was produced by Attur Krishna Pisharoti.[4] John Brough was to publish an edition of the Sanskrit text, as well as a part of the translation in 1947. His edition/translation is based on Pisharoti's.[5] Four manuscripts should be accessible in India, probably copied from the same original.[6]

We do not know if the name *Līlātilakam*, which literally signifies 'Ornament of leisure', is the original title of the treatise and/or of the *Vṛtti*—it sounds more like the title of a commentary than anything else. The first *śilpa* ends with the following mention: *iti līlātilakē*[7] *maṇipravāḷa-lakṣaṇaṃ prathama-śilpaṃ* and some scholars consider *maṇipravāḷa-lakṣaṇaṃ* ('definition of Maṇipravāḷam') to be the original title of the whole work.[8]

The *Līlātilakam* does not actually constitute a grammar of Maṇipravāḷam; it is a poetical manual intended for those composing in Maṇipravāḷam. But, insofar as a good composition necessarily requires correct morphology and syntax, the text provides some considerations concerning the functioning of the language.

The text and its *Vṛtti*—of the same authorship, according to some[9]—, both entirely in Sanskrit, take the form of a *śāstra* in aphoristic *sūtras*. The resort to this form of composition may probably be explained by the attempt to confer *śāstric* status on the work and the authority which proceeds from such status. It is well known that, by this time, Sanskrit still represents a descriptive apparatus or a discursive model of compositions for the most part (technical as well as literary).

[3]Gopala Pillai (1985: 23–31) reviews the different theses supported (and provides a summary of them [26]). According to him, the author of the *Līlātilakam* would have been a Nambutiri brahmin (29). See also Freeman 1998.

[4]See Gopala Pillai 1985: 5.

[5]Ezhuthacchan would provide an English translation of the first three chapters between 1964 and 1968. See Gopala Pillai 1985: 9.

[6]See Gopala Pillai 1985: 11–13.

[7]Not all the editions seem to have the word *līlātilake*; Brough's edition does.

[8]See Gopala Pillai 1985: 6–7.

[9]Gopala Pillai (1985: 32–38) reviews some contradictions between the *sūtras* and the *Vṛtti*.

The *Līlātilakam* consists of 151 *sūtras*—most of them followed by a *Vṛtti*—organized in eight chapters (*śilpa*):

1) *maṇipravāḷa-lakṣaṇam* ('definition/description of Maṇipravāḷam'): definition and division into nine types

   = eleven *sūtras*

2) *śarīra-nirūpaṇam* ('examination of constituent elements'): nominal and verbal morphology

   = twenty-five *sūtras* (2.1–2.5: words composing the *bhāṣā* (*deśī*, *saṃskṛtabhava*, *saṃskṛtarūpa*); 2.6: two varieties of *bhāṣā* (*apakṛṣṭā*, *utkṛṣṭā*); 2.7–2.8: sanskritized *bhāṣā*; 2.9–2.23: nominal endings (cases, genders, numbers); 2.24–2.25: expression of gender and number in verbs)

3) *sandhi-vivaraṇam* ('description of junctions'): phonetics/phonology

   = twenty-nine *sūtras* (3.1–3.6: vocalic junctions; 3.7–3.12: vocalic-consonantic junctions; 3.13–3.19: nasal junctions; 3.20–3.28: glide junctions; 3.29: list of phonetical operations which are to be known from usage)

4) *dōṣa-ālōcanam* ('survey of faults'): faults of poetical composition

   = twenty-seven *sūtras*

5) *guṇa-nirūpaṇam* ('examination of qualities'): qualities of poetic composition

   = five *sūtras*

6) *śabdālaṅkāra-vivecanam* ('discussion of figures of speech'): figures of speech relative to the form of words

   = nine *sūtras*

7) *arthālaṅkāra-vivaraṇam* ('description of figures on meaning'): figures of speech relative to the meaning of words

   = thirty *sūtras*

8) *rasa-prakaraṇam* ('explanation of *rasa*'): discussion of *rasa*

   = fifteen *sūtras*

What we may call the "grammatical section" is then restricted to the second and third chapters.

2. An example from the second *śilpa*

L 2.9 *arthaviśēṣē 'syāḥ parabhāgaviśēṣaḥ.*

"When there is a difference in meaning, there is a difference in the last part [of words] of the [*bhāṣā*]."

Vṛtti: *samprati bhāṣāyā vibhaktyādyaṃśō nirūpyatē. arthaviśēṣaḥ prātipadikamātrādiḥ liṅgavacanē ca. asyāḥ bhāṣāyāḥ.*

"Now, the part [of the word] of the *bhāṣā* which is the ending, etc.[10] is considered. The difference in meaning consists in the group [of eight items] beginning with *prātipadikamātra* (i.e. the use of the mere nominal base, which characterizes the nominative case),[11] as well as in gender and number. *asyāḥ* [stands for] *bhāṣāyāḥ*."

L 2.10 *sō 'ṣṭadhā tridhā dvidhā ca.*

"The [difference in the last part of words] is of eight kinds, of three kinds and of two kinds."

Vṛtti: *saḥ parabhāgaviśēṣaḥ. aṣṭadhā vibhaktayaḥ. tridhā liṅgaṃ. dvidhā vacanaṃ.*

"*saḥ* [stands for] *parabhāgaviśēṣaḥ*. Endings are of eight kinds. Gender is of three kinds. Number is of two kinds."

---

[10]The word 'etc.' (*-ādi*) means '*liṅga* and *vacana*'; the *parabhāga* ('suffixes') category is then divided into three sub-types of units: nominal endings (*vibhakti*), gender suffixes (*liṅga*) and number suffixes (*vacana*). Malayāḷam nominal morphology is mainly of the agglutinating type: one marker is used for the case, another marker is used for gender and another one is used for number. Examples: *ava-n-uṭe* (3rd sing. pers. base, masc., gen.) 'his', *ava-ḷ-uṭe* (3rd sing. pers. base, fem., gen.) 'her', *ava-n-il* (3rd sing. pers. base, masc., loc.) 'on/in him', *ava-ḷ-il* (3rd sing. pers. base, fem., loc.) 'on/in her'.

[11]The use of the expression *prātipadikamātra* seems to echo a passage of the *Collatikāram* of the *Tolkāppiyam*. The commented *sūtra* is *avaṟṟuḷ // eḻuvāy vēṟṟumai peyar tōṉṟu nilai ē* (*sūtra* 65 according to Cēṉāvaraiyar); the commentary reads: "What [we call] 'situation where appears the name only' is the situation where, without any association with case endings or the vocative mark, the name is not combined with something else." [based on the French translation by Chevillard (1996: 144)]

L 2.11 *pēr, e, oṭu, kkŭ,*[12] *ninṟŭ, nnŭ, il viḷīty aṣṭakaṃ.*[13]

"The group of eight [nominal endings is]: *pēr, e, oṭu, kkŭ, ninṟŭ, nnŭ, il, viḷi.*"[14]

Vṛtti: *atra prathamāṣṭamāv arthau. anyē śabdāḥ. tatra prathamaḥ parabhāgaviśēṣō yathā—kaṇṭan, āna, maraṃ. atra prātipadikamātram ēvārthaḥ. tad ēva pēr ity ucyatē. tasya nāmaśabdavācyatvāl.* [...]

"Here, the first and the eighth [elements of the list] are meanings (i.e. they express the meaning of the first and the eighth endings, that is: 'name' for *pēr* and 'call' for *viḷi*). The other [elements of the list] are forms (i.e. they are the endings themselves). The first difference in the last part of words (i.e. the first nominal ending) [is], for example: *kaṇṭan* (name of a man), *āna* ('elephant'), *maram* ('tree').[15] Here, the meaning [consists] precisely [in the one of] the nominal base only. This [first nominal ending] is called *pēr* ('name') because it has the property of being the meaning of the word 'name'. [...]"

L 2.12 *ṣaṣṭhaṃ samāsē vā lupyatē.*

"The sixth [ending] is optionally elided in a compound."

Vṛtti: *yathā—pulivāl, māntōl.*

"For example: *puli-vāl* ('tiger's tail'), *mān-tōl* ('deer's skin')."

L 2.13 *saptamaś ca.*

"The seventh [ending] also."

[12]The letter *ŭ* is used to indicate a half-vowel—the shortest vocalic sound in Malayāḷam—which stays at the end of many words.

[13]In the edition by Iḷaṅkuḷaṃ Kuññan Piḷḷa (1985), this is not a *sūtra* but part of the *Vṛtti*. I would like to take the opportunity to warmly thank Rich Freeman for having indicated to me some of the variants adopted in I. Kuññan Piḷḷa's edition, to which I had no access.

[14]Ezhuthachan (1975: 91) writes: "The first, i.e. *pēr* (noun), denotes the primary word with no suffix. The last word *viḷi* (call) [...] denotes the vocative." This way of naming cases follows a Tamil method. The *sūtra* 64 of the *Collatikāram* of the *Tolkāppiyam*: *avai-tām peyar ai oṭu ku iṉ atu kaṇ viḷi ˜eṉṉum īṟṟa* states: "These [cases are]: the nominative (*peyar*), *ai, oṭu, ku, iṉ, atu, kaṇ* and they have the vocative (*viḷi*) as the end of their enumeration." [based on the French translation by Chevillard (1996: 143)]

[15]There are two suffixes for the nominative case: *-m* and zero. The *-m* suffix is found in di- and poly-syllabic non-human nouns with bases in *-a*. Other nouns are used with a zero suffix.

Vṛtti: *yathā—kaṭalāna, malayiñci.*

"For example: *kaṭal-āna* (litt. 'elephant of the sea', 'whale'), *malay-iñci* ('mountain ginger')."

L 2.14 *dvitīyam asamāsē vā.*

"The second [ending] is optionally [elided] when it is not in a compound."

Vṛtti: *yathā—māla kaṇḍu, mālayekkaṇḍu. puli konṟu, puliye-kkonṟu. acētanē tiraści cāyaṃ vikalpaḥ. anyatra na lupyatē. amātyanekkaṇḍu.*

"For example: *māla kaṇḍu* [and] *mālaye-kkaṇḍu* ('he saw the garland'), *puli konṟu* [and] *puliye-kkonṟu* ('he killed the tiger'). This is an option which concerns inanimate beings and animals. Elsewhere, there is no elision: *amātyane-kkaṇḍu* ('he saw the minister')."

L 2.15 *strīpunnapuṃsakaṃ trikaṃ.*

"The three [genders are] feminine, masculine, neuter."

L 2.21 *ēkānēkaṃ dvikaṃ.*

"The two [numbers are] singular [and] plural."[16]

3. Pāṇinian features of the *Līlātilakam*

The influence of *Vyākaraṇa*, and more precisely, of Pāṇini, on the *Līlātilakam*, is evident at two levels: 1) at the metalinguistic level, that is to say, at the level of the organization of rules and of the technical terminology; 2) at the linguistic level, that is to say, at the level of the described facts of language.

3.1. Typology of borrowings

I have tried to establish a typology of borrowings by the *Līlātilakam* from the *Aṣṭādhyāyī*, which are observed in the second and third chapters of the former. This includes the given borrowing, its localization in the *Līlātilakam*,

[16]In the *Tolkappiyam*, the category of words denoting human beings is divided into three *pāls*: *āṇpāl* (word denoting a male), *peṇpāl* (word denoting a female) and *palarpāl* (word denoting more than one male or female). The category of words denoting objects other than human beings is divided into two *pāls*: *oṉṟaṉpāl* (word denoting one object other than a human being) and *palaviṉpāl* (word denoting more than one object other than a human being). See Subrahmanya Sastri 1997: 107–108.

its level (metalinguistic or linguistic) and its modality, that is to say, whether it is indicated as a borrowing or not.

	borrowing	localization	level	modality of the borrowing
1	*sUBanta—tiṄanta* 'term ending in a nominal ending'—'term ending in a verbal ending'	V *ad* 2.7	M[17]	NI[18]
2	A 7.1.1 *yuvōr anākāv iti*[19]	V *ad* 2.7	L[20]	NI (*iti*)
3	*prātipadika* 'nominal base'	V *ad* 2.9 and 2.11	M	NI
4	*karman* 'object'	V *ad* 2.11	M	NI
5	A 2.3.5 *kālādhvātyantasaṃyōgādikam*[21]	V *ad* 2.11	L	NI (-*ādikam*)

[17] M stands for 'metalinguistic level'.

[18] NI stands for 'not indicated'.

[19] Close to the canonical form of the rule. The context of the quotation is the following: in the Kēraḷabhāṣā, the distinction between alveolar and dental nasals is relevant (though not represented in the writing system), in contrast to the Pāṇḍyabhāṣā (where it is represented in the writing system but no longer pronounced by this time) and Sanskrit (where it is not represented in the writing system and of course not pronounced since it is irrelevant). To show that alveolar and dental nasals are mere allophones in Sanskrit, the author quotes the rule A 7.1.1. According to him, the *n* in *anākau* is alveolar; if this alveolar nasal were really different from the dental one, these two phonemes would not have a similar allophone *ṇ* as in *karaṇa*, *haraṇa*, etc. Therefore, alveolar and dental nasals in Sanskrit are mere allophones and not phonemes.

[20] L stands for 'linguistic level'.

[21] The canonical form of the rule is A 2.3.5 *kālādhvanor atyantasaṃyoge* "[The second ending is used with words denoting] time or distance to express total connection." The context of the borrowing is the following: in the edition presently used, the rule L 2.11 provides the list of the nominal endings. The *Vṛtti* describes them successively, on the formal and the semantic levels. It is when the semantic value of the second ending (-*e*) is under consideration that the *Vṛtti* quotes the rule A 2.3.5. *Vṛtti ad* L 2.11: *atra punar 'e' ity asya nirvarttyavikāryaprāpyātmakaṃ karmārthaḥ. na tu kālādhvātyantasaṃyōgādikaṃ.*

6	*kāndanōkkinōṭu utsukam iti* (form which would be generated by A 2.3.44)[22]	V *ad* 2.11	L	NI
7	*kāndannu kōpikkinṟitu kānda ityādi* (form which would be generated by A 1.4.37)[23]	V *ad* 2.11	L	NI
8	*avaṅgalninṟŭ payaṟṟi (ityādi)* (form which would be generated by A 1.4.29)[24]	V *ad* 2.11	L	NI
9	*puliyiṅgalninṟŭ pēṭiccu ityādi* (form which would be generated by A 1.4.25)[25]	V *ad* 2.11	L	NI

[22]The context of the quotation is the following: the *Vṛtti* deals with the third ending (*-oṭu*/*-ōṭu*). Several examples are given, as well as a counterexample *kāndanōkkinōṭu utsukam* ('one is eager for the glance of his beloved'), which would be generated if the rule A 2.3.44 *prasitotsukābhyāṃ tṛtīyā ca*, which states that the third ending is also used after a nominal base co-occurring with *prasita* and *utsuka*, were applied. But *kāndanōkkinōṭu utsukam* is not considered as correct in the Kēraḷabhāṣā.

[23]The context of the quotation is the following: the *Vṛtti* deals with the fourth ending (*-kkŭ*/*-nnŭ*). Several examples are given, as well as a counterexample *kāndannu kōpikkinṟitu kānda* ('the lady is angry with the lover'), which would be generated if the rule A 1.4.37 *krudhadruherṣyāsūyārthānāṃ yaṃ prati kopaḥ* were applied. This rule provides that the technical term *sampradāna* denotes the person towards whom anger is felt in relation with verbal roots having the meaning of 'feel anger' (*krudh-*), 'injure' (*druh-*), 'not tolerate' (*īrṣy-*), 'find fault with' (*asūy-*). But *kāndannu kōpikkinṟitu kānda* is not considered as correct in the Kēraḷabhāṣā.

[24]The context of the quotation is the following: the *Vṛtti* deals with the fifth ending (*-ninṟŭ*). Several examples are given, as well as a counterexample *avaṅgalninṟŭ payaṟṟi* ('studied from him'), which would be generated if the rule A 1.4.29 *ākhyātopayoge*, which states that the technical term *apādāna* denotes a reciter when instruction is intended, were applied. But *avaṅgalninṟŭ payaṟṟi* is not considered as correct in the Kēraḷabhāṣā.

[25]The context is the same as in the previous case. The *Vṛtti* deals with the fifth ending and gives another counterexample *puliyiṅgalninṟŭ pēṭiccu* ('got afraid of the tiger'), which would be generated if the rule A 1.4.25 *bhītrārthānāṃ bhayahetuḥ*, which provides that the technical term *apādāna* denotes a cause of fear in relation with [verbal roots] having the meaning of 'fear' or 'protection', were applied. But *puliyiṅgalninṟŭ pēṭiccu* is not considered as correct in the Kēraḷabhāṣā.

10	*kāṇkekku pōyi (ityādi)* (form which would be generated by A 2.3.38)[26]	V *ad* 2.11	L	NI
11	*maraṅṅaḻuṭe māvu ninṟu ityādi* (form which would be generated by A 2.3.41)[27]	V *ad* 2.11	L	NI
12	*udikkinṟa ādityanil piṟannān ityādi* (form which would be generated by A 2.3.37)[28]	V *ad* 2.11	L	NI
13	*vā* 'or rather, preferably'[29]	2.12 *et passim*	L	NI
14	*maṇḍūkapluti* process	2.16–18–19–23	M	NI
15	*aT* /a/	2.19	M	NI
16	*aC* 'vowels'	3.1	M	NI
17	*haL* 'consonants'	V *ad* 3.1	M	NI

[26]The context of the quotation is the following: the *Vṛtti* deals with the sixth ending (*-nnŭ/-kkŭ*, *-uṭe/iṭe/eṭe*). Several examples are given, as well as a counterexample *kāṇkekku pōyi* ('he went away without caring for the onlookers'), which would be generated if the rule A 2.3.38 *ṣaṣṭhī cānādare* were applied. This rule provides that the sixth ending is also used after a nominal base to express the meaning of 'notwithstanding'. But *kāṇkekku pōyi* is not considered as correct in the Kēraḷabhāṣā.

[27]The context is the same as in the previous case. The *Vṛtti* deals with the sixth ending and gives another counterexample *maraṅṅaḻuṭe māvu ninṟu* ('a mango tree is the best among trees'), which would be generated if the rule A 2.3.41 *yataś ca nirdhāraṇam* were applied. The rule provides that the seventh as well as the sixth endings are used after a nominal base denoting something from which something else is set apart. But *maraṅṅaḻuṭe māvu ninṟu* is not considered as correct in the Kēraḷabhāṣā.

[28]The context of the quotation is the following: the *Vṛtti* deals with the seventh ending (*-il*). Several examples are given, as well as a counterexample *udikkinṟa ādityanil piṟannān* ('he was born when the sun was rising'), which would be generated if the rule A 2.3.37 *yasya ca bhāvena bhāvalakṣaṇam* were applied. This rule states that the seventh ending is used after a nominal base denoting an action which serves to characterize another action. But *udikkinṟa ādityanil piṟannān* is not considered as correct in the Kēraḷabhāṣā.

[29]*na vā* 'or rather not' is used in the *Vṛtti ad* L 3.7.

18	*saṃjñā* 'technical term'	V *ad* 3.1	M	NI
19	A 1.1.66 *tasminn iti nirdiṣṭe pūrvasya (ityādi)*[30]	V *ad* 3.1	M	I[31] *saṅkēta-vyavahāraḥ pāṇinīyavat*[32]
20	A 1.1.67 *tasmād ity uttarasya ityādi*	V *ad* 3.1	M	I *saṅkēta-vyavahāraḥ pāṇinīyavat*
21	*anuvṛtti* process	3.4–5 *et passim*[33]	M	NI
22	substitution process *x* (gen. case)—*y* (nom. case)[34]	3.14 *et passim*	L	NI

3.2. Comments

Concerning the metalinguistic level, we may say the following.

First, the technical terminology includes a significative number of "Pāṇinian basics" like *sUBanta* 'term ending in a nominal ending' and *tiṄanta* 'term ending in a verbal ending',[35] *karman* ('object'), *aC* ('vowels') and *haL* ('consonants') and the notion of *saṃjñā* ('technical term').

Secondly, one typical Pāṇinian way of describing linguistic facts is also used: substitution (in the phonetic/phonology section).[36]

I call these elements "Pāṇinian basics" because they are not used in

[30]The context of the quotation is the following: the third chapter is devoted to *sandhis*. *Sūtras* start *in media res* and it is the *Vṛtti* which explains the conventions and organization of the chapter.

[31]I stands for 'indicated'.

[32]The full sentence is as follows: *acam, halam ityādisaṃjñāvyavahāraḥ 'tasminn iti nirddiṣṭē pūrvasya, tasmād ity uttarasya' ityādisaṅkētavyavahāraḥ pāṇinīyavad iha draṣṭavyaḥ* "The use of technical terms such as *aC* and *haL*, [as well as] the use of conventions such as *tasminn iti nirddiṣṭē pūrvasya* [and] *tasmād ity uttarasya*, as in the Pāṇinian grammar, is observed here."

[33]The *Vṛtti* often gives the element(s) to be supplied (*x ity adhikārāt, x ity anuṣajyatē/anuṣaṃgaḥ, x iti prastāvāt sidhyati, x iti varttatē*, etc.).

[34]The rule is: *ṇas tasya ṭaḥ* "After *ṇ*, *ṭ* is substituted for *t*."

[35]The author of the *Vīracōḻiyam* also used these two terms. Later grammairians (from the 13th century onwards) sometimes use *nāman* in place of Tamil *peyar*. See Subrahmanya Sastri 1997: 104–106

[36]It is important to note that the technical terminology in the *Līlātilakam* is more *Vyākaraṇic* than strictly Pāṇinian (e.g. *akṣara, apaśabda, udāharaṇa, oṣṭhyatva, karmasādhana, kriyā, deśī, nāman, prakṛti, rūḍhā, liṅga, vacana, x-kāra*, etc.), though this does not appear in the table above.

works of other grammatical schools such as, for instance, some *Śīkṣās* and *Prātiśākhyas*, the *Kātantra*, the *Mugdhabodha*, the *Tolkāppiyam*, the *Śabdamaṇidarpaṇa*, the *Kalāpasūtra*, the grammar of Kaccāyana, etc.; these works, according to some scholars,[37] would pertain to an "Aindra school"—but I know that the question is controversial and I do not intend to discuss it here. The use of these "Pāṇinian basics" in the *Līlātilakam* (*sūtras* and *Vṛtti*) seems to imply a strong affinity for the Pāṇinian treatise and—maybe even more—for the language it describes and normalizes. We find indeed most of these "Pāṇinian basics"[38] in contexts where Sanskrit is clearly in the mind of the author. I will come back to the relation between Sanskrit and Maṇipravāḷam in a moment.

Thirdly, the functioning of the rules is clearly based on the Pāṇinian model (except for the generative pattern, which is absent from the *Līlātilakam*): we find the *anuvṛtti* process, the *maṇḍūkapluti* process and the metalinguistic use of cases (cf. A 1.1.66–67).

Concerning the linguistic level, we may observe the following: among the nine Pāṇinian rules—dealing with linguistic facts—to which the *Vṛtti* refers in the grammatical section, seven (cf. rows six to twelve) are indirectly quoted. Let us take just one example. The rule L 2.11 gives the eight nominal endings; the *Vṛtti* describes each of them successively at the formal and semantic levels. Let us look at the description of the third ending:

> *Vṛtti ad* L 2.11: *tṛtīyō yathā—avanoṭu, avaroṭu, nampiyoṭu, marattoṭu. atrāpi kāndanōkkinōṭu utsukam ityādi na bhavati.*
>
> "The third [ending], for example: *avanoṭu* ('with him'), *avaroṭu* ('with them'), *nampiyoṭu* ('with [a] Nampi'), *marattoṭu* ('with [a] tree'). Here also, there is no [expression] like *kāndanōkkinōṭu utsukaṃ* ('one is eager for the glance of his beloved')."

The expression *kāndanōkkinōṭu utsukam* would be generated if the Pāṇinian rule A 2.3.44 *prasitotsukābhyāṃ tṛtīyā ca*, which provides that the third ending is also used after a nominal base co-occurring with *prasita* and *utsuka*, were applied. What does this mean? It seems to imply that the *Līlātilakam*—or, at least, the *Vṛtti* on its grammatical section—was composed with the *Aṣṭādhyāyī* in mind or before the eyes. When one reads again the first three chapters of the *Līlātilakam* with this in mind, one observes that the manual presupposes a perfect knowledge of Sanskrit[39] as well as of its grammatical and literary culture. I have already emphasized that Sanskrit was a descriptive apparatus or a discursive model for Maṇipravāḷam,

[37]See Burnell 1991.

[38]Exceptions are: *aC*, *aT*, *haL* and *vā*. They are used in every kind of context.

[39]More than that: knowledge of Sanskrit is a prerequisite insofar as the manual is composed in Sanskrit.

but its role does not stop here. Three other reasons explain its more or less manifest omnipresence.

3.2.1. First reason: Sanskrit is one of the two linguistic components of Maṇipravāḷam, the second being the *bhāṣā*. Insofar as Sanskrit is "substantively installed *in* the composition of the language itself,"[40] the shadow of the *Aṣṭādhyāyī* is justified right away. However, it is not really as such, i.e. as one of the linguistic components, that Sanskrit is the most present in the *Līlātilakam* for, obviously, it does not need to be described—Pāṇini had already done this, magisterially. What is—partially—taught in the grammatical section of the *Līlātilakam* concerns exclusively the second linguistic component of Maṇipravāḷam, that is to say, the Keralite regional language. As Freeman relevantly remarks (1998: 45): "*bhāṣā* could refer generally to any spoken language."[41] Guidelines are therefore needed for the Kēraḷabhāṣā, not for Sanskrit. The latter is none the less present, but as the well-known component which is already in the mind of Maṇipravāḷam authors. I quote a few instances illustrating this constant though discreet presence:

> 1) *Vṛtti ad* L 2.7 reads: "Here, in the *bhāṣā*, there are four phonemes which do not exist in Sanskrit: *nṟŭ, ṟṟŭ, ṟŭ* et *ḻŭ*."
>
> 2) *Vṛtti ad* L 3.1 reads: "This sandhi concerns the *bhāṣā*. It is not [a sandhi] of Sanskrit, etc. [...]."
>
> 3) *Vṛtti ad* L 3.2 reads: "It is said: only the *a* which has the meaning of the word *tad* and the *i* which has the meaning of *idam*."

3.2.2. Second reason: Sanskrit often overwhelms the Kēraḷabhāṣā. The first three chapters of the *Līlātilakam* provide a good overview of the characteristics of the Kēraḷabhāṣā, which make this different not only from other Dravidian languages such as the Pāṇḍyabhāṣā, but also, I would say, above all, from Sanskrit. For the domain of the Sanskrit component and the domain of the *bhāṣā* component are not clearly delimited. Very frequently, indeed, in early texts of Maṇipravāḷam, *bhāṣā* words are used as if they were Sanskrit words, that is to say, with Sanskrit endings.[42]

---

[40]Freeman 1998: 45.

[41]Freeman adds (1998: 46): "Indeed, as the text progresses, this assertion for the distinctive autonomy of Kēraḷa-bhāṣā, directly against the Tamil spoken in the adjoining kingdoms, becomes increasingly marked."

[42]L 2.7 reads: *sandarbhē saṃskṛtīkṛtā ca* "And, in compositions, it (i.e., the *bhāṣā*) is sanskritized." On this point, Andronov (1996: 61) notes: "There are

Let us consider a few examples:

1) *koṅkayā* 'by the breast'

koṅka is taken as a Sanskrit base ending in the third ending -*ā*.[43]

2) *ūṇ-uṟakkau* 'food and sleep'

The Sanskrit dual ending -*au* is added to the compound though the dual does not exist in the Kēraḷabhāṣā.[44]

3) *pōkkāṃ cakṟē* 'I have sent'

The Sanskrit form of the periphrastic perfect, which does not exist in the Kēraḷabhāṣā, is added here to the root *pōkk-*.[45]

The description of nominal endings—we saw the example of the third ending—perfectly illustrates this continuous intrusion of Sanskrit which has to be kept within limits.

3.2.3. Third reason: By this time, Sanskrit was very often considered as the source of all languages, and this is explicitly stated in the *Līlātilakam*:

> *Vṛtti ad* L 2.4: *saṃskṛtam anādi. anyad ādimat. tasya saṃskṛtāt prabhavaḥ syāt.*
>
> "Sanskrit is beginningless. Other [languages] have a beginning. Their source is Sanskrit."[46]

3.2.4. For all these reasons, Pāṇinian features of the *Līlātilakam*—features which represent the guarantee of the purest form of Sanskrit—are clear evidence. As shown above, 1) Sanskrit plays a model role at discursive, literary and grammatical description levels; 2) Sanskrit is one of the two linguistic components of Keralite Maṇipravāḷam; 3) in Keralite Maṇipravāḷam compositions, *bhāṣā*'s words are very frequently sanskritized; and 4) Sanskrit is considered as the source of all languages, including the Kēraḷabhāṣā.

cases in early texts when nouns of the Dravidian stock take Sanskrit desinences [...]," and (131): "In early texts Ma. verbs of the Dravidian stock can also take the Sanskrit grammatical forms [...]." Concerning compounding and sandhi, we find the following combinations: Kēraḷabhāṣā word + Kēraḷabhāṣā word = Kēraḷabhāṣā rules; Sanskrit word + Sanskrit word = Sanskrit rules; Kēraḷabhāṣā word + vernacularized Sanskrit word = Kēraḷabhāṣā rules; Kēraḷabhāṣā word + pure Sanskrit word = Sanskrit rules. See Ramaswami Aiyar 1944: 79.

[43]Non-sanskritized form: *koṅkayāl*.

[44]Non-sanskritized form: *ūṇuṟakkamār* (with the suffix of plural).

[45]Non-sanskritized form: *pōttēn* (verbal base with the past tense suffix and the suffix of the first person of singular).

[46]L 2.4 introduces *saṃskṛtabhavas*, that is to say, *tadbhavas*, *bhāṣā*'s words which are derived from Sanskrit. The *Vṛtti* starts with the remark quoted.

4. *Līlātilakam* and Prakrit grammars

A final remark before concluding. Several characteristics of the *Līlātilakam* remind us of Prakrit grammars: 1) the use of Sanskrit as a metalanguage, 2) the aim of the work: a manual intended for those who, knowing Sanskrit, want to compose in a linguistic variety different from it, 3) the grammatical description dealing exclusively with morphology and phonology/phonetics, 4) the omnipresent shadow of the *Aṣṭādhyāyī*: the same number of chapters, similarities in the technique of description, etc. But there are also two major differences: 1) Prakrit grammars are real grammars in the sense that they describe constituent elements and operations they are submitted to; the *Līlātilakam* is, above all, a poetical manual, only two chapters out of eight deal with grammatical description; 2) rules of the grammatical section of the *Līlātilakam* are not formulated on the model 'instead of *a*, one says *b*' which characterizes rules of Prakrit grammars, probably because the *bhāṣā* component is not considered to be derivable from Sanskrit—though it is said that Sanskrit is the source of all languages. In the *Līlātilakam*, indeed, Sanskrit and *bhāṣā* are in a relationship of combination, not of derivation.[47]

Concluding remarks

To conclude very briefly, I would say that Keralite Maṇipravāḷam strongly incorporates Sanskrit influence. Because it is a hyper-sanskritized variety, and because of the reasons mentioned above, the appropriateness of the Sanskrit descriptive model was undoubtedly perceived in the Keralite grammatical tradition more strongly than in any other.

This high hybridization of the regional language with Sanskrit was probably authorized, regulated and claimed as part of the struggle against the hegemony of the Pāṇḍya literary tradition.[48]

References and abbreviations

A: *Aṣṭādhyāyī*. See Katre.

Andronov, Mikhail Sergeevich
1996 *A Grammar of the Malayalam Language in Historical Treatment.* Wiesbaden: Harrassowitz Verlag.

Brough, John
1947 Līlātilaka: A Sanskrit tract on Malayalam grammar and poetics. *Bulletin of the School of Oriental and African Studies* 12 (1): 148–162.

[47] Or of substitution. See Kahrs 1992: 229–234.

[48] See Freeman 1998: 41.

Burnell, Arthur Coke
1991 *On the Aindra School of Sanskrit Grammarians.* 1875. Reprint, Delhi: Bharatiya Book Corporation.

Chevillard, Jean-Luc
1996 *Le commentaire de Cēṉāvaraiyar sur le Collatikāram du Tolkāppiyam: Sur la métalangue grammaticale des maîtres commentateurs tamouls médiévaux.* Vol. I. Pondichéry: Institut français de Pondichéry, École française d'Extrême-Orient.

Ezhuthacchan, K. N.
1975 *The History of the Grammatical Theories in Malayalam.* Part I. Trivandrum: University of Kerala, Dravidian Linguistics Association.

Freeman, Rich
1998 Rubies and coral: The lapidary crafting of language in Kerala. *The Journal of Asian Studies* 57 (1): 38–65.

Gopala Pillai, A. R.
1985 *Linguistic Interpretation of Līlātilakam.* Trivandrum: University of Kerala, Dravidian Linguistics Association.

Kahrs, Eivind G.
1992 What is a *tadbhava* word? *Indo-Iranian Journal* 35: 225–249.

Katre, Sumitra Mangesh
1987 *Aṣṭādhyāyī of Pāṇini.* Austin: University of Texas Press. Reprinted with corrections, 1989, Delhi: Motilal Banarsidass.

Kuññan Piḷḷa, Iḷaṅkuḷaṃ
1985 *Līlātilakam: Maṇipravāḷalakṣaṇam.* Kottayam: National Book Stall.

Kuññan Piḷḷa, Śūranāṭṭu
1985 *Līlātilakam: Paṭhaṇavuṃ Vyākhyānavum.* 1955. Trivandrum: State Institute of Languages.

L: *Līlātilakam.* See Kuññan Piḷḷa, Śūranāṭṭu.

Monius, Anne
2001 *Imagining a Place for Buddhism: Literary Culture and Religious Community in Tamil-Speaking South India.* Oxford: Oxford University Press.

Ramaswami Aiyar, L. V.
1944 *Grammar in Līlātilakam: A Critical and Comparative Study.* Trichur: The Saraswathi Ptg. and Pbg. House.

Subrahmanya Sastri, P. S.
1997 *History of Grammatical Theories in Tamil.* Chennai: The Kuppuswami Sastri Research Institute.

Traditional Stocks of Examples and Their Influence on the First Prakriyā Grammars*

MARIA PIERA CANDOTTI

1.1. Since the very beginning of grammatical tradition examples have been considered a core part of the exegetical method. In a frequently quoted passage of the *Mahābhāṣya* an explanation is said to be made of three components: example (*udāharaṇa*), counterexample (*pratyudāharaṇa*) and completion of the utterance (*vākyādhyāhāra*).[1] In the common practice of commentaries examples are a crucial pedagogical device too. The recurrent question *kim udāharaṇam* is generally asked of a rule and answered by the quotation of a linguistic form showing the desired result of the application of that rule. The question is thus an alternative to and almost synonymous with *kiṃ prayojanam* 'what is the aim [of the rule]?' Note, on this point, Patañjali's alternate use of the term while commenting on A 1.1.29 *na bahuvrīhau* "(Words of the list beginning with *sarva* 27) do not (get the name *sarvanāman*) in a bahuvrīhi:"

> M on A 1.1.29 (I.91.2–4): *kim udāharaṇam* | *priyaviśvāya* | *naitad asti prayojanam* | *sarvādyantasya bahuvrīheḥ pratiṣedhena bhavitavyam* | *vakṣyati caitad* | *bahuvrīhau sarvanāma-saṃkhyayor upasaṃkhyānam iti* | *tatra viśvapriyāyeti bhavitavyam* ||
>
> "What example is there [for this rule]? *priyaviśvāya* 'to one who is fond of/dear to all'.[2] This is not the aim [of the rule]. The prohibition concerns a bahuvrīhi ending in *sarva* and so on. Now [Kātyāyana] will say [in vt. 1 on A 2.2.35] *bahuvrīhau*

*This research was made possible by financial aid from The Gonda Foundation and the International Institute for Asian Studies (IIAS), Leiden, the Netherlands.

[1]M (I.11.20–23): *na hi sūtrata eva śabdān pratipadyante* | *kiṃ tarhi* | *vyākhyānataś ca* | *nanu ca tad eva sūtraṃ vigṛhītaṃ vyākhyānaṃ bhavati* | *na kevalāni carcāpadāni vyākhyānaṃ vṛddhiḥ āt aij iti* | *kiṃ tarhi* | *udāharaṇam pratyudāharaṇam vākyādhyāhāra ity etat samuditaṃ vyākhyānaṃ bhavati* ||

[2]That is, a bahuvrīhi where *viśva*, although included in the list of pronominal forms quoted in A 1.1.27, does not get pronominal declension.

> *sarvanāmasaṃkhyayor upasaṃkhyānam* 'There shall be an additional mention of pronouns and names of numbers [as having the first place] in a bahuvrīhi.' Then, the [correct] form must be *viśvapriyāya*."

Yet this is not the only type of exemplification used by commentaries. If linguistic forms of the object language are the aim or the examples of the rules, the rules themselves are the domain of application (*pradeśa*) of names and metalinguistic devices. The *Kāśikā* is particularly scrupulous in specifying for each name its domain of application, that is, the rules where it occurs.[3] Rules are thus framed by two domains: they are the scope of application of metalinguistic elements and have the object language as their own scope.

These very well known facts are briefly mentioned here simply in order to remind readers of the importance of this device and of its import for studying the history of grammatical tradition: examples are somehow the distillate of the scholastic knowledge concerning a given rule and the language it describes. Some recent enterprises in the indological field, above all the project named *La Grammaire Paninéenne par ses Exemples / Pāṇinīyavyākaraṇodāharaṇakośa* based at the Institut Français de Pondichéry,[4] consider explicitly the transmission of examples and of the derivations (*prakriyā*) attached to them as a way to preserve traditional grammatical knowledge as a whole.

1.2. The question at stake in this paper is whether this practice has influenced the prakriyā-method which, structuring the rules around some derivative patterns, highlights the link between each grammatical rule and the final output which is expected from it. Then, should the answer to this first question be positive, whether it is possible to identify different sources for this influence. In other words, it seems sound to suppose that in everyday pedagogical practice (just as is often done nowadays) each rule was commented on and explained through its insertion in one or more derivations and that this way of proceeding was transmitted from teacher to pupil, thus

---

[3]This domain of rules is then divided between rules where the name is specifically enjoined (*vidhi*) and rules where it is simply repeated to establish some context of the rule (*anuvāda*). The *Kāśikā* points out that those two different contexts may entail different interpretations of a given term. For example K on A 1.1.45: *tatra vidhau vākyārtha upatiṣṭhate—ṣyaṅaḥ saṃprasāraṇaṃ putrapatyos tatpuruṣe, vasoḥ saṃprasāraṇam iti | anuvāde varṇaḥ—saṃprasāraṇāc ca iti |* Cf. also P on vt. 8 to A 1.1.1 (I.133): *vidhau cāyaṃ doṣo nānuvāde* and *Pbh* 93: *vidhau paribhāṣopatiṣṭhate nānuvāde |*

[4]See Grimal et al. 2006, 2007, 2009.

contributing to crystallizing different sets of examples in different schools.[5] This kind of practice may be at least one of the factors determining the specific arrangement of rules adopted by grammarians using the prakriyā arrangement of rules and may thus show us some kind of affiliation of those same grammarians. It is a matter of looking at the rule order adopted by each grammar from a philological point of view, as a hint of the author's personal history and training besides his cultural references and models.[6]

More specifically we will deal with data coming from the analysis of the metalinguistic rules of the *Aṣṭādhyāyī*[7] as they are dealt with in three texts, namely Rāmacandra's *Prakriyākaumudī*, Nārāyaṇa Bhaṭṭa's *Prakriyāsarvasva* and Bhaṭṭoji Dīkṣita's *Siddhāntakaumudī*, that is, the first two prakriyā-grammars arranging the totality of the rules of the *Aṣṭādhyāyī* and their nearer model and forerunner.

1.3. The choice of working specifically on these rules is justified by some considerations concerning the nature of those same rules and of the 'metalinguistic chapters' in the three grammars under consideration. Let us begin with some facts:

- In our grammars the metalinguistic chapters are a kind of survivors of the old Pāṇinian order. Of the approximately 351 rules composing the first adhyāya in the *Aṣṭādhyāyī*, the *Prakriyākaumudī* has preserved only 32 forming a kind of start-up set for the following chapter on sandhi rules.[8] The *Siddhāntakaumudī*'s chapter is made of 46 rules and Nārāyaṇa's is the bulkiest with 74 rules.

- The other Pāṇinian metalinguistic rules have been shifted next to operational rules that require them for their correct interpretation. Yet, more than one place is generally eligible for each rule: a saṃjñāsūtra can soundly be placed beside any occurrence (*pradeśa*) of the term

[5]Bali states (1976: 89): "There is, however, an important reason why Bhaṭṭoji Dīkṣita did not pick up new words for the purpose of illustrations. It is a convention among Sanskrit grammarians that they illustrate their interpretation of *sūtras* by quoting examples from old texts of grammar. Patañjali makes it clear, while interpreting A 1.1.50 that the illustration should be *mūrdhābhiṣikta*, and Kaiyyaṭa explains *mūrdhābhiṣikta* as that which is illustrated in all *vṛtti*-works. Thus, Bhaṭṭoji Dīkṣita only follows a well-established tradition when he reproduces old examples."

[6]This is not to say that the two are bound to be different but that, at least to some degree, they might be.

[7]Precisely from pādas 1 and 2 as the classification of data coming from the whole first adhyāya is not finished yet.

[8]The chapter is traditionally known as *sandhyupayogisaṃjñāprakaraṇam*.

it teaches and, of course, there are plenty of places where a given paribhāṣā may be of help.

- Moreover it can be proved that no purely mechanical interpretation of these shifts works. For example, saṃjñāsūtras are not always mentioned at the first occurrence of the term.[9]

The above-mentioned facts show that we can assume that there was a certain degree of freedom for the authors in choosing where to place a metalinguistic rule and it is particularly in the context of this, albeit limited, freedom that each choice may become significant.

2.1. What were the reasons that regulated the shift of the metalinguistic rules in their specific locations? In fact, having a look at the strategies adopted by the three authors, it is possible to point out at least three different lines of acting. First of all it cannot be denied that there was probably some kind of automatism compelling them to state the metalinguistic rules as soon as possible. There were numerous exceptions to that, as we have already pointed out, yet there is no doubt that a number of metalinguistic rules are found in the very first chapters of our prakriyā-grammars.

2.2. Another rationale behind the choice to put a metarule in some specific location may be the wish to offer a solution to some difficulty pointed out by earlier commentators. I have already discussed the point elsewhere[10] and will not repeat the whole argument here. It is quite evident, for example, that the beginning of all the three grammars is—even though differently—influenced by some passages of Patañjali where he resorts to a fixed order of rule application in order to avoid some difficulties relating to the usage of markers, particularly to their usage in condensed forms (*pratyāhāra*).

[9]For example, SK 2003 (= A 1.1.22) *taraptamapau ghaḥ* immediately precedes SK 2004 (= A 5.4.11) *kimettiṅavyayaghād āmv adravyaprakarṣe* in which the term *gha*, which has already occurred in SK 975 (= A 6.3.17) and 975 (= A 6.3.43), occurs. Similarly SK 2373 (= A 1.1.20) *dādhā ghv adāp* which precedes immediately A 6.4.67 with an instantiation of the term *ghu* already mentioned in SK 2223 (= A 2.7.77) and 2285 (= A 8.4.17). It may also happen that a sūtra for a saṃjñā is not quoted beside a rule quoting the saṃjñā but rather beside a rule helping in the derivation of what has the saṃjñā (saṃjñin): PS 1742 (= A 5.2.27) *vinañbhyāṃ nānāñau nasaha* is immediately followed by A 1.1.38 *taddhitaś cāsarvavibhaktiḥ* through which the name of *avyaya* is given to the output of the rule itself, that is, the indeclinable forms *vinā* and *nānā*.

[10]See Candotti forthcoming. The rationale behind Bhaṭṭoji Dīkṣita's choices had already been pointed out by Bali (1976: 62).

One initial difficulty concerns the risk that condensed forms denote, together with the sounds, also the markers internal to the recitation of the akṣarasamāmnāya. This may be solved, following one of Patañjali's suggestions, considering that the rule teaching the substitution with zero of markers is stronger (*balavattara*) than the other rules and is thus applied right at the beginning of any derivation.[11] The usage of markers is also impaired by a risk of circularity between their definition, where Pāṇini uses a condensed form, and their usage in the definition of condensed forms themselves. In this case also, one of Patañjali's (and before him Kātyāyana's) proposals is to interpret *hal* in A 1.3.3 *hal antyam* as an ekaśeṣa meaning *hal* (= the last akṣasamāmnāya) *ca hal* (= the abridged form) *ca*.[12] The first *hal* gives the name of marker (*it*) to the sound *l*; with this information it is possible to apply A 1.1.71 and obtain ***hal*** as a condensed form meaning the whole set of consonants and thus, through a fresh interpretation of A 1.3.3 give the name of marker to any consonant. Last of all, there might be circularity between the rule teaching the notion of homogeneity (*sāvarṇya*)—again through the usage of the condensed form—and its usage in the definition of condensed forms, circularity which is solved by applying A 1.1.9 and 10 before A 1.1.69.[13] Summing up the results of the different passages we may consider that the rule order suggested by Patañjali is the following:

> M: Akṣarasamāmnāya → A 1.3.3 (*hal antyam*) → 1.3.9 (*tasya lopaḥ*) → 1.1.71 (*ādir antyena sahetā*) → [1.3.3 repeated] 1.3.2 (*upadeśe 'j anunāsika it*) → 1.3.4–8 (*na vibhaktau tusmāḥ*; ...; *laśakv ataddhite*) → 1.1.9 (*tulyāsyaprayatnaṃ savarṇam*) → 1.1.10 (*nājjhalau*) → 1.1.69 (*aṇudit sarvarṇasya cāpratyayaḥ*).

[11] M on śl., akṣarasamāmnāya 5 (I.32.13–25).

[12] M on vt. 5 to A 1.3.3 (I.261.16).

[13] M on vt. 4 to A 1.1.10 (I.64.12–14): *varṇānām upadeśas tāvat* | *upadeśottarakāletsaṃjñā* | *itsaṃjñottarakāla ādir antyena sahetā iti pratyāhāraḥ* | *pratyāhārottarakālā savarṇasaṃjñā* | *savarṇasaṃjñottarakālam aṇudit savarṇasya cāpratyayaḥ iti savarṇagrahaṇam* | *etena sarveṇa samuditena vākyenānyatra savarṇānāṃ grahaṇaṃ bhavati* | "First, the sounds are taught. After this teaching there is the name *it* (marker). Having defined the name *it* there is the definition of abridged forms as taught by A 1.1.71 'The first [element] together with the last marker [of a list is a name of itself] and also of all the elements in between.' Following the abridged forms we have the definition of the name *savarṇa* and after the name *savarṇa* there is the teaching on the denotation of homogeneous sounds through A 1.1.69 'Any vowel, semivowel or *h*, and any sound followed by the marker *U* is a name of itself and of the sounds homogeneous with it.' It is by all these elements altogether that we understand homogeneous sounds in other rules."

If we now check the rule order adopted by our three authors we see that the *Prakriyākaumudī* has:

> PK 1–13 (I.11–29): Akṣarasamāmnāya → A 1.3.2 (*upadeśe 'j anunāsika it*) → 1.3.9 (*tasya lopaḥ*) → 1.3.3 (*hal antyam*) → 1.1.71 [...] (*ādir antyena sahetā*) → 1.1.69 (*aṇudit sarvarṇasya cāpratyayaḥ*) → 1.1.70 (*taparas tatkālasya*) → 1.1.9 (*tulyāsya-prayatnaṃ savarṇam*),

from which we may surmise that Rāmacandra considered crucial the issue of getting rid of markers as soon as possible and put the substitution with zero just after the very first rule of definition. A 1.3.3 is somehow still linked with A 1.1.71 even though the aim of this placement is not commented upon by the author. On the other hand Rāmacandra does not consider relevant the order of application of rules to solve the second problem of circularity, so much so that he places A 1.1.9 right *after* A 1.1.69 and A 1.1.10 outside the metalinguistic chapter. Both the *Siddhāntakaumudī* and the *Prakriyāsarvasva* show a much stricter adherence to the rule order recommended by Patañjali:

> PS 1–9: Akṣarasamāmnāya → A 1.3.3 (*hal antyam*) → 1.1.71 (*ādir antyena sahetā*) → 1.3.9 (*tasya lopaḥ*) → 1.1.60 (*adarśanaṃ lopaḥ*) → 1.3.2 (*upadeśe 'j anunāsika it*) → 1.1.69 (*aṇudit sarvarṇasya cāpratyayaḥ*) → 1.1.70 (*taparas tatkālasya*) → 1.1.9 (*tulyāsyaprayatnaṃ savarṇam*) → 1.1.10 (*nājjhalau*)

and

> SK 1–15: Akṣarasamāmnāya → A 1.3.3 (*hal antyam*) → 1.1.71 (*ādir antyena sahetā*) [→ 1.3.3[14]] → 1.3.2 (*upadeśe 'j anunāsika it*) [...] → 1.1.9 (*tulyāsyaprayatnaṃ savarṇam*) → 8.4.68 (*a a*) → 8.2.1 (*pūrvatrāsiddham*)[15] → 1.1.10 (*nājjhalau*) → 1.1.69 (*aṇudit sarvarṇasya cāpratyayaḥ*) → 1.1.70 (*taparas tatkālasya*).

2.3. Another good example of the influence that traditional debates may have exerted over the authors' choice on where to put some metarules is that of the placement of A 1.1.23 by Rāmacandra and Bhaṭṭoji Dīkṣita.

[14]The repetition of the sūtra is stated by the commentary. Rules stated by the commentaries as pertaining to a given prakriyā are written in square brackets.

[15]Particularly interesting here is the placement of A 8.2.1 *purvātrasiddham* immediately before the couple of rules A 1.1.10 and 1.1.69 which highlights the fact that the order of enunciation reflects in this case the order of application.

A 1.1.23 *bahugaṇavatuḍati saṃkhyā* gives the name *saṃkhyā* 'number' to the linguistic forms *bahu, gaṇa,* forms ending in ***vatu*** and ***ḍati***. Now this metarule is not shifted in any context showing the usage of the technical name itself. On the contrary our two authors insert it in a derivation of a form which is at the same time the name bearer of *saṃkhyā* and of the following technical term *ṣaṭ*:

> PK 198–220 (I.152–60) / SK 241–63: A 7.3.109 *jasi ca* "(A guṇa vowel occurs in place of a short vowel final of an aṅga) before the ending ***jas***." [. . .] → 1.1.23 *bahugaṇavatuḍati saṃkhyā* "The linguistic forms *bahu* and *gaṇa* and bases ending with ***vatu*** and ***ḍati*** are called *saṃkhyā*." → 1.1.25 *ḍati ca* "Bases ending with ***ḍati*** also (are called *ṣaṭ*)." → 1.1.61 *pratyayasya lukślulupaḥ* "A phonic zero called ***luk***, ***ślu*** and ***lup*** occurs in place of an affix." → 7.1.22 *ṣaḍbhyo luk* "After a base called *ṣaṭ* a phonic zero called ***luk*** occurs (in place of the endings ***jas*** and ***śas***)." → 1.1.62 *pratyayalope pratyayalakṣaṇam* "In the case of rules concerning the zero substitution of an affix, rules conditioned by that suffix [are still valid]." → 1.1.63 *na lumatāṅgasya* "But not rules concerning a preaffixal base (*aṅga*) (in the case of a zero substitution) made by a name in *lu*."[16]

Here, the main focus of the prakriyā is, without doubt, that of explaining the functioning of A 1.1.63. Yet, inside this derivation Rāmacandra and Bhaṭṭoji Dīkṣita place the two rules A 1.1.23 and 25 and while the second one is placed near one of its pradeśas (A 7.1.22 using the name *ṣaṭ*) the first one seems completely out of context. The *Kāśikā* which is unusually rich in information for this saṃjñā says that the aim of the metalinguistic rule A 1.1.23 is to help in creating linguistic forms like *bahukṛtvas* 'many times' (A 5.4.17 *saṃkhyāyāḥ kriyābhyāvṛttigaṇane kṛtvasuc*), *bahudhā* 'in many ways' (A 5.3.42 *saṃkhyāyā vidhārthe dhā*), *bahuka-* 'consisting of many' (A 5.1.22 *saṃkhyāyā atiśadantāyāḥ kan*), *bahuśas* 'many by many'(A 5.4.43 *saṃkhyaikavacanāc ca vīpsāyām*) and that its pradeśas are rules from A 2.1.19 onwards.[17] None of these rules is to be found in the prakriyā we are dealing with. Why is the definition of *saṃkhyā* put in this context? We may get a first clue of this in Patañjali's commentary to A 1.1.25 where the author emphasizes the fact that the ***ḍati*** mentioned in A 1.1.25 is the same

[16]The specific role of A 1.1.63 is to negate the validity of guṇa-replacement taught in A 7.3.109 *jasi ca* in the case of zero substitution of the endings ***jas*** and ***śas*** after a base called *ṣaṭ*. A 1.1.63 thus grants the correct form *kati*.

[17]K on A 1.1.23: *saṃkhyāpradeśāḥ saṃkhyā vaṃśyena* (A 2.1.19) *ity-evamādayaḥ* |

ḍati mentioned in A 1.1.23; but the author seems to make no sense of this repetition and even proposes getting rid of one of the two:

> M on A 1.1.25 (I.84.9): *idam ḍatigrahaṇam dviḥ kriyate saṃkhyā-saṃjñāyām ṣaṭsaṃjñāyāṃ ca | ekaṃ śakyam akartum*
>
> "This mention of *ḍati* is made twice, once in the [rule of] the name *saṃkhyā* and once in the [rule of] the name *ṣaṭ*. It is possible to omit one."

Yet the debate among commentators must have continued on this point as we can see both with Jinendrabuddhi's *Nyāsa* and Kaiyaṭa in his *Pradīpa*. Both authors underline the fact that only the bases ending with the taddhita affix *ḍati* should be called *ṣaṭ* and not forms derived with the uṇādi affix *ḍati* (*Uṇādisūtra* 506 *pāter ḍatiḥ*). Now this information may be got only if the second *ḍati* is considered as the same as the first one. Let us follow Jinendrabuddhi's reasoning, at once the more ancient and the clearer on this specific point:

> *Nyāsa* on A 1.1.25: *saṃkhyāgrahaṇenehāpi saṃkhyānuvartata iti darśayati | kimartham punaḥ sehānuvartate | pāter ḍatiḥ pataya ity atra mā bhūt | atha saṃkhyānuvṛttāv api kasmād evātra na bhavati, yāvatāyam api saṃkhyāsaṃjña eva, sāmānyena hi pūrvaṃ ḍateḥ saṃkhyāsaṃjñā vihitā | naitad asti, vatunā sāhacaryāt taddhitasyaiva ḍates tatra grahaṇam, na kṛtaḥ; kṛc cāyam ||*
>
> "By mentioning of *saṃkhyā* [the author] shows that *saṃkhyā* recurs here also. [Question] But for what purpose does it recur here? [Answer] Lest [the name *ṣaṭ*] should apply [to the verbal base *pā*] as taught by [*Uṇādisūtra* 506] *pāter ḍatiḥ* whence the nom. pl. form *patayaḥ*.[18] [Objection] Now, even though [*saṃkhyā*] recurs by anuvṛtti, how is it possible that [the name *ṣaṭ*] does not apply here (i.e. in *pati* derived from *pāter ḍatiḥ*) as long as this item also gets the very name *saṃkhyā*? For it has previously been provided in general that an item ending in the affix *ḍati* is assigned the name *saṃkhyā*. [Answer] It is not so: (in A 1.1.23), because of the close connection with the [taddhita affix] *vatu*, only the taddhita [form ending in] *ḍati* is mentioned, not the kṛt; and this (i.e. the one in the uṇādisūtras) is a kṛt."

It is worth noting that Nārāyaṇa Bhaṭṭa, though placing A 1.1.25 in the same prakriyā as Rāmacandra and Bhaṭṭoji Dīkṣita, does not feel the urge to link it with A 1.1.23 which is placed in the metalinguistic chapter.

[18] Without the substitution with zero of *jas* and *śas* endings taught for *ṣaṭ* bases by A 7.1.22 *ṣaḍbhyo luk*.

2.4. Of course caution is necessary in discriminating whether some given rule order is significant or not. Sometimes the correct interpretation of a prakriyā is impossible without the commentary that integrates some rules in the derivation itself. One example should suffice. As far as pure surface rule ordering is concerned, A 1.1.59 *dvirvacane 'ci* seems to be treated in the *Prakriyākaumudī* as in connection with A 7.4.66 *ur at*, a rule which is not generally linked by traditional examples to the problem tackled by the metarule:

> PK 1444–8 (II.66-70): A 3.1.36 *ijādeś ca gurumato 'nṛcchaḥ* "(The affix *ām*) is introduced (before a *liṭ* affix) also after a verbal base beginning with an ***ic*** vowel provided the vowel is heavy and with the exception of *ṛcch-*." → 2.4.81 *āmaḥ* "(Zero replacement by ***luk*** substitutes *li* affixes) after *ām*." → 3.1.40 *kṛñ cānuprayujate liṭi* "Verbal roots of the group ***kṛñ*** also (are added after a form ending in *ām*) (when they are followed by *liṭ* affixes." → 7.4.66 *ur at* "A short *a* is substituted to the *ṛ* (of a reduplication)." → 1.1.59 *dvirvacane 'ci* "(A unit specifically instructed in place of a vowel is like the place-holder) before a vowel in the domain of doubling."

Yet, the commentary helps us in understanding that A 7.4.66 is not linked with A 1.1.59, on the contrary it marks the end of a prakriyā as shown by the example *indāṃ cakāra*. And A 1.1.59—interpreted following strictly Patañjali[19]—forms in itself a small prakriyā accounting for the specific forms where A 6.1.77 *iko yaṇ aci* can apply before the doubling (taught in A 6.1.8 *liṭi dhātor anabhyāsasya*) on account of its being subsequent (*paratvād ādau yaṇādeśaḥ*). From the verbal base *kṛ* followed by the vowel ending *-atus* we would thus get *kr-atus* which, being devoid of a vowel, would not be reduplicated by A 6.1.8. The metarule is not used to grant the application

[19] The exact interpretation of the sūtra is given by Rāmacandra in the commentary thereon: *rūpātideśo 'yam | dvitvanimitte 'ci yo 'jādeśaḥ sa sthānivat syāt dvitve kartavye iti |* The mention of the extension of form (*rūpātideśa*) and the double meaning of the restriction *dvirvacane* qualifying at the same time the vowel ('before a vowel causing a doubling') and the scope of the rule ('in the context of doubling') is an evident reminder of Patañjali's interpretation of the rule (cf. M on vts. 1–8 to A 1.1.59 [I.155.8–156.27]). The difficulties in extending only the operations are already pointed out by the second vārttika and exemplified by forms like *cakratus* where the monovocalic verbal base *kṛ* is entitled to doubling but not the form *kr* the base assumes, for example, before the ending *-atus*. By extending the sole operation the rule A 1.1.59 might grant doubling, yet not the correct one as we would get **kr-kr-atus*. Thus, to get the correct result one must extend not only the operations pertaining to the place-holder but also its form (i.e. *kṛ*).

of 7.4.66 which would apply anyway, being subsequent to 6.1.77. The 'real' prakriyā, integrated with rules quoted in the commentary, would thus be:

> PK 1444–8: A 3.1.36 (*ijādeś ca gurumato 'nṛcchaḥ*) → 2.4.81 (*āmaḥ*) → 3.1.40 (*kṛñ cānuprayujate liṭi*) → 7.4.66 (*ur at*).
>
> Ex. *indāṃ cakāra.*
>
> → [6.1.8 (*liṭi dhātor anabhyāsasya*) → 6.1.77 (*iko yaṇ aci*)] 1.1.59 (*dvirvacane 'ci*).
>
> Ex. *indāṃ cakratuḥ; indāṃ cakruḥ.*

Thus interpreted Rāmacandra's choices are much more in line with traditional interpretation which lists the semivowel substitution taught by A 6.1.77 as one of the rules whose conflict with the doubling rule is taken care of by A 1.1.59.[20]

The positioning of the rule in the *Siddhāntakaumudī*, even though different at the surface level,[21] is similar if we take into account the rules evoked by the commentary:

> SK 2237–85: A 3.1.36 (*ijādeś ca gurumato 'nṛcchaḥ*) → 2.4.81 (*āmaḥ*) → 3.1.40 (*kṛñ cānuprayujate liṭi*) → 1.3.63 (*āmpratyayavat kṛño 'nuprayogasya*) → 3.4.81 (*liṭas tajhayor eśirec*) → 1.2.5 (*asaṃyogāl liṭ kit*) → [6.1.8 (*liṭi dhātor anabhyāsasya*) → 6.1.77 (*iko yaṇ aci*)] → 1.1.59 (*dvirvacane 'ci*) → 7.4.66 (*ur at*) → 7.4.62 (*kuhoś cuḥ*).

[20]M on vt. 8 to A 1.1.59 (I.157.1–3): *kāni punar asya yogasya prayojanāni | papatuḥ papuḥ tasthatuḥ tasthuḥ | jagmatuḥ jagmuḥ | āṭitat āśiśat | cakratuḥ cakrur iti | āllopopadhālopaṇilopayaṇādeśeṣu kṛteṣv anackatvād dvirvacanaṃ na prāpnoti* "Now, what are the aims of this rule? [They are:] *papatuḥ papuḥ tasthatuḥ tasthuḥ* (i.e. *pa-p-atus*; *pa-p-us* with substitution with zero of the *ā* of the verbal base); *jagmatuḥ jagmuḥ* (i.e. *ja-gm-atus ja-gm-us* with substitution with zero of the penultimate vowel of the verbal base); *āṭitat āśiśat* (i.e. *ā-ṭi-ṭ-a-t* with substitution with zero of *ṇi*); *cakratuḥ cakrus* (i.e. *ca-kr-atus* with substitution of vocalic *ṛ* with semivocalic *r*). Once the zero substitute of *ā* (A 6.4.64 *āto lopa iṭi ca*), of the penultimate vowel (A 6.4.98 *gamahanajanakhanaghasāṃ lopaḥ kṅiti anaṅi*) of *ṇi* (6.4.51 *ṇer aniṭi*) and the substitute with a semivowel (6.1.77 *iko yaṇ aci*) are made, because of the absence of the vowel, the doubling cannot be obtained."

[21]The prakriyā of the *Prakriyākaumudī* concerns the formation of periphrastic perfect in the context of teaching perfect endings for verbs of the first class (yet the rules quoted are extensible also to verbs of other classes) and specifically for verbs beginning with a vowel, whilst the prakriyā of the *Siddhāntakaumudī* is collocated inside the same chapter in the subgroup of verbs beginning with *edh-* and getting ātmanepada endings. The key rule in this context is thus A 1.3.63 teaching that when the principal verb taking the affix *-ām* is ātmanepadin, then also the auxiliary verb will take ātmanepada endings: *edhāṃ cakrire.*

Ex. *edhāṃ cakrire.*[22]

The quotation of A 1.1.59 in both cases is, so to say, out of context or, better said, it creates its own context by recalling a well known set of rules, A 6.1.8 → 6.1.77, bound together by an extension procedure or the imposition of a specific order of application.[23] Thus, in both cases there is a much stricter adherence to traditional themes than it might have seemed at first sight. In fact there is an oddity in the choice of these prakriyās to illustrate A 1.1.59 but it is more the fact that the pretty wide scope of the metarule is exemplified by the very marginal forms of the so-called periphrastic perfect: *indāṃ cakratuḥ, indāṃ cakruḥ, edhāṃ cakrire.* There is of course a great deal that is arbitrary in this collocation, and that asks for an explanation. Bhaṭṭoji Dīkṣita has surely taken the lead from the *Prakriyākaumudī*, as he often does, but for Rāmacandra the problem remains.

3.1. In fact, as it has been suggested at the beginning of this paper, the personal training of each author, the specific teaching tradition he became acquainted with as a brahmacārin may also have had its role in determining the placement of metarules in their specific context. Of course, to be significant hints of the influence of authors' personal history and training, the above-mentioned rule placements must really prove to be otherwise arbitrary, the result of a mostly unconscious drive. In other words, cases like the prakriyā in which rule A 1.3.3 is inserted are more likely to be implicit, voluntary quotations of some well known passages. Similarly, to be considered significant, the placement shall of course not be the only or one of the few possible ones. The rule teaching the technical term *pragṛhya*, A 1.1.11 *īdūded dvivacanaṃ pragṛhyam*, is placed by the *Prakriyākaumudī* next to A 6.1.125 *plutapragṛhyā aci nityam* which is the pradeśa explicitly mentioned in the *Kāśikā*. Yet, as there are only three occurrences of the term in the whole *Aṣṭādhyāyī* and the other two (namely A 8.2.107 *eco 'pragṛhyasyādūrāddhūte pūrvasyārdhasyāduttarasyedutau* and 4.57 *aṇo*

[22]But the commentary brings to light a fundamental difference from the *Prakriyākaumudī*. The metarule is interpreted by Bhaṭṭoji Dīkṣita not as an extension rule but as a negation rule: *dvitvanimitte 'ci pare aca ādeśo na syād dvitve kartavye.* This interpretation is clearly indebted to a vārttika quoted by Patañjali as a possible (albeit weaker) alternative to formulating A 1.1.59. M on vt. 8 to A 1.1.59 (I.157.4–5): *dvirvacanaṃ yaṇyavāyāvādeśāllopopapadhālopaṇilopakikinoruttvebhya iti* | "Doubling [prevails over] the substitutes *yaṇ, ay, av, āy, āv*, the zero substitute of *ā*, of a penultimate vowel, of *ṇi*, and of *ut* in place of *ki* and *kin*." The vārttika recalled here is vt. 9 on A 6.1.12 (III.17.12).

[23]In the *Prakriyāsarvasva* also the two rules at stake, namely A 6.1.8 and 6.4.64, are not stated at the surface level of the prakriyā but simply recalled by the very presence of A 1.1.59.

'pragṛhyasyānunāsikaḥ) are occurrences of *apragṛhya*, the choice of the author is less significant than it might have been.[24] Lastly, relevant occurrences should preferably be traced to one text only: the link between A 1.1.59 *dvirvacane 'ci* and A 6.1.77 *iko yaṇ aci*, for example, is so common that it is difficult to identify any specific source for it. Of course all this is extremely restrictive and good examples are not so frequent. Less good examples nevertheless must not be discarded but interpreted in the light of the global figures and may at the end strengthen some position.

3.2. What would be good hints of a specific scholastic affiliation for a given author? Three of them will be discussed in detail. The first one concerns the placement in the *Prakriyāsarvasva* of the metarule A 1.1.4 *na dhātulopa ārdhadhātuke* which negates substitution with guṇa and vṛddhi when an ārdhadhātuka affix follows which conditions partial deletion of the root. The most immediate link, a link highlighted by our three authors, is with the rule A 2.4.74 *yaṅo 'ci ca* teaching variously (*bahulam*) zero substitution by ***luk*** of the deverbative ***yaṅ*** before the affix ***ac*** providing us with a partial deletion caused by an ārdhadhātuka affix. The authors then interpret the mention *bahulam* as meaning that the zero substitution mentioned above may take place also in the absence of the affix ***ac***. Nārāyaṇa, while introducing his *yaṅluganta* section, recalls in the commentary the rule A 2.4.74:

> PS on 3379 (= A 7.3.94): *atha yaṅluk | yaṅo 'ci ca* (A 2.4.74) *iti cakārād anacy api yaṅ bahulaṃ luk* ... |
>
> "Now [the section] with zero substitution by ***luk*** of [the affix] ***yaṅ***. In the rule *yaṅo 'ci ca* because of the particle *ca* ***luk*** is obtained variously also when non-***ac*** follows."

In fact this rule *in its extended interpretation* is a key point for the whole *yaṅluganta* section as it is the only one teaching the substitution with zero of the affix ***yaṅ***. Rāmacandra and Bhaṭṭoji Dīkṣita put this rule at the head of the whole chapter and use it to derive forms like *totorti* (SK: without application of A 1.1.4, as the zero of ***yaṅ*** is conditioned by sārvadhātuka endings) or *bebhiditā* (PK: with A 1.1.4).[25] Nārāyaṇa also accepts the ex-

[24]Both the *Prakriyāsarvasva* and the *Siddhāntakaumudī*, although they show A 1.1.11 under the heading of A 6.1.125, insert a whole section on the derivation of prolated vowels. This recalls Patañjali's discussion on whether A 1.1.11 includes also prolated vowels or not.

[25]PK: A 2.4.74 *yaṅo 'ci ca* → 7.3.94 (*yaṅo vā*) → 8.2.65 (*mvoś ca*) → 1.1.4 (*na dhātulopa ārdhadhātuke*). Ex. *bebhiditā* / *marīmṛjitā* vs *bebetti* / *marīmārṣṭi*.

SK: A 2.4.74 (*yaṅo 'ci ca*) → 7.3.94 (*yaṅo vā*) → 7.4.91 (*rugrikau ca luki*) → 7.4.92 (*ṛtaś ca*) → 6.4.20 (*jvaratvarasrivyavimavām upadhāyāś ca*) → 6.4.21 (*rāl lopaḥ*) → 1.1.4 (*na dhātulopa ārdhadhātuke*). Ex. *totorti* vs *totūrtaḥ*.

tended interpretation of the rule, as it is evident from his commentary, but puts it, together with A 1.1.4, in a completely different context, that of primary derivates with optional augment *iṭ*:

> PS 357–61: A 3.1.134 *nandigrahipacādibhyo lyuṇinyacaḥ* "The affixes ***lyu***, ***ṇin***^{i} and ***ac*** occur after verbal bases of the groups beginning with *nandi*, *grah* and *pac*." → 6.1.45 *ād eca upadeśe 'śiti* "The sound *ā* occurs in place of a verbal base ending with a diphthong in the first teaching except before [an affix] marked by *ś*." → 2.4.74 *yaṅo 'ci ca* "(Zero substitution by ***luk***) occurs also (variously) in place of ***yaṅ*** before the suffix ***ac***." → 1.1.61 *pratyayasya lukślulupaḥ* "(Zero substitution) of an affix is called ***luk***, ***ślu*** and ***lup***." → 1.1.4 *na dhātulopa ārdhadhātuke* "There is no substitution with guṇa and vṛddhi of an ***ik*** vowel before an ārdhadhātuka affix causing [partial] zeroing of a verbal base."[26]

The choice of this specific prakriyā can hardly be justified by the need of higlighting any specific interpretation either of A 2.4.74 or of A 1.1.4. On the contrary it is the most straightforward example of application of A 1.1.4, which the *Kāśikā* illustrates almost step by step:

> K on A 1.1.4: *loluvaḥ, popuvaḥ, marimṛjaḥ | lolūyādibhyo yaṅ-antebhyaḥ pacādyaci* (3.1.134) *vihite yaṅo ci ca* (2.4.74) *iti yaṅo luki kṛte tam evācam āśritya ye guṇavṛddhī prāpte tayoḥ pratiṣedhaḥ |*
>
> "[Examples are] *loluvaḥ, popuvaḥ, marimṛjaḥ*.[27] At the stage where, after verbal bases ending in ***yaṅ***, like *lolū-ya-*, the rule teaching the affix ***ac*** after the bases of the group beginning with *pac* (A 3.1.134) is prescribed and the affix ***yaṅ*** is substituted by zero (***luk***) through A 2.4.74 *yaṅo 'ci ca* (*lolū* + ϕ + ***ac***), guṇa[28] and vṛddhi[29] substitutions result on the basis of that same ***ac***; prohibition is made of these substitutions by this rule."

Here the placement does not hint at some interpretative difficulty nor is it linked with some long lasting commentarial debate. Even in Patañjali's view these forms are not problematic but may simply be accounted for without having recourse to A 1.1.4. It is also difficult to consider it as an explicit

[26]Nārāyaṇa paraphrases the rule as follows: *dhātvaṃśalopanimitte ārdhadhātuke pare iko guṇavṛddhī na staḥ |*

[27]These examples are already quoted by Patañjali (M on vt. 7 to A 1.1.4 [I.52.25]) but in the context of a proposal of getting rid of the metarule itself.

[28]A 7.3.84 *sārvadhātukārdhadhātukayoḥ ||*

[29]A 7.2.114 *mṛjer vṛddhiḥ ||*

quotation of the *Kāśikā* by the author of the *Prakriyāsarvasva*. It seems more a reflex, caused by some deep-rooted knowledge.

3.3. Of course, interesting as it may be, this example tells us nothing if it stands alone. But one is then justified in looking for other similar occurrences in order to strengthen the case. This kind of reasoning may gain some plausibility only from accumulation. Let us consider, for example, the placement of the rule A 1.1.20 *dādhā ghv adāp* teaching the name *ghu* for the set of verbs *dā* and *dhā*. It is quite a straightforward rule and the difficulties brought out by commentators concern principally the denotatum of the terms *dā, dhā* and *dā**p***. Rāmacandra, followed again by Bhaṭṭoji Dīkṣita, quotes the saṃjñāsūtra in close relationship with the rule A 6.4.67 *er liṅi* in the context of the derivation of forms like *deyāt/dheyāt*, that is, they choose quite a prototypical example of formation of a *ghu* verbal base. Nārāyaṇa's choice is more bewildering:

> PS 482–4: A 3.2.74 *āto maninkvanibvanipaś ca* "Also the affixes *man*^{i}***n***, *kvan*^{i}***p*** and *van*^{i}***p*** occur (in the hymns) after verbal bases ending in *ā* (co-occurring with an inflected word or a preverb)." → 1.1.20 *dādhāghv adāp* "Verbal bases [of form] *dā* and *dhā* with the exception of *dā**p*** are called *ghu*)."[30] → 6.4.66 *ghumāsthāgāpājahātisāṃ hali* "(The sound *ī*) occurs (in place of the final *ā* of the verbal aṅgas) *ghu, mā, sthā, gā, pā, hā, sā* before (an ārdhadhātuka affix) beginning with a consonant (and marked by *k* or *ṅ*)."
>
> Ex. *sudīvā* 'giving liberally', *veṇudhīvā* 'holding a cane/fisherman', *kṣīrapīvā* 'drinking milk/water' (affix *kvan*^{i}***p***), *sudāvā* 'giving liberally' (affix *van*^{i}***p***).

Such a placement seems arbitrary and casual. It is true that it is the first occurrence of the term in the *Prakriyāsarvasva*[31] but there were some other twelve rules with explicit mention of the term. Nor did Rāmacandra or Bhaṭṭoji Dīkṣita feel the need to yield to such a constraint on this point. In fact, in this case again Nārāyaṇa seems to be echoing the *Kāśikā*:

> K on A 1.1.20: *ghupradeśāḥ ghumāsthāgāpājahātisāṃ halītyevam-ādayaḥ* |
>
> "The applications of the name *ghu* are [rules like] *ghumāsthāgāpā-jahātisāṃ hali* (A 6.4.66) and so on."

[30] Nārāyaṇa's paraphrase: *lavanaśodhanārthau dāpdaipau muktvā dādhārūpā dhātavo ghusaṃjñāḥ* |

[31] Even good examples are rarely absolutely flawless.

3.4. Let us consider briefly one last example. The extension rule A 1.2.1 *gāṅkuṭādibhyo 'ñṇin ṅit* tells us that after the verbal base ***gāṅ*** and those of the group beginning with ***kuṭa*** affix which are not marked with *ñ* nor *ṇ* are considered as marked with *ṅ*. The aim of the rule is to extend to the above-mentioned cases the prohibition of *guṇa* taught by A 1.1.5 *kṅiti ca*. But none of our three authors put the extension next to the rule it is supposed to extend. Bhaṭṭoji Dīkṣita puts it inside a derivation concerning the verbal base ***gāṅ***, which conditions the extension, and accounts for the form *adhyagīṣyata* with *ī* substitution of the base vowel in front of affixes marked with *ṅ*.[32] Nārāyaṇa, on the contrary, puts the rule at the very end of a chapter dedicated to primary derivatives with compulsory and optional augment ***iṭ***.

> PS 350: A 7.2.48 *tīṣasahalubharuṣariṣaḥ* "After the verbal bases *iṣ*, *sah*, *lubh*, *ruṣ* and *riṣ* (the augment ***iṭ***) occurs before an affix beginning with *t*."
>
> Ex.: *eṣitā* vs *eṣṭā* and so on.

The link with the prakriyā to derive *kuṭitā* (which, by the way, has a compulsory ***iṭ***) is made by opposition, in the sense that by A 1.2.1–3 forms with augment ***iṭ*** without guṇa of the base are accounted for. This is hinted at by Nārāyaṇa, who introduces the rule with the words *kuṭa kauṭilye | kuṭ i tṛ* '***kuṭa*** in the sense of being crooked: *kuṭ* + *i* + *tṛ*', thus recalling the verbal base quoted in A 1.2.1:

> PS 351: A 1.2.1 *gāṅkuṭādibhyo 'ñṇin ṅit* "An affix not marked by *ñ* nor *ṇ* and occurring after ***gāṅ*** and the verbal bases beginning with ***kuṭa*** are treated as being marked with *ṅ*."[33]
>
> Ex. *kuṭitā*, *puṭitā*.

Then the two other extension rules immediately follow:

> PS 352: A 1.2.2 *vija iṭ* "Affixes with the initial increment ***iṭ*** (are treated as if marked with *ṅ*) after the verbal base *vij*."

[32]SK 2459–62: A 2.4.49 (*gāṅ liṭi*) → 2.4.50 (*vibhāṣā luṅlṛṅoḥ*) → 1.2.1 (*gāṅkuṭādibhyo 'ñṇin ṅit*) → 6.4.66 (*ghumāsthāgāpājahātisāṃ hali*). Ex. *adhyagīṣṭa*, *adhyāgīṣyata*.

[33]Nārāyaṇa's paraphrase: *iṅādeśād gāṅaḥ kuṭādibhyaś ca paro ñṇidvarjitaḥ pratyayo ṅit syāt | iti tṛco ṅittvād guṇābhāvaḥ* "After the verbal base ***gāṅ*** specifically instructed in place of ***iṅ*** and after the bases beginning with ***kuṭa*** let a subsequent affix, with the exclusion of those marked by *ñ* or *ṇ*, be treated as if marked by *ṅ*. Thus the affix ***tṛc***, because of the condition of being marked by *ṅ*, does not get the guṇa."

Ex. *udvijitā.*

A 1.2.3 *vibhāṣorṇoḥ* "(Affixes with the initial increment *iṭ* are) optionally (treated as if marked with *ṅ*) after the verbal base *ūrṇu.*"

Ex. *ūrṇavitā* vs *ūrṇuvitā.*[34]

Now, these are exactly some of the examples the *Kāśikā* gives for our three rules, namely, for A 1.2.1 *adhyagīṣṭa, adhyāgīṣātām adhyāgīṣyata* (with application of A 6.4.66 *ghumāsthāgāpājahātisāṃ hali*) and *kuṭitā, kuṭitum, kuṭitavyam* (with application of A 1.1.5); for A 1.2.2 *udvijiitā, udvijitum, udvijitavyam* (with application of A 1.1.5); for A 1.2.3 *prorṇuvitā* vs *prorṇavitā* (again 1.1.5). On the other hand, Bhaṭṭoji Dīkṣita, who had put A 1.2.1 in the context of the derivation of *gāṅ* substitute of *iṅ*, mantains also the other two rules in the context of verbal derivation, namely *udvijitā* and *udivijiṣyate*[35] and *ūrṇunuvitha* vs *ūrṇunavitha, ūrṇuvitā* vs *ūrṇavitā, ūrṇautu ūrṇotu, ūrṇavāni ūrṇavai*[36] where *Kāśikā* forms are mentioned among others without putting particular emphasis on them.

4. At this point the question whether this way of reasoning may prove fruitful and help us in the interpretation of the authors we are dealing with cannot be avoided further. More specifically, the question is whether this method may help in discovering links of affiliation that would otherwise pass unnoticed if tackled with more traditional philological tools (like looking for quotations). Of course, a sound answer will be possible only once the totality of the data is processed. Yet, there is enough material to test at least the tool and its capacity of bringing to light new facts..

We have concentrated on the role of the *Kāśikā* whose influence both on Nārāyaṇa and Bhaṭṭoji Dīkṣita is well known and it would hardly be necessary to have recourse to such a complicated procedure to uncover it.[37] Nevertheless, the depth and strength of this influence may vary. Let us imagine evaluating the influence of the metalinguistic chapters of the *Kāśikā* simply by looking for quotation from it in the metalinguistic chapters of the *Prakriyāsarvasva* and the *Siddhāntakaumudī.* Figures are in both cases very low; in PS 16 (= A 8.4.68) we have the only explicit quotation of the *Kāśikā*;[38] in SK none.

[34]By A 6.4.77 *aci śnudhātubhruvāṃ yvoe iyaṅuvaṅau.*

[35]SK 2356 in the section dedicated to verbal bases of the sixth class.

[36]SK 2447 in the section dedicated to verbs of the second class.

[37]See at least Bali 1976: 89 for Bhaṭṭoji Dīkṣita's work and Iyer 1972: 37–8 for Nārāyaṇa's.

[38]PS 16 on A 8.4.68: *ralayor aikyam icchanti kecid ity āha vṛttikṛt* | "The author of the *vṛtti* says: some support the oneness of *r* and *l.*"

On the other hand we have seen that Nārāyaṇa very often places metarules inside derivations explicitly quoted in the *Kāśikā* as prototypical examples of the application of that given metarule. Besides the three cases we have discussed we can find at least six similar cases in the placement of the sole rules of pāda 1.1 of the *Aṣṭādhyāyī*. Nothing similar is to be found in Bhaṭṭoji Dīkṣita's practice. If we thus want to weight the influence of the *Kāśikā*, the accurate study of the rationale behind the shift of metarules in specific 'times of operation' allows us to discriminate between two situations that, at a surface level, seemed similar. A thorough and complete scrutiny of all relevant data is needed before one can present interesting results, nonetheless the data presented here are hopefully sufficient to show the potential benefits of this way of looking at the texts.

References and abbreviations

A: *Aṣṭādhyāyī*. See Böhtlingk.

Abhyankar, Kashinath Vasudev

1962 *Paribhāṣenduśekhara of Nagojībhaṭṭa, edited critically with the commentary Tattvādarśa of MM. Vasudev Shastri Abhyankar.* Part 1. Poona: Bhandarkar Oriental Research Institute.

1962–72 *The Vyākaraṇa-mahābhāṣya of Patañjali, edited by F. Kielhorn, third edition, revised and furnished with additional readings, references and select critical notes by K. V. Abhyankar.* 3 vols (1: 1962; 2: 1965; 3: 1972). Pune: Bhandarkar Oriental Research Institute.

Bāli, Suryakant

1976 *Bhaṭṭoji Dīkṣita: His Contribution to Sanskrit Grammar.* New Delhi: Munshiram Manoharlal Publishers Pvt.Ltd.

Böhtlingk, Otto

1887 *Pâṇini's Grammatik, herausgegeben, übersetz, erläutert un mit verschiedenen Indices versehen von Otto Böhtlingk.* Leipzig: Hassel. Reprint, Delhi: Motilal Banarsidass, 1998.

Candotti, Maria Piera

forthcoming The role and import of the metalinguistic chapters in the new 'pāṇinian' grammars. In *Saṃskṛta-sādhutā: Studies in Honour of Professor Ashok Aklujkar*, edited by Chikafumi Watanabe, Yoshichika Honda, and Michele Desmarais, 68–81. New Delhi: D.K. Printworld.

Grimal, F., V. Venkataraja Sarma, V. Srivatsankacharya, and S. Lakshminarasimham

2006 *Pāṇinīyavyākaraṇodāharaṇakośaḥ: La grammaire paninéenne par ses exemples; The Paninian grammar through its examples.* Vol. 1, *Udāharaṇasamāhāraḥ: Le livre des exemples: 40000 entrées pour un texte; The book of examples: 40,000 entries for a text.* Tirupati: IFP/EFEO/Rashtriya Sanskrit Vidyapeetha.

Grimal, F., V. Venkataraja Sarma, and S. Lakshminarasimham

2007 *Pāṇinīyavyākaraṇodāharaṇakośaḥ: La grammaire paninéenne par ses exemples; The Paninian grammar through its examples.* Vol. 2, *Samāsaprakaraṇam: Le livre des mots composés; The book of compound words.* Tirupati: IFP/EFEO/Rashtriya Sanskrit Vidyapeetha.

2009 *Pāṇinīyavyākaraṇodāharaṇakośaḥ: La grammaire paninéenne par ses exemples; The Paninian grammar through its examples.* Vol. 3. 2, *Tiṅantaprakaraṇam 2: Le livre des formes conjuguées 2; The Book of Conjugated Forms 2.* Tirupati: Rashtriya Sanskrit University; Pondichéry: Ecole française d'Extrême-Orient, Institut français de Pondichéry.

Iyer, Venkitasubramonia S.

1972 *Nārāyaṇabhaṭṭa's Prakriyāsarvasva: A Critical Study.* Trivandrum: Department of Sanskrit, University of Kerala.

K: *Kāśikāvṛtti.* See Sharma.

M: *Mahābhāṣya.* See Abhyankar 1962–72. [References are to volume, page, and line.]

N: *Nyāsa* on *Kāśikāvṛtti.* See Tripathi.

P: *Pradīpa* on *Mahābhāṣya.* See Vedavrata.

Pbh: *Paribhāṣenduśekhara.* See Abhyankar 1962.

Pisharoty, K. P. Narayana

1998 *The Prakriyāsarvasva of Melputtur Nārāyanabhaṭṭathiri.* Guruvayur: Guruvayur Devaswom.

PK: *Prakriyākaumudī.* See Trivedi. [References are to serially numbered sūtras, volumes, and pages.]

PS: *Prakriyāsarvasva.* See Pisharoty. [References are to serially numbered sūtras.]

Sharma, Aryendra, Khanderao Deshpande, and D. G. Padhye

1969–70 *Kāśikā: A Commentary on Pāṇini's Grammar by Vāmana and Jayāditya (Śrīvāmanajayādityaviracitā pāṇinīyāṣṭādhyāyīsūtravṛttiḥ kāśikā).* 2 vols. Hyderabad: Sanskrit Academy, Osmania University.

SK: *Siddhāntakaumudī.* See Vasudev Lakshman Shastri. [References are to serially numbered sūtras.]

Tripathi, J. Sh. L., and S. Malaviya

1984–94 *Śrīmadvāmanajayādityaviracitā pāñinīyāṣṭādhyāyīsūtravṛttiḥ kāśikā śrījinendrabuddhiviracitayā nyāsāparaparyāyakāśikāvivaraṇapañjikākhyayā. . . .* 9 vols. Varanasi: Tara Printing Works.

Trivedi, Kamalashankar Pranashankar
1925 *The Prakriyākaumudī of Rāmachandra (in two parts): Part I with the Commentary Prasāda of Viṭṭhala.* Bombay Sanskrit and Prakrit Series 78. Poona: Bhandarkar Oriental Research Institute.

Uṇādisūtra. See Vasudev Lakshman Shastri.

Vasudev Lakshman Shastri, Panashikar
2002 *Siddhāntakaumudī with the Tattvabodhinī Commentary of Jñānendra Sarasvatī and the Subodhinī Commentary of Jayakṛṣṇa.* Delhi: Chaukhamba Sanskrit Pratishthan.

Vedavrata
1962–63 *Śrībhagavatpatañjaliviracitaṃ Vyākaraṇamahābhāṣyam (Śrīkaiyaṭakṛtapradīpena nāgojībhaṭṭa-kṛtenabhāṣyapradīpoddyotena ca vibhūṣitam).* 5 vols. Gurukul Jhajjar (Rohatak): Hairyāṇā-Sāhitya-Saṃsthānam.

pūrvatrāsiddham and *āśrayāt siddham*[*]

George Cardona

पुराणमित्येव न साधु सर्वं न चापि काव्यं नवमित्यवद्यम् ।
सन्तः परीक्ष्यान्यतरद्भजन्ते मूढः परप्रत्ययनेयबुद्धिः ॥
(Mālavikāgnimitra, introduction 2)

1. Rule suspension and its consequences

1.1. Rule suspension

Pāṇini divides his Aṣṭādhyāyī into two major groups of sūtras, set apart by the heading-metarule

[R1] 8.2.1: *pūrvatrāsiddham*.[1]

By this rule, a sūtra in the Tripādī, the last three quarter chapters of the grammar, is suspended (*asiddham*) with respect to anything that precedes (*pūrvatra*); that is, the Tripādī as a whole is suspended with respect to the preceding seven and one-quarter pādas of sūtras (*sapādasaptādhyāyī*) and within the Tripādī each rule is suspended with respect to any sūtra that precedes. Accordingly, an order of application is established: if a situation arises such that a rule R_2 of the Tripādī and an earlier rule R_1 could possibly be considered for application, only R_1 can apply. For, at

*I owe a debt of gratitude to several scholars who read and commented on a version of this paper: Ashok Aklujkar, Sharon Ben Dor, Deven Patel, and Peter Scharf.

[1]For a summary discussion of how rule suspension provided by this rule operates, see PWT **655–58**. References of the type '8.2.1: *pūrvatrāsiddham*' are to sūtras of Pāṇini's Aṣṭādhyāyī. Additional numbered references within parentheses are to sūtras or parts of sūtras understood to recur in the rule referred to. For example, '[R5] 7.3.102: *supi ca* (*ato dīrgho yañi* 101)' refers to Aṣṭādhyāyī sūtra 7.3.102 in which the entire preceding sūtra is understood to recur and [R7] 6.1.220: *anto'vatyāḥ* (*sañjñāyāṁ striyām* 219) refers to rule 6.1.220 in which *sañjñāyāṁ striyām* is understood from the preceding rule. Except for Vedic accentuation (see PWT **li–lxiv**), I follow the standard system for transliterating Devanāgarī, but also have used a dieresis to distinguish a sequence of vowels in, e.g., *kaü*, as opposed to a diphthong *au* (कउ versus कौ).

the time one considers what the operations stated by these rules might apply to, one cannot consider both the rules eligible for application, since one is suspended, hence non-existent, with respect to the other. On the other hand, if a particular item is such that only a rule of the Tripādī can apply to it, this rule of course does take effect. The result of applying the rule, however, cannot be considered subject to a provision made in a prior rule, since the Tripādī rule is suspended, hence non-existent, with regard to that sūtra. The second situation can be illustrated by the derivation of *rājabhyām* (instr.-dat.-abl. du.), *rājabhis* (instr. pl.), *rājasu* (loc. pl.) from *rājan* 'king' (see **1.2**); the first situation may be illustrated by *amuṣmai* (dat. sg. m.-nt.), *amuṣmāt* (abl. sg.), *amuṣmin* (loc. sg.), *amuyoḥ* (gen.-loc. du.), *amuyā* (instr. sg. f.) and other forms of the pronominal *adas* 'that' (see **1.3**).

1.2. Restricting suspension in respect of particular rules

Pāṇini is required not only to operate with rule suspension as formulated in [R1] (**1.1**) but also to specify that the suspension of a particular rule in the Tripādī applies with respect only to particular rules of the preceding seven and one-quarter pādas. Thus,

[R2] 8.2.2: *nalopaḥ supsvarasañjñātugvidhiṣu kṛti*

provides that a rule for *n*-deletion (*nalopaḥ*) is suspended with respect to rules which provide operations related with nominal endings (*sup*) as well as to rules which introduce particular accents (*svara*), assign a class name (*sañjñā*), and introduce the final augment ***tuk*** to a sound when a kṛt suffix follows (*kṛti*).[2] This concerns the sūtra

[R3] 8.2.7: *nalopaḥ prātipadikāntasya*

[2] My paraphrase is intended to reflect that the term *vidhi*, a compound (by 2.2.19: *upapadam atiṅ* [PWT **315**]) of the preverb *vi* and the derivate *dhi* from the base *dhā* (3.3.92: *upasarge ghoḥ kiḥ* [PWT **295**]), is not only construed with each term of the dvandva *supsvarasañjñātuk-* in the tatpuruṣa *supsvarasañjñātugvidhi-* but also has two values according to the term with which it is construed. In construction with *sup*, *vidhi* is an object noun denoting any operation that is provided for (*vidhīyate*) and *sup* reflects an underlying genitive referring to nominal endings relative to which such operations are provided; accordingly, *subvidhi-* refers to the introduction of an ending as well as to an operation on a stem conditioned by an ending. Construed with *svara*, *sañjñā*, and *tuk*, on the other hand, *vidhi* is an action noun equivalent to *vidhāna* ('providing by rule'), and the terms in construction with this have the syntactic value of genitives signifying objects which are provided by rules.

whereby replacement by zero applies to *n* which is the final sound of a pada that is also a nominal base (*prātipadikāntasya*).[3] Consider the examples *rājabhyām*, *rājabhis*, *rājasu*; *rājavatī* (woman's name); *daṇḍidattau/datta-daṇḍinau* 'staff bearer and one that has been granted' (nom.-acc. du. m.); *vṛtrahabhyām* (instr.-dat.-abl. du. [*vṛtrahan-* 'one who has slain Vṛtra']), *vṛtrahabhiḥ* (instr. pl.).

The derivation of the first three examples involves [R3] in connection with

[R4] 7.1.9: *ato bhisa ais*

[R5] 7.3.102: *supi ca* (*ato dīrgho yañi* 101)

[R6] 7.3.103: *bahuvacane jhaly et.*

According to [R4], the ending *bhis* is replaced by *ais* after a stem ending in short *a* (*ataḥ*); e.g., *puruṣa-bhis* → *puruṣa-ais* → *puruṣais*[4] 'men'. The next two sūtras state replacements for the final *-a* (*ataḥ*) of a stem before certain nominal endings (*supi*). By [R5], a long *ā* substitutes for the stem vowel if the ending begins with one of the consonants denoted by *yañ*, that is *y v r l jh bh*; e.g., *puruṣa-bhyām* → *puruṣābhyām*. [R6] has *-e* (*et*) substitute for *-a* before a plural ending (*bahuvacane*) that begins with a consonant other than a nasal or a semivowel (*jhali*); e.g., *puruṣa-su* → *puruṣe-su* → *puruṣeṣu*.[5] Now, the base *rājan* is classed as a pada when followed by a consonant-initial nominal ending such as *bhyām*, *bhis*, or ***sup***[6] so that its *-n* is deleted according to [R3]. Once deletion has taken place in *rājan-bhyām*, *rājan-bhis*, and *rājan-su*, the substitution of *bhis* for *ais* by [R4] and the replacements for stem-final *-a* provided for in [R5]–[R6] do not apply to *rāja-bhyām*, *rāja-bhis*, *rāja-su* since [R3] is suspended with respect to [R5]–[R6].

The derivate *rā́javatī-*, formed with the taddhita affix *ma**tup***,[7] is accented as shown. Once the *-n* of *rā́jan-* has been deleted, the possibility arises of applying

---

[3][R3] comes under the heading of [R39] 8.1.16: *padasya* (**2.2.3**), so that it applies to a pada. The class name *pada* is assigned, to begin with, to an item that terminates in a nominal or verbal ending (1.4.14: *suptiṅantam padam* [PWT **49**]). If a pada consists of a nominal base and a nominal ending and its ending is deleted, one has a nominal base which also bears the class name *pada* even after the deletion of the ending (1.1.62: *pratyayalope pratyayalakṣaṇam* [PWT **140**]).

[4]6.1.88: *vṛddhir eci* (PWT **529**).

[5]8.3.59: *ādeśapratyayayoḥ* (PWT **563**).

[6]1.4.17: *svādiṣv asarvanāmasthāne* (PWT **75**).

[7]*rājan-s-mat* (5.2.94: *tad asyāsty asminniti matup* [PWT **346**]) → *rājan-mat* (2.4.71: *supo dhātuprātipadikayoḥ* ([PWT **278**]) → *rājan-mat-ī* (4.1.6: *ugitaś ca* ([PWT **271**]) → *rāja-matī* ([R3]) → *rājavatī* (8.2.11: *saṁjñāyām*).

[R7] 6.1.220: *anto'vatyāḥ* (*sañjñāyāṁ striyām* 219).

According to this rule, the final (*antaḥ*) vowel of a item that ends with *avatī* (*avatyāḥ*) is high-pitched if the term in question is used to name a particular person or thing; e.g., *haṁsavatī́* '(a verse) in which there is the word *haṁsa*'. Were [R7] to apply in *rājavatī*, the result would be a wrongly accented derivate. Since [R3] is suspended with respect to a rule that provides for a particular accent, however, *rāja-* resulting from deletion of *-n* by this sūtra cannot be considered for applying the accent provided for in [R7]. The suffix *ma**tup*** is marked with *p* to show that it does not have a high-pitched vowel,[8] so that *rā́javatī-* has high pitch on the syllable which the first constituent has originally.

In a dvandva compound such as *hariharau* 'Hari and Hara', a constituent that ends in *-i* or *-u*, assigned to the class of nominals called *ghi*,[9] occurs first, as provided for in

[R8] 2.2.32: *dvandve ghi* (*pūrvam* 30).

On the other hand, a dvandva compound like *daṇḍidattau/dattadaṇḍinau* should not be subject to this restriction. Since the deletion of the *-n* in *daṇḍin-* by [R3] is suspended with respect to 1.4.7 (note 9), *daṇḍi* resulting from this deletion is not subject to being classed as a ghi element.

vṛtrahabhyām (instr.-dat.-abl. du.) and *vṛtrahabhiḥ* (instr. pl.) contain a stem that originally ends with *-n*: *vṛtrahan-*. A nominal followed by the endings *bhyām* is classed as a pada[10] so that the *-n* of *vṛtran-* is dropped. Now, the constituent *-han* 'one who has killed' is derived by introducing the agentive kṛt suffix ***kvip*** to the verbal base *han* construed with a form of *vṛtra-* signifying an object that was slain.[11] In addition, a short vowel (*hrasvasya*) preceding a kṛt suffix marked with *p* (*piti kṛti*) receives the final augment ***tuk***, as in *āhatya* 'after striking, directly', *nicitya* 'after collecting', *prastutya* 'after presenting', where the bases *ha*, *ci*, and *stu* precedes the kṛt suffix ***lyap***.[12] This augment is provided for in

[R9] 6.1.71: *hrasvasya piti kṛti tuk*.

[8] 3.1.4: *anudāttau suppitau* (PWT **592**).

[9] 1.4.7: *śeṣo ghy asakhi* (PWT **57**).

[10] 1.4.17 (note 6).

[11] 3.2.87: *brahmabhrūṇavṛtreṣu kvip* (PWT **295**).

[12] 7.1.37: *samāse'nañpūrve ktvo lyap* (PWT **491**). *ha* in turn derives from *han*. However, the deletion of *-n* here is not by [R2] 8.2.2 but by 6.4.37: *anudāttopadeśavanatitanotyādīnam anunāsikalopo jhali kṅiti* (PWT **448**), which provides, among other things, for deleting the final nasal consonant of a verbal base before a suffix that begins with a consonant other than a semivowel or a nasal and is marked with *k* or *ṅ*.

Since [R3] is suspended with respect to [R9], the *-a* of *ha-* that results from applying this rule is not available to receive the augment.

[R2] specifies that [R3] is suspended with respect to a rule which introduces ***tuk*** in the context of a kṛt suffix marked with *p*. Accordingly, [R3] is not suspended with respect to

[R10] 6.1.73: *che ca*

whereby ***tuk*** is also introduced to a short vowel followed by *cha*, e.g., *svāmicchatram*[13] 'master's umbrella'. Similarly, since [R2] restricts the suspension of [R3] to rules which concern nominal endings and rules which provide for particular accents and class names, this suspension does not hold with respect to other rules. Thus, the derived verbal bases *rājīya-* 'wish for a king', *rājāya-* 'act like a king' are formed with the suffixes ***kyac*** and ***kyaṅ***.[14] Certain operations apply to final vowels of stems before *y-* of a following suffix that does not belong to the kṛt or sārvadhātuka class (*akṛtsārvadhātukayoḥ*), two of which are stated in

[R11] 7.4.25: *akṛtsārvadhātukayor dīrghaḥ*

[R12] 7.4.33: *kyaci ca* (*asya* 32, *ī* 31).

A vowel is lengthened (*dīrghaḥ* 'long vowel') before such a suffix, and an *a*-vowel (*asya*) in particular is replaced by *ī* before ***kyac*** (*kyaci*). These operations can apply to the *-a* of *rāja-* because [R3] is not suspended with respect to [R11] and [R12], so that it can supply items subject to the operations in question:

(1) *rājan-am-ya* → *rājan-ya* (2.4.71 [note 7]) → *rāja-ya* → *rājīya*

(2) *rājan-s-ya* → *rājan-ya* → *rāja-ya* → *rājāya*.

In the absence of [R2], the general rule [R1] would let [R3] be suspended with respect to all preceding rules. The implicit effect of stating [R2] is thereby to restrict the suspension of [R3] only with respect to the specified rules, so that [R3] is not suspended in respect of other rules.

1.3. Negating suspension

In another case, Pāṇini has to exclude suspension by [R1] 8.2.1 (**1.1**) for one rule of the Tripādī with respect to a single prior rule, thereby having the Tripādī sūtra suspended in respect of other preceding sūtras. According to

[13] *-i-ch-* → *-it-ch-* → *-icch-* ([R31] 8.4.40 [**2.1.3**]).

[14] 3.1.8: *supa ātmanaḥ kyac*, 3.1.11: *kartuḥ kyaṅ salopaś ca* (PWT **283**).

[R13] 8.2.3: *na mu ne*

the sūtra which provides for replacement such that *mu* occurs in forms of *adas* 'that' is not (*na*) suspended with respect to the sūtra whereby *nā* substitution applies. The rules in question are

[R14] 8.2.80: *adaso'ser dād u do maḥ*

[R15] 7.3.120: *āṅo nāstriyām* (*gheḥ* 19).

By [R14], an *u*-vowel (*u*) substitutes for the vowel which follows the *-d-* (*dāt*) of *adas* (*adasaḥ*) once the *s* of this pronominal has been replaced[15] (*aseḥ* 'without *s*'); simultaneously, the *d* (*daḥ*) of *adas* is replaced by *m* (*maḥ*). [R15] provides that the third-triplet ending ***āṅ*** (*āṅaḥ*) is replaced by *nā* following a base of the ghi class,[16] except in the feminine (*astriyām*); for example, *agninā*, *vāyunā*, instrumental singular forms of *agni* 'fire, Agni' and *vāyu* 'wind, Vāyu', as opposed to *kṛtyā* and *dhenvā*, corresponding forms from the feminine bases *kṛti* 'doing, deed', *dhenu* 'cow'. If [R14] were suspended with respect to [R15], at the stage of derivation where *ada-* is followed by the third-triplet ending *ā*, this ending would be subject to replacement by *ina*,[17] as it is in deriving *tena* 'that' from *tad-ā*.[18]

On the other hand, other forms of the pronominal *adas* require that [R14] be suspended with respect to preceding sūtras. Consider first non-feminine singular forms with endings that include *-sm-*: *amuṣmai* (dat.), *amuṣmāt* (abl.), and *amuṣmin* (loc.), derived from *adas-e*, *adas-as*, and *adas-i*. These forms are comparable to *tasmai*, *tasmāt*, and *tasmin* from *tad-e*, *tad-as*, and *tad-i*. The required results are accounted for if [R14] is suspended with respect to

[R16] 7.1.14: *sarvanāmnaḥ smai* (*ataḥ* 9, *ṅeḥ* 13)

[R17] 7.1.15: *ṅasiṅyoḥ smātsminau*

whereby *smai* replaces the fourth-triplet ending ***ṅe*** and the fifth- and seventh-triplet endings ***ṅasi*** and ***ṅi*** are respectively replaced by *smāt* and *smin* after a pronominal (*sarvanāmnaḥ*) stem that ends in *-a*. Since [R14] is suspended with respect to these last two rules, at the stage where *ada-* is followed by the endings in question, the replacements provided for in [R16]–[R17] apply first and [R14] comes into play subsequently:

---

[15] *adas* is part of the subgroup of pronominals that begins with *tyad* 'that', so that its *-s* is replaced by *-a* before an ending (7.2.102: *tyadādīnām aḥ* [PWT **476**]): *adas-* → *adaa-* → *ada-* (6.1.97: *ato guṇe* [PWT **531**]).

[16] 1.4.7 (note 9).

[17] [R22] 7.1.12 (see below).

[18] *tad-ā* → *taa-ā* → *ta-ā* (see note 15) → *ta-ina* → *tena* ([R40] 6.1.87 [**2.2.3**]).

(3) *ada-e* → *ada-smai* → *amu-smai* → *amuṣmai* (8.3.59 [note 5])

(4) *ada-as* → *ada-smāt* → *amu-smāt* → *amuṣmāt*

(5) *ada-i* → *ada-smin* → *amu-smin* → *amuṣmin.*

If [R14] were not suspended in respect of [R16]–[R17], it would block the application of these rules, giving **amu-e*, **amu-as*, **amu-i*, so that the required forms would be disallowed and incorrect forms allowed.

The feminine counterparts of the forms considered above are *amuṣyai*, *amuṣyāḥ*, and *amuṣyām*. According to

[R18] 7.3.114: *sarvanāmnaḥ syāḍ ḍhrasvaś ca* (*āpaḥ* 113, *ṅitaḥ* 111)

[R19] 7.3.116: *ṅer ām nadyāmnībhyaḥ*

after a pronominal stem that ends with a feminine affix designated by ***āp***, an ending marked with *ṅ* (*ṅitaḥ*) receives the initial augment *syāṭ*, with simultaneous shortening of the stem vowel;[19] and the ending ***ṅi*** is replaced by *ām* after stems of the nadī class, stems that end in a feminine suffix designated by ***āp***, and the particular stem *nī* ('one who leads, heads'). The derivations for the feminine forms of *adas* noted above start with *adas* followed by the endings ***ṅe***, ***ṅas***, ***ṅi***, and proceed as follows:

(6) *adas-e* → *adaa-e* → *ada-e* → *adaā-e*[20] → *adā-e*[21] → *ada-syāe* → *ada-syai* (6.1.88 [note 4]) → *amu-syai* → *amuṣyai*

(7) *adas-as* → *adaa-as* → *ada-as* → *adaā-as* → *adā-as* → *ada-syāas* → *ada-syās* (6.1.101 [note 21]) → *amu-syās* → *amuṣyās*

(8) *adas-i* → *adaa-i* → *ada-i* → *adaā-i* → *adā-i* → *adā-ām* → *ada-syāām* → *ada-syām* → *amu-syām* → *amuṣyām.*

---

[19] [R18] is an exception to 7.3.113: *yāḍ āpaḥ* (PWT **499**), whereby an ending marked with *ṅ* receives the initial augment *yāṭ* after a stem with a feminine affix ***āp***, e.g., *senā-e* → *senā-yāe* → *senāyai* (6.1.88 [note 4]) 'army.'

[20] Part of the semantics in the derivation of an utterance containing *adas-ā* in its initial string is that something feminine is referred to. Accordingly, once a base form *ada* is arrived at, the conditions are met which serve to introduce the feminine affix ***ṭāp*** (4.1.4: *ajādyataṣ ṭāp* [PWT **271**]): this suffix follows a base in *-a* used in the feminine (*striyām*).

[21] 6.1.101: *akaḥ savarṇe dīrghaḥ* (PWT **532**). The single replacement for a preceding and following segment ([R42] 6.1.84 [R**2.2.3**]) provided for in this rule is treated as the final of a larger unit that precedes another unit and the initial of the latter (6.1.85: *antādivac ca* [PWT **110**]), so that *-ā* of *adā-* from *ada-ā* is treated as the final sound of the pronominal stem and the initial of a feminine suffix; hence, *adā-* has the status of a stem ending in a feminine suffix referred to by the cover term ***āp***.

Similarly, *amuyoḥ* and *amuyā* require that [R14] be suspended with respect to

[R20] 7.3.104: *osi ca* (*et* 103)

[R21] 7.3.105: *āṅi cāpaḥ*.

[R20] provides that stem-final *-a* is replaced by *-e* before the ending *os*. According to [R21], replacement with *-e* also applies before the third-triplet ending ***āṅ***, if this ending follows a stem with a feminine suffix ***āp***. Since [R14] is suspended with respect to these sūtras, *amuyoḥ* and *amuyā* are derived as follows:

(9) *adas-os* → *adaa-os* → *ada-os* → *adaā-os* → *adā-os* → *ade-os* → *aday-os*[22] → *amuyoḥ*

(10) *adas-ā* → *adaa-ā* → *ada-ā* → *adaā-ā* → *adā-ā* → *ade-ā* → *aday-ā* → *amuyā*.

Other forms of *adas* also require that [R14] be suspended with respect to prior rules. Thus, the sixth-triplet ending ***ṅas*** is regularly replaced by *sya* after a stem in *-a*, but not after a stem in *-u*. Accordingly,

[R22] 7.1.12: *ṭāṅasiṅasām inātsyāḥ* (*ataḥ* 9)

provides for replacing ***ṭā***, ***ṅasi*** and ***ṅas*** respectively by *ina*, *āt* and *sya* if they follow a stem in *-a* (*ataḥ*); for example, *devena* (instr. sg.), *devāt* (abl. sg.), *devasya* (gen. sg.), as opposed to *vāyunā* (see above), *vāyoḥ*, *vāyoḥ*.[23] However, *amuṣya* (gen. sg. m.-nt.) does have *sya*. This situation is accounted for if [R14] is suspended with respect to [R22], so that the latter applies first:

(11) *adas-as* → *adaa-as* → *ada-as* → *ada-sya* → *amu-sya* → *amuṣya*.

Similarly, long-vowel substitution before *bhyām* applies to stem-final *-a*, but not to *-u* (*vāyubhyām*), so that [R14] is appropriately suspended with respect to [R5] 7.3.102 (see above):

[22] 6.1.78: *eco'yavāyāvaḥ* (PWT **524**).

[23] *vāyu-as* (***ṅasi/ṅas***) → *vāyo-as* (7.3.111: *gher ṅiti* [PWT **484**]) → *vāyos* (6.1.110: *ṅasiṅasoś ca* [PWT **583**]).

(12) *adas-bhyām* → *adaa-bhyām* → *ada-bhyām* → *adā-bhyām* → *amūbhyām*.[24]

In accordance with the fact that [R14] is suspended with respect to earlier rules concerning *adas*, Pāṇini presumes the application of such earlier rules also in accounting for *amī* (nom. pl. m.), *amībhiḥ* (instr. pl. m.-nt.), *amībhyaḥ* (dat.-abl. pl. m.-nt.), *amīṣām* (gen. pl. m.-nt.), *amīṣu* (loc. pl. m.-nt.), comparable to forms of *idam* ('this'), which have e: *ime*, *ebhiḥ*, *ebhyaḥ*, *eṣām*, *eṣu*. To account for *amī* and so on,

[R23] 8.2.81: *eta īd bahuvacane* (*adaso'ser dāt, do maḥ* 80)

provides that, along with the replacement of *-d-* by *-m-*, an *e* following the *-d-* of *ada* is replaced by *ī* in forms signifying plurality; for example:

(13) *adas-as* → *adaa-as* → *ada-as* → *ada-ī*[25] → *ade* → *amī*.

2. Implied nonsuspension of sūtras in the Tripādī

In still other instances where a sūtra occurs in the Tripādī but is nevertheless not suspended with respect to a preceding rule or rules, Pāṇini neither specifies the particular sūtras with respect to which such a Tripādī rule is suspended nor denies its suspension. Instead, he allows the status of these rules as being unsuspended (*siddhatva*) to be inferred.

2.1. General rules and related exceptions within the Tripādī

There are sūtras in the Tripādī which are intrinsically related to other sūtras as general rules (*utsarga*) and exceptions (*apavāda*). The larger domain in which a general rule applies includes the domain of a related exception, so that the latter is vacuous (*anavakāśa* 'without a space [of its own]') unless it captures its proper domain from that of the related general rule, wherein it

[24]Since the vowel replaced by an *u*-vowel as provided for in [R14] is long, the corresponding long *ū* replaces it (1.1.50: *sthane'ntaratamaḥ* [PWT **92**]). Similarly, *-ū* replaces the *-au* of *adau* ← *ada-au* (nom. acc. du.), where *-au* is the single replacement for stem final *-a* (m.-nt.) and *-ā* (f.) and the endings *au*, *auṭ*; the *-ā-* of *-ān* in *adān* (acc. pl. m.), *-ās* in *adās* (nom.-acc. pl. f.), and *adāni* (nom.-acc. pl. nt.), which account for *amū*, *amūn*, *amūs*, *amūni*. In all these instances, [R14] is suspended with rules that apply first to result in *adau* and so on. It is not necessary to deal here with all the rules in question.

[25]The first-triplet ending *jas* is replaced by *śī* following a pronominal stem in *-a*: 7.1.19: *jasaḥ śī* (PWT **493**).

blocks the application of this rule.[26] That an exception is formulated, then, serves to make known that it applies—by virtue of being an exception—despite what might provisionally take effect by [R1] 8.2.1 (**1.1**). Just as Pāṇini does not explicitly formulate a metarule stating that an exception should block a related general rule, assuming this to be a principle known from what obtains in the real world, so does he allow one to imply that in the Tripādī also this relation holds, counter to the provision made in [R1]. Let us consider now examples of this situation.

2.1.1. Consider first the pair of sūtras

[R24] 8.2.31: *ho ḍhaḥ* (*jhali* 26, *padasya* 8.1.16, *ante ca* 29)

[R25] 8.2.32: *dāder dhātor ghaḥ*.

These rules state replacements for *h* (*haḥ*): *ḍh* substitutes for this sound if it occurs at the end (*ante*) of a pada (*padasya*) as well as before a consonant other than a semivowel or nasal stop (*jhali*); if *h* is part of a verbal base (*dhātoḥ*) which begins with *d* (*dādeḥ*), it is replaced by *gh* under the same conditions. Clearly, the domain in which [R25] can apply is totally included in the domain for [R24], so that it is an exception to this rule. If, by virtue of being stated later in the Tripādī, [R25] were considered suspended with respect to [R24], the latter would apply first under these conditions, rendering [R25] vacuous: there remains no purpose for stating this sūtra. Consequently, where its conditions are met, [R25] alone applies. Only if this relation is maintained, do the sūtras in question account for the required results, for example, *leḍhum* 'to lick', *dogdhum* 'to milk' (inf.), derived as follows:

(14) *lih-tum* → *leh-tum*[27] → *leḍh-tum* → *leḍh-dhum*[28] →

[26]This holds for total blocking. There are also instances where a subdomain of a general rule includes an even narrower domain in which a related exception applies; this is limited blocking. For example, 7.3.113 (see note 19) applies to endings that follow any stem with a feminine affix denoted by ***āp***, and [R18] 7.3.114 (**1.3**) applies for such endings and stems where the latter is a pronominal. [R19] 7.3.116 applies for a particular ending marked with *ṅ*, the seventh-triplet ending ***ṅi***, after stems that have a feminine suffix ***āp*** as well as others. The stems other than those with ***āp*** constitute a domain for [R19] that is independent of the domain covered by 7.3.113. The particular ending ***ṅi*** following a stem with ***āp***, however, constitutes a domain that is included in the domain of 7.3.113; where the stem is a pronominal, this particular domain is included in that of [R18].

[27]7.3.86: *pugantalaghūpadhasya ca* (PWT **127**).

[28]8.2.40: *jhaṣas tathor dho'dhaḥ* (PWT **547**).

leḍh-ḍhum[29] → *leḍhum*[30]

(15) *duh-tum* → *doh-tum* → *dogh-tum* → *dogh-dhum* → *dog-dhum.*[31]

2.1.2.

[R26] 8.2.23: *saṁyogāntasya lopaḥ* (*padasya* 8.1.16)

[R27] 8.2.29: *skoḥ saṁyogādyor ante ca* (*lopaḥ* 26, *padasya* 8.1.16, *jhali* 26)

concern pada-final consonant clusters (*saṁyoga*): the last sound of a pada (*padasya*) ending with such a cluster (*saṁyogāntasya*) is replaced by zero (*lopaḥ*); *s* and *k* (*skoḥ*) are replaced by zero if they are the first sounds of a consonant cluster (*saṁyogādyoḥ*) with which a pada ends, and also within a pada if the cluster occurs before a consonant other than a semivowel or nasal stop. It is clear that one domain in which [R27] applies—word-final clusters—is included in the larger domains of [R26], so that it is an exception to the latter, which it blocks.[32] Only if this relation obtains do the rules

[29][R32] 8.4.41; see **2.1.3**.

[30][R33] 8.3.13; see **2.2.1**.

[31]8.4.53: *jhalāṁ jaś jhaśi* (PWT **577**).

[32][R24]–[R25] (**2.1.1**) and [R26]–[R27] are the two pairs of rules that Patañjali brings in during the discussion of Kātyāyana's first two vārttikas on [R1] (8.2.1.vtt. 1–2: *pūrvatrāsiddhe nāsti vipratiṣedho'bhāvād uttarasya* | *apavādo vacanaprāmāṇyāt* |). Kātyāyana remarks that in the section headed by [R1] 8.2.1 (*pūrvatrāsiddhe*), there is no conflict (*nāsti vipratiṣedhaḥ*) between an earlier and later sūtra allowing one to invoke the generalized metarule 1.4.2: *vipratiṣedhe paraṁ kāryam* (PWT **110**) such that, where there is conflict (*vipratiṣedhe*) between two sūtras, what is provided by the later (*param*) rule is to be effected (*kāryam*). The reason Kātyāyana gives for the impossibility of conflict here is the absence (*abhāvāt*) of a later rule (*uttarasya*). Despite this, he goes on to say, an exception (*apavādaḥ*) does exist in relation to an earlier general rule, and he gives a reason for this: because the statement of an exception has the property of making this known (*vacanaprāmāṇyāt*). That is, if an exception were not considered available to interact with a preceding general rule, its statement would be purposeless. Patañjali fleshes this argument out as follows. There is conflict between two rules which have their own independent domains (*sāvakāśayoḥ*) and come together possibly to apply in a given situation (*samavasthitayoḥ*). In the section headed by [R1] 8.2.1, a later sūtra (*param*) does not exist (*na bhavati*) with respect to a prior rule (*pūrvaṁ prati*). If this holds for [R25] and [R27], instead of replacement by *gh*, replacement by *ḍh* obtains for *h* in derivations which should result in *dogdhā* 'one who milks' (nom. sg. m.), *dogdhum*; and the deletion of a cluster-final consonant obtains instead of the deletion of cluster-initial *k* in derivation which should result in *kāṣṭhtaṭ*, *kūṭataṭ* ('one who cuts a mass'). This

in question apply properly to derive forms such as *gomān* 'rich in cattle' (nom. sg. m.), and *kāṣṭhataṭ* 'wood cutter' (nom. sg. m.):

(16) *gomat-s* → *gomat-ϕ*[33] → *gomāt*[34] → *gomānt*[35] → *gomān*

(17) *kāṣṭhatakṣ-s* → *kāṣṭhatakṣ-ϕ* → *kāṣṭhataṣ* → *kāṣṭhataḍ*[36] → (optionally) *kāṣṭhataṭ*.[37]

2.1.3. A variation on this theme involves a general rule that, for other reasons, follows exceptions in the Tripādī. Thus,

[R28] 8.2.30: *coḥ kuḥ* (*jhali* 26, *padasya* 8.1.16, *ante ca* 29)

[R29] 8.2.36: *vraścabhrasjasṛjamṛjayajarājabhrājacchaśāṁ ṣaḥ* (*jhali* 26, *padasya* 8.1.16, *ante ca* 29)

[R30] 8.2.39: *jhalāṁ jaśo'nte*

also are related rules. The first two concern replacements that take effect when there follows a consonant other than a semivowel or nasal (*jhali*) as well as in pada final position. As shown, *jhali* of 8.2.26 (*jhalo jhali* [PWT **543**]) and *ante ca* of [27] 8.2.29 (**2.1.2**) are understood to recur

---

is because the rules that provide for *gh*-substitution and cluster-initial deletion follow those which provide for *h*-replacement and cluster-final deletion, hence are suspended with respect to the prior sūtras. Patañjali then notes, in the Bhāṣya on 8.2.1 vt. 2, that the two rules in question lack domains of their own (*anavakāśāv etau*), so that the operations in question will apply because of the very formulation of these rules make this known (*vacanapāmāṇyāt*): that the rules are stated requires that they apply in their proper domains. [Bh. III. 385.15–18, 20–21: *pūrvatrasiddhe nāsti vipratiṣedhaḥ | kiṁ kāraṇam | abhāvād uttarasya | dvayor hi sāvakāśayoḥ samavasthitayor vipratiṣedho bhavati na ca pūrvatrāsiddhe paraṁ pūrvaṁ prati bhavati | yady evaṁ dogdhā dogdhum ghatvasyāsiddhatvād ḍhatvaṁ prāpnoti kāṣṭhataṭ kūṭataṭ saṁyogādilopasyāsiddhatvāt saṁyogāntalopaḥ prāpnoti ... anavakāśāv etau vacanaprāmāṇyād bhaviṣyataḥ* |] The Bhāṣya on 8.2.6 vt. 6 (*saṁyogādilopaḥ saṁyogāntalope*)—where Kātyāyana claims that [R27] should be declared not to be suspended with respect to [R26]—cites 8.2.1 vt. 2 and gives the examples cited earlier.

[33] 6.1.68: *halṅyābbhyo dīrghāt sutisy apṛktaṁ hal* (PWT **404**).

[34] 6.4.14: *atvasantasya cādhātoḥ* (PWT **404**). This provides for the penultimate vowel of a stem in *-atu* or *-as*, provided this is not part of a verbal base, to be replaced by a long vowel *ā* if the stem occurs before the ending ***su*** except where this is used in a vocative. By convention (1.1.62, see note 3) an operation that is conditioned by an affix takes effect even after this affix has been dropped.

[35] 7.1.70: *ugidacāṁ sarvanāmasthāne'dhātoḥ* (PWT **488**).

[36] [R30] 8.2.39 (see **2.1.3**).

[37] 8.4.56: *vāvasāne* (PWT **578**).

in subsequent sūtras, through 8.2.37 (*ekāco baśo bhaṣ jhaṣantasya sdhvoḥ* [PWT **545**]), including [28] and [29] but not [30]. By [R28], any palatal stop (*coḥ*) is replaced by a corresponding velar stop (*kuḥ*). According to [R29], however, *ṣ* substitutes for final segments of particular verbal bases in these contexts: *vraśc* 'hew', *bhrasj* 'fry', *sṛj* 'let loose', *mṛj* 'wipe clean', *rāj* 'shine', *bhrāj* 'shine'; in addition, *tch* (*ch* augmented with *t*) and *ś* undergo replacement by *ṣ* in the same contexts. [R30] provides that in pada-final position voiced unaspirated stops (*jaśaḥ*) substitute for corresponding consonants other than semivowels and nasal stops (*jhalām*). Those bases covered specifically by [R29] that end in a palatal stop would otherwise be susceptible to velar replacement by the general rule [R28]. In accordance with [R30], a base ending with *ś* would be susceptible to replacement in pada final position by the corresponding unaspirated palatal stop *j*. Pāṇinīyas have correctly recognized and explicitly noted that [R28] and [R29] thereby constitute exceptions to [R30].[38] Having the sūtras thus interact, despite their being included in the Tripādī, headed by [R1] 8.2.1, accounts for the proper derivations in examples such as the following:

(18) *vac-tum* → *vaktum* 'say, speak' (inf.)

(19) *vāc-s* → *vāc-ϕ* → *vāk* → *vāg* ([R30]) → (optionally) *vāk* 'voice, speech, word' (nom. sg.)

(20) *yaj-tum* → *yaṣ-tum* → *yaṣṭum* ([R32]) 'venerate, perform a rite' (inf.)

(21) *suyaj-s* → *suyaj-ϕ* → *suyaṣ* → *suyaḍ* ([R30]) → (optionally) *suyaṭ* 'one who performs the ritual well'.

All these rules are included in the Tripādī, wherein

[R31] 8.4.40: *stoḥ ścunā ścuḥ*

[R32] 8.4.41: *ṣṭunā ṣṭuḥ* (*stoḥ* 40)

are suspended with respect to them. The last two sūtras concern *s* and dental stops (*stoḥ*). [R31] provides that these sounds are replaced respectively by *ś* and a corresponding palatal stop (*ścuḥ*) when in contact with *ś* and a palatal stop (*ścunā*). According to [R32], the same sounds are replaced respectively by *ṣ* and a corresponding retroflex stop (*ṣṭuḥ*) when in contact with *ṣ* and a retroflex stop (*ṣṭunā*). Since [R31] is suspended with respect to [R28] and [R29], it cannot apply in *vac-tum* or *yaj-tum* to give, wrongly, **vac-cum*, **yaj-cum*.[39]

---

[38]Cf. N VI.400 (ad 8.2.36): *atra ca śakārasya jaśtve prāpte itareṣāṁ tu kutve tadapavādaḥ ṣakāro vidhīyate*; similarly, PM VI.400. The blocking of [R30] 8.2.39 is limited blocking (see note 26).

[39]Cf. Buiskool 1939: 94–95, who remarks, in the context of 8.4.40, that *yuj-ta* and *rāj-tra* 'become **yugta* and **rāṣtra* respectively, not *-jc-* according to

2.2. Nonsuspension due to dependence

There are also instances where a given rule R_2 in the Tripādī is not suspended with respect to an earlier sūtra R_1, either within the Tripādī or in the previous adhyāyas, although it is not an exception to R_1. Instead, R_2 is not suspended because of R_1's depending (*āśrayāt*) on R_2 for its application: because R_2's applying supplies the only domain in which R_1 can apply. This situation is obviously comparable to what obtains in the case of related general rules and exceptions within the Tripādī as discussed above (**2.1.1**–**2.1.3**). Here also, a sūtra R_2 must not be suspended with respect to R_1 because if it were, the latter would be purposeless, since it would have no scope of application.

2.2.1. As an example of this situation, consider again the derivation of *leḍhum* (**2.1.1**(14)). At the stage *leḍh-ḍhum*,

> [R33] 8.3.13: *ḍho ḍhe lopaḥ*

takes effect, whereby *ḍh* (*ḍhaḥ* 'in place of *ḍh*') is deleted (*lopaḥ* 'zero') before *ḍh* (*ḍhe*). In order to have a sequence -*ḍhḍh*-, however, [R32] 8.4.41 (**2.1.3**) has to apply. In fact, the retroflex substitution provided for in this sūtra has to take place for [R33] to apply at all. Thus, if by virtue of [R1] 8.2.1, [R32] 8.4.41 were suspended with respect to [R33] 8.3.13, the latter could not apply at all. It would lack any domain of application. Consequently, one must conclude that, because of the dependence (*āśrayāt*) of [R33] on [R32], the latter is not suspended with respect to the former.[40]

2.2.2. Consider now the derivation of the past participle *līḍha*-, from the base *liḥ* 'lick' with the suffix ***kta***:

the present sūtra (*pūrva-vipratiṣedha* in either case).' The appeal to conflict is inappropriate, since, by [R1] 8.2.1, a later rule of the Tripādī is non-existent with respect to an earlier sūtra of this section; see note 32.

[40]This is explicitly recognized by Pāṇinīyas. For example, Kāś. 8.3.13 notes that retroflexion by 8.4.41 is to be considered nonsuspended with respect to 8.3.13 because of dependence: *ṣṭutvasyātra siddhatvam āśrayād draṣṭavyam* | Jinendrabuddhi elucidates as follows. *ḍh* is depended upon as a condition. In addition, there is no instance where a nonsuspended *ḍh* can occur such that it would be the cause of carrying out the deletion of *ḍh* by this rule. Therefore, because of the dependence on *ḍh* as a condition for deletion, one has to recognize the nonsuspension of retroflexion. For otherwise, the formulation of this rule would be purposeless because of its having no scope of application. [N VI.493: *ḍhakāro'tra ḍhalopanimittatvenāśrīyate na cāsau kvacit siddhaḥ sambhavati yatrānena ḍhalopaḥ kartavyaḥ* | *tasmāḍ ḍhakārasya nimittatvenāśrayād eva ṣṭutvasya siddhatvaṁ veditavyam* | *anyathā hy asya vacanasya vaiyarthyaṁ syād anavakāśatvāt* ||]

(22) *lih-ta* → *liḍh-ta* ([R24]) → *liḍh-dha* (8.2.40 [note 28]) → *liḍh-ḍha* ([R32]) → *li-ḍha* ([R33]) → *līḍha*.

Long -*ī*- substitutes for -*i*- by

[R34] 6.3.111: *ḍhralope pūrvasya dīrgho'ṇaḥ*.

This rule provides that a vowel *a i u* (*aṇaḥ*) is replaced by a corresponding long vowel (*dīrghaḥ*) when there follows a sound before which *ḍh* or *r* is deleted (*ḍhralope*). This rule presupposes that a consonant *ḍh* or *r* has indeed been dropped before another consonant. That is, the deletion of $ḍh_1$ before $ḍh_2$ provided by [R33] 8.3.13 (**2.2.1**) is assumed to have taken effect, as a condition for the long-vowel replacement. Accordingly, due to dependence, although [R33] is stated in the Tripādī, it is not suspended with respect to [R34]. Otherwise, the latter could not apply to allow the replacement before $ḍh_2$.

Long-vowel substitution by [R34] covers also the case where *r* is dropped. This deletion is provided for in another rule of the Tripādī:

[R35] 8.3.14: *ro ri* (*lopaḥ* 13)

according to which *r* (*raḥ*)[41] is replaced by zero (*lopaḥ*) if an *r* follows (*ri*). For example, the -*r* of *agnir*[42] 'Agni' (nom. sg.) and *punar* 'again' is deleted, with consequent long-vowel substitution, in:

(23) *agnir rakṣāṁsi* → *agni rakṣāṁsi* ([R35]) → *agnī rakṣāṁsi* ([R34])[43]

(24) *punar raktam* → *puna raktam* → *punā raktam* 'dyed anew'.

Now, one condition [R34] specifies is that a consonant follows which determines the dropping of *r*. This condition is met only if [R35] applies first. Consequently, unless this sūtra is not suspended with respect to [R34] despite its being stated in the Tripādī, the deletion of *r* by this sūtra has no scope. Therefore, because of dependence, [R35] is not suspended with respect to [R34].

---

[41] [R35] 8.3.14 provides for deleting any *r*, whether it is an original *r* in a base or the particular *r*—marked with *u* (***ru***)—that substitutes for -*s* by [R36] 8.2.66 (**2.2.3**).

[42] ← *agni-s* ([R36]), with the nominal ending ***su***.

[43] Ṛ̣V 7.15.10a: *agnī rakṣāṁsi sedhati* 'Agni will turn away the demons.'

2.2.3. Similarly, let us consider now

[R36] 8.2.66: *sasajuṣo ruḥ* (*padasya* 8.1.16)

in relation to

[R37] 6.1.113: *ato ror aplutād aplute* (*ati* 109, *ut* 111)

[R38] 6.1.114: *haśi ca.*

[R36] is part of a long section of rules headed by

[R39] 8.1.16: *padasya.*

Unless otherwise specified, these rules state operations relative to a pada. Accordingly, [R36] provides that pada-final *-s* as well as the final sound of *sajuṣ* 'companion' are replaced by ***ru***. By [R37]–[R38] *u* substitutes for this *r* (*roḥ*) if it is preceded by non-pluta (*aplutād*) *a* (*ataḥ*) and followed by such a vowel (*ati aplute*) *a* as well as by a voiced consonant (*haśi*). For example, the *-s* of *kas* (nom. sg. m.) 'who?' is replaced by *-r*, which is then subject to replacement by *-u*. In addition, by

[R40] 6.1.87: *ād guṇaḥ* (*aci* 77, *ekaḥ pūrvaparayoḥ* 84)

an *a*-vowel (*āt*) and an immediately following (*pūrvaparayoḥ*) vowel (*aci*) are both replaced by a single substitute (*ekaḥ*), namely a guṇa vowel, that is, one of the vowels *a e o*.[44] Thus, a complex *a*+*i* is replaced by *e*, and *o* substitutes for *a*+*u*. Further, if pada-final (*padāntāt*) *-e* or *-o* (*eṅaḥ*) is followed by *a-* (*ati*), the first (*pūrvaḥ* 'prior') of the two contiguous vowels replaces both these vowels:

[R41] 6.1.109: *eṅaḥ padāntād ati* (*pūrvaḥ* 107, *ekaḥ pūrvaparayoḥ* 84)

As shown, [R40] and [R41] are two rules of a group headed by

[R42] 6.1.84: *ekaḥ pūrvaparayoḥ*

according to which a single (*ekaḥ*) sound takes the place of both preceding and following sounds (*pūrvaparayoḥ*). Thus, starting with strings in which *kas* precedes *atra* ('here') and *gacchati*,[45] the following replacements occur to arrive at the final utterances shown:

[44] 1.1.2: *adeṅ guṇaḥ* (PWT **9**). The choice of which guṇa vowel occurs as a replacement is made according to phonetic proximity (1.1.50: *sthāne'ntaratamaḥ* [PWT **92**]).

[45] The derivational history of *atra* and *gacchati* is irrelevant to the present discussion.

(25) *kas*[46] *atra* → *kar atra* ([R36]) → *kaŭ atra* ([R37]) → *ko atra* → *kotra* ([R41]) 'Who is here?'

(26) *kas gacchati* → *kar gacchati* → *kaŭ gacchati* ([R38]) → *ko gacchati* 'Who is going?'

[R37] 6.1.113 and [R38] 6.1.114 obviously presuppose ***ru*** as the sound for the replacement of which they provide. Unless [R36] 8.2.66 is available to supply this sound, then, these rules have no scope for applying, hence are vacuous. Due to dependence, then, although [R36] 8.2.66 is stated in the Tripādī it is not suspended with respect to [R37] 6.1.113 and [R38] 6.1.114. Pāṇinīyas recognize this from earliest times. Kātyāyana takes it for granted,[47] and later Pāṇinīyas agree.[48]

2.2.4. Another possibility which Pāṇinīyas entertain is changing the position of [R37] to a place in the grammar after [R36]. However, this avenue leads to intolerable difficulties.

Kātyāyana and Patañjali already considered this possibility, as is clear from vārttika 5 on 1.1.12 (*adaso māt*). Following his paraphrase of 1.1.12 vt. 4 (see note 47), Patañjali asks why one should conclude that ***ru*** substitution is not suspended with respect to substituting *u* for ***ru*** by [R37] 6.1.113 because of dependence; why, instead, is the latter not stated in a place in the grammar where ***ru*** is not suspended?[49] That is, [R37] 6.1.113 and [R38] 6.1.114 would be transposed to a position within the Tripādī, somewhere after [R36] 8.2.66, so that *ru* would be available for replacement. Neither Kātyāyana nor Patañjali suggests precisely where in the Tripādī these

[46] *kim-s* → *ka-s* (7.2.103: *kimaḥ kaḥ* [PWT **487**]).

[47] 1.1.12 vt. 4: *āśrayāt siddhatvaṁ ca yathā ror uttve* |

[48] For example, Kāś. 6.1.113 remarks that, since substitution of ***ru*** is the basis on which 6.1.113 depends, it is not suspended by virtue of 8.2.66 coming under the heading of 8.2.1: *rutvasyāśrayatvāt pūrvatrāsiddham ity asiddhatvaṁ na bhavati* | As elsewhere, Jinendrabuddhi (N IV.586–587) explains clearly what is at issue: if ***ru***-substitution were suspended, then it would serve no purpose to depend on ***ru*** as a substituend in 6.1.113, since no *r* distinguished by the marker *u* would be possible here. Therefore, because of dependence on it, there is no suspension of ***ru***. [*yadi rutvam asiddhaṁ syāt tadā sthānitvena ror āśrayaṇam anarthakaṁ syāt kasyacid ukārānubandhaviśiṣṭasya ror asambhavāt* | *tasmād āśrayād eva ror asiddhatvaṁ nāsti* ||] Some modern scholars also have accepted this. See Buiskool 1939: 87, 98–99, Cardona 1997a: 346, 1999: 239. The Kāśikā on [R37] 6.1.113 also appropriately notes that 6.1.113 is an exception to [R43] 8.3.17 (**2.2.5**): the first rule provides for replacement by ***ru*** countering replacement by *y*, which would apply according to the second sūtra in the absence of the first rule. [*bhobhago-aghoapūrvasya yo'śīty asmin prāpta utvaṁ vidhīyate* ||]

[49] Bh. I.69.6–7: *kiṁ punaḥ kāraṇaṁ rur uttva āśrayāt siddho bhavati na punar yatraiva ruḥ siddhas tatraivottvam ucyate* |

sūtras would be placed, but later Pāṇinīyas do deal with this issue. Kaiyaṭa considers stating 6.1.113 immediately after 8.3.16[50] and in a reformulated form: *8.3.16a: *ata ur ati* ('*u* in place of *ru* that is preceded and followed by *a*').[51] This reformulation has an obvious advantage of economy: since *roḥ* is available from 8.3.16 (note 50) to carry over into *8.3.16a, the latter need not overtly state the sound to be replaced. In addition, *8.3.16a does not have to include the qualifiers *aplutāt* and *aplute*. This sūtra follows the set of rules providing for pluta substitution,[52] so that extra-long *a*-vowels are available here for consideration; since *8.3.16a refers specifically to short *a* (***at***) extra-long *a*-vowels are thereby excluded.[53] Whether Kaiyaṭa himself noticed any difficulty in this reformulation but remained silent or was unaware of such problems I cannot tell. However, Nāgeśa astutely sees a problem with this reordering. [R38] 6.1.114 should of course accompany [R37] 6.1.113, so that a reordered [R38] must also come after *8.3.16a, as *8.3.16b. This means that *8.3.16b now follows [R35] 8.3.14, so that, by [R1] 8.2.1, it is suspended with respect to this rule. Accordingly, given a sequence *-ar r*, such that *-r* derives from *-s* by [R36] 8.2.66, instead of *8.3.16b applying to replace *-r* with *u*, [R35] should apply to delete this consonant. Hence, the grammar would not provide for derivates like *mano-ratha-* 'wish', *mano-rama-* 'charming', in accounting for which the following operations should apply: *-as r-* → *-ar r-* ([R36] 8.2.66) → *-aü-r-* ([R37] 6.1.113) → *-o r-* ([R40] 6.1.87). In view of this, Nāgeśa notes, one has to consider that the intent in suggesting a change of rule position is that not only should [R37] 6.113 and [R38] 6.1.114 be restated within the Tripādī but also that [R33] 8.3.13 and [R35] 8.3.14 should be transposed to the very latest part of the grammar, immediately preceding 8.4.45 (*yaro'nunāsike 'nunāsiko vā*).[54]

These are fairly drastic reorderings. And they still do not confront the

[50] 8.3.16: *roḥ supi* (PWT **557**). This rule provides that *ḥ* replaces ***ru*** before a nominal ending (*supi*), e.g., *payaḥsu* (loc. pl.): *payas-su* → *payar-su* → *payaḥsu*; contrast *gīrṣu* 'words, speeches', with *-r* that is not a substitute for *-s*.

[51] Pr. I.223: *na punar yatraiveti* : *roḥ supītyanantaram ata ur atīti vaktavyam* |

[52] The set of rules headed by 8.2.82: *vākyasya ṭeḥ pluta udāttaḥ* (PWT **621**).

[53] Pr. I.223: *evaṁ cāsiddhatvaṁ na bādhitaṁ bhavati atra pāṭhakrame'siddhatvasya prāptyabhāvāt plutasya cotve siddhatvāt tatkālatvābhāvād aplutād apluta iti na vaktavyaṁ bhavati* | It is not necessary to consider here additional details concerning this point.

[54] Ud. I.223: *roḥ supīty asyānantaram iti* : *na caivaṁ haśi cety asyaitaduttaratvād ro rīti dṛṣṭyāsiddhatvāpattau manorathāsiddhiḥ* | *ḍho ḍhe lopaḥ ro rīty anayor yaro'nunāsike'nunāsika ity ataḥ pūrvaṁ pāṭhaḥ kārya ity āśayāt* | Note that this additional transposition eliminates the economy gained in Kaiyaṭa's reformulation, since *roḥ* is now no longer available to carry over into *8.3.116a. It is possible that, by omitting *iti* after *manoratha*, Nāgeśa is being humorous.

major problem, which Kātyāyana immediately brings up in his fifth vārttika: if the rules providing the substitution of *u* for ***ru*** are placed in the section of rules that are suspended with respect to prior rules, so that this replacement is suspended, the grammar fails to account for guṇa replacement by [R40] 6.1.87.[55] Although Kātyāyana does not say more about this point, it is clear that additional reordering to remedy the situation would not do much at all. Suppose that [R40] 6.1.87 also were transposed to the Tripādī and suppose that, following Kaiyaṭa and Nāgeśa, this were located near the repositioned [R37] 6.1.113 and [R38] 6.1.114, thus keeping the relative positioning of the sūtras as in Pāṇini's formulation. This has serious consequences. For these sūtras would now occur in a section headed by [R39] 8.1.16, so that guṇa replacement for *-aŭ* would apply only to pada-final segments. Yet this and the following rule, whereby vṛddhi vowels are single substitutes for *a*-vowels and *e o ai au* following them,[56] apply without regard for pada boundaries. For example, the guṇa vowel *-e* replaces *-a-* and *-i-* of *paca-iyta* within a pada in deriving *paceta* (3 sg. opt. mid.)[57] 'should cook'. Moreover, these two rules are part of a group headed by [R42] 6.1.84. This heading and [R39] 8.1.16 are incompatible. [R42] states simply that two sounds are both replaced by a single substitute, and [R39] provides for operations to apply relative to a pada.

It is appropriate, then, that in his last comments on 1.1.12 vt. 5 Patañjali concludes that in the case of *u* substitution for ***ru*** one must accept nonsuspension because of dependence.[58] In view of the difficulties noted, it is also proper for modern scholars to conclude that one must keep the Pāṇinian order of rules and accept that [R36] 8.2.66 is indeed not suspended with respect to [R37] 6.1.113 and [R38] 6.1.114.

2.2.5. As shown earlier (**2.1.1–2.1.3**), in cases where rules R_1 and R_2 are related as general rule and exception respectively, although the rules occur in the Tripādī, R_2 is not suspended with respect to R_1. For, if the exception were suspended with respect to the related general rule, then the latter would apply in the total general domain, including the subdomain of R_2, leaving the exception without a domain of its own. In the same vein consider

[R43] 8.3.17: *bhobhagoaghoapūrvasya yo'śi* (*roḥ* 16)

[R44] 8.3.18: *vyor laghuprayatnataraḥ śākaṭāyanasya*

[R45] 8.3.19: *lopaḥ śākalyasya*

[55] 1.1.12 vt. 5: *asiddhe hy uttva ādguṇāprasiddhiḥ* |

[56] 6.1.88 (note 4).

[57] *paca-iyta* → *paceyta* → *paceta* (6.1.66: *lopo vyor vali* [PWT **522**]).

[58] Bh. I.69.10–11: *tasmāt tatrāśrayāt siddhatvam eṣitavyam* |

[R46] 8.3.22: *hali sarveṣām* (*lopaḥ* 19).

By [R43], before a vowel or a voiced consonant (*aśi*), *y* (*yaḥ*) substitutes for ***ru*** (*roḥ*) that is preceded by *bho*, *bhago*, *agho* (in the terms of address *bhos*, *bhagos*, *aghos*) or an *a*-vowel. [R44]–[R45] state substitutions for pada-final *v* and *y* (*vyoḥ*) in the same contexts. According to Śākaṭāyana, each of these consonants is replaced by a glide with very light articulatory effort (*laghuprayatnataraḥ*), and according to Śākalya they are deleted (*lopaḥ*). Moreover, all scholars (*sarveṣām*) agree that *-v*, *-y* are deleted before a consonant (*hali*). Accordingly, *-v*, *-y* and the attenuated glides provided for by [R43]–[R44] as well as the deletion of *-v*, *-y* by [R45] apply before vowels. For example:

(27) *te*[59] *āsate* → *tay*[60] *āsate* → *ta*^{y}/*ta āsate* ([R44], [R45]) 'They are sitting'

(28) *te iha* → *tay iha* → *ta*^{y}/*ta iha* 'They are here'

(29) *tās*[61] *āsate* → *tār āsate* ([R36]) → *tāy āsate* ([R43]) → *tā*^{y}/*tā āsate* 'They are sitting'

(30) *tās iha* → *tār iha* → *tāy iha* → *tā*^{y}/*tā iha* 'They are here'

(31) *tās gacchanti* → *tār gacchanti* → *tāy gacchanti* → *tā gacchanti* ([R46]) 'They are going.'

As shown, [R43] 8.3.17 lets *-y* substitute for *-**ru*** preceded by any *a*- (*-apūrvasya*) before any voiced segment (*aśi*), while [R37] 6.1.113 (**2.2.3**) provides for the same sound to be replaced by *u* if it occurs after short *a* (*ataḥ*) and is followed also by a short *a* (*ati*). Thus, the domain of [R37] is totally included in one of the domains of [R43]. Even though this sūtra is stated in the Tripādī, it is not suspended with respect to [R37], not only because the latter depends on it for the substituend ***ru*** but also because it meets the main criterion for being an exception to [R43]: in the absence of [R37], [R43] would necessarily apply (*yena nāprāpte*) by virtue of its domain being included in that of [R43].[62]

[59] *te* 'those, these' (nom. pl. m.): *tad-as* → *taa-as* → *ta-as* → *ta-ī* → *te*; cf. (13).

[60] 6.1.78 (note 22).

[61] *tās* 'those, these' (nom. pl. f.): *tad-as* → *taa-as* → *ta-as* → *taā-as* → *tā-as* → *tās* (6.1.102: *prathamayoḥ pūrvasavarṇaḥ* [PWT **532**]).

[62] This too is explicitly recognized by Pāṇinīyas. For example, Kāś. 6.1.113 remarks that *u*-replacement (*utvam* 'the property of being *u*') is provided (*vidhīyate*) by this rule, it being given that [R43] would otherwise apply (*bhobhagoagho-apūrvasy yo'śīty asmin prāpta utvaṁ vidhīyate* |).

2.3. As has been illustrated above, there are good reasons for Pāṇini's letting the sūtras he states in the Tripādī be suspended with respect to earlier rules. Given Buiskool's (1939) study of this set of rules, it is not necessary to consider in general possible rearrangements of rules. Nevertheless, it will be useful to consider in more detail [R36] 8.2.66 and [R37] 6.1.113 (**2.2.3**).

[R36] concerns padas that end in *-s*. This rule is included both in the set of sūtras headed by [R1] 8.2.1 (**1.1**) and in the set which [R39] 8.1.16 heads. The padas in question can be either syntactic units, which terminate with nominal and verbal endings,[63] or nominal bases that precede particular affixes.[64] For example, *kas* of (25), (26) (**2.2.3**) is a pada with the first-triplet nominal ending ***su***, and *payobhis* (instr. pl.) contains the pada *payas* 'water, milk' followed by the third-triplet ending *bhis*:

(32) *payas-bhis* → *payar-bhis* → *payaŭ-bhis* → *payobhis*.

manas (nom. sg. n.) 'mind' is also a pada that originally includes the ending ***su***. After the neuter base *manas*, however, this ending is replaced by zero.[65] The nominative singular *sumanās* 'benevolent' also is a pada such that the ending ***su*** following *sumanas-* has been deleted.[66] The *-s* of both *manas* and *sumanās* is subject to operations that apply to pada-final *-s*; e.g., *mano me* 'my mind' has *-o* before the voiced consonant of *me* (enclitic gen. sg.), and *sumanā* occurs before *g-* in *sumanā gacchati* 'The benevolent one is going.' On the other hand, *sumanās* has a long penultimate vowel that *manas* does not have. By 6.4.14 (see note 34), before the ending ***su***, a long vowel (*dīrghaḥ*) replaces the penult (*upadhāyāḥ*) of a stem in *-a**tu*** or *-as* (*atvasantasya*), provided the segment in question is not part of a verb (*adhātoḥ*). Although ***su*** following *sumanas* is dropped, by convention (1.1.62 [note 3]), the operation conditioned by this affix nevertheless applies, so that the penultimate *-a-* of *sumanas* is replaced by *-ā-*. The ending of *manas-s* also is dropped, but the zero replacement here is *luk*, so deleting the ending precludes applying the operation which would take place in its presence.[67] Hence, long-vowel substitution by 6.4.14 does not take effect in *manas*.

Now, although both 6.4.14 and [R36] 8.2.66 have to do with final *-s*, the larger units in question are distinct. [R36] applies for a pada ending in *-s*, but 6.4.14 applies for a presuffixal stem (*aṅga*)[68] in *-s*. In Pāṇini's derivation system, operations within padas, affecting stems and affixes, regularly

[63] 1.4.14 (note 3).
[64] 1.4.17 (note 6).
[65] 7.1.23: *svamor napuṁsakāt* (PWT **495**).
[66] 6.1.68 (note 33).
[67] 1.1.63: *na lumatāṅgasya* (PWT **103**).
[68] 6.4.14 comes under the heading of 6.4.1: *aṅgasya* (PWT **105**).

precede operations involving padas in the context of other padas. It is understandable, then, that [R36] 8.2.66 occurs within the Tripādī, along with rules such as [R3] 8.2.7 (**1.2**), which have to be suspended with respect to prior rules.

2.4. The matters considered above have theoretical consequences which bear noting.

2.4.1. It is noteworthy that Pāṇini specifies in [R2] 8.2.2 (**1.2**) the particular rules relative to which [R3] 8.2.7 is suspended and denies in [R13] 8.2.3 (**1.3**) the suspension of [R14] 8.2.80 with respect to one particular rule. This is worthy of note because in most cases—including those considered in sections **2.2.1**–**2.2.3**—he excludes suspension without such specification and solely by implication: the application of a rule R_1 depends on the application of a rule R_2 which would otherwise be suspended.[69] In order that R_1 not be vacuous, one must infer that R_2 is in fact not suspended with respect to R_1. This apparent discrepancy calls for clarification.

What sets apart the rules relative to which [R2] and [R3] provide for non-suspension is that they have domains of application independent of those which arise due to the application of rules in the Tripādī. Thus, any stem with primitive *-a*, such as *puruṣa*, is a context for the substitution of *ais* for *bhis* by [R4] 7.1.9 and is subject to the replacements provided for in [R5] 7.3.102 and [R6] 7.3.103. Derivates like *haṁsavatī*, where *-avat-* does not have *-a-* due to the deletion of *n*, supply a domain for the accentuation covered by [R7] 6.1.220 independent of derivates like *rājavatī*, where *-avat-* has *a* before *vat* resulting from such deletion. Any ghi base, such as *hari*, supplies a domain for the constituent order provided for in [R8] 2.2.32 independent of instances where *-i* derives from *-in*. And there is an ample number of instances where [R9] 6.1.71 and [R10] 6.1.73 can apply and the short vowel preceding a kṛt suffix or *ch* does not involve the deletion of *n* by [R3] 8.2.7, for example *āhatya*, *nicitya*, *prastutya*, *gacchati*, *icchati* ('wishes'). Similarly, [R15] 7.3.120 applies to derive instrumental singular forms of any non-feminine stem in *-i*, *-u*, like *agninā*, *vāyunā*, independently of *amu* gotten by applying [R14] 8.2.80. Thus, the rules in question are not vacuous if these rules of the Tripādī remain suspended with respect to them.

[69] In order to keep within space limits, I have dealt only with three examples of this, which are particularly clear and recognized explicitly by Pāṇinīyas. There are more instances, some of which involve details that would entail a more extended discussion than is possible here. Let me merely mention here the set of rules headed by 8.2.82 (note 52), which provide for pluta substitution, and 8.4.66 (*udāttād anudāttasya svaritaḥ* [PWT **622**]), which substitutes a svarita syllable for a low-pitched syllable.

It is appropriate to conclude from the above that Pāṇini specifies in [R2] 8.2.2 and [R13] 8.2.3 particular rules with respect to which certain Tripādī rules are or are not suspended because he cannot depend on implication to show this. In other cases where particular sūtras are vacuous unless related Tripādī rules are not suspended, he allows it to be implied, by dependence, that the Tripādī sūtras in question are not suspended.

2.4.2. Another situation where a Tripādī rule is not suspended with respect to a prior sūtra involves general rules and related exceptions (**2.1.1–2.1.2**). Here again, Pāṇini has no need to specify explicitly that certain Tripādī rules are not suspended with respect to earlier rules to which they are exceptions. He proceeds in this way because he assumes as a principle that an exception must have a domain proper to it and that it does so by interacting with a related general rule, removing from the general domain of such a rule the subdomain proper to itself. Pāṇini also does not state this principle explicitly in his Aṣṭādhyāyī. Nor does he have to. It is a principle known to any one studying this grammar, from practice in everyday life.[70]

[70]This is exemplified by the situation where two commands are made: that yogurt should be given to brāhmaṇas and that buttermilk be given to a particular brāhmaṇa, Kauṇḍinya. Although it is possible for both commands to be carried out, so that buttermilk is given to Kauṇḍinya, the command concerning the particular brāhmaṇa counters the general command. Patañjali prefaces his allusion to this situation with the remark that neither does the lord command nor the authors of sūtras on dharma say in their texts that general rules should be blocked by exceptions, since this is known from the real world. [Bh. I.114.24–115.3 (ad 1.1.47): *naiveśvara ājñāpayati nāpi dharmsūtrakārāḥ paṭhanty apavādair utsargā bādhyantām iti kin tarhi laukiko'yaṁ dṛṣṭāntaḥ | loke hi saty api sambhave bādhanaṁ bhavati | tad yathā dadhi brāhmaṇebhyo dīyatām takraṁ kauṇḍinyāyeti | saty api sambhave dadhidānasya takradānaṁ nivartakaṁ bhavati* |] Patañjali also notes that in certain instances Pāṇini makes special provision for countering an indecisiveness that would apply if one followed common usage. Thus, for example if one says *ajāvidhanau devadattayajñadattau* ('Devadatta and Yajñadatta have wealth consisting of goats and sheep'), using the bahuvrīhi compound *ajāvidhanau*, this does not make known which of the two persons spoken of has wealth consisting of goats and which has sheep. Such an indecisiveness is countered by the metarule 1.3.10: *yathāsaṅkhyam anudeśaḥ samānām* (PWT **91**), which provides for relating terms in order. Thus, 1.1.46: *ādyantau ṭakitau* (PWT **17**), where the dvandvas *ādyantau* and *ṭakitau* are used, provides that augments bearing the markers *ṭ* and *k* respectively are initial and final segments of items to which they are introduced. [Bh. I.112.19–22 (on 1.1.46): *samāsanirdeśo'yam | tatra na jñāyate ka ādiḥ ko'nta iti | tad yathā : ajāvidhanau devadattayajñadattāv ity ukte na jñāyate kasyājā dhanaṁ kasyāvaya iti | yady api tāval loka eṣa dṛṣṭāntas tathāpi puruṣārambho nivartako bhavati | asti ceha kaścit puruṣārambhaḥ | astīty āha | kaḥ | saṅkhyānudeśo nāma* |]

One's inferring that certain rules of the Tripādī, though governed nominally by the heading [R1] 8.2.1, are not suspended with respect to certain prior rules because of dependence is also connected with cultural factors that involve common sense. The Aṣṭādhyāyī is accepted as the grammar (*vyākaraṇa*) that plays the role of an ancillary to the Vedas (*vedāṅga*). In addition, Pāṇini is granted the exalted status of a teacher who, sitting facing eastward in a pure place, with a ring of holy kuśa grass round his ring finger, composed a set of sūtras with great effort, such that there cannot be in this work any useless part, not even a sound, much less a sūtra.[71] The point is not, of course, that any one should blindly accept any statement merely on faith in a tradition. The point is rather that the author of the Aṣṭādhyāyī could count on recognized cultural factors to mediate how this work was approached by students. With these factors in mind, when faced with situations such as those considered here, a student of Pāṇini's work does not jump to the conclusion that somehow Pāṇini has been inconsistent. Instead, one infers that the particular Tripādī sūtras in question are in fact not suspended with respect to certain rules.

2.4.3. There are, in addition, instances where a sūtra of the Tripādī is not suspended and this is known through implication but in a manner different from what I have discussed thus far. Consider, for example, the derivation of aorist forms like *alāvīt* (3 sg.) '... (has) cut':

(33) *lū-l*[72] → *lū-ti*[73] → *lū-t*[74] → *lū-l-t*[75] → *lū-s-t*[76] → *lū-is-t*[77] → *lū-is-īt*[78] → *alū-is-īt*[79] → *alau-is-īt*[80] → *alāv-is-īt*[81]

[71]Bh. I.39.10–13 (ad 1.1.1): *pramāṇabhūta ācāryo darbhapavitrapāṇiḥ śucāv avakāśe prāṅmukha upaviśya mahatā yatnena sūtraṁ praṇayati sma | tatrāśakyaṁ varṇenāpy anarthakena bhavituṁ kim punar iyatā sūtreṇa* | Recall that NS 1.1.7 (*āptopadeśaḥ śabdaḥ*) defines that means of gaining correct knowledge (*pramāṇa*) which is verbal testimony (*śabda*) as what a trustworthy person says (*āptopadeśa*).

[72]L-affix ***luṅ*** (3.2.110: *luṅ* [PWT **233**]).

[73]3.4.77–78: *lasya, tiptasjhisipthasthamibvasmastātāñjhathāsāthāndhvamiḍvahimahiṅ* (PWT **232**).

[74]3.4.100: *itaś ca* (PWT **400**).

[75]With affix ***cli***, introduced after a verbal base when a sārvadhātuka suffix follows which derives from ***luṅ*** (3.1.43: *cli luṅi* [PWT **236**]).

[76]3.1.44: *cleḥ sic* (PWT **236**).

[77]7.2.35: *ārdhadhātukasyeḍ valādeḥ* [PWT **145**].

[78]7.3.96: *astisico'pṛkte* (PWT **440**).

[79]6.4.71: *luṅlaṅlṛṅkṣv aḍ udāttaḥ* (PWT **238**).

[80]7.2.1: *sici vṛddhiḥ parasmaipadeṣu* (PWT **412**).

[81]6.1.78 (note 22).

→ *alāv-i-īt*[82] → *alāvīt*[83]

alāvīt has the augment *aṭ*, introduced as the initial segment of a stem. This augment is not introduced, however, to a verb stem construed with the negative particle *mā*,[84] as in *mā làvīt* 'may ... not cut'. Where a finite form follows a nominal, moreover, the entire verb form lacks a high-pitched vowel;[85] for example *làvīt* following *mā* starts with two low-pitched syllables, the first of which is replaced by a svarita after the high-pitched vowel of *mā*.[86] This lack of high pitch holds, however, only in general. In particular constructions a finite verb form does not conform to this pattern. One of these constructions involves a verb used with the particle *hi*.[87] For example, *lāvīt* following *mā hi* retains an accented syllable: *mā hi lāvīt/mā hi lāvīt*. As shown, the accentuation is variable, with either the first or second syllable of *lāvīt* bearing high pitch. Accordingly, Pāṇini provides that the first syllable of a verb form derived with the suffix ***sic*** is optionally high pitched.[88]

As shown in (33), the derivation of *alāvīt* involves not only having ***sic*** following *lū* but also introducing initial augments: ***iṭ*** to ***sic*** and ***īṭ*** to the ending *t* which follows this suffix; the same operations apply in deriving *lāvīt*. The augmented suffix *-iṣ-* (← *-is*) appears in forms such as *alāviṣṭām* (3 du.), so that Pāṇini has to account for *-ī-* in forms such as *alāvīt*. He does so by providing, in 8.2.28 (note 82), that *-s-* is deleted if it occurs between the preceding augment *iṭ* and the following augment *īṭ*. Once *-s-* has been deleted, a single long vowel *-ī-* should replace both the contiguous vowels *-i-ī*. Further, if one of the two vowels is high pitched, the single replacement for both of them is also high pitched.[89] Thus, the single substitute *-ī* which replaces *-íī-* has high pitch: *lāvīt*.

Now, the substitution of *-ī-* for *-iī-* is provided for in 6.1.101 (note 21). However, 8.2.28 is nominally suspended with respect to this rule, so that one must inquire how the result of applying this sūtra could be subject to 6.1.101. Kātyāyana simply states that the deletion of ***sic*** is to be considered not suspended with respect to the rule whereby a single vowel replaces two contiguous vowels,[90] and later Pāṇinīyas follow suit. But there is more. Note that ***sic*** is marked with *c*. Pāṇini marks items in this way to indicated

[82] 8.2.28: *iṭa īṭi* (PWT **543**).
[83] 6.1.101 (note 21).
[84] 6.4.74: *na māṅyoge*.
[85] 8.1.28: *tiṅṅatiṅaḥ* (PWT **615**).
[86] 8.4.66: *udāttād anudāttasya svaritaḥ* (PWT **622**).
[87] 8.1.34: *hi ca* (PWT **616**).
[88] 6.1.187: *ādiḥ sico'nyatarasyām* (PWT **600**).
[89] 8.2.5: *ekādeśa udāttenodāttaḥ* (PWT **610**).
[90] 8.2.6 vt. 5: *sijlopa ekādeśe*.

that the vowel of such an item is high-pitched.[91] The only vowel in question with regard to ***sic*** is the augment *iṭ*. In addition, although in general an affix bears high pitch on its first vowel,[92] the vowels of augments are regularly low-pitched.[93] Marking ***sic*** with *c* thus indicates the high-pitched property of the augment in *is*,[94] and Kātyāyana also recognizes that this is the purpose in marking this affix with *c*:[95] it is only if ***sic*** is augmented with high-pitched *iṭ* that forms like *lāvīt* can be derived appropriately, by deleting *-s-* between the augments *i* and *ī*, then letting the two contiguous vowels be replaced by a single long *ī*, which is high-pitched since the first of the vowels is high-pitched.[96]

Accordingly, one can infer that 8.2.28 is not suspended with respect to 6.1.101. For only if this is true, does marking ***sic*** with *c* in order to show that *i* of augmented *is* has high pitch have a purpose: this is necessary for 8.2.5 (note 89) to apply, and in turn this requires that there be a single replacement for contiguous vowels, by 6.1.101.

---

[91] 6.1.163: *citaḥ* (PWT **599**).

[92] 3.1.3: *ādyudāttaś ca* (PWT **592**).

[93] Accordingly, in 3.4.103 (*yāsuṭ parasmaipadeṣūdātto ṅic ca* [PWT **401**]) Pāṇini specifies that the initial augment *yāsuṭ* that is added to parasmaipada endings which derive from ***liṅ*** has a high-pitched vowel. Pāṇinīyas consider that this sūtra shows (*jñāpayati* 'makes known') that augments regularly have low-pitched vowels. It is not necessary to consider here details of arguments presented in the Mahābhāṣya and elsewhere.

[94] The genitive *citaḥ* ('of an item marked with *c*') in 6.1.163 (note 91) is construed with *anta udāttaḥ*, understood to recur from 6.1.159: *karṣātvato ghaño 'nta udāttaḥ*. Although *antaḥ* 'final' is used, this does not require that the vowel in question be the final segment of the unit to which it belongs; it can be the last vowel. In addition, an element that is the only vowel of a grammatical item can be treated as though it were the final vowel of that unit. The syntax of 6.1.163 is comparable to that of 6.1.166 (*tisṛbhyo jasaḥ*), where *anta udāttaḥ* is also understood and construed with the genitive *jasaḥ*. This sūtra provides that the vowel of the nominal ending ***jas*** (nom. pl.) is high-pitched when it follows the feminine number word *tisṛ* 'three' (*tisraḥ*). The vowel of *as* is thus spoken of as final (*antaḥ*).

[95] 3.1.44 vt. 2: *arthavat tu citkaraṇasāmarthyād dhīṭa udāttatvam* | I do not consider it necessary to take up here the full argument of which Kātyāyana's second vārttika on 3.1.44 is a part and which involves the marking of ***cli*** also with *c*.

[96] At the end of his comments on 8.2.6 vt. 5 (see note 90), Patañjali argues thus and cites 3.1.44 vt. 2 (note 95): *iṭi punaḥ saty uktam etad arthavat tu citkaraṇasāmarthyād dhīṭa udāttatvam iti* | *tatraikādeśa udāttenodātta ity udādattvaṁ siddhaṁ bhavati* (Bh. III.391.21–22). This follows the rejection of an alternative interpretation of 8.2.28 (note 82) under which *iṭaḥ* is a genitive, so that the sūtra provides for deleting *s* with the augment *iṭ* (*-is-ī-* → *-ī*).

2.4.4. Pāṇini's depending on one's inferring something instead of explicitly stating it in the Aṣṭādhyāyī clearly plays an important role in this work. The contrast between the two procedures is vividly illustrated by another example.

[R47] 3.1.95: *kṛtyāḥ* (PWT **66**)

is a heading whereby affixes introduced in rules that follow bear the class name *kṛtya*. [R47] does not specify the range of this heading. In his two vārttikas on this sūtra, Kātyāyana takes up alternative ways in which it may be made known where the heading ceases to have effect. First, he suggests that one should state explicitly *prāṅ ṇvulaḥ* (*prāṅṇvulvacanam*).[97] That is, [R47] should be reformulated as

[R48] *3.1.95: *kṛtyāḥ prāṅ ṇvulaḥ*

so that the heading extend only up to

[R49] 3.1.133: *ṇvultṛcau* (PWT **248**).

In this way, the name *kṛtya* does not apply to the suffix ***ṇvul***.[98] Kātyāyana next notes that Pāṇini's saying *kṛtyatṛcaḥ* ('kṛtya affixes and ***tṛc***') in

[R50] 3.3.169: *arhe kṛtyatṛcaś ca* (PWT **294**)

makes it known that it is not necessary (*ānarthakyasya* 'of having no purpose') to state *prāṅ ṇvulaḥ* as in [R48].[99] That is, [R50] provides not only for affixes called *kṛtya* but also for ***tṛc***. One must infer thereby that ***tṛc*** is not an affix with the name *kṛtya*, so that the name introduced by [R47] extends only up to but not including *ṇvul* of [R49].[100] Moreover, since [R49] introduces ***ṇvul*** and ***tṛc*** as affixes which alternate with each other, by virtue of excluding the latter, this sūtra also excludes the former, so that the *kṛtya* is introduced by rules prior to [R49] as a whole.[101]

Clearly, there are two opposed approaches involved: one, which may be considered appropriate for relatively slow witted (*mandabuddhi*) students who require that everything be spelled out for them, envisages [R 48];[102] an-

[97]3.1.95 vt. 1: *kṛtyasañjñāyāṁ prāṅṇvulvacanam |*

[98]Bh. II.81.9–10: *kṛtyasajñāyāṁ prāṅ ṇvula iti vaktavyam | kiṁ prayojanam | ṇvulaḥ kṛtyasañjñā mā bhūt |*

[99]3.1.95 vt. 2: *arhekṛtyatṛjvacanaṁ tu jñāpakaṁ prāṅṇvulvacanānarthakyasya |*

[100]Bh. II.81.12–13: *yad ayam arhe kṛtyatṛcaśceti tṛjgrahaṇaṁ karoti taj jñāpayaty ācāryaḥ prāṅ ṇvulaḥ kṛtyasañjñā bhavatīti |*

[101]Patañjali makes this point when he ends his discussion of 3.1.95 vt. 2 by bringing up an objection and answering it (Bh. II.81.13–14): *evam api ṇvulaḥ kṛtyasañjñā prāpnoti | yogāpekṣaṁ jñāpakam* 'Even so, the name *kṛtya* obtains for ***ṇvul***. The indication (*jñāpakam* '... which makes known') is with respect to the rule.'

[102]This is in fact the formulation adopted in the Kāśikāvṛtti.

other, which can be considered appropriate to more astute students, leaves the range of the heading in question to be inferred from the manner in which another sūtra is formulated. Equally clearly, Pāṇini adopted the second approach, not only in the present instance but, as had been shown, more generally.

2.5. In brief, Pāṇini operates with assumed principles governing how rules relate with one another and he can assume that students of his work—native speakers of Sanskrit—recognize these principles. He also assumes that the same students could infer from the manner in which particular rules are formulated certain things that are not stated explicitly.

3. Pāṇini and the text of the Ṛgveda

3.1. Introduction

The matters I have discussed above and the conclusions to be reached from these also have consequences for what one may say justifiably about the text of the Ṛgveda known to Pāṇini.

Pāṇini knew both the saṁhitāpāṭha of the Ṛgveda and the corresponding padapāṭha composed by Śākalya. This is generally accepted for good reasons which need not be rehearsed. In recent times, the view has been advanced that the version of the Ṛgveda known to Pāṇini was more archaic in some respects than the transmitted version which is accounted for by rules of Śaunaka's Ṛgvedaprātiśākhya. In particular, the claim has been made that, contrary to the norm known from Śākalya's Ṛgveda text, accounted for in the Ṛgvedaprātiśākhya, Pāṇini knew and accounted for by rules in his Aṣṭādhyāyī, a Ṛgveda version where one recited *-ay a-* instead of *-o a-* or *-o-* for original *-as a-*. This claim is demonstrably unacceptable because it is based on misunderstandings of the pertinent Pāṇinian sūtras. Although at an earlier time I argued against the claim at issue and presented evidence showing why it is unacceptable,[103] it is appropriate and, I think, necessary to come back to the issue in view of the recent repetition of this claim by its proponent.[104] In considering the issue once more, I have also to rehearse evidence which is—or should be—well known to well informed Sanskritists who deal with Pāṇini and the Veda. This is necessary, in my opinion, not only because the evidence has been misunderstood on more than one occasion but also because in arguing against it and attempting to justify his original view, the scholar in question brings up the

[103]See Cardona 1999: 235–40.

[104]Bronkhorst 2007: 336, 343–47.

issue of an "orthodox", "traditional" interpretation of Pāṇini,[105] as though Pāṇinīyas themselves somehow were slaves to a rigid interpretational tradition from which they did not veer and a modern scholar who accepts certain siddhāntas now deemed "orthodox" and "traditional" also would fall prey to such enslavement.

3.2. Sequences *-e a-*, *-o a-* in the Ṛgveda

The facts concerning the treatment of sequences *-e a-*, *-o a-* in the Ṛgveda are well known. In the modern tradition of Vedic exegesis, these facts were explained in exemplary fashion by Oldenberg and Wackernagel, and later modern scholars have added historical explanations accounting for the development to *-e-*, *-o-*.[106] The prevalent treatment of sequences *-e a-* and *-o a-* is to retain vowels in hiatus, even where the first vowel in question does not belong to the pragṛhya class. There are, nevertheless, irrefutable examples of abhinihitasandhi, with *-e-* (← *-e a-*), *-o-* (← *-o a-*). The usages are distributed among three general groups, as follows.[107]

A. Hiatus without metrical deviation. For example:

(34) *te àgre̱pā ṛ̀bhavo mandasā̱nāḥ*[108] (ṚV 4.34.10c)

(35) *vra̱taiḥ sīkṣànto avra̱tam* (ṚV 6.14.3d).

These are respectively a triṣṭubh and an anuṣṭubh pāda, with the required eleven and eight syllables.

B. Abhinihitasandhi without metrical deviation. For example:

(36) *yam aicchàma manàsā̱ sò̱3yam āgàt* (ṚV 10.53.1a)

(37) *tè'vadan pratha̱mā bràhmakilbi̱ṣe* (ṚV 10.109.1a)

[105]Bronkhorst 2007: 336 n. 4: 'Cardona (1999: 239), while reviewing this passage, draws attention to the orthodox interpretation of the rules concerned and maintains without argument that this orthodox interpretation has to be followed. He seems to overlook the fact that an historical approach sometimes carries the obligation to question traditional interpretations.' In saying 'without argument', Bronkhorst chooses not to mention that Cardona argued from evidence, namely that [R37] 6.1.113 is an exception to [R43] 8.3.17, a fact Bronkhorst himself ignored in his earlier article and continues to ignore, and that [R37] and [R38] 6.1.114 would be vacuous if [R36] 8.2.66 were suspended with respect to them.

[106]For literature on the issues, see Cardona 1987 (references, 64 n. 12), 1997b: 36 n.14.

[107]In order to avoid questions of interpretation, I cite examples (34)–(45) without translation.

[108]I cite the pāda with *-ḥ* in *mandasā̱nāḥ*, although in close junction with the initial of the following pāda the actual form is *mandasā̱nā*. Similarly, in (42) I cite *naraḥ*, with *-ḥ*, although the actual saṁhitā text has *nara*.

are triṣṭubh pādas, which ideally require eleven syllables. This requirement is met with *sò3yam* (← *saḥ ayam*)[109] and *tèvadan* (← *te avadan*).

C. Abhinihitasandhi or praśliṣṭasandhi in a hypometrical pāda. For example:

(38) *dadhāsi ratnan draviṇañ ca dāśuṣegnè sakhye mā rìṣāmā vayan tavà* (ṚV 1.94.14cd)

(39) *atrà cin no madho pitoràm bhakṣāyà gamyāḥ* (ṚV 1.187.7cd)

(40) *yuvaṁ śvetam pedavè'śvināśvàm* (ṚV 10.39.10a)

(41) *tam pṛcchantovàrāsaḥ paràṇi* (ṚV 6.21.6a).

(38) contains two pādas of a set of verses in jagatī metre, which ideally requires twelve syllables; the first pāda, ending with *dāśuṣe*, has the requisite number of syllables, but the second, beginning with *gnè*, has only eleven syllables. (39) consists of two pādas in a set of anuṣṭubh verses, which ideally have octosyllabic sections; the first pāda meets this requirement, but the next one, beginning with *ràm*, has only six syllables. (40) and (41) are hendecasyllabic and decasyllabic pādas of jagatī and triṣṭubh verses, which ideally require twelve and eleven syllables in a pāda. Similarly,

(42) *pretā jayàtā naraḥ* (ṚV 10.103.13a)

is an anuṣṭubh pāda with seven syllables, although ideally such a pāda requires eight syllables.

3.3. Resolution of sandhi

Modern scholars have recognized that the metrical deviation in examples such as (40)–(41) can be eliminated by doing away with abhinihita sandhi, reading *pedavà aśvināśvàm* and *pṛcchanta avàrāsaḥ*. Similarly, (42) can be made metrically regular by eliminating praśliṣṭa sandhi: *pra itā* instead of *pretā*. This possibility is known to Śaunaka, who states[110] that in order to allow the perfection (*sampade*) of pādas which are deficient by having less syllables than those required for the ideal pādas of particular metres (*pādeṣūneṣu*), one should separate (*vyūhet*) into constituent vowels the single vowels that result from fusion (*ekībhāvān*). Commenting on the prātiśākhya sūtra in question, Uvaṭa cites (42). That is, one breaks up the vowel *-e-* of *pretā* into the segments *-a* and *i-*, as they appear in the padapāṭha:

[109] I have given underlying forms with *-ḥ* in accordance with the practice of the padapāṭha; see **3.4** with note 115.

[110] ṚPr. 17.22: *vyūhed ekākṣarībhāvān pādeṣūneṣu sampade* |

(42a) *pra* | *i͟ta͟* | *jayàta* | *na͟ra͟ḥ* | (ṚV 10.103.13a padapāṭha).

Now, modern scholars eliminate such sandhi modifications in order to arrive at metrically correct pādas, under the assumption that the original text had such lines and that these were modified in the course of transmission by later reciters, who observed the phonological operations applicable in their own speech. Śaunaka does not have the same purpose or premise. For him, the Ṛgveda text as handed down in the Śākala tradition of recitation stands as accepted. Accordingly, the Ṛgvedaprātiśākhya recognizes hypometric (*nicṛt*) and hypermetric (*bhurik*) pādas. Undoing the results of praśliṣṭa sandhi combinations such as *-e-* into *-a i-*, as well as restoring *-iy-* and *-uv-* for *-y-* and *-v-*, in clusters where kṣaipra sandhi change has applied[111] then serves a purpose other than providing ideal lines that are actually recited in ritual performance.[112] Metrically ideal lines thus posited allow the formulation of generalized rules of metrical lengthening. For example, the padapāṭha text from which (42) is formally derived through the application of phonological rules has *jayàta*, with *-a*, as opposed to *jayàtā* in the saṁhitāpāṭha. Śaunaka formulates a rule[113] according to which the sixth syllable in an eight-syllable pāda is subject to lengthening. In the idealized pāda *pra ìta͟ jayàta naraḥ*, *ta* occurs as the sixth syllable.[114]

In this vein, consider again (37). It is of course possible to undo the sandhi here, as in (40): *ta àvadan pratha͟mā bràhmakilbi͟ṣe*. The pāda also has the cadence of a jagatī. On the other hand, this change results in a contextual anomaly. For we have now a jagatī pāda in the midst of triṣṭubh verses. Moreover, with abhinidhāna at the juncture of the final *-e* of the first pāda and the *a-* of the second, the latter is a hypometric triṣṭubh pāda *kùpāraḥ sali͟lo màta͟riśvā̀*. Even with sandhi resolution in this pāda, the result is an eleven-syllable pāda with a triṣṭubh cadence: *akùpāraḥ sali͟lo màta͟riśvā̀*. Thus, while undoing sandhi changes in cases such as (38)–(42) resolves anomalies, the same procedure results in an anomaly for (37). It is understandable, then, that the Śākala recension has (37) as shown, that Śaunaka's formulation for abhinihita sandhi acknowledges this (see **3.4.1**, note 119), and that Pāṇini also recognizes this state of affairs (see **3.4.2**, note 126). Examples such as (37) and (38), from the tenth maṇḍala, represent the result of historical developments such that the phonological

[111]ṚPr. 17.23 (*kṣaipravarṇāṁś ca saṁyogān vyaveyāt sadṛśaiḥ svaraiḥ* |) also provides that, to bring a pāda to fullness, one should separate clusters with *y*, *v* from *i*, *u* by a similar vowel; that is, one should insert *i*, *u* to yield *iy*, *uv*.

[112]For a discussion of these issues, see Cardona 1998.

[113]ṚPr. 8.39: *ṣaṣṭhañ cāṣṭākṣare'kṣaram* |

[114]The metrical lengthening that applies to yield *pretā͟* is provided for by another sūtra (ṚPr. 8.31: ... *itā jayatā* ...). Details concerning this and other rules of metrical lengthening are not pertinent to the present paper.

adjustments typical of Sanskrit in Pāṇini's time had been established for the received recension of the Ṛgveda.

3.4. Rules accounting for Vedic usage

Pāṇini and Śaunaka equally recognize that in Vedic usage one has both hiatus sequences *-e a-*, *-o a-* and abhinidhāna, as in *-e-* (← *-e a-*), *-o-* (← *-o a-*), although they differ in their formulations. Pāṇini sets out to describe the accepted spoken language of his time, and deals with usage proper to sacred literature (*chandasi*) in particular rules associated with those that describe the usage of his time. Pāṇini and Śaunaka agree also that the normal outcome for *-as* followed by a voiced consonant is *-o*,[115] and again they differ in procedure. Starting from the padapāṭha, Śaunaka provides for *-aḥ* to change to *-o* before a voiced consonant.[116] Pāṇini, on the other hand, starts from *-as* and provides for a series of replacements leading to *-o*: *-as* → *-ar* → *-aü* → *-o* (see **2.2.3** (25)).

3.4.1. The Ṛgvedaprātiśākhya on usage in the Ṛgveda

Śaunaka recognizes not only that the Ṛgveda recitation in the Śākala tradition involves sequences of the types shown under **3.2 A–C** but also acknowledges that hiatus sequences *-e a-*, *-o a-* are the general rule. Thus, his statement of abhinihita sandhi is preceded by a rule[117] which provides that *-aḥ* changes to *-o* (*o bhavati*) before *a-* (*akāre*), and *-e*, *-o* remain in their original forms (*prakṛtyā*) before *a-*. In a set of rules (ṚPr. 2.34–50) that follows, he goes on to give the various contexts in which *-e a-* and *-o a-* change to *-e-*, *-o-*.

This group of rules begins[118] with a statement of a heading: 'Now (*atha*) begins the section in which the juxtaposition called *abhinihitaḥ sandhiḥ* is formulated.' To start with, Śaunaka provides that pāda-initial *a-* (*pādādir*

[115]As in (34) *ṛ̀bhavo mandasā̱nāḥ* ← *ṛ̱bha̱va̱ḥ ma̱nda̱sā̱nāḥ* (ṚV padapāṭha 4.34.10: *ṛ̱bha̱va̱ḥ* | *ma̱nda̱sā̱nāḥ* |).

[116]According to ṚPr. 4.25 (*okāraṁ hrasvapūrvaḥ* [*visarjanīyaḥ arephī ghoṣavatparaḥ* 24]), *-ḥ* which is not susceptible to changing to *-r* before voiced segments changes to *-o* before a voiced consonant, provided it is preceded by the short vowel *a*. By ṚPr. 1.67 (*sahopadho'riphita ekavarṇavad visarjanīyaḥ svaraghoṣavatparaḥ* |), a *-ḥ* not subject to changing to *-r*, when it is followed by a vowel or a voiced consonant, behaves as a single sound in conjunction with the preceding vowel, so that the change is of *-aḥ* to *-o*.

[117]ṚPr. 2.33: *udgrāhāṇām pūrvarūpāṇy akāre prakṛtyā dve o bhavaty ekam ādyam* | *prācyapañcālapadavṛttayas tāḥ pañcālānām oṣṭhyapūrvā bhavanti* | See Cardona 1987: 60–61.

[118]ṚPr. 2.34: *athābhinihitaḥ sandhir etaiḥ prākṛtavaikṛtaiḥ* | *ekī bhavati pādādir akāras te'tra sandhijāḥ* |

akāraḥ) fuses (*ekī bhavati* 'becomes one') with the aforementioned vowels whether they are original or result from change (*prākṛtavaikṛtaiḥ*), that is, with original -*e*, -*o* and with -*o* that derives from -*aḥ*. For example, in *dā̱śuṣegnè* and *pi̱toràm* of (38) and (39), pāda-initial *a*- has fused with -*e* and -*o* of the preceding pāda. The next Ṛgvedaprātiśākhya sūtra[119] begins the set of rules providing for the fusion of *a*- with preceding -*e*, -*o* in the interior of a pāda (*antaḥpādam*). This rule states that the change in question applies if, in the saṁhitā, *a*- is a light syllable after which (*laghoḥ param*) there occurs a light (*laghu*) syllable (*akṣaram*) beginning with *y* (*yakārādi*) or *v* (*vakārādi*). For example, (36) and (37) have *sò̱3yam* and *tè'vadan* in the interior of pādas. On the other hand, vowel fusion does not apply in *sī́kṣànto avra̱tam* of (35), where *a*- is followed by a cluster -*vr*-, so that it is not light.

After such general rules, Śaunaka goes on to state more particular contexts in a group of rules,[120] and this includes listing specific instances. For example, *stotàva a̱mbyàm* of

(43) *veti̱ stotàva a̱mbyàm* (ṚV 8.72.5c)

has -*a a*- instead of -*e a*- (*stotàve* 'to praise') or -*e*- (← -*e a*-), and Śaunaka lists this sequence amid a group of sequences that do not conform to norms.[121] Uvaṭa notes[122] that abhinihita sandhi fails to apply and -*e* changes to -*a* here.

Śaunaka also takes note of a usage particular to the elder Śākalya (*śākalyasya sthavirasya*) and remarks that the established norm (*sthitiḥ*) of recitation is otherwise (*itarā*).[123] According to the elder Śākalya, instead of -*e a*- and -*o a*- in examples such as

(44) *sujā̀te̱ aśvàsūnṛte* (ṚV 5.79.1e–10e [refrain])

(45) *adhvàryo̱ adrìbhiḥ su̱taṁ somàm pa̱vitra̱ ā sṛ̀ja* (ṚV 9.51.1ab)

one recited -*e ĕ*- (*sujā̀te̱ ĕśva̱sūnṛte*) and -*o ŏ*- (*adhvàryo̱ ŏdrìbhiḥ*), with short vowels *ĕ*- and *ŏ*-.[124]

[119] ṚPr. 2.35: *antaḥpādam akārāc cet saṁhitāyāṁ laghor laghu | yakārādy akṣaraṁ paraṁ vakārādy api vā bhavet |*

[120] Space considerations preclude considering here even a sample of these rules; see note 126.

[121] ṚPr. 2.73: *aśvineva ... stotava ambyaṁ ...*

[122] ṚPrU 2.73: *stotava ambyaṁ ca | abhinihitābhāva ekārasya ca attvam |*

[123] ṚPr. 2.81–82: *prācyapañcāla upadhānibhodayāḥ śākalasya sthavirasya | itarā sthitiḥ |* See Cardona 1987: 60–1.

[124] This mode of pronouncing such sequences is known also within particular branches of the Taittirīya and Sāmaveda traditions. In addition, commentators differ concerning precisely how these were pronounced; see Cardona 1987: 60–3.

3.4.2. Pāṇinian rules

Pāṇini also deals with pertinent phenomena of Vedic usage and, as one should expect, he does so in a manner that differs from Śaunaka's. Since the first concern of his grammar is the standard usage of his time and area, Pāṇini accounts for the more general abhinihita sandhi by providing[125] that the first vowel of sequences *-e a-*, *-o a-* with pada-final *-e*, *-o* is the single replacement for both vowels. In addition, he provides[126] that the replacements provided for sequences *-e a-*, *-o a-* do not apply within a metrical pāda of a Vedic text, provided the second vowel in question is not followed by *v* or *y* (*avyapare*).

3.5. A novel proposal

In 1981, J. Bronkhorst proposed that the Ṛgveda text known to Pāṇini antedated the accepted redaction by Śākalya. One of Bronkhorst's arguments (1981: 85–87) was that Pāṇini's rules show that in the text of the Ṛgveda which he knew, abhinihita sandhi of the type illustrated here in section **3.2** was not present and that, instead, the text had *-ay a-*. In a recent work, Bronkhorst (2007: 337–339) has reiterated his arguments, nearly verbatim and without considering any additional evidence. He begins his presentation of this, the third of his topics, saying (336), 'The third case rests upon a somewhat unorthodox interpretation of some rules of the Aṣṭādhyāyī, an interpretation which, however, has rather strong arguments in support of it. They will be discussed below.'[127] After taking up (2007: 337 [= 1981: 85]) Pāṇini's sūtras 8.3.17–19 ([R43]–[R45], **2.2.5**), Bronkhorst goes on (2007: 338 [= 1981: 86]) as follows:

> The example *-as+a-* would yield *-o-* according to the orthodox interpretation of Pāṇini's grammar, in the following manner: *-as+a-* > *-a-rU+a-* (8.2.66) > *-a-u+a-* (6.1.113) > *-o+a-* (6.1.87) > *-o-* (6.1.109). There can be no doubt that this form of sandhi was *also* accepted by Pāṇini, for his own grammar makes abundant use of it, e.g., in P 8.3.17 (see above), which has *yośi* for *yas+aśi*. The question is if *only* this form was accepted. Some circumstances indicate that such is not the case.

[125] [R41] 6.1.109; see **2.2.3**.

[126] 6.1.115: *nāntaḥpādam avyapare*; the sūtra is also known in the form *prakṛtyāntaḥpādam avyapare*, and Patañjali cites it in both forms. I cannot take up in the space available other sūtras of the relevant section in the Aṣṭādhyāyī (6.1.116–121), which concern also usage in yajus, or the Vedic materials in question. The most thorough discussion to date of these data is Thieme's (1935: 46–62).

[127] This is identical with what was said earlier (Bronkhorst 1981: 85) except for a trivial detail: in his later restatement he says 'below'; in 1981 he referred to a later section.

> The fact is that a strict application of the principles of Pāṇini's grammar can *not* lead to *-o-* but *only* to *ay+a* (with normal or lighter *y*) and *-a+a-*! To understand why, we must recall that the substitute *rU* for *s* is introduced in P 8.2.66, a rule which is part of the last three sections of the Aṣṭādhyāyī, the so-called "Tripādī", which has a linear rule ordering (Bronkhorst 1980: 72f.). Use of P 8.2.66 can therefore only be followed by application of a rule which comes after P 8.2.66, certainly not by application of P 6.1.113, which would be necessary to obtain *-o-*.

After remarking (Bronkhorst 2007: 339 [= 1981: 86]), 'The location of P 6.1.113 is the most flagrant violation of the principle of linear ordering of the Tripādī which there is in the Aṣṭādhyāyī (cf. Buiskool, 1939: 83, 99)', Bronkhorst cites and explains [R37] 6.1.113 (see **2.2.3**), then continues:

> This rule presupposes the presence of the substitute *rU*. But *rU* is not introduced except in the Tripādī. Strictly speaking, P 6.1.113 should never apply, and be superfluous. Why was P 6.1.113 not located in the Tripādī, somewhere after P 8.2.66 and before P 8.3.17?
>
> I think that there are two answers to this question and they may be valid simultaneously. The first is that P 6.1.113 has to "feed" P 6.1.87 in the derivation of *-o-* out of *-as+a-* (see above). This answer is not fully satisfying, for if the linear ordering of the Tripādī was to be broken, then why not *after* the application of P 6.1.113? The second answer is that if P 6.1.113 were located in the Tripādī, it would make the derivation of *-ay+a-/ay̆*[128]*+a-/-a+a-* out of *-as+a-* impossible. That this second answer leads to a result which agrees so well with the original Ṛgveda only confirms that it is most probably correct.

Bronkhorst concludes (2007: 339 [= 1981: 86–87]), 'The above shows that Śākalya was not the final redactor of the Ṛgveda . . . .' In an accompanying note (2007: 339 n. 7 [= 1981: 86 endnote 7 (on p. 93)]), he remarks:

> As far as I can see, no difficulties would arise if P 6.1.113 *and* 6.1.87—but then also P 6.1.109 and 6.1.87—were taken into the Tripādī, in this order (after 8.2.66 and before 8.3.19, of course). If this is correct, the riddles surrounding P 6.1.113 intensify and depend for their solution exclusively on the second answer.

For a serious observer, I think the riddle actually is how Bronkhorst could tolerate obvious inconsistency. First he says, correctly, that [R37] 6.1.113 has to "feed" [R40] 6.1.87. For Bronkhorst, however, this reason 'is not fully satisfying'. Hence, he not only also observes that if [R37] 6.1.113 were in the

[128] Bronkhorst 2007: 339 has *-ày̆*, which I have corrected in accordance with 1981:86.

Tripādī, Pāṇini would not account for *-ay a-*, *-a^y a-*, and *-a a-* as outcomes of *-as a-*, but also finds this a more satisfactory reason for having this sūtra prior to the Tripādī, because it 'agrees so well with the original Ṛgveda'. Moreover, despite the unsatisfactory status of the first answer, Bronkhorst considers that both of his answers 'may be valid simultaneously'. Now, there is a choice that must be made: either (a) [R36] 8.2.66 is suspended with respect to [R37] 6.1.113 or (b) it is not. If (a), then [R37] is vacuous and cannot apply to supply *a* followed by *u*, which alone can allow [R40] 6.1.87 to replace the two contiguous vowels with *o*. If (b), then [R37] 6.1.113 blocks [R43] 8.3.17, so that *-ay a-* cannot be derived from *-as a-*. Bronkorst has not shown that his compromise is justifiable. He also seems unaware of an obvious point. As has been shown, Pāṇini accounts for *-o a-*, with hiatus, in Vedic (see **3.4.2** with note 126), in addition to *-o-* in current usage. Accordingly, had he intended to account also for *-ay a-* and *-a^y a-* as Vedic realizations of original *-as a-*, one might reasonably expect that he would have provided for such usage explicitly. He could have formulated a sūtra [R37a] **yo vā chandasi* in the vicinity of [R37] 6.1.113, providing that in Vedic (*chandasi*), ***ru*** preceded and followed by *a* is optionally replaced by *y*.

Of course, the additional sūtra [R37a] presupposes, as does [R37], that ***ru*** is available to be replaced, so that [R36] 8.2.66 should not be suspended with respect to these rules. Nor can one reasonably resort to transposing [R37], [R37a], and [R38] into the Tripādī at a place following [R36] (see **2.2.4**). To be sure, Bronkhorst remarks that, as far as he can see, 'no difficulties would arise' if both [R37] 6.1.113 and [R40] 6.1.87 were transposed so as to occur 'after 8.2.66 and before 8.3.19', but he does not see very far. If [R40] were put in the Tripādī where Bronkhorst suggests, this rule would then be placed in the midst of a set of rules which, according to [R39] 8.1.16, are applicable to pada-final segments. This would also entail bringing into this group another, incompatible, set of rules, headed by [R42] 6.1.84.

In addition, Bronkhorst appears to overlook another aspect of his thesis that is not justified by the evidence. As pointed out earlier (see **2.2.5** with note 62), [R 37] is an exception to [R 43]. It blocks the replacement of ***ru*** by *y*. If, [R 36] is suspended with respect to [R37], the substitution of *y* for *ru* applies when this is both preceded and followed by *a*. This is what Bronkhorst claims should apply. But now [R 36] is also suspended with respect to [R 38], so that the same replacement by *y* should apply before a voiced consonant. The *y* which is thus brought in is subject to the replacements provided for in [R44]–[R 46], so that it is deleted before a consonant. Consequently, one could consider that Pāṇini's rules would now provide only for juxtapositions of the type **ka gacchati* instead of *ko gacchati* (see (26), **2.2.3**), which is certainly the norm both in the bhāṣā of Pāṇini's time and area and in Vedic.[129] What is more, even this consequence results under the assumption that [R46] 8.3.22 takes precedence over [R43] 8.3.17 by virtue of being an exception to this general rule. Bronkhorst does not consider the relation of exceptions to general rules in the Tripādī. Hence, I cannot know whether or not he would accept the traditional position that general rules stated in the Tripādī are blocked by exceptions to them stated later in this section in spite of [R1] 8.2.1 (see **2.1.1**–**2.1.2**). Should one reject this "traditional" position, however, one would be forced to accept juxtapositions of the type **kay gacchati*, possibly as alternants of **ka gacchati*. And the compromise position Bronkhorst takes with respect to the type *-ay a-* from *-as a-* should envision these as possibilites in addition to the only regular juxtaposition.

It is clear, I think, that Bronkhorst's departure from what he dubs the "orthodox" interpretation has serious undesirable consequences and also is based on misunderstandings of Pāṇini's grammar. Repeating the same arguments twenty-six years after proposing them in no way makes them any less unacceptable on the evidence. Nor does asserting 'the fact that an historical approach sometimes carries the obligation to question traditional interpretations' excuse ignorance of that evidence.

So far as concerns the particular sandhi in question, one must accept that the recited text of the Ṛgveda known to Pāṇini is the one attested by the Śākalya tradition as represented by Śaunaka's Ṛgvedaprātiśākhya.

4. Summary

[R1] 8.2.1 (**1.1**) heads a set of rules—traditionally called the Tripādī—such that, unless otherwise provided for, a rule R_2 is suspended (*asiddham*) with respect to a prior rule R_1, whether within the Tripādī or in the preceding seven and one quarter adhyāyas. There are also Tripādī rules which are not suspended relative to other rules. Pāṇini allows for the unsuspended status of such Tripādī sūtras in two ways: explicitly and through implication. Thus, he specifies that a particular Tripādī rule, [R3] 8.2.7, is suspended only with respect to certain sūtras (**1.2**), and that another Tripādī rule, [R14] 8.2.80, is not suspended with respect to a particular rule of the preceding sections (**1.3**). Further, in order to account for accepted usage, Pāṇini must allow other sūtras within the Tripādī not to be suspended relative to prior rules of this section. An exception stated later than a general rule which it should block would be vacuous if it were suspended with respect to this rule (see **2.1.1**–**2.1.2**). By implication, then, an exception is not suspended. Similarly, there are rules whose application depends solely on the prior

[129]As in *no madho* of example (38) (**3.2 C**), the padapāṭha to which has *naḥ* | *madhọ*; see note 116.

application of rules in the Tripādī, so that, if the latter were suspended with respect to them, they too would be vacuous (see **2.2.1**–**2.2.3**). These Tripādī rules also are not suspended with respect to the sūtras that depend on them. Pāṇini explicitly specifies that particular Tripādī rules are not suspended only if he cannot allow the unsuspended status of such sūtras to be known by implication. His depending on implication is not surprising, since Pāṇini also sees no need to say explicitly that an exception blocks the general rule to which it is related (see **2.4.2**).

[R36] 8.2.66 (**2.2.3**) is one rule that is not suspended, by implication, with respect to a set of prior sūtras, [R37] 6.1.113–[R38] 6.1.114: in order to apply, these last rules require that [R36] first take effect to supply the sound ***ru*** for which they provide a replacement. If [R36] were suspended relative to [R37] and [R38], these rules would be vacuous. These rules together with [R40] 6.1.87 and [R41] 6.1.109 serve to account for *-e-* and *-o-* as an outcome of underlying *-e a-* and *-as a-*.

The sūtras of the Aṣṭādhyāyī as formulated and interpreted in the manner shown above account not only for the usage in the current language of Pāṇini's era and later but also for the early Vedic known from texts such as the Ṛgveda as reflected in Śākalya's padapāṭha and accounted for in Śaunaka's Ṛgvedaprātiśākhya (see **3.1**–**3.4**). The recitation of *-e ĕ-* and *-o ŏ-* instead of *-e a-* and *-o a-* (see **3.4.1**) allows one to consider reconstructing early texts with **-ĕy ĕ-* and **-ŏv -ŏ* as intermediate stages in developments that led to the later regular *-e-* and *-o-*.[130] The attested Vedic texts, moreover, do have juxtapositions such as *-ay ā-*, which persisted dialectally in Pāṇini's time. On the other hand, there is no evidence to indicate that Pāṇini knew a Ṛgvedic recitation tradition in which **-ay a-* or **-a^y a-* occurred as a development from original *-as a-*.

In sum, the available evidence and the rules of the Aṣṭādhyāyī as traditionally arranged accord with the known Vedic materials and the later Sanskrit developments.

---

[130] **-ay a-* > **-ĕy ĕ-* > **-ĕ ĕ-* > *-e-*, **-av a-* > **-ŏv ŏ-* > **-ŏ ŏ-* > *-o-*.

References and abbreviations

Bh. Mahābhāṣya (volume, page, line of Kielhorn's edition, revised by K. V. Abhyankar).

Bronkhorst, Johannes

1981 The orthoepic diaskeuasis of the Ṛgveda and the date of Pāṇini. *Indo-Iranian Journal* 23: 83–95.

2007 *Greater Magadha, Studies in the Culture of Early India* (Handbook of Oriental Studies, Section Two, India, volume 19). Leiden/Boston: Brill. [Appendix IV. The form of the Ṛgveda known to Pāṇini, pp. 335–47]

Buiskool, H. E.

1939 *The Tripādī, Being an Abridged Recast of Pūrvatrāsiddham (An Analytic-Synthetical Inquiry into the System of the last three Chapters of Pāṇini's Aṣṭādhyāyī)*. Leiden: E. J. Brill.

Cardona, George

1970 Some principles of Pāṇini's grammar. *Journal of Indian Philosophy* 1: 40–74.

1987 Some neglected evidence concerning the development of abhinihita sandhi. *Studien zur Indologie und Iranistik* 13/14: 59–67.

1997a *Pāṇini, his Work and its Traditions. Volume I : Background and Introduction*. Second edition. Delhi: Motilal Banarsidass.

1997b Vedic tradition and descriptions of grammarians, in Michael Witzel (ed.), *Inside the Texts and Beyond the Texts, New Approaches to the Study of the Vedas*, Harvard Oriental Series, Opera Minora, vol. 2, Cambridge, MA: Department of Sanskrit and Indian Studies, Harvard University, pp. 33–8.

1998 Ideal and performance in Sanskrit, in Rajendra I. Nanavati (chief editor), *Purāṇa-Itihāsa-Vimarśaḥ, Essays in Honour of Prof. S. G. Kantawala*, Delhi/Varanasi: Bhartiya Vidya Prakashan, pp. 313–35.

1999 *Recent Research in Pāṇinian Studies*. Delhi: Motilal Banarsidass (second edition 2004).

Kāś. Kāśikāvṛtti (Osmania edition).

N Kāśikāvivaraṇapañjikā alias Nyāsa on Kāśikāvṛtti (volume, page of edition by Dwarikadas Shastri and Kalikaprasad Shukla).

NS Nyāyasūtra (see Thakur).

PM Padamañjarī on Kāśikāvṛtti (volume, page of edition by Dwarikadas Shastri and Kalikaprasad Shukla).

Pr. Pradīpa on the Mahābhāṣya (volume, page of the Rohtak edition).

PWT Cardona 1997a.

ṚPr. Ṛgvedaprātiśākhya (paṭala, sūtra in Mangal Deva Shastri's edition).

ṚPrU Uvaṭa's commentary on the Ṛgvedaprātiśākhya (Mangal Deva Shastri's edition).

ṚV Ṛgveda

Thakur, Anantalal
1997 *Gautamīyanyāyadarśana with Bhāṣya of Vātsyāyana.* New Delhi: Indian Council of Philosophical Research.

Thieme, Paul
1935 *Pāṇini and the Veda: Studies in the early history of linguistic science in India.* Allahabad: Globe Press.

Ud. Uddyota on the Pradīpa (volume, page of the Rohtak edition).

Studies in India's Vedic Grammarians, 1: Nārāyaṇa Bhaṭṭa's *Prakriyā-sarvasva* and Pāṇini's *Śe**

JAN E. M. HOUBEN

To Dr. J. A. F. Roodbergen,
profound *pāṇinīya*, on the occasion of his 88th birthday

1. Introduction of the problem area: *vyākaraṇa* and Vedic grammar

The earliest more or less datable events in the cultural history of India, the death of the Buddha[1] and the composition of Pāṇini's grammar,[2] antedate

---

*I thank Prof. Cardona for valuable critical comments on an earlier version of this paper which have led to several improvements.

[1]The date of the Buddha's *mahāparinibbāna* is now considered to be around 400 B.C.E.: Bechert 1991–1997; Cousins 1996.

[2]For the date of Pāṇini wild guesses need no more be entertained as his grammar points to certain types of coins (cf. already Agrawala 1953: 258ff, 471f, suggested dates now open to revision). Thus, both von Hinüber 1989: 34 and Falk 1993: 304, refer to AA 5.2.120 and currently available reasonably secure datings in numismatics (Cribb 1985; cf. now 2005) to arrive at a date for Pāṇini around 350 B.C.E. (von Hinüber: "kaum lange vor etwa 350 v. Chr."; Falk: "in den Jahrzehnten nach 350 v. Chr." Since Pāṇini belonged to the north-west of the Indian subcontinent—Śalātura, north of the Kabul river and west of the Indus, is mentioned as his native place—he must have been well aware of the political and economic importance of Persia. It therefore cannot be entirely excluded that his *rūpya* (formed according to AA 5.2.120) referred to Persian or Greek coins as Scharfe (2009: 28) pointed out. In view of Pāṇini's linguistic and cultural orientation towards the east and north of the Indian subcontinent it would nevertheless be more likely that reference is made to an Indian coin, perhaps still locally issued but with "pan-Indian" circulation (cf. Cribb 2005: 69). Cardona (forthc.) reviews the relevant passages of Pāṇini and his early commentators, numismatic evidence, and the arguments of Agrawala and von Hinüber to arrive at the conclusion that Pāṇini is to be placed between the mid-fourth century B.C.E. and 500 B.C.E.

with one to two centuries a slow and hesitant shift from orality to the written transmission of sacred and literary texts.[3] These same events presuppose a long and solid tradition of Vedic texts, and Pāṇini's grammar moreover presupposes a long tradition of grammatical and linguistic concerns with details in these texts—details in accent and phonetic variation which are so minute that the overarching stability of the main texts is all the stronger confirmed.

We are therefore confronted with a solid tradition of Vedic texts stretching over at least around two and a half millennia, out of which only the last few centuries show a text transmission in written form, usually parallel with a gradually weakening tradition of oral transmission of the core texts that to varying degrees takes occasional or even systematic support from in the course of time available written manuscript sources for the transmission of ancillary texts.[4]

---

[3]Early Buddhist canonical texts clearly indicate a completely oral monastic culture. Several examples are given by Falk 1993: 285–288, 322–323 and Hartmut Scharfe 2002: 23–25. Harry Falk (1993: 266–267) demonstrated that Pāṇini's grammar cannot have been composed in writing for the simple reason that the script attested soon after the date at which we have to place him (mid fourth century B.C.E.), namely the script in Aśoka's inscriptions of the mid third century B.C.E., was not yet suitable for representing Sanskrit phonetics but was adapted to the requirements of Sanskrit in the course of a considerable period.

[4]Staal (1986: 262–263) depicted the position of the early western discoverers and explorers of the Ṛgveda as follows: "the brahmins who preserved the 'text' did no[t] possess any 'text'; they had committed the entire Rigveda to memory as they had learned it from their teachers, who had committed the entire Rigveda to memory as they had learned it from their teachers—and so on ... All this sounded unbelievable, nay absurd. And yet, the language of the entire composition conformed in every detail to the state of Indo-European that comparative and historical philology had postulated. Everything fitted perfectly and the Rigveda precisely filled a gap that philology [JH: and esp. linguistics], history and geography had left open. The only thing lacking was an acceptable hypothesis about feasible channels of transmission. At this point most Western scholars, more interested in Indo-European than in India, left it at that, vaguely assuming that some written sources must have existed at some time or other to safeguard the purity of the text and its characteristic lack of corruption."

The earliest available manuscript of a text belonging to the category of Vedic literature is a Nakṣatrakalpa (Falk 1993: 284): a peripheral text from the point of view of those which are generally accepted as central for the Vedic tradition, the mantra collections (Saṁhitās) and Brāhmaṇas (cf. ĀpŚS 24.31 *mantrabrāhmaṇayor vedanāmadheyam*). The latter became available in manuscript form much later, in the course of the second millennium C.E. (cf. Witzel 1974).

Both the date of Pāṇini and its original (predominantly) oral environment have been the subject of controversies since the beginnings of Sanskrit studies. Pāṇini was familiar with writing (*lipi*), but his grammar was meant for memorization and oral transmission: the Brāhmī attested in the Aśokan inscriptions, a century or so after Pāṇini's date, was suitable for the Middle Indo-Aryan dialects of Aśoka's time but was not yet able to represent Sanskrit phonetics adequately, and would be adapted for this task only in the course of several centuries.[5]

Since transmission through manuscripts came relatively late in the formation and transmission both of Vedic texts and of grammar, there must have been an alternative device for sufficiently reliable transmission. This role was fulfilled, at least to a very large extent, by a sophisticated memory culture (mnemotechnics) about which at present we can get an understanding only on the basis of hints and indications in ancient texts and isolated practices in Vedic schools (*pāṭhaśālās*). During a great part of the oral transmission of these traditions, grammatical treatises such as the Prātiśākhyas and the Aṣṭādhyāyī—the main representative of the traditional discipline of *vyākaraṇa*—have supported the transmission of the Vedic texts in an important, but at present not entirely clear manner. Analysis of the relationship between (a) Pāṇinian and other grammatical treatises and (b) the Vedic texts is therefore of utmost importance and has consequences both for the analysis of Vedic texts and for our understanding of Pāṇinian and other grammars. The remarkable contributions of Thieme (1935) and Bronkhorst (2007) are still only pioneering works that have explored only part of the problem area.

The fact, for instance, that Pāṇini devotes a considerable number of rules specifically to Vedic forms and prescribes other rules apparently in order to cover both the current high standard language—*bhāṣā*—and Vedic usage undermines the position defended in recent decades that pure semantics or meaning conditions would be the starting point of Pāṇini's grammar: the Pāṇinian consultation cycle must have started with a preliminary statement (cf. Houben 1999, 2003, 2009b). This may be a statement from Vedic or current usage. Pāṇini's grammar can confirm such statement as it is or, when needed, give it a "polished" (*saṁskr̥ta*) form, by the application of rules with reference to problematic aspects in the statement, in the case of Vedic forms especially the accentuation, the linguistic intuition for which

[5] Falk 1993: 267. Scharfe 2009: 66–84 devotes a chapter to the "inadequacies of early writing" for the representation of crucial details in Pāṇini's grammar. For instance, the writing of the *pratyāhāra-sūtras a-i-u-Ṇ* etc., and of a *pratyāhāra* such as *aC*, would have been problematic in Kharoṣṭhī with its single sign for the intitial vowel or vowel onset (2009: 29 note 8).

was on the verge of extinction in Pāṇini's time.[6] There is no dispute whether the application of rules is unidirectional within the grammar (body of rules) once the derivation of a form has started (although one may have different views on the exact nature and number of the levels involved) but rather whether the starting point is in semantics (meaning elements, meaning conditions, etc.) or in a preliminary statement. Pāṇini's system is indeed to a large extent "synthetic" but this is only part of the truth: in a larger perspective it is "reconstitutive," and this has important consequences for our understanding of the aim and context of the grammar and of the function of specific rules.

If placing "semantics" as the starting point is in conflict with the presence of a considerable number of rules, namely the specifically Vedic ones (and moreover with the majority of the explicit aims mentioned in the Paspaśāhnika: *rakṣā* "preservation of the Veda," *ūha* "ritual modification," etc.[7]), how can it be that this view has become so widespread among Pāṇini

[6] If Pāṇini's grammar is used for a statement from current usage (see my brief remark in Houben 2009b: 14) we should imagine a user of the language who wants to "polish" a sentence the "correctness" of which may vary from fully "Pāṇinian" to that of the usage found, for instance, in an inscription of Aśoka, *dhramacaraṇaṁ pi ca na bhoti aśilasa* (Bloch 1950: 100). The latter is regarded as a different language by us, but was not necessarily so considered by contemporaries (cf. Houben 1996 for the non-perception of strict divisions of languages in sociolinguistic circumstances such as those apparently pertaining in ancient India). This user must have sufficient active and passive knowledge both of what we consider Sanskrit and of Aśokan dialects and must be well familiar with Pāṇini's grammar in order to take this sentence as a starting point, understand *bhū* as the root semantically and formally closest to *bhoti* and, answering the semantic and syntactic questions asked by the grammar with reference to the word and the preliminary sentence, to derive the "polished" form *bhavati*; the same procedure is to be followed for other problematic words to arrive at the *saṁskṛta* version of the quoted line, *dharmacaraṇam api ca na bhavati aśīlasya.*

[7] The MBh (I:1.14–2.2) mentions and explains five aims of the study of grammar: (1) *rakṣā* "the preservation (of the Vedic texts of one's tradition)"; (2) *ūha* "modification (of a Vedic mantra according to a modified ritual context)"; (3) *āgama* "(the fulfilment of) the Vedic injunction (to study the Veda and its ancillaries, including grammar)"; (4) *laghu* "simplicity in knowing correct word forms in a specific context"; (5) *asaṁdeha* "removal of doubts (regarding words in Vedic sentences." All these aims suggest that grammar is invoked to reconstitute a (problematic) word given in Vedic passages; in the case of *ūha* 'modification' there is reconstitution with modification according to the variation of a semantic, grammatically relevant variable, for instance gender, number. Neither here nor in any of the secondary aims next mentioned in the Mahābhāṣya (I:2.3–5.12), a semantic level or semantic conditions are the starting point in the derivation of correct linguistic forms.

specialists (cf. Houben 1999: 23–26)? Part of the explanation is no doubt the brilliant article by Paul Kiparsky and Frits Staal on "Syntactic and semantic relations in Pāṇini" (1969), which by analyzing Pāṇini's grammar against the background of then current developments in transformational generative (Chomskian) grammar proved a great stimulus for fresh research.

At present, looking back at the history of transformational generative and esp. Chomskian grammar[8] it may seem unlikely that it could have encouraged placing semantics first in Pāṇini's grammar, as Chomsky never focused on semantics. The latter half of the 1960s and early 1970s was, however, precisely the time when Chomsky had introduced the suggestive concept of "deep structure" which some of his students (e.g., Chomsky's former student Lakoff in 1971) understood and developed in a semantic sense. In Kiparsky's and Staal's model of Pāṇinian grammar (1969), a level of "semantic representations" underlies and precedes the one of "deep structures" which is followed by "surface structures" and, finally, "phonological representations." After having initially remained unpronounced on the exact nature of this "deep structure" Chomsky started to evade a "semantic" interpretation[9] of his "deep structure" in language and later on the entire concept disappeared from his models. Together with Chomsky also one of the two authors of the influential 1969 article, Frits Staal, became gradually averse to semantics not only in his approach to Indian linguistics but also with regard to ritual.[10] In the study of Pāṇinian grammar, however, the fascination with and overemphasis on semantics, meaning elements and meaning conditions as starting point of linguistic derivations has remained (in spite of its contradiction with Vedic rules and the explicit aims attributed to grammar by the ancients).

Whatever historical reasons and temporary advantages there may have been for the postulation of levels starting with "semantics," it contributes to a marginalization of the study of Vedic sections and rules.[11] To redress

---

[8]Cf. Joshi 2009, Kaldewaij 1986, Searle 2002 and Seuren 1998.

[9]This move was in line with the linguist who was in several respects Chomsky's predecessor, Leonard Bloomfield, and who evinced a "rather pessimistic attitude towards semantics" (Robins 1979: 208); "Bloomfieldian" linguists from the 1930s to ca. 1957 preferred to concentrate their attention on the formal analysis of language (Robins 1979: 209).

[10]As for language, a sequel to Staal's "Indian Semantics I" (1966) was never published. In his endeavour to study "meaningless ritual" without semantics but with syntax, Staal (1989) explicitly invoked Chomsky's theories.

[11]A corollary to the relative neglect of India's Vedic grammarians is the unsatisfactory condition of editions of primary sources. With regard to the Prakriyā-sarvasva (see abbreviations under PS) there is one edition that covers the Vedic or *chāndasa* chapter (khaṇḍa 20), viz., the edition of Trivandrum (fascicule 7 by Madhavan Unni). The sūtras are here not consecutively numbered (consecutive

the balance it is therefore high time to make a fresh study of the nature, function and context of the Vedic rules in Pāṇini's grammar and, more generally, of Indian treatises on Vedic grammar. In the context of Indian cultural history in which orality and manuscript culture have dominated till at least the beginning of the nineteenth century, this requires the study not only of the most ancient authors but, necessarily, also of more recent authors in the grammatical tradition to whom we owe the transmission and, in an important way, the presentation and interpretation of the older authors. It is not only important *what* a certain pre-modern or ancient author understands in his dealing with Pāṇini's grammar and its application to Vedic, but also *how* he understands it and which knowledge domains are invoked or presupposed. This applies even to our understanding of the same.[12] In this first article of a proposed series of studies on India's Vedic grammarians, I would like to introduce Nārāyaṇa Bhaṭṭa of Melputtūr as a Vedic grammarian and evaluate the treatment by him and his predecessors of a technical expression which remains somewhat obscure in Pāṇini: *Śe*.

2. Nārāyaṇa Bhaṭṭa as grammarian and as Vedic grammarian

Born in 1560 in his family's village Melputtūr (sanskritized as *uparinava-grāma*), Nārāyaṇa Bhaṭṭa had a long literary productive period between ca. 1580 and 1650.[13] His works comprise (a) the devotional poem Nārāyaṇīya, completed in 1586 and still famous throughout India; (b) numerous literary and scholarly works; (c) a grammar, the Prakriyā-sarvasva. His main patron was king Devanārāyaṇa of Ampalapuḻa (1566–1622) in current Kerala. It was this king who encouraged Nārāyaṇa Bhaṭṭa to compose the Prakriyā-sarvasva.

numbering is absent in the entire Trivandrum edition), which would have been a minimum aid for the reader to find his way in the ca. 600 grammatical sūtras of this chapter, the phiṭ-sūtras and the commentary with its quotations of Vārttikas etc. The compilation (by Nārāyaṇa Pisharoti, 1998) is particularly careless in the 20th khaṇḍa. The sūtras plus commentary on p. 58 and 59 of fasc. 7 of the Trivandrum edition are omitted in this compilation and replaced by a repetition of earlier matter.

[12]From our exploration of India's Vedic grammarians we do not expect—nor entirely exclude—substantially new and more authoritative interpretations (cf. Kuiper 1965); we rather can look forward to arrive at a better appreciation of the understanding of the Vedic texts that conditioned their remarkable transmission over at least around two and a half millennia.

[13]Kunjunni Raja 1958: 119–152; Venkitasubramonia Iyer 1972: 21–23 defends, contra Kunjunni Raja who argues that he died before 1655, the traditional view that Nārāyaṇa Bhaṭṭa lived from 1560–1666, reaching the age of 106.

Major features of the Prakriyā-sarvasva are as follows. Like its predecessor the Prakriyā-kaumudī of Rāmacandra (14th–15th century), its backbone is formed by a rearrangement of Pāṇini's sūtras. For the determination of complex ellipses (anuvr̥tti[14]) the sūtras are still dependent on the sequence they have in the sūtra-pāṭha that goes back to Pāṇini.[15] The re-ordering can hence be seen as a "commentary" on the sūtras that tells something on the (primary) topic and function accepted for a specific sūtra. In its rearrangement the Prakriyā-sarvasva follows Rāmacandra's Prakriyā-kaumudī to a great extent. Unlike the Prakriyā-kaumudī it endeavors to give a place to *all* sūtras of Pāṇini. Nārāyaṇa Bhaṭṭa shows no familiarity with Bhaṭṭoji Dīkṣita who would compose his own re-ordered Pāṇinian grammar, the Siddhānta-kaumudī, in Benares at around the same time.[16] Bhaṭṭoji Dīkṣita, too, follows the organization of Rāmacandra's Prakriyā-kaumudī, and he too tried to use all sūtras of Pāṇini. The comments in Nārāyaṇa Bhaṭṭa's Prakriyā-sarvasva are not exegetic or polemical but straightforward, pragmatic and in a lucid Vr̥tti-style (often partly in verse) so that usually no further commentary is needed. Grammatical examples in the Prakriyā-sarvasva are often original statements dealing with the life of Kr̥ṣṇa. Otherwise there is no interference of theology in grammar: Pāṇini and other grammarians are not deified, *pratyāhāra*-sūtras are not *śiva-* or

[14]In the grammar of the Prakriyā-sarvasva, as in the Prakriyā-kaumudī and other reordered Pāṇinian grammars, anuvr̥tti functions according to the sequence in the original sūtra-pāṭha. For the principles of anuvr̥tti see Joshi and Bhate 1984. Moreover, a verb form of *as* or *bhū* is understood (*gamyate*) as recognized, for instance, in Vārttika 11 on AA 2.3.1 (MBh 1:443.5–8). This usage is, in fact, normal in Sanskrit syntax. Speijer (1886: 1–2) points out that the form that is understood is generally a present tense, but it may also be a form in the imperative or optative. Earlier authors such as those of the Kāśikā supply a verb in the present tense and Bhartr̥hari in his Mahābhāṣya-dīpikā explains (MBhD 7: 1.8): *sopaskāratvāt sūtrasya 'bhavati' vākyaśeṣatvena samarthayiṣyāmahe* "because a sūtra needs supplements, we will corroborate it with the word 'is' as a *vākyaśeṣa* 'part of the sentence that is left out'." In the Prakriyā-kaumudī of Rāmacandra, a major example for Nārāyaṇa (and for Bhaṭṭoji), an optative is supplied (starting with the sūtra corresponding to AA 1.3.2, PK I: 15). The general need to provide a sūtra with supplements is expressed by Bhartr̥hari as follows (MBhD 4: 9.13): *sopaskāratvāt sūtrasya vākyaśeṣo 'dhyāhriyate* "as the sūtra needs supplements, we supply a *vākyaśeṣa* 'part of the sentence that is left out'."

[15]As is clear from his commentary on sūtras such as 20-4 (AA 1.1.18), Nārāyaṇa Bhaṭṭa accepts Pāṇini as original author of the sūtras, but takes an "updated" version as the basis of his work. Important observations on Nārāyaṇa's version, often but not always similar to that in the Kaśika-vr̥tti, are provided by Venkitasubramonia Iyer (1972: 56–59).

[16]Nārāyaṇa Bhaṭṭa and Bhaṭṭoji Dīkṣita can be contrasted in several respects: cf. Houben 2008.

māheśvara-sūtras. In contrast with Bhaṭṭoji's school, there is no passion for presenting grammar as a closed system in the Prakriyā-sarvasva: there are rules of thumb (*nyāyas*) to help in the interpretation, but there is no attempt to construct an explicit, logically tight system of metarules as in Nāgeśa's Paribhāṣenduśekhara. Lists of verbal roots and other linguistic items are principally open-ended, with additions explicitly attributed to specific post-Pāṇinian authorities inserted in the list or added in a separate section at the end. More than to "generative grammar" this is congenial to "construction grammar" (cf. Houben 2009a and 2009b).

At the end of chapter XI on verbal endings, Nārāyaṇa gives a verse (in the Sragdharā metre) that, in a nutshell, explains his view on the position of Pāṇini. For Nārāyaṇa Pāṇini was obviously a grammarian of great importance, but his authority—or that of Kātyāyana and Patañjali—was not absolute. The verse is repeated at the beginning of a small tract by Nārāyaṇa Bhaṭṭa, the Apāṇinīya-pramāṇatā, where the argument is expanded. With the rhetorical question *pāṇineḥ prāk kathaṁ vā* contained in this verse, Nārāyaṇa indicates that there must have been language use also before Pāṇini and that even without Pāṇini's grammar people could speak correctly.

Nārāyaṇa Bhaṭṭa, famous throughout India for his devotional poem the Nārāyaṇīya, has been little studied as grammarian, and even less as Vedic grammarian.[17] The chapter on Vedic language is the last out of 20 chapters. Chapters 1–19 deal with Pāṇini's rules for the current language (*bhāṣā*) under the headings: 1. *sañjñā-* "technical terms"; 2. *pari-bhāṣā-* "metarules"; 3. *sandhi-* "phonetic modifications where words and morphemes meet"; 4. *kr̥t-* "primary suffixes"; 5. *taddhita-* "secondary suffixes"; 6. *samāsa-* "compounds"; 7. *strī-pratyaya-* "feminine suffixes", 8. *sub-artha-* "the meaning of nominal endings", 9. *sub-vidhi-* "rules for nominal endings", 10. *ātmanepada-parasmaipada-vibhāga-* "distinction active and medium"; 11. *tiṅ-* "verbal endings (according to ten present-classes & ten formal categories (*la-kāra*) of times and modes"; 12. *lārtha-viśeṣa-* "particularities in the meaning of the *la-kāras*"; 13. *san-anta-* "desideratives"; 14. *yaṅ-* "intensives"; 15. *yaṅ-luk-* "intensives without *-ya-*"; 16. *sub-dhātu-* "denominatives"; 17. *nyāya-* "rules and general principles in the derivation of forms"; 18. *dhātu-* "verbal stems"; 19. *uṇādi-* "suffixes for the formation of nominal stems".

In introductory verse no. 5 (in the Śārdūlavikrīḍita metre), placed in the mouth of king Devanārāyaṇa, the features of the Prakriyā-sarvasva which Nārāyaṇa is requested to compose, are contrasted with those of other works:

[17] Venkitasubramonia Iyer undertook a study of the Prakriyā-sarvasva which was published in 1972 when the edition of the text was still far from complete and did in any case not cover the last or *chāndasa* chapter.

> *vr̥ttau cāru na rūpasiddhi-kathanā[>naṁ] rūpāvatāre punaḥ kaumudyādiṣu cātra sūtram akhilaṁ nāsty eva tasmāt tvayā / rūpānīti-samasta-sūtra-sahitaṁ spaṣṭaṁ mitaṁ prakriyā-sarvasvābhihitaṁ nibandhanam idaṁ kāryaṁ mad-uktādhvanā //*
>
> In the (Kāśikā-)Vr̥tti the description of the formation of the form (of words) is not nice; and again in the Rūpāvatāra (of Dharmakīrti) and in works such as the (Prakriyā-) kaumudī (of Rāmacandra), in these the text of the sūtras is not complete; that is why you (Nārāyaṇa Bhaṭṭa) should compose, according to the way which I (Devanārāyaṇa) tell you, this clear and moderate (neither excessively long nor too short) work called Prakriyā-sarvasva that contains all sūtras and the formation of forms.

Elsewhere in the Prakriyā-sarvasva, at the end of the chapter on Kr̥t, we find a more detailed and partly overlapping list of works that formed his principal sources: *vr̥ttiṁ tad-dharadatta-rāma-vivr̥tī bhāṣyādikaṁ kaumudīṁ ... bhojokti-dvaya-daṇḍanātha-vivr̥tī ...* "The (Kāśikā-)Vr̥tti; its two commentaries, namely the one by Haradatta (the Padamañjarī) and the one by Rāma (the Vr̥ttipradīpa by Rāmadeva or Rāmamiśra); the (Mahā-)Bhāṣya, etc. (i.e., the Mahābhāṣya and its commentaries, esp. the one by Kaiyaṭa); the (Prakriyā-)Kaumudī; ... the two works of Bhoja (his grammar Sarasvatīkaṇṭhābharaṇa and his work on Alaṅkāraśāstra, Śr̥ṅgāraprakāśa) and the commentary by Daṇḍanātha (the Hr̥dayahāriṇī on Bhoja's grammar) ..." Moreover, at the end of some chapters, the chapter on Nyāyas and the Uṇādi-chapter, Nārāyaṇa mentions the works that have been of importance to him when working on a specific chapter. Since a probably quite small portion is missing at the end of chapter 20, we do not know whether specific sources had been mentioned there or not.

While chapter 20 basically deals with those rules which Pāṇini intended as applicable for Vedic (*chandas*) only, Nārāyaṇa did not hesitate to occasionally discuss Vedic rules in one of the preceding chapters if their usage in current language (*bhāṣā*) is attested.[18] Conversely, although Pāṇini presents accents as applicable to both current language and Vedic, Nārāyaṇa Bhaṭṭa gives the section on accents within the twentieth chapter. In view of Nārāyaṇa Bhaṭṭa's interest in Vedic ritual attested in some of his other works we should expect him to be well familiar with major Vedic texts which he quotes in his brief comments on chapter 20. It is further to be noted that in Nārāyaṇa's immediate environment remarkably strong traditions of Vedic

[18]For instance, *havyavāhana*, though Nārāyaṇa mentions it in the chapter on Kr̥t under 478 (AA 8.4.56), is for Pāṇini a Vedic form (AA 3.2.63, 66); this and other examples are briefly discussed in Iyer (1972): 65–66.

textual learning and ritual performance were still available. On the basis of the presence of rare traditional experts of Vedic recitation, chant and ritual, Frits Staal was able first to encourage and next to record and study in detail an extensive and complicated Soma sacrifice, the Agnicayana, in Kerala some three hundred years after Nārāyaṇa Bhaṭṭa of Melputtūr, in 1975 (Staal 1983).

3. Nārāyaṇa and Pāṇini's technical expression *Śe*

3.1 The very first sūtra of the Vedic or *chāndasa* chapter of the Prakriyā-sarvasva consists of the single, one-syllable word *śe*. What is this *śe*, what does it mean? In Pāṇini's Aṣṭādhyāyī (AA) this is sūtra 1.1.13 and, in order for the statement to make any sense, we have to start by supplying a word from the preceding sūtra 1.1.11 in accordance with the principles of anuvṛtti. This is the word *pragṛhyam* "to be kept separate (without applying sandhi)," which has a specialized, technical sense in Pāṇini's system. Showing the word supplied through anuvṛtti and its source, Nārāyaṇa Bhaṭṭa's sūtra at the beginning of the Vedic chapter can be represented as:

PS 20-1 *śe* [*pragṛhyam* (AA 1.1.11)] (AA 1.1.13).

Nārāyaṇa Bhaṭṭa comments on this as follows:

> *śe iti sub-ādeśaś chāndaso vakṣyate / sa pragṛhya-saṁjñaḥ syāt / asme indrā-bṛhaspatī / yuṣme id vaḥ / tve iti.*
>
> The Vedic replacement *Śe* for nominal endings will be stated. Let that (Vedic replacement *Śe*) bear the name *pragṛhya*. (Examples are) *asmé indrā-bṛhaspatī* (ṚV 4.49.4a), *yuṣmé íd vaḥ* (ṚV 8.18.19c), *tvé íti* (e.g., ṚV 1.26.6c pada-pāṭha).

In order to interpret this sūtra and the commentary we should first of all identify the subsequent passage or statement to which Nārāyaṇa referred when he said *vakṣyate* "will be stated." We expect to find it in a subsequent sūtra.[19] Indeed, we find *Śe* in one single other sūtra in chapter 20, PS

[19]Elsewhere, however, Nārāyaṇa uses *vakṣyate* to refer to a subsequent supplement to a gaṇa: under PS 20-328 [p. 71] (AA 6.2.81) he writes *gaṇaśeṣaḥ samāse vakṣyate*. This refers to the discussion of members of the *yuktārohyādi*-gaṇa under a statement following PS 20-411 [p. 86] (AA 6.2.74), *yuktārohyādiṣu matsye vā*. Since this statement is commented upon as a sūtra and since it starts a new topic after PS 20-411 it is to be considered part of the sūtrapāṭha of Nārāyaṇa. It is perhaps the only case where Nārāyaṇa accepts in his sūtrapāṭha a sūtra found only in SKĀ (8.4.89–90) but not in the Kāśikā or Mahābhāṣya. Even then, gaṇaśeṣa under PS 20-328 refers to the members of the gaṇa rather than to this (gaṇa-) sūtra.

20-184 [p. 39], which corresponds to Pāṇini's AA 7.1.39. This is the only other occurrence of this term in the entire Aṣṭādhyāyī. As we will see in more detail in a moment, sūtra AA 7.1.39 teaches various replacements of (unspecified) nominal endings (*sUPām*), among them *Śe*. As it is a replacement for nominal endings we infer that *Ś* in *Śe* must be an anubandha or "tag-phoneme" (by convention often put in capital) which indicates that the entire substituend is replaced (cf. AA 1.1.55). In other words, we interpret *śe* as the replacement (ādeśa) *Śe*; the replacement that will remain after taking away the "tag-phoneme" *Ś* is *e*.

We should next find out what it means, concretely, if a term such as *Śe* is labeled *pragr̥hya*. This was explained in chapter 3 on *sandhi* "phonetic modifications where words and morphemes meet". The relevant sūtra is PS 3-142 which is equivalent to AA 6.1.125 *pluta-pragr̥hyā aci nityam*. It states that prolated and *pragr̥hya* forms always retain their original form before a vowel. A crucial part in this statement is based on a supplied word, *prakr̥tyā*, which derives through anuvr̥tti from a sūtra that precedes in Pāṇini's sūtra-pāṭha. This sūtra, AA 6.1.115 *prakr̥tyāntaḥpādam avyapare*, applies exclusively to Vedic language or *chandas* and is hence found in chapter 20 in the Prakriyā-sarvasva (PS 20-139), but in its repetition through anuvr̥tti in AA 6.1.125 it applies to both chandas and secular language on account of *sarvatra* "everywhere" in AA 6.1.122 (PS 3-136).

Finally, we have to identify the quotations that should illustrate this grammatical rule. The first two Vedic quotations in Nārāyaṇa's commentary can be identified as:

> R̥V 4.49.4 *asmé indrā-br̥haspatī rayím̐ dhattam̐ śatagvínam áśvāvantam̐ sahasríṇam.*

K. F. Geldner translates: "Bringet uns Reichtum, Indra und Br̥haspati, in hundert Kühen bestehend, in Rossen bestehend, tausendfältigen!" And Louis Renou, ÉVP XV p. 62: "Conférez nous, ô Indra et Br̥haspati, la richesse faite de cent,/ faite de chevaux, faite de mille!" The other example is:

> R̥V 8.18.19 *yajñó hīḷó vo ántara ā́dityā ásti mr̥ḷáta yuṣmé íd vo ápi ṣmasi sajātyè.*

Geldner's translation: "Das Opfer tritt schützend zwischen uns und euren Zorn, ihr Āditya's; seid barmherzig! Wir finden nur in eurer Bekanntschaft Zuflucht." Renou, ÉVP V p. 106: "Le sacrifice est (placé par nous) entre votre courroux (et nous-mêmes), ô Āditya's, ayez pitié! C'est à vous que nous adhérons, pour (attester notre) communauté-de-race (avec vous)."

R̥V 4.49.4 we find quoted in earlier commentaries on AA 1.1.13, from the Kāśikā-vr̥tti (seventh cent.[20]) onwards, but the commentary on PS 20-1 (AA 1.1.13) is the only one among major commentarial texts citing a Vedic example to illustrate non-sandhi after *yuṣmé*. If the verse is not quoted from a lesser known commentary, we have here a small but significant independent contribution by Nārāyaṇa. Still the question remains: what is this *śe* which Nārāyaṇa interprets as the replacement *Śe*; more concretely, what is substituted by it and what are the conditions for its occurrence?

3.2 The Mahābhāṣya on AA 1.1.13 does not help for our purpose: Patañjali only finds it necessary to silence the apprehension (*śaṅkā*) that the rule might be improperly formulated (*durukta*) and that *śe* might also stand for *śe* in *kāśe* (loc. sg. of *kāśa* "appearance" or a species of grass); *hariśe* (loc. sg. of *hariśa* "greenish (?)"[21]).

3.3 The Kāśikā on AA 1.1.13 is the earliest Pāṇinian text that provides more information about *Śe*, this technical term which appears out of the blue near the beginning of the Aṣṭādhyāyī and as the very first sūtra of the Vedic chapter of the Prakriyā-sarvasva. According to the Kāśikā, sūtra AA 1.1.13 is concerned with four forms that are concerned in this sūtra: *yuṣme, asme, tve, me*. As examples it cites R̥V 4.49.4 (see above) and another Vedic stanza:

> R̥V 8.68.19 *ná yuṣmé vājabandhavo ninitsúś caná mártyaḥ avadyám ádhi dīdharat.*

The latter is an example of *yuṣmé* but not of non-sandhi before vowel. This example is suitable for AA 7.1.39 but hardly relevant here. On the other hand, the example selected by Nārāyaṇa, R̥V 8.18.19, is entirely appropriate for this sūtra. Geldner translates R̥V 8.68.19 as follows: "Auch ein tadelsüchtiger Mensch soll euch, ihr Beutegenossen, keinen Tadel anhängen."

The Kāśikā on AA 7.1.39, when it comes to speak of *Śe*, cites again this R̥V 8.68.19, and then R̥V 4.49.4, both examples which it had already cited

[20]Discussions on the date of the Kāśikā-vr̥tti (which shows familiarity with the late 6th cent. poet Bhāravi), converge on the (early) seventh century as its date: Cardona 1976: 280–282; Haag & Vergiani 2009: 15 and note 1. The Chinese Buddhist monk I-Tsing was aware of a text which has been identified with the Kāśikā-vr̥tti: it occupied an important place in the curriculum of a grammar student and it was attributed to a single author, Jayāditya, who would have died a little before I-Tsing's arrival in India, ca. 660 C.E. (Takakusu 1896: 176).

[21]*hariśa*, not attested in literature, is a derivation from *hari* (member of *lomādi-gaṇa*) acc. to AA 5.2.100.

with regard to AA 1.1.13. It adds: *yūyaṁ vayam iti prāpte / yūyādeśo vayādeśaś ca chāndasatvān na bhavati*, to which we will return below.

3.4 Böhtlingk (1887) mentions in his paraphrase of AA 1.1.13 only *yuṣme* and *asme* and omits *tve* and *me* mentioned in addition in the Kāśikā. Thieme (1935) points out that this is a mistake due to a wrong way of reading the Kāśikā. Indeed, AVPrāti 1.77 indicates that *asme*, *yuṣme*, *tve* and *me*, carrying the *udātta* accent, are termed *pragr̥hya* (so that they do not lead to sandhi with a following vowel). The mentioned forms and their non-sandhi, as Thieme demonstrates in detail (1935: 1–8), are attested in the R̥g-veda and in other Saṁhitās and in corresponding Pada-pāṭhas. The Kāśikā mentions only R̥V 4.49.4 as Vedic example for this non-sandhi and says explicitly that it is the only *chāndasa* example, its other examples, viz., *yuṣmé íti*, *tvé íti*, *mé íti*, it refers to as *laukika*; Thieme shows that the latter must derive from Pada-pāṭhas (regarded not as revealed text but as human creation).

3.5 Perhaps encouraged by Thieme's demonstration of the value of the Kāśikā, modern interpreters and translators follow the Kāśikā, unfortunately uncritically, also under AA 7.1.39, the only other sūtra where *Śe* occurs. This is what also Böhtlingk (1887) did before them. In his *Pāṇini and the Veda* Thieme did not touch on AA 7.1.39 so there was no direct occasion for him to analyze it (and correct Böhtlingk there too).

AA 7.1.39 is as follows: *supāṁ sulukpūrvasavarṇāccheyāḍāḍyāyājālaḥ*. If we isolate the relevant linguistic forms (resolving compound-internal sandhis) and indicate the "tag-phonemes" by putting them in capital we get:

sUPāṁ sU-luK-pūrvasavarṇa[-ā]-āt-Śe-yā-Ḍā-Ḍyā-yāC-āL-aḥ.

For us, the relevant part of the sūtra is *supāṁ* ... *Śe*. Böhtlingk (1887) translates: "Für verschiedene Casusendungen werden im Veda folgende unregelmässige Endungen substituirt: ... *e* für die Endung des Nomin. Pl. ..." This means that Böhtlingk took *ś* in *śe* (*Śe*) correctly as anubandha. However, the identification of the case to be substituted, which Pāṇini has left undetermined, as "Nomin. Pl." is wrong in the light of attested usage in the Veda and its modern linguistic understanding.

Vasu (1891–1898) translates and commits the same mistake: "The following irregular endings are substituted for the various case endings in the Veda: ... *e* (*śe*) for the ending of the Nom. Plural ..." Vasu's explanation of the two examples of the Kāśikā: "*śe—na yuṣme* (for *yūyam*) *vājabandhavaḥ*, Rig VIII.68.19. *asme* (for *vayam*) *indrābr̥haspatī*; Rig IV.49.4, the *yūya* and *vaya* substitution has not taken place as a Vedic usage."

Katre (1987): "[In the Chándas 38] the substitute elements ... Śe ... replace the sUP triplets [introduced after 3.1.2 a nominal áṅga 6.4.1]." With regard to *Śe* as a replacement of "sUP triplets" the two examples of the Kāśikā are cited and provided with a brief—but, as we will see, equally wrong—explanation: "*ná yuṣm-é vāja-bandhavaḥ* (ṚV 8.68.19) = *yūy-á-m*; *asm-é indrā-bṛhas-patī* = *vay-ám*."

Sharma (2003: 39): "Affixes denoted by the abbreviatory term *sUP*, when occurring after an *aṅga* in the Vedic, are replaced with ... [*Ś*]*e*[22] ..." with an explanatory note: "Refer to the derivational details of *yuṣme* and *asme* (II:350–52), as against *yuṣmāsu* and *asmāsu*, where *Śe* replaces *suP* 'locative plural'. A lack of replacement in *yūya* and *vaya*, for *yuṣm* and *asm*, is also a Vedic peculiarity." Among the examples for this sūtra Sharma (2003: 40) cites "*na* [sic] *yaṣmé* [sic] *bājabandhavaḥ* [sic]" for which he provides the fanciful translation: "you do not have associates in battle."

Joshi and Roodbergen (2003): "(in the Vedic language) ... *Śe* ... (comes) in place of (the endings called) *sUP* (added after a nominal base *aṅga*)." Their explanatory note shows the same mistakes in their understanding of *Śe* and its traditional examples: "*na yuṣme vājabandhavaḥ* 'not you (pl. acc.) who share in the booty' (ṚgV 8.68.19) and *asme indrabṛhaspatī* 'to us, o Indra and Bṛhaspati' (ṚgV 4.49.4), for what in Sanskrit should be *yūyam* and *vayam*. The substitutions of *yūya* and *vaya* (by P. 7.2.93) are not applied because the forms belong to *chandas*."

3.6 All these modern interpreters, apparently following the Kāśikā under AA 7.1.39,[23] understand that *yuṣmé, asmé* may stand for, among other things, nominative plural *yūyám* and *vayám*. This is also accepted in the oldest available commentary on the Kāśikā, the Kāśikā-vivaraṇa-pañcikā or Nyāsa by Jinendrabuddhi (ca. 700[24]).[25] However, this use of *yuṣmé* and *asmé* as equivalent to the nominative plural of the first and second personal pronoun is entirely unattested in the extant Vedic literature (and

[22] In the light of Sharma's use of capitals in *Ḍā*, *Ḍyā* in his translation of the same sūtra and *Śe* on p . 41 the employment here of *śe* instead of *Śe* must be by mistake.

[23] The Mahābhāṣya (MBh III: 256.12) does discuss some Vedic examples under this sūtra but none concerning *Śe*.

[24] This date can be inferred if the reference in Māgha's Śiśupālavadha to a Nyāsa is indeed to this commentary (Cardona 1976: 281). Steinkellner, Krasser & Lasic (2005) show, moreover, that the Kāśikā-commentator Jinendrabuddhi was probably identical with the author of a commentary on Diṅnāga's Pramāṇasamuccaya which would confirm this date.

[25] The Nyāsa explains that the examples of the Kāśikā presuppose that Pāṇini's *Śe* is a replacement of *Jas*, the nominative plural ending (*yuṣmad-asmac-chabdābhyāṁ parasya ca jasaḥ śe ity ayam ādeśaḥ*).

unlikely from the point of the modern understanding of *asmé* and *yuṣmé* as originally dative or locative, Wackernagel and Debrunner 1930: 470).

Did modern Vedicists miss something very important, or did something go seriously wrong in the Kāśikā? The 17th century Prakriyā-sarvasva understands AA 7.1.39 (PS 20-184) quite differently and in complete accord with modern understanding of the Veda. First, Nārāyaṇa gives a general explanation of the sūtra without going into details: *supāṁ sthāne yathādarśanam ete syuḥ* "in place of the nominal endings *sUP*, the following endings are substituted according to observation." Since we are in the chāndasa chapter, it is for Nārāyaṇa not necessary to specify that this rule applies in the Veda (*chandas*). Next, commenting on the relevant part of the sūtra and indicating the outlines of the derivation of *yuṣmé* and *asmé* he states:

> *śe*[26]*—śi[t]tvāt sarvasya*[27] */ yuṣma e / ato guṇe* [/] *na yuṣme vājabandhavaḥ*[28] */ asme indrābr̥haspatī / yuṣmāsu asmabhyam iti cārthaḥ /*

There is here no trace of *yuṣmé, asmé* standing for *yūyam* and *vayam*. Nārayaṇa refers here clearly to a suitable example for *yuṣmé* (R̥V 8.68.19[29]) *tva*) and *asmé* (R̥V 4.49.4[30]) and understands them as, respectively, locative pl. and dative pl.

Also the contemporaneous work of Bhaṭṭoji Dīkṣita, the Siddhānta-kaumudī, avoids the strange[31] mistake of taking *yuṣmé, asmé* as Vedic substitutes for *yūyam* and *vayam*. SK 3561 is thus similar but more terse than in PS 20-187: *ná yuṣmé vājabandhavaḥ / asmé indrābr̥haspatī / yuṣmāsu asmabhyam iti prāpte śe.*[32]

---

[26]In the light of the structure of Nārāyaṇa's discussion of other substitutes mentioned in this sūtra, read thus instead of *śeḥ*.

[27]AA 1.1.55 *anekāl-śit sarvasya.*

[28]The editors give: *ato guṇena yuṣme / vājabandhavaḥ* (PS 20, p. 39) which also appears in the compilation (PS 1998 ed. p. 778).

[29]Cited by the Kāśikā under AA 1.1.13 although it is not suitable to illustrate the consequences if a form bears the technical name *pragr̥hya.*

[30]Nārāyaṇa appropriately quoted it under PS 20-1 as well.

[31]Strange, especially for the modern scholars who followed the Kāśikā uncritically (see paragraph 3.9). For the ancient situation see the observations below, in paragraph 3.10.

[32]Although it applies only to the Vedic language, Bhaṭṭoji gives AA 1.1.13 in the *ac-sandhi* chapter as SK 102, where it is followed by the comment ; *ayaṁ pragr̥hyaḥ syāt / asme indrābr̥haspatī.*

3.7 Apart from the question how so many modern interpreters, East and West, could have followed the Kāśikā entirely uncritically, we are entitled to ask how such an evidently wrong statement could ever have been made by the author(s) of the Kāśikā. Apparently, the same question occurred around a millennium ago to Haradatta, the author of the Padamañjarī, another major subcommentary on the Kāśikā perhaps belonging to the tenth century.[33] His conclusion:

> *yūyam vayam iti prāpte iti* (in the Kāśikā-vr̥tti): *pramādapāṭho 'yam / tathā hi—'na yuṣme vājabandhavaḥ' ity atra mantre r̥kṣāśvamedhanāmno rājñor dānaṁ stūyate / vyatyayena dvayor bahuvacanam / vājam ity annanāma / annapradānena sarveṣāṁ bandhavas* [/] *teṣāṁ sambodhanaṁ he vājabandhavaḥ / yuṣme yuṣmāsu* [/] *adhīty asyānena sambandhaḥ / sa ca saptamyarthānuvādī / ninitsuś ca nindanaśīlo'pi martyo yuṣmāsu avadyaṁ na dhārayati nāvadhārayati / avadyābhāvād ity arthaḥ / asme indrābr̥haspatī ity atrāpi rayiṁ dhattam iti kriyā / dadhātiś ca dānārthaḥ/ tasmād yuṣmāsu asmabhyam iti yuktaḥ pāṭhaḥ / yūyādeśa ityādy api na paṭhitavyam / yūyam vayam iti prāpte* (in the Kāśikā-vr̥tti):
>
> This reading is madness.[34] To explain. In the Vedic stanza *ná yuṣmé vājabandhavaḥ* [R̥V 8.68.19 *ná yuṣmé vājabandhavo ninitsúś caná mártyaḥ avadyám ádhi dīdharat* "Even a censorious mortal should put no blame on you, booty fellows"], the gift of the two kings named R̥kṣa and Aśvamedha is praised; instead of the dual there is the plural through interchange; *vāja* (in *vāja-bandhavaḥ*) is a word for food; by giving food they (the kings) are friends to all. (It is) these (kings who) are addressed: *he vājabandhavaḥ* "o booty fellows"; *yuṣme* (is here in the sense of) *yuṣmāsu* 'you' (loc. pl.); *adhi* 'on': the syntactic connection of this (word *adhi*) is with this (*yuṣme*), and accordingly it gives additional expression to the sense of the seventh nominal ending

[33] It was customary to place Haradatta in the thirteenth century (e.g. Tripathi 1981), but Dharmakīrti, the author of a grammar, the Rūpāvatāra, refers to Haradatta (Cardona 1976: 281, 285). At least two eleventh century inscriptions and one twelfth century inscription refer to endowments for the teaching of the Rūpāvatāra (Scharfe 2002: 173, 181, 182) so that the latter cannot be later than the eleventh century.

[34] Despite appearances, an English sentence of this pattern does not express an identity relation. As for the Skt. compound, it is to be understood as *pramādena pāṭhaḥ*, with *pramāda* used in a relatively strong sense as 'complete foolishness', 'madness': Haradatta identifies problems which are evidently not just a matter of *pramāda* in the weak sense of the word, 'negligence'.

(loc.). Even a mortal who is *ninitsu* 'censorious', i.e., who has a tendency to critisize, does not put, i.e., does not find, blame in you. What is meant is: because of the absence of blame. Also with regard to this (stanza), *asmé indrābr̥haspatī* [R̥V 4.49.4 *asmé indrā-br̥haspatī rayím̐ dhattam̐ śatagvínam áśvāvantam̐ sahasríṇam* "Bring us richess, o Indra and Br̥haspati, consisting of a hundred cows, consisting in horses, thousandfold!"], (the Kāśikā reading *yūyam vayam iti prāpte* is inappropriate, because) the verbal action is expressed in *rayím̐ dhattam* "bring (imperative 2nd dual) richess" and the verb *dadhāti* is in the sense of giving.

Therefore a correct reading (instead of *yūyam vayam iti prāpte* would be): *yuṣmāsu* (loc. pl.), *asmabhyam* (dat. pl.) *iti* (*prāpte*). Also one should not read *yūyādeśa* etc. [*yūyādeśo vayādeśaś ca chāndasatvān na bhavati* "the linguistic form *yūya* and the linguistic form *vaya* are not there because it is Vedic language]."

3.8 The textcritical implications of Haradatta's discussion are as follows. For the first part, *yūyam vayam iti prāpte*, he proposes a correct reading, *yuṣmāsu asmabhyam iti* (*prāpte*). Regarding the second part he only states it should not be read, so that he perhaps only wants to see it deleted. From Haradatta's formulation we do not understand that he has actually found the correct reading in any of his sources, presumably one or more manuscripts. Hence, we infer that it is Haradatta's personal emendation for which he adduces precise reasons.

Haradatta's discussion presupposes four derivations (*prakriyā*) of *yuṣmé* and *asmé*, two which he considers correct and two incorrect ones which he thinks are implied in the reading which he found in the Kāśikā, namely, after the citation of two Vedic stanzas where *Śe* (-*e*) occurs in one of their words: *yūyam vayam iti prāpte / yūyādeśo vayādeśaś ca chāndasatvān na bhavati*. With regard to *yuṣmé* the outlines of the correct *prakriyā* apparently presupposed by Haradatta are as follows.

Step 1. Selection of a statement, in our case the R̥g-vedic stanza 8.68.19, which can be understood preliminarily with regard to its form (including the accent) and semantics, and which contains a word with the affix under discussion, *Śe* (-*e*), in our case *yuṣmé*.

Step 2. The user of the grammar[35] searches a verbal and nominal base (*dhātu*) or a nominal stem (*prātipadika*) at the basis of the problematic word. In our case he should not have much difficulty to find *yuṣmad* as the corresponding basis for deriving *yuṣmé*.

Step 3. *yuṣmad* is considered a meaningful linguistic unit with reference to the stanza in which it is used, and as such a nominal stem by AA 1.2.45 *arthavad adhātur apratyayaḥ prātipadikam*.

Step 4. First the number of the word to be reconstituted is to be determined with reference to the stanza in which it is used: there it refers to many (according to Haradatta it refers to two, but the plural is used through interchange).[36] With reference to the syntactic (*ádhi*)[37] and semantic context of the word in the stanza, it is further decided that the meaning of the seventh case ending is required, and hence the seventh ending. By AA 4.1.1 *ṅyāp-prātipadikāt*, AA 4.1.2 *svaujasamauṭ...*, AA 1.4.102–103 *tāṅy ekavacana ... supaḥ*, we therefore have to select *suP* (*bahuvacanam, saptamī*) among the *sUP*-endings enumerated in AA 4.1.2.

Step 5. All decisions regarding semantic and syntactic conditions have now been taken and we turn to the "automatic" morpho-phonological rules that produce the final ending. The form that might be derived without AA 7.1.39, according to Haradatta, is *yuṣmāsu*, but at present we have only *yuṣmad* + *suP*. The rest of the prakriyā is then:

[35]The user of the grammar is well familiar with: (a) Sanskrit in various styles and registers; (b) the archaic language of Vedic mantras and other texts; (c) the lists and rules of Pāṇini's grammar; (d) finally—and this is at the basis of his motivation to consult the grammar—he is familiar, at least passively but most probably also actively, with numerous "undesirable" linguistic forms, which from a current perspective we may categorize as forms belonging to Prakrits or Middle Indo-Aryan dialects. These may seem excessive demands to us, but they are reasonable requirements easily met with in the educated circles to which Pāṇini belonged. On the sociolinguistic context of early speakers of Sanskrit and of Pāṇini's *bhāṣā* see: Renou 1956; Deshpande 1979, 1993; Aklujkar 1996, 2003; Houben 1996; Pollock 2006.

[36]Haradatta wants the verse to refer only to two kings, Ṛkṣa and Aśvamedha (or the latter's son, Āśvamedha, as the difference between short and long *a* is not seen in the compound). This is in accordance with Bṛhad-devatā 6.92.

[37]The construction of *ádhi* 'on' with locative is normal in Vedic—an example is found in ṚV 10.71.2d cited in the Paspaśāhnika, MBh I:4.11—next to the use with ablative in the sense 'from'; cf. Delbrück 1888: 441–443. In classical Sanskrit the use of *ádhi* with locative is more restricted. Pāṇini, in AA 1.4.97, recognizes the use in connection with the possessor-possessed relationship.

yuṣmad + *Śe* (AA 7.1.39 *sUPām suluk* ...; 1.1.55; 1.3.9)
yuṣma + *é* (AA 7.2.90 *śeṣe lopaḥ*; accent: Thieme 1935: 2)
yuṣmé (AA 6.1.97 *ato guṇe*)

Step 6. Re-appreciation and (in our case) confirmation of formal and semantic aspects of the problematic word in the preliminary statement, (in our case) *yuṣmé* in R̥V 8.68.19.

3.9 What is, then, the derivation which Haradatta apparently rejects? The form that is—erroneously—regarded as the one that might be derived is *yūyam*, and AA 7.1.39 *sUPām suluk* ... would intervene even before *yuṣm* of *yuṣmad* is replaced by *yūya* before ending *Jas* (AA 7.2.93). In view of the unspecified *sUP* in AA 7.1.39 there is not much that can be objected to such a derivation, except for one important point: it is impossible to match this with the context of the word to be derived, *yuṣmé*, in the preliminary statement that is the starting point, the cited stanza, R̥V 8.68.19 (or to match it with *yuṣmé* in any other available Vedic sentence). In other words, what went wrong in the derivation rejected by Haradatta went wrong, thoroughly, at the very first step: the preliminary statement was entirely misunderstood with the interpretation of *yuṣmé* as a form somehow representing a nom. pl. All subsequent steps may be entirely correct according to Pāṇinian rules, but they are wrong only with reference to the preliminary statement selected in Step 1.

With regard to the modern translators and interpreters quoted above we have to conclude that they have unfortunately completely overlooked the relevance of Thieme 1935 for AA 7.1.39 and have dealt with the interpretation of a Vedic rule in Pāṇini in a most careless and uncritical way. We may only add that Wackernagel & Debrunner have made proper use of the commentarial tradition when they write, with reference to *asmé* and *yuṣmé*, that "die Padamañjarī die Beispiele der Kāśikā für Nominativbedeutung beseitigt" (1930: 469). Their reference to "P 7, 1, 36" is apparently to be corrected to 7.1.39.[38] When Haradatta refutes the "Nominativbedeutung" for the two R̥g-vedic examples, does it imply a rejection of the nominative interpretation for all Vedic occurrences, also outside the R̥g-veda? The Nirukta (6.7) cites *asmé te bándhuḥ* as example where *asmé* would stand for the nominative plural first person pronoun. This phrase occurs in several Vedic texts, for instance, MaitrS 1.2.5, KS 2.6, TS 1.2.7.1 and VS 4.22,

[38]Wackernagel and Debrunner (1930: 469–470) recognize the Vedic use of *asmé* and *yuṣmé* as datives, genetives, locatives and perhaps as intrumentals, but think that as locatives they are originally to be associated with Vedic locatives such as *mé* and *tvé*, and elsewhere with the enclitics *me* and *te*. Szemerenyi 1996: 214–215 in a similar vein thinks of two pairs of underlying forms: on the one hand **n̥smei* **usmei*, on the other hand **asmayi* and **yuṣmayi*.

in a context that is everywhere similar, the buying of the Soma with the Soma-cow.[39] It is easy to translate not "we are thy kinsmen" in accordance with the analysis of the Nirukta, but "in us is thy kinship" or "with us be union with thee."[40] Here the interpretation of the Nirukta can be avoided according to the context but it is not excluded either. In two other Vedic places, however, an interpretation according to Haradatta is confirmed and the Nirukta interpretation is excluded: KS 24.6 and ŚB 3.3.1.6, which are the Brāhmaṇa-passages that briefly explain the mantras of their tradition. The first explains *asme te bandhur ity ātmann evāsyā vīryaṁ dhatte* from which we in any case infer that *asme* is not understood as nominative plural but rather as locative plural.[41] The second explains *asmé te bándhur íti yájamāne te bándhur íty evaìtád āha*[42] which also implies that *asmé* is locative plural.

3.10 With regard to the ancient commentators and interpreters a similar question is to be asked before we can feel confident to have solved the problem of their way of dealing with *Śe* in Pāṇini's grammar: how could the mistake come about and be relatively persistent (as the Kāśikā's interpretation of *Śe* as nom. pl. ending is accepted in the Nyāsa). Or, to approach the matter from the other side, how could Haradatta, more than 1000 years after Pāṇini, "suddenly" arrive at a correct interpretation of *Śe* with regard to the Kāśikā examples when his predecessors as far as known to us, the Kāśikā itself and the Nyāsa, gave what we have to consider a wrong interpretation? Haradatta may not have convinced Vedic commentators,[43] but he convinced

[39]For the context see Caland & Henry 1906: 43ff. Details of the procedure differ according to different Śrauta-sūtras.

[40]These are the translations, resp., of Eggeling for this phrase in VS 4.22 (quoted ŚBr 3.3.1.6) and Keith for this phrase in TS 1.2.7.1.

[41]Does *asyāḥ* refer here to the Soma-cow? Mahīdhara on VS 4.22 makes *te* refer to the "footstep of the cow" (*somakrayaṇīpada*) which is contextually equally possible.

[42]The accentuation is transcribed following the principles proposed by Hoffmann 1960, with the understanding that the original accent-system was not basically different from the one current in other Vedic texts and presupposed by Pāṇini, that the writing down and accentual notation of the ŚB, as of all Vedic texts, are relatively late, and that the Bhāṣika-sūtra, a *pariśiṣṭa* to a *pariśiṣṭa* (Pdt. Yugal Kishore Pāṭhak in VS, p. 412), is not indicative of a dialectal development in ancient India: it rather is a late text that tries to give a systematic account of a recitation style that developed in Śukla Yajurveda pāṭhaśālas, independent of any linguistic practice in wider circles of Sanskrit speakers (to the extent these were still available in restricted niches). Differently: Chaubey 1975 and Cardona 1993.

[43]Bhaṭṭabhāskara and Sāyaṇa on TS 1.2.7.1 and Uvaṭa and Mahīdhara on VS 4.22 all accept *asmé* as standing for, inter alia, the nom. pl. first person pronoun.

Nārāyaṇa Bhaṭṭa, Bhaṭṭoji Dīkṣita and Nāgeśa.[44] A contemporaneous user of Pāṇini's grammar (above, footnote 30) must be considered to have been familiar, at least passively but most probably also actively, with numerous "undesirable" linguistic forms, which from a current perspective we may categorize as forms belonging to Prakrits or Middle Indo-Aryan dialects. For *asmé* there is a corresponding Prakritic word that formally looks similar, *amhe*, but which is used equally or even preferably for nom. and acc. pl.[45] For *yuṣmé* the correspondence is more distant, with *tumhe* being the nom. and acc. pl. As already suggested by Wackernagel & Debrunner 1930: 470, the *-e* of these Prakritic forms has a different background than Vedic *asmé* and *yuṣmé*. Apparently either the author(s) of the Kāśikā or someone whose annotation got inserted into the main text was influenced by these Prakritic forms when accepting *Śe* as a replacement for the nominal ending *Jas* in *asmé* and *yuṣmé* (wrongly) understood as nominatives.

Or was the Kāśikā influenced by the Nirukta which in 6.7 gives examples of *asmé* for all cases of the first person plural, according to Wackernagel and Debrunner (1930: 469) "mit oft falscher Erklärung vedischer Stellen"? Can we exclude that Pāṇini's understanding regarding *asmé* (and *yuṣmé*) was in accordance with this passage of the Nirukta (whether or not we consider the latter as [partly] earlier or later than Pāṇini); or even that Pāṇini wanted to incorporate forms which to us would be Prakritic (or hybrid Sanskrit?) forms in *-e*,[46] since his grammar gives only the rule with the unspecified *supām* and no textual example? The case which would be most "wrong" from our current perspective is the nominative pl. of the two pronouns. It is also the case which required the clarification *yūyādeśaḥ, vayādeśaś ca chāndasatvān na bhavati* in the Kāśikā.[47] The absence of a provision for this in the sūtras or in a Vārttika under AA 7.2.93—a provision that would apparently have been desirable at least in the perception of the

Bhaṭṭabhāskara and Mahīdhara explicitly refer to AA 7.1.39 to justify what they see as a substitution of *Jas* with the *ādeśa Śe*.

[44]Kulkarni 2002: 71 notes that Nāgeśa in his Bṛhacchabdenduśekhara on AA 7.1.39 (SK 3561) quotes the Vṛtti passage discussed above and rejects it in words that echo those of Haradatta: *yat tu vṛttau yūyaṁ vayam iti prāpte ity uktam tat prāmādikam.*

[45]Rhys-Davids 1923: 91 records not only *amhe* but also *asme* as accusative pl. in a Jātaka. Pischel 1981: 347 notes the use of *asme* as acc. pl. in the Veṇīsaṁhāra 36.5. Cf. also von Hinüber 2001: 252 para. 369.

[46]Cf. von Hinüber 2001: 123 on the closeness of Pāṇini to Pāli.

[47]From this statement we can infer (a) that the Kāśikā-authors saw a possible conflict between AA 7.2.93 that prescribes the replacements *yūya* and *vaya* on account of the ending *Jas* and AA 7.1.39 that in their view would prescribe or allow the replacement of *Jas* by *Śe* and (b) that they thought that usual conflict solving procedures would be unable or insufficient to guarantee the desired results.

Kāśikā authors—may be taken as a reason to believe that the nom. pl. ending *Jas* (as implied in *sUPām*) was not envisaged as the substituend for *Śe* with regard to the first and second plural personal pronouns. As for the Vedic examples cited, the Kāśikā passage as it was received and discussed by Jinendrabuddhi and by Haradatta was wrong, as Haradatta demonstrated. If the "foolish reading" goes indeed back to the Kāśikā-authors, did the Kāśikā inherit correct examples but explain them in an erroneous way? How wide-spread was the "wrong" understanding of *asmé* and *yuṣmé* before Haradatta: were the views of the Nirukta, the Kāśikā and the Nyāsa really generally accepted without critical comments?

4. Conclusion and discussion

4.1 With his largely acceptable analysis of the cited Vedic verses a few centuries before Sāyaṇa and the resolute rejection of wrong interpretations, Haradatta shows himself to have been a most alert and critical student not only of Pāṇinian grammar but also of Vedic literature. His remarkably well reasoned rejection of the problematic Kāśikā passage is unequivocal, and it is in accordance with observed usage in Vedic texts and with the interpretation of an occurrence of *asmé* in the KS and in the ŚB that the Nirukta took as a nom. pl. Jinendrabuddhi had before him commented on it as if it were a passage without any problem. Nārāyaṇa, Bhaṭṭoji, Nāgeśa may well have read Haradatta's comments and have accepted his argument without mentioning him explicitly. It is indeed a remarkable achievement that Haradatta, more than 1000 years after Pāṇini and after a wrong intepretation had been accepted for centuries, could establish an interpretation and understanding of *Śe* that later specialists would accept as exclusively correct and that is also in line with our modern linguistic understanding, taking into account early Brāhmaṇa comments and Pāṇini's formulation of AA 7.2.93 etc. In addition, Bhaṭṭoji Dīkṣita and especially also Nārāyaṇa Bhaṭṭa deserve to be appreciated not only as grammarians in the Pāṇinian tradition but also as Vedic grammarians.

Nārāyaṇa's interpretation and brief comments on AA 1.1.13 and 7.1.39 are not spoiled by the acceptance of the spurious examples (or spuriously interpreted examples) of *yuṣmé* and *asmé* for *yūyam* and *vayam*. For *Śe* he provides an example, R̥V 8.18.19, which is most appropriate to illustrate *pragr̥hya -é* in *yuṣmé* but which is not known from major texts such as the Kāśikā-vr̥tti where an illustration of *pragr̥hya -é* in *yuṣmé* is anyway missing.

4.2 We further note that without recognizing Step 1, the selection of a preliminary statement, in our case the Ṛg-vedic stanza, as a necessary first step in the derivation, the basis of the problem discussed by Haradatta would have remained invisible, and an adequate analysis of the accepted and rejected prakriyās and of their discussion by Haradatta's commentary would have remained impossible. Similarly, the basis for a controversy such as the one between Cardona (1999: 202–204: the derivational system starts with semantics, also for Vedic usage) and Palsule (1991: judgement of Pāṇini's system with regard to morphological elements, tense-stems, recognized in western grammars of Vedic[48]) disappears if it is realized that neither semantics nor abstracted and isolated morphological elements—nor even abstracted and isolated words such as *piba* and *pāhi* investigated by Palsule—are the starting point of a Pāṇinian derivation but rather a preliminary statement, for instance in the form of a selected Vedic sentence. The reconstitution of a problematic word would normally aim at clarifying details that may remain unclear or problematic from the perspective of someone receptively familiar with Vedic (for instance in the repetition and ritual employment of inherited stanzas) and actively conversant with the post-Vedic classical language. Since, next to the preliminary statement, the then current use of post-Vedic classical Sanskrit forms the frame of reference, it suffices to the grammar user contemporaneous to Pāṇini to understand *pāhi* as a Vedic (*chāndasa*) equivalent of *piba* and it would be of no interest to search for an aspectual distinction which the current language would anyhow not be able to express. Similarly, in AA 7.1.39 *sUPām suluk* ... *Śe* ... there is no need to specify the endings that are substituted by *Śe* since the resulting forms are limited to Vedic and are not available in the current language. Scharfe (2009: 86) finds it unlikely that Pāṇini's grammar would have served any practical purpose, even the relatively modest one of verifying and, when needed, polishing a preliminary statement (Houben 1999, 2003). The "formidable problems of interpretation" and "the great number of topics Pāṇini did not cover (e.g. nominal clauses, gender, irregularly formed nouns, etc.)" would go against this. It is to be noted, however, that next to the exegetical tradition of Kātyāyana and Patañjali in which minute problems of exegesis are put under the microscope, there was an ancient, pragmatic *vṛtti*-tradition of straightforward interpretation and application that is reflected in the Kāśikā and, at a much later stage, in the Prakriyā-sarvasva. The "topics Pāṇini did not cover" were either dealt with elsewhere or they concerned distinctions important in the confrontation of Vedic with other Indo-european and modern western languages but to Pāṇini and his contemporaries without sufficient practical consequence and below the threshold of interest.

---

[48] See also Palsule 1978: 229, 232–236.

An underlying question is whether the derivation of Vedic forms in Pāṇini's grammar is indeed basically similar to the derivation of forms in the current language. According to Joshi and Roodbergen (1992: 10), the Aṣṭādhyāyī deals, "as a whole," "with the speech called *bhāṣā*." According to them, "Vedic peculiarities merely form an appendage." They give three reasons: (1) the relatively small number of rules dealing with Vedic matter; (2) their usually unspecific and often sweeping formulation; (3) a difference in the application of these rules in accordance with Vārttika 1 on AA 1.1.6, *dṛṣṭānuvidhitvāc ca cchandasaḥ*, which they translate as: "and because with regard to *chandas* rules are applied following (the form) observed (in usage)."[49] From this they make a text critical inference (1992: 10): "This difference in formulation and rule-application, in combination with other facts, leads us to assume that the rules dealing with *chandas* come from a different source and have been incorporated in the *A.*(Aṣṭādhyāyī) by a later redactor, in the period between Pāṇini and Kātyāyana."

It is not necessary to draw such a drastic conclusion if a preliminary statement, whether from the domain of Vedic literature or from the current language, is the starting point of the derivation. Indeed, it would *a priori* be more attractive to follow Wilhelm Rau's suggestion (1985: 104) and to see the language described by Pāṇini as a continuum with, as two opposed extremes, on the one hand the Vedic domain (*chandas*), on the other the current language (*bhāṣā*), and in the middle a large area where rules apply to both current and Vedic language. With regard to both exclusively *chandas* and exclusively *bhāṣā* language, and also with regard to language in a domain of overlap, the starting point of the analysis of a word is a "Step 1": the selection of a preliminary statement, which will remain the frame of reference throughout the derivation, especially with regard to the semantic and syntactic questions asked by the grammar. We may want to see Pāṇini's grammar as "a device for the derivation of words from given initial elements" with "syntax ... entering into word-derivation" (Roodbergen 1974: vi), but then it is to be admitted that syntax enters into word-derivation precisely because there was a preliminary "Step 1," whether acknowledged or unacknowledged, which provides the frame of reference for the syntax that enters into the derivation of the word. It should be clear that accepting a preliminary sentence as the starting point does not render the grammar circular, as there is a difference between the preliminary, possibly partly substandard sentence and the confirmed, correct, *saṁskṛta* sentence. We should also assume that, after Step 1 and before reaching the stage of the confirmed, correct sentence, "General principles govern the ap-

[49] Accordingly, Nārāyaṇa comments on AA 7.1.39 (PS 20-187): *supāṁ sthāne yathādarśanam ete syuḥ* "in place of the nominal endings *sUP*, the following endings are substituted according to observation."

plication of rules, which account for the desired results, without circularity" (Cardona 1997: xiv). As I have indicated elsewhere (Houben 2009a), this understanding of the derivational practice in Pāṇinian grammar is perfectly in accordance with the theoretical position of Bhartṛhari. Is it also suitable to the grammatical practice and theory of Nārāyaṇa Bhaṭṭa? A (too) brief answer would be that Nārāyaṇa often, and in chapter 20 usually, takes short sentences, Vedic or colloquial, as examples to demonstrate the derivation of words, as in the case of the first two Vedic quotes cited under PS 20-1. In fact, however, this is one of the many points where a closer study of the Prakriyā-sarvasva is still required and where the available philological tools are still very insufficient.[50]

Abbreviations

AA[51] = Pāṇini's Aṣṭādhyāyī: (a) ed. and German translation, O. Böhtlingk, Leipzig 1887; (b) ed. and English translation, extracts from Kāśikā, S. C. Vasu, Allahabad-Banaras 1891–1898; (c) ed. and French translation, extracts from the commentaries, L. Renou,

[50] If we concentrate on the Vedic chapter of the Prakriyā-sarvasva, we note that a most interesting section for our problem starts towards the end, namely the section dealing with *ekaśruti*, the monotonous pronunciation of a sentence at a single high tone. As Nārāyaṇa remarks, rules for *ekaśruti* concern the sentence and are discussed after having first explained the accents that are based on the word (*svarān padāśritān evam uktvā saṁkṣepataḥ punaḥ / ekaśrutyādikān vākyaviṣayān brūmahe'dhunā*). Unfortunately, this section is incomplete. Although only a small portion may be missing, this renders the Vedic chapter and hence also the Prakriyā-sarvasva incomplete. From the point of view of the Pāṇinian sūtras the section (and the chapter) may be complete as all sūtras of the sequence directly dealing with *ekaśruti* (AA 1.2.33–38) are present, and in addition AA 8.2.100 and 8.2.102. The sūtra that follows this sequence in the Aṣṭādhyāyī, AA 1.2.39, occurs earlier in the chapter, and that even two times (PS 20, p. 63 and 66), out of which one must be a quotation that should not count for the sūtrapāṭha (the fact that the commentary on both occurrences is for 90 percent identical also points to a mistake at some point in the constitution of the text). Because the last but one sūtra of this section receives a discussion that refers extensively to Bhoja's SKĀ, the commentary on the very last sūtra might also have been long enough for Nārāyaṇa to insert quotations and to give his own point of view in witty formulations as we find them so abundantly especially at the beginning and conclusion of the preceding nineteen chapters..

[51] Current abbreviations for Pāṇini's work, P and A, are inconsistent, confusing and unsatisfactory; hence this abbreviation that evokes the derivation of Aṣṭādhyāyī as *aṣṭan* + *adhyāya* + *ṄīP* and that is parallel to the generally accepted abbreviation VP for the Vākyapadīya.

Paris 1966; (d) translation, S. M. Katre, Delhi 1989; (e) translation and analysis, S. D. Joshi and J. A. F. Roodbergen, Delhi 1992–. . . ; (f) translation, analysis and extracts from commentaries, Ram Nath Sharma, Delhi 1987–2003.

AV = Atharva-veda: ed. of saṁhitā and pada texts, with Sāyaṇa's commentary: Vishva Bandhu, Hoshiarpur 1960–1964.

AVPrāti = Atharvaveda-prātiśākhya: ed. and tr. W. D. Whitney, New Haven 1862.

Br̥had-devatā = Br̥had-devatā attributed to Śaunaka: (a) ed. and tr. A. A. Macdonell (vols. 1–2), Cambridge, Mass. 1904; (b) Muneo Tokunaga, Kyoto 1997. References are to "vulgate" of (a).

Kāśikā = Kāśikā or Kāśikāvr̥tti of Vāmana and Jayāditya: (a) ed. Aryendra Sharma and Khanderao Deshpande, Hyderabad 1969, repr. 2008; (b) ed., with the Nyāsa or Pañcikā commentary of Jinendrabuddhi and the Padamañjarī of Haradatta, Dwarikadas Shastri and Kalikaprasad Shukla, Varanasi 1965–1967.

KS = Kāṭhaka-saṁhitā: ed. L. von Schroeder, Leipzig 1900–1910 (3 vols.)

MaitrS = Maitrāyaṇī-saṁhitā: ed. L. von Schroeder, Leipzig 1881-1886 (4 vols.).

MBh = (Vyākaraṇa-) Mahābhāṣya of Patañjali: ed. F. Kielhorn (vols. I–III), Bombay 1880–85; Third revised edition K.V. Abhyankar, Poona 1962–1972. References are to volume, page, and line.

MBhD = Mahābhāṣya-dīpikā of Bhartr̥hari: edition by a team of scholars (V.B. Bhagavat et al.), Poona, 1985–1991. References are to āhnika, page, and line.

Nirukta = Yāska's Nirukta: (a) ed. Rudolph Roth, Goettingen 1852; reprint Darmstadt 1976; (b) ed. and tr. L. Sarup, 1920–1927; reprint Delhi: Motilal Banarsidass, 1967, 1984.

PK I = Rāmacandra's *Prakriyākaumudī*, with the commentary *Prasāda* of Viṭṭhala, ed. by K.P. Trivedi, pt. I, Bombay 1925. Reference is to page.

PS = Prakriyā-sarvasva of Melputtūr Nārāyaṇa Bhaṭṭa: (a) ed.: Trivandrum: Thiruvananthapuram : Oriental Research Institute, Manuscripts Library, 1931–1992 (Trivandrum Sanskrit Series 106, 139, 153, 174, 258, 262, 263), by Sambasiva Sastri (fasc. 1–2 [1931, 1938]), Ramaswamy Sastri (fasc. 3 [1947], introduction by S. Venkitasubramonia Iyer), Suranad Kunjan Pillai (fasc. 4 [1954]), Madhavan Unni (fasc. 5, 7 [1987, 1992]), Visweswari Amma (fasc. 6 [1989]); (b) synthetic volume ("compiled by") K. P. Narayana Pisharoti, Guruvayur: Guruvayur Devaswom, 1998. Page numbers refer to this work.

R̥V = R̥g-veda (-saṁhitā): ed.: (a) F. M. Müller, (a) saṁhitā and pada texts (2 vols), 3rd reprint Varanasi 1965; (b) N. S. Sontakke, C. G. Kashikar, et al., saṁhitā and pada texts, with Sāyaṇa's commentary, indices (5 vols), Pune, Vaidika Saṁśodhana Maṇḍala, 1933–1951; translation (a) into German, K. F. Geldner 1951; (b) into French, partly: L. Renou in *Études Védiques et Pāṇinéennes* I–XVII, Paris 1955–1969.

ŚB = Śatapatha-brāhmaṇa with Vedarthaprakash commentary: ed. by several learned persons. Kalyan-Bombay : Laxmi Venkateshwar Steam press, Samvat 1997 / San 1940. (The Bhāṣika-sūtra in vol. 5: 300-320); transl. Julius Eggeling, Sacred Books of the East 12, 26, 41, 43, 44 (Oxford, 1882–1900).

TS = Taittirīya-saṁhitā: ed. with the comm. of Bhaṭṭabhāskara and Sāyaṇa, in various volumes, N. S. Sontakke and T. N. Dharmadhikari, Poona, 1970–; tr. A. B. Keith, Harvard Oriental Series 18–19, 1914.

SK = (Vaiyākaraṇa-)Siddhānta-Kaumudī of Bhaṭṭoji Dīkṣita: (a) Siddhānta-Kaumudī with Tattvabodhinī commentary of Jñānendra Sarasvati and the Subodhinī commentary of Jayakṛṣṇa, ed. Vāsudev Lakṣmaṇ Shāstrī Paṇsīkar, Bombay: Nirnaya-Sagar Press; (b) The Siddhānta Kaumudī of Bhaṭṭoji Dīkṣita, ed. and tr. Śrīśa Chandra Vasu. 2 vols. Allahabad: 1906.

SKĀ = Sarasvatī-Kaṇṭhābharaṇa of Bhoja: ed. with Daṇḍanātha Nārāyaṇa's Hṛdaya-hāriṇī Vyākhyā, by V.A. Ramaswami Sastri, Trivandrum: 1948–.

VPr = Vājasaneyi-prātiśākhya: ed. by Pt. Yugal Kishore Pāṭhaka, Benares 1888.

VS = Vājasaneyi-saṁhitā: ed. with the Mantra-bhāṣya of Uvaṭa and the Veda-dīpa-bhāṣya of Mahīdhara by Wasudev L. Shastri Paṇsīkar, Bombay 1912.

References

Agrawala, V. S.

1953 *India as Known to Pāṇini*. Lucknow: University of Lucknow.

Aklujkar, Ashok

1996 The early history of Sanskrit as supreme language. In *Ideology and Status of Sanskrit: Contributions to the History of the Sanskrit Language*, edited by J. E. M. Houben, 59–85. Leiden: E.J. Brill.

2003 A different sociolinguistics for Brahmins, Buddhists and Jains. In *Contemporary Views on Vedic Civilization*, edited by BhuDev Sharma, 54–69. N.p.: World Association for Vedic Studies.

Bechert, Heinz, ed.

1991–1997 *The Dating of the Historical Buddha—Die Datierung des Historischen Buddhas*. 3 vols. Göttingen: Vandenhoeck & Ruprecht.

Bloch, Jules

1950 *Les Inscriptions d'Aśoka, traduites et commentées*. Paris: Société d'édition "les belles lettres."

Böhtlingk, Otto

1887 *Pāṇini's Grammatik, herausgegeben, übersetzt, erläutert und mit verschiedenen Indices versehen*. Leipzig: Haessel. Reprint, Hildesheim: Olms, 1964.

Bronkhorst, Johannes
2007 *Greater Magadha: Studies in the Culture of Early India.* Leiden: E.J. Brill.

Caland, Willem, and V. Henry
1906 *L'Agniṣṭoma. Description complète de la forme normale du Sacrifice de Soma dans le culte védique. Tome I, Tome II.* Paris: Ernest Leroux.

Cardona, George
1976 *Pāṇini: A Survey of Research.* The Hague: Mouton.
1993 The bhāṣika accentuation system. *Studien zur Indologie und Iranistik* 18: 1–40.
1997 *Pāṇini: His Work and Its Traditions*, vol. 1, *Background and Introduction.* 2nd ed. Delhi: Motilal Banarsidass.
1999 *Recent Research in Pāṇinian Studies.* Delhi: Motilal Banarsidass.
forthcoming Pāṇini's dates and the evidence of coinage. Prof. Ranganath Ramachandra Deshpande memorial volume.

Chaubey, Braj Bihari
1975 *Bhāṣikasūtra of Maharṣi Kātyāyana with the Commentaries of Mahāsvāmin and Anantabhaṭṭa.* Panjab University Indological Series 4. Hoshiarpur: Vishveshvaranand Vishva Bandhu Institute of Sanskrit and Indological Studies, Panjab University.

Cousins, L. S.
1996 Review of *The Dating of the Historical Buddha*, ed. Heinz Bechert. *Journal of the Royal Asiatic Society*, series 3, 6.1: 57–63.

Cribb, Joe
1985 Dating India's earliest coins. In *South Asian Archeology—1983*, edited by M. Taddei and J. Schotsmans, 535–554. Napoli: Istituto Universitario Orientale, Dipartimento di Studi Asiatici.
2005 *The Indian Coinage Tradition: Origins, Continuity & Change.* Nashik: IIRNS Publications.

Delbrück, Berthold
1888 *Altindische Syntax.* Halle a/d Saale: Waisenhaus.

Deshpande, Madhav M.
1979 *Sociolinguistic attitudes in India: A historical reconstruction.* Linguistica Extranea Studia, 5. Ann Arbor: Karoma.
1993 *Sanskrit and Prakrit: Sociolonguistic Issues.* Delhi: Motilal Banarsidass.

Falk, Harry
1993 *Schrift im alten Indien: Ein Forschungsbericht mit Anmerkungen.* Tübingen: Gunter Narr Verlag.

Geldner, K. F.
1951 *Der Rig-Veda aus dem Sanskrit ins Deutsche übersetzt und mit einem laufenden Kommentar versehen.* Harvard Oriental Series 33–35. Cambridge, Mass.: Harvard University.

Haag, Pascal, and V. Vergiani, eds.
2009 *Studies in the Kāśikāvr̥tti: The Section on Pratyāhāras. Critical Edition, Translation and Other Contributions.* Florence: Società Editrice Fiorentina.

Hinüber, Oskar von
2001 *Das ältere Mittelindisch im Überblick.* Vienna: Austrian Academy of Sciences.

Hoffmann, Karl
1960 Buchbesprechung: Wackernagel, *Altindische Grammatik* ... *Zeitschrift der Deutschen Morgenländischen Gesellschaft* 110: 175–182.

Houben, Jan E. M.
1996 Sociolinguistic attitudes reflected in the work of Bhartr̥hari and some later grammarians. In *Ideology and Status of Sanskrit: Contributions to the History of the Sanskrit Language*, edited by J. E. M. Houben, 157–193. Leiden: E.J. Brill.
1999 'Meaning statements' in Pāṇini's grammar: On the purpose and context of the Aṣṭādhyāyī. *Studien zur Indologie und Iranistik* 22: 23–54.
2003 Three myths in modern Pāṇinian studies. (Review of *Recent Research in Pāṇinian Studies*, by George Cardona.) *Asiatische Studien/Études Asiatiques* 57.1: 121–179.
2008 Bhaṭṭoji Dīkṣita's 'small step' for a grammarian and 'giant leap' for Sanskrit grammar. *Journal of Indian Philosophy* 36: 563–574.
2009a Bhartr̥hari as a 'cognitive linguist'. In *Bhartr̥hari: Language, Thought, Reality: Proceedings of the International Seminar on Bhartr̥hari, New Delhi, December 2003*, edited by Mithilesh Chaturvedi, 523–543. Delhi: Motilal Banarsidass.
2009b Pāṇini's grammar and its computerization: A construction grammar approach. In *Proceedings of Sanskrit Computational Linguistics, Third International Symposium, Hyderabad, India, 2009*, LNCS 5406, edited by A. Kulkarni and G. Huet, 6–25.

Joshi, S. D.
2009 Background of the Aṣṭādhyāyī. In *Proceedings of Sanskrit Computational Linguistics, Third International Symposium, Hyderabad, India, 2009*, LNCS 5406, edited by A. Kulkarni and G. Huet, 1–5.

Joshi, S. D., and Saroja Bhate
1984 *The Fundamentals of Anuvr̥tti.* Pune: University of Poona.

Joshi, S. D., and J. A. F. Roodbergen
1992– *The Aṣṭādhyāyī of Pāṇini with Translation and Explanatory Notes.* Vol. I (1.1.1–1.1.7): 1992; vol. II (1.2.1–1.2.73): 1993; vol. III (1.3.1–1.3.93): 1994: vol. IV (1.4.1–1.4.110): 1995: ... vol. XI (2.4.1–2.4.85): 2004. Delhi: Sahitya Akademi.

Kaldewaij, Jelle
1986 Structuralisme en transformationeel generatieve grammatica. PhD diss., Utrecht University.

Katre, Sumitra M.
1989 *Aṣṭādhyāyī of Pāṇini: Roman Transliteration and English Translation.* Delhi: Motilal Banarsidass.

Kiparsky, Paul
2009 On the architecture of Pāṇini's grammar. In *Revised Selected and Invited Papers: Sanskrit Computational Linguistics, First and Second International Symposia, Rocquencourt, France, 2007 and Providence, RI, USA, 2008*, LNCS 5402, edited by A. Kulkarni, G. Huet and P. Scharf, 33–94.

Kiparsky, Paul, and Frits Staal
1969 Syntactic and semantic relations in Pāṇini. *Foundations of Language* 5: 83–117. (= Staal 1988: 184–218.)

Kuiper, F. B. J.
1965 Review of *The Soma-Hymns of the R̥gveda ... Part III*, by S. S. Bhawe. *Indo-Iranian Journal* 8: 245–247.

Kulkarni, Malhar
2002 *The Quotations of the Kāśikāvr̥tti (with Special Reference to the Pāṇinian Grammatical Literature).* Pune: Vidyanand Prakashan.

Kunjunni Raja, K.
1958 *The Contribution of Kerala to Sanskrit Literature.* Madras: University of Madras.

Lakoff, George
1971 On generative semantics. In *Semantics: An Interdisciplinary Reader in Philosophy, Linguistics and Psychology*, edited by D. D. Steinberg & L. A. Jakobovits, 232–296. Cambridge: Cambridge University Press.

Palsule, G. B.
1978 *Verbal Forms in the R̥gveda (Maṇḍala VI).* Pune: University of Poona.
1991 Pāṇini and the Vedic verbal system with special reference to the modal forms. In *Panels of the VIIth World Sanskrit Conference, Vol. V: Pāṇini and the Veda*, edited by M. M. Deshpande, 55–64. Leiden: E.J. Brill.

Pischel, Richard
1981 *A Grammar of the Prākrit Languages.* Translated from German [and thoroughly revised] by Subhadrā Jhā. Delhi: Motilal Banarsidass.

Pollock, Sheldon
2006 *The Language of the Gods in the World of Men: Sanskrit, Culture, and Power in Premodern India.* Berkeley: University of California.

Rau, Wilhelm
1985 *Die vedischen Zitate im Vyākaraṇa-Mahābhāṣya.* Stuttgart: Franz Steiner.

Renou, Louis
1955–1969 *Études védiques et pāṇinéennes.* Paris: E. de Boccard.
1956 *Histoire de la Langue Sanskrite.* Lyon: Editions IAC.
1966 *La Grammaire de Pāṇini: Texte sanskrit, traduction française avec extraits des commentaires.* 2 vols. 2nd ed. Paris: Ecole française d'Extrême-Orient.

Rhys-Davids, Thomas, and William Stede
1923 *Pali-English Dictionary.* London: Pali Text Society.

Robins, R. H.
1979 *A Short History of Linguistics.* 2nd ed. London: Longman.

Roodbergen, J. A. F.
1974 *Patañjali's Vyākaraṇa-Mahābhāṣya: Bahuvrīhidvandvāhnika (P. 2.2.23–2.2.38); Text, Translation and Notes.* Poona: University of Poona.

Scharfe, Hartmut
2002 *Education in Ancient India.* Leiden: E.J. Brill.
2009 *A New Perspective on Pāṇini.* Reprinted from *Indologica Taurinensia*, vol. XXXV (2009). Torino: Comitato AIT.

Searle, John R.
2002 End of the revolution. *The New York Review of Books*, February 28: 33.

Seuren, Pieter A. M.
1998 *Western Linguistics: An Historical Introduction.* Oxford: Blackwell.

Sharma, Ram Nath
1987–2003 *The Aṣṭādhyāyī of Pāṇini.* 6 vols. New Delhi, Munshiram Manoharlal.

Staal, Frits
1966 Indian semantics I. *Journal of the American Oriental Society* 86: 304–311.
1986 *The Fidelity of Oral Tradition and the Origins of Science.* Amsterdam: North-Holland Publishing Company.
1983 (Ed.) *Agni: The Vedic Ritual of the Fire Altar.* 2 vols. Berkeley: University of California.
1988 *Universals.* Chicago: University of Chicago.
1989 *Rules without Meaning: Ritual, Mantras and the Human Sciences.* New York: Peter Lang.

Steinkellner, Ernst, H. Krasser, and H. Lasic
2005 *Jinendrabuddhi's Viśālāmalamatī Pramāṇasamuccaya-ṭīkā, Chapt. I*, Pt. I: *Critical Edition, with an Introduction by Ernst Steinkellner.* Beijing/Vienna: China Tibetology Publishing House/Austrian Academy of Sciences Press.

Szemerenyi, Oswald J. L.
1996 *Introduction to Indo-European Linguistics.* Oxford: Oxford University.

Takakusu, J.
1896 *The Buddhist Religion as Practiced in India and the Malay Archipelago, by I-Tsing (A.D. 671–695).* Translated by J. Takakusu. Oxford. Reprint, Delhi: Motilal Banarsidass, 1966, 1982.

Thieme, Paul
1935 *Pāṇini and the Veda: Studies in the Early History of Linguistic Science in India.* Allahabad: Globe Press.

Tripathi, Tirth Raj
1981 *Haradatta's Padamañjarī: A Critical Study (Śrīharadattācārya-praṇītāyāḥ padamañjaryāḥ paryālocanam).* New Delhi: Bhavana Prakashan.

Vasu, Śrisa Chandra
1891–1898 *The Aṣṭādhyāyī of Pāṇini, Edited and Translated into English.* (In 32 fascicules or eight volumes.) Allahabad/Benares: the Panini Office. Reprint in 2 volumes, Delhi: Motilal Banarsidass, 1962, 1988.

Venkitasubramonia Iyer, S.
1972 *Nārāyaṇabhaṭṭa's Prakriyāsarvasva: A critical study.* Trivandrum: University of Kerala.

Wackernagel, Jakob, and Albert Debrunner
1930 *Altindische Grammatik, Band III: Nominalflexion–Zahlwort–Pronomen.* Göttingen: Vandenhoeck & Ruprecht.

Witzel, M.
1974 On some unknown systems of marking the Vedic accents. *Vishveshvaranand Indological Journal* 12: 472–502.

‘Subject’ in English is *abhihita*[*]

Akshar Bharati[†] and Amba Kulkarni

1. Introduction

Pāṇini’s method of grammatical description of the Sanskrit language is an important landmark in the history of language science. His grammar has continued to have influence not only upon the grammars of Prākṛta languages like Mahārāṣṭrī (Scharfe 1977: 192), but also on the grammars of modern Indian languages such as the *Līlātilakam* of Malayālam (Pillai 1955), the *Āndhraśabdacintāmaṇi* of Telugu (Nannayya 1932), and the *Mahārāṣṭraprayogacandrikā* of Marāṭhī (Arjunwadkar 1970), to name a few. During the eighteenth and nineteenth centuries, when modern linguistics was taking shape, focus among Pāṇinian scholars shifted to comparison of various modern linguistic theories with the Pāṇinian system and thus the development of grammars utilizing Pāṇini’s method for modern languages took a back seat.

The discovery of computers and advancements in computational linguistics have opened up new avenues to show the relevance of Pāṇini’s grammar for developing computational grammars of modern languages. The current trend in computational linguistics is either to develop parsers based on dependency grammar formalisms or to map native output of parsers (which is typically in terms of phrase structure rules) to a dependency format. Dependency format is preferred over the constituency not only from an evaluation point of view (Lin 1998: 323) but also because of its suitability (Marneffe 2006: 449) for a wide range of Natural Language Processing tasks such as machine translation, information extraction, question answering, etc. However, no two dependency output formats match each other. There is no consensus among dependency parser developers on the number

[*]Amba Kulkarni thanks Gautam Sengupta, Peter Scharf and Korada Subrahmanyam for their valuable feedback and suggestions. Her special thanks are also due to George Cardona for valuable discussions and suggestions.

[†]Akshar Bharati is the personification of the group working on Natural Language Processing giving due attention to the traditional Indian theories of grammar and languages.

of dependency relations and the names of these relations. One way to bring uniformity to output formats is to map dependency relations to Pāṇinian relations. Thus Pāṇinian grammar, the foremost dependency grammar, has a major role to play.

Akshar Bharati group has been developing a Language Accessor named Anusaaraka[1] that facilitates a Hindi reader to access English content through Hindi. The Anusaaraka uses freely available English parsers such as link parser[2] and Stanford parser.[3] These parsers show the parse of an English sentence as dependency relations. However they differ in the number of relations used and their labels. Anusaaraka provides a Pāṇinian interface to the output of these parsers that maps these outputs to Pāṇinian relations. The advantage of having an interface is that further processing is independent of the parser being used and one can plug and play with various parsers without the necessity of rewriting later modules. In an effort to develop such an interface to the output of two English parsers viz. link parser and Stanford parser, it was necessary to understand concepts used by various Western grammar formalisms such as Chomsky's minimalism (Radford 1997), Link grammar (Sleator 1993) and Phrase Structure Grammars in terms of Pāṇinian concepts.

The notion of subject is an important notion in these grammar formalisms. There have been efforts to provide a universal definition of *subject* (Keenan 1975) and also to locate the subject in various languages including modern Indian languages as well as Sanskrit. The notion of subject is alien to most Indian languages. Cardona (1976a: 11) writes:

> In sum, it is not obvious that one can best describe Sanskrit in terms of subjects of sentences, defined by the relation of elements in a derivational scheme (a "tree") and correlated with subjects of predication. Nor, of course, is it necessarily true a priori that all sentences of any language should be analyzed to conform with the semantics of subject and predication.

This conclusion holds good for modern Indian languages as well. This poses a problem when an English parser output is to be mapped to any modern Indian languages. In this paper we look at the concept of subject in English afresh from the point of view of information coding. We start with typologists' classification of English as SVO and thus assume that pre-verbal and post-verbal positions in English code information about grammatical relations. On the basis of counter examples, we revise our hypothesis and show that the subject in English is *abhihita* 'already expressed' and that

[1] `http://anusaaraka.iiit.ac.in`

[2] `http://www.link.cs.cmu.edu/link/`

[3] `http://nlp.stanford.edu/software/lex-parser.shtml`

it occupies a fixed position known as the subject position. Since English codes the information about declarativeness and interrogativeness in the subject-auxiliary order, it imposes a constraint that subject position cannot be empty. This leads to a deviation from the observation that subject (occupant of subject position) is abhihita. Further this also breaks the usual *sannidhi* 'proximity' between an auxiliary and a verb. We show how the *gamakatva* 'ability to convey the desired meaning' in all these cases helps in comprehension. Instead of formulating the information content in the notion of subject in the form of a definition,we state it in the form of rules. These rules are ordered as a general (*utsarga*) rule followed by its exception (*apavāda*). The information in the form of rules is more appropriate for computer implementation than definition.

2. Subject in English: an investigation

The most frequently noted properties of subject that apply to English (Keenan 1975, Harley 1995) are the following:

1. Every sentence must have a subject, either overt or covert. (Keenan 1975: A.2[4])
2. The unmarked position for overt subjects is pre-verbal. (Keenan 1975: A.3.12)
3. In interrogative sentences, the subject and the finite verb are inverted, except for wh-questions with the subject as wh-element.
4. In an imperative, there is no overt subject, but the subject is understood to be the addressee. (Keenan 1975: C.3)
5. The subject triggers agreement with the verb. (Keenan 1975: A.3.3)
6. The subject is associated with certain semantic roles: for example, in the active voice it is an agent. (Keenan 1975: C.2)
7. Subjects undergo raising. (Keenan 1975: A.3.16)

    (a) It seems the boys have eaten fruits.

    (b) The boys seem to have eaten fruits.

8. The controlled argument of a subordinate clause is its subject. (Keenan 1975: A.3.4.2)

    John wanted to read the letter.

9. The subject is stranded in VP preposing constructions. (Harley 1995: 18)

[4]The reference is to the serial number in the Subject Property List under II 3.1.

Jane said John would write that letter, and write that letter John did.

10. The subject is shared by coordinated clauses. (Keenan 1975: A.3.4.3)

    I came in and was asked where I had put the keys.

We observe:

- 2 and 3 indicate that information about subjecthood is coded in position, and in the case of declarative sentences its position is pre-verbal. But 9 exhibits a different behavior: the subject is not before the main verb but before an auxiliary verb.
- 4 and 5 are in favor of the position that a subject is expressed (abhihita) by the verbal suffix.
- 6 states that the subject is associated with certain semantic roles, but 7(b) again is an exception, because *the boys* which is in the subject position of *seem* does not have any semantic relation to the verb *seem*.

3. Information in position

Language typologists classify English as an SVO (Comrie 1983: 6) and Indian languages as SOV languages (Comrie 1983: 208). However, comparing English and Indian languages on the basis of word order is like comparing apples and oranges! The reason is: English uses position to code crucial information of the grammatical relation. So when one says English is an SVO language, one is asserting a fact about the encoding of grammatical relations, viz. subject and object, with respect to a verb. On the other hand, in the case of Sanskrit, a relatively free word order language, when one says Sanskrit is an SOV language, one is just stating a statistical fact about the order of words in a typical Sanskrit sentence.

To make the point clear: the following two English sentences have exactly opposite meanings:

- Rats kill cats.
- Cats kill rats.

The following two Sanskrit sentences, on the other hand, have the same meaning (ignoring the topicalization, of course):

- Skt: *rāmaḥ phalaṁ khādati.*
- gloss: Rama {nom. sg.} fruit {acc. sg.} eat {3rd sg. pres.}.
- Eng: Rama eats a fruit.

- Skt: *phalaṁ rāmaḥ khādati.*
- gloss: Fruit {acc. sg.} Rama {nom. sg.} eat {3rd sg. pres.}.
- Eng: Rama eats a fruit.

In order to understand the concept of subject in English, we start with the typologists' classification of English as SVO and the assumption that both the subject and the object position mark grammatical relations. Thus our initial hypothesis is:

H_1: In English, both pre-verbal as well as post-verbal positions mark grammatical relations.

However, we come across such sentences as

1. Mrs. Venables turned a little pale.
   Lord Peter presented no difficulties,
   but *Bunter* she found rather *alarming.*
   (Sayers 1972: 221)

where an argument (*Bunter*) which is expected to be in post-verbal position is not in that position. Therefore, we conclude that the information that *Bunter* is an argument of the verb *alarm* is not coded in the position. Thus it follows that the post-verbal position does not invariably mark a grammatical relation. This leads us to reframe our hypothesis as:

H_2: In English, pre-verbal position marks the grammatical relation.

But there are examples going against this hypothesis as well.

2. Uneasy lies *the head* that wears a crown.
3. Never was *the sea* so calm!
4. Here comes *the bus*!
5. On the bed, hung *a mosquito net.*

In the above examples, *head*, *sea*, *bus* and *net*, which are the arguments for the verbs *lies*, *was*, *comes*, and *hung* respectively, are not in pre-verbal position. Further, all these verbs are monovalent. That is, each of these verbs has an expectancy of only one argument. The argument (viz. *head*, *sea*, *bus* or *net*) agrees with the verb in number and person and thus may be considered to be abhihita (expressed) by the verbal suffix.

In Sanskrit, where an abhihita argument, which is already expressed by the verb, does not need any special vibhakti and hence takes *prathamā* vibhakti (nominative case ending), in the case of a transitive verb which needs two arguments, if one argument shows agreement with the verb and thus is abhihita, we expect the other argument to be marked explicitly. In English, on the contrary, we observe that the second argument of a transitive verb, unless it is a pronoun, does not have any specific marker—neither a morphological formative nor any fixed position and that an abhihita argument is always in the pre-verbal position. Hence we revise our hypothesis as follows:

H_3: In the case of a transitive verb, S-V order invariably marks a grammatical relation.

There is also evidence against this observation. Consider the following sentences:

6. She could only hope that Harriet was mistaken in his feelings ....
   Wish it **she** *must*, for his sake .... (Austen 1867: 385)
7. **Ride** in the same taxi with Pamela Dean and Bredon **he** *could not.* (Sayers 1933: 60)

In both these examples, the abhihita argument is post-verbal. But at the same time, we also note that it is always followed by an auxiliary. So finally we conclude that it is the abhihita-auxiliary proximity (*sannidhi*) that is invariant in English. As a result, in English, the normal proximity between auxiliary verbs and the main verb is weakened,[5] and a new proximity comes into existence between an abhihita and an auxiliary verb.

This leads to a new concept, a concept of 'subject position'. The subject position is the position which is to the immediate left (*avyavahita-pūrva*) of a verb group.[6] And thus, we revise our hypothesis as follows:

H_4: In the case of a transitive verb, an abhihita always occupies a special position called the subject position; or the subject (occupant of the subject position) is abhihita.

The *avyavahitatva* (uninterrupted-ness) between the subject noun phrase and the verb phrase leads to a new meaning over and above the meanings of its constituents. For example, the group of words *Rama laughs* also indicates

[5]For example, in sentence 6 *must* and *wish* are separated and in sentence 7 *could not ride* is split as *ride* and *could not.*

[6]A verb group consists of a verb or a main verb followed by either a modal or one or more auxiliaries. *Goes*, *am going*, *would have gone*, *can go*, etc. are examples of verb groups.

the grammatical relation between *Rama* and *laughs* in addition to the meanings of individual words (*padas*) *Rama* and *laughs*. A complex unit, which is derived from components and which has a single complex meaning, different from the meanings of the components, is termed *vṛtti* in the Pāṇinian grammar.[7] Five types of vṛttis are recognized and discussed by Bhaṭṭojidīkṣita in his *Siddhāntakaumudī*.[8] They are *kṛdanta*, *taddhitānta*, *samāsa*, *ekaśeṣa*, and *sanādyantadhātu*. For example, the kṛdanta *pācaka* is derived from the verb *pac* 'to cook' with the kṛt affix ***ṇvul*** signifying a kartṛ-kāraka. The meaning of *pācaka* is 'one who cooks'. Similarly, the samāsa 'compound' *rājapuruṣa* 'king's man' is derived from the padas *rājñaḥ* (*rājan-ṅas*) 'king's' and *puruṣaḥ* (*puruṣa-**su***) 'man' whose endings, ***ṅas*** and ***su***, are deleted. The compound thus denotes a single complex meaning which also includes the grammatical relation between its constituents, *rājan* 'king' and *puruṣa* 'man'. The avyavahitatva between the subject noun phrase and the verb phrase comes close to the concept of a compound. However, this calls for a detailed comparative study of the two concepts, viz. that of an avyavahitatva and that of a samāsa. Nonetheless, to present English grammar in the framework of Pāṇini, we need a vṛtti, viz. avyavahitatva between an NP and a VP. Whether the vṛtti of this type is different from the five vṛttis described in the Pāṇinian grammar or not needs further investigation.

4. *Ānupūrvī* or information in order

Consider the following two sentences in English:

8. *Rama is* going to school.
9. *Is Rama* going to school?

As is obvious from these sentences, the information of interrogativeness and declarativeness of a sentence is marked in the abhihita-auxiliary order. The concept of avyavahitatva and the fact that the abhihita-auxiliary order codes a certain kind of information put several constraints on the sentence construction. We discuss below the consequences thereof.

[7] MBh on vt. 2 to A 2.1.1 (II.238): *parārthābhidhānaṁ vṛttiḥ*. In his *Pradīpa* (II.28) Kaiyaṭa explains: *parasya śabdasya yo 'rthas tasyābhidhānaṃ śabdāntareṇa yatra sā vṛttir ity arthaḥ*.

[8] SK (Sarvasamāsaśeṣaprakaraṇa) [341]: *kṛttaddhitasamāsaikaśeṣasanādyantadhāturūpāḥ pañcavṛttayaḥ* |

4.1. Consequences of information coding in position and order

• Subject position cannot be empty.

For, if it were empty, it would not be clear whether the given sentence is an interrogative or a declarative.

• Insertion of auxiliary *do* in interrogatives.

If a verb group does not have an auxiliary verb, then dummy *do* is inserted, as shown below.

10. He goes to school.
11. *Does* he go to school?

Here *goes* has two morphemes: *go-* and *-es*. The morpheme *-es* marks the tense and hence should get inverted with *he*. But *-es*, being a bound morpheme, requires a verb to which it should get attached. The auxiliary *do*[9] satisfies the requirement, and thus the auxiliary *does* then is inverted with the subject to give an interrogative sentence. The verb *be*[10] is an exception as shown below.

12. It is there.
13. Is it there?

• Extra overheads: dummy *it* and expletive *there*

(1) In the case of verbs with implicit (*antarbhūta*) arguments, the subject position, which cannot be empty, is occupied by dummy *it*[11] as in:

14. It is raining.

---

[9]In his *Śṛṅgāraprakāśa* Bhoja classifies verbal bases into three types: *astyartha*, *bhavatyartha*, and *karotyartha*. *Śṛṅgāraprakāśa* (I.194): *dhātavaś ca tredhā—astyarthāḥ, bhavatyarthāḥ, karotyarthāś ca | tatra yeṣāṁ kartāra udāsate te astyarthāḥ—yathā asti vidyate dhriyate tiṣṭhati āste vartate ityādi | yeṣāṁ vikurvate te bhavatyarthāḥ yathā bhavati saṁjāyate vardhate vipariṇamate apakṣīyate vinaśyati ityādi | yeṣāṁ prayuñjate te karotyarthāḥ yathā—karoti vidhatte janayati nirvartayati sādhayati utpādayati |* Further, he says that all the *karotyartha* verbs can be paraphrased with *karoti*: e.g., *pacati* = *pākaṃ karoti*. *Śṛṅgāraprakāśa* (I.323): *tasmāt pākaṃ karotīti padadvayasya yo'arthas sa eva pacatīty ekapadasyeti |*

[10]This is again in accordance with Bhoja's distinction between *karotyartha* verbs and *astyartha* verbs. The distinction between *bhavatyartha* and *karotyartha* verbs however does not hold good in English. English allows *Does it grow?*, whereas Sanskrit does not allow *kiṁ vardhanaṁ karoti?* The latter uses *bhavati* as in *kiṁ vardhanaṁ bhavati?*

[11]This *it* is termed 'dummy *it*' since it, being just a place holder, does not convey any information.

(2) The word or phrase that is to be focused is normally placed into a focus position at the front of a clause in order to highlight it. When a verb is to be focused, it is not possible to bring it to the front, since then either the subject position will be empty or the sentence with the verb in the front will become an interrogative sentence. Hence in such cases the subject position is filled with expletive *there*, as in:

15. *There* are flowers in the garden.
16. *There* could have occurred a diplomatic incident. (Radford 1997: 211)

The expletive *there* thus serves as a focus element to express the 'factuality' or 'happeningness' of the event.

It is interesting to note that certain transitive verbs also have the expletive *there* to express the happeningness. For example,

17. Suddenly *there* entered the hall an ugly old man. (Levin 1993: 90)

In the case of a verb group involving one or more auxiliaries, the main verb assumes the focus position, leaving the subject-auxiliary vṛtti intact as in sentences 6 and 7. If the manner of the activity is to be focussed, then the subject position is occupied by the adverb expressing the manner as in sentences 2 and 3.

4.2. *asamarthaḥ padavidhiḥ*?

The dummy *it* does not carry any lexical information, and hence it is an extra overhead. So there is a tendency to drop it. This is natural and consistent with the principle of economy (*lāghava*). In such cases then the subject (and in some cases the object) of the subordinate clause is moved to the subject position of the main verb. The raised subject, though it shows agreement with the verb, is not semantically related to the verb.

In order to interpret this phenomenon from the Pāṇinian perspective, we look at the constraints imposed by Pāṇini on the grammatical operations (*vidhi*) concerning finished words (*pada*). Patañjali interprets Pāṇini's sūtra A 2.1.1 *samarthaḥ padavidhiḥ* as 'wherever a grammatical operation (*vidhi*) concerning finished words (*pada*) is prescribed, it must be applied to words which are semantically connected (*samartha*)' (Joshi 1968: v). Patañjali further discusses the example *asūryampaśyāni mukhāni* 'faces that do not see the sun'. This is an example of an *asamartha* compound,[12] where the

[12] A compound whose components are semantically not connected.

negative particle *a-*, in spite of being semantically related to the verb *dṛś* of *paśya*, gets compounded with the noun *sūrya*. Such usages are still accepted because they convey the desired meaning. This leads to the acceptance of gamakatva as a criterion for accepting such syntactic constructions. Gamakatva 'the ability to convey the desired meaning' is not accepted in standard speech, as is evident from the mention of *akiṁcit kurvāṇam* in the *Mahābhāṣya* as being regarded as ungrammatical. Only the constructions which are in usage in spite of being asamartha are accepted on the basis of gamakatva.

In the light of this discussion, let us now discuss two English constructions, which fall under the category of asamartha syntactic constructions but are in usage because of their gamakatva.

4.2.1. *Seem* type of verbs

Consider the following two English sentences with the same meaning:

18. It seems that the boys have eaten fruits.
19. The boys seem to have eaten fruits.[13]

In sentence 19, *the boys* is in the subject position of *seem* and also abhihita, as it shows person-number agreement with the verb *seem*. However, semantically, *the boys* does not have any relation with the verb *seem*. This is clear from sentence 18 in which *the boys* is semantically related to the verb *eat* and the *that* clause is an argument of *seem*. The sentence structure in sentence 19 thus seems to be asamartha to convey the desired meaning.[14]

But then the following questions arise. How is it that an English reader does not find such constructions odd? How is it that the sentence is acceptable to a native speaker? How does a language allow proper communication in spite of apparent incomprehensibility of the sentence at the structural level? It is gamakatva (*arthabodhakatva*, the ability to convey the desired meaning) that takes care of proper communication. The gamakatva of the construction is justified by the expectancy of the verb *eat* in the subordinate clause and the fact that the verb *seem* does not have an expectancy of a subject.

---

[13]This is an example of subject-subject raising, where the subject in the subordinate clause has been moved to the subject position of the main verb.

[14]Naiyāyikas, who hold the *prathamāntamukhyaviśeṣyakaśābdabodha*-view, may not consider the two sentences to differ significantly; *the boys* is *prathamānta* 'ending in the nominative case' in both the cases. But they will have difficulty in explaining the kārakatva of a prathamānta in the following sentence:

The prisoners are alleged to have been ordered to pick up the money.

Here *the prisoners* is semantically related to the verb *order* and not to the verb *allege*.

4.2.2. *Tough* type of adjectives

Consider the following pair of sentences that convey the same meaning.

20. It is hard to see John.
21. John is hard to see.

In sentence 21, the object *John* of the subordinate verb is moved to the subject position of the main verb *is* which was occupied by dummy *it*. This is again a case of *asāmarthya* (the state of being asamartha). Because, though *John* is not an argument of the verb *is*, there is an agreement between *John*, which is an occupant of the subject position, with the verb *is*.

Not only objects but also complements of prepositions can move to the subject position. However, when the complement of a preposition moves to the subject position, the preposition is left behind. This then leads to the violation of normal proximity (*sannidhi*). For example, the dummy *it* in 22 is replaced by the noun phrase *this violin* in 23 leaving the preposition *on* in situ.

22. It is tough to play these sonatas on this violin.
23. This violin is tough to play these sonatas on.

Thus the normal sannidhi between the preposition *on* and the noun *violin* is violated.

4.2.3. Exceptional case marking (subject-object raising)

Another phenomenon in English is the raising of a subject to the object position, which is termed 'exceptional case marking' (ECM). Consider the following sentence:

24. I want him to go there.

Here the pronoun *he*, which is an argument of the verb *go* of the subordinate clause, gets case-marked by the main verb *want*. From the point of view of the Pāṇinian grammar, there are two problems in this sentence.

(1) In the case of verbs signifying desire (*icchārthakadhātu*), if a subordinate verb is an infinitive (terminates in the suffix ***tumun***), then it shares kartṛ-kāraka with the main verb which signifies desire,[15] as in:

Skt: *aham bhoktum icchāmi.*

gloss: I to_eat desire {1st sg.}

Eng: I desire to eat.

---

[15]A 3.3.158 *samānakartṛkeṣu tumun.*

But in 24 the subject of the verb *want*, an *icchārthakadhātu*, is different from the subject of *go*.

(2) The second problem is with the accusative form of *he*. *He* is an argument of the verb *go* which is in infinitive form. Hence according to A 2.3.65 *kartṛkarmaṇoḥ kṛti*[16] the kartṛ-kāraka of *go* should take the sixth case ending. But *him* is not in the genitive case.

In his *Vākyapadīya* Bhartṛhari states (3.7.81–82):

> *pradhānetarayor yatra dravyasya kriyayoḥ pṛthak* |
> *śaktir guṇāśrayā tatra pradhānam anurudhyate* ||
>
> *pradhānaviṣayā śaktiḥ pratyayenābhidhīyate* |
> *yadā guṇe tadā tadvad anuktāpi prakāśate* ||

According to Bhartṛhari, if x is an argument of both a main verb and a subordinate verb, it is the main verb that assigns case to x, and the relation of the subordinate verb to x gets manifested even without any marking.

But we cannot adopt this way of looking at the problem since there lie the following discrepancies:

- The argument of *want* is not *he* but the clause *him to go there*.
- The relation of *want* with *him to go there* is not the same as that of *go* with *he*.

A native speaker understands such constructions, because they contextually have the property of making the meanings understood (gamakatva). For example, in this case, the object position of *want* overlaps with the subject position of *go* and this overlapping acts as a clue for gamakatva. Because now a native speaker of English finds *he* in the subject position of *go* helping him get the desired meaning. Further, since *he* also occupies the object position of *want*, *want* assigning the accusative case to *he* looks natural.

Thus sentence 24 is a case of exceptional case marking or anomalous behavior or a grammatical operation between two words that are not related semantically. And hence this is an example of *asamarthaḥ padavidhiḥ*. In spite of the asāmarthya the native speakers understand such usages because of gamakatva.

---

[16] If a kartṛ or karman has not been expressed already, the sixth case ending is added to a prātipadika to denote the kartṛ or karman given a kṛt suffix construction.

5. Subject in English: a Pāṇinian viewpoint

Our observations may be summarized in the form of a set of rules as follows:

1. Modern English exhibits a special vṛtti, avyavahitatva, between an NP and a VP. The position that immediately preceeds a VP is called 'subject position'.
2. Abhihita—the kāraka which has been expressed by the verbal suffix—occupies the subject position. (Hence the abhihita is also called 'subject'.)
3. If a verb is to be focussed, then the subject position is occupied by either *there* or *here*.

   Here comes the bus!

   Suddenly there entered the hall an ugly man!
4. If the manner of an activity is to be focussed, then the subject position is occupied by the adverb expressing the manner.

   Never was the sea so calm.

   Uneasy lies the head which wears a crown.
5. If a verb has an implicit kartṛ, then the subject position is occupied by *it*.

   It is raining.
6. If the main verb is *seem*, then the subject of the subordinate verb optionally occupies the subject position of the main verb.
7. In such a case the verb of the subordinate clause takes an infinitive form.

   The boys seems to have eaten fruits.
8. If the subject of a verb signifying desire (*iccārthakadhātu*) is the same as that of the secondary verb in infinitive, the subject is shared.

   I want to go.
9. If the subject of the main verb signifying desire (*iccārthakadhātu*) differs from that of the secondary verb (which is in infinitive), then the subject of the secondary verb takes an accusative marker.

   I want him to go.

6. Conclusion

The purpose of the foregoing exercise is to look at the concept of subject in English from a Pāṇinian viewpoint. It has been shown that English exhibits a special vṛtti, avyavahitatva, between an NP and a VP, and also that English codes information in the NP-VP order. These two factors, taken together, explain the sacrosanctness of the subject position in English. Since the subject position cannot be empty, it leads to an introduction of dummy *it* and expletive *there*. Further, the natural tendency of a language towards lāghava introduces a kind of asāmarthya in sentences involving verbs like *seem* and adjectives like *tough*. The overlapping of the object position of the main verb with the subject position of the subordinate verb provides the gamakatva for sentences with exceptional case marking.

References and abbreviations

A: Pāṇini's *Aṣṭādhyāyī*. See Pande 2004.

Abhyankara, Vāsudevaśāstrī
2007 *Vyākaraṇamahābhāṣya, mūḷa āṇi marāthī bhāṣāntara.* Part 2. Poona: Sanskrit Vidya Parisamsthana.

Arjunwadkar, K. S.
1970 *Veṃkaṭamādhavakṛta-Mahārāṣṭra-Prayogacandrikā.* Poona: Deshmukh and Co.

Austen, J.
1867 *Emma: A Novel.* Boston: Ticknor and Fields.

Bharati, Akshar, and Rajeev Sangal
1990 A karaka based approach to parsing of Indian languages. In *COLING 90: Proceedings of International Conference on Computational Linguistics*, vol. 3, 25–29. Helsinki: Association for Computational Linguistics.

Bharati, Akshar, Rajeev Sangal, and Vineet Chaitanya
1990 Natural language processing, complexity theory and logic. In *Foundations of Software Technology and Theoretical Computer Science* 10, Lecture Notes in Computer Science 472, 410–420. Berlin: Springer Verlag.

Bharati, Akshar, Vineet Chaitanya, and Rajeev Sangal
1994 *NLP: A Paninian Perspective.* Delhi: Prentice Hall of India.

Bharati, Akshar, and Amba Kulkarni
2007 English grammar from Hindi speaker's point of view in the light of Paaninian grammar. In *English Grammar from Paninian Perspective*, 34–59. Tirupati: Rashtriya Sanskrit Vidyapeetham.
2008 English from Hindi viewpoint: A Paninian perspective. In *Papers on Language Technology*, 1–20. Kuppam: Dravidian University.

Cardona, George
1976a Subject in Sanskrit. In *The Notion of Subject in South Asian Languages*, South Asian Studies Publication Series 2, 1–38. Madison: Wisconsin University.
1976b *Pāṇini: A Survey of Research.* Hague-Paris: Mouton.
1997 *Pāṇini: His Work and Its Tradition; Volume One: Background and Introduction.* 2nd ed. Delhi: Motilal Banarsidass.

Comrie, B.
1983 *Language Universals and Linguistic Typology.* 1981. Reprint, with corrections and additions, England: Basil Blackwell Publisher Limited.

Dwivedī, Rewāprasāda, and Sadāśivakumāra Dwivedī
2007 *Śṛṅgāraprakāśa [Sāhityaprakāśa] by Bhojarāja; Volume-I [1–14 Prakāśa].* New Delhi: Indira Gandhi National Center for the Arts.

Gillon, Brendan S.
2002 Bhartṛhari's rule for unexpressed kārakas: The problem of control in Classical Sanskrit. In *Indian Linguistic Studies: Festschrift in Honor of George Cardona*, edited by Madhav M. Deshpande and Peter E. Hook, 93–111. Delhi: Motilal Banarasidass.

Guruprasad Shastri
2006 *Patañjali's Vyākaraṇamahābhāṣya with Kaiyaṭa's Pradīpa and Nāgojibhaṭṭa's Uddyota with the Notes by Pandit Guruprasad Shastri: (Adhyāya 2).* Delhi: Rashtriya Sanskrit Sansthan.

Harley, H.
1995 Subjects, events, and licensing. PhD diss., MIT.

Jigyasu, Brahmadatt
1979 *Aṣṭādhyāyī (Bhāṣya) Prathamāvṛtti.* 3 vols. Sonapat: Ramlal Kapoor Trust Bahalgadh.

Joshi, S. D.
1968 *Patañjali's Vyākaraṇa-Mahābhāṣya: Samarthāhnika (P. 2.1.1).* Pune: University of Poona.

Joshi, S. D., and J. A. F. Roodbergen
1998 *The Aṣṭādhyāyī of Pāṇini with Translation and Explanatory Notes: Volume VII (2.3.1–2.3.73).* Delhi: Sahitya Akademy.

Keenan, E. L.
1975 Towards a universal definition of 'subject of'. In *Syntax and Semantics: Subject and Topic*, edited by C. Li, 303–333. New York: Academic Press.

Kiparsky, Paul
2009 On the architecture of Pāṇini's grammar. In *Proceedings of the Sanskrit Computational Linguistics*, edited by G. Huet, A. Kulkarni, and P. Scharf, Springer-Verlag Lecture Notes 5402, 33–94. Berlin: Springer.

Levin, B.
1993 *English Verb Classes and Alternations: A Preliminary Investigation.* Chicago: University of Chicago Press.

Lin, D.
1998 Dependency-based evaluation of MINIPAR. Paper presented at the Workshop on the Evaluation of Parsing Systems, Granada.

Marneffe, M., B. MacCartney, and C. D. Manning
2006 Generating typed dependency parsers from phrase structure parsers. In *the Proceedings of the 5th International Conference on Language Resources and Evaluation (LREC, 2006)*, 449–454.

MBh: Patañjali's *Mahābhāṣya.* See Abhyankara.

Nannayya
1932 *Āndhra-śabda-cintāmaṇi: A Treatise on Telugu Grammar.* Madras.

Pande, Gopal Dutt
2000 *Vaiyākaraṇa Siddhāntakaumudī of Bhattojidikshita.* Varanasi: Chowkhamba Vidyabhavan.
2004 *Aṣṭādhyāyī of Pāṇini, elaborated by M. M. Panditaraj Dr. Gopal Shastri.* Varanasi: Chaukhamba Surbharati Prakashan.

Pillai, E. P. N. Kunjan
1955 *Līlātilakam: Maṇipravāḷalakṣaṇam.* Kottayam: National Book Stall.

Pradīpa. See Guruprasad Shastri.

Radford, Andrew
1997 *Syntax: A Minimalist Introduction.* Cambridge: Cambridge University Press.

Raghunātha Śarmā
1979 *Vākyapadīyam [Part III, Vol. II]: Bhūyodravya-Guṇa-Dik-Sādhana-Kriyā-Kāla-Puruṣa-Sankhyā-Upagraha and Liṅga Samuddeśa, with the Commentary 'Prakāśa' by Helārāja and Ambākartrī by Pt. Raghunātha Śarmā.* Varanasi: Sampurnanand Sanskrit Visvavidyalaya.

Sayers, D. L.
1933 *Murder Must Advertise: A Detective Story.* New York: Harcourt, Brace and Co.
1972 *The Nine Tailors.* London: New English Library.

Scharfe, H.
1977 *A History of Indian Literature.* Vol. 5, fasc. 2, *Grammatical Literature.* Wiesbaden: Otto Harrassowitz.

SK: Bhaṭṭojidīkṣita's *Siddhāntakaumudī.* See Pande 2000.

Sleator, D. D., and D. Temperley
1993 Parsing English with a link grammar. Paper presented at the Third International Workshop on Parsing Technologics. Tilburg, Netherlands.

Śṛṅgāraprakāśa. See Dwivedī.

Taverniers, Miriam
2005 Subjecthood and the notion of instantiation. *Language Sciences* 27: 651–678.

Vākyapadīya. See Raghunātha Śarmā.

Some Issues in Editing the *Gaṇapāṭhas* in the *Kāśikāvṛtti*[*]

MALHAR KULKARNI

Introduction

The *Kāśikāvṛtti* is one of the most important texts of the Pāṇinian grammatical tradition. Its importance is once again highlighted recently by Bronkhorst (2009: 129) in the following words:

> The importance of the *Kāśikā* for Indological research is not in doubt. It is the oldest surviving commentary on the whole of Pāṇini's *Aṣṭādhyāyī*. It is our earliest testimony for all those *sūtras* of Pāṇini's text that are not cited, used or referred to in Patañjali's *Mahābhāṣya*. It is also the earliest text in the Pāṇinian tradition that contains a full *Gaṇapāṭha*, i.e., a complete collection of the lists (*gaṇa*) of words that accompany many *sūtras*.

It is this aspect of *Gaṇapāṭhas* which is the subject matter of the current article. The importance of the *Kāśikāvṛtti* in this aspect is reiterated by Radicchi (1991: 66) in the following words: "One can not escape the historical truth that the first *gaṇapāṭha* to reach us is the one the *Kāśikā* supplies . . . ."

There are a number of issues related to *Gaṇapāṭhas* which have drawn scholastic attention so far. They can be summarized as follows:

[*]I express my gratitude towards Prof. Johannes Bronkhorst, and the Authorities of the University of Lausanne as well as my parent organization, IIT Bombay for having given me an opportunity to spend three months in Lausanne, starting from June 2010 which gave me some space to revise my paper. I also wish to thank Prof. Surendra Mohan Misra, Dr. Irawati Kulkarni, Mrs. Amruta Kulkarni, Ms. Anuja Ajotikar, Ms.Tanuja Ajotikar and Ms. Trupti Kulkarni for their assistance in collecting some references which I needed for this article. I take this opportunity to thank Dr. Chaitali Dangarikar for the help I have been receiving from her in converting my handwritten 'trees' into the electronic format; one such 'tree', I have used in this paper.

1. What is the exact number of words in the *gaṇa*?
2. How do we decide this number?
3. Are the words recorded in the *gaṇas prātipadikas* or *padas*?
4. What are the possible sources of the words?
5. Is there an order in which the words appear in a particular *gaṇa*?
6. Can the words in the *gaṇas* be translated?

One of the examples of the study which tries to address itself to the first question is Bloomfield (1927), which critically examines the number of words in the *sarvādigaṇa* as found in the textual resources for P.1.1.27. Bloomfield concludes that the list of words in *sarvādigaṇa* should be read without certain words which are found in the resources. He also argues to ascertain this conclusion on the basis of textual evidence culled from texts from the *Vyākaraṇamahābhāṣya* of Patañjali onwards, up to Nāgeśa's *Paribhāṣenduśekhara*. Thus he addresses in a certain way the second question.

Brough (1973: 253, n. 25) addresses the third question and remarks: "I-ching's brief remarks, however, suffice to indicate that he did not understand the nature of the *Gaṇapāṭha*." Brough admits that there are *gaṇas* of both kinds. Some have to have *prātipadikas* as their constituents and some have to have *padas*.

Birwé (1961) is an important work that has addressed more or less all the issues mentioned above. In the words of Schwarzschild (1964: 459), Birwé establishes: "...the forms of *Gaṇapāṭha* given in the non-Pāṇinian schools are only varying recensions of the same basic lists that are found in Pāṇinian school." And she further remarks (1964: 460):

> Birwé also shows that some minor problems are still insoluble, as for instance the question of the order of words within a *gaṇa*.... Birwé has undertaken a critical edition not only of those *gaṇas* that are available only in manuscripts ..., but he has also corrected the text of extant editions with the help of manuscripts, as in the case of the *gaṇas* of *Jainendra* and the *Kāśikā*. ...The synoptic tables clearly show the historical evolution of the *gaṇas*: how for instance additions appear in the later texts, and how some of these may be due to spelling and other errors.

On another occasion, Birwé (1964) used a manuscript of the *Kāśikāvṛtti* and compared the *Gaṇapaṭha* on P.2.1.71 as found in it with that of Bhoja's *Sarasvatīkaṇṭhābharaṇa* and its commentary written by Nārāyaṇadaṇḍanātha. He published the entire text of the *Kāśikāvṛtti* on P.2.1.71 including the entire *gaṇa* and also showed discrepancies in the texts compared.

In all these and many other works dealing with the *Gaṇapāṭha*, the absence of a critical edition of the *Kāśikāvṛtti* is indicated as one of the major handicaps in determining the exact text of the *gaṇas*, as Radicchi (1991: 67) puts it:

> . . . one can not fail to recall the old, unsatisfied desideratum for a critical edition of the *Kāśikā*. And also the correlated yet distinct and specific task of critically editing the *Kāśikā gaṇas* is still to be carried out.

So far, the text of the *Kāśikāvṛtti* has been printed more than ten times. The edition published by Osmania University, Hyderabad, claims to be a critical edition.[1] In number as well as in scripts, this edition takes into account very few mss. The *Gaṇapāṭhas* edited in the edition thus need to be re-edited in the light of wider mss material. Kapila Deva Shastri who has published the *Gaṇapāṭha* as ascribed to Pāṇini (1967) has also used some manuscripts of the *Kāśikāvṛtti* in the process. He has also highlighted the importance of the *Kāśikāvṛtti* in the following words (1967: 69):

> . . . the published editions of the *Kāśikā* often differ in the readings of the *Gaṇapāṭha* from some of its manuscripts. In the manuscripts, we come across words which are absent in the published editions and *vice versa*.

In this paper, an attempt is made to present a critical edition of the text of the *Kāśikāvṛtti* that includes a *gaṇa*, taking into account all the known manuscript tradition that has come down to us. As Birwé has dealt with *gaṇas* in the 4th and 5th *adhyāyas* in his book, it is decided to present material on a *sūtra* about which not much material has been brought to light and discussed.

Radicchi (1991: 70–72) has studied individual *gaṇas* from P.2.1 and 2.2 except the one selected for discussion in this paper. She has argued (1991: 66): "It seems more reasonable to believe that all the grammarians of that period drew on a common store of *gaṇas*."[2]

The *sūtra* selected here is P.2.2.31: *rājadantādiṣu param*. This *sūtra* is accompanied by *rājadantādigaṇa*, which is an *ākṛtigaṇa* and not a closed one. P.2.2.31 is not commented upon in the *Mahābhāṣya* and therefore in its commentaries. There is a problem of justification of *anuvṛtti* in its case. Joshi and Roodbergen (1997: 76) say: "It seems, therefore, that P.2.2.31 is an inserted rule."

This paper is divided into five parts:

[1] For critical comments on and shortcomings of the Osmania University edition, see Birwé 1973, Kulkarni 2000, Haag and Vergiani 2009: 22–26.

[2] See also Cardona 2004: 144.

The first presents manuscript material used, with brief descriptions.[3]
The second deals with the edition of KV on P.2.2.31, with critical apparatus.
The third provides notes and discusses different issues regarding variants.
The fourth presents a general rooted tree showing interrelation of mss.
The fifth presents conclusions and also sketches the directions for future work.

Five appendices are added. In the first, a concordance of the available non-Pāṇinian traditions on P.2.2.31 is presented. In the second, the remarks found in the *Gaṇaratnamahodadhi* and a commentary on the *Siddhahaimaśabdānuśāsana* about variations and the precise nature of words as found in this *gaṇa* are recorded. The third presents the texts of the *Nyāsa* and the *Padamañjarī* on P.2.2.31 with my translations.[4] The fourth presents the data on the relation of P.2.2.31 with P.2.2.32–38 (this will be helpful in deciding the composition of this *gaṇa*). The fifth presents the analyzed data from two important groups of mss.

About P.2.2.31

According to P.1.2.43: *prathamānirdiṣṭaṁ samāsa upasarjanam*, an element referred to by a nominative form in a rule of composition is assigned the name *upasarjana*; the general rule P.2.2.30: *upasarjanaṁ pūrvam* provides that an *upasarjana* is the prior component of a compound; P.2.2.31: *rājadantādiṣu param* is an exception to this general rule and states that an *upasarjana* occurs in later position within items of the set referred to by *rājadantādi*. For example, *ṣaṣṭhī* in P.2.2.8: *ṣaṣṭhī* is a nominative form, so that a *pada* with a genitive ending subject to compounding by this rule generally occupies first position in the compound derived. For example, *mṛgarājaḥ* 'king of the beasts', equivalent to *mṛgāṇāṁ rājā*, is a form of the compound *mṛgarāja*, with the constituent that derives from a genitive in first position. *rājadantaḥ*, equivalent to *dantānāṁ rājā*, is a form of the compound *rājadanta*, derived from the *padas danta-ām rājan-s*. Instead of occuring in first position, the constituent that derives from a genitive *pada*, *danta-* (← *danta-ām*) is now the second constituent.

Another important factor to note here is that this rule is stated by the tradition to be an exception not only of P.2.2.31 but also of the exceptions to this main *sūtra*, which are stated in P.2.2.32–38. An important feature of the associated *gaṇa* is that it is stated to accommodate those words to which

[3] A detailed description of all the mss used is given in Kulkarni 2000a.

[4] I have given relevant passages only.

no position prescribing rule is applicable. Thus in the case of a dvandva compound, the compound prescribing rule, P.2.2.29: *cārthe dvandvaḥ*, leads to a position where all the compounding words are referred to by the word *anekam*. Thus there is no clear directive concerning the position of the word in a dvandva compound. The same is the case with the bahuvrīhi compounds which come under the rule P.2.2.24: *anekam anyapadārthe*. In all such cases, according to the commentators, it is P.2.2.31 which decides the position of the constituent word.[5]

It is to be noted here that in this section only two words, *pūrva* 'preceding/earlier' and *para* 'following/later', are used to indicate the position of the constituent in the compound. This indicates that this section deals only with compounds having two constituents. In the case of more than two constituents the words in question do not have any use for the determination of the precise position. If we look at other *sūtras* in the same group of *sūtras*, P.2.2.32–2.2.38, which are also exceptions to P.2.2.30, the fact reveals itself that most of the examples of these exception rules are two-membered compounds only.

Although P.2.2.31 is not commented upon in the *Mahābhāṣya*, the *gaṇa* on P.2.2.31 is referred to there in the course of other discussions, twice. In the *Mahābhāṣya* on P.5.4.7: *aṣaḍakṣāśitāṅgvalaṅkarmālampuruṣādhyuttarapadāt khaḥ*, it is suggested that a compound *rājādhīna* be derived with an avyayībhāva equivalent to *rājani adhi*. This is subject to the objection that *adhi* would then be made a prior constituent, as in *adhistri*. To counter this objection, a pūrvapakṣin suggests that *rājādhīnaḥ* be included in the *gaṇa* to P.2.2.31: *rājadantādiṣu pāṭhaḥ kariṣyate*.[6] Similarly, in connection with a compound *alābukarkandhudṛnbhuphala*, in order to account for the short final vowel of *alābu*-and *karkandhu*- (← *alābū*-, *karkandhū*-) in the dialect of Gālava, according to P.6.3.6: *iko hrasvo 'ṅyo gālavasya*, it is first suggested that instead of a dvandva *alābūkarkandhūdṛnbhū*- one have first a two-membered dvandva *alābukarkandhū* (*alābukarkandhvau*), which then forms another dvandva with *dṛnbhū* (*alābukarkandhudṛnbhvaḥ*), which then forms a tatpuruṣa with *phala*. This meets with the objection that, by P.2.2.34: *alpāctaram*, the constituent with lesser number of syllables, namely *dṛnbhū*, would occupy prior position. This is countered with the suggestion that the item in question be included in the *gaṇa* to P.2.2.31: *rājadantādiṣu pāṭhaḥ kariṣyate*.[7] Obviously, Patañjali knew of this *gaṇa*. Moreover, he considered that one could add to it (*ākṛtigaṇa*).

---

[5]For details, see Appendix IV.
[6]Mbh (II.431.22).
[7]Mbh (III.164.12–13).

Structure of the text of the *Kāśikāvṛtti*

I have shown (Kulkarni: 1999) that the text of the *Kāśikāvṛtti* for most *sūtras* exhibits a certain structure. The text consists of:

1. An introductory sentence, which contains the explanation of a word used in the *sūtra* either in the form of a gloss of the word or a grammatical explanation of the formation of the word, the *anuvṛtti* and the nature of the *sūtra*.
2. The explanation of the sūtra in a full sentence with a verbal form like *bhavati* at the end;
3. Examples of the *sūtra*, their possible explanations, and some comment on them that highlights a grammatical point;
4. Counter examples with a question and a possible explanation in terms of *prakriyā*;
5. Important relevant discussion from the Mbh as well as other *jñāpakas* and *paribhāṣās* and other views about formations of different word forms etc.

Let us look at the text of KV on P.2.2.1 as an example:[8]

> P: पूर्वापराधरोत्तरमेकदेशिनैकाधिकरणे । २ । २ । १ ।
>
> KV: (1) एकदेशोऽस्यास्तीत्येकदेशी अवयवी । तद्वाचिना सुबन्तेन सह पूर्व अपर अधर उत्तरशब्दाः सामर्थ्याद् एकदेशवचनाः समस्यन्ते तत्पुरुषश्च समासो भवति । (2) एकाधिकरणग्रहणम् एकदेशिनो विशेषणम् । (3) एकं चेदम् अधिकरणम् एकद्रव्यम् एकदेशि भवति । (4) षष्ठीसमासापवादोऽयं योगः । (5) पूर्वं कायस्य पूर्वकायः । (6) अपरकायः । (7) अधरकायः । (8) उत्तरकायः । (9) एकदेशिनेति किम् ? पूर्वं नाभेः कायस्य । (10) एकाधिकरण इति किम् ? पूर्वं छात्राणाम् आमन्त्रय । (11) कथं मध्याह्नः सायाह्न इति । संख्याविसायपूर्वस्याह्नस्याहन्नन्यतरस्यां ङौ इति ज्ञापकात् सर्वैणैकदेशशब्देनाह्नः समासो भवति ।

We can say that sentence (1), *ekadeśo 'syāstīty ekadeśī avayavī*, corresponds to 1 as it contains a grammatical explanation of the word *ekadeśī* that is used in the sūtra. The remaining part of that sentence as well as sentences (2), (3) and (4) corresponds to 2 as they explain the meaning of the *sūtra*. Sentences (5)–(8) correspond to 3 as they contain the examples of this *sūtra*. Sentences (9) and (10) correspond to 4 as they contain counter examples. The last sentence (11) corresponds to 5 as it explains compounds like *madhyāhna* and *sāyāhna*, which are not explicitly stated by this *sūtra*, with the help of a *jñāpaka*.

---

[8] Sharma et al. 2008: 119. Numbers to senteces are given by the present author.

The text of the *Kāśikāvṛtti* on a sūtra containing a *gaṇa* follows more or less the same pattern, having hardly any counter examples but a list of words instead. Thus 4 and 5 are replaced by a list of words.

The *gaṇa* accompanying a sūtra has its own internal structure, so that words are arranged in the *gaṇa* not at random but for a practical purpose. Certain statements are made to explain the nature of the words yet to be enumerated. Certain *vārttikas* are found usually at the end. When the *gaṇa* is an *ākṛtigaṇa*, a list of words is interspersed with the statements describing why such words are put in the list in question, and at the end there is a tag in the form of the phrase *ākṛtigaṇo'yam*. In the absence of such a tag, there is found a statement within the *gaṇa* which says that all the words sharing similar morphological features that cannot be accounted for by any of the *sūtras* of Pāṇini can be accommodated in the *gaṇa*.[9]

[9]KV on P.2.2.71: *avihitalakṣaṇas tatpuruṣo mayūravyaṁsakādiṣu draṣṭavyaḥ* |

I

A brief description of the manuscripts used for *Kāśikā* 2.3.31

The sigla used in this edition are shown followed by brief descriptions: name of the library, place, accession number of the ms.,[10] which are accompanied by the sigla used in my unpublished PhD dissertation submitted to the University of Pune, 2000. The number of mss used in Kulkarni 2005 are 67. In the present article, however, I have used 3 more mss, which were not used in the dissertation. They were used in Kulkarni 2007. These three mss are not used by Haag and Vergiani 2009. The mss are referred to by the scripts in which they are written: B stands for *Bengali*, D for *Devanāgarī*, G for *Grantha*, M for *Malayalam*, N for *Nandināgarī*, S for *Śarādā* and T for *Telugu*.

B1- The Asiatic Society of Bengal, Calcutta 700016. No. G3816. (c6).

D1- The Asiatic Society of Bombay, Mumbai 400023. No. 35. (asb).

D2- Bhandarkar Oriental Research Institute, Pune 411004. No. 64. (bh8).

D3- University of Mumbai, Mumbai. No. 1552. (bu1).

D4- The India office library, London. Bühler133, IOL 4064. (io1).

D5- Shri Ranabir Sanskrit R. Institute, Jammu. No. 4k, k, g, G, x, c, C, j. (jm6).

D6- Vaidik Samshodhan Mandal, Pune. No. 11809. (v1).

D7- Ganganath Jha Research Institue, Allahabad. (gjri). Not catalogued.

D8- Bhandarkar Oriental Research Institute, Pune-4. No. 65/532/1895–98. (bh1).

D9- Bhandarkar Oriental Research Institute, Pune-4. No. 63/234/1895–98. (bh4).

D10- L.D. Institute of Indology, Ahmedabad. No. LD5451, Patra265. (ld0).

D11- Bhandarkar Oriental Research Institute, Pune-4. No. 62/34/1882–1883. (bh2).

D12- Bhandarkar Oriental Research Institute, Pune-4. No. 66/533/1889–91. (bh5).

D13- V.V.R. Institute, Hoshiarppur. No. 3112-3-4-5-6-7-8-9. (hp1).

D14- Hindi Sahitya Sammelan, Allahabad. No. 7247/4102. (hss).

D15- Bhandarkar Oriental Research Institute, Pune-4. No. 61/1868–69. (bh6).

D16- Shri Ranabir Sanskrit R. Institute, Jammu. No. 145 1K, 2K, G. (jm3).

[10] Wherever available. Some mss have not been cataloged. See D7.

D17- Rajasthan Oriental Research Institute, Jodhpur. No. 16577. (rj).

D18- Sampurnananda Sanskrit Visvavidyalaya, Varanasi. No. 38896. (ss14).

D19- National Archives, Kathmandu. (n1).

D20- Rajasthan Oriental Research Institute, Alwar. No. 3199, 3200, 3201–2, 3, 4, 5, 6. (r1).

D21- Rajasthan Oriental Research Institute, Alwar. No. 3207-8-9-10-11-12-13-14. (r2).

D22- Sampurnananda SanskritVishvavidyalaya, Varanasi. No. 38676. (ss12).

D23- Asiatic Society of Bengal, 1, Park Street, Calcutta 700016. No. G8862. (c10).

D24- The India Office Library, London. No. IOL 4084. (io5).

D25- Bibliothèque Nationale Universitaire de Strasbourg, Strasbourg, France. No. 4575. (st3).

D26- Sampurnananda Sanskrit Vishvavidyalaya, Varanasi. No. 39365. (ss15)[11].

D27- Ananadashrama, Pune. No. 6004. (aa).

D28- Asiatic Society of Bengal, Calcutta. No. G9735. (c11).

D29- Niedersächsische Staats- und Universitätsbibliothek, Göttingen. No. cod. Ms. sanscr. 183. (g1).

D30- The India Office library, London. IOL 4087. (io2).

D31- The India Office Library, London. IOL 593, 594, 595. (io4).

D32- Oriental Research institute, Mysore. No. 33688. (my11).

D33- Sarasvati Mahal Library, Thanjavur. No. 872. (th2).

D34- Sarasvati Mahal Library, Thanjavur. No. 5434. (th5).

D35- Prajna PathashalaMandal Wai, Maharashtra. No. 9138/9–6/509. (wai2).

D36- Niedersächsische Staats- und Universitätsbibliothek, Göttingen. No. cod. Ms. sanscr. 184. (g2).

D37- The India Office Library, London. No. IOL 4086. (io6).

G1- Adyar Library, Chennai. No. 69208. (a5).

G2- Adyar Library, Chennai. No. 69213. (a6).

G3- Adyar Library, Chennai. No. 69214. (a7).

G4- Oriental Research Institute, Baroda. No. 6613. (ba1).

G5- Government Oriental Manuscripts Library, Chennai. No. 4761. (m7).

G6- Oriental Research Institute, Mysore. No. 33679. (my2).

M1- Adyar Library, Chennai. No. 70128. (a10).

M2- O.R.I. and Manuscripts Library, Kariavottam, Thiruvananthapuram. No. 18857. (tri47).

[11]This is a ms used by Kapila Deva Shastri 1967.

M3- O.R.I. and Manuscripts Library, Kariavottam, Thiruvananthapuram. No. 25A. (tri1).

M4- O.R.I. Baroda. No. 25421. (ba6).

M5- O.R.I. and Manuscripts Library, Kariavottam, Thiruvananthapuram. No. 82. (tri3).

M6- O.R.I. and Manuscripts Library, Kariavottam, Thiruvananthapuram. No. 22409. (tri55).

M7- O.R.I. and Manuscripts Library, Kariavottam, Thiruvananthapuram. No. 28B. (tri2).

M8- O.R.I. and Manuscripts Library, Kariavottam, Thiruvananthapuram. No. 11035A. (tri21).

M9- O.R.I. and Manuscripts Library, Kariavottam, Thiruvananthapuram. No. 14959. (tri32).

M10- O.R.I. and Manuscripts Library, Kariavottam, Thiruvananthapuram. No. 13476A. (tri26).

M11- O.R.I. and Manuscripts Library, Kariavottam, Thiruvananthapuram. No. 18530. (tri41).

M12- O.R.I. and Manuscripts Library, Kariavottam, Thiruvananthapuram. No. 17440. (tri37).

N- Bibliothèque Nationale Universitaire de Strasbourg, Strasbourg. No. 4563. (st1).

S1- Bhandarkar Oriental Research Institute, Pune. No. 60/283/1875–76. (bh7).

S2- Central Library, B.H.U. Varansi. No. C921, 2A/747. (bhu1).

S3- Central Library, B.H.U. Varansi. No. C4452, 2A/745. (bhu2).

S4- The India Office Library, London. No. IOL 4089. (io7).

S5- Shri Ranabir Research Institute, Jammu. No. 20bhu. (jm1).

S6- Niedersächsische Staats- und Universitätsbibliothek, Göttingen. No. cod. Ms. sanscr. Mu. I, 94. (g3).

S7- Iqbal Library, University of Kashmir, Srinagar. No. 779.[12]

S8- Iqbal Library, University of Kashmir, Srinagar. No. 931.

S9- Iqbal Library, University of Kashmir, Srinagar. No. 1015. Folio- 259.

T1- Adyar Library, Chennai. No. 69206. (a3).

T2- Adyar Library, Chennai. No. 69215. (a8).

T3- G.O.M.L. Chennai. No. D-1313, 1314, 15667. (m1).

T4- Sarasvati Mahal Library, Thanjavur. No. D5430. (th1).

[12] I newly discovered S7–9 after completing my dissertation.

A note on variants and abbreviations used to note them

The variants are noted under four heads: omitted (*om*), added (*add*), change of a word (*cw*), change in the place of a word (*cpw*). Sometimes the place of the letter in the variation is marked with the following signs: *lm*- left margin of the folio; *otl*- on top the line; *rm*- right margin of the folio; *bl*- below the line.

II

Edited text of the *Kāśikāvṛtti* on P.2.2.31

राजदन्तादिषु परम्[*1)] । २.२.३१

पूर्वनिपाते[*2)] प्राप्ते परप्रयोगार्थं[*3)] वचनम् । राजदन्तादिषु[*4)] उपसर्जनं[*5)] परं प्रयोक्तव्यम्[*6)] । न[*7)] केवलम्[*8)] उपसर्जनस्य[*9)] अन्यस्यापि[*10)] यथालक्षणं[*11)] विहितस्य[*12)] पूर्वनिपातस्य अयम्[*13)] अपवादः[*14)] परनिपातो विधीयते। दन्तानां राजा[*15)] राजदन्तः । वनस्य अग्रे अग्रेवणम्[*16)] । निपातनाद्[*17)] अलुक्[*18)] ।

---

*1) add : पूर्वेण in M4, 5.

*2) cw : पूर्वनपाते in G6.

*3) add : इदम् in D22 ; cw: परनिपातप्रयोगार्थं D32, T3.

*4) add : परं in G-1, 2; S-1, 2, 5, 6; D-1, 2, 4, 8, 9, 11, 12, 14–17, 20–31, 34–37, M-10, 11.

*5) add : प्रयोक्तव्यम् in G1, 6; D-2, 4, 6, 9, 10, 11, 12, 14, 15, 17, 20, 21, 22, 25, 27, 28, 30, 31, 34, 37; S-1, 3; cw: अपसर्जनं in D6.

*6) om: in M-1, 3, 6.

*7) om : D25; cw: तेन in D23.

*8) om: D23–26.

*9) add: पूर्वत्र in D33; cw: उपसर्जनं in D30.

*10) om: D33, add: घ्यादेर् in D-8, 9, 11, 12, 14–18, 27, 29, 30, 31, 34, 35; G-1, 2, 4; M-1, 3, 4, 5, 12; तेन उपसर्जनस्यापि घ्यादेर् in D25; स्यात् in D36, 37; G6; T3; व्याघ्रादे in M6 and S1, 4; व्याघ्रादेर् in S-2, 3, 5; देर् in D20 ; cw: अपि तु in B1, अपि in D23, अस्यापि in D29, अन्यसापि in D17 (अन्य in lm), T3(न्य otl).

*11) om: D33: add: घ्यादेः in B1; cw: यथालक्षण in B1, D29 (with ण bl), 35, G2, S-1–5.

*12) add: घ्यादेः in M-8, 10, 11; cw: विहित in B1, D-11, 12, 16, 17, 25, 29, 33; M1, S1.

*13) illegible till 16 in G1; om: B1, D-1–4, 8, 9, 11, 12, 20–37; G-1, 2, 4, 6; M-1, 3, 5, 6, 8, 10–12; S, T3.

*14) om: same as in 13.

*15) add: इति in D25.

*16) cw: अग्रेवर्ति in D35, अग्रेवनम् in D20, 37; M4, S.

*17) om : in M3 ; add : सप्तम्या in B1, S2, 4.

*18) add: वनं पुरगेत्यादिना णत्वम् in D34.

राजदन्तः[*19)]। अग्रेवणम्[*20)]। लिप्तवासितम्[*21)]। नग्नमुषितम्[*22)]। सिक्तसंमृष्टम्[*23)]। मृष्टलुञ्चितम्[*24)]। अवक्लिन्नपक्कम्[*25)]। अर्पितोप्तम्[*26)]।

[*19)] om: in B1, D2, 34, G1, M3; cw: राजदन्तम् in D30.

[*20)] om: in B1, D2, 34, M3; add: अर्पितोप्तम् उप्तगाढम् शूद्रार्यम् सिक्तसंमृष्टम् in M4, अर्पितोप्तम् उप्तगाढम् आश्मादयः सिक्तसंमृष्टम् in M6, : उप्तगाढम् अर्पितोप्तम् शूद्रार्यम् सिक्तसंमृष्टम् in M5, निपातनाद् अलुक् राजदन्तः अग्रेवणम् in D16; cw: अग्रेवनम् in S1, 3, 4, 6–9 ; T3.

[*21)] cw: लिप्तवासित in D33, विप्रवासितम् in D27.

[*22)] cw: नग्नमुखितम् in D25, 34, 35; नग्नमुषित in D33, मासेमुषितम् in D37, मासेमूषितम् in D36, नग्नमुमिपितम् in D31, नग्नमुस्रितम् in D30; नयग्रमुषितम् in D2, 4; लग्नमुषितम् in D11, 12, 14, 15, 17; नग्नमुह्यितम् in D23, नग्नमुञ्चितम् in T3.

[*23)] om: in M4–6; cw: सिक्तं संसृष्टम् in D35, सिक्तसंसृष्टम् in D3–5, 8, 11, 12, 14–18, 23; G1, S1; सिक्तसमृष्टम् in D33, 34 ; सिक्तसंक्रष्टम् in D9, 25; सित्तसंदृष्टम् in S3.

[*24)] add: हृष्टमुषितम् in M4.; cw: क्रष्टलुञ्चितम् in D35, सृष्टलुञ्चितम् in D34, भ्रष्टलुपितम् D33, भ्रष्टलुचितम् in D36, 37; , भ्रष्टाचितम् in D30, मृष्टलुचितम् in B1, D15, 27, G6, S5; भ्रष्टलुञ्चितम् in S1; भृष्टरुचितम् in D9; हृष्टमुदितम् in M1, 4, 5, 12; पृष्टरुचितम् in M11 ; दृष्टलुठितम् in S3, 4; तृष्टलुठितम् in S2; म्रष्टलुठितम् in D20; भृष्टलुञ्चितम् in D1, 3; पृष्टकुपितम् in M10; हृष्टरुपितम् in M8; भृष्टलुम्पितम् in M3; पृष्टलुञ्चितम् in G2; दृष्टमुषितम् in M6, मृष्टविमृष्टम् in D22; मृष्टलुपितम् in D21.

[*25)] illegible till 39 in G1; cw: अपक्लिन्नपक्कम् in G2, M4, S1-3, 5–9; अरक्लिन्नपक्कम् in D23; अवक्लिनपक्कम् in D21, अविक्लिन्नपक्कम् in M4, 5.

[*26)] om: M4–6; add: ऋणग्रहणं नियोगोपलक्षणार्थम् इहापि समासो भवति पूर्वाह्णेगेयं साम प्रातरध्येयोनुवाकः ।ऋण इति किम्। मासे देया भिक्षा।संज्ञायाम्। संज्ञायाम् विषये सप्तम्यन्तं सुपा सह समस्यते तत्पुरुषश्च समासो भवति। संज्ञायाम् इति समुदायोपाधिस्तेन नित्यसमास एवायं न हि वाक्येन संज्ञा गम्यते अरण्येतिलकाः अरण्येमाषकाः वनेकशेरुकाः वनेबिल्वकाः कूपेपिशाचिकाः । हलदन्तात्सप्तम्या संज्ञायाम् इत्यलुक्। क्तेनाहोरात्रावयवाः । अहरवयवा रात्र्यवयवाश्च सप्तम्यन्ताः क्तान्तेन समस्यन्ते तत्पुरुषश्च समासो भवति। पूर्वाह्णेकृतम् अपराह्णेकृतम् पूर्वरात्रकृतम्। अवयवग्रहणं किम् उलूकल्हलैर् आभरणैः पिशाची यदभाषत एतत्तु ते दिवा नृत्तम् रात्रौ नृत्तम् क्व द्रक्ष्यसि। तत्र। तत्रेत्येतत् सप्तम्यन्तं क्तान्तेन समस्यते तत्पुरुषश्च समासो भवति। तत्रकृतम्। तत्रभुक्तम्। तत्रपीतम्। ऐकपद्यमैकस्वर्यमेकविभक्तित्वं च समासाद् भवति। क्षेपे। क्षेपो निन्दा। क्षेपे गम्यमाने सप्तम्यन्तं क्तान्तेन सह समस्यते तत्पुरुषश्च समासो भवति। अवतप्तेनकुलस्थितम्। चापलमेतत् तवेत्यर्थः । उदकेविशीर्णम्। प्रवाहेमूत्रितम्। भस्मनिहुतम्। निष्फलं यद् क्रियते तदेवमुच्यते। पात्रेसमितादयश्च। समुदाया एव निपात्यन्ते पात्रेसमितादयः शब्दास्तत्पुरुषसंज्ञा भवन्ति क्षेपे गम्यमाने ये चात्र क्तान्तेन सह समस्तास्तेषां पूर्वेणैव सिद्धे वचनमिदं युक्तारोह्यादिपरिग्रहार्थं पूर्वपदाद्युदात्तत्वं यथा स्यादिति। युक्तारोह्यादिषु तु हि पात्रेसमितादयश्चेति पठ्यते। पात्रेसमिताः । पात्रेबहुलाः । आवधारणेन क्षेपो गम्यते पात्र एव समिताः न पुनः क्वचित् कार्य इति। उदुम्बरमषकादिषु तूपमया क्षेपः ।

उप्तगाढम्[*27)]। पूर्वकालस्य[*28)] परनिपातः[*29)]। उलूखलमुसलम्[*30)]।

मातरिपुरुष इति प्रतिषिद्धसेवनेन पिण्डीशूरादिषु निरिहतया अवृत्कृतत्वाद् वाकृतिगणो'यम्। पात्रेसमिताः ।पात्रेबहुलाः ।उदुम्बरमषकः ।उदुम्बरक्रिमिः ।कूपकच्छपः ।कूपमण्डूकः । कुम्भमण्डूकः । नगरकाकः । नगरवायसः । मातरिपुरुषः । पिण्डीशूरः । गेहेक्ष्वेडी। गेहेनर्तकी। गेहेनटी। गेहेविजिति। गेहेव्याथः । गेहेतृप्तः । अहनिकबकः । गोष्ठेशूरः । गोष्ठेविजिति। गोष्ठेक्ष्वेडी। गेहेमेहि। गेहेदाहि। गोष्ठेपटुः । गोष्ठेपण्डितः । गोष्ठेप्रगल्भः । कर्णेटिरिटिरिका। कर्णेदुरुच्चरुका। चकारो'वधारणार्थः । समासान्तरं न भवति। परमपात्रेसमिताः । पूर्वकालैकसर्वजरत्पुराणनवकेवलाः समानाधिकरणेन। सुप्सुपेति वर्तते। तस्य विशेषणं चैतत्। पूर्वकाल एक सर्व जरत् पुराण नव केवल इत्येते सुबन्तास्समानाधिकरणेन सुपा सह समस्यन्ते तत्पुरुषश्च समासो भवति। भिन्नप्रवृत्तिनिमित्तस्य शब्दस्य एकस्मिन् अर्थे वृत्ति सामानाधिकरण्यम्। पूर्वकाल इत्यर्थनिर्देशः । परिशिष्टानां स्वरूपग्रहणम्। पूर्वकालो परकालेन सह समस्यते। स्नातानुलिप्तः ।वृष्टसमीकृतम्। दग्धप्ररूढम्। एकशाटी। एकभिक्षा। सर्वदेवाः ।सर्वभिक्षा। जरस्त्रि। जरधृतिः । पुराणान्नम्। पुराणावसधम्। नवान्नम्। नवावसधम्। केवलम् in D33; cw: अर्पितोदम् in D33, 35; अस्फीत्तमम् in D30, अर्पितोत्तसम् in S1, अर्पितोप्तः in D11, 12, 14, 16; अर्पितोत्तप्तम् in S2, 4; सर्पिर्हेमि in D23; सर्पिर्होमम् in D26; अर्पितोत्तमम् in S3, अर्पितोतम् in B1.

[*27)]om: in D22, M4–6; cw: उप्तगारम् in D6, गुप्तगाठम् in D34, गुप्तगाढम् in D33, 36, 37; गुप्तगूढम् in D30, उप्तगढम् in D18.

[*28)]om: in D22, M12; cw: पूर्ववलस्य in D34, पूर्वकास्य in T3.

[*29)]om: in D22, M12; add: गाधोपगूढम् in T3, भाधोपगृमविम् in G6, : गाधोपद्रधम् मिझ्नास्थि M4, : गाधोपग्रधम् G2, M3, 8, 10, 11; गावोपगूढम् शिझ्नास्थि M6; गाधोपगूढः अशिझ्नास्थि आरग्वायनिबन्धकी गजवाजिनौ आवन्त्यश्मकः पूलासकुण्डकम् आरग्वायनबन्धकी गोपालिधानी पूलासकुण्डक शिरोविङ्ग तण्डुलकिण्वः उलूखलमुसलम् स्नातकराजानौ दृषदुपलम् केशश्मश्रू चित्रास्वाती दारगवा स्थूलपूलासम् लौकारिमतम् अक्षिभ्रुवम् विष्वक्सेनार्जुनौ चित्ररथबाल्हीकम् उशीरबीजम् पुत्रपतिः शब्दार्थौ अर्थकामौ तत् कथम् वक्तव्यम् इदम् धर्मादिषु उभयम् इति भार्यापती पुत्रपशू जम्पति दम्पति भार्याजायाशब्दस्य जम्भावो दम्भावश्च निपात्यते in M5; cw: निपातः in S1, 3; पूर्वनिपातः in S2, 4; परनिपातः in S5 (with पर otl).

[*30)]illegible in G6; om: M4–6; cw: उलूखलमुशलम् in D18, 27, 35; उदूखलमुसलम् in D12; उलूखलमुश in D1; उलूखलमुसुलम् in S3.

तण्डुलकिण्वम्[*31)] । दृषदुपलम्[*32)] । आरग्वायनबन्धकी[*33)] । चित्ररथबाल्हीकम्[*34)] । आवन्त्यश्मकम्[*35)] । शूद्रार्यम्[*36)] । स्नातकराजानौ[*37)] । विष्वक्सेनार्जुनौ[*38)] ।

[*31)]om: in M4–6; cw: तणुलकिवम् in D6; तण्डुलकणम् in D33; तड्डुलकिण्वम् in D31; तण्डुलकिम् in M3; तण्डूलकिण्वम् in D17; तण्दुलकिण्वम् in D21.

[*32)]om: D 30, G2, M3–6 ; cw: पृषदुपलम् in D33, दृष्टदुपलम् in D37, द्रषदुपलम् in D1.

[*33)]om: in D30, M5; add: गजवाजिन् गोपालिधानी in M4; cw: आरग्वायनिबन्धकी in D35, G2, M4; आरदायानबन्धकी in D6; आरखट्वायनिवासन्धकी in D33; आरियनम् ब-न्धुकी in D34; आद्याजनबन्धुकी in D25; : आरग्वायवानान्धकी in D37; आरदायनिबन्धकी in D2, 4, 5, 8; आरग्वायनिबधनी in B1; आरग्वायनिचान्धकी in S1; आरग्वाथनिबान्ध-की in D14, 15; आग्वाथनिबान्धकी in D12; आरदायनबन्धकी in D9; आरग्वाथनवान्धकी in D11; आरव्यायनबन्धकी in D27; आरग्वायवनान्धकी in G6; आरग्वटायानिचाटन्धकी in G4; अरक्षयतवान्धकी in M11; आरज्ञायनिचन्धकी in S4; अरीद्वापनिबन्धकी in D1; आरषान्धकिः in m12; आरक्षायतवान्धकी in M10; जारपतिन्धकी in D23; आरग्वायव-नन्धकी in D36; आरक्षायाटवान्धकी in M8; आरक्षायनः in M3; आट्वायनिबन्धकी M1; आरग्वायनिबन्धकी in D26; आरग्वायनिबान्धकी in D29; आरग्वायनिवान्धकी in D20; आरट्टायनिबन्धकी in D3; आरग्वषनिबानद्यायनवबन्धकी in D22; आरग्वावद्यायनिवाधकी in D18; आरग्वायविहन्धकी in T3; आरग्वाघनिवान्धकी in D17(with र otl); आरज्गाय-निचातकी in S2; आरज्वायनिवाकी in S3; आरध्यायनिवान्धकी in D7; आग्वापनिवान्धकी in D21; आग्व्याधनिवाधकी in D16; आलद्वायनिचल्लकी in S5.

[*34)]page is cut in G2; om: M4, 5; add: उशीरबीजम् पुत्रपति in M6; cw: चित्ररथबा-हिकम् in D36, 37; चित्ररथबाल्हीको in B1; चित्ररथवाल्हीकम् in D11, 12, 14, 16, G4; चित्ररबाल्हीकम् in D23; चित्ररथहाहाकम् in T3; चित्ररथवान्हीकम् in D17; चित्ररथबाल्ह-कम् in S3.

[*35)]om: in G6, M5, 6, T3; add: अधरोष्ठम् in D9, M4; cw: आवन्त्यस्मकम् in D35, आवन्त्यशकम् in D6, G4, अवन्त्यशकम् in D33, 34; अवन्त्याश्मिकम् in D25; अवन्त्यशा-कम् in D37; , आवन्त्याश्मकः in D30; अवन्त्यश्मकम् in D-1, 3, 8, 9, 11, 12, 14, 15, 21, 23, 27, 29; M3, 11; S1, 5; आवन्त्याश्वकम् in M12; आवन्त्यसाकम् in D36; अवन्त्यस्मकम् in D20; अवन्तीस्माकम् D7.

[*36)]om: in B1, D7, M4–6; cw: शूद्राचार्यम् in G4, M11; शूद्रार्थम् in D8, 25; शूद्रार्थः in D30; शूद्रार्यकम् in G2; शूद्रार्ये in D17.

[*37)]om: in B1, M4–6; cw: सूतकराजानौ in D33; स्नातराजानौ in D36, 37, G6, T3.

[*38)]om: in B1, D33, M4–6; cw: विष्वनाक्सेनार्जुनौ in D1; विष्वक्सेना in D5 (with र्जुनौ in Rm), M12.

अक्षिभ्रुवम्[*39)]। दारगवम्[*40)]। शब्दार्थौ[*41)]। धर्मार्थौ[*42)]। कामार्थौ[*43)]। अनियमश्[*44)] चात्रेष्यते[*45)]। अर्थशब्दौ[*46)]। अर्थधर्मौ[*47)]। अर्थकामौ[*48)]। तत्[*49)] कथम्[*50)] वक्तव्यम्[*51)] इदम्[*52)] धर्मादिषु[*53)] उभयम्[*54)] इति[*55)]।

[*39)]illegible till 46 in G1; om: in B1, M4–6; add: उत्तगाढम् in D22; cw: अक्षिभ्रवम् in D37; अक्षिषणुव in D30.

[*40)]om: in B1, D5, M4–6; cw: दारुगवम् in T3.

[*41)]om: in B1, M4, 5; add: अर्थशब्दौ अर्थधर्मौ अर्थकामौ चन्द्रार्कौ अर्कचन्द्रौ आद्यन्तौ अन्तादी भीष्मद्रोणौ द्रोणभीष्मौ चन्द्रादित्यौ आदित्यचन्द्रौ चन्द्रराहू राहुचन्द्रौ ग्रीष्मवसन्तौ वसन्तग्रीष्मौ शुक्रशुची शुचिशुक्रौ करभरासभौ रासभकरभौ गुणवृद्धी वृद्धिगुणौ समीरणाग्नी अग्निसमीरणौ सर्पिर्मधुनी मधुसर्पिषी दीर्घलघु लघुदीर्घौ पाणिनीयरौढीयाः रौढीयपाणिनीयाः अर्जुनभीमसेनौ भीमसेनार्जुनौ कपित्थाश्वत्थौ अश्वत्थकपित्थौ देवापीशंतनु शंतनुदेवापी in D9

[*42)]om: in B1, D8, 9, 23; M3, 4, 5, 8; add: अर्थधर्मौ in M6.

[*43)]om: in B1, D9, 11, 12, 16, 17, 29, 33; G2, 4; M3, 4, 5, 12; add: अर्थकामौ in M6

[*44)]om: in B1, D25, M4–6.

[*45)]om: in B1, D25, M4–6.

[*46)]page is cut in G6; om: B1, D9, 20; M1, 4–6, 12; S3.

[*47)]om: B1, D9, 20, 26; M1, 4–6, 12; S3; add: कामार्थौ in M6.

[*48)]om: B1, D9, 29, 33; G4; M1, 4–6, 12; S3; add: चन्द्रार्कौ अर्कचन्द्रौ आद्यन्तौ अन्तादी भीष्मद्रोणौ द्रोणभीष्मौ चन्द्रादित्यौ आदित्यचन्द्रौ चन्द्रराहू राहुचन्द्रौ ग्रीष्मवसन्तौ वसन्तग्रीष्मौ मुक्तशुची शुचिमुक्तौ करभरासभौ रासभकरभौ गुणवृद्धी वृद्धिगुणौ समीरणाग्नी अग्निसमीरणौ सर्पिर्मधुनी मधुसर्पिषी दीर्घलघु लघुदीर्घौ पाणिनीयरौढीयाः रौढीयपाणिनीयाः अर्जुनभीमसेनौ भीमसेनार्जुनौ कपित्थाश्वत्थौ अश्वत्थकपित्थौ देवापीशंतनु शंतनुदेवापी अनियमश् चात्रेष्यते in D25.

[*49)]om: B1, M4, 5.

[*50)]om: B1, M4, 5, 12 ; add: दंमि in D23 ; 3 illegible letters in S5.

[*51)]om: B1, D23, M4, 5; cw: भवति in S1–5, 7–9.

[*52)]illegible in D8; om: in B1, D23, 33; M1, 4–6, 12, S4, 5, T3.

[*53)]om: in B1, M4, 5; cw: धर्मार्थादिषु in D1, 5, 9, 11, 14, 16–18, 30, 31, 36; M8, 10, 11.

[*54)]om: B1, M4, 5.

[*55)]om: B1, M4, 5.

वैकारिमतम्[*56)] । गजवाजम्[*57)] । गोपालधानीपूलासम्[*58)] । पूलासकुरण्डम्[*59)] । स्थूलपूलासम्[*60)] । उशीरबीजम्[*61)] । सिञ्जास्थम्[*62)] । चित्रास्वाती[*63)] ।

[*56)]om: B1, M4–6; cw: वेकारिकमतम् in D35, M3; वैकारिकमतम् in D-1–7, 11, 12, 14–17, 29, 36, 37; G1, 2, 4; M1, 8, 10, 12; S4, T3; वैयाकरणमतम् in D9, 20, 23, 25, 26, 31, 34; वैराकिकिमतम् in D33; वैकारिकतम् in D28, M11; वैकायिकमतम् in D8; वैकारिकतमम् in D27; बौधकारिमतम् in D22; वैयाकारिणकमतम् in D18; वैधकारिमतम् in D21.

[*57)]om: B1, M4–6; cw: गोजविजम् in D35, G1; गोजवाजम् in D1, 4-7, 11, 12, 14–17, 25, 27, 29, 31; गोजाविजम् in D34, 36, 37, G2, 4, 6 ; T3; गोजाविकम् in D33, S2–5, 7–9; गोजविकम् S1; गोचवाजम् in D2, 4; गाजवाजम् in D8; गजवाजि in D30, M8, 11, 12; गोवाविकम् in D23; गजवाजिम् in M1; गोवालम् in D22.

[*58)]om: B1, D30, M4, 5: cw: गोवालिधानि in D35; गोवालधानि in S5; गोवालधानी in D1, 6, 7, 11, 12, 15–18; गोपालधानी D2–5, 9, 14, 26, 31, 34; M1, 8, 10, 11; गोपालिपान in D33; गोआलधानी in D25; गोवालिधान्यपूला in D37; गोपालधानीपूलास in G2; गोपालधान्य in S1, 2, 3; गोपालधान्यपूलासी in S5, गोपालिधानम् in D8; गोपाल-धानम् in M3; गोपालिधान्य in G6, T3; गोपालिधानी in G4; गोपालधानी (illegible) G1; गोपालधीनी M23; गोवालिधान्यपूलासम् in D36; गोवालधानम् in D29; गोपालीधानीपूला-सकरण्डकम् in D22; गोवालाभिधानी in D20; गोवालीलीधानी D21.

[*59)]om: B1, D22, 30, M5; cw: पूलाषकरण्डम् in D6; पूलासकरण्डकम् in D20, 21, 29, 33, 34; M1; पूलाषकरण्टकम् in D25; सकरण्डम् in D36, 37; पूलासककरण्डम् D28; पलासकरण्डम् in D2; पूलासकुरण्डकम् in S1; पूलासोकुरण्डकम् in S5; पूलासकुरम्भिकम् in D9; पूलासम् कुरण्ड in D8; पूलासकुरण्यनम् in G6.

[*60)]om: in B1, G6, M5, 6, T3; add: लैकारिमतम् अक्षिभ्रुवम् विष्वक्सेनार्जुनौ चित्ररथबा-ल्हीकम् उशीरबीजम् पुत्रपती दिष्टभयम् इति in M4; स्थालीपूलासम् D21; cw: स्थलपूलासम् in D12, 14, 16, 17, 25, 27; S1, M10; फलपलाशम् D30; स्थलप्रपलासम् in D4; स्थूलप्र-जासम् in D2; स्थलीकुलासम् in M3; cpw: M4 (after चित्रास्वाती which follows).

[*61)]om: B1, M4, 5; add: शक्ष्य D33; जिज्ञास्थि in D31; cw: उसीरबीजम् in D18, 20, 33; उशीरवीजम् in 12; उशश्वीरबीजम् G6; उशीरपूलीलम् in G1; उशीरवीणम् in S3.

[*62)]om: B1, D20, 22, 33; M4–6; add: तमालसिक्तरम्यम् in D3; cw: सिजास्थम् in D35; सिञ्जाश्वथम् in D7, 9, 12, 13, 15–18, 25, 27, 31, 34; सञ्जाश्वथम् in D11; शीताश्वर्यम् in D6; सिक्षास्थि in D23, 37, G4; भिक्षास्थि in D26; सिक्षास्थिम् in D36; शिक्षास्थि in G1, 2, 6, S5, T3; राजस्थलम् in D30; तिक्ताश्वथम् in D2–5, तिक्तावत्थम् in D1; सिक्षास्ति in S1; शिक्षास्ति in D29, S2, 3; चिञ्चास्थलम् in M8, 11; सिञ्जास्थिम् in S4; शिखास्थयम् in M12; शिक्षास्थलम् in M1; शिक्षास्थालम् in M10; शिञ्जास्थम् in M3.

[*63)]om: in B1, M5, 6; add: दार्गवम् in M4; cw: चित्रस्वाती in D35; चितास्वाती in D6; चित्रास्वादी in G1; कुरण्डकम् in G2; पूलीसकुरण्डम् in D1; ककरण्डम् in M12; पूला-सककुरण्टकम् in D23; पूलासुकुरुण्डम् in M3; पूलासकुरुण्डनम् in T3; पूलासीकुरुण्डकम् in

भार्यापती[*64)] । जायापती[*65)] । जम्पती[*66)] । दम्पती[*67)] । जायाशब्दस्य[*68)] जम्भावो[*69)] दम्भावश्च[*70)] निपात्यते[*71)] । पुत्रपती[*72)] । पुत्रपशू[*73)] । केशश्मश्रू[*74)] । श्मश्रुकेशौ[*75)] । शिरोबीजम्[*76)] । सर्पिर्मधुनी[*77)] । मधुसर्पिषी[*78)] । आद्यन्तौ[*79)] । अन्तादी[*80)] । गुणवृद्धी[*81)] । वृद्धिगुणौ[*82)] ॥

S2, 3; कुकरण्डकम् in S4; पूलासकुण्डकम् in M6; अलासकरण्डम् in M11;

[*64)]om: in D18, M5, S1–5, 6–9; add: पुत्रपशू in M4, 5.

[*65)]om: in B1, D7, 14, 30, 35; M5; जायापती in Rm in D29.

[*66)]page cut in G6 upto 70; om: in B1, D1, 2, G1, M3, 5, 6; cw: ज in S1; cpw: after दम्पती which follows D20–22.

[*67)]om: in B1, G1, S3, 4, M5; add: दम्पती in D35.

[*68)]page cut in D17; om: in B1, D33, M5, S3; cw: जायाशब्दश्चस्य in G1; जायाया in D22.

[*69)]om: in B1, M5; cw: जम्भावश्च in M6; जम् in M4.

[*70)]om: in B1, M5, 6.

[*71)]om: in B1, M5; add: पुत्रपशा in D35; जम्पती in G1; cw: निपाद्यते in G1; निपात्यतते in D8; निपात्येति in G6.

[*72)]om: in B1, D9, M5, 6; cw: युवपती in D23-26; cpw: in D36, 37 after पुत्रपशू which follows.

[*73)]om: in B1, D35, M5, 6; cw: पुत्रपशु in D26.

[*74)]om: in B1, M5, 6; cw: केशश्मश्रुणी in D2, 4–6; केशश्मश्रुकेणी in D1; केशस्मश्रू in D22.

[*75)]om: in B1; D7, 8, 10, 11, 12, 14, 16, 23, 29, 30, 35, 36; G1, 4; M1, 3, 6, 11, 12.

[*76)]om: in B1, D27, G1, M5, 6; add: शिक्षास्थि काकमयूरम् in D25; शिक्षाण्डि काकमयूरम् in D9; शिक्षास्थि in D20; शिषास्थि in D21; cw: सरोबीजम् in D16; शिरोधीजम् in S5; शिरोवीजुः in D33 ; शिरोविज in D30 ; शिरोग्रीवम् in D9, S1–4, 7–9; श्रोग्रीवम् in D8; शिरोवीजम् in G4; शिरोवबीजम् in D1; शिरो शिखास्थि in M12; शिरोवजू in D21

[*77)]om: in B1, D9, 25: cw: सर्पिमधुनी D12, 15, 27, 28, 30, 35; S1. सपिमधुनी in D6; सर्पिर्मधु in D33.

[*78)]om: in B1; D9, 25, 35; S3; cw: मधुसर्पिषि in D33; । मधुसमर्पिषी in D1.

[*79)]page cut in D17; om: in B1, D9, 25; cw: आद्यन्तम् in D33.

[*80)]om: in B1, D9, 25, 30; cw: अन्तदी in D6, 11, 35; अन्तादि in D1.

[*81)]om: in B1, D9, 25.

[*82)]om: in B1, D9, 25, 30; cw: वृद्धीगुणौ in D1, 2, 4, 11, 12, 15, 28, 33, 35, 37.

III

Important Notes on some variants and discussion

1

It is quite clear that not all the variants noted down carry equal weight. Some variants can be easily dispensed with as scribal errors and hence very minor errors. For example, **pūrvanapāte* in place of *pūrvanipāte* as noted in *2 is a case of such a sribal error. Moreover, a long addition noted in *26 which contains the text of KV on P.2.1.43–P.2.1.49 can as well be regarded as a minor variant. This variant reproduces the text of KV on P.2.1.43, which starts in between, continues upto P.2.1.49 and ends abruptly without going to the end of the text of KV on 2.1.49. However, the entire text of this variation had to be reproduced as it might contain a piece of variation on the text of the *Kāśikāvṛtti* on P.2.1.43–P.2.1.49. It was, however, kept in mind as a policy that other seeming errors of scribal omission in terms of *n* > *ṇ*, *s* > *ś*, *b* > *v*, etc. need to be handled carefully, as in a grammatical text such variations could ultimately prove to be major variations. Thus *agrevaṇam*, when found to be *agrevanam*, is considered to be an important variant and is rated slightly above **pūrvanapāte*. The most important variants, however, are:

1. Those for which independent evidence is available to ascertain the exact nature of the text;
2. Those found in a list of words in the form of words and statements.

2

2.1. Examination of material: variants 1
P.2.2.31 is not commented upon in the *Mahābhāṣya*, which removes the possibility of the existence of this *gaṇa* as such in commentaries of the *Mahābhāṣya*, like the *Pradīpa* and the commentaries thereupon. The first and foremost important independent source of information about the *sūtra* is the two commentaries of the *Kāśikāvṛtti*, *Nyāsa* and *Padamañjarī*. These two commentaries offer an invaluable aid to us in that they give the *pratīka*s of the *Kāśikāvṛtti* in the form of statements as well as words listed. A glance at the texts of both these commentaries, presented in Appendix III, supports the following observations:

1. They show awareness of certain words as members of the *rājadantādi-gaṇa*;
2. They know a certain order of the words;
3. They show some awareness of the demarcation of words within the *gaṇa*;

4. They recognize that certain compounds included in the *gaṇa* can be left out because the order of their constituents can be accounted for by other *sūtras*;
5. The *Nyāsa* and the *Padamañjarī* show awareness of readings in the text of the *Kāśikāvṛtti*.

2.1.1

Let us first consider the fifth point.

Variant *12 shows that the *Padamañjarī* definitely knows that there are two readings: *vihitapūrvanipātasya* and *vihitasya pūrvanipātasya*. The first reading is a compounded form while the second one is not. Although explaining the formation of the compound, most importantly, the *Padamañjarī* passes judgement on a reading to be accepted. According to the *Padamañjarī*, the second reading *vihitasya pūrvanipātasya* is generally accepted.

If we look at the mss data, we notice that indeed the majority of the mss have the reading which the *Padamañjarī* says is predominant. However, there are other mss as well which do record a reading which according to the *Padamañjarī* is less acceptable. There are 10 such mss: 1 written in B, 7 in D, 1 in M and 1 in S. The dates of some of them are available. The following is the table of dates of these mss.

No.	Mss	Date (CE)
1	B1	17th c.
2	D11	-
3	D12	-
4	D16	-
5	D17	1258
6	D25	1632
7	D29	1408
8	D33	-
9	M1	1547
10	S1	1660

Except for the 10 mss, all the other mss seem to have accepted the reading preferred by the *Padamañjarī*. D17 is the oldest dated available ms used in my editing above. We can claim from this fact that there is a stream of mss within the material consulted which shows its link with a version of the *Kāśikāvṛtti* different from the one known to the *Padamañjarī*. If the *Padamañjarī* is dated in the 11th century, this link becomes more probable as our oldest ms is not far in time from the *Padamañjarī*. We can clearly say that these mss do seem to show a feature, namely the preservation of an independent mss tradition, when a celebrated author like Haradatta clearly records that the generally accepted reading is something else. This can indeed be a very useful clue in showing interrelations of mss.

2.2. Examination of material: variants 2

Now let us consider points 1–4.

The following are the words which, according to the *Nyāsa* and the *Padamañjarī*, are certainly members of the *rājadantādigaṇa*:

No.	Description	Words
1	Directly quoted by both	3 (*dṛṣadupalam, akṣibhruvam, dāragavam*)
2	Directly quoted by N but not by Pm as *pratīka*	1 (*sthūlapūlāsam*)
3	Directly quoted by Pm but not by N as *pratīka*	1 (*agrevaṇam*)
4	Mentioned only by N as member of this *gaṇa*	2 (*liptavāsitam, uptagāḍham*)
5	Mentioned only by Pm as a member of this *gaṇa*	–
6	Mentioned by both as a member of the *gaṇa*	1 (*ulūkhalamusalam*)
7	Not explicitly mentioned by both but can be inferred from the existing statements of either (with no certainty about sequence in occurrence, but at least one member of each item)	5 (*nagnamuṣitam, siktasammṛṣṭam, mṛṣṭaluñcitam, avaklinnapakvam, arpitoptam*)[13] 4 (*bhāryāpatī,*[14] *śūdrāryam,*[15] *taṇḍulakiṇvam,*[16] *citrāsvātī*[17])
8	Not quoted by both as a member of this *gaṇa* but stated in the sūtra, quoted by both N and Pm	1 (*rājadantaḥ*)

[13] *liptavāsitādyuptagāḍhaparyanteṣu.* See Appendix III (N).

[14] *kvacid ghyantatvāt.* See Appendix III (Pm).

[15] *kvacid ajādyadantatvāt.* See Appendix III (Pm).

[16] *tatra kvacid alpāctaratvāt.* See Appendix III (Pm).

[17] *kvacit tulyatvād aniyamaḥ.* See Appendix III (N).

Thus we can be sure that at least 18 words are members of this *gaṇa*, on the basis of the statements made by the *Nyāsa* and the *Padamañjarī*.

2.2.1

Even a cursory glance at the variants recorded from the mss tradition reveals that most of the mss tradition does follow the *Nyāsa* and the *Padamañjarī* on the membership of the 18 words. We notice that many more words, 31 maximum, are added to the *gaṇa*. This suggests that, as pointed out by Kapila Deva Shastri (1967: 65), by the time of the *Kāśikāvṛtti* the number of interpolations must have considerably increased.

Almost all mss, with few exceptions, do show the existence of all the 18 words. The few mss that do not have those words are very important for our analysis. There are 4 such mss: B1 and M4–6. They can be shown to be following a certain pattern after comparing various other passages in the *Kāśkāvṛtti*.[18] The number of words found in B1 and M4–6 are 14 and 33 respectively. If we look at B1, we see that it contains even less number of words than the *Nyāsa* and the *Padamañjarī*. Of these 14 words, 11 are known to the *Nyāsa* and the *Padamañjarī* and 3 (11–13 in Appendix V) are not. The *Nyāsa* and the *Padamañjarī* have 18 words. Thus 7 words, which are known to the *Nyāsa* and the *Padamañjarī*, are not members of the *gaṇa* in B1. Now if we look at the 3 other mss, we come to know that only 8 (1, 2, 3, 4, 5, 6, 16, 19 in Appendix V) of these 33 words are the ones known to the *Nyāsa* and the *Padamañjarī*. This fact can be said to represent the tradition which was pre-Nyāsa/Padamañjarī or an independent tradition not known to either the *Nyāsa* or the *Padamañjarī*.

The other explanation is that the 4 mss represented the tradition that was influenced by the remarks of the two commentaries about the unnecessary membership of words in this *gaṇa*. The *Nyāsa* mentions two such words: *dṛṣadupalam* and *sthūlapulāsam* and the *Padamañjarī* three: *dṛṣadupalam*, *akṣibhruvam*, and *dāragavam*.[19] Thus in all there are four such words about whose membership strong objections were raised by the *Nyāsa* and the *Padamañjarī*. We notice that B1 does mention *dṛṣadupalam* but not the other three and that M4–6 mention *sthūlapulāsam* but not the other three. Thus we see that the words to whose membership to this *gaṇa* was objected by the *Nyāsa* are available in B1 and M4–6, but none of the two whose membership to the *gaṇa* was denied by the *Padamañjarī* found their place in the *gaṇa* in these mss. This is very significant. It may strengthen the point that these mss do represent partly the tradition which was influenced by the remarks of the *Padamañjarī*. We say 'partly' because not all words known to the *Nyāsa* and the *Padamañjarī* as members of this *gaṇa* are found

[18] See Kulkarni 2000a; 2000b; forthcoming.

[19] See Appendix III.

in B1 and M4–6. We have to conclude that these two groups of mss represent in themselves partly a tradition that can be called 'pre-Nyāsa/Padamañjarī' and partly influenced by both. Except for B1 and M4–6, all other mss have the 4 words in question. It seems that they were not under the influence of the remarks of the *Nyāsa* and the *Padamañjarī*.

It is important to note that of the 33 words mentioned in M4–6 only the first and last 6 words are accepted as members of this *gaṇa* by all the three mss. In the case of the remaining 21 middle words there is no uniformity among the three mss. These words are found in any two of the three mss of this group. Mostly M5 seem to be omitting these 21 middle words consistently. It is possible to say that this indicates another intermediary stage in the development of the size of this *gaṇa*.

A further important feature is the omission of the following 10 words:

> *śabdārthau, dharmārthau, kāmārthau, arthaśabdau, arthadharmau, arthakāmau, ādyantau, antādī, guṇavṛddhī, vṛddhiguṇau.*

B1 does not record all these words. We have to note that except for *śabdārthau* and *arthaśabdau*, all other words are given as examples of the vārttika on P.2.2.34 in the *Mahābhāṣya*.[20] As Kapila Deva Shastri puts it (1967: 289):

> Nāgeśa regards the expression *dharmādiṣūbhayam* to be a *gaṇa-sūtra* under the *Rājadantādi-gaṇa*. But in the *Mahābhāṣya*, it is treated and explained as a *Vārtika*, and words from *śabdārthau* to *artha-dharmau* and from *ādyantau* to *vṛddhi-guṇau* of this *gaṇa* are given as illustration. This shows that after Patañjali, the so called sūtra and the aforesaid words got mixed up with the *gaṇa* by commentators.

B1 seems to represent a tradition which does not know that the words quoted in the *Mahābhāṣya* are members of this *gaṇa*. M4–6 do not have the first 6 words. But they do have the last four. Thus the 3 mss can be said to show an intermediary stage where some words discussed in the *Mahābhāṣya* were not yet members of the *gaṇa* as found in the text of the *Kāśikāvṛtti* and at the same time some words discussed in the *Mahābhāṣya* had already become members of the *gaṇa* as found in the text of the *Kāśikāvṛtti*.

2.2.2

Now if we look at some peculiar words in this *gaṇa*, especially the ones which are not in the list of words known to the *Nyāsa* and the *Padamañjarī*, and compare with the lists preserved in other mss traditions, we may be able to

[20]Mbh (I.437).

throw some more light on another stage of development of the size of this *gaṇa*. In this case, the other traditions are the sources presented in Appendix II: quotations culled from the *Gaṇaratnamahodadhi* (1140 CE) and the *Nyāsānusandhāna* on the *Siddhahaimaśabdānuśāsana* with its commentary *Svopajñatattvaprakāśikāprakāśa* (12th century CE)[21] and the *Nyāsa*.

These sources reveal that the following 5 words are members of the *rājadantādi gaṇa*. They are:

> *uśīrabījam, siñjāstham, siñjāśvattham, āraṭvāyanibandhakī, citrarathabāhlīkam.*

The word *uśīrabījam* is accepted by the mss tradition with minor variations in very few mss. So also is the case with *citrarathabāhlīkam*. The word *siñjāśvattham*, however, is not found in the mss tradition except in 11 D mss. The 11 mss can not be said to share features consistently. Among them is the oldest available ms, D 17 (1258 CE). Hemacandra says that it is not proper to state this word in the *gaṇa*. He remarks that this word could have entered the *gaṇa* by a scribal error. This remark indicates the following:

a. The *gaṇa* received by Hemachandra as a Pāṇinīya *gaṇa* had this word;
b. Probably he had access to at least two mss of the *Kāśikāvṛtti* and compared them;
c. He found out that this reading *siñjāśvattham* was not supported uniformally by the mss tradition.

Further, we notice that this reading *siñjāśvattham* has not received any support in other mss written in D or mss written in other scripts. All these facts render the value of this reading sub-regional.

In the case of *āraṭvāyanibandhakī*, there are three similar readings found in the *Gaṇaratnamahodadhi*:

> 1. *āraṭvāyanibandhakī*, 2. *āraṭvāyanicāndhanī* and 3. *āraṭvāyanibandhanī.*

The *Gaṇaratnamahodadhi* derives *āraṭvāyanicāndhanī* from two words: *āraṭvāyani* and *cāndhani*. None of the extant mss of the *Kāśikāvṛtti* knows of the three words. Therefore, we may deduce the following:

a. The known mss tradition of the *Kāśikāvṛtti* did not come into contact with the *Gaṇaratnamahodadhi*;
b. It did not come into contact with that ms whose reading is recorded in the *Gaṇaratnamahodadhi* as Pāṇini's.

[21] Belvalkar 1976: 73.

There are 40 different variations of *āragvāyanabandhakī*. We notice that there are only three cases where the same variant is copied down: 1) *āragvāyanibandhakī* is copied in D35, G2 and M4; 2) *āradāyanibandhakī* in D2, 4, 5 and 8; 3) *āragvāthanibāndhakī* in D14 and 15. All other variations are found in single mss.

We notice that B1 is the only ms that reads *arpitotam* in place of *arpitoptam*. The reading found in B1 is attested only in the *Gaṇaratnamahodadhi*.

These particulars make it clear that the readings of the mss tradition that has come down to us can indeed be confirmed by two external sources (the *Gaṇaratnamahodadhi* and the *Nyāsānusandhāna*) to a significant extent. However, the sources do not show any direct awareness of the words as members of the *gaṇa* except for a few words. We also notice that the words which are now found in the *gaṇa* and which are not explicitly supported by the *Nyāsa* and the *Padamañjarī* are found in the *gaṇa* as preserved in the specified sources. It is also plain that B1 and M4–6 do not have some words as members of the *gaṇa* which are found in the *Nyāsa* and the *Padamañjarī*. But we have to note that there is no adequate evidence available to us to determine why the relevant mss omit those words which are acknowledged by the *Nyāsa* and the *Padamañjarī* or why the same mss omit words found in other sources like the *Gaṇaratnamahodadhi*.

2.2.3

Further we notice that D4 and D25 add a list of 32 words at variant *41 and *48. The words added by the two mss are:

> *candrārkau arkacandrau ādyantau antādī bhīṣmadroṇau droṇabhīṣmau candrādityau ādityacandrau candrarāhū rāhucandrau grīṣmavasantau vasantagrīṣmau muktaśucī śucimuktau karabharāsabhau rāsabhakarabhau guṇavṛddhī vṛddhiguṇau samīraṇāgnī agnisamīraṇau sarpirmadhunī madhusarpiṣī dīrghalaghu laghudīrghau pāṇinīyaraudhīyāḥ rauḍhīyapāṇinīyāḥ arjunabhīmasenau bhīmasenārjunau kapitthāśvatthau aśvatthakapitthau devāpīśaṁtanu śaṁtanudevāpī.*

These words are similar to *dharmārthau* and *arthadharmau* mentioned in the *gaṇa* by the *Kāśikāvṛtti*. We notice that some of the already accepted pairs of words like *ādyantau antādī*, *guṇavṛddhī vṛddhiguṇau* and *sarpirmadhunī madhusarpiṣī* are listed here. Except for these 6, the other 26 can be said to be fresh additions. It is to be noted that all these 26 words are indeed noted by the *Gaṇaratnamahodadhi*. These are not accepted by the main stream mss tradition and have been kept out of the Pāṇinian tradition.

However, we cannot deny the possibility that these additions made under the influence of the *Gaṇaratnamahodadhi* might have come in as part of the text of the KV and got absorbed into the tradition of mss so much that not even a trace of their earlier unacceptability remains behind.[22]

On the basis of the above discussion, we can show the stages of composition of the *rājadantādigaṇa* in the following way:

Layer	Description
1	Pre/independent of N and Pm, without any influence of Mbh
2	Known to N and Pm
3	Words known to Mbh
4	Words known to GRM and a subcommentary on *Siddhahaimaśabdānuśāsana*
5	Words that can be said to have been added because of contact with other traditions

It is to be noted that there is not a single ms which represents any of these stages independently and completely. We have to admit that we have received this *gaṇa* through the extant mss tradition of the *Kāśikāvṛtti* in such a way that all these layers are removed and one consolidated list of words remains.

[22]Kulkarni (2003), discussing such a case, has shown by means of using the available dates how a reading which was earlier given on the margin had later become part of the main text of the *Kāśikāvṛtti* and how, on account of the remarks of the *Śabdakaustubha*, the later mss tradition removed such a reading from the main body of the text of the *Kāśikāvṛtti*.

IV

Stemma: P.2.2.31

1. The text of KV on P.2.2.31 presented here is admittedly not different from the one available in the Osmania edition of the *Kāśikāvṛtti*. There are many instances where the text of the *Kāśikāvṛtti* edited with mss used in this paper matches exactly with the one available in the Osmania edition. But this cannot be considered to be a problem as we notice that an increased number of mss actually strengthen the readings adopted in the Osmania edition and provide a decisive clue about the common ancestor of the mss used.

KV on P.2.2.6 *nañ* is an important instance in this regard, which has been discussed in Kulkarni 2005. Except for 8 mss (D1–7 and S6), all other mss do not have in the body of the text of the *Kāśikāvṛtti* the following *vārttika* and its example:

> *naño nalopas tiṅi kṣepe | apacasi tvaṁ jālma |*

All the printed editions except for Osmania and Bahalgarh do have this *vārttika* in the main body of the text of the *Kāśikāvṛtti*. Kulkarni (2002), discussing the possible reasoning behind the addition of this *vārttika* in the 8 mss and a number of printed editions, has concluded that the reading in the Osmania edition is justified. It has also been shown in Kulkarni 2005 that the group of 8 mss, which adds the above-mentioned *vārttika*, is of the later period, the 19th century, that the 8 mss do not share any other variant exclusively as a group, and that we can postulate a source ms for the 8 mss to account exclusively for this addition.

Further, it has been shown in Kulkarni (2000a) that the first ever printed edition of the *Kāśikāvṛtti* uses 3 mss, one of which is traced as S6 which appears in the group of 8 mss adding this *vārttika*. On the basis of these facts, we can now trace how the addition entered in the main body of the text of the *Kāśikāvṛtti* in the first ever printed edition. The later editions of the *Kāśikāvṛtti* were based on the first edition and hence kept reprinting the *vārttika* in the text of KV on P.2.2.6. The Osmania edition also used the first edition of the KV as its source. But this edition used some mss in which the *vārttika* was not found in the main body of the text of the *Kāśikāvṛtti*, so that it does not have the *vārttika* there.[23]

2. The variant readings we have discussed give us a clue as to the common ancestor of all the mss that we have used. 62 mss—6 in Grantha, 12 in Malayalam, 4 in Telugu, 1 in Begali, 1 in Nandināagarī, 8 out of 9 in Śāradā,

[23] See Kulkarni 2002; 2005.

and 10 out of 37 in Devanāgarī—do point towards a common ancestor. The addition found in the remaining 8 mss (D1–7 and S6) points towards another source which has to be considered relatively very modern. The addition is seen supported neither by the oldest known mss written in each of the scripts nor by any external evidence that it is mentioned in the *Nyāsa* and the *Padamañjarī* and in the quotations of the *Kāśikāvṛtti* found in other texts. This reduces the value of the addition and that of the source which added it. It has been shown in Kulkarni (2007) that S6 can be said to share some common features not only with all the remaining mss written in Śāradā script but also with another source which could be related to the source adding the *vārttika* to the text.

Kulkarni (2000) has shown that all the mss, including the 8 mentioned above, share a common variant in the text of KV on P.2.2.4. They have *vidhānasāmarthyāt* in place of *samāsavidhānāt*. This reading points towards a common ancestor of all the mss. We name it *The KV*.

Kulkarni (2000) has discussed several other significant variants which force us to postulate common sources from which certain mss are seen to have been copied down. Kulkarni (2000) has presented a list of all dated mss, which is presented below in a reformulated way:

Dates (CE)	Name of ms
1258	D17
1408	D29
1443	D28
1479–86	D15
1478–1538	D19
1533	D35
1547	M1
1632	D24, 25
1660	S1
17th century	B1
1732	D20
1756	D13
1769	D5
18th century	D30
18th century	D31
18th–19th century	S4
18th century	D21
1809	S6
1863–64	D4
1867	D1
1868	D2
1868–69	D37

Now let us consider the following points pertaining to the present edition of KV on P.2.2.31 which are helpful in determining a stemma of all the mss used.

1. Addition of *ghyāder/vyāghrāder* in *10.
2. *vihita-* in place of *vihitasya* in *12.
3. Omission of *ayam apavādaḥ* in *13 and *14.
4. Omission of *śmaśrukeśau* in *75.

1. Addition of *ghyāder/vyāghrāder* in *10
The adopted reading runs as follows:

> *na kevalam upasarjanasya anyasyāpi yathālakṣaṇaṃ vihitasya pūrvanipātasya ayam apavādaḥ paranipāto vidhīyate* |

The word *ghyāder/vyāghrāder* occurs after *anyasyāpi*. The sentence states, as the purpose of P.2.2.31, that this *sūtra* is an *apavāda* of the other *sūtras* stated in the section P.2.2.30–38. P.2.2.32 *dvandve ghi* states that in a *dvandva* compound the word termed as *ghi* takes prior position. P.2.2.33 *ajādyadantam* states that in a dvandva compound the word which begins with a vowel and ends in short *a* takes prior position. The sentence under discussion says that P.2.2.31 is an *apavāda* to all such conditions stated in P.2.2.32, 33 and so on. It is natural, therefore, that the sentence has a word referring to such conditions mentioned in *sūtras* from P.2.2.32 onwards of which P.2.2.31 is an *apavāda*. However, we also notice that this reading is not supported by either the *Nyāsa* or the *Padamañjarī*, though the *Padamañjarī* mentions this word in its effort to explain the meaning of the sentence in question. The reading *anyasyāpi ghyāder* is found in the group of 22 mss. Thus we may postulate a common source for all the 22 mss. It is to be noted that, out of the 22, 3 mss (D17, D29 and M1) preserve the variant known to the *Padamañjarī* discussed earlier.[24] We have shown that D17 is the oldest known ms used for this edition. We will have to show that the 22 mss have one common source.

The group of 3 Śāradā mss (S2, 3 and 5) has the addition *vyāghrāder*. This addition is found with a minor variation in another group of 3 mss (S1, 4 and M6), two of which are written in Śāradā script. It is important that the reading, though obviously an interpolated one, helps to show a relation between mss written in Śāradā script.

[24]See 2.1.1.

2. *vihita-* in place of *vihitasya* in *12

As mentioned before, the variant *vihitapūrvanipātasya* is found in 10 mss.[25] The importance of this variant forces us to postulate a common source from which 10 mss must have been copied. It is to be noted that, out of the 10 mss, 2 mss—from M and S—are the oldest known mss and that these 2 mss share several other features with other mss from M and S. We do not see the particular reading *vihitapūrvanipātasya* copied from the 2 mss by the remaining ones in the respective scripts.

3. Omission of *ayam apavādaḥ* in *13 and *14

The omission of *ayam apavādaḥ* in *13 and *14 is found in mss written in almost all the scripts except for N. We can thus call the reading without *ayam apavādaḥ* 'a pan-indian reading'. It is noteworthy that the omission is present in all mss written in S. The reading without the phrase certainly shows a common source for all the 48 mss.

4. Omission of *śmaśrukeśau* in *75

The omission in question is found in a number of manuscripts in all scripts. Moreover most of the mss which omit the word *śmaśrukeśau* omit *ayam apavādaḥ* also.

Of the four points made above, point 2 is the most significant, as it is discussed in the *Padamañjarī*.

3. On the basis of the preceding points, we can construct the stemma of the mss used for the present edition. As regards KV on P.2.2.31, on the basis of words which do not have any variation at all and the other words which have minor scribal errors, we can postulate that all the mss emanate from one common source. We can get further support for this postulation from the variants found in other parts of KV on P.2.2. Concerning KV on P.2.2.6, it has been shown that all the mss except for 8 do not have a *vārttika* in the text, from which it follows that all the mss emanate from one common source, and that the remaining 8 mss can also be shown to have another source which is relatively modern.

Let us now construct a stemma for the mss whose dates are known to us. The following table should give us a clear picture of what the dated mss tell us about the four significant variants mentioned above.

---

[25] See §2.1.1.

Date (CE)	Ms	1. addition of *ghyāder* /*vyāghrāder* in *10	2. *vihita* in place of *vihitasya* in *12	3. omission of *ayam apavādaḥ* in *13 and *14	4. omission of *śmaśrukeśau* in *75
1258	D17	Y	Y	N	N
1408	D29	Y	Y	Y	Y
1443	D28	N	N	Y	N
1479–86	D15	Y	N	N	N
1478–1538	D19	N	N	N	N
1533	D35	Y	N	Y	Y
1547	M1	Y	Y	Y	Y
1632	D24	N	N	Y	N
1632	D25	Y	Y	Y	N
1660	S1	N	Y	Y	N
17th c.	B1	N	Y	Y	Y
1732	D20	N	N	Y	N
1756	D13	N	N	N	N
1769	D5	N	N	N	N
18th c.	D30	Y	N	Y	Y
18th c.	D31	Y	N	Y	N
18th c.	D21	N	N	Y	N
18–19th c.	S4	N	N	Y	N
1809	S6	N	N	Y	N
1863–64	D4	N	N	Y	N
1867	D1	N	N	Y	N
1868	D2	N	N	Y	N
1868–69	D37	N	N	Y	N

(Y refers to the presence of the variant and N refers to the absence of the same variant.)

If we focus on #2, the most significant variant, we can construct the following tree:

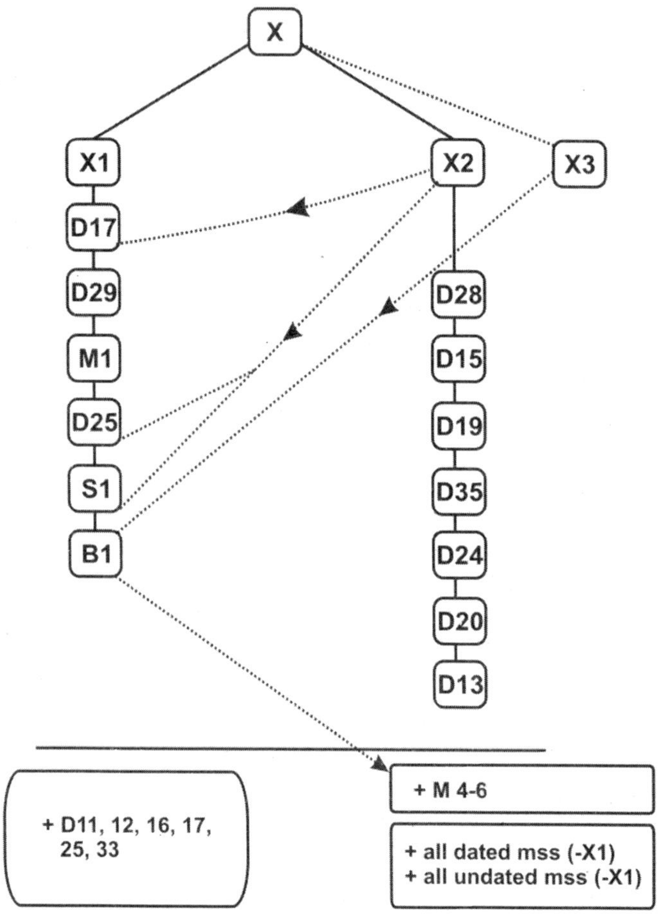

In this tree, X1 refers to the tradition of mss which was known to the *Padamañjarī* and X2 refers to that which the *Padamañjarī* followed as a generally accepted tradition. We can place X1 in the 11th century or even before the 11th century on the basis of the date of the *Padamañjarī*. Now we can add all the undated mss on either side. Then if we focus on #1 and the dated mss, we see that till 1632 mss from X1 have one reading. But from 1660 onwards mss from the same postulated source have the reading of X2. So they must be shown to be related to X2. Further, if we look at variants #3 and #4, we notice that several mss from X1 copy readings of X2. Therefore the relation of X1 to X2 has to be shown in the tree. We have to note that D29 and M1 follow X1 in all details. These two remain unrelated to X2.

All the four variants occur in D29 (1408) and M1 (1547). It is noteworthy that 'no occurrence' of any of these four variants is found in D19 (1478–1538), D13 (1756) and D5 (1769). We notice that from 18th century onwards a uniform picture is given as far as the four variants are concerned.

In the edited text of the KV, we have the reading which is said to be generally acceptable to Pm, in other words, to X2. However, the development of X2 is a complicated matter and will be taken up for detailed discussion in the future.

Thus, in the compiling of the *rājadantādigaṇa*, we notice that we have the evidence that B1 belongs to X1. In addition, M4–6, which can be said to be following X2 with respect to variant #1, can be shown to be related to X1 through B1. We also notice that B1, D25 and M4–6 share the omission of the statement *aniyamaś cātreṣyate* in the *gaṇa*. In order to account for the common features, we may postulate X3 which can be shown to be related with the *Gaṇaratnamahodadhi*, as discussed in Appendix III.

4. I have restricted myself to a general tree. For a detailed tree, a few more variants, such as *22 and *23 in D, which point towards certain common sources within the same script mss and inter-script mss, such as *17 in B and S, will have to be taken into consideration.

I have not presented variants by grouping the mss sharing common features and labeling them with a certain siglum. After studying evidence presented in Kulkarni (2000) and Deo (2001),[26] I have come to the conclusion that different and more complicated grouping patterns are visible among the mss of the *Kāśikāvṛtti* on the different sections of the *Aṣṭādhyāyī*. Thus, the evidence given in Appendix III shows that we may group M4–6 together in the tree which shows interelation of mss of KV on P.2.2.31. But Haag and Vergiani (2009) do not group them together, They have not shown that the mss are related directly to one another.

[26]Both are not referred to by Haag and Vergiani 2009.

IV

Conclusion

From what we have discussed about the text of KV on P. 2.2.31 and the *rājadantādigaṇa*, the following points should become clear:

1. Most of the mss traditions show that the words quoted in Mbh on P.2.2.34 are now members of the *rājadantādigaṇa*. However, there is manuscript evidence for a stage where this *gaṇa* lacked the MBh-quoted words. In addition, there is ms evidence to show that some of the quoted words got into the mss tradition of the *Kāśikāvṛtti* while others were left out of the same tradition. Later on, all the words came to be members of the *gaṇa*.

2. According to Schwarzschild (1964: 459), Birwé establishes that non-Pāṇinian *gaṇapāṭhas* are mere variations of Pāṇinian *gaṇapāṭhas*. But it might be argued on the basis of detailed evidence that the Pāṇinian *gaṇapāṭha* as found in the *Kāśikāvṛtti* took the shape of today, perhaps, because of its interaction with the non-Pāṇinian *gaṇapāṭhas*.

3. Variations in the mss tradition were known to the *Padamañjarī*. A certain mss tradition preserves the readings which this commentary does not consider to be acceptable.

4. The Source-Text of all the mss that we have examined can certainly be shown to be pre-Padamañjarī. The *Padamañjarī* can explain the loss of circulation of readings in the majority of mss.

Appendix 1

A detailed account of the 49 words of 2.2.31 in Non-Pāṇinian sūtra traditions

KV = Kāśikāvṛtti
Ś = Śākatāyana
KT = Kātantra
J = Jainendra
C = Cāndra
H = Haima
G = Gaṇaratrnamahodadhi

No.	KV	Ś	KT	J	C	H	G
1	*rājadantaḥ*	Y		Y	Y	Y	Y
2	*agrevaṇam*	Y		Y			Y
3	*liptavāsitam*	Y		Y	Y (... *taḥ*)	Y	Y (... *taḥ*)
4	*nagna-muṣitam*	Y		Y	Y (... *taḥ*)	Y	Y (... *taḥ*)
5	*sikta-sammṛṣṭam*	Y		Y	Y (... *ṣṭaḥ*)	Y	Y (*sikta-samsṛṣṭam ity anye*)
6	*mṛṣṭa-luñcitam*	*bhṛṣṭa-luñcitam*		*bhṛṣṭa-luñcitam*	*bhṛṣṭa-luñcitaḥ*	*bhṛṣṭa-luñcitam*	*bhṛṣṭa-luñcitam*
7	*avaklinna-pakvam*	Y		Y	Y (..*kvaḥ*)	Y	Y
8	*arpitoptam*	Y		Y	Y (..*taḥ*)	*arpitotam*	*arpitotam*
9	*uptagāḍham*	Y		Y	Y (..*ḍhaḥ*)	Y	Y
10	*ulūkhala-musalam*	... *le*	(*le*)*	Y	(... *le*)	Y (... *ś* ...)	Y
11	*taṇḍula-kiṇvam*	Y			Y	Y	Y
12	*dṛṣadupalam*						Y
13	*āragvāya-nabandhakī*			*āragvāya-nibandhakī*		*araṭāya-nicāndhani*	*āraṭvāya-nicāndhani*
14	*citraratha-bāhlīkam*	Y		Y	Y	Y (... *au*)	Y
15	*āvantyā-śmakam*			*avantya-kṣamakam*		*avantyā-śmakāḥ*	Y
16	*śūdrāryam*			Y	Y	Y (... *ryau*)	Y (... *ryau*)
17	*snātaka-rājānau*			Y	Y	Y	Y
18	*viśvaksenā-rjunau*			Y		Y	Y
19	*akṣibhruvam*			Y	Y		Y
20	*dāragavam*			Y	Y		Y
21	*śabdārthau*			Y	Y		Y
22	*dharmārthau*			Y	Y		Y
23	*kāmārthau*			Y	Y		Y
24	*arthaśabdau*			Y	Y		Y

25	*arthadharmau*			Y	Y		Y
26	*arthakāmau*			Y	Y		Y
27	*vaikārimatam*	*vaiyākaraṇamatam*		*vaiyākaraṇamatam*		Y	Y
28	*gajavājam*					Y (27 & 28 together)	(*gājavājam*)
29	*gopāladhānipulāsam*	Y		Y		Y	*gaupālidhānapulāsam*
30	*pulāsakaradaṇḍam*			Y			*pulāsakuradaṇḍam*
31	*sthūlapulāsam*					*kuradaṇḍasthalapulāsam*	*sthalapulāsam*
32	*uśīrabījam*	*uśīrabīja*		Y		*uśīrabīja*	Y
33	*siñjastham*	together with 32		Y		32 & 33 together	Y
34	*citrāsvātī*	Y		Y	Y		Y
35	*bhāryāpati*	Y		Y	Y		Y
36	*jāyāpati*	Y		Y			Y
37	*jampatī*	Y		Y	Y		Y
38	*dampatī*	Y		Y	Y		Y
39	*putrapatī*	Y		Y	Y		Y
40	*putrapaśū*	Y		Y	Y		Y
41	*keśaśmaśrū*	Y		*keśaśmaśruḥ*	Y (. . . *śru*)		Y
42	*śmaśrukeśau*						Y
43	*śirobījam*	*śirobinduḥ*		*śirobinduḥ*	*śiroviju*		*śiroviju*
44	*sarpirmadhunī*			Y	Y		Y
45	*madhusarpiṣī*			Y	Y		Y
46	*ādyantau*			Y	Y		Y
47	*antādī*			Y	Y		Y
48	*guṇavṛddhī*			Y	Y		Y
49	*vṛddhiguṇau*			Y	Y		

(Y indicates the occurrence of the word, blank space indicates the absence of the word.)

Appendix II

Comments of various traditions on the words in this *gaṇa* in the Pāṇinīya tradition

Nyāsānusandhāna on *Siddhahaimaśabdānuśāsana* with *Svopajñatattvaprakāśikāprakāśa* (12th century CE)[27] and *Nyāsa*

> उशीरबीजशिञ्जास्थम् इति समासः। उशीरबीजो नाम पर्वतः शिञ्जास्थोऽपि स एव तयोः समाहार इति लघुन्यासः। पाणिनीये गणे तु उशीरबीजमिति पृथगेव पठ्यते। तत्रोशीरं च बीजं चेति द्वन्द्वे अल्पस्वरत्वाद् बीजस्य पूर्वनिपाते प्राप्ते उशीरस्य पूर्वनिपातः । शिञ्जास्थम् इति तालव्यादेः स्थाने सिञ्जास्थम् सिञ्जाश्वत्थम् इति द्वौ दन्त्यादी द्वन्द्वौ पठ्येते ...एवं सिञ्जास्थम् इति पाठस्यावश्यकत्वेऽपि सिञ्जाश्वत्थम् इति पाठे न प्रयोजनं पश्यामः ...तथासौ पाठः सन्दिग्धप्रयोजनक एव लेखकप्रमादकृतो वा। एवम् अन्योऽपि गणपाठे भेदो दृश्यते। तदीययुक्तायुक्तत्वविचारो न लक्षणैकचक्षुष्कविषयः। **(255.75–256.8)**[28]

Gaṇaratnamahodadhi of Vardhamāna (1140 AD)[29]

1. भोजस्तु शिरोविजू इत्याह। (p. 122)
2. शाकटायनस्तु वैकरेर् मतो वैकारिमतः। गाजयतीति गाजः। वाजयतीति वाजः। गाजस्य वाजः गाजवाजः। वैकारिमतश्च गाजवाजश्च वैकारिमतगाजवाजमित्याह । (p.123)
3. केशश्मश्रू इति भोजः। (p. 123)
4. शाकटायनस्तु कुरण्डानां स्थलं कुरण्डस्थलम्। कुरण्डस्थलम्। कुरण्डस्थलं च पूलासश्च कुरण्दस्थलपूलासमित्युवाच। (p. 124)
5. पाणिनिस्तु आरट्वायनिबन्धकीत्याह। (p. 124)
6. शाकटायनस्तु उशीरं बीजं यस्मिन् उशीरबीजो नाम पर्वतः। सिञ्जायां तिष्ठतीति सिञ्जास्थः पर्वतः। उशीरबीजश्च सिञ्जास्थश्च उशीरबीजसिञ्जास्थम्। (p. 124)
7. चित्ररथश्च बाल्हीकश्च चित्ररथबाल्हीकौ राजानौ। अल्पाज्द्वारेण। पाणिनिवामनमतेन। (p. 126)
8. शाकटायनस्तु बल्हो'स्यास्तीति बल्ही। बल्हीव बल्हिकः। संज्ञाप्रकृत्योरित्यनेन के चित्ररथबल्हिकम्। (p. 126)
9. भोजस्तु चित्ररथबाल्हिकावस्मिन् गणे पपाठ। (p. 126)

---

[27] Belvalkar 1976: 61.

[28] This reference is to page and line.

[29] Kapila Deva Shastri 1967: 55.

Appendix III.

Nyāsa and *Padamañjarī* on P.2.2.31

Nyāsa

Text

राजदन्तादिषु परम्॥ पूर्वस्य परनिपात इति लिप्तवासिताद्युप्तगाढपर्यन्तेषु। उदूखलमुसलादयो ये द्वन्द्वाः तत्र क्वचिद् अल्पाच्तरत्वात् पूर्वनिपातः प्राप्नोति क्वचिद् घ्यन्तत्वात् पूर्वनिपातः क्वचिद् अजाद्यदन्तत्वात् क्वचित् तुल्यत्वादनियमः। दृषदुपलमिति। प्रमादाच्चायं पाठो लक्ष्यते। अल्पाच्तरत्वाद् दृषत्शब्दस्य पूर्वनिपातः सिद्धः। अक्षिभ्रुवम् दारगवमिति। अचतुरादिसूत्रेणाच् समासान्तः। स्थूलपूलासमिति। प्रमादपाठोऽयमिति लक्ष्यते। पूर्वोक्तादेव कारणात्।

Translation

rājadantādiṣu param ||
The statement *pūrvasya paranipātaḥ*[30] applies to the set of words beginning with *liptavāsita* and ending with *uptagāḍha*.

Of *dvandva* compounds, such as *udūkhalamusala*, to some, *pūrvanipāta* is applicable because of prior constituents [such as *musala*] having less vowels, by P.2.2.34 ; to some, *pūrvanipāta* [is applicable] because [of a prior constituent] ending in *ghi*, by P.2.2.32 ; to some, [*pūrvanipāta* is applicable] because [of a prior constituent] beginning with a vowel and ending in short *a*, by P.2.2.33; to others, [*pūrvanipāta*] is applicable without restriction because of equal number of [syllables], by P.2.2.30.

The reading *dṛṣadupalam* is seen here due to some mistake. The preceding position of the word *dṛṣad* is established because it contains less number of vowels (and P.2.2.34 applies).

In the words *akṣibhruvam dāragavam*, there is the suffix *aC* by P.5.4.77.[31] The reading *sthūlapūlāsam* is seen here due to some mistake because of the reason mentioned earlier (namely that the preceding position of the word *sthūla* is established because it contains less number of vowels [and P.2.2.34 applies]).

[30]It is to be noted that the text of the *Kāśikāvṛtti* reads: *pūrvakālasya paranipātaḥ*. The reading *pūrvasya paranipātaḥ* is not supported by any ms evidence of the *Kāśikāvṛtti*.

[31]P.5.4.77 *acaturavicaturasucaturastrīpuṁsadhenvanaḍuharksāmavāṅmanasākṣibhruvadāragavorvaṣṭhīvapadaṣṭhīvanaktaṁdivarātriṁdivāhardivasarajasaniḥśreyasapuruṣāyuṣadvyāyuṣatryāyuṣargyajuṣajātokṣamahokṣavṛddhokṣopaśunagoṣṭhaśvāḥ* |

Padamañjarī

Text

राजदन्तादिषु परम्॥ न केवलमित्यादि। अत्र विहितपूर्वनिपातस्येति पाठे विहितः पूर्वनिपातो यस्य तस्येत्यर्थः। प्रायेण तु विहितस्येति पाठः। तत्रापवाद इति शेषः। अन्यस्यापि घ्यादेर् यः पूर्वनिपातो यथालक्षणं विहितस् तस्याप्यपवाद इत्यर्थः। ...उलूखलमुसलादिद्वन्द्वेषु क्वचिद् अल्पाक्षरत्वात् क्वचिद् घ्यन्तत्वात् क्वचिद् अजाद्यदन्तत्वात् पूर्वनिपातप्रसङ्गः क्वचित् अनियमः। दृषदुपलमिति प्रमादपाठः अल्पाच्तरत्वाद् ।अक्षिभ्रुवम् दारगवमिति। अचतुरादिसूत्रे अच् समासान्तः निपातितः। तेन परनिपातस्यापि सिद्धत्वादिह पाठः शक्योऽकर्तुम् ॥

Translation

rājadantādiṣu param ||
To explain a passage beginning with *na kevalam.* In the case of the reading *vihitapūrvanipātasya* the meaning would be 'to that whose preceding position is prescribed'. But the reading *vihitasya* is generally accepted. There the remaining part [of the sentence] is [the word] *apavādaḥ* '[is] exception'.[32] The meaning [of the sentence] is that this *sūtra* states exception to the preceding position prescribed, according to rules, with regard to other words like the one termed *ghi.*

Of *dvandva* compounds, such as *udūkhalamusala*, to some, *pūrvanipāta* is applicable because of prior constituents [such as *musala*] having less syllables by P.2.2.34; to some, *pūrvanipāta* [is applicable] because [of a prior constituent] ending in *ghi*, by P.2.2.32; to some, [*pūrvanipāta* is applicable] because [of a prior constituent] beginning with a vowel and ends in short *a*, by P.2.2.33; to others, [*pūrvanipāta*] is applicable without restriction because of equal number of [syllables] by P.2.2.30.

The reading *dṛṣadupalam* is a mistaken one since [the word in the initial position *dṛṣad*] contains less vowels [and thereby by the application of P.2.2.34 its preceding position is alredy established].

In the words *akṣibhruvam* and *dāragavam*, the suffix *aC* at the end of the compound is stated by P.5.4.77, so that, because the later position has been established, it is possible not to list them here.

[32]That is, *apavādaḥ* is supplied to have the sentence *vihitasya pūrvanipātasya apavādaḥ.*

Appendix IV

P.2.2.31 and other sūtras in P.2.2.30–2.2.38

S1 = Sūtra prescribing the order of words which is affected by membership of this gaṇa.
S2 = Sūtra prescribing the compound.
N = Name of the compound.
ṢT = *ṣaṣṭhītatpuruṣa.*
KDh = *karmadhāraya.*
ID = *itaretaradvandva.*

No.	Word	Relation	S1	S2	N
1	*rājadantaḥ*	*apavāda*	2.2.30	2.2.8	ṢT
2	*agrevaṇam*	*apavāda*	2.2.30	2.2.8	ṢT
3	*liptavāsitam*	*apavāda*	2.2.30	2.1.49	KDh
4	*nagnamuṣitam*	*apavāda*	2.2.30	2.1.49	KDh
5	*siktasaṁmṛṣṭam*	*apavāda*	2.2.30	2.1.49	KDh
6	*mṛṣṭaluñcitam*	*apavāda*	2.2.30	2.1.49	KDh
7	*avaklinnapakvam*	*apavāda*	2.2.30	2.1.49	KDh
8	*arpitoptam*	*apavāda*	2.2.30	2.1.49	KDh
9	*uptagāḍham*	*apavāda*	2.2.30	2.1.49	KDh
10	*ulūkhalamusalam*	*apavāda*	2.2.34	2.2.29	ID
11	*taṇḍulakiṇvam*	*apavāda*	2.2.34	2.2.29	ID
12	*dṛṣadupalam*	*apavāda*	2.2.34	2.2.29	ID
13	*āragvayanabandhakī*	*apavāda*	2.2.34	2.2.29	ID
14	*citrarathabālhīkam*	*apavāda*	2.2.34	2.2.29	ID
15	*āvantyāśmakam*	*niyama*	2.2.33	2.2.29	ID
16	*śūdrāryam*	*apavāda*	2.2.33	2.2.29	ID
17	*snātakarājānau*	*apavāda*	2.2.34	2.2.29	ID
18	*viṣvaksenārjunau*	*apavāda*	2.2.34	2.2.29	ID
19	*akṣibhruvam*	*apavāda*	2.2.34	2.2.29	ID
20	*dāragavam*	*apavāda*	2.2.34	2.2.29	ID
21	*śabdārthau*	*apavāda*	2.2.33	2.2.29	ID
22	*dharmārthau*	*apavāda*	2.2.33	2.2.29	ID
23	*kāmārthau*	*apavāda*	2.2.33	2.2.29	ID
24	*arthaśabdau*	*apavāda*	2.2.33	2.2.29	ID
25	*arthadharmau*	*apavāda*	2.2.33	2.2.29	ID
26	*arthakāmau*	*apavāda*	2.2.33	2.2.29	ID
27	*vaikārimatam*	*apavāda*	2.2.34	2.2.29	ID
28	*gajavājam*	*apavāda/ niyama*	2.2.30	2.2.29/ 2.2.8	ID/ṢT
29	*gopāladhānīpulāsam*	*apavāda*	2.2.34	2.2.29	ID
30	*pulāsakaraṇḍam*	*apavāda*	2.2.34	2.2.29	ID
31	*sthūlapulāsam*	*apavāda*	2.2.34	2.2.29	ID

32	*uśīrabījam*	*apavāda*	2.2.34	2.2.29	ID
33	*siñjāstham*	*apavāda*	2.2.33	2.2.29	ID
34	*citrāsvātī*	*niyama*	2.2.30	2.2.29	ID
35	*bhāryāpatī*	*apavāda*	2.2.32	2.2.29	ID
36	*jāyāpatī*	*apavāda*	2.2.32	2.2.29	ID
37	*jampatī*	*apavāda*	2.2.32	2.2.29	ID
38	*dampatī*	*apavāda*	2.2.32	2.2.29	ID
39	*putrapatī*	*apavāda*	2.2.32	2.2.29	ID
40	*putrapaśū*	*apavāda*	2.2.32	2.2.29	ID
41	*keśaśmaśrū*	*apavāda*	2.2.32	2.2.29	ID
42	*śmaśrukeśau*	-	2.2.32	2.2.29	ID
43	*śirobījam*	*niyama*	2.2.30	2.2.29	ID
44	*sarpirmadhunī*	-	2.2.32	2.2.29	ID
45	*madhusarpiṣī*	-	2.2.32	2.2.29	ID
46	*ādyantau*	-	2.2.32	2.2.29	ID
47	*antādī*	*apavāda*	2.2.32	2.2.29	ID
48	*guṇavṛdhī*	*apavāda*	2.2.32	2.2.29	ID
49	*vṛdhiguṇau*	-	2.2.32	2.2.29	ID

Note: The words in front of which no relation is stated are the ones in which no restricted position is determined by this particular sūtra. They are the forms which are derived by application of both the rules, a. one mentioned in the next column as well as b. the general rule. This amounts to say that the constituents in this compound will have both positions alternatively.

Appendix V

List of words found in various mss groups

(Numbers in the round brackets refer to the number of the word as mentioned in Appendix I.)

1. M4–6

33 words

1. *rājadantaḥ* (1)
2. *agrevaṇam* (2)
3. *liptavāsitam* (3)
4. *nagnamuṣitam* (4)
5. *mṛṣṭaluñcitam* (6)
6. *avaklinnapakvam* (7)
7. *āragvayana-bandhakī* (13)
8. *citrarathabālhīkam* (14)
9. *āvantyāśmakam* (15)
10. *śabdārthau* (21)
11. *dharmārthau* (22)
12. *kāmārthau* (23)
13. *arthadharmau* (25)
14. *gopāladhānīpūlāsam* (29)
15. *pulāsakaraṇḍam* (30)
16. *sthūlapulāsam* (31)
17. *uśīrabījam* (32)
18. *citrāsvātī* (34)
19. *bhāryāpatī* (35)
20. *jāyāpatī* (36)
21. *jampatī* (37)
22. *dampatī* (38)
23. *putrapatī* (39)
24. *putrapaśū* (40)
25. *keśaśmaśrū* (41)
26. *śmaśrukeśau* (42)
27. *śirobījam* (43)
28. *sarpirmadhunī* (44)
29. *madhusarpiṣī* (45)
30. *ādyantau* (46)
31. *antādī* (47)
32. *guṇavṛddhī* (48)
33. *vṛddhiguṇau* (49)

All the three mss (M4–6) omit statement 1 omitted by B1 (as shown below). M4 and 5 omit statement 2 which is omitted by B1. M5 omits statement 3 which is omitted by B1.

B1

14 words

1. *liptavāsitam* (3)
2. *nagnamuṣitam* (4)
3. *siktasaṁmṛṣṭam* (5)
4. *mṛṣṭaluñcitam* (6)
5. *avaklinnapakvam* (7)
6. *arpitotam* (8)

7. *uptagāḍham* (9)	8. *ulūkhalamusalam* (10)
9. *taṇḍulakiṇvam* (11)	10. *dṛṣadupalam* (12)
11. *āragvayana-bandhakī* (13)	12. *citrarathabālhīkam* (14)
13. *āvantyāśmakam* (15)	14. *bhāryāpatī* (35)

This is the only ms that omits all the three statements mentioned below found interspersed with words explaining them.

1. *aniyamaś cātreṣyate* |
2. *tat kathaṁ vaktavyam idaṁ dharmādiṣu ubhayam iti* |
3. *jāyāśabdasya jambhāvo dambhāvaś ca nipātyate* |

References and abbreviations

Bāla Śāstrī
1876–1878 *Kāśikā: A commentary on Pāṇini's Grammatical Aphorisms by Vāmana and Jayāditya.* 2 vols. Benares: Medical Hall Press.

Belvalkar, S. K.
1976 *Systems of Sanskrit Grammar.* Reprint, Delhi: Bharatiya Vidya Prakashan.

Birwé, Robert
1961 *Der Gaṇapāṭha zu den adhyāyas IV und V der Grammatik Pāṇinis.* Wiesbaden: Otto Harrassowitz.
1964 Nārāyaṇadaṇḍanātha's commentary on rules III.2, 106–121 of Bhoja's *Sarasvatīkaṇṭhābharaṇa. Journal of the American Oriental Society* 84-2: 150–162.
1973 Review of volume 1 of the Hyderabad edition of the Kāśikā. *Zeitschrift der Deutschen Morganlandischen Gesellschaft* 123: 427–441.

Bloomfield, Leonard
1927 On some rules of Pāṇini. *Journal of the American Oriental Society* 47: 61–70.

Böhtlingk, Otto
1971 *Pāṇini's Grammatik.* Hildesheim: Georg Olms Verlag, 1887. Reprint, New York.

Bronkhorst, Johannes
1983 On the history of Pāṇinian grammar in the early centuries following Patañjali. *Journal of Indian Philosophy* 11: 357–412.
2009 The importance of the Kāśikā. In *Studies in the Kāśikāvṛtti: The Section on Pratyāhāras; Critical Edition, Translation and Other Contributions*, edited by Pascale Haag and Vincenzo Vergiani, 129–140. Firenze: Societa Editrice Fiorentina.

Brough, John
1973 I-ching on the Sanskrit grammarians. *Bulletin of the School of Oriental and African Studies* 36-2: 248–260.
Cardona, George
2004 *Recent Researches in Pāṇinian Studies*. 2nd ed. Delhi: Motilal Benarsidass.
Chatterji, K. C.
1953 *Cāndra Vyākaraṇa of Candragomin*. Part I. Poona: Deccan College Post Graduate and Research Institute.
1961 *Cāndra Vyākaraṇa of Candragomin*. Part II. Poona: Deccan College Post Graduate and Research Institute.
Deo, Puja Vinayak
2001 Critical edition of Kāśikā (3.1). Ph.D. diss., University of Pune, Pune.
Dvivedi, Janakiprasad
1997 *Kātantravyākaraṇam with Durgasiṁhakṛta-Kātantravṛttiṭīkā, Trilocanadāsakṛta-Kātantravṛttipañjikā, Suṣeṇakṛta-Kalāpacandraṭikā*. Part I. Varanasi: Sampurnanda Sanskrit Vishvavidyalalya.
Eggeling, Julius
1963 *Gaṇaratnamahodadhi of Vardhamāna*. 1879. Reprint, Delhi: Motilal Benarsidass.
GRM: *Gaṇaratnamahodadhi*. See Eggling.
Haag, Pascale, and Vincenzo Vergiani
2009 *Studies in the Kāśikāvṛtti: The section on Pratyāhāras; Critical Edition, Translation and Other Contributions*. Firenze: Societa Editrice Fiorentina.
Joshi, S. D., and J.A.F. Roodbergen
1997 *The Aṣṭādhyāyī of Pāṇini: Vol. VI (2.2.1–2.2.38)*. New Delhi: Sahitya Academi.
KV: *Kāśikāvṛtti*. See Sharma et al.
Katre, S. M.
1971 *Dictionary of Pāṇini: Gaṇapāṭha*. Poona: Deccan College Post Graduate and Research Institute.
Kapila Deva Shastri
1967 *The Gaṇapāṭha: Ascribed to Pāṇini*. Kurukshetra: Kurukshetra University.
Kielhorn, Franz
1970 *Vyākaraṇamahābhāṣya of Patañjali*. 3 vols. 1880–1885, Reprint, Osnabruk: Otto Zeller Verlag.

Kulkarni, Malhar
1999 The shortest manuscript of the Kāśikāvṛtti. In *Tattvadīpaḥ*, vol.3, edited by H. V. Nagraj Rao, 19–27. Melcote: Academy for Sanskrit Research.
2000a Critical edition of Kāśikā (2.2). Ph.D. diss., University of Pune, Pune.
2000b On identifying the manuscripts at the base of the first ever printed edition of *the Kāśikāvṛtti*. *Annals of the Bhandarkar Oriental Research Institue* 81: 203–212.
2002a On a vārttika on P.2.2.6 in the *Kāśikāvṛtti*. *Annals of the Bhandarkar Oriental Research Institute* 83: 201–205.
2002b A study of the quotations of the *Kāśikāvṛtti* in the late Pāṇinian grammatical literature. *Saṁbhāṣā (Nagoya Studies in Indian Culture and Buddhism, Nagoya University)* 23: 73–78.
2005 A sample of the new edition of the Kāśikāvṛtti. In *Bharatiya Vidya* LXV/1–4, edited by J. H. Dave and S. A.Upadhyaya, 116–127. Mumbai: Bharatiya Vidya Bhavan.
2007 Śāradā manuscripts of the Kāśikāvṛtti: A study- II. In *Linguistic Traditions of Kashmir: Essays in Memory of Pandit Dinanath Yaksha*, edited by Mrinal Kaul and Ashok Aklujkar, 432–441. New Delhi: DK Printworld.
forthcoming *Malyalam manuscripts of the Kāśikāvṛtti*. *Annals of the Bhandarkar Oriental Research Institute.*

Mbh: *Vyākaraṇamahābhāṣya*. See Kielhorn.

N: *Nyāsa*. See Swami Dwarika Das Shastri and Pt. KalikaPrasad Shukla.

P: Pāṇini's *Aṣṭādhyāyī*. See Böhtlingk.

Pm: *Padamañjarī*. See Swami Dwarika Das Shastri and Pt. KalikaPrasad Shukla

Radicchi, Anna
1991 On gaṇapāṭhas and the gaṇapāṭha ascribed to Pāṇini. In *Panels of the VIIth World Sanskrit Conference, Vol. V: Pāṇini and the Veda*, edited by Madhav Deshpande, 65–73. Leiden: E.J.Brill.

Scharfe, Hartmut
1977 *A History of Indian Literature*. Vol. 5, fasc. 2, *Grammatical Literature*. Wiesbaden: Otto Harrassowitz.

Schwarzschild, L. A.
1964 Review of Birwé (1961), Der Gaṇapāṭha zu den adhyāyas IV und V der Grammatik Pāṇinis. *Journal of the American Oriental Society* 84-4: 459–460.

Sengupta, Sailendranath
1961 Contribution towards a critical edition of the Gaṇapāṭha. *Journal of the Asiatic Society, Calcutta* III.3–4: 89–186.

Sharma, Aryendra, Khanderao Deshpande, and D. G. Padhye
2008 *Kāśikāvṛtti*. 1969–1976. Reprint, Hyderabad: Osmania University.

Sūri Vijayalāvaṇya
1960 *Śrī-Siddha-Hemecandra-Śabdānuśāsana with Bṛhadvṛtti and Nyāsa: tṛtīyādhyāyasya prathamapādaḥ*. Bombay: Śrīsiddha-hema-prakāśana-samitiḥ.

Swami Dwarika Das Shastri and Pt. Kalika Prasad Shukla
1985 *Kāśikāvṛtti with Nyāsa and Padamañjarī.* 6 vols. Varanasi: Sudhi Prakashan.

Tripathi, Shambhunath
1971 *Śākaṭāyana-vyākaraṇa.* Varanasi: Bharatiya Jnanapitha Prakashana.

Tripathi, Shambhunath, and Mahadev Chaturvedi
1956 *Jainendra-Vyākaraba with Jainendramahāvṛtti.* Kashi (Banaras): Bharatiya Jnanapitha.

Vijaypal, Vidyavaridhi
1997 *Kāśikāvṛtti.* Sonipat: Ramalal Kapur Trust.

Paulinus a Sancto Bartholomaeo and Sanskrit Grammar*

CARMELA MASTRANGELO

1. The aim of this paper is to cast light upon the history of the studies on Sanskrit grammar in the West, through the works of Father Paulinus a Sancto Bartholomaeo. Without the analysis of his writings a history of the knowledge of Sanskrit grammar in Europe would be incomplete. In fact, Staal (1972: 30–32) starts his survey of Western scholars researching in the field of Sanskrit grammar with Father Jean François Pons. He then maintains that Charles Wilkins was the first European who knew Sanskrit well, and that William Jones, chairman of the Asiatic Society, was the founder of Sanskrit studies in the West (Staal 1972: 33). Jean François Pons, a French Jesuit missionary who worked in Southeast India, made an abridgment of a Sanskrit grammar in 1733. This manuscript, discovered by Jean Filliozat in the Bibliothèque du Roi in Paris in 1937, referred to a non-Pāṇinian school of grammar called *Sārasvata*, traditionally considered as founded by Anubhūtisvarūpācārya after the 13th century. As for Charles Wilkins, he wrote *A grammar of the Sanskrita language*, which was published in London in 1808, but whose first printed sheet was destroyed by fire in 1795. This grammar, as the other earliest grammars written by Englishmen, was based on a work in the non-Pāṇinian tradition, the *Mugdhabodha* of Vopadeva, probably of the 13th century. English scholars of the Asiatic Society studied the Pāṇinian tradition as well, namely the KV by Jayāditya and Vāmana of the 7th century, and the *Siddhāntakaumudī* by Bhaṭṭojidīkṣita of the 18th century.

2. So far, this is what we learn from Staal's book. On the other hand, Paulinus' Sanskrit grammars—*Sidharùbam seu grammatica Samscrdamica* published in 1790 and *Vyàcarana seu locupletissima Samscrdamicae linguae institutio* published in 1804—refer to an original Indian grammar called

*I would like to express my deepest thanks to Raffaele Torella, Jan Houben, Rich Freeman, Bruno Lo Turco and Gianni Pellegrini for their precious suggestions.

Sidharùbam, i.e. *Siddharūpa*, copied together with *Vyágarná*, i.e. *Vyākaraṇa*, and *Amarasinha*, i.e. the Sanskrit dictionary called *Amarakoṣa*, by the Jesuit Johann Ernst Hanxleden from a palm leaf manuscript found in Trichur. More specifically, according to the VLS (p. xiv):

> Vyàcaranam *ipsam ex codice* ms. *R. P. Joannis Ernesti* Hanxleden, *Samscrdamici Sermonis peritissimi viri, qui eam ex codicibus palmeis* Granthamicis *Academiae Brahmanicae* Triciurensis *accuratissima manu descripsit, deprompsi, atque ad codicem* chart. ms. *Francisci* Texeira, *indigenae Indi, rite contuli, quem ego mea manu jam anno 1778 descripseram.*[1]

Furthermore, according to DMC (p. 6):

> *Descripsit ille* [i.e. Hanxleden] *manu propria ex codicibus palmarum Brahmanicae academiae* Tritschuricensis *grammaticam samscrdamicam magnam* Sidharúbam *dictam, qua ipsi Brahmanes in addiscenda samscrdamica lingua utuntur. Haec grammatica minutissimis characteribus exarata numerat, ut ajunt, in quarto paginas quadraginta quatuor;* Amarasinha seu Dictionarium Samscrdamicum *versibus scriptum, quod grammaticae annexum est, occupat in eodem quarto paginas centum et sex; syntaxis,* Vyágarná *nuncupata, paginas bis centum decem; sententiae gymnosophisticae,* Shlóga *dictae, occupant paginas duodecim.*[2]

Father Hanxleden, well known among the Indians as Arnos Pathiri,[3] was himself the author, in the early 18th century, of a grammar called *Samskruthavyaakaranam*,[4] and even before him, in 1660, in Agra, the Jesuit mis-

[1] "I derived this *Vyàcarana* itself from a manuscript codex by Reverend Father Johann Ernst Hanxleden, great expert in the Sanskrit language, who painstakingly copied it from palm leaf manuscripts in Grantha script held by the Brahmanical Academy of Trichur. Then, I accurately collated it with the paper codex by Francisco Texeira, a native of India, which I myself copied in 1778."

[2] "He himself copied the great Sanskrit grammar called *Sidharúbam*, used by Brahmins themselves for learning the Sanskrit language, from palm leaf manuscripts held by the Academy of Trichur. This grammar, written in very small characters, is a quarto edition, as they say, which has forty-four pages; *Amarasinha seu Dictionarium Samscrdamicum*, written in verse, attached to the grammar, is also a quarto edition, which has one hundred six pages; a syntax, called *Vyágarná*, has two hundred ten pages; the gymnosophists' sentences, called *Shlóga*, have twelve pages." See also ASP, p. vi.

[3] On the life of Hanxleden and on his contribution to Indian literature, see Mundadan 1988.

[4] As for Hanxleden's manuscript works, cf. DMC and IOC, pp. 191–192.

sionary Heinrich Roth wrote a Sanskrit grammar in Latin, whose manuscript was discovered in 1967 by Arnulf Camps in the National Library in Rome.[5]

3. The Discalced Carmelite Paulinus a Sancto Bartholomaeo, in the world known as Johann Philip Wesdin, an Austrian friar of Croatian origin, author of the first Sanskrit grammar ever printed in Europe, settled in Kerala from 1776 to 1789.[6] There, he could learn Malayalam and Sanskrit with the help of pandits Kr̥ṣṇa Vāriar and Kuñji Menon,[7] studying directly or indirectly works in the Indian grammatical tradition. As we have seen, this tradition was a peculiar one, different from those mentioned by Staal (1972), and attested in the works of Paulinus' predecessor in Southwest India, but unknown to French missionaries in Tamil Nadu and to Englishmen in Bengal.

Paulinus' VLS was printed almost fifteen years after the publication of SGS, which had been wrongly considered by Englishmen as a manual of some vernacular language of South India. Western scholars criticized the way in which the friar presented grammatical rules, which was—they said—"non-European".[8] After the exposition of the alphabet, namely Grantha-Malayalam script, SGS is divided into four chapters dealing with declension, compounds, conjugation and case syntax. On the other hand, VLS is divided into seven chapters—the first on alphabet, the second on declension of vowel stems, the third on declension of consonant stems, the fourth on conjugation, the fifth on syntax, the sixth on *sandhi* rules, the seventh on indeclinable words. As a supplement to this grammar there is a glossary based on the first section of the *Amarakoṣa*.

In his preface to VLS (p. xiv), Paulinus states that his work is a sort of abridgement of a grammar by Pāṇini, "primaevus auctor magnae Brahmanicae Grammaticae", i.e. primeval author of the great Brahmanical grammar. He then writes that VLS is the *syntaxis* of SGS, but here it is not clear what is meant by the word 'syntaxis'. In his preface to SGS (p. 63), the friar explains the meaning of the title as "forma nominum seu vocabulorum in

---

[5]See Camps 1969.

[6]A detailed biography of Paulinus (born on April 25, 1749, in Hof; dead on January 7, 1806, in Rome) is Barone 1888; see also Franolic 1991.

[7]See VLS, p. xx: *Denique mea schediasmata, quae ex lectionibus a Brahmane Krshna Vàriar et a Cugni Mènon auditis, confeci et asservavi.* "Finally, my annotations, which I adjusted and kept from the readings I heard from Brahmin Kr̥ṣṇa Vāriar and from Kuñji Menon."

[8]See VLS, p. xi: *Cur, dicebant aliqui, cur eidem* [i.e. SGS] *nullus europaeus color et cultus?* "Why—they said—why has it nothing European in color and style?" See also p. 52 note: *Duo eruditi viri ... conquesti sunt, quod eam* [i.e. SGS] *necessitati hominum Europaeorum ... non accomodaverim.* "Two scholars complained about the fact I did not adapt it to the needs of Europeans."

mente retinendorum", i.e. noun or verb forms to be learned by heart. He also mentions a text called *Vyàgarna* with "syntaxeos praecepta", i.e. syntax rules (SGS, p. 65). But, as we have seen, an entire chapter of SGS—as well as one of VLS—deals with the explanation of Sanskrit syntax.

In the fourth chapter of VLS (p. 80), we read about the perfect tense that its formation could be learned through the rules of *syntaxis*.[9] Here Paulinus refers to sound changes due to vowel or consonant clusters, and hence the word 'syntaxis' seems to mean *sandhi*. Nevertheless, a section of the second chapter of SGS deals with "coniunctio et separatio dictionum", i.e. internal and external *sandhi* rules.

In his survey of Indian literature Lanjuinais (1832: 47) mentioned *Vyākaraṇa* and *Siddharūpa*, and maintained that the former was "l'explication de l'écriture", while the latter "la forme des noms et verbes connue". Adelung (1832: 23) referred to a text called *Vyākaraṇa* as "a treatise on the formation of simple and compound words ... and on the manner of using them in speech". In later times, we find a survey of education in Kerala in Wood 1985. There, we can read the memoir of Kāṇippayūr Śaṅkaran Nampūtirippāṭū, a Brahmin born in 1891 in what was then Cochin State, who wrote that "*Siddharūpam* was the verse text traditionally used for teaching Sanskrit grammar ... with the conjugation of many verbs ... but no instruction as to their meaning" (Wood 1985: 33; see also 47, 48, 50). He also said that he studied *Siddharūpam* using a printed book. Furthermore, we can read that, after a primary education, a Brahmin student had "to recite by heart an entire dictionary [i.e. *Amarakoṣa*] composed in verse" (Wood 1985: 9). Hence, we may assume that Paulinus' SGS is actually a sort of translation in Latin of the Sanskrit manual traditionally used in Kerala. By the word 'syntaxis' Paulinus could have meant 'explication', so that *Vyākaraṇa* could be the explanation of grammatical rules presented in *Siddharūpa* in a *sūtra* style. *Siddharūpa* was used and printed as well till the 20th century, and, together with the dictionary *Amarakoṣa*, had to be learned by heart, i.e. "in mente retinendum". Hence, the manuscript copied by Father Hanxleden with *Sidharùbam*, *Vyàgarnà* and *Amarasinha*, and used by Paulinus in writing his grammars, was the basic text for learning Sanskrit in Kerala.

4. We should now try to understand on which grammatical sources this text was based. If we take into consideration the chapters dealing with declension, the terminology used in both Paulinus' grammars seems to be the traditional one: for example, the seven case endings are called *prathamā vibhakti* etc., the vocative is *sambodhana*, the three genders are

[9] *Ex* vyàcarana *seu* syntaxi *huiusmodi formatio* [i.e. the perfect tense] *addisci poterit.*

called *puṃliṅga*, *strīliṅga* and *napuṃsaka*, the number is *vacana*, the noun-base is called *prādipadika*, i.e. *prātipadika*, vowel and consonant stems are respectively called *ajanda* and *halanda*, i.e. *ajanta*, *halanta* (VLS, pp. 20–22; SGS, *passim*). As for the declension patterns, most of the examples given by Paulinus are taken from Pāṇini's grammar. For instance, according to A. 7.1.95, 97 (*tr̥jvat kroṣṭuḥ*, *vibhāṣā tr̥tīyādiṣu*), *kroṣṭu-* is treated as though it were a derivate with *tr̥c* when it occurs with sarvanāmasthāna endings, and optionally so before endings of the third through seventh triplets, while Paulinus discusses this noun as exceptionally declined in the manner of a *nomen agentis.*[10] Moreover, the word for ox, *anaḍuh*, is dealt with in A. 7.1.98, 99, 82 (*caturanaḍuhor ām udāttaḥ*, *aṃ sambuddhau*, *sāv anaḍuhaḥ*) as formed with the high-pitched augment *ām* before a sarvanāmasthāna ending, with the augment *am* before the sambuddhi ending, and with the addition of *num* before the endings of nominative and vocative singular. Furthermore, in A. 8.2.72 (*vasusraṃsudhvaṃsvanaḍuhāṃ daḥ*), it is said that in *pāda*-final position *d* replaces the *-h* of *anaḍuh*. These are exactly the cases which Paulinus discusses as exceptions in his grammar.[11] Note also that the friar gives such examples as *khalapū* (VLS, p. 30), which is given in the KV as well to comment on A. 6.1.175 and 8.2.4 about accentuation rules. In general, most of the stems and the declension patterns proposed in SGS and VLS are essentially Vedic and often discussed as exceptions in Indian grammars with a high circulation such as Kale's.

As for the section about conjugation, the terminology is traditional as well: for example, the verb-base is called *dhādu*, i.e. *dhātu*, the conjugational affixes are called *śabvikaraṇa* etc. (VLS, pp. 20, 72–74; SGS, *passim*). Paulinus explains verbal forms by a *śloka* which, he maintains, is traditionally used by pandits for teaching *lakārārthas* (VLS, p. 73):

> *Lal vartamànè, lang, lil, lung bhùdè;*
>
> *Lul, lirl tscha bhàvini, vidhyàdau*
>
> *Lol, lingau lirngtscha crià niszpadya sambhavè.*[12]

Here, as usual, Paulinus transliterates the final retroflex stop as the Roman *l*, and replaces the voiceless dental stop /*t*/ with the voiced /*d*/, but the meaning of the *śloka* is quite clear: i.e. *laṭ* in the sense of present, *laṅ liṭ luṅ* in the sense of past, *luṭ* and *lr̥ṭ* in the sense of future, *loṭ* and *liṅ* in the sense of command and so on. As for the fourth *pāda* about the use of the conditional

[10] VLS, p. 30: *Excipitur ab hac regula nomen Kròshtu, quod significat Adibe, Malabarice Curuken, animal orientale, ab Europaeis Schakal dictum.*

[11] VLS, p. 51: *Ita pariter differt Anadvàn, ortum ex Anaduh, Taurus. 1 Anadvàn. Hè anadvan. 3 Anaduhà. Anadudbhyàm. Anadudbhi<ḥ>.*

[12] *laḍ vartamāne laṅ liḍ luṅ bhūte luḍ lr̥ṭ ca bhāvini / vidhyādau loḍliṅau lr̥ṅ ca kriyāniṣpa[d]<tt>yasambhave //*

(*lr̥ṅ*), the compound *kriyāniṣpadyasambhava* could be emended and read *kriyāniṣpattyasambhava*. For metrical reasons, it could stand for *kriyātipatti*, used in A. 3.3.139 (*liṅnimitte lr̥ṅ kriyātipattau*), quoted by Paulinus later on in his grammar, to signify the non-occurrence or non-achievement of an action. This rule introduces the L-affix *lr̥ṅ* under the conditions which determine the introduction of *liṅ*—that is, if two actions are related as cause and effect (*hetuhetumator liṅ*, A. 3.3.156)—but do not actually take effect; that is, in contrary-to-fact conditional sentences, conditional forms occur instead of optatives. As we can see, in this *śloka* the technical terms for the L-affixes, as well as the use of *vartamāna*, *bhūta* and *bhāvin* for present, past and future time are evidence of Paulinus' knowledge of traditional Sanskrit grammar. On the other hand, *vidhyādau lolliṅau* in the third *pāda* could be completed by A. 3.3.173 *āśiṣi liṅloṭau*, in the sense that the optative and the imperative are alternately used to express a wish and a command as well. The use of *śloka*s to explain grammatical rules is quite common in the so-called *prakriyā* grammars, which arrange the content of A. according to general topics; see, in particular, the *Prakriyāsarvasva* by Nārāyaṇa Bhaṭṭa, a 17th century grammar from Kerala.[13]

Moreover, the friar quotes word-for-word some of Pāṇini's *sūtra*s dealing with L-affixes. These *sūtra*s are A. 3.2.123 *vartamāne laṭ* about the present tense (VLS, p. 74), A. 3.2.111 *anadyatane laṅ* about the first past, which "excludes today" (VLS, p. 74), A. 3.3.139 *liṅnimitte lr̥ṅ kriyātipattau* about the use of the conditional—as we have seen—(VLS, pp. 75–76), A. 3.2.115 *parokṣe liṭ* about the second past, which is "beyond direct perception" (VLS, p. 75), and A. 3.3.15 *anadyatane luṭ* about the periphrastic future (VLS, p. 76).

5. After this brief survey of the stems and grammatical rules presented in SGS and VLS, we may assume that the textual sources used by Paulinus were in the Pāṇinian tradition. It is now of some interest to try to understand how the friar approached this tradition. In this respect, we can review some "mistakes" in the transliteration of Sanskrit into Roman characters. These "mistakes" were the principal cause of Paulinus' quarrel with Englishmen of the Asiatic Society ("Angli Calcuttenses",[14] as he contemptuously called them) and of the lack of interest on part of the international scholarship (see Rocher 1977: xviii, xix)—indeed, it is difficult to read and understand Sanskrit words transliterated in Paulinus' grammars, and sometimes they rather seem Malayalam. Paulinus felt that he had to somehow justify himself for his own transliterations in a polemical footnote addressed

[13]For instance: *daśa tatra lakārāḥ syur laṭ ca liṅ loṭ ca laṅ kamāt / luṅliḍāśīrliṅo luṭ ca lr̥ṭ ca lr̥ṅ ceti laukikāḥ //* (PS, p. 13).

[14]See, for instance, VLS, p. 10.

to other contemporary scholars (VLS, p. 94):

> *Verba et nomina Samscrdamica ubique latinis literis scribimus, sicut ea scripsere R. P. Joannes E. Hanxleden, R. P. de Nobilibus, et D. G. Jones, olim Academiae Anglo-Calcuttanae Praeses; hi enim viri alios omnes linguae Samscrdamicae peritia, et sana orthographia longe superarunt. Wilkins, Anquetil du Perron, Hodges, Dow, aliique, qui Samscrdamica attigerunt, projectitia, corrupta, et plerumque erronea methodo et arte vocabula Samscrdamica exprimunt et describunt.*[15]

As we have seen, the most common peculiarity in Paulinus' transliteration is the replacement of an intervocalic voiceless stop by its voiced equivalent: for example *sidharūbam* stands for *siddharūpam*, and *bhūde* stands for *bhūte*. The same applies to voiceless stops following a homorganic nasal—see, for instance, *ajanda*, *halanda*. This is due to the influence of Dravidian languages, in which the distinction between voiced and voiceless stops, as well as between aspirate and non-aspirate, was not phonemic.[16] This fact also explains another kind of "mistake", which is sometimes[17] found in Paulinus' transliteration, namely the transgression of Bartholomae's Law—according to which in a cluster of two or more stops, anyone of which is a voiced aspirate, the whole cluster becomes voiced and aspirated (i.e. *budh-ta > buddha)—as well as Grassmann's Law—according to which an aspirated consonant followed by another aspirated consonant in the next syllable loses its aspiration. In fact, in Paulinus' VLS we find *nactum* (p. 82) instead of *naddhum*—according to A. 8.2.34 (*naho dhaḥ*)—and *tattvabhudh* (p. 43), with *bh* and *dh* both aspirated. Obviously, Paulinus studied Sanskrit with the help of local pandits, who cannot correctly pronounce these phonemes. As for the declension and conjugation patterns, a particular kind of misunderstanding is often found, namely the systematic exchange of the quantity of some vowels. The graphic device by which Paulinus marks a long vowel is an accent, but nevertheless there is sometimes an accent on short vowels as well, as for instance the vowel *a* of the verbal endings -*mahe* and -*vahe*. Here

[15] "We always transliterate Sanskrit words by Latin characters, like Hanxleden, De Nobili and William Jones, former chief of the Asiatic Society [*Academia Anglo-Calcuttana*], did; these scholars outclassed everyone in the Sanskrit language and orthography. Wilkins, Anquetil du Perron, Hodges, Dow and the others who touched upon Sanskrit pronounce and write Sanskrit words in a featureless, rough and often wrong way."

[16] In Proto-Dravidian, voiced stops were allophones of their voiceless counterparts. According to Caldwell's Law, voiced stops occur when they are intervocalic or when they follow a homorganic nasal (see Steever 1998: 15).

[17] Actually, Paulinus is quite uncertain about this kind of sound laws, which demonstrates that his teachers had difficulty in pronouncing these phonemes.

perhaps the accent was meant to mark the syllable stressed by the *udātta*. The pandits with whom Paulinus studied probably retained the memory of the Vedic accent.

6. These remarks are evidence of the fact that Paulinus first studied this tradition orally with the pandits. Nevertheless, he also himself copied texts written in Grantha-Malayalam script. This is why he often mistakes *p* for *v* and vice versa—for example *yupadi* for *yuvati* (VLS, p. 35), and *prāval* for *prāpat* (VLS, p. 60)—, in fact the Grantha-Malayalam letters *p* and *v* are very similar. These mistakes are often found in the examples derived by the friar from the *Bhāgavatapurāṇa* and the *Yudhiṣṭhiravijaya*, whose manuscripts were brought by Paulinus to Rome (see VLS, p. xx). The Grantha script, also known as *Ārya-eḻuttu*, has evolved out of two Dravidian scripts known as *Vaṭṭeḻuttu* and *Koleḻuttu*, which do not have symbols for voiced and aspirated sounds, but show a few special characters for those sounds which do not have parallels in Indo-Āryan languages. Eventually, some 'transitional' scripts have evolved showing the special characters of *Ārya-eḻuttu* and *Vaṭṭeḻuttu* as well (see Mangalam 1988: v). In fact, the alphabet expounded by Paulinus at the beginning of SGS and of VLS as well is also provided with the characters for the alveolar liquid [ṟ], for the retroflex lateral [ḷ] and for the retroflex fricative [ḻ]. Some peculiarities in transliterating into Roman characters are due to the fact that Paulinus read texts written in *Vaṭṭeḻuttu*, which is why the consonants are systematically doubled after *r*[18]—for example, *svargga* for *svarga* (VLS, p. 7). Moreover, the friar mistakes the double voiced aspirated dental for the single, and, conversely, the single voiced aspirated velar for the double—for example, *sidha* for *siddha*, and *magghavan* for *maghavan* (VLS, p. 44). This kind of reduplication is quite common in the Grantha script, both in print and manuscripts (see Venugopalam 1983: 6). Another peculiarity of Paulinus' transliteration is the use of the Roman *l* in word-final position instead of dental *t* or retroflex *ṭ*—we have seen, for example, *prāval* for *prāpat*, and *lal* for *laṭ*. If we take into consideration those words which have been transliterated by Paulinus into Roman characters and into Grantha-Malayalam as well, we can note that in word-final position the Roman *l* transliterates two different Grantha letters, namely the dental lateral [*l*] and a special character of *Koleḻuttu* (see Grandhavali 1971: 18, 34 note 1), i.e. the *ardhākṣara* of the retroflex lateral [ḷ] used instead of the retroflex stop [ṭ]. In Malayalam language, dental and retroflex stops are not allowed in word-final position. Consequently, whenever these sounds occur as the terminal consonant of a Sanskrit word, they are substituted by their lateral equivalent in both pro-

[18]Optionally admitted by A. 8.4.46 *aco rahābhyāṃ dve* (*yaraḥ vā* 45).

nunciation and writing.[19] Paulinus' transliteration is once again evidence of a peculiar pronunciation of his teachers.

7. In spite of these peculiarities in the orthography, SGS and VLS are grammars of pure Sanskrit, as Ludo Rocher (1977) pointed out in his translation of the preface to SGS. Nevertheless, Rocher considered it impracticable to study Paulinus' grammars due to these peculiarities and to the fact that these texts were mostly written in Latin. But, as we have seen, Paulinus' works are maybe the first document of the grammar known in Kerala as *Siddharūpa* and used—and printed as well—up to the present time for teaching Sanskrit. Moreover, SGS and VLS are proof of a local pronunciation of Sanskrit, influenced by Dravidian languages in the phonology but not in the morphology. Last of all, Paulinus' grammars help to reconstruct the history of the knowledge of Sanskrit in Europe: even Kant (1802: 157) cited *Grammatica Samsordamica*—which was actually Paulinus' SGS—in his lecture notes on physical geography.

References and abbreviations

A: Aṣṭādhyāyī of Pāṇini. See Katre.

Adelung, Friedrich von
1832 *An Historical Sketch of Sanscrit Literature: With Copious Biographical Notices of Sanscrit Works and Traditions.* Oxford: D. A. Talboys.

ASP: *Amarasinha. Sectio prima de caelo ex tribus ineditis codicibus Indicis manuscriptis.* See Paulinus a Sancto Bartholomaeo 1798.

Barone, Giuseppe
1888 *Vita, precursori ed opere del P. Paolino da S. Bartolommeo (Filippo Werdin): Contributo alla storia degli studi orientali in Europa.* Napoli: A. Morano.

Bhaskaran, T.
1987 *Prakriyāsarvasvam: Melputtūr Nārāyaṇabhaṭṭatiri.* 5th vol. Trivandrum: University of Kerala.

[19] The same applies to dental and retroflex stops occurring as the first consonant of a cluster. See, for instance, Staal 1961: 38.

Camps, Arnulf
1969 Father Heinrich Roth s.j. (1620–1668) and the history of his Sanskrit manuscripts. *Zeitschrift für Missionswissenschaft und Religionswissenschaft* 53: 185–195. Revised version in *The Sanskrit Grammar and Manuscripts of Father Heinrich Roth s.j. (1620–1628): Facsimile Edition of Biblioteca Nazionale, Rome, Mss. Or. 171 and 172; With an Introduction by Arnulf Camps and Jean-Claude Muller*, edited by Arnulf Camps, 5–12. Leiden: Brill, 1988. Now in *Studies in Asian Mission History, 1956–1998*, 90–102. Leiden: Brill, 2000.

DMC: *De manuscriptis codicibus Indicis R. P. Joan Ernesti Hanxleden epistola ad R. P. Alexium Mariam a S. Joseph carmelitam excalceatum.* See Paulinus a Sancto Bartholomaeo 1799.

Franolic, Branko
1991 *Filip Vezdin's Contribution to Indic Studies in Europe at the Turn of the 18th Century.* Paris: Nouvelles Editions Latines.

Grandhavali, Rama Varma
1971 *Prācīna Kēraḷa Lipikaḷ.* Trichur: The Kerala Sahitya Akademi.

IOC: *India orientalis christiana: Continens fundationes ecclesiarum, seriem episcoporum, missiones, schismata, persecutiones, reges, viros illustres.* See Paulinus a Sancto Bartholomaeo 1794.

Kant, Immanuel
1802 *Physische Geographie: Auf Verlangen des Verfassers, aus seiner Handschrift und zum Theil bearbeitet von D. Friedrich Theodor Rink*, 1st vol. Königsberg: Göbbels und Unzer.

Katre, Sumitra Mangesh
1987 *Aṣṭādhyāyī of Pāṇini.* Austin: University of Texas Press. Reprinted with corrections, 1989, Delhi: Motilal Banarsidass.

KV: Kāśikāvr̥tti of Vāmana and Jayāditya. See Sharma.

Lanjuinais, Jean Denis
1832 *Œuvres de J. D. Lanjuinais*, ed. by Victor Ambroise Lanjuinais and Bon Joseph Dacier. Paris: Dondey-Dupré.

Mangalam, S. J.
1988 *Paleography of Malayalam Script.* Delhi: Eastern Book Linkers.

Mundadan, Anthony Mathias
1988 John Ernest Hanxleden (*Arnos Pathiri*): His contributions to the Sanskrit and Malayalam languages and literatures. In *Jesuit Presence in Indian History: Commemorative Volume on the Occasion of the 150th Anniversary of the New Madurai Mission, 1838–1988*, edited by Anand Amaladass, 182–204. Anand: Gujarat Sahitya Prakash.

Paulinus a Sancto Bartholomaeo
1790 *Sidharùbam seu grammatica Samscrdamica: Cui accedit dissertatio historico-critica in linguam Samscrdamicam, vulgo Samscret dictam; In qua huius linguae existentia, origo, praestantia, antiquitas, extensio, maternitas ostenditur, libri aliqui ex ea exarati critice recensentur, et simul aliquae antiquissimae gentilium orationes liturgicae paucis attinguntur, et explicantur.* Roma: S. C. de Propaganda Fide.
1794 *India orientalis christiana: Continens fundationes ecclesiarum, seriem episcoporum, missiones, schismata, persecutiones, reges, viros illustres.* Roma: Typis Salomonianis.
1798 *Amarasinha: Sectio prima de caelo ex tribus ineditis codicibus Indicis manuscriptis.* Roma: Antonio Fulgoni.
1799 *De manuscriptis codicibus Indicis R. P. Joan Ernesti Hanxleden epistola ad R. P. Alexium Mariam a S. Joseph carmelitam excalceatum.* Wien.
1804 *Vyàcarana seu locupletissima Samscrdamicae linguae institutio.* Roma: S. C. de Propaganda Fide.

PS: Prakriyāsarvasva of Nārāyaṇa Bhaṭṭa. See Bhaskaran.

Rocher, Ludo
1977 *Dissertation on the Sanskrit Language.* Amsterdam: John Benjamins B. V.

Sharma, Aryendra, Khanderao Deshpande, and D. G. Padhye
1969–70 *Kāśikā: A Commentary on Pāṇini's Grammar by Vāmana and Jayāditya.* 2 vols. Hyderabad: Sanskrit Academy, Osmania University.

Staal, Johan Frederik
1961 *Nambudiri Veda Recitation.* Den Haag: Mouton & Co.
1972 *A Reader on the Sanskrit Grammarians.* Cambridge (MA): MIT.

SGS: *Sidharùbam seu grammatica Samscrdamica: Cui accedit dissertatio historico-critica in linguam Samscrdamicam, vulgo Samscret dictam; In qua huius linguae existentia, origo, praestantia, antiquitas, extensio, maternitas ostenditur, libri aliqui ex ea exarati critice recensentur, et simul aliquae antiquissimae gentilium orationes liturgicae paucis attinguntur, et explicantur.* See Paulinus a Sancto Bartholomaeo 1790.

Steever, Sanford B.
1998 Introduction to the Dravidian languages. In *The Dravidian Languages*, edited by Sanford B. Steever, 1–39. London: Routledge.

Venugopalam, K.
1983 *A Primer in Grantha Characters.* St. Peter: James H. Nye.

VLS: *Vyàcarana seu locupletissima Samscrdamicae linguae institutio.* See Paulinus a Sancto Bartholomaeo 1804.

Wood, Ananda
1985 *Knowledge Before Printing and After: The Indian Tradition in Changing Kerala.* Delhi: Oxford University Press (electronic version prepared by Ananda Wood, 2002, www.advaitin.net/Ananda/KnowledgeBeforePrinting&After.pdf).

Can We Describe the *Grammar* of the Language of Hand Gestures in Indian Dancing as *vyākaraṇa*?*

BILIANA MÜLLER

1. The use of the word *grammar*

The use of the word *grammar* in contemporary literature on sign-systems in general and the arts in particular is nowadays influenced by a rather metaphoric understanding. This can be illustrated by a quotation from an interview with Werner Herzog, who says: "I'm looking for a new *grammar* of images, for images that fit our era, images never yet seen."[1] On the other hand, theoretical literature in the field of linguistics continues to consider *grammar* as a technical term. Consequently, we can observe a two-pronged tendency in the use of the word *grammar*: it is used as a metaphor for certain qualities and as a technical term adopted from the field of linguistics.

1.1. The use of the word *grammar* as a metaphor

The metaphoric use of the word *grammar* is extremely frequent in contemporary literature on Indian dance in India, in print and on the internet. To illustrate this better two examples can be quoted.

(1) In the recently published material on the use of hand gestures, *Hastha Prayogaah: Vocabulary of Hand Gestures in Bharatanatyam* by the contemporary bharatanāṭyam-dancer Jayalakshmi Eshwar, we read:

---

*This question was raised by Prof. Klaus Butzenberger, external referee at the viva voce examination of my thesis "Structure of Hand Gestures in Indian Dancing," and, due to its controversial character, led me to investigate the subject further. I would like to thank the organizers of the vyākaraṇa section of the 14th WSC for giving me the opportunity to share the results of this investigation.

[1]Werner Herzog, interview, *Programme 2009* (New Delhi. Goethe-Institut). Emphasis mine.

"The viniyogas form the essential *grammar* for the dance and constitute an essential aspect of Bharatanatyam."[2]

(2) The second example is from the internet, where we read: "Kuchipudi has a well-defined *grammar* and every essay of human expression is covered in the comprehensive treatise written by Bharatamuni. Swami Siddhendra Yogi has culled out the *grammar* of Nāṭyaśāstra and defined the *grammar* of this classical form."[3]

We can see that in the two quotations the word *grammar* is used each time in a different sense and that the four usages have little in common. In the first quotation *grammar* is related to the *viniyogas* in a particular dance style, bharatanāṭyam, and in the second to a particular dance style, kuchipuḍi. But three additional different meanings are also ascribed to the word *grammar*. In this paper we will not go into details about the differences in those metaphoric applications. For, in taking up the question whether *vyākaraṇa* is appropriate as a Sanskrit term with reference to the language of hand gestures in Indian dancing, it is not the metaphoric use of the word *grammar* but its use as a technical term towards which our analysis will be directed. The direction we get from the observation on its metaphoric use is to reconsider the database on Indian dance from a linguistic point of view while applying *grammar* as a technical term. The use of this technical term will be examined thereafter, dealing with its equivalence with the technical term *vyākaraṇa* in the grammar tradition of the Sanskrit language.

1.2. The use of *grammar* as a technical term

The first investigation in literature on Indian dance where the word *grammar* is used as a technical term borrowed from the field of linguistics was undertaken by Yoshihiko Ikegami, a student of Sydney Lamb. Influenced by his teacher, known as the 'father' of stratificational grammar, Ikegami applies to the system of hand gestures in Indian dancing the method of stratificational grammar in accordance with his objective "to show that the theory of stratificational grammar can successfully be applied to communication systems other than natural language."[4] His investigation is very precise from the perspective of stratificational grammar and achieves the aim of meeting the objectives stated by the author, but due to lack of indological background it is not a big contribution to indological discourse. It is a matter of fact that this first proposal for a grammar model for the language of hand gestures in Indian dance has remained a rather isolated attempt for over four decades and even Ikegami himself has not elaborated

[2] Jayalakshmi 2006: Introduction on the DVD cover. Emphasis mine.

[3] `http://www.kuchipudi.com/htmlfiles/grammar.htm`. Emphasis mine.

[4] Ikegami 1973: 365.

further on this idea in his later studies. Nevertheless, this investigation is an example of the fact that, when applied to the language of hand gestures in Indian dancing, the word *grammar* can be used as a technical term and not as a metaphor.

2. The use of the word *vyākaraṇa* in the text tradition on Indian dance

Although body language in Indian dance in general and the language of hand gestures in particular have frequently been described as 'having a grammar'—be it in a metaphorical or strictly technical sense—nowhere have these been described as *vyākaraṇa*, either in Indian or non Indian literature.

Some possible reasons for this observation could be explained with the common understanding of the word *vyākaraṇa* and the ground it provides for metaphoric interpretations. This will be elaborated next.

2.1. The use of the word *vyākaraṇa* as a metaphor

A possible reason for avoiding the word *vyākaraṇa* in theoretical discourse on Indian dancing could be the interpretation of this term as signifying separation, division and the like: this would be in contradiction with the holistic principles in Indian dance, where any utterance in a dance performance is supposed to be seen as part of an integrated whole. The interpretation of *vyākaraṇa* as *separation* is supported by the etymological derivation of *vyākaraṇa* from the verbal root $\sqrt{kṛ}$, meaning 'to do', 'to make', 'to perform', 'to accomplish', with the prefixes *vi-* and *ā-*; the verbal root and the prefixes, taken together, lead to a common understanding of the word *vyākaraṇa* as signifying 'making apart', 'separating' and the like. On the other hand, exactly this one interpretation of *vyākaraṇa* as *separation* etc. underlies the meaning of the word as a technical term in Sanskrit linguistics, where the process of dividing a language unit into its constituents defines the *analytic approach*. Pāṇini's system presupposes the analysis of utterances into components. This is pointed out by George Cardona, who says: "Pāṇini's derivational system presupposes the analysis of utterances into components: padas, stems, bases, affixes and augments."[5] Kashinath Vasudev Abhyankar also interprets *vyākaraṇa* as *analysis*, translating the Mahābhāṣya passage: *vyākriyate anena iti vyākaraṇam*[6] as 'analysis or explanation by analysis'.[7]

[5]Cardona 1988: 499 (**666**) [Second edition (1997): 428 (**666**)].
[6]Abhyankar 1977: 377.
[7]Abhyankar 1977: 376.

2.2. The use of *vyākaraṇa* as a technical term

It is a matter of fact that the first grammars of the Sanskrit language were not described as *vyākaraṇa* by their authors. It is in examples to A 4.3.101 *tena proktam* that the work of Pāṇini is described as *pāṇininā proktam* = *pāṇinīyam* 'the Aṣṭādhyāyī which was expounded by Pāṇini'.[8] As Rama Nath Sharma points out (1999: 314), a twofold classification is traditionally made: (1) texts which are qualified as *proktam* (A 4.3.101): for example, the Aṣṭādhyāyī; (2) other texts, which are qualified as *kṛte granthe* (A 4.3.116). The first evidence for using *vyākaraṇa* as a technical term in the grammar discourse on Sanskrit linguistics is to be found in the Mahābhāṣya. A systematic overview for using the word *vyākaraṇa* as a technical term in the field of Sanskrit linguistics was suggested by Kashinath Vasudev Abhyankar. He enumerated (1977: 376–77) seven different usages of *vyākaraṇa* as a technical term and supported this enumeration by quotations from Sanskrit grammatical tradition.

(a) analysis or explanation by analysis;
(b) rules of explanation;
(c) specific rules explaining the formation of words;
(d) explanation of the formation of rules;
(e) a treatise in which such an explanation is given;
(f) a collection of such treatises;
(g) a systematic explanation of the formation of words in a language.

In order to examine whether these meanings of the technical term *vyākaraṇa*, or at least one of them, is applicable to the *grammar* of the body language in Indian dancing in general and the language of hand gestures in particular, we will focus here on the data from Indian dance tradition.

3. Data sources for proposing a grammar model for the language of hand gestures in Indian dancing

There are two main sources for transmitting knowledge about the symbolic interaction in Indian dancing, which have developed separately from each other: the oral tradition of knowledge transfer and the written tradition of texts on dance.

3.1. Oral sources

In the oral tradition knowledge has been transmitted through personal intercourse between the teacher (*guru*) and the student (*śiṣya*). As a result, memory about the system in question is preserved only in the present phase

[8] Sharma 1999: 313.

of the contemporary dancing generation. There are no records about its earlier phases. This tradition is known as *guruśiṣyaparamparā*, or *sampradāya* or, in modern Indian Languages such as Urdu and Hindi, by the Arabic word *silsilā*.

3.2. Written sources

The second tradition of knowledge transfer is through written sources in the form of texts, didactic literature described as *śāstra*, *sūtra* and the like. The written tradition of knowledge transfer has preserved several phases of the system in question. Unfortunately, however, the oldest texts are corrupted and suffer from many interpolations, repetitions and omissions. Consequently, attempts to reconstruct a knowledge system amount to solving a puzzle.

The mutual links between Indian grammar tradition and Indian dance tradition go back in time as early as the earliest texts preserved. Evidence can be provided from the Aṣṭādhyāyī of Pāṇini. A 4.3.110 *pārāśaryaśilālibhyāṃ bhikṣunaṭasūtrayoḥ* provides that those who study the *naṭasūtra* expounded by Śilālin are called *śailālin*[9] and A 4.3.111 *karmandakṛśāśvād iniḥ* provides that those performers who study the *naṭasūtra* expounded by Kṛśāśva are called *kṛśāśvin.*[10]

In terms of the terminological description of *grammar* at this time as *proktam* we can observe that, according to the Aṣṭādhyāyī, the Naṭasūtra of Śilālin and the Naṭasūtra of Kṛśāśva are of the same status of being *proktam* ('expounded') as the Aṣṭādhyāyī of Pāṇini, because the application of A 4.3.101 *tena proktam* is not disconnected till A 4.3.111 and has to be supplied both in A 4.3.110 and in A 4.3.111. As a result of that application, we may conclude that the way of expounding a text described in Sanskrit as *naṭasūtra* and ascribed to Śilālin and Kṛśāśva is identical with the way of expounding a text as done by Pāṇini in the Aṣṭādhyāyī. Hence the status of authorship in all the cases mentioned is to be considered in the same terms: Śilālin, Kṛśāśva and Pāṇini are equally *pravaktāraḥ*.

At this point we can consider that the Aṣṭādhyāyī clearly acknowledges texts described as *naṭasūtra* to be of the same type as texts on Sanskrit grammar. This supports in general the idea of using Sanskrit terminology for grammar to describe both a text on grammar of the Sanskrit language and a text on the symbolic interaction in Indian dance. Unfortunately the texts described in the Aṣṭādhyāyī as *naṭasūtra* and ascribed to Śilālin and Kṛśāśva have not been preserved. The earliest text preserved on body language in general and the language of hand gestures in particular is the Nāṭyaśāstra, which is ascribed to Bharata and dated in the period between

---

[9]Sharma 1999: 320.
[10]Sharma 1999: 321.

the 2nd century B.C. and the 2nd century A.D. We will take here this text as the main data source for further analysis.

3.3. The relationship between written and oral traditions of knowledge transfer in Indian dance in general and the system of hand gestures in particular

It is a matter of fact that knowledge about Indian dance in general and the system of hand gestures in particular has been transmitted separately in both traditions through a period of 2 millennia and covering a territory of 3.3 million square kilometers. Considering this fact, one should be more surprised by similarities preserved in both traditions than by differences. A comparison of those traditions shows that the differences are restricted to number, name and meaning of the hand gestures included and most of all remaining features of the system in question are surprisingly similar. But contemporary discourse on Indian dance in general and on hand gestures in particular is focused on pointing out the differences and not the similarities in the information received by the teacher and the information found in the texts. Regarding the system of hand gestures there is a slogan postulated in the discourse: *lakṣaṇaṃ lakṣyaviruddhaṃ*, which implies that the information about a particular meaning of a hand gesture as explained by the teacher is seen in *contradiction* (*viruddha*) to the information about this meaning preserved in the text tradition. As a result of this development the discussion on symbolic interaction in dance started focusing on the proper meaning and the correct hand form of a particular hand sign.

This attitude towards the language of hand gestures in Indian dance resembles the attitude in the *vyākaraṇa* tradition of the Sanskrit language in terms of 'defining' and teaching 'the correct forms' as for example the understanding of *vyākaraṇa* as teaching the correct speech forms (*śabdānuśāsana*). Due to the different mode of articulation between a spoken and a sign language, in the latter the formal is carried out through the hand form hasta and not through a speech form *śabda*. Therefore the prescription for the 'correct speech form' (*śabdānuśāsana*) is seen here as functionally identical with the prescription for the 'correct hand form' (*hastānuśāsana*).

To remedy the apparent contradictory (*viruddha*) status of the oral and the written traditions we will consider their differences to be due to changes in a genealogical model. The situation is comparable to that of genetically related languages in a language family. For illustrating the genealogy of the languages in the Indo-European language family the picture of a tree with different branches is commonly used. Here we will apply the same picture (see figure 1 below) to the language system of hand gestures in Indian dancing, where the different branches will represent the languages used and taught in the different chains of a *guruśiṣyaparamparā*. For representing the written tradition of knowledge transfer the following texts will be taken into account in chronological order:

(1) the Nāṭyaśāstra ascribed to Bharata (NŚBh);
(2) the Abhinavabhāratī ascribed to Abhinavagupta, 950–1020 (AB);
(3) the Abhinayadarpaṇa ascribed to Nandikeśvara, 11th century (ADN);
(4) the Saṅgītaratnākara ascribed to Śārṅgadeva, 1210–1247 (SRŚ);
(5) the Nṛttaratnāvalī ascribed to Jaya Senāpati, 13th century (NRJ);
(6) the Hastamuktāvalī (HM) and the Saṃgītadāmodara (SD)—both ascribed to Śubhaṅkara Kavi, 14th century;
(7) the Abhinavacandrikā ascribed to Śrī Satyanātha Tīrtha, 1660–1673 (AC):
(8) the Bālakrīḍā edited by Madhusudan Shastri in 1975 together with the commentary Madhusūdanī (BKMS).

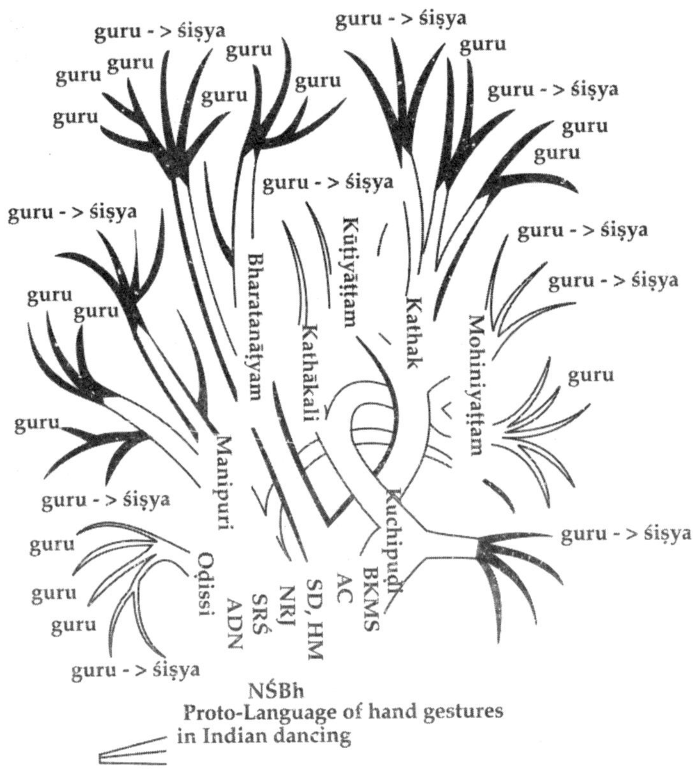

Fig. 1: Genealogy of the language of hand gestures in Indian dancing regarding the written and the oral tradition of knowledge transfer

4. The system of hand gestures in Indian Dancing

It is the 9th chapter of the Nāṭyaśāstra of Bharata that describes the performance, the meaning and the use of hand gestures in the symbolic interaction of dance. The first main feature of this description is the invention of a special nomenclature for the hand forms (*hasta*), which, while used as a gesture in dance, can convey a particular meaning. This special nomenclature describes 64 hand forms by names (*nāmatas*) as said in NŚBh 9.17: *catuṣṣaṣṭikarā hy ete nāmato 'bhihitā mayā.* These hand forms are further divided into three types:

(i) hand forms performed with one hand (*asaṃyuta-hasta*);
(ii) hand forms performed with two hands (*saṃyuta-hasta*);
(iii) hand forms which do not convey a predefined meaning (*nṛtta-hasta*).

The distinction between (i) and (ii) is obviously a formal one and has consequences on the syntactic level. But the distinction between (i) and (iii) is a semantic one as the distinction between (ii) and (iii). Examples of such names are:

> *patāka*, *tripatāka*, *kartarīmukha*, *ardhacandra*, *arāla*, *śukatuṇḍa*, *alapadma*, *catura*, *bhramara*, *haṃsapakṣa*, *sandaṃśa*, *mukula*, *ūrṇanābha*, *añjali*, *kapota*, *karkaṭa*, *svastika*, *utsaṃga*, etc.

The crucial point about this nomenclature is that the names build a kind of a meta-language, which is invented for the purpose of enabling the discourse about the units in the system of symbolic interaction and are not the units themselves. For example, in relation to the already quoted hand form *arāla*, the text describes 25 different meanings, which can be represented in dance. The first seven are described as (1) *sattva* 'being, existence, reality', (2) *śauṇḍīrya* 'haughtiness, pride', (3) *vīrya* 'manliness, strength, heroism', (4) *dhṛti* 'satisfaction, content', (5) *kānti* 'beauty, splendor', (6) *divya* 'heavenly, divine' and (7) *gāmbhīrya* 'deepness, depth' (NŚBh. 9.46cd: ... *sattvaśauṇḍīryavīryadhṛtikāntidivyagāmbhīryam*). It is obvious that these descriptions are different enough not to be complementary explanations of one and the same meaning. Consequently, the conclusion can be drawn that any separate verbal description is to be attributed to a different sign. As a result of this observation, we can say that according to the Nāṭyaśāstra there are 25 different signs which can be performed with the hand form *arāla*.

This procedure proved to be applicable to all the hand forms described in the 9th chapter of the Nāṭyaśāstra. As a result we could distinguish a total number of approximately 500 hand signs for representing 500 concepts explicitly described in the text. The name which the Nāṭyaśāstra introduces for every particular hand form can be considered as a name of a class of signs where all the signs share the common formal feature to be performed by the same hand form (*hasta*). Due to the fact that both descriptions are provided in the same language, Sanskrit, and in the same text, the 9th chapter of the Nāṭyaśāstra, it has not been pointed out with sufficient clarity, that a distinction is to be made between the inventory of the meta-language, consisting of the names invented by the author with respect to a formal feature of the units of the system in question, and the inventory of the language itself, consisting of approximately 500 units described in the text through the concept they are supposed to represent in dance.

5. A grammar model for the language of hand gestures in Indian dancing

If we apply the methodology of stratificational grammar, we can propose a *four strata*[11] grammar model[12] for the language of hand gestures in Indian dancing. The data provided by the 9th chapter of the Nāṭyaśāstra can be ascribed to the different levels as follows.

The *names* introduced for the hand forms are given by the author with respect to a formal feature of the hand sign and are to be identified with the morphemes of a spoken language and to be mapped on the second level—the *morphemic stratum*. The next higher level—the *lexemic stratum*—consists of the elements, which in a spoken language are the lexemes. For the language of hand gestures in Indian dancing we collect those elements through the descriptions in the text where the meaning which a hand form can convey in dance is explained. The interpretation of this meaning is in a four strata language model equal with the interpretation of the meaning of a lexeme and to be mapped here on the next higher level—the *sememic stratum*.

The 9th chapter of the Nāṭyaśāstra provides approximately 500 descriptions which are attributed to 37 hand forms. For the hand forms described as *nṛttahasta* there are also particular names in the text but no explanation for the meanings they should convey in dance. Consequently they will have no representations on the *sememic stratum* and will not be included in the grammar model proposed here.

In order to distinguish the different elements on the third level, the *lexemic stratum*, we introduce numbers after the name of the hand form: for

[11] "Four strata have been recognized for English, and it is probable that all languages may have at least these four: the sememic, the lexemic, the morphemic, and the phonemic strata." (*Encyclopedia Britannica* on line: 'stratificational grammar')

[12] A first idea about such a model was proposed in Müller 2007 and finalized in Müller 2008.

example, the already quoted hand form *arāla* will have 25 'realizations' on the next higher level, namely, *arāla*/01, *arāla*/02, *arāla*/03, *arāla*/04, ..., *arāla*/25.

The formal distinction between the different elements which are performed by the same hand form is made by different movements and by different positions in relation to the body. But the text does not always provide this information. Concerning the movement of the hand while performing a particular gesture, the text introduces the technical term *karaṇa* and explains that it can be of four types:

1) *apaveṣṭita*; 2) *udveṣṭita*; 3) *vyāvartita* and 4) *parivartita*.

The text does not explain how the four different types of movement influence the meaning of a particular hand sign but only introduces their metalanguage descriptions. As we can observe, these descriptions in Sanskrit use the same verbal root with different prefixes. This clearly conveys the idea of minimal pair relations since those movements are described twice by the derivation of the same verbal root with a different prefix. The opposing semantic relations associated with *apa-veṣṭita* and *ud-veṣṭita* are linked with the semantic relations conveyed by the meanings of the prefixes *apa* and *ut*. Similarly, the relation between *vyāvartita* and *parivartita* is associated with a contrast of the prefixes: *vyā* (= *vi-ā*) versus *pari*.

For several signs there are explicit explanations of the movements in question; for example the antonyms 'opening' and 'closing' performed with the same hand form called *patāka*. The semantic opposition is formally carried out by the opposite direction of the movement. Such explanations, however, are rather exceptions in the text tradition and derive mainly from the oral tradition of knowledge transfer of the system in question.

Another formal aspect of the hand sign in relation to the structural character of the data base is its position in relation to the performing body. Here again, instead of all the information required, the text provides only some examples. These include three signs performed with the hand form called *añjali*: *añjali*/01 is performed at the forehead, *añjali*/02 in front of the face, and *añjali*/03 at the chest. These convey respectively greetings to gods, respected persons, and friends. The three signs can be distinguished by a particular position of the sign with respect to a particular part of the body.

The elements of the first stratum are explained neither in the text nor in the oral tradition of knowledge transfer. They are to be elaborated by a detailed analysis of the hand form and a possible division in its constituting elements. In our approach we will apply the methodology and the terminology from contemporary literature on gesture studies as established since Birdwhistell, Ekman and Friesen. For the proposed analysis we will implement the 'model of genesis of emblematic gestures' by Roland Posner where he distinguishes six stages in the development of any emblematic gesture from an everyday gesture.[13]

Our starting point will be what the author describes in his work as 'Stage 4: Designation of a potential cause (as well as abstract predication with a directive function)'.[14] This stage will be identified here with the description of the meaning of a hand gesture in the text and the lexemic stratum in the grammar model. Our direction of analysis will be reversed—aiming at finding out what Posner describes as 'Stage 1: Self-oriented body movements produced with a physical purpose'[15] which will provide the basis for defining the elements of the first stratum in the grammar model proposed here.

As an example, we will take the hand form (*hasta*) introduced in the text by the name *bhramara*. The Nāṭyaśāstra gives a clear instruction as to how to perform the *hasta*. NŚBh. 9.102: *madhyamāṅguṣṭha-sandaṁśo vakrā caiva pradeśinī / ūrdhvam anye prakīrṇe dvyaṅgulyau bhramare kare //* It is illustrated here in figure 2.

Fig. 2: *bhramara*

The first concepts which can be performed by this hand form in dance are described in the text as 'holding, grasping or putting behind one's ear flowers such as padma, utpala, kumuda or flowers with a long stem'. NŚBh. 9.102: *padmotpalakumudānām anyeṣāṃ caiva dīrghavṛntānām / puṣpāṇāṃ grahaṇavidhiḥ kartavyaḥ karṇapuraś ca //*

On the basis of this description we separate three different elements for the lexemic stratum: *bhramara*/01, *bhramara*/02 and *bhramara*/03, which have their representations on the sememic stratum as shown on the table below.

[13] Posner 2001; 2003.

[14] "Stadium 4: Designation einer potentiellen Wirkung (sowie abstrakte Prädikation)" in Posner 2001: 14.

[15] "Stadium 1. Auf einen physischen Zweck gerichtete selbstbezogene Körperbewegungen" in Posner 2001: 11.

STRATA	ELEMENT 1	ELEMENT 3	ELEMENT 3
Description in the Nāṭyaśāstra	*padmotpala-kumudānām anyeṣāṃ caiva dīrghavṛntānām puṣpāṇāṃ* ***grahaṇavidhiḥ***	*padmotpala-kumudānām anyeṣāṃ caiva dīrghavṛntānām puṣpāṇāṃ* ***grahaṇavidhiḥ***	*padmotpala-kumudānām anyeṣāṃ caiva dīrghavṛntānām puṣpāṇāṃ* ***karṇapuraḥ***
IV: sememic stratum	**to hold** flowers as *padma, utpala, kumuda* and the like or flowers with a long stem	**to grasp** flowers as *padma, utpala,* ...	**to put** flowers as *padma, utpala,* ... **behind one's ear**
III: lexemic stratum	*bhramara*/01	*bhramara*/02	*bhramara*/03

The descriptions 'to hold flowers as ...' (... *puṣpāṇāṃ grahaṇavidhiḥ*), 'to grasp flowers as ...' (... *puṣpāṇāṃ grahaṇavidhiḥ*), and 'to put flowers as ... behind one's ear' (... *puṣpāṇāṃ karṇapuraḥ*) are obviously descriptions for movements where a flower is held, picked, or put behind one's ear. The descriptions of these movements lead us to what Posner (2001: 11) describes as 'Self-oriented body movements produced with a physical purpose'. Essential element for performing the movements here seems to be the touch between thumb and middle finger (*madhyamāṅguṣṭhasandaṁśa*), which also indicates the physical purpose of the movements: the fingers touch each the same way as they would do if there were holding a flower with a long stem.

Fig. 3: *madhyamāṅguṣṭhasandaṁśa*

On the basis of this analysis we distinguish one element of the hand form *bhramara* on the first level—'touch between thumb and middle finger', shown here in figure 3.

The same element we can recognize in another hand form described in the text with the name *tāmracūḍa* 'rooster', shown in figure 4. To perform this element in both hand forms, the text repeats the same instruction: it is 'to be performed separating the fingers with a sound, as in threatening and the like' (NŚBh 9. 103ab, 123ab: *vicyutaś ca saśabdaś ca kāryo nirbhartsanādiṣu*).

Fig. 4: hand form *tāmracūḍa*

This observation makes us assume that we have a single element on the first stratum that is shared by two representations on the next higher stratum: pressing the middle finger with the thumb (*madhyamāṅguṣṭhasandaṁśa*), than separation accompanied by a sound (*vicyutaś ca saśabdaś ca*); this element is common to the hand forms *bhramara* and *tāmracūḍa*. A proposal for mapping this observation is shown here in figure 5:

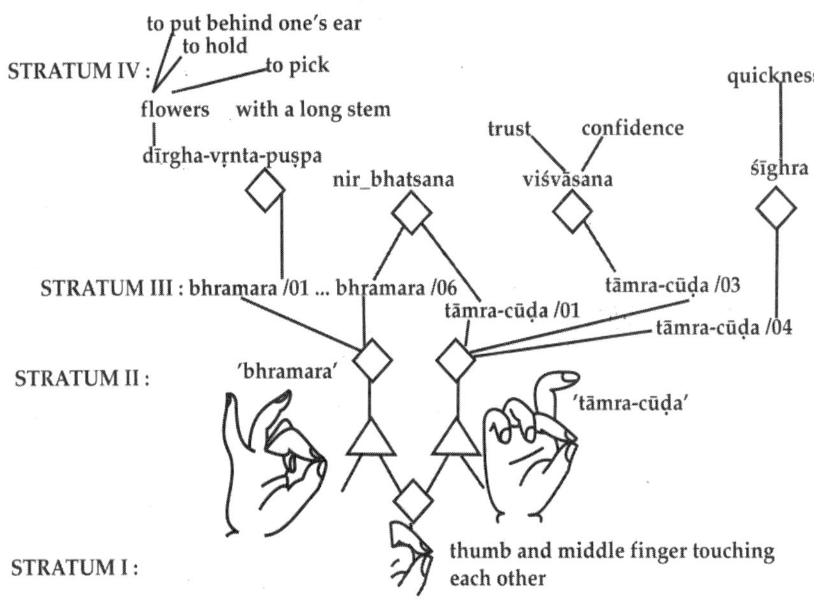

Fig. 5: Graph mapping on a four strata grammar model some realizations of the hand forms *bhramara* and *tāmracūḍa*

6. Conclusion

The investigative study presented here has shown that a morphological analysis of the language of hand gestures in Indian dancing leads us to a grammar model where, as practiced in the tradition of stratificational grammar, a four strata division of the constituting elements is suggested. The demonstrated morphological analysis of the constituting elements is identified with the analytical approach in the *vyākaraṇa* tradition regarding the Sanskrit language. Based on this comparison, the Sanskrit description as *vyākaraṇa* for the grammar of the hand gestures in Indian dance is regarded as appropriate though never used in such a context before. The probable reason why there has not been a single quotation where the word *vyākaraṇa* is used for denoting the grammar of the body language in Indian dance in general and the language of hand gestures in particular is found in the etymological explanation of the meaning of *vyākaraṇa* in terms of separating which places the meaning of this word into a semantic opposition to the holistic principles of Indian dance according to which any utterance in dance should be seen as an indivisible whole.

It was shown that 'not describing' the treatise on body language in general and the language of hand gesture in particular as *vyākaraṇa* meets again the attitude in the early *vyākaraṇa* tradition towards the *grammar* of the Sanskrit language which also was not described as *vyākaraṇa* but as *proktam*—a metalanguage description which is used in the same text for describing both the treatise—on Sanskrit language and on the symbolic interaction in dance.

References and abbreviations

A: Aṣṭādhyāyī of Pāṇini. See Sharma.

Abhyankar, Kashinath Vasudev
1977 *A Dictionary of Sanskrit Grammar*. Baroda: Oriental Institute.

Cardona, George
1988 *Pāṇini: His Work and Its Traditions; Volume One: Background and Introduction*. Delhi: Motilal Banarsidass.
1997 *Pāṇini: His Work and Its Traditions; Volume One: Background and Introduction*. 2nd ed. Delhi: Motilal Banarsidass.

Chakravarty, Shrutidhara
2008 *Paninian Influence on Sanskrit Poetics*. Delhi: Pratibha Prakashan.

Ekman, Paul, and Wallace Friesen
1969 The repertoire of nonverbal behaviour. *Semiotica* 1: 49–98.

Ikegami, Yoshihiko
1971 A stratificational analysis of the hand gestures in Indian classical dancing. *Semiotica* 4: 365–391.

Jayalakshmi, Eshwar
2006 *Hastha Prayogaah: Vocabulary of Hand Gestures in Bharatanatyam.* With DVD and CD. Delhi: Vedams Books.

Lamb, Sydney M.
1966 *Outline of Stratificational Grammar.* Washington, D.C.: Georgetown University Press.

Madhusudan Shasti, Acharya
1975 *Nāṭyaśāstram with the Comm. Abhinavabharati, Madhusudani and Balakrida.* Varanasi: Banaras Hindu University Press.

Monier-Willims, Monier
1964 *Sanskrit-English Dictionary: Etymologically and Philologically Arranged with Special Reference to Cognate Indo-European Languages.* 1899. Oxford: Oxford University Press.

Müller, Biliana
2007 Codes for performing the Old Indian Epics: Language typology of propositions. Paper presented at the 13th WSC, Edinburgh, 2007.
2008 *Die Struktur der Handgesten im indischen Tanz nach dem ‚Nāṭya-Śāstra'des Bharata (NŚBh).* Berlin: TUB.

NŚBh: Nāṭyaśāstra ascribed to Bharata. See Madhusudan.

Posner, Roland
1986 Systematik der Beschreibung verbaler und nonverbaler Kommunikation. In *Perspektiven auf Sprache*, edited by Hans-Georg Bosshardt. Berlin/New York: de Gruyter.
2001 Alltagsgesten als Ergebnis von Ritualisierung. *Forschungsberichte des Instituts für Phonetik und Sprachliche Kommunikation der Universität München (FIPKM)* [= „Human and Machine Perception in Acoustic and Visual Communication (HAMP)"Conference Proceedings] 37: 5–24.
2003 Everyday gestures as a result of ritualization. In *Gestures: Meaning and Use*, edited by Rector/Poggi/Trigo. Oporto: Fernando Pessoa University Press.

Posner, Roland, and Cornelia Müller
1998 *The Semantics and Pragmatics of Everyday Gestures: Proceedings of the Berlin Conference, April 1998.* Berlin: Weidler.

Ragini Devi
1972 *Dance Dialects of India.* Delhi: Vikas Publishing House.

Rao, U. S. Krishna
1980 *Dictionary of Bharata Natya.* Bombay: Longman.

Sequeira, A. Ronald
1977 *Spielende Liturgie Bewegung neben Wort und Ton im Gottesdienst am Beispiel des Vaterunsers.* Freiburg: Herder.
1978 *Klassische indische Tanzkunst und christliche Verkündigung eine vergleichende religionsgeschichtlich-religionsphilosophische Studie.* Freiburg: Herder.

Sharma, Rama Nath
1987–2003 *The Aṣṭādhyāyī of Pāṇini.* 6 vols. Vol. 1 (1987); vol. 2 (1990); vol. 3 (1995); vol. 4 (1999): vol. 5 (2001); vol. 6 (2003). Delhi: Munshiram Manoharlal.

Simon-Vandenbergen, Anne-Marie, Miriam Taverniers, and Louise Ravelli
2003 *Grammatical Metaphor: View from Systemic Functional Linguistics.* Amsterdam: John Benjamins Publishing Company.

Srivastava, Harishchandra
1986 *Kathak Nṛtya Paricay.* Gandharva Niketan: Mandal Publications.

Zeshan, Ulrike
2000 *Sign Language in Indo-Pakistan: A Description of a Signed Language.* Philadelphia: John Benjamins.

Bhartṛhari on *A* 1.1.45 *ig yaṇaḥ saṃprasāraṇam**

HIDEYO OGAWA

0. Introduction

A 1.1.45 is known as the rule which provides that *i*-, *u*-, *ṛ*-, and *ḷ*-vowels (***ik***) that replace *y*-, *v*-, *r*-, *l*-semivowels (*ya**ṇ***) are called *saṃprasāraṇa*, and this term denotes also the replacement of those semivowels by those vowels (*ubhayasaṃjñā*).[1] This interpretation of the rule in question is based on the third vārttika on the rule: *vibhaktiviśeṣanirdeśas tu jñāpaka ubhayasaṃjñātvasya*. In this vārttika Kātyāyana proposes that *A* 1.1.45 is to assign the name *saṃprasāraṇa* both to a set of sounds (*varṇasaṃjñā*; [Bhāṣya] *ig yo yaṇaḥ sthāne varṇaḥ sa saṃprasāraṇasaṃjño bhavati*) and to a sentence (*vākyasaṃjñā*; [Bhāṣya] *ig yaṇa ity etad vākyaṃ saṃprasāraṇasaṃjñam bhavati*).

This paper is concerned with Bhartṛhari's treatment of issues concerning the *vākyasaṃjñā*-view, to which he resorts in order to illustrate the point that a sentence meaning is single and indivisible. It can easily be imagined that the idea that the sentence *ig yaṇaḥ [bhavati]* is referred to by the term *saṃprasāraṇa* strongly attracted him when he developed his theory of a sentence and a sentence meaning. The aim of this paper is to see how he incorporates the *vākyasaṃjñā*-view into his arguments about what a sentence and a sentence meaning are. It will be shown that Bhartṛhari holds the *vākyasaṃjñā*-view to be a direct indication (*liṅga*) to show that the tradition of Pāṇini's grammar declares that a sentence meaning is single, impartite, and indivisible.

*The present paper is one of the outcomes of the seminar on the second kāṇḍa of the *Vākyapadīya*, conducted by Professor Ashok Aklujkar, Kyoto, October 2003–February 2004. I would like to express my gratitude to Professor Aklujkar for providing me with the text of the *Vṛtti* on the second kāṇḍa of the *Vākyapadīya*, critically edited, though unpublished, by him. Thanks are also due to Professor Brendan S. Gillon for reading the draft and making a number of helpful suggestions.

[1] See PWT 38.

1. *MBh* on *A* 1.1.45

Let us first look at how, in his Bhāṣya on *A* 1.1.45, Patañjali presents the *vākyasaṃjñā*-view. He says the following:

> *MBh* on *A* 1.1.45 (I.111.2–3): *ig yaṇa ity etad vākyaṃ samprasāraṇasaṃjñaṃ bhavati /*

Kaiyaṭa gives two interpretations to this statement of Patañjali's.

> *Pradīpa* on *MBh* to *A* 1.1.45 (I.342): (a) *vākyaśabdena vākyārtha ucyate / ig yaṇa ity atra bhavatīty adhyāhārād ig yaṇo bhavatīti yo 'yaṃ vākyārthas tasyeyaṃ saṃjñety arthaḥ /*
> (b) *athavā vākyasyaiveyaṃ saṃjñā, tatpratipāditaṃ ca vākyaṃ svārtham api pratipādayati /*
>
> "(a) [Interpreation 1] Patañjali means a sentence meaning (*vākyārtha*) by the word *vākya*. Because of supplying the verb form *bhavati* 'occurs' in the string *ig yaṇaḥ*, Patañjali's statement means that the name [*samprasāraṇa*] is a technical one for the meaning of the sentence *ig yaṇo bhavati*.
>
> (b) [Interpretation 2] Alternatively, this name is given to the sentence *ig yaṇo bhavati* itself; the sentence understood from the name conveys its own meaning as well."

In the *vākyasaṃjñā*-view the item *iti* is considered to recur in *A* 1.1.45 from *A* 1.1.44 *na veti vibhāṣā*.[2] When the item *iti* recurs in *A* 1.1.45, we have the string *ig yaṇa iti*. The item followed by *iti* denotes either its meaning (*arthapadārthakatā*) or its own form (*śabdapadārthakatā*) as in *gaur ity arthaḥ* or *gaur iti śabdaḥ*.[3] Patañjali states: *ig yaṇa ity etad vākyam*.

According to interpretation 1, what is assigned the name *samprasāraṇa* is the meaning conveyed by the sentence *ig yaṇo bhavati* 'There occurs ***ik*** in place of *yaṇ*, to which the verb form *bhavati* is supplied. From the

[2] *Uddyota* on *MBh* to *A* 1.1.45 (I.342): *pūrvasūtrād itīty anuvartya ig yaṇa iti samprasāraṇasaṃjñam ity arthād iti bhāvaḥ / svaṃ rūpam ity ukteḥ śāstre śabdaparatvasyautsargikatvenetisamabhivyāhāraṃ vinārthaparatvāsambhavād iti bodhyam /*

[3] *MBh* on vt. 3 to *A* 1.1.44 (I.102.5–10): *loke gaur ity ayam āheti gośabdād itikraṇaḥ paraḥ prayujyamāno gośabdaṃ svasmāt padārthāt pracyāvayati / so 'sau svasmāt padārthāt pracyuto yāsāv arthapadārhakatā tasyāḥ śabdapadārthakaḥ sampadyate / evam ihāpi navāśabdād itikaraṇaḥ paraḥ prayujyamāṇo navāśabdaṃ svasmāt padārthāt pracyāvayati / yo 'sau svasmāt padārthāt pracyuto yāsau śabdapadārthakatā tasyā laukikam arthaṃ sampratyāyati /*

Pāṇinīyas' point of view, the sentence meaning is paraphrased as *yaṇsthānikegbhavana*, that is, ***ik***'s action of occurring in place of *yaṇ*.[4]

According to interpretation 2, what is named *samprasāraṇa* is the sentence *ig yaṇo bhavati* itself; the name *samprasāraṇa* conveys indirectly, through the intermediary of this sentence, the meaning of the sentence. Nāgeśa denies this interpretation for the reason that a sentence conveys its own form (*svarūpa*) and its own meaning (*svārtha*) only when it is uttered.[5] In his *Vṛtti* on *VP* 2.40 Bhartṛhari discusses this interpretation, which shall be dealt with later.[6]

2. *MBhD* on *A* 1.1.45

In his *Mahābhāṣyadīpikā* Bhartṛhari explains how *A* 1.1.45 can be a rule which provides that a sentence is named *saṃprasāraṇa*.

2.1. To begin with, Bhartṛhari states that one has to supply not the verb form *asti* 'is, exists' but the verb form *bhavati* to the string *ig yaṇaḥ* in order to have a sūtra statement that serves for rules, such as *A* 6.1.13 *ṣyaṅaḥ samprasāraṇaṃ putrapatyos tatpuruṣe*,[7] to take effect.

---

[4] *Uddyota* on *MBh* ad *A* 1.1.45 (I.342): *nanu yaṇsthānikatvopalakṣita ig eva vākyārtha iti varṇapakṣād asya ko bheda ity ata āha—bhavatīti / evaṃ cegbhavanaṃ vākyārtha iti bhāvaḥ /* If the verb form *bhavati* is not supplied, the meaning of a complex of words *iko yaṇaḥ* will be 'the vowels denoted by ***ik*** that are qualified by the extrinsic property of occurring in place of the semivowels denoted by *yaṇ*' (*yaṇsthānikatvopalakṣita ik*).

[5] *Uddyota* on *MBh* ad *A* 1.1.45 (I.342): *pratipādayatīti / ṣyaṅaḥ samprasāraṇam ityādau / uccāritasyaiva pratyāyakatvam ity aṇudit iti sūtrasthabhāṣyaviruddham idam / MBh* on *A* 1.1.68 (I.175.26): *śabdenoccāritenārtho gamyate /*

[6] See §4.2.3.

[7] Of the tatpuruṣa compound *kaumudagandhīputra* 'a son of a female descendant of Kumudagandhi', the first member *kaumudagandhyā* is a patronymic derived with the taddhita affix *aṇ* (*A* 4.1.92 *tasyāpatyam*; *kumudagandhi* + *aṇ*). The base *kumudagandhi* 'one who smells like a white lily' is a bahuvrīhi compound (*vt.* 12 on *A* 2.2.24: *saptamyupamānapūrvapadasyottarapadalopaś ca*): *kumudagandha iva gandho yasya sa kumudagandhiḥ* → *kumudagandha-su* + *gandha-su* → *kumudagandha-φ* + *gandha-φ* (*A* 2.4.71 *supo dhātuprātipadikayoḥ*) → *kumudagandha-φ* → *kumudagandha* → *kumudagandhi* (*A* 5.4.137 *upamānāc ca*). *kaumudagandhyā* is derived as follows: (1) *kumudagandhi-ṅas* + *aṇ* → (2) *kumudagandhi-φ* + *a* (*A* 2.4.71 *supo dhātuprātipadikayoḥ*) → (3) *kumudagandhi* + *ṣyaṅ* (*A* 4.1.78 *aṇiñor anārṣayoḥ gurūpottamayoḥ ṣyaṅ gotre*) → (4) *kumudagandhφ* + *ya* (*A* 6.4.148 *yasyeti ca*) → (5) *kaumudagandhya* (*A* 7.2.117 *taddhiteṣv acām ādeḥ*) → (6) *kaumudagandhya* + ***cāp*** (*A* 4.1.74 *yaṅaś cāp*) → (7) *kaumudagandhyā* (*A* 6.1.101 *akaḥ savarṇe dīrghaḥ*)

MBhD on *A* 1.1.45 (VIII.VII.1.4–7): (1) (a) *nanu cākhyātaṃ saviśeṣaṇaṃ vākyam ity uktam / nākhyātapadaṃ śrūyate /*
(b) *athaivaṃ kalpyate astir bhavantīpara iti,*
(c) *evam api vipratiṣiddhatvam āpadyate—samprasāraṇaṃ bhavatīti samprasāraṇapradeśeṣu idam upatiṣṭhate ig yaṇo 'stīti; yady asti na tarhi bhavati, atha bhavati na tarhi astīti /*
(d) *ucayte / sopaskāratvāt sūtrasya bhavatiṃ vākyaśeṣatvena samarthayiṣyāmahe—ig yaṇo bhavatīti /*

"(a) [Objection] It is said that a finite verb form with qualifiers constitutes a sentence.[8] The verb form (*ākhyātapada*), however, is not directly stated in *A* 1.1.45.

(b) [Solution suggested] In such a case [the verb form *asti* 'is, exists'] is assumed to occur, as *ig asti* '***ik*** exists', by the statement *astir bhavantīparaḥ [prathamapuruṣo 'prayujyamāno 'py asti].*[9]

(c) [Difficulty pointed out] Even so, conflict (*vipratiṣiddhatva*) results. To explain: In rules, [such as *A* 6.1.13 *ṣyaṅaḥ samprasāraṇaṃ putrapatyos tatpuruṣe*], which provide that the replacement of ***yaṇ*** by ***ik***, denoted by the name *samprasāraṇa*, occurs (*samprasāraṇaṃ bhavati*), the meaning understood from the sentence *ig yaṇo 'sti* 'There exists ***ik*** in place of ***yaṇ***' is called

By *A* 6.1.13, when *kaumudagandhyā* is followed by *putra* 'son' in a tatpuruṣa compound, the samprasāraṇa replacement takes place for the semivowel *y* of ***ṣyaṅ*** which replaces ***aṇ*** at stage (3). The tatpuruṣa compound *kaumudagandhīputra* is derived as follows. (8) *kaumdagandhyā-**ṅas** + putra-**su*** → (9) *kaumudagandhyā-ϕ + putra-ϕ* (*A* 2.4.71 *supo dhātuprātipadikayoḥ*) → (10) *kaumudagandhi-ā + putra* → (11) *kaumudagandhi + putra* (*A* 6.1.108 *samprasāraṇāc ca*) → (12) *kaumudagandhī + putra* (*A* 6.3.139 *samprasāraṇasya*) → (13) *kaumudagandhīputra*

Kātyāyana distinguishes rules such as *A* 6.1.13 from those like *A* 6.1.108. *A* 6.1.108 provides that if a vowel follows a samprasāraṇa vowel the first vowel replaces both (PWT 533). Suppose that with reference to element x operation y takes place: if the term *samprasāraṇa* refers to x, then the *varṇasaṃjñā*-view is acceptable; on the other hand, if the same term refers to y, then the *vākyasaṃjñā*-view is acceptable. *Vts.*1–2 on *A* 1.1.45: *samprasāraṇasaṃjñāyāṃ vākyasya saṃjñā ced varṇasaṃjñā; varṇasaṃjñā cen nirvṛttiḥ* // Element x is what is stated as something known in a rule (*anuvāda*) and operation y is what is stated as something unknown in a rule (*vidhi*). See *Kāśikāvṛtti* on *A* 1.1.45.

[8] *MBh* on *A* 2.1.1 (I.367.15): *ākhyātaṃ saviśeṣaṇam /*

[9] Vt. 11 on *A* 2.3.1: *avakāśo 'kārakam iti cen nāstir bhavantīparaḥ prathamapuruṣo 'prayujyamāno 'py asti* // Pāṇinīyas recognize that verb forms are to be supplied for sūtras in accordance with everyday usage, in which, according to Kātyāyana, the verb *as* followed by a third-person (*prathamapuruṣa*) present ending (*bhavantīpara*) is understood to occur even if this verb is not overtly used (*aprayujyamāno 'pi*). See PWT 13.

to mind (*upatiṣṭhate*). If [*ik*] is what exists, then it is not what occurs; but if it is what occurs, then it is not what exists.

(d) [Answer] Because a sūtra statement needs supplements (*sopaskāra*), we will establish, according to the context, that the verb form *bhavati* is a word needed to complete the elliptical sentence in the form of the sūtra (*vākyaśeṣa*), to have the sentence *ig yaṇo bhavati*."[10]

As in the string *rājñaḥ puruṣaḥ* 'the king's man' the verb form *asti* is expected to be supplied so as to have the sentence *rājñaḥ puruṣo 'sti* 'There is the king's man', so also in the string *ig yaṇaḥ* '***ik*** related to *yaṇ*' it might be expected to be supplied so as to have the sentence *ig yaṇo 'sti* 'There is ***ik*** related to *yaṇ*. According to Bhartṛhari, however, one has to have the sentence *ig yaṇo bhavati* not by taking note of the first-triplet form *ik* (*ik-**su***) in the sūtra but by considering *A* 1.1.45 to be a sūtra statement.[11] It goes without saying that, when an operational rule provides for replacement, the operation (*kārya*) is something to be brought to accomplishment (*nirvṛtti*).[12] This is the reason that the verb form *bhavati* 'occurs' is supplied here instead of *asti*.

2.2. Bhartṛhari then goes on to discuss whether what is given the name *saṃprasāraṇa* is the sentence *ig yaṇo bhavati* or the meaning of this sentence.

MBhD on *A* 1.1.45 (VIII.VII.1.10–13): (2) (a) *evam api yaugapadyābhāvād asya vākyasya saṃjñitvam anupapannam / prathamānto hi saṃjñī ṣaṣṭhyanto vā, na ca vākyaṃ prathamāntaṃ ṣaṣṭhyantaṃ vā /*
(b) *ucyate / vākyārtho vākyam ity abhidhīyate, yathā matvartho matupśabdenocyate matau chaḥ sūktasāmnoḥ iti /*

"(a) [Objection] Even so, since this sentence has no qualification as a pada to be used in a rule (*yaugapadyābhāvāt*), it is improper to say that the sentence [which is referred to by that sentence]

[10]That is, on the assumption that a sūtra statement contains ellipsis, the verb form *bhavati* is thought of as something omitted from the statement of *ig yaṇaḥ*.

[11]A sūtra statement needs supplements necessary for explaining lucidly correct speech forms (*sopaskāra*). *VP* 3.14.464ab: ***sopaskāreṣu sūtreṣu vākyaśeṣaḥ*** *samarthyate* / *Prakāśa* on *VP* 3.14.464: ***iha sūtravākyānāṃ*** *kriyāpadāśravaṇāt sādhyāhāratvam avasīyate* / ***lakṣyānuguṇyena ca lakṣaṇa****praṇayanād yathāyathaṃ lakṣyabhedānusāreṇa kriyāpadam* ***adhyāhartavyam*** /

[12]In his second vārttika Kātyāyana points out that if the name *saṃprasāraṇa* is given to a set of sounds replacing semivowels, the replacement itself is not brought about (*varṇasaṃjñā cen nirvṛttiḥ*). See note 7.

is the bearer of the name.[13] For, a name bearer is referred to by a first-triplet form or a ṣixth-triplet form;[14] but the sentence [which refers to itself] does not end in a first-triplet or sixth-triplet ending.

(b) [Answer] A sentence meaning is denoted by the word *vākya* 'sentence', as in *A* 5.2.59 *matau chaḥ sūktasāmnoḥ* the meaning of the affix *ma**tup*** is meant by the word *matup*.[15]"

A 1.1.68 *svaṃ rūpaṃ śabdasyāśabdasaṃjñā* provides that an item which is not a technical term (*śabdasaṃjñā*) of grammar refers to itself.[16] If *A* 1.1.45 states that the name *samprasāraṇa* is assigned to the sentence *ig yaṇo bhavati*, the sentence given in the rule (sentence 1) must refer to itself (sentence 2). According to Bhartṛhari, before the name-named relation (*saṃjñāsaṃjñisambandha*) is established between the term *samprasāraṇa* and the sentence *ig yaṇo bhavati*, this term, serving as a name, denotes its own form.[17] The item *samprasāraṇa* that is referred to by the term *samprasāraṇa* given in the rule is the name and sentence 2 *ig yaṇo bhavati* that is referred to by sentence 1 *ig yaṇo bhavati* given in the rule is the bearer of this name.[18]

In Pāṇini's grammar, an item which refers to a name bearer ends in a first-triplet or sixth-triplet ending. According to Bhartṛhari, sentence 1

[13]Palsule/Bhagavat (1991) suggests emending *yaugapadyābhāvād* to *padatvābhāvād*, rendering (1991: 43): "Even then, this sentence cannot be the named because of the absence of the designation *pada* (for the sentence)." I have taken the word *yaugapadya* to be derived from *yogapada* 'a pada in a rule' with the taddhita affix ṣya**ñ** (*A* 5.1.124 *guṇavacanabrāhmaṇādibhyaḥ karmaṇi ca*). By *A* 1.4.14 *suptiṅantaṃ padam* an item that ends in a nominal or verbal ending is called *pada* (PWT 49). The pada in question is this very pada.

[14]For example, in *A* 1.1.1 *vṛddhir ādaic* a set of sounds to be given the name *vṛddhi* are denoted by the first-triplet form *ādaic* (PWT 9) and in *A* 1.1.69 *aṇ udit savarṇasya cāpratyayaḥ* a specific sound to be given the name *aṇ* is referred to by the sixth-triplet form *savarṇasya* (PWT 84).

[15]*A* 5.2.59 provides that the taddhita affix *cha* occurs after the nominal base to denote the meaning of the taddhita affix *ma**tup*** when a hymn or a melody is to be signified.

[16]See PWT 29.

[17]*VP* 1.60: *vṛddhyādayo yathā śabdāḥ svarūpopanibandhanāḥ / ādaicpratyāyitaiḥ śabdaiḥ sambandhaṃ yānti saṃjñibhiḥ // VP* 1.67ab: *prāk saṃjñābhisambandhāt saṃjñā rūpapadārthikā /*

[18]This is comparable to the case in which, in *A* 1.1.22 *taraptamapau ghaḥ* which provides that the affixes *tarap* and *tamap* are given the name *gha*, the item *gha* referred to by the term *gha* in the rule is the name and the items *tarap* and *tamap* referred to by the terms *tarap* and *tamap* in the rule are the bearers of this name (PWT 73).

that refers to sentence 2, which is the bearer of the name *samprasāraṇa*, is not an item that ends in such a nominal ending (*sup*). Neither *A* 1.2.45 *arthavad adhātur apratyayaḥ prātipadikam* nor *A* 1.2.46 *kṛttaddhitasamāsāś ca*[19] allows a sentence to be termed *prātipadika*, so that a nominal ending cannot be introduced after sentence 1. Thus, Bhartṛhari denies that the sentence is named *samprasāraṇa*, arguing that the meaning of the sentence is the bearer of this name.

2.3. However a difficulty arises. Bhartṛhari states:

> *MBhD* on *A* 1.1.45 (VIII.VII.1.14–18): (3) (a) *nanu cārtho 'py asattvabhūto 'yam iti [kim iti] vākyasyeti vākyārthopalakṣitam [/]*
> (b) *ucyate / saṃjñāsambandhakāle pratyavamṛṣṭaḥ[,] sarvanāmnā vasturūpeṇopasaṃhṛtaḥ, idaṃ tad iti vyapadeśārhaḥ,*
> (c) *saṃjñitvam anubhūya pradeśeṣu svena vyāpāreṇa pravṛtto 'sattvabhūta evopatiṣṭhate iti [/]*
> (d) *ig yaṇo bhavatīty asya yo 'rthas tasya samprasāraṇasaṃjñāyāṃ pradeśeṣv idam upatiṣṭhate, ig yaṇo bhavatīg yaṇo jāyate ig yaṇo niṣpadyate iti /*
>
> "(a) [Objection] Even if this name bearer is the meaning of the sentence, this meaning does not have the status of a being (*asattvabhūta*) [since it is an action (*kriyā*), so that it cannot be signified by the nominal form *samprasāraṇa*]; therefore, when the sentence *ig yaṇo bhavati* is said to have the name *samprasāraṇa*, [the sentence which] is qualified by the meaning of the sentence, something extrinsic to that sentence (*vākyārthopalakṣita*), [is meant by the word *vākya* 'sentence'].[20]
>
> (b) [Answer] When the relation with the name is established, [the meaning of the sentence is treated like *sattva*, something that has the status of a being, so that the meaning is that which

[19]See PWT 48.

[20]Palsule/Bhagavat (1991: 43): "How is it then, that the 'sentence-meaning' is (supposed to be) indicated by 'sentence'?" It is important to note that, in Bhartṛhari's theory of denotation, an adventitious qualifier (*upalakṣaṇa*) cannot be regarded as being signified by the name but functions as the application cause of the name. *VP* 3.2.3: *adhruveṇa nimittena devadattagṛhaṃ yathā / gṛhītaṃ gṛhaśabdena śuddham evābhidhīyate //*

I have not read the latter half of passage (a) as *...iti kim iti vākyasyeit vākyārthopalakṣaṇam*, which can be rendered as follows: 'Therefore how could it be that [*samprasāraṇa*] is [the name of] the sentence? Accordingly, [the sentence qualified by its meaning, something extrinsic to the sentence, is named *samprasāraṇa*'.

is referred to, as a substance (*vasturūpeṇa*), by a pronominal (*sarvanāman*), which is something [whose sequence is] taken away (*upasaṃhṛta*), and which is capable of being denoted by *idam* 'this' or *tad* 'that'.[21]

(c) When, after undergoing the state of being named *samprasāraṇa*, this sentence meaning occurs in operational rules by virtue of the denotative function of the name's own, it is called to mind precisely as what does not have the status of a being (*asattvabhūta*).

(d) Consequently, if the name *samprasāraṇa* is given to the meaning of the sentence *ig yaṇo bhavati*, this sentence meaning is called to mind in operational rules in the following manner: '***ik*** occurs in place of *yaṇ*' (*ig yaṇo bhavati*); '***ik*** arises in place of *yaṇ*' (*ig yaṇo jāyate*); '***ik*** comes into being in place of *yaṇ*' (*ig yaṇo niṣpadyate*)."

The difficulty lies in the principal meaning of the verb form *bhavati* being not *sattva*. As is well known, in his *Nirukta* Yāska states: *bhāvapradhānam ākhyātam / sattvapradhānāni nāmāni* 'A verb form is that whose principal meaning is *bhāva*; nominal forms are those whose principal meanings are *sattvas*'.[22] According to Patañjali, the term *sattva* means a substance (*dravya*) and the term *bhāva* an action (*kriyā*).[23] Bhartṛhari's characterization of *sattva* here well accords with that given by him in his *Vākyapadīya*.[24]

Suppose that the sentence *ig yaṇo bhavati* denotes the action of occurring qualified, through the kriyā-kāraka relation, by *ik*, which in turn is quali-

---

[21]The essential feature of what is understood to be an action (*kriyā*) is that it has sequence (*krama*) and is accordingly spoken of as something to be brought to accomplishment (*sādhya*). *VP* 3.8.1: *yāvat siddham asiddhaṃ vā sādhyatvenābhidhīyate / āśritakramarūpatvāt tat kriyeti pratīyate //* The action is treated like a substance (*dravya*, *sattva*) if its sequence is taken away. *VP* 3.8.30 might give a good account of this point. According to Bhartṛhari, with reference to an entity occurring before the stage where the word *jāta* '...has been born' is used, one can use the finite verb form *jāyate* '...is being born' and the nominal *janman* 'birth'; when one uses the former one regards the entity as having sequence and when one uses the latter one regards it as something whose sequence is taken away. *VP* 3.8.30: *ākhyātaśabdair artho 'sāv evaṃbhūto 'bhidhīyate / nāmaśabdāḥ pravartante saṃharanta iva kramam //* (pāda b: *evaṃbhūtaḥ* = *VP* 3.8.29c: *āśritakramarūpeṇa*.) *Prakāśa* on *VP* 3.8.30: *sa eva ca pūrvabhāgo janmeti nāmapdena saṃhṛtakramarūpatayā dravyāyamāṇaḥ siddharūpo 'bhidhīyate /*

[22]*Nirukta* 1.1..

[23]*MBh* on *A* 5.3.66 (II.16–17): *kriyāpradhānam ākhyātaṃ bhavati dravyapradhānaṃ nāma /*

[24]*VP* 3.4.3: *vastūpalakṣaṇaṃ yatra sarvanāma prayujyate / dravyam ity ucyate so 'rtho bhedyatvena vivakṣitaḥ //*

fied, through the substituend-replacement relation, by *yaṇ*. The action per se cannot be the bearer of the name *samprasāraṇa* since this term is a nominal base (*prātipadika*) whose significand is in general a substance. Thus Bhartṛhari argues that at the time of giving the name *samprasāraṇa* to the meaning of the sentence, the action in question is treated like a substance so that the relation of the name and the named may be established between the term *samprasāraṇa* and the action; but, at the time when the action is called to mind in operational rules, it is called to mind as an action per se so that a grammatical operation may be brought to accomplishment.

This is all that is said by Bhartṛhari in his *Mahābhāṣyadīpikā* about the question of how the *vākyasaṃjñā*-view is formed. In terms of the Pāṇinian system of grammar, I think, he explains the view convincingly.

3. *VP* 2.444

Now let us turn to the *Vākyapadīya* and the *Vṛtti*. The important point to note is that in his *Vākyapadīya* and the *Vṛtti* thereupon Bhartṛhari attempts to illustrate, by this *vākyasaṃjñā*-view, the theory that a sentence meaning is single and undivided.

What Bhartṛhari states in *VP* 2.444 is this.

> *VP* 2.444: *anekaśakter ekasya pravibhāgo 'nugamyate / ekārthatvaṃ hi vākyasya mātrayāpi pratīyate //*
>
> "Of a single indivisible entity with multiple powers, its division is uderstood. Indeed, a sentence signifies a single indivisible meaning, which is understood from the fact that a sentence meaning is conveyed even by a smaller unit (*mātrā*)."

3.1. *Ṭīkā* on *VP* 2.444

Before coming to the *Vṛtti*, let us see what Puṇyarāja says on this kārikā. He explains the first line of the kārikā as follows:

> *Ṭīkā* on *VP* 2.444: (1) (a) *tathābhūtasya ca vākyārthasya nānāśaktikhacitasya nirvibhāgasyopādhikṛtaḥ padārthadvārakaḥ pravibhāgo nānārūpatvam anugamyate /*
> (b) *pratīyate paramārthatas tv eka evāsāv ity āha /*
>
> "(a) In addition, of such a sentence meaning which is combined with multiple powers and which is indivisible, division (*pravibhāga*), or multiplicity (*nānārūpatva*), is understood; the division is made on the basis of delimiting factors relating to it (*upādhikṛta*) and hence is established through [the abstraction

of] the meanings to be denoted by constituent words (*padārtha-dvāraka*).[25]

(b) In the final analysis, however, it is understood that the sentence meaning is precisely a single indivisible entity. This is what Bhartṛhari intends to say in *VP* 2.444."

Puṇyarāja then explains the second line of the kārikā. First he comments on the phrase *ekārthatvaṃ hi vākyasya pratīyate.*

> *Ṭīkā* on *VP* 2.444: (2) *vākyasya sphoṭātmano vācakarūpasyaikārthatvam eka eva nirvibhāgasvarūpo vācyārtho yasya tat tathā, tasya bhāvas tattvaṃ pratīyate,*
>
> "The word *ekārthatva* is the one in which the affix *tva* follows the sixth-triplet form of the bahuvrīhi *ekārtha*.[26] Thus Bhartṛhari intends to say: It is understood that a sentence which consists in sphoṭa and which is in essence a meaning-conveyer has, for its meaning to be conveyed, precisely a single, essentially indivisible, meaning."

Puṇyarāja continues to interpret the phrase *mātrayāpi.*

> *Ṭīkā* on *VP* 2.444: (3) (a) *katham mātrayāpi iti / yadā tasya mātrayā niyatasaṃkhyākenālpīyasā śabdena yogo 'bhisambandho dṛśyate / yathoktam—ig yaṇa iti yoge sthānyādeśabhāvalakṣaṇo vākyārthaḥ sa samprasāraṇam iti vyapadiśyate / ataḥ samprasāraṇam ity evam ekasaṃkhyena laghīyastvān mātrayā vyapadiśyate /*
> (b) *tasya yogo yadātra paridṛṣṭas tadaitad avagamyate yad utānaṃśa eka evākhaṇḍasvarūpo 'sau vākyārtho 'nyathā samprasāraṇam ity anenaikasaṃkhyākena kathaṃ yujyeta vaktum //*
>
> "(a) How is it that Bhartṛhari says *mātrayāpi*? The word *mātrā* refers to a linguistic unit (*śabda*) which is smaller than a sentence (*alpīyas*) and whose number is limited (*niyatasaṃkhyāka*). When the connection (*yoga*) of the sentence meaning with such a smaller linguistic unit, or the identity relation (*abhisambandha*) of the sentence meaning with the smaller linguistic unit, is observed, [it is understood that a sentence denotes a single indivisible meaning]. As stated [by Kātyāyana], in the rule (*yoga*)

[25] A sentence is divided into component parts on the basis of the abstraction of their meanings. In Helārāja's view, the abstraction of words from a sentence is preceded by the abstraction of partial meanings from the meaning of a sentence. *Prakāśa* on *VP* 3.1.1: *arthāpoddhāra eva hi padāpoddhārasya nimittam /*

[26] *A* 5.1.119 *tasya bhāvas tvatalau //* See PWT 348.

> *ig yaṇaḥ samprasāraṇam* the sentence meaning which is characterized by the substituend-replacement relation (*sthānyādeśabhāva*) is spoken of by the term *samprasāraṇa*. In this case, therefore, [the sentence meaning is said to be] spoken of by a smaller linguistic unit since such a single (*ekasaṃkhya*) word as *samprasāraṇa* is smaller (*laghīyas*) [in number than the sentence *ig yaṇo bhavati* which consists of three words].
>
> (b) When the connection of the sentence meaning with such a smaller linguistic unit is observed in this instance, then the following is understood: The sentence meaning is precisely a single indivisible entity; otherwise, how could one speak of the sentence meaning by using such a single word as *samprasāraṇa*?"

According to Puṇyarāja, Bhartṛhari makes the following point: A sentence meaning is a single indivisible entity which has multiple powers, so that it is variously differentiated on the conceptual level. The unity of the sentence meaning is indicated by Pāṇini's formulation of *A* 1.1.45. Consider the following two cases:

1. The meaning is denoted by the sentence *ig yaṇo bhavati*;
2. The same meaning is denoted by the word *samprasāraṇa*.

According to Puṇyarāja, the word *samprasāraṇa* is defined as *mātrā* a 'smaller unit' in the sense that in 1 the meaning is denoted by a sentence consisting of three words, while in 2 the same meaning is denoted by a single word.

3.2. *Vṛtti* on *VP* 2.444

Now let us consider what Bhartṛhari says in his *Vṛtti* on *VP* 2.444.

> *Vṛtti* on *VP* 2.444: *ekatvanityatvadarśinas tu manyante /*
> (a) *viśiṣṭā hi kriyā yathāsambhavaṃ kālasādhanadravyapuruṣopagrahādibhir anugatā vākyenābhidhīyate /*
> (b) *sa ca ekaḥ śabdo vyavahārāya pravibhaktoddeśaḥ*[27] *sarvaviśeṣaviśiṣṭe parikalpitaviśeṣaṇaviśeṣyabhede ekasminn arthe vartate /*
> (c) *tasya śaktīr apoddhṛtya vyāvahāriko vibhāgo 'nugamyate /*
> (d) *tena vākyārthas tv ekaḥ samprasāraṇādiprakārayā mātrāparimāṇayā vibhāgoddeśam antareṇa pratyāyyate*[28] */*
> (e) *vākyārthasya hi samprasāraṇasaṃjñā vibhāgoddeśena vinā sambandhinī vijñāyate //*

[27]Iyer: *pravibhaktoddeśyaḥ*. I have adopted Aklujkar's reading.
[28]Iyer: *pratyāpyate*. I have adopted Aklujkar's reading.

"Those who hold the view that a sentence is a single indivisible entity and that it is perennial (*ekatvanityatvadarśin*) think as follows:

(a) Indeed, a sentence denotes a specific action,[29] attended as far as possible by time (*kāla*), a substance functioning as what brings the action to accomplishment (*sādhanadravya*), a person (*puruṣa*), an aspect (*upagraha*), and so on.[30]

(b) The single indivisible utterance (*ekaḥ śabdaḥ*), which, for grammatical talk (*vyavahārāya*), is divided into discrete parts (*pravibhaktoddeśa*),[31] signifies a single indivisible meaning, which is differentiated from all other particular actions (*sarvaviśeṣa-viśiṣṭa*), with respect to which particular qualifiers and a particular qualificand are assumed (*parikalpitaviśeṣaṇaviśeṣyabheda*), and which is qualified by all that differentiates it from others (*sarvaviśeṣaṇaviśiṣṭa*).[32]

(c) After abstracting multiple powers of such a sentence meaning, one understands its division into constituent elements, which yield to grammatical talk (*vyāvahārika*).[33]

---

[29] *Vṛtti* on *VP* 1.24–26: *sthitalakṣaṇas tu vākyarūpopagrahaḥ kalpitoddeśa-vibhāgo viśiṣṭa ekaḥ kriyātmā vicchinnapadārthagrahaṇopāyapratipādyaḥ* . . . / The meaning whose character is fixed (*sthitalakṣaṇa*) is what a sentence accepts as its own significand (*vākyarūpopagraha*). Such a meaning is that in which the division into discrete parts is an assumption (*kalpitoddeśavibhāga*). Moreover, the meaning is in essence an action (*kriyātman*), which is differentiated from other actions (*viśiṣṭa*) and which is one (*eka*).

[30] From a verbal form one understands an action, what brings the action to accomplishment, time, a person, and an aspect. *Vṛtti* on *VP* 1.24–26: *kriyā-sādhanakālādayo 'pi kaiścit kathaṃcid abhidheyatvena pravibhaktāḥ* / *Paddhati* on *Vṛtti* to *VP* 1.24–26: *tiṅanteṣv āha kriyāsādhanakālādayaḥ iti* / *ādiśabdāt saṃkhyāpuruṣopagrahāḥ* /

[31] The term *uddeśa* here means *avaccheda* 'a part, portion'. *Vṛtti* on *VP* 1.49: *sa tadānīm eko 'pi vibhaktoddeśāvaccheda iva pratyavabhāsate* / *Paddhati* on *Vṛtti* to *VP* 1.49: *eko 'pi iti* / *akramaḥ* / *vibhaktoddeśa iti* / *uddeśas teṣām avacchedaḥ parasparavyāvṛttatā* / *te ca kvacid avibhāgenāpy avatiṣṭhanta iti vibhaktagrahaṇam* / *uddeśarūpā ye 'vacchedās te vibhaktāḥ parasparavyāvṛttākāreṇāsyeti* /

[32] *VP* 2.71ab: *viśiṣṭaiva kriyā yena vākyārthaḥ parikalpyate* / A sentence meaning is said to be assumed to be an action with qualifiers and hence a specific action because the action as a qualificand and its qualifiers are merely those which are mentally constructed. *Vṛtti* on *VP* 2.71: *yasya tu pūrvoktena dharmeṇa kriyāviśeṣaḥ śaktidravyasaṃsargabhinna eko vākyārthaḥ tasyāvibhakta-śabdārthatvād* . . . /

[33] *Prakāśa* on *VP* 3.1.1: *vākyārthaś ca sthitalakṣaṇo niraṃśaḥ kārakotkalita-*

(d) Therefore, a sentence meaning is a single indivisible entity. One understands this meaning from [names (*saṃjñayā*)] which are linguistic units of smaller size (*mātrāparimāṇā*), such as *samprasāraṇa* and the like. [In this case the linguistic items which serve as such names are] without division and their discrete parts (*vibhāgoddeśam antareṇa*).

(e) For, it is known [from *A* 1.1.45 *ig yaṇaḥ samprasāraṇam*] that the ṇame *samprasāraṇa*, without division and its discrete parts, is related to a sentence meaning."

As said earlier, in Bhartṛhari's view, a sentence meaning is a single indivisible enity. In (a) it is stated that such a single indivisible meaning is simply a specific action with qualifiers. What is stated in (b) is that although a specific action qualified by its qualifiers is said to be denoted by a sentence, the qualifier-qualificand relation is merely an assumption since an action as a qualificand and its qualifiers are mental constructs. The reason is stated in (c) that a single indivisible meaning is divided into parts: one can have the abstraction of such parts from the sentence meaning, which has multiple powers to bring about multiple conceptualizations. An action as the meaning of a sentence is fused in a single whole meaning together with its qualifiers, so that, with reference to the single whole meaning, one can have the conceptual cognition 'This is an action as what is to be brought to accomplishment', the conceptual cognition 'This is a kāraka as what brings the action to accomplishment', and so on.[34]

We have to note (d) and (e). In (e) the *vākyasaṃjñā*-view is adduced. The name *samprasāraṇa* is referred to by the term *mātrāparimāṇā*, which means 'the name whose quantity (*parimāṇa*) is smaller (*mātrā*)'. It is important to note that Bhartṛhari states that from the name *samprasāraṇa*, without assuming its division and its discrete parts, one understands the single meaning denoted by the sentence *ig yaṇo bhavati*. This implies that the term *samprasāraṇa* is not susceptible to division into putative parts that have posited corresponding partial meanings.

It is also important to note that if one can speak of the name *samprasāraṇa* as *mātrāparimāṇā* with respect to the string *ik yaṇo bhavati*, one can, as a logical consequence, speak of a single phoneme, serving as a name, as *mātrāparimāṇā* with respect to the stretch of sound *samprasāraṇa*.

śarīrakriyāsvabhāvaḥ / tatra cāṃśāṃśikalpanayā apoddhāre kārakātmā kriyātmā cāṃśo vibhāgārha iti siddhasādhyalakṣaṇāṃśadvayaviṣayaḥ . . . / See also note 49.

[34] *Paddhati* on *VP* 1.13: *vyākhyāntaram āha saṃsargaḥ iti / saṃsargānupahitasyārthasyāśakyavyavahāratvāt sa eva tattvam / sa hi kriyākārakayoḥ parasparātmānupraveśalakṣaṇaḥ / artho hi sādhyasādhanabhedād dvividhaḥ / śeṣasya sādhanāntarbhūtatvāt /*

4. *VP* 2.40

Thus in *VP* 2.40 Bhartṛhari states that the meaning conveyed by a sentence can be denoted by a single phoneme (*ekavarṇa*). In the *Vṛtti* on *VP* 2.40, it is important, the question of how the meaning denoted by a sentence can be denoted by a smaller linguistic unit is discussed in detail.

VP 2.40 goes as follows:

> *VP* 2.40: *so 'yam ity abhisambandho buddhyā prakramyate yadā / vākyārthasya tadaiko 'pi varṇaḥ pratyāyakaḥ kvacit //*
>
> "In some cases, when, with a sentence meaning, the identity relation in the form 'this is that' is intended to be established by the mind, even a single phoneme becomes a conveyer of the sentence meaning."

4.1. *Ṭīkā* on *VP* 2.40

Let us first consider here also what Puṇyarāja says on this kārikā, which he introduces by saying the following:

> *Ṭīkā* on *VP* 2.40: (1) *ataś ca niraṃśa evāyaṃ padārthaśūnyo vākyārtho 'dhyāsamātrasambandhagarbha ekasmād api varṇāt pratīyata evety abhidhātum āha—*
>
> "For this reason, moreover, this sentence meaning, which is absolutely indivisible and hence devoid of word meanings (*padārtha-śūya*), is indeed understood even from a single phoneme. For the sentence meaning has the possibility (*garbha*) of being related to the single phoneme by mere superimposition (*adhyāsa*) of the identity between the sentence meaning and this single phoneme. In order to convey this, Bhartṛhari states *VP* 2.40."

Puṇyarāja gives the following interpretation:

> *Ṭīkā* on *VP* 2.40: (2) (a) *so 'yam ity abhisambandho 'dhyāsarūpo vākyārthasya vākyena saha yadā vaktrā prakramyate tadaiko 'pi varṇo vākyārthasya vācako bhavaty eva,*
> (b) *kiṃ punar anekam aśeṣaviśeṣābhidhānavivakṣayodīritaṃ padam iti /*
> (c) *evam adhyāsavaśād vākyavākyārthayor abhinnasvarūpatvād vākyārthābhivyaktau vākyam api sphoṭātmakam abhivyaktam evety uktam—vākyārthasya tadaiko 'pi ityādi //*
>
> " (a) When, between the meaning of a sentence and the sentence, the relation in the form 'this is that' (*so 'yam ity abhisambandha*), which consists in superimposition of identity (*adhyāsa*),

is intended to be established by a speaker, even a single phoneme does indeed become a signifier of the meaning of the sentence;

(b) [If even a single phoneme which is generally meaningless can become a signifier of the meaning of the sentence,] then how much more so a word (*pada*), which is a multiple entity (*aneka*), when it is uttered with the intention of expressing a specific complete meaning.

(c) This being the case, since a sentence and its meaning are regarded as being in essence identical with each other because of the superimposition of identity, once the meaning of a sentence manifests itself, the sentence, which consists in sphoṭa, also definitely manifests itself. This is what is meant by the latter half of the kārikā."

Note (b). Puṇyarāja seems to miss the point made by Bhartṛhari here. Bhartṛhari never intends to imply that if even a single phoneme, which is in general meaningless, denotes a sentence meaning, then how much more so a word, which is a larger and meaningful linguistic unit. As is clear from the *Vṛtti* on *VP* 2.40, what he means to say here is the contrary. Note (c) also. What Puṇyarāja intends to say is: When the meaning of a sentence manifests itself, the sentence, which consists in sphoṭa, also manifests itself on account of the identity between them; the sentence manifests itself as what is single and undivided, so that its meaning must also manifest itself as what is single and undivided. This exploits the possibility that the same meaning can be signified by a phoneme, which is single and undivided, when by superimposition the relation of identity is established between the former and the latter.

4.2. *Vṛtti* on *VP* 2.40

Now let us turn to the *Vṛtti* on *VP* 2.40. For convenience, I have split up the text into several parts.

4.2.1

40.1 *nāvaśyaṃ vicchinnapadarūpopagraha*[35] *eva śabdaḥ paurvāparyayuktam anugatavibhāgam evārthaṃ pratyāyayati* /

"It is not necessarily true that only a linguistic item which is susceptible of being divided into separate words (*vicchinna-*

[35] Iyer: *vicchinnapadarūpavigraha*. I have adopted Aklujkar's reading.

> *padarūpopagraha*)[36] conveys precisely the meaning whose division is conceptually posited (*anugatavibhāga*)[37] and which has sequence (*paurvāparyayukta*) [when its putative partial meanings are separately grasped]."

It is highly important to note that Bhartṛhari here declares that a sentence is not the only unit to convey the meaning which is supposed to be signified by the sentence.

A sentence and its meaning are indivisible, but they are subject to having partial elements extracted. This point is also emphasized here. Only under the assumption that a sentence is a composite of words, obviously, can one have the sequence in which words are used (*śabdapaurvāparyaprayoga*) and the one in which meanings are conveyed (*arthapaurvāparyābhidhāna*).[38]

4.2.2

> 40.2 (a) *yadā hi vākyārthasyaiveg yaṇaḥ sthāne bhavatītyevamāder buddhiviṣayaḥ sampraśāraṇam iti vā ṭīti vā*[39] *so 'yam ity abhisambandhaḥ kriyate*
> (b) *atho*[40] *yathaiveg yaṇa ity anena paurvāparyānupātinī pratipattir bhavati / evam apaurvāparyayā bha mi ity ekavarṇayā tasyārthasya saṃjñayā pratyastamitapaurvāparyaḥ sa evārthātmā pratīyate /*
>
> "The reason is as follows: (a) Of a sentence meaning, such as the one understood from the sentence *ig yaṇo bhavati* 'There occurs ***ik*** in place of *yaṇ*', the identity relation with the word *samprasāraṇa* or *ṭi* in the form 'this is that' is mentally posited (*buddhiviṣayaḥ ... so 'yam ity abhisambandhaḥ kriyate*).[41]

---

[36] *Paddhati* on *VP* 1.26: *vākyarūpopagrahaḥ iti / vākyarūpa upagraho 'sya, upagrahaṇam upagrahaḥ svīkāraḥ, sa ca vākyarūpāśrayatvād vākyarūpaśabdenoktaḥ / tad dhi tāṃ kriyām ātmānam abhidheyatayā svīkaroti upagṛhṇāti vā / kartary acam eke kurvanti vākyarūpam upagrāhakam asyeti / granthakāreṇa vākyam eva vācakam ity uktam /*

[37] See *VP* 2.444, in which Bhartṛhari states: *vibhāgo 'nugamyate.*

[38] *MBh* on vt. 5 ad *A* 2.2.29 (I.431.21–24): *evam api śabdapaurvāparyaprayogād arthapaurvāparyābhidhānam / śabdapaurvāparyaprayogād arthapaurvāparyābhidhānaṃ prāpnoti / ataḥ kim / yugapadadhikaraṇavacanatāyā anupapattiḥ / plakṣanyagrodhau, plakṣanyagrodhā iti / yathaiva hi śabdānāṃ paurvāparyaṃ tadvad arthānām api bhavitavyam /*

[39] Iyer: *samprasāraṇam iti vādīti vā.*

[40] Aklujkar: *tho.* I have adopted the reading given by Iyer.

[41] According to the *Vṛtti*, we may have the rules formulated as *ig yaṇas ṭi* ; *ig yaṇo bha* ; *ig yaṇo ma* instead of *ig yaṇaḥ samprasāraṇam.* It must be recalled

(b) In that case (*atho*), just as, from the sentence *ig yaṇaḥ [bhavati]*, its putative partial meanings are assumed to be understood in the sequence in which its putative component words are uttered (*paurvāparyānupātinī pratipattiḥ*), so, from a name, such as *bhA* or *mI*,[42] the very essence of the meaning whose sequence has gone (*pratyastamitapaurvāparya*) is understood. For such a name consists of a single phoneme (*ekavarṇā*), has no sequence, and is related to the meaning of the sentence.

We have to recall that in the *Vṛtti* on *VP* 2.444 it is said that from the name *samprasāraṇa* one understands the meaning denoted by the sentence *ig yaṇo bhavati* without assuming its division and its discrete parts (*vibhāgoddeśam antareṇa, vibhāgoddeśena vinā*). It is simply because a sentence admits of the abstraction of component words from it that the understanding of the meaning of the sentence seems to have sequence. If one understands the meaning denoted by the sentence *ig yaṇo bhavati* from the name *samprasāraṇa* without assuming its division into discrete parts, how much more one should understand its meaning without assuming its division into discrete parts from the name *bh* or *m*. In this case it is clear that one cannot assume distinct meanings corresponding to distinct linguistic elements. This is the point made here.

4.2.3

40.3 *na cāvaśyaṃ śabdavyavahitaiva tatra pratipattir bhavati / kṛtābhyāsānāṃ hi śabdāntareṇārthapratipattir na vyavadhīyate /*

"It is not necessarily true, in addition, that the meaning of the sentence is understood indirectly from the term consisting of a single phoneme from which the meaning is separated by a different linguistic item, the sentence itself. This is because, for speakers among whom the term in question has gained established status through continuous transmission (*kṛtābhyāsa*), the meaning of the sentence, not being separated from the term by a different linguistic item, is understood directly from the term."

---

here that *Jainendravyākaraṇa* 1.1.45 runs: *ig yaṇo jiḥ*. See also §5. It is also to be noted that in a rule such as *A* 1.1.64 *aco 'ntyādi ṭi* (PWT 41) a term serving as a name is given with the first-triplet ending -***su*** deleted (*ṭi-su* → *ṭi*; *A* 7.1.39 *supāṃ sulukpūrvasavarṇāccheyāḍāḍyāyājālaḥ*).

[42]The final vowels of *bha* and *mi* are considered to be used merely to facilitate pronunciation (*uccāraṇārtha*). In *A* 3.4.77 *lasya* 'in place of an L-affix' (PWT 232), for example, Pāṇini uses the term *la*, the sound *a* of which is added to *l* for this purpose.

The question posed here is this. Now we have the following three cases:

1. The replacement of *yaṇ* by ***ik*** is signified by the sentence *ig yaṇo bhavati*;
2. The replacement of *yaṇ* by ***ik*** is signified by the word *samprasāraṇa*;
3. The replacement of *yaṇ* by ***ik*** is signified by the phoneme *bh*.

A question arises: Even if it is accepted that the word *samprasāraṇa* or the phoneme *bh* signifies the replacement of *yaṇ* by ***ik*** which is signified by the sentence *ig yaṇo bhavati*, is it not the case that the replacement is signified by this word or this phoneme indirectly, as separated from its signifier by the sentence, which directly signifies it?[43] The answer given is that such a smaller linguistic unit does not signify indirectly, through the intermediary of the sentence; when having gained established status through continuous transmission, the unit conveys the meaning directly, without calling to mind the sentence. Here we notice that Bhartṛhari sets forth the same argument in dealing with the question of whether an incorrect term (*apaśabda*) is a direct signifier or not. In *VP* 1.181 he states that for speakers among whom corrupted terms (*apabhraṃśa*) have become established, they signify and correct terms (*sādhuśabda*) do not.[44]

4.2.4

40.4 (a) *yadi ca laghūpāyaṃ sāmānyaviśeṣayuktaṃ*
(b) *śāstraṃ sadṛśasaṃvyavahāram*[45] *alasa itīva mithyābhyāsa-viparyastadarśano*[46] *loko*[47] *nānupatet tataḥ*[48] *pratipattāras tam*[49] *evākramaṃ pratipadyeran* /

"(a) Grammar (*śāstra*), a set of rules concerning what is general and what is particular (*sāmānyaviśeṣayukta*), is a brief means (*laghūpāya*) of knowing correct speech forms.

[43]Bhartṛhari admits that, as in gestures, in some cases one understand the meaning of an item indirectly through the intermediary of the item. *VP* 2.328: *śabdavyavahitā buddhir aprayuktapadāśrayā / anumānāt tadarthasya pratyaye hetur ucyate //* See §1: interpretation 2.

[44]*Vṛtti* on *VP* 1.181: *pāramparyād apabhraṃśā viguṇeṣv abhidhātṛṣu / prasiddhim āgatā yena teṣāṃ sādhur avācakaḥ //*

[45]Aklujkar: *śāstrasadṛśaṃ saṃvyavahāram.* I have adopted the reading given by Iyer.

[46]Iyer: *mithyābhyāsaviparyayas taddarśino.*

[47]Iyer: *loke.*

[48]Iyer: *tadā.*

[49]Aklujkar: *pratipattāraḥ sa[rvam].* I have adopted the reading by Iyer.

(b) If, as if at the thought of having no energy (*alasa itīva*), the world (*loka*) whose perspective is distorted (*viparyastadarśana*) by continuous repetition of faults (*mithyābhyāsa*) had not taken into consideration (*anupatet*, lit. 'follow') grammar and the everyday talk which is similar to the grammatical talk of the grammar (*sadṛśasaṃvyavahāra*),[50] it would be established that in everyday interaction hearers understand the very sequenceless (*akrama*) meaning from the sentence."

The fact that the meaning signified by a sentence is capable of being signified by any smaller linguistic unit—in an extreme case, even by a single phoneme which has no parts—indicates that a sentence meaning is essentially without parts.

Grammarians abstract component elements assumed to occur in what is actually an impartite linguistic unit and they do this for the purpose of carrying out grammatical operations which account for such whole units. They also adopt partial meanings as what is signified by these abstracted component elements. However, even the world whose perspective is distorted, when finding no interest in grammar or grammatical talk, tends to understand from a sentence its meaning without sequence. This also provides conclusive evidence that a sentence meaning is essentially without parts. It is to be noted that Bhartṛhari states that grammarians establish assumed forms following their fancies, in accordance with what they have understood following traditions and exposing themselves to them so repeatedly as to have their latent traces. In this sense grammarians also have to be said to be those whose perspective is distorted with respect to a sentence and its meaning insofar as they are involved in conceptualizing them.

[50] *Vṛtti* on *VP* 1.24–26: *so 'yam apoddhārapadārthaḥ śāstravyavahāram anupatati, śāstravyavahārasadṛśasṃ ca laukikaṃ bhedavyavahāram /* ("This abstracted meaning yields to (*anupatati*) grammatical talk [since it is established by grammarians for the purpose of carrying out grammatical operations], and also everyday talk which is similar to that of a grammar (*śāstravyavahārasadṛśa*) and in which speakers speak of distinct meanings [such as an agent and an action] (*bhedavyavahāra*).") *Paddhati* on *Vṛtti* to *VP* 1.24–26: *yo 'yaṃ loke pravibhāgaḥ ayaṃ kartā aparā kriyā . . . /*

4.2.5

40.5 (a) *bhedarūpeṇa caikatvaṃ saṃkīrṇavat*[51] /
(b) *tena sāparādhaiva prakarṣaviniveśinyā[ḥ]*[52] *prāptakramarūpopaplavāyā vāco vṛttiḥ* /
(c) *sā hi sāparādheṣu puruṣeṣv anyathaivātmānaṃ darśayati* /
(d) *atas tām*[53] *eke paśyanto 'pi na paśyanti, śṛṇvanto 'pi na śṛṇvanti* /
(e) *tāṃ tu vaiyākaraṇā vāgyogavidaḥ śabdātmānam abhisambhūtā bhedadarśanam atītya svena svarūpatattvenopalabhante* /
(f) *sā ca tebhya evātmānaṃ vivṛṇoti* /
(g) *uktam idam—arthaṃ kathaṃcit puruṣaḥ kaścit sampratipadyata*[54] *iti* / *ataḥ puruṣapratipattibhedānāṃ parimāṇavikalpānāṃ*[55] *nidarśanamātraṃ kriyate* //

"(a) And the unity (*ekatva*) appears as though mingled with division (*bheda*).[56]

(b) Therefore, speech (*vāc*) that has entered into a preeminent state (*prakarṣaviniveśinī*), when suffering the distress (*upaplava*) of attaining sequence (*prāptakramarūpa*), does indeed have a deceptive appearance (*sāparādhā vṛttiḥ*)."

(c) For the speech quite differently shows itself to persons who have faults.

(d) For this reason, some, seeing the speech, do not see it; others, hearing the speech, do not hear it.

(e) However, grammarians who know the property of speech (*vāgyogavid*)[57] and who have attained unity with the essence of

---

[51] Aklujkar suggests reading this passage as *bhedarūpeṇa caikatvaṃ saṃkīrṇa[m i]va*.

[52] Iyer: *prakarṣaviniveśinyā*.

[53] Iyer: *ataś ca tām*.

[54] Iyer: *sampratidyate*.

[55] Aklujkar suggests the reading: *[a]parimāṇavikalpānāṃ*.

[56] The passage literally means: 'The unity occurs as unity mingled with division does'. What is meant is that the unity is not preceded by actual division. It is useful to note that Bhartṛhari distinguishes between *atyantasaṃsṛṣṭa* and *saṃsṛṣṭa*. The word *atyantasaṃsṛṣṭa*, with *atyanta* 'absolutely', is used to exclude a whole preceded by distinct parts which are combined. *Vṛtti* on *VP* 1.24: *tatrāpoddhārapadārtho nāmātyantasaṃsṛṣṭaḥ saṃsargād anumeyena parikalpitena rūpeṇa prakṛtavivekaḥ sann apoddhriyate* / *Paddhati* on *VP* 1.24: *vibhāgapūrvakasaṃsarganiṣedhāyātyantagrahaṇam* /

[57] *Paddhati* on *VP* 1.159: *vāgyogavidām* / *te hi tām akramāṃ vācaṃ vedayante* / *apabhraṃśair vācaṃ viviktāṃ yathā vaiyākaraṇāḥ* /

the word (*śabdātmānam abhisambhūtāḥ*) perceive (*upalabhante*) the speech in its own essential, constant, nature (*svarūpatattva*), beyond the experience of dividing the speech into components (*bhedadarśanam atītya*).[58]

(f) And the speech unfolds itself precisely to the grammarians.[59]

(g) This has been said [in *VP* 2.39ab]: 'A certain grammarian understands a given object in a certain way and another grammarian understands it in another way'.[60]

(h) For this reason [grammar] affords a mere instance that shows that human beings differently understand speech to posit conceptually linguistic units of different sizes (*parimāṇavikalpa*)."

As said above, in Bhartṛhari's view, the same single meaning is signified by linguistic units of different sizes. The next question is how to account for such diversity of linguistic units to signify the same single meaning. The *Vṛtti* introduces the concept of *vāc*, speech-reality, the one, imperishable, non-dual, absolute; which in Bhartṛhari's system, being called sphoṭa, is identical with Brahman.

---

[58] Vṛṣabha's interpretation of the expression *kālabhedadarśanābhyāsa* in the *Vṛtti* may help account for what is meant by the expression *bhedadarśana* here. *Paddhati* on *VP* 1.1: *kālabhedadarśanābhyāsena iti / tatra kālabhedo yuge bhavati na bhaviṣyatīti / tasya darśanam anubhavaḥ, tasyābhyāsaḥ punaḥpunarutpattiḥ /*

[59] In (d)–(f) Bhartṛhari alludes to the Bhāṣya in which Patañjali cites *Ṛgvedasaṃhitā* 10.71.4 to give a reason for studying grammar. Paspaśā (I.4.4–8): *api khalv ekaḥ paśyann api na paśyati vācam / api khalv ekaḥ śṛṇvann api na śṛṇoty enām / avidvāṃsam āhārdham / uto tv asmai tanvaṃ visasre / tanuṃ vivṛṇute / jāyeva patya uśatī suvāsāḥ / tadyathā jāyā patye kāmayamānā suvāsāḥ svam ātmānaṃ vivṛṇuta evaṃ vāg vāgvide svātmānaṃ vivṛṇute / vāṅ no vivṛṇuyād ātmānam ity adhyeyaṃ vyākaraṇam /* In his *Mahābhāṣyadīpikā* Bhartṛhari comments simply on the passage *paśyann api na paśyati / śṛṇvann api na śṛṇoti. MBhD* IV.1.12.9–10: *vyākaraṇādhyāyino vāca īśate prabhutvaṃ yeṣāṃ vāci bhavatīti /* ("Those who study grammar rule over speech since mastery over speech accrues to them.")

[60] *VP* 2.39: *arthaṃ kathaṃcit puruṣaḥ kaścit sampratipadyate / saṃsṛṣṭā vā vibhaktā vā bhedā vākyanibadhanāḥ //* The *Vṛtti* illustrates the point by saying the following. *Vṛtti* on *VP* 2.39: *tad yathā—śrotriyaṃś chando 'dhīte iti vākyārthe padavacanaṃ chandaso vā śrotrabhāvaḥ ghaṃś ca pratyayaḥ, śrotrābhyāṃ kṛtaṃ karmeti va /* The *Vṛtti* here refers to two vārttikas on *A* 5.2.84 *śrotriyaṃś chando 'dhīte*: *vt.* 1–2: *śrotriyaṃś chando 'dhīta iti vākyārthe padavacanam; chandaso vā śrotrabhāvas tad adhīta iti ghaṃś ca.* On the interpretation of *VP* 2.39 and on the *Vṛtti* thereupon, see Ogawa (forthcoming).

Consider the following kārikā:

> *VP* 3.9.66: *evaṃ mātrāturīyasya bhedo dāśatayasya vā / parimāṇavikalpena śabdātmani na vidyate //*
>
> "Similarly, the difference between a quarter of a mora (*mātrāturīya*) and the *Ṛgveda* consisting of ten maṇḍalas (*dāśataya*) is based on the conceptualization of linguistic units of different sizes (*parimāṇavikalpa*) and not on the essence of the word."

As short, long, and extra-long vowels do not differ from one another, so also a quarter of a mora and the text of the *Ṛgveda* do not differ from each other. Articulated sounds (*dhvani*, *nāda*), which manifest the essence of the word, have distinctions based on time; it takes some time to articulate a certain stretch of sound, so that they can be of greater or lesser quantity. The differentiation of the essence of the word is thus due to the attribution of distinctions based on time to it (*kālaparimāṇabheda*).[61] The point the *Vṛtti* tries to make is clear: In order to convey the replacement of *yaṇ* by ***ik***, some use the sentence *ig yaṇo bhavati*, some the word *samprasāraṇa*, and others the phoneme *bh*. This replacement is capable of being conveyed by any linguistic unit, which is possible precisely because a meaning conveyer, that is, speech-reality, is undifferentiated. Which linguistic unit is used to convey the meaning, therefore, depends on a grammarian's choice.

5. Houben on *VP* 2.40, 444

Jan E.M. Houben (2009) also dealt with Bhartṛhari's treatment of issues concerning the *vākyasaṃjñā*-view. In the article Houben makes an attempt to show that Bhartṛhari referred in *VP* 2.40 and 444 to the fact that 'a whole sentence was conventionally equated with a single phoneme'[62] by the influence of the *Jainendravyākaraṇa*'s formulation of the rule 1.1.45: *ig yaṇo jiḥ*.

[61] *Prakāśa* on *VP* 3.9.66: *mātrāyāś caturthasya bhāgasyāpacitataradhvanivyaṅgyasya, daśa avayavā yeṣāṃ te daśatayāḥ samudāyāḥ ṛgātmānaḥ teṣāṃ samūhasya dāśatayasya catuṣṣaṣṭyātmakasya vedarāśeḥ pracitataradhvanivyaṅgyasya kālaparimāṇabhedena viśeṣo nāsti /* Helārāja clearly states that speech reality does not differ from a word to a sentence. *Prakāśa* on *VP* 3.9.66: *na kevalaṃ hrasvadīrghādāv eva śabdatattvam abhinnaṃ yāvat sarvatraiva padavākyaviṣaye /* Bhartṛhari says that although a phoneme, word, and sentence have no difference in time, they seem to have time because of the difference in time of the manifesting sounds (*nāda*). *VP* 1.104: *tasmād abhinnakāleṣu varṇavākyapadādiṣu / vṛttikālaḥ svakālaś ca nādabhedād vibhajyate //*

[62] Houben 2009: §4.10. See §5.2.

5.1. *mātrā*

In Houben (2009: §4.4) the following is stated:

> ". . . . This is the interpretation of the later commentator Puṇyarāja when he explains 2.444. But then it remains a bit strange that the long term *saṁprasāraṇa* is called a *mātrā* in the kārikā. After all, *mātrā* is not only the general word for 'measure' or 'small element', but it is also the term for a single prosodic unit equivalent to the time needed to pronounce a short vowel. According to Puṇyarāja, the term *saṁprasāraṇa* is called a *mātrā* in the kārikā because it is just a single, small element. The reference to *saṁprasāraṇa* would in this way be unsuitable in kārikā 40, which speaks of a single phoneme that is expressive of the sentence meaning. Puṇyarāja has therefore to keep his explanation of this kārikā very abstract.
>
> The Vr̥tti on 40, however, does refer to the term *saṁprasāraṇa*. In addition, it seems to give two times an example of the 'single phoneme' mentioned in the kārikā. . . . ."

As shown in §3.1, Puṇyarāja glosses the term *mātrā* in *VP* 2.444 as *niyatasaṃkhyākenālpīyasā śabdena* 'a linguistic unit (*śabda*) which is smaller than a sentence (*alpīyas*) and whose number is limited (*niyatasaṃkhyāka*)'. It is certain that he takes this term in a different sense from that in which it is used in the expression *mātrāturīya* 'a quarter of a mora' in *VP* 3.9.66.[63] But we have to note that under *VP* 2.444 the *Vṛtti* makes the following statement.

> *Vṛtti* on *VP* 2.444 (d): *tena vākyārthas tv ekaḥ saṃprasāraṇādiprakārayā mātrāparimāṇayā vibhāgoddeśam antareṇa pratyāyyate* /[64]

Houben here does not refer to this *Vṛtti* statement. The expressions *saṃprasāraṇādiprakārā* and *mātrāparimāṇā* both refer to the name (*saṃjñā*): The name *saṃprasāraṇa* is *mātrāparimāṇā* or '[the name] whose *parimāṇa* is *mātrā*'.[65] I have rendered the expression *mātrāparimāṇā* as '[names] which are linguistic units of smaller size'. The important point to note here is that the *Vṛtti* uses the term *parimāṇa*, which has an intimate bearing on what Bhartṛhari states in *VP* 3.9.66.[66] Clearly the *Vṛtti* understands that the

[63] See §4.2.5.

[64] See §3.2.

[65] In his *Amarakoṣa* Amarasiṃha says that the word *mātrā* has the meanings *paricchada* 'personal property', *alpa* 'a small portion, little', and *parimāṇa* 'measure'. *Amarakoṣa* 3.3.177–78: . . . *mātrā paricchade // alpe ca parimāṇe syān* . . . /

[66] See §4.2.5.

name *samprasāraṇa* can be referred to by the term *mātrā* in *VP* 2.444. It is also important to note that the *Vṛtti* considers that the linguistic item referred to by the expression *mātrāparimāṇā* here can have its division and its discrete parts (*vibhāgoddeśa*). If the linguistic item is not assumed to have its division and its discrete parts, it is taken to be a single entity (*eka*).

In Houben (2009: §4.8), however, he refers to the *Vṛtti* statement mentioned above.

> "Puṇyarāja, oblivious of the JV's technical term *ji*,[67] is forced to interpret *mātrayā* in the kārikā unconvincingly as a reference to the whole term *saṁprasāraṇa* as a single unit (*ataḥ saṁprasāraṇam ityevam ekasaṁkhyena laghīyastvān mātrayā vyapadiśyate*). Something similar was already done by the author of the Vr̥tti, but he explained *mātrā* as a reference to '*saṁprasāraṇa* and so forth' (Iyer, 1983: 314.5)."

It is true that the *Vṛtti* explains the term *mātrā* in *VP* 2.444 as a reference to *samprasāraṇādiprakārā [saṃjñā]*. As is clear from the *Vṛtti* passage given above, however, the *Vṛtti* also takes the very term as referring to *mātrāparimāṇā [saṃjñā]*, which Houben does not mention. Houben makes a rough translation of the phrase *samprasāraṇādiprakārā*: '*saṁprasāraṇa* and so forth'. The term *prakāra* here means 'similarity' (*sādṛśya*).[68] Therefore the phrase *samprasāraṇādiprakārayā mātrāparimāṇayā* literally means: 'from [names] like *samprasāraṇa* and so on whose *parimāṇa* is *mātrā*'. Thus the term *mātrā* in the kārikā must refer primarily to what is meant by the expression *mātrāparimāṇā [saṃjñā]*. In my opinion, this point is crucially important. According to the *Vṛtti*, a linguistic unit, as a name, can have *parimāṇa* 'quantity, size': a certain linguistic unit may be said to be of smaller size than another linguistic unit. Undoubtedly, the *Vṛtti* here holds that the term *samprasāraṇa* is a smaller unit than the sentence *ig yaṇo [bhavati]*. What is a smaller unit than the single term *samprasāraṇa*? It is a phoneme (*varṇa*). It is said in *VP* 2.40 that a single phoneme can denote the meaning of a sentence. When a single phoneme serves as a name, the phoneme can properly be said to be *mātrāparimāṇā [saṃjñā]* with respect to the single term *samprasāraṇa*. This is how the following argument made by Houben (2009: §4.8) turns out to be unsound.

> "The crucial step of the example of *ji* is presupposed but no longer emphasized in the Vr̥tti on 2.444 and was completely forgotten since Puṇyarāja. As explained above (section 3.3 and

[67] *Jainendravyākaraṇa* 1.1.45: *ig yaṇo jiḥ*. See note 41.

[68] *Kāśikāvṛtti* on *A* 8.1.12 *prakāre guṇavacanasya*: *prakāro bhedaḥ sādṛśyaṃ ca* /

note 24), the word *mātrā* may refer to any (small) unit, but in the context of linguistic units it denotes especially a well-defined prosodic unit."

The *Vṛtti* on *VP* 2.444 says:

> *Vṛtti* on *VP* 2.444 (e): *vākyārthasya hi samprasāraṇasaṃjñā vibhāgoddeśena vinā sambandhinī vijñāyate* /[69]

A single phoneme has neither division nor parts. Thus the present passage amounts to saying the following:

> *vākyārthasya apravibhaktoddeśa*[70] *eko varṇaḥ sambandhī* /
>
> "A single phoneme, which is not divided into discrete parts, is related to a sentence meaning."

This is precisely what *VP* 2.40 says. The *Vṛtti* on this kārikā also provides a parallel.

> *Vṛtti* on *VP* 2.40 [2.(b)]: *evam apaurvāparyayā bha mi ity ekavarṇayā tasyārthasya saṃjñayā pratyastamitapaurvāparyaḥ sa evārthātmā pratīyate* /[71]

5.2. *MBhD*

Houben (2009: §4.10) says:

> "While the interest shown in the MBhD for the problem of how a single term may refer to a complex expression or sentence corresponds with the two kārikās and the theme of the second Kāṇḍa of the VP, we miss in the MBhD any reference to the extreme case of only one single phoneme referring to a whole sentence meaning. If the MBhD is accepted as Bhartṛhari's earlier work, we may surmise that Bhartṛhari, while writing that work, was not yet acquainted with the JV. This could either mean that Bhartṛhari had not yet widened his horizon to include the grammar of the Jainas in all its technical details, or that that grammar was at that time not yet written. Once Bhartṛhari became familiar with that grammar, the fact that a whole sentence was conventionally equated with a single phoneme impressed so much that he referred to it in two kārikās."

[69] See §3.2.

[70] See §3.2 [*Vṛtti* on *VP* 2.444 (b)].

[71] See §4.2.2. We have to note that in his *Ṭīkā* on *VP* 2.40 [(1)] Puṇyarāja says that a sentence meaning has the possibility (*garbha*) of being related to a single phoneme. See §4.1.

What impressed Bhartṛhari is the *vākyasaṃjñā*-view maintained by Kātyāyana on *A* 1.1.45. Bhartṛhari derived the theory of *parimāṇavikalpa* possibly from this view also, so that he could naturally conceive that a linguistic unit characterized as *mātrāparimāṇā* can denote the meaning of a linguistic unit of larger size, to which we may refer as *mahāparimāṇa*. Irrespective of whether he knew of *Jainendravyākaraṇa* 1.1.45: *ig yaṇo jiḥ*, *A* 1.1.45 and its one possible interpretation must have impelled Bhartṛhari to compose the two kārikās, *VP* 2.40 and 444, and opened up the possibility of his arguing that even a single phoneme name (*eko 'pi varṇaḥ*), or, even a *mātrāpariṇāmā* (*mātrayāpi*) with respect to *samprasāraṇa*, can denote the meaning of the sentence *ig yaṇo [bhavati]*. The argument is of course meant for showing that a sentence meaning is single, impartite, and indivisible and is based on the principle that any single impartite linguistic unit must be related to any single impartite meaning and vice versa.

It is to be noted in passing that, as shown in §2, the interest shown in the *Mahābhāṣyadīpikā* on the *vākyasaṃjñā*-view is not for the problem of how a single term may refer to a sentence but for the problem of how the *vākyasaṃjñā*-view can be justified in terms of Pāṇini's derivational system. In the *Mahābhāṣyadīpikā*, to be sure, there is no reference to the case in which a single phoneme refers to a sentence meaning. In the *Mahābhāṣyadīpikā* in question, however, Bhartṛhari did not feel it necessary to bring in the idea that even a single phoneme can denote the meaning of the sentence *ig yaṇo [bhavati]*, for the task to be carried out by him there was merely to explain the Bhāṣya passage: *ig yaṇa ity etad vākyaṃ samprasāraṇasaṃjñaṃ bhavati*. The fact is simply that the *Mahābhāṣya* on which Bhartṛhari comments does not demand that he be involved in discussing such a case.

6. Conclusion

We have seen how in his *Mahābhāṣyadīpikā* and the *Vṛtti* on the second kāṇḍa of his *Vākyapadīya* Bhartṛhari deals with the *vākyasaṃjñā*-view advanced by Kātyāyana under *A* 1.1.45. In the former Bhartṛhari discusses how the *vākyasaṃjñā*-view is established and in the latter how this view serves to establish the theory that a sentence meaning is a unity. We know that in *VP* 1.26 Bhartṛhari says that the eight topics (*aṣṭaka*) to be dealt with in the *Vākyapadīya* are described in grammar both through indirect indications (*liṅga*) and direct statements (*svaśabda*) and that they are followed according to tradition (*yathāgamam*), to memorialize them.[72] The *vākyasaṃjñā*-view is thus an indirect indication to show that the tradition

[72] *VP* 1.26: *te liṅgaiś ca svaśabdaiś ca śāstre 'sminn upavarṇitāḥ / smṛtyartham anugamyante ke cid eva yathāgamam //*

of Pāṇini's grammar tells that a sentence and its meaning are indivisible. If we accept this, the well-known theory about a sentence and its meaning could not be an invention by Bhartṛhari but the theory worked up by him in accordance with tradition.

In his *Mahābhāṣyadīpikā* Bhartṛhari confines himself to justifying the *vākyasaṃjñā*-view within the framework of Pāṇini's derivational system and in his *Vākyapadīya* and the *Vṛtti* thereupon he goes deep into the philosophical import of this view, the discussion about which he keeps beyond the scope of the *Mahābhāṣyadīpikā*. It is not likely that in discussing the view in the *Mahābhāṣyadīpikā* he could not grasp the difficulty that the meaning of a sentence is conveyed by a single word. It cannot be emphasized too strongly that Bhartṛhari is an *apoddhārapadavādin* as well as an *akhaṇḍavākyavādin*.

The *Vṛtti* I have considered shows the author's great and deep insight into language. Going beyond the confines of being a commentary on the *Vākyapadīya*, obviously, the *Vṛtti* tries to amplify on a subject.

I believe that what is now asked for regarding the study of Bhartṛhari is none other than the keen-eyed reading of the *Vṛtti* that is made in a steady manner.

References and abbreviations

A: Pāṇini's *Aṣṭādhyāyī*.

Abhyankar, Kashinath Vasudev

1962–72 *The Vyākaraṇa-mahābhāṣya of Patañjali, edited by F. Kielhorn, third edition, revised and furnished with additional readings, references and select critical notes by K. V. Abhyankar.* 3 vols. Poona: Bhandarkar Oriental Research Institute. 1: 1962; 2: 1965; 3: 1972.

Amarakoṣa: Amarasiṃha's *Amarakoṣa*. See Dādhimatha 1987.

Bronkhorst, Johannes

1987 *Mahābhāṣyadīpikā of Bhartṛhari, Fascicule IV: Āhnika I.* Post-Graduate and Research Department Series 28. Poona: Bhandarkar Oriental Research Institute.

Cardona, George

1997 *Pāṇini, His Work and Its Traditions. Volume I: Background and Introduction.* 2nd ed. Delhi: Motilal Banarsidass.

Dādhimatha, M. M. Pandit Sivadatta

1987 *Nāmaliṅgānuśasana alias Amarakosa of Amarasiṁha with the commentary Vyakhyāsudhā or Rāmāśramī of Bhānuji Dīksita.* 2nd ed. Revised by Pt. Vāsudeva Laksmana Panaśīkara. Delhi: Chaukhamba Sanskrit Pratishthan.

Houben, Jan E.M.
2009 Bhartṛhari and the Jainas. In *Bhartṛhari: Language, Thought and Reality*, edited by Mithilesh Chaturvedi. Delhi: Motilal Banarsidass.

Jainendravyākaraṇa: Pūjyapāda Devanandin's *Jainendravyākaraṇa*. See Tripathi 1956.

Kāśikāvṛtti: Vāmana and Jayāditya's *Kāśikāvṛtti*. See Miśra 1985.

MBh: Patañjali's *Vyākaraṇamahābhāṣya*. See (1) Vedavrata 1962–63 and (2) Abhyankar 1962–72. [References of the text of the *Mahābhāṣya* are to volumes, pages, and lines of Abhyankar 1962–72.]

MBhD: Bhartṛhari's *Mahābhāṣyadīpikā*. See Bronkhorst 1987 and Palsule/Bhagavat 1991.

Miśra, Śrīnārāyaṇa
1985 *Kāśikavṛtti of Jayāditya-Vāmana, along with Commentaries Vivaraṇapañcikā-Nyāsa of Jinendrabuddhi and Padamañjarī of Haradatta Miśra*. 6 vols. Ratnabharati Series 5–10. Varanasi: Ratna Publications.

Nirukta: Yāska's *Nirukta*. See Sarup 1927.

Ogawa, Hideyo
forthcoming "Abstraction (*apoddhāra*) theory and a sentence meaning: a study of the *Vṛtti* on *VP* 2.39." Festschrift Ashok Aklujkar.

Paddhati: Vṛṣabhadeva's *Paddhati*. See Subramania Iyer 1966.

Palsule/Bhagavat (Palsule, G. B., and V. B. Bhagavat)
1991 *Mahābhāṣyadīpikā of Bhartṛhari, Fascicule VIII: Āhnika VII*. Post-Graduate and Research Department Series 37. Poona: Bhandarkar Oriental Research Institute.

Pradīpa: Kaiyaṭa's *Pradīpa*. See Vedavrata 1962–63. [References of the text of the *Pradīpa* are to volumes and pages of Vedavrata 1962–63.]

Prakāśa: Helārāja's *Prakāśa*. See Subramania Iyer 1963, 1973.

PWT: See Cardona 1997.

Raghunātha Śarmā (Sharmā)
1968 *Vākyapadīyam, part II (Vākyakāṇḍam), with the commentary Ambākartrī by Pt. Raghunātha Sharmā*. Sarasvatī Bhavana Granthamālā 91. Varanasi: Vārāṇaseya Saṃskṛta Viśvavidyālaya.

Rau, Wilhelm
1977 *Bhartṛharis Vākyapadīya: Die Mūlakārikās nach den Handschriften herausgegeben und mit einem Pāda-Index versehen*. Abhandlungen für die Kunde des Morgenlandes XLII, 4. Wiesbaden: Franz Steiner Verlag.

Sarup, Lakshman

1927 *The Nighaṇṭu and the Nirukta, the oldest Indian treatise on etymology, philology and semantics; critically edited from original manuscripts and translated for the first time into English, with introduction, exegetical and critical notes, three indexes and eight appendices; Sanskrit text, with an appendix showing the relation of the Nirukta with other Sanskrit works.* Lahore: University of the Panjab. Reprint: Delhi: Motilal Banarsidass, 1967.

Subramania Iyer, K. A.

1963 *Vākyapadīya of Bhartṛhari with the Commentary of Helārāja, Kāṇḍa III, Part 1.* Deccan College Monograph Series 21. Poona: Deccan College.

1966 *Vākyapadīya of Bhartṛhari with the Commentaries Vṛtti and Paddhati of Vṛṣabhadeva.* Deccan College Monograph Series 32. Poona: Deccan College.

1973 *Vākyapadīya of Bhartṛhari with the Commentary of Helārāja, Kāṇḍa III, Part II.* Poona: Deccan College.

1983 *The Vākyapadīya of Bhartṛhari (An Ancient Treatise on the Philosophy of Sanskrit Grammar), Containing the Ṭīkā of Puṇyarāja and the Ancient Vṛtti, Kāṇḍa II, with a Foreword by Ashok Aklujkar.* Delhi: Motilal Banarsidass.

Ṭīkā: Puṇyarāja's *Ṭīkā*. See Subramania Iyer 1983.

Tripathi, Shambhu Nath, and Mahadeo Chaturvedi

1956 *Jainendra Vyākaraṇam by Pūjyapāda Devanandin with Jainendra Mahāvritti of Shri Abhayanandi.* Jñānapītha Mūrtidevī Jaina Granthamālā Saṃskrit Grantha 17. Banaras: Bhāratīya Jñānapītha Kāshī.

Uddyota: Nāgeśa's *Uddyota*. See Vedavrata 1962–63.

Vedavrata

1962–63 *Śrībhagavatpatañjaliviracitaṃ Vyākaraṇamahābhāṣyam (Śrīkaiyaṭakṛtapradīpena nāgojībhaṭṭa-kṛtenabhāṣyapradīpoddyotena ca vibhūṣitam).* 5 vols. Gurukul Jhajjar (Rohatak): Hairyāṇā Sāhitya Saṃsthānam.

VP: Bhartṛhari's *Vākyapadīya*. See Rau, Subramania Iyer. [References to kārikās of the *Vākyapadīya* are made according to Rau 1977, so that kārikā numbers are given according to his edition.]

Vṛtti: *Vākyapadīya Vṛtti*. See Subramania Iyer 1966, 1983.

"Rule Selection in the Aṣṭādhyāyī," or "Is Pāṇini's Grammar Mechanistic?"

PETER M. SCHARF

I Total blocking

Cardona (1970; 1997: 401–427) discusses general principles that determine precedence in the application of rules in Pāṇini's grammar. Primary among these principles is that an exception (अपवाद) takes precedence over a general rule (उत्सर्ग) that operates in the same domain. An exception whose domain of application is wholly included within the domain of application of a general rule would have no scope at all if it did not take precedence; hence there would have been no reason to formulate it. The very fact that the wholly included exception has been stated (वचनसामर्थ्यात्) therefore demonstrates that Pāṇini operated with the principle that exceptions take precedence over their related general rules. The precedence of an exception wholly included within the domain of a rule with broader scope Cardona terms 'simple blocking'.

An example of simple blocking is afforded by *A.* 6.1.87 आद्गुणः and *A.* 6.1.88 वृद्धिरेचि. The first of these two rules provides that the sequence of a short or long अ and a following vowel is replaced by the closest guṇa vowel. The latter provides that the sequence of a short or long अ and a following ए, ओ, ऐ, or औ is replaced by the closest vṛddhi vowel. Since ए, ओ, ऐ, and औ constitute a subset of vowels, the domain of *A.* 6.1.88 is wholly included within the domain of *A.* 6.1.87 and is therefore an exception to it. (See Figure 1.)

II Overlapping domains

The situation is more complicated, however, where the domains of operation of two rules overlap, yet neither is wholly included within the other so that each rule finds scope in the domain exclusive to it. The problem is in determining which rule takes precedence in the shared domain. The two

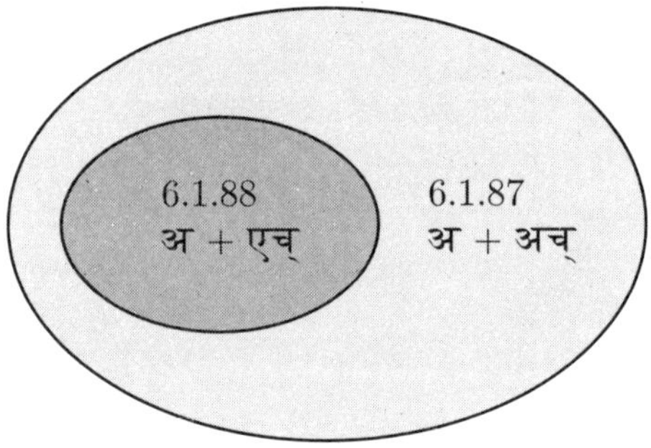

Figure 1: Simple blocking

Light gray: 6.1.87 आद्गुणः (अचि 77). The sequence of a vowel of the class अ followed by a vowel (अच्, i.e. अ, इ, ..., औ) is replaced by the guṇa vowel corresponding to the latter. Gray: 6.1.88 वृद्धिरेचि. The sequence of a vowel of the class अ followed by a vowel in the pratyāhāra एच् (i.e. ए, ओ, ऐ, औ) is replaced by the वृद्धि vowel corresponding to the latter. 6.1.88 blocks 6.1.87 because, due to the inclusion of its domain within the domain of 6.1.87, 6.1.88 would have no scope otherwise.

rules *A.* 6.1.77 इको यणचि and *A.* 6.1.101 अकः सवर्णे दीर्घः demonstrate the situation of overlapping domains. *A.* 6.1.77 provides that a simple vowel other than short or long अ, followed by a vowel, is replaced by its corresponding semivowel. *A.* 6.1.101 provides that the sequence of two like simple vowels (a simple vowel and a following simple vowel produced at the same place of articulation as the preceding vowel) is replaced by their corresponding long vowel. The domains of application of the two rules overlap, but neither is wholly included within the domain of the other. The domains overlap where a simple vowel other than short or long अ is followed by its like simple vowel. Yet each rule has its exclusive domain. *A.* 6.1.77 alone applies to simple vowels other than short or long अ followed by unlike vowels, and *A.* 6.1.101 alone applies to short or long अ followed by अ. (See Figure 2.) Since the domain of neither rule is wholly included within the domain of the other, simple blocking does not apply; neither is an exception to the other. Considering the initial context in each rule, since the domain of any simple vowel other than short or long अ is included within the domain of any simple vowel, *A.* 6.1.77 would have the narrower domain and would block *A.* 6.1.101, but considering the subsequent context, since the domain of the like simple vowel is included within the domain of vowels, *A.* 6.1.101 would have the narrower domain and would block *A.* 6.1.77. There does not appear to be any factor with respect to the domains of the two rules that

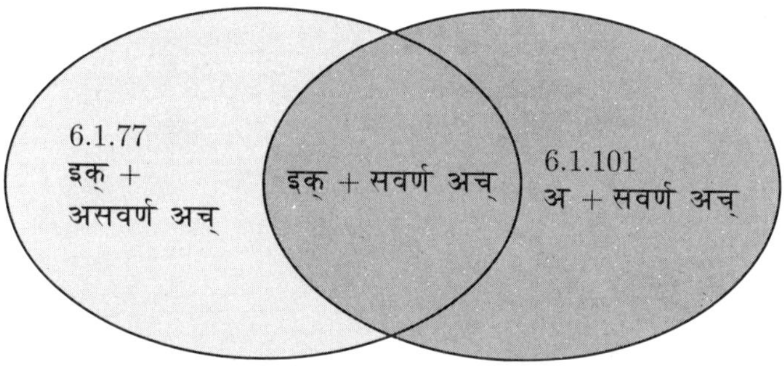

Figure 2: Overlapping domains. Example 1

6.1.77 इको यणचि. Followed by a vowel (अच्), a simple vowel other than अ (इक्) is replaced by its corresponding semivowel (यण्). 6.1.101 अकः सवर्णे दीर्घः. A sequence of a simple vowel (अक्) followed by a homorganic simple vowel is replaced by their corresponding long simple vowel. 6.1.77 domain: इ, उ, ऋ, or ऌ + any vowel (अच्). 6.1.101 domain: अ, इ, उ, ऋ, or ऌ + a homorganic (सवर्ण) vowel. 6.1.77 exclusive domain: इक् + असवर्ण अच्, i.e.: इ + अ, इ + उ, इ + ऋ, इ + ऌ; उ + अ, उ + इ, उ + ऋ, उ + ऌ; etc. 6.1.101 exclusive domain: अ + सवर्ण अच्, i.e.: अ + अ. Shared domain: इक् + सवर्ण अच्, i.e.: इ + इ, उ + उ, ऋ + ऋ, ऌ + ऌ. Problem: Neither domain is wholly included within the other. 1. The scope of इक् is included within the scope of अक्, i.e. इ, उ, ऋ, ऌ is included within अ, इ, उ, ऋ, ऌ implying that 6.1.77 has the narrower domain and that by simple blocking it would take precedence over 6.1.101. 2. The scope of the terms सवर्ण अच् is included within the scope of अच् implying that 6.1.101 has the narrower domain and that by simple blocking it would take precedence over 6.1.77. The two implications are contradictory.

determines the precedence of application. Each rule has its own exclusive scope. Neither is left without scope if the other takes precedence. Hence one cannot resort to the principle that one or the other takes precedence by virtue of the fact that it has been stated (वचनसामर्थ्यात्). There is a conflict regarding which of the rules applies.

III Vipratiṣedha

Patañjali refers to the conflict of rules with overlapping domains as विप्रतिषेध. In such cases, he appeals to *A.* 1.4.2 विप्रतिषेधे परं कार्यम् as the grounds for resolving conflict. *A.* 1.4.2 states that when two rules are in conflict, the latter rule applies. Commenting on Kātyāyana's first vārttika on *A.* 1.4.2 (द्वौ प्रसङ्गावन्यार्थावेकस्मिन्, स विप्रतिषेधः। MBh. 1.304.13), Patañjali explains that conflict occurs where two rules that have independent domains have the opportunity to apply simultaneously to the same domain (द्वौ प्रसङ्गौ यदान्यार्थौ भवत एकस्मिंश्च युगपत्प्राप्नुतः, स विप्रतिषेधः। MBh. 1.304.14). Patañjali applies the principle that the rule which is stated later (परत्व 'being later') prevails in cases of conflict (विप्रतिषेधे) throughout the grammar where other principles of rule precedence, such as being more internally conditioned (अन्तरङ्गत्व), precedence in condition elimination (नित्यत्व), and rule suspension (असिद्धत्व), are inapplicable. In the above example, applying the principle that the later rule takes precedence produces the correct result. As shown by the same shade of gray in the intersection of ellipses in Figure 2, *A.* 6.1.101 takes precedence over *A.* 6.1.77 in the domain common to the two rules where a simple vowel other than short or long अ is followed by a like vowel. For example, in दधि इन्द्रः, the sequence of the final इ of दधि and the initial इ of इन्द्रः is replaced by their single corresponding long vowel ई yielding दधीन्द्रः.

Patañjali's solution would settle some other cases of विप्रतिषेध besides that in Example 1 as well. As shown in Figure 3, *A.* 7.3.102 सुपि च and *A.* 7.3.103 बहुवचने झल्येत् apply in overlapping domains. The former provides that the final sound of a stem ending in short अ is replaced by its corresponding long vowel when followed by a nominal termination beginning with य्, न्, or भ्. The latter provides that the final sound of a stem ending in short अ is replaced by ए when followed by a plural nominal termination beginning with भ्, or स्. Neither domain is wholly included within the other; each rule has its exclusive domain. The former alone applies when the nominal termination begins with य्, or न्, or with भ् in the dual, that is, when the nominal terminations य, नाम्, or भ्याम् follow the stem. The latter alone applies when the nominal termination begins with स्, that is, when the nominal termination सु follows. Yet the domains overlap. Both have scope when the nominal termination begins with भ् in the plural, that is, when the nominal termination भ्यस् follows the stem. भ्यस् is equally as well included within the referents of यञ् सुप् as within the referents of झल् बहुवचन सुप्.

As Patañjali writes under *A.* 1.4.2, the two rules apply to independent domains, *A.* 7.3.102 to वृक्ष + भ्याम्, and *A.* 7.3.103 to वृक्ष + सु; they both apply simultaneously to वृक्ष + भ्यस्. (वृक्षाभ्यां वृक्षेष्वित्यन्यार्थौ वृक्षेभ्य इत्यत्र युगपत्प्राप्नुतः। MBh. 1.304.15–16.) Patañjali determines which of the two rules applies by virtue of the principle stated in *A.* 1.4.2 विप्रतिषेधे परं कार्यम्; the latter rule takes precedence. Thereby, he argues, the correct form वृक्षेभ्यः is obtained. The solution is stated by Kātyāyana as well under *A.* 7.3.103. He writes in vārttika 1, in place of short अ before a plural nominal termination, replacement by ए occurs in precedence to replacement by a long vowel by the principle that the latter rule applies in cases of conflict (अतो दीर्घाद्बहुवचन एत्त्वं विप्रतिषेधेन MBh. 3.340.2). In that context Patañjali reit-

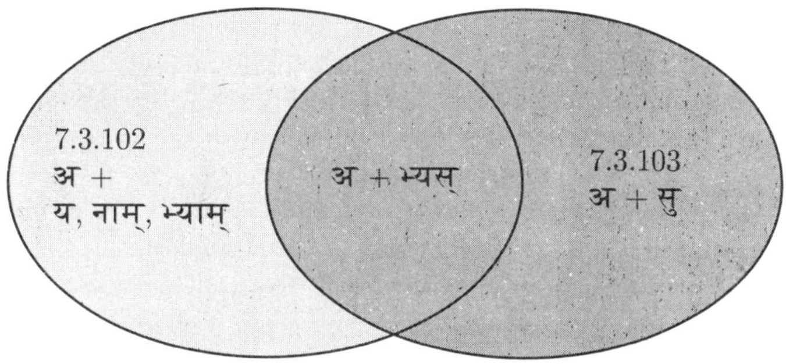

Figure 3: Overlapping domains. Example 2

7.3.102 सुपि च (अतो दीर्घो यञि 101). Followed by a nominal termination (सुप्) beginning with a sound in the pratyāhāra यञ्, the final sound of a stem ending in अ is replaced by its corresponding long vowel. 7.3.103 बहुवचने झल्येत्. Followed by a plural nominal termination beginning with the pratyāhāra झल्, the final sound of a stem ending in अ is replaced by ए. 7.3.102 domain: अ + य, नाम्, भ्याम्, भ्यस्, defined by the terms यञ् सुप्. 7.3.103 domain: अ + भ्यस्, सु defined by the terms झल् बहुवचन सुप्. 7.3.102 exclusive domain: अ + य, नाम्, भ्याम्. 7.3.103 exclusive domain: अ + सु. Shared domain: अ + भ्यस्.

erates Kātyāyana's comment (अतो दीर्घाद्बहुवचन एत्त्वं भवति विप्रतिषेधेन) and then explains as follows: The scope of *A.* 7.3.102 is वृक्षाभ्याम् प्लक्षाभ्याम्. The scope of *A.* 7.3.103 is वृक्षेषु प्लक्षेषु. Both have scope here: वृक्षेभ्यः, प्लक्षेभ्यः. Replacement by ए occurs by the principle that the latter applies in cases of conflict. (अतो दीर्घो यञि सुपि च [7.3.101–102] इत्यस्यावकाशः — वृक्षाभ्याम् प्लक्षाभ्याम्। बहुवचने झल्येदित्यस्यावकाशः — वृक्षेषु प्लक्षेषु। इहोभयं प्राप्नोति — वृक्षेभ्यः प्लक्षेभ्यः। एत्त्वं भवति विप्रतिषेधेन॥ MBh. 3.340.3–5.)

A third example of the resolution of conflicting rule application in overlapping domains by the principle that the latter rule takes precedence appears in the application of *A.* 7.3.113 याडापः and *A.* 7.3.116 ङेराम्नद्याम्नीभ्यः (see Figure 4). *A.* 7.3.113 provides that a nominal termination marked with ङ् that occurs after a stem ending in a feminine affix आ receives the initial augment या. *A.* 7.3.116 provides that the singular seventh triplet nominal termination ङि, when it occurs after a stem termed नदी, a stem ending in a feminine affix आ, or a nominal that ends in the root नी, is replaced by आम्. (Feminine stems ending in short and long इ and उ are termed नदी under certain conditions by *A.* 1.4.3–6.) The former rule applies to a stem ending in the feminine affix आ followed by any of the singular nominal terminations of the 4th–7th triplets, i.e. ङे, ङसि, ङस्, or ङि. The latter applies to the singular seventh triplet nominal termination ङि preceded by a feminine stem termed नदी, a nominal stem ending in a feminine affix आ, or a nominal stem ending in the root नी. As shown in Figure 4, the domains overlap but neither is wholly included within the other. *A.* 7.3.113 alone applies to the dative, ablative, and genitive singular terminations ङे, ङसि, and ङस् following a stem ending in the feminine affix आ, producing forms such as the feminine dative singular खट्वायै and the feminine ablative and genitive singular खट्वायाः, both from the stem खट्वा 'cot'. *A.* 7.3.116 alone applies to the locative singular termination ङि following feminine stems in short or long इ and उ termed नदी, and stems ending in the root नी, producing locative singular forms such as कुमार्याम् (< कुमारी 'girl'), and सेनान्याम् (< सेना-नी 'army-leader'). Both rules have scope where the locative singular termination ङि follows a stem ending in the feminine affix आ. The fact that ङि is included within the domain of nominal terminations marked with ङ् would imply that *A.* 7.3.116 takes precedence over *A.* 7.3.113 by simple blocking. However, the fact that आप् is included within the domain of नदी, आप्, नी, would imply that *A.* 7.3.113 takes precedence over *A.* 7.3.116 by simple blocking. The two implications are contradictory. Patañjali determines that the latter of the two rules takes precedence by virtue of the principle stated in *A.* 1.4.2 that the latter of two rules takes precedence in cases of conflict. *A.* 7.3.113 then applies after the application of *A.* 7.3.116. Thereby the correct forms, such as the feminine locative singular खट्वायाम् are obtained (< खट्वा-या-आम् (*A.* 7.3.113) < खट्वा-आम् (*A.* 7.3.116) < खट्वा-ङि).

IV Pūrvavipratiṣedha

The preceding sections have shown that the principle that the latter rule takes precedence in cases of conflict provides a solution to a number of cases of conflict. There is a problem, however, in determining the precedence of conflicting rules by the principle of later occurrence stated in *A.* 1.4.2. There are cases of conflict where the earlier rule must take precedence in order to account for the proper forms. Consider the two rules *A.* 7.3.111 घेर्ङिति and *A.* 7.1.73 इको ऽचि विभक्तौ (see Figure 5). *A.* 7.3.111 provides that the final vowel of a stem termed घि is replaced by its corresponding गुण vowel before a nominal termination marked with ङ्. *A.* 7.1.73 provides that the last vowel of a neuter stem that ends in a simple vowel other than अ and is followed by a vowel-initial nominal termination receives the augment न्. *A.* 7.3.111 has as its exclusive domain masculine stems (except सखि, and uncompounded पति under certain circumstances; see *A.* 1.4.7–9), and feminine stems not termed नदी, ending in इ, or उ followed by any of the singular nominal terminations of the 4th–7th triplets, that is, ङे, ङसि, ङस्, or ङि. *A.* 7.1.73

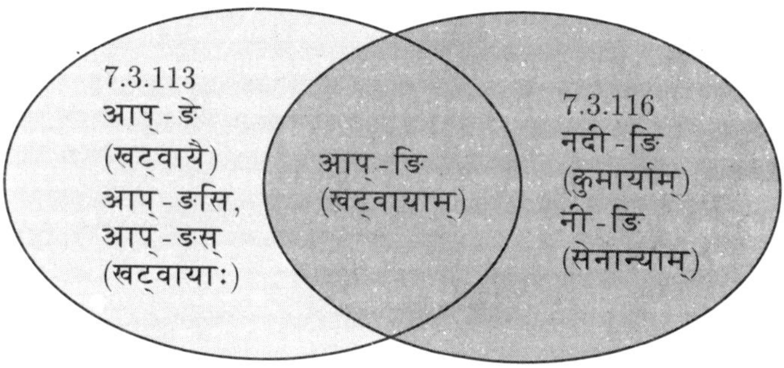

Figure 4: Overlapping domains. Example 3

7.3.113 याडापः (ङिति 111). After a stem ending in the feminine affixes आप् (i.e. टाप् 4.1.4, डाप् 4.1.13, चाप् 4.1.74), a nominal termination marked with ङ् receives the initial augment याट्. 7.3.116 ङेराम्नद्याम्नीभ्यः. After a stem termed नदी (1.4.3–6), the feminine affixes आप् (i.e. टाप् 4.1.4, डाप् 4.1.13, चाप् 4.1.74), or a nominal stem ending in the root नी, the singular seventh triplet nominal termination ङि is replaced by आम्. 7.3.113 domain: आप्-ङे, आप्-ङसि, आप्-ङस्, आप्-ङि. 7.3.116 domain: नदी-ङि, आप्-ङि, नी-ङि. 7.3.113 exclusive domain: आप्-ङे, आप्-ङसि, आप्-ङस् (खट्वायै f4s, खट्वायाः f5/6s). 7.3.116 exclusive domain: नदी-ङि, नी-ङि (कुमार्याम्, सेनान्याम् f7s). Shared domain: आप्-ङि (खट्वायाम् f7s).

has as its exclusive domain neuter stems ending in ऋ followed by the vowel-initial nominal terminations of the nominative and accusative dual ई, and genitive and ablative dual ओस्.[1] The overlapping domain of the two rules is neuter stems ending in इ or उ termed घि, followed by any of the singular nominal terminations of the 4th–7th triplets, i.e. ङे, ङसि, ङस्, or ङि. As shown in Figure 5, neither domain is wholly included within the other. The fact that nominal terminations marked with ङ् (ङित्) are included among the referents of the term विभक्ति and the fact that the referents of the term घि are included among stems ending in इ and उ both imply that *A.* 7.3.111 has the narrower domain and blocks *A.* 7.1.73. Conversely, neuter stems are included among stems of any gender, implying that *A.* 7.1.73 has the narrower domain and blocks *A.* 7.3.111. There is no criterion to determine which of the two rules takes precedence by simple blocking. To account for the desired forms, for example the neuter dative singulars त्रपुणे (< त्रपु 'tin' + ङे) and जतुने (< जतु 'lac' + ङे), the rule providing the augment न् (*A.* 7.1.73) must apply, not the rule providing guṇa (*A.* 7.3.111). The earlier rule must take precedence, not the later rule. Therefore one cannot invoke the principle stated in *A.* 1.4.2 that the later rule takes precedence over the former to resolve the conflict.

V The desired operation takes precedence

In such cases, where the earlier of two conflicting rules must apply, the initial solution proposed in the *Mahābhāṣya* is to state that the opposite principle to *A.* 1.4.2 applies in those cases. Kātyāyana states that the augment नुम् occurs in precedence over guṇa in cases such as Example 4 [Figure 5] by virtue of the principle that the prior rule applies in cases of conflict. (गुणवृद्ध्यौत्त्वतृज्वद्भावेभ्यो नुम्पूर्वविप्रतिषिद्धम् *A.* 7.1.96 vt. 10, MBh. 3:275.23.)

Patañjali specifically adduces examples illustrating Example 4. First he describes the exclusive domain of *A.* 7.3.111 and *A.* 7.1.73, and their overlapping domain. In that case, he states, the exclusive domain of guṇa (*A.* 7.3.111) is the dative through locative singular of इ-final and उ-final stems termed घि such as the masculine dative singulars अग्नये (< अग्नि 'fire' + ङे) and वायवे (< वायु 'wind' + ङे). The exclusive domain of the augment नुम् is the nominative/accusative duals of neuter stems such as त्रपुणी (< त्रपु 'tin' + ई) and जतुनी (< जतु 'lac' + ई). Both rules obtain in the dative through

[1] The singular third-triplet termination आ is replaced by the न्-initial ना by *A.* 7.3.120; the plural sixth-triplet termination gets an initial augment न् (नुट्) by *A.* 7.1.54–57; the neuter nominative, vocative, and accusative plural stem (preceding the सर्वनामस्थान termination शि) gets the augment नुम् already by *A.* 7.1.72.

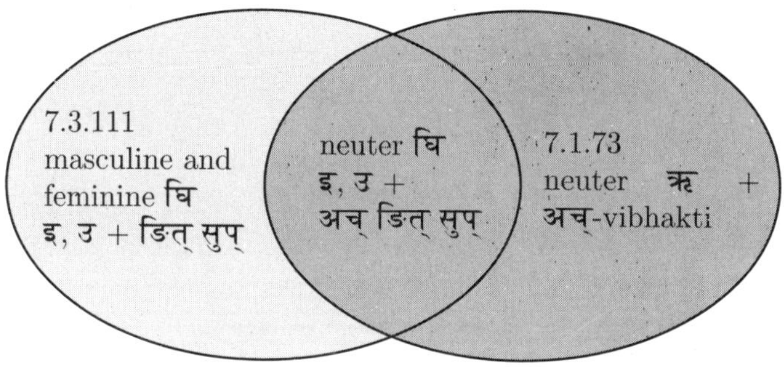

Figure 5: Overlapping domains.
Example 4: Earlier rule takes precedence over later rule.

7.3.111 घेर्ङिति (गुणः 108). Followed by a nominal termination marked with ङ्, the final vowel of a stem termed घि is replaced by its corresponding गुण vowel. 7.1.73 इकोऽचि विभक्तौ (नपुंसकस्य 72, नुम् 58). Followed by a vowel-initial nominal termination, the last vowel of a neuter stem ending in a vowel in the pratyāhāra इक् receives the augment न् (नुम्). 7.3.111 domain: masculine, feminine, and neuter stems ending in इ or उ that are termed घि + ङित् (4–7s) सुप्. 7.1.73 domain: neuter stems in इ, उ, ऋ + अच् vibhakti. 7.3.111 exclusive domain: masculine and feminine इ and उ stems termed घि + ङित् (4–7s) सुप्. 7.1.73 exclusive domain: neuter ऋ + अच्-initial vibhakti. Shared domain: neuter stems ending in इ, उ termed घि + अच्-initial ङित् (4–7s) सुप्.

locative singular of neuter stems such as त्रपुणे (< त्रपु + ङि) and जतुने (< जतु + ङि). (गुणवृद्ध्यौत्त्वतृज्वद्भावेभ्यो नुम्भवति पूर्वविप्रतिषेधेन॥ तत्र गुणस्यावकाशः — अग्नये वायवे। नुमो ऽवकाशः — त्रपुणी जतुनी। इहोभयं प्राप्नोति — त्रपुणे जतुने॥ MBh. 3.275.24–25.) As shown in the examples of the overlapping domain त्रपुणे and जतुने, the augment नुम् provided by the earlier of the two rules, namely *A.* 7.1.73, takes precedence.

To justify the prior rule taking precedence, Patañjali states that in the section of rules governed by the heading *A.* 6.4.1 अङ्गस्य, that is, the fourth pāda of adhyāya six through the end of the seventh adhyāya, the prior of two conflicting rules takes precedence. It is objected that there are conflicting rules in that section, where the latter rule must apply to account for proper forms. Witness examples 2–3 (figures 3–4). In addition, to state such a principle would require emending *A.* 1.4.2. (विप्रतिषेधे परमित्युक्त्वाङ्गाधिकारे पूर्वमिति वक्तव्यम्। किं कृतं भवति। पूर्वविप्रतिषेधा न पठितव्या भवन्ति। गुणवृद्ध्यौत्त्वतृज्वद्भावेभ्यो नुम्पूर्वविप्रतिषिद्धम्। नुमचिरतृज्वद्भावेभ्यो नुडिति। कथं ये परविप्रतिषेधाः। इत्त्वोत्त्वाभ्यां गुणवृद्धी भवतो विप्रतिषेधेनेति। सूत्रं च भिद्यते॥ MBh. 1.306.1–4.)

Patañjali concludes that everything is in order even with the sūtra left as it is. Among the many meanings of the term पर is the meaning *desired* (इष्टवाची परशब्दः) such as in the phrase, "Gone to the supreme abode" (परं धाम गतः), and it is the term पर having that meaning that is used in *A.* 1.4.2 (तस्येदं ग्रहणम्). The meaning of *A.* 1.4.2 is therefore that the rule which is supreme, that is, which is desired, takes precedence where there is conflict between rules with overlapping domains (विप्रतिषेधे परं यदिष्टं तद्भवति). (यथान्यासमेवास्तु। कथं ये पूर्वविप्रतिषेधाः। विप्रतिषेधे परमित्येव सिद्धम्। कथम्। परशब्दो ऽयं बह्वर्थः। ... अस्तीष्टवाची परशब्दः। तद्यथा। परं धाम गत इति। इष्टं धामेति गम्यते। तद्य इष्टवाची परशब्दस्तस्येदं ग्रहणम्। विप्रतिषेधे परं यदिष्टं तद्भवति॥ MBh. 1.306.4–10.) That Patañjali's final conclusion is that the desired rule applies in cases of conflict is shown by its frequent invocation. Patañjali repeats his interpretation that the term पर in *A.* 1.4.2 विप्रतिषेधे परं कार्यम् means *desired* (इष्ट) rather than *subsequent* (MBh. 1.46.14, etc.) and his assertion that in cases of conflict the desired rule applies (MBh. 1.46.15, etc.) in numerous discussions in the *Mahābhāṣya*.

Cardona (1976: 189–191) and other scholars do not accept Patañjali's interpretation of the term पर, nor do they accept his extension of the scope of *A.* 1.4.2 to the whole grammar. They consider that the scope of *A.* 1.4.2 is limited to the section of rules headed by *A.* 1.4.1 आ कडारादेका संज्ञा and ending with *A.* 2.2.38 कडाराः कर्मधारये. *A.* 1.4.2 determines that only the latter of two conflicting technical terms (संज्ञा) applies in the fourth pāda of the first adhyāya and the first two पादs of the second अध्याय. *A.* 1.4.2 does not apply as a decision-making device concerning the precedence of rules throughout the grammar. Nor is it desirable that there be a decision-making device that selects the preferred rule. Such a principle departs from a mechanistic procedure for determining the application of rules and relies rather on knowledge of the desired outcome of the generative grammar to determine rule ordering. Such a departure would be a shortcoming in the grammar. Cardona (1976: 191) states, "I think that such a procedure would weaken the grammar. .... I think this can and should be avoided. Cardona (1970a) has discussed how this can be done in the context of principles seen to operate in the *Aṣṭādhyāyī*." Indeed, if the grammar were meant to validate correct speech forms, it would be circular for knowledge of correct speech forms to be required in order to comprehend what the grammar provided.

VI Topicality

Cardona has sought other principles that might determine the ordering of rules in cases of conflict. He asserts (1997: 406) that "the rule concerning the narrower part of the overlapping domain blocks the other by what I call partial limited blocking." Kiparsky (1991) rejects limited blocking and denies that it is a principle accepted by Patañjali. In each of the four examples Cardona (1997: 406–409) provided — the same four examples discussed above and shown in figures 2–5 — a cursory distribution of rule conditions into domains appears to justify the application of the undesired rule equally as much as the desired one, just as Kiparsky objected. However, careful attention to the statement of the rules in question, the terms used, and their contexts does reveal means to determine the blocking relationship of overlapping domains without invoking the principle stated in *A.* 1.4.2 outside its proper scope. In particular, the terms used in the formulation of certain rules justifies domain inclusion within an overlapping domain and bears out the concept of limited blocking.

In the case of Example 1 (Figure 2), Kiparsky himself (1991: 358–359) proposes a solution that he calls 'collective blocking' rather than invoking the principal that the later rule takes precedence. Kiparsky's solution requires recognizing that *A.* 6.1.101 is wholly included within the combined domains of two rules, *A.* 6.1.77–78. Because of this total inclusion, in order to have scope, *A.* 6.1.101 must take precedence over both. It therefore takes precedence over each. As shown in Figure 1, *A.* 6.1.87 states that the sequence of a short or long अ and a following vowel is replaced by the single closest गुण vowel. *A.* 6.1.88 states an exception to *A.* 6.1.87. It states that the sequence of a short or long अ and a following ए, ओ, ऐ, or औ is replaced by the single closest वृद्धि vowel. By simple blocking, *A.* 6.1.87 has its scope limited to the sequence of a short or long अ and a following simple

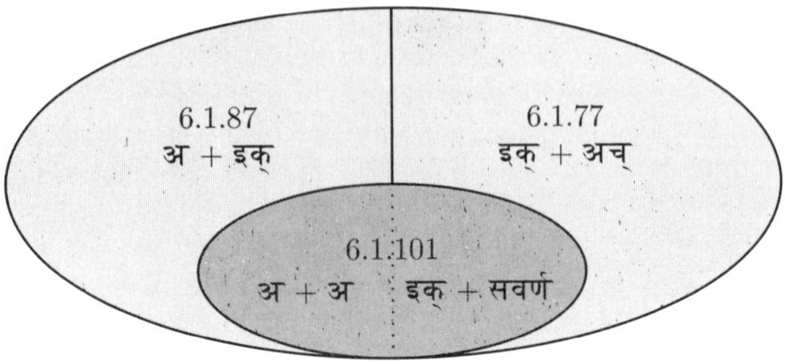

Figure 6: Solution to Example 1

(cf. Figure 2. See Cardona 1997: 406; Kiparsky 1991: 358–359.) 6.1.77 इको यणचि has domain: इक् + अच्. 6.1.87 आद्गुणः has domain: अ + अक्. 6.1.78 एचो ऽयवायावः has domain: एच् + अच्. 6.1.88 वृद्धिरेचि has domain: अ + एच्. The domains of the four rules constitute the combined domain अच् + अच्. Considering rules in pairs, अ + अ in 6.1.101 is an exception to 6.1.87 leaving it with the scope अ + इक्. इक् + सवर्ण इक् in 6.1.101 is an exception to 6.1.77. Alternatively, 6.1.101 has domain अक् + सवर्ण अक्, which is an exception to the combined domains of the two rules 6.1.77 and 6.1.87.

vowel. The combined domains of application of the four rules *A.* 6.1.77–78, 87–88 constitute the conjunction of two vowels. The combined domains of the two rules *A.* 6.1.77, 87 constitute the domain of a simple vowel followed by a vowel. *A.* 6.1.101 is an exception to this combined domain. The conjunction of short or long अ with short or long अ is a subset of the conjunction of short or long अ with any vowel so that part of the domain of *A.* 6.1.101 is wholly included within the domain of *A.* 6.1.87. Similarly, the conjunction of a simple vowel other than short or long अ with a following like simple vowel is a subset of the domain of the conjunction of a simple vowel other than short or long अ with any vowel, so the other part of the domain of *A.* 6.1.101 is wholly included within the domain of *A.* 6.1.77. *A.* 6.1.101 is therefore an exception to the combined domains of *A.* 6.1.77, 87. (See Figure 6.) Patañjali states under *A.* 6.1.102 vt. 3 that *A.* 6.1.77 and *A.* 6.1.87 (आद्गुणयणादेशौ) are general rules (उत्सर्गौ) and that, among others, *A.* 6.1.101 providing सवर्णदीर्घ is an exception to them. (*A.* 6.1.102 vt. 3 आद्गुणयणादेशयोरपवादा वृद्धिसवर्णदीर्घपूर्वसवर्णादेशास्तेषां पररूपं स्वरसन्धिषु MBh. 3.79.1–2. आद्गुणयणादेशावुत्सर्गौ। तयोरपवदा वृद्धिसवर्णदीर्घपूर्वसवर्णादेशाः। MBh. 3.79.3.)

Kiparsky's solution requires examining the domain structure of all rules pertaining to a domain together in order to determine blocking relationships. He does not propose solutions to the other cases considered in this paper. Cardona prefers to consider the blocking relation between two rules at a time. He treats *A.* 6.1.101 as an exception to *A.* 6.1.77 and to *A.* 6.1.87 individually.[2] Rather than simply examining the ultimate referents of terms stated in सूत्रs in a set-theoretic framework to determine what constitutes the domain of each rule, a more nuanced approach is required.

First, let us consider the terms used to describe elements within the conflicting domain in their contexts and make a judgement concerning the topic of Pāṇini's description. Terms in earlier sūtras in a single context determine the topic. Terms introduced in later sūtras in the same context specify additional restrictions. The order is therefore significant, in spite of the fact that rule *A.* 1.4.2 is not allowed to apply outside its proper scope. Although later rules may include some terms that have broader reference than some others, if they are still governed by the same topic of other terms, the new broader terms do not change the topic. With respect to the shared domain, the earlier terms with narrower reference do not serve to limit the scope of the terms introduced later. The later rules therefore constitute exceptions to the earlier rules in the shared domain, but not vice versa. In the case of *A.* 6.1.77 and *A.* 6.1.101, the term अचि in the former rule opens the topic by stating the broader domain. The term सवर्णे in the latter rule qualifies the term अचि and therefore states an additional restriction. Although the term अक् refers to a broader context than the term इक् does, it does not change the topic. The fact that the term सवर्ण restricts अच् therefore determines that *A.* 6.1.101 is an exception to *A.* 6.1.77. The case of conflict of the two rules *A.* 6.1.87 and *A.* 6.1.101 is similar.

The topical approach to determining the precedence of rule application just sketched in regard to *A.* 6.1.77 or *A.* 6.1.87 and *A.* 6.1.101 works where the two conflicting rules occur in close contiguity in the same section, where a term at the beginning of that section determines the topic common to the two conflicting rules, and where it is the latter rule that is desired to take precedence. Such is the case for Example 2 (Figure 3) and for Example 3 (Figure 4). In Example 2, *A.* 7.3.101 अतो दीर्घो यञि determines the topic of the section with the terms अतः 'in place of the final sound of a stem ending in short अ', and यञि 'before a sound in the pratyāhāra यञ्'. The term सुपि in *A.* 7.3.102 सुपि च limits this context to nominal terminations that begin

[2]Cardona has expressed additional thoughts concerning rule precedence both in an unpublished typescript composed thirty-four years ago (1976) and in recent private conversations on the matter during the preparation of the present paper. Although these may not be his final conclusions on this complex issue, I attempt to articulate and explore them here.

with यञ्. The terms झलि and बहुवचने in *A.* 7.3.103 बहुवचने झल्येत् further limit this context to a nominal termination beginning with झ् or भ् in the plural, namely to the termination भ्यस्. Although the scope of the terms झल् and बहुवचन include the termination सु not included within the scope of the term यञ्, the terms do not change the topic; the fact that the scope of its reference includes sounds within the domain of the term यञ् makes *A.* 7.3.103 an exception to *A.* 7.3.102 within the domain common to the two rules.

In Example 3, The term ङित् 'an affix marked with ङ्' in *A.* 7.3.111 घेर्ङिति determines that the topic of the section is the singular dative through locative terminations. The term recurs in *A.* 7.3.113 याडापः (ङिति 111). The term ङि in *A.* 7.3.116 ङेराम्नद्याम्नीभ्यः refers to just one of these affixes, the locative. The fact that ङि in *A.* 7.3.116 is an added term that narrows the domain dictates that the later rule constitutes an exception to the earlier one. The fact that the term नद्याम्नी in *A.* 7.3.116 is broader than the term आप् in *A.* 7.3.113 does not reverse rule precedence because it is not the topic.

The topical solution works for other cases in which two rules have overlapping domains as well. These include *A.* 3.1.97 अचो यत् and *A.* 3.1.124 ऋहलोर्ण्यत् where the term अच् in the former determines the topic, *A.* 6.1.97 अतो गुणे and *A.* 6.1.102 प्रथमयोः पूर्वसवर्णः where the term अच् in *A.* 6.1.77 determines the topic, *A.* 6.4.144 नस्तद्धिते and *A.* 6.4.155 टेः where the term तद्धिते in *A.* 6.4.144 determines the topic, etc.

The topical solution has some complications, however. The criteria for determining the topic are not clear. What makes the subsequent context a more suitable topic than the preceding context in Example 1 (figures 2 and 6)? How can the term यञ् in *A.* 7.3.102 determine the topic of *A.* 7.3.103 when the term झल् in the latter is not included within its scope? The determination of inclusion is likewise not clear where several limiting terms occur together in a sūtra, often in compounds. Is there significance to considering the scope of terms individually? The scope of ऋहल् in *A.* 3.1.124, for example, is not wholly included within the scope of the term अच् in *A.* 3.1.97; the scope of ऋ is. What justifies selecting अच् as the topic when हल् is not included within that topic but the sūtra in which it occurs is yet included within the section? Furthermore, if topic were determined by terms in preceding sūtras, topicality would be able to determine rule precedence only in cases where later rules take precedence over earlier rules; not in cases such as Example 4 (Figure 5) where an earlier rule takes precedence over a later rule. The principle would achieve no more than the extension of the विप्रतिषेध principle stated in *A.* 1.4.2 to the whole grammar.

Instead of determining domain inclusion on the basis of a topic stated at the beginning of a section of rules, selection of the domains to compare may

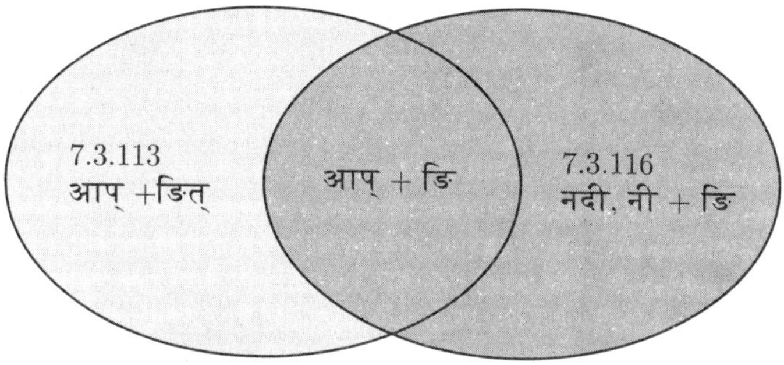

Figure 7: Solution to Example 3

(Cf. Figure 4. See Cardona 1997: 409 "limited blocking".) 7.3.116 ङेराम्नद्याम्नीभ्यः takes precedence over 7.3.113 याडापः (ङिति 111) because the scope of 7.3.116, defined by the term ङि, is a limitation of the domain of 7.3.113 (ङे, ङसि, ङस्, ङि) defined by the term ङित्.

be determined by the terms used to describe the overlapping domains. It appears to be necessary to determine the overlapping domain and then to examine just the terms used to describe that domain. Considering compound elements as separate terms, the broader term is then selected as designating the more general scope; the narrower term then states the exception, and the rule that includes the term with the narrower scope takes precedence in the shared domain. This procedure justifies setting the compound element हल् aside in *A*. 3.1.124, comparing the scope of the two terms ऋ and अच्, and selecting the latter as the topic without reference to the order of the rules. Similarly, regarding the solution to Example 3 (see Figure 7; cf. Figure 4) this procedure justifies breaking up the compound नदी-आप्-नी in *A*. 7.3.116, considering just the term आप् in the rule since it alone describes the domain that overlaps with that of *A*. 7.3.113, selecting the term ङि in *A*. 7.3.116 for comparison with the term ङित् in *A*. 7.3.113, and determining general scope and domain inclusion on the basis of that comparison. Since the terms नदी and नी are irrelevant to the shared domain and the term आप् is common to both rules, these terms are not pertinent to determining precedence of rule application on the basis of domain inclusion. *A*. 7.3.116 takes precedence because the term ङि has narrower scope wholly included within the scope of the term ङित् in *A*. 7.3.113.

VII Specificity hierarchy

As was stated above, the approach of determining the precedence in rule application by examining the topic of a section leads to proper results where the two conflicting rules occur in close contiguity in the same section, where a term at the beginning of that section determines the topic common to the two conflicting rules, and where it is the latter rule that is desired to take precedence. However, this solution does not work where the former rule is desired to apply. There are likewise difficulties with the approach of determining precedence in rule application just by considering the scope of terms that describe the overlapping domain of two conflicting rules. These difficulties arise where the relation of inclusion does not hold between the scope of terms in the conflicting rules, regardless of whether the two conflicting rules are in completely different sections or occur in close contiguity.

As an example of the circumstance in which consideration of the scope of terms alone will not succeed in determining a solution for rules in completely different sections, take Example 4 (Figure 5). The overlapping domain is neuter stems ending in इ or उ termed घि before vowel-initial nominal terminations marked with ङ्. The scopes of the terms घि and ङित् in *A.* 7.3.111 घेर् ङिति are wholly included within the scopes of the terms इक् and अच् विभक्ति respectively in *A.* 7.1.73 इको ऽचि विभक्तौ. The scope of the term नपुंसक, which recurs in *A.* 7.1.73 from *A.* 7.1.72 नपुंसकस्य झलचः, is neither wholly included within (see the discussion of the compound अतिसखि in the neuter below) nor wholly includes the scope of the term घि in *A.* 7.3.111. The scope of terms in one of the two rules is neither wholly included within nor wholly includes the scope of terms in the other.

It is sometimes the case that consideration of the scope of terms alone will not succeed in determining a solution for rules in close contiguity either. For example, the rules *A.* 7.1.70 उगिदचां सर्वनामस्थाने ऽधातोः and *A.* 7.1.72 नपुंसकस्य झलचः come into conflict because they have overlapping domains. *A.* 7.1.70 provides that a stem (other than a root) marked with उ, ऋ, or ऌ, and the root अन्च् receive the augment न् after their last vowel before a nominal termination termed सर्वनामस्थान. (The neuter plural termination शि that replaces the plural first and second triplet terminations in the neuter, and the first triplet and second triplet singular and dual terminations are termed सर्वनामस्थान by *A.* 1.1.42–43.) *A.* 7.1.72 provides that a neuter stem ending in a non-nasal stop or spirant or in a vowel receives the augment न् after its last vowel before a termination termed सर्वनामस्थान. As shown in Figure 8, neither domain is wholly included within the other; each rule has its exclusive domain. The former alone applies when a masculine stem is marked with उ, ऋ, or ऌ. The latter alone applies when a neuter stem is not so marked. Yet the domains overlap. Both have scope when a

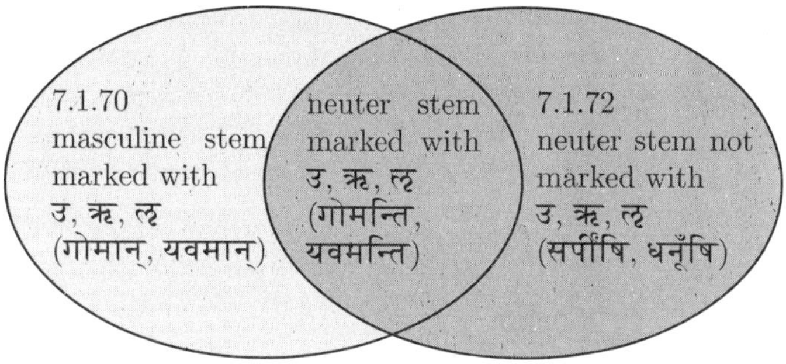

Figure 8: Overlapping domains. Example 5

7.1.70 उगिदचां सर्वनामस्थाने ऽधातोः. A stem, other than a root, marked with उ, ऋ, or ऌ, and the root अन्च् receive the augment नुम् before a nominal termination termed सर्वनामस्थान. 7.1.72 नपुंसकस्य झलचः. A neuter stem ending in a non-nasal stop or spirant or in a vowel receives the augment नुम् before a termination termed सर्वनामस्थान. 7.1.70 exclusive domain: masculine stem marked with उ, ऋ, ऌ: गो - मत्, यव - मत् end in मतुप् marked with उ. 7.1.72 exclusive domain: neuter stem not so marked: सर्पिस्, धनुस्. Shared domain: neuter stem marked with उ, ऋ, ऌ: श्र - ईयस् (5.3.60), भूयस्. The affix ईयसुन् is marked with उ.

neuter stem is marked with उ, ऋ, or ऌ.

Kātyāyana and Patañjali count Example 5 as another case of conflict in which the latter rule takes precedence due to the application of *A.* 1.4.2. Vārttika 2 on *A.* 7.1.72 states, "It works because (the latter rule applies in cases) of conflict." (vt. 2 विप्रतिषेधात्सिद्धं MBh. 3.264.4.) Patañjali comments,

> It works because (the latter rule applies in cases) of conflict. In case of the conflict between the augment नुम् occurring because the stem terminates in a non-nasal stop or spirant, or because the stem is marked with उ, ऋ, or ऌ, the augment will occur because the stem terminates in a non-nasal stop or spirant because (the latter rule applies in cases) of conflict. The scope of the augment due to the stem terminating in a non-nasal stop or spirant is, for example, सर्पींषि (< सर्पिस् 'ghee') and धनूंषि (< धनुस् 'a bow'). The scope of the augment due to the stem being marked with उ, ऋ, or ऌ is, for example, गोमान् (< गोमत् 'possessing cattle') and यवमान् (< यवमत् 'possessing barley'). Both have scope here for example: गोमन्ति ब्राह्मणकुलानि 'Brahmin families

possessing cattle', यवमन्ति ब्राह्मणकुलानि 'Brahmin families possessing barley,' श्रेयांसि (< श्रेयस् 'very splendid'), भूयांसि (< भूयस् 'very abundant'). The augment will occur because the stem terminates in a non-nasal stop or spirant. (विप्रतिषेधात्सिद्धमेतत्। झल्लक्षणः क्रियतामुगिल्लक्षण इति झल्लक्षणो भविष्यति विप्रतिषेधेन। झल्लक्षणस्यावकाशः — सर्पींषि धनूंषि। उगिल्लक्षणस्यावकाशः — गोमान् यवमान्। इहोभयं प्राप्नोति। गोमन्ति ब्राह्मणकुलानि। यवमन्ति ब्राह्मणकुलानि। श्रेयांसि भूयांसीति। झल्लक्षणो भविष्यति विप्रतिषेधेन॥ MBh. 3.264.5–8.)

Instead of resolving the conflict by applying the principle that the latter rule takes precedence in cases of conflict, which does not apply universally, one could attempt to resolve the conflict by determining which of the terms that describes the shared domain has narrower scope as demonstrated above regarding Example 3. Since only stems that end in non-nasal stops are marked with उ, the term अच् in *A.* 7.1.72 is not relevant to the consideration of the scope of terms that apply to the overlapping domain; the overlapping domain includes only neuter stems marked with उ that end in non-nasal stops. Yet the scope of the term उगित् in *A.* 7.1.70 is neither wholly included within nor wholly includes the scope of the term नपुंसक, even limited to the domain of the term झल् which it qualifies in *A.* 7.1.72. For there are stems marked with उ that are not neuter (गोमान्), and there are neuter stems ending in a non-nasal stop that are not marked with उ (सर्पींषि). The term उगित् in *A.* 7.1.70 and the term नपुंसक, as a qualifier of the term झल् in *A.* 7.1.72, both refer to specific sets of stems that end in non-nasal stops. The domains of the two terms intersect, yet neither is wholly included within the other, so no clear criterion emerges to determine precedence in the shared domain. Consideration of the scope of terms alone does not succeed in determining rule precedence.

Where the relation of total inclusion does not hold between the scope of terms that describe the shared domain of conflicting rules, regardless of whether the two conflicting rules occur in close contiguity or in different contexts in the *Aṣṭādhyāyī*, a specificity ranking may help to determine rule precedence. The scope of technical terms and qualifiers used to describe the shared domain is still relevant in determining which of two rules that have overlapping domains more specifically describes the overlapping region. Yet an additional factor may be considered. In determining specificity of reference one may establish a hierarchy in which certain types of reference are considered more specific than others. One possible scale of specificity is from concrete to abstract. In linguistics, most concrete is phonetics. More abstract is phonology: phonetic terms that depend on a greater degree of phonological classification are more specific than phonetic terms that do not. More concrete still is morphology: terms that describe contexts morphologically with reference to larger, fixed sequences of phonetic elements with functional or semantic properties, such as terms for stems and affixes, are more specific than terms that describe contexts purely phonetically. Finally more specific still are terms that describe contexts semantically, such as terms for gender and number. Within this hierarchy, clearly certain phonetic terms are more specific than other phonetic terms, certain morphological terms are more specific than other morphological terms, etc. The hierarchy of specificity therefore is

$$\textit{phonetic} < \textit{phonological} < \textit{morphological} < \textit{semantic} \qquad (1)$$

Specificity ranking could account for rule application correctly in examples 1 and 2 in section II and III above. In Example 1 (see Figure 2), the term सवर्णे in *A.* 6.1.101 is higher in specificity rank than the other terms in the two sūtras. Rules *A.* 6.1.77 and *A.* 6.1.101, which have overlapping domains, describe their domains exclusively in phonetic terms. Yet the latter rule describes the overlapping domain using the very specific phonological term सवर्ण 'belonging to the same class' in addition to the simpler phonetic terms अक् + अच्. *A.* 6.1.77 describes the overlapping domain simply in general phonetic terms: इक् + अच्. Although the phonetic term इक् in *A.* 6.1.77 is narrower than the phonetic term अक् in *A.* 6.1.101, the phonological term सवर्णे in the latter is more restrictive. The domain referred to does not consist merely of one set of sounds plus another independent set of sounds. It is restricted to abstract relations between the phonetic features of sounds in one set and the sounds in the other. Phonological abstraction is more restrictive than simple phonetics. Both rules apply within the phonetic domain of इक् + इक्; only the latter rule contains an additional restriction that the subsequent इक् be the same as the preceding इक्.

Specificity ranking similarly could account for rule application correctly in Example 2 as well (see Figure 9; cf. Figure 3). Both rules occur within the section headed by *A.* 6.4.1 अङ्गस्य and therefore deal with morphology: they both concern operations on stems (अङ्गस्य) followed by nominal terminations (सुपि). Yet most of the other terms that restrict which stems and affixes are involved are phonetic. The term अतः, stated in the first and recurring in the second, limits the domain of the rules to stems that are अ-final. The term यञि in the first rule limits its domain to contexts in which affixes begin with a sound in the pratyāhāra यञ्. The term झलि in the second rule similarly limits its scope to contexts in which affixes begin with a sound in the pratyāhāra झल्. Since the intersection of यञ् and झल् is the sounds झ् and भ्, and no nominal terminations begin with the former, just considering the intersection of the domains described by these terms, the overlapping domain is that in which a stem ending in अ is followed by

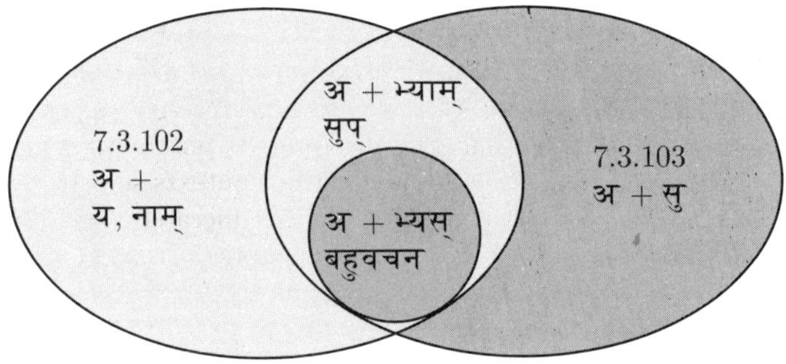

Figure 9: Solution to Example 2

(Cf. Figure 3. See Cardona 1997: 407.) 7.3.102 has domain य, नाम्, भ्याम् defined by the term यञ्. 7.3.103 has domain सु, भ्यस् defined by the term झल्. 7.3.102 exclusive domain: य, नाम्. 7.3.103 exclusive domain: सु. Shared domain: भ्याम्, भ्यस्. In the conflicting domain, बहुवचन (103) is wholly included within सुप् (102), so 103 takes precedence. Examination of the terms used, rather than simply the ultimate referents of the statements, justifies Cardona's description of the solution as domain inclusion within an overlapping domain.

a nominal termination beginning with भ्. Even without the term बहुवचने, the term झल् in *A.* 7.3.103 and the term यञ् in *A.* 7.3.101 constitute overlapping domains. The term बहुवचने in *A.* 7.3.103 is a semantic term that carves out a subdomain within the overlapping domain described by the other terms. Hence *A.* 7.3.103 takes precedence by virtue of having the narrower scope. The rule has narrower scope by virtue of the principle of the specificity ranking described above in (1).

Now let us consider the applicability of specificity ranking to the conflict of *A.* 7.1.70 and *A.* 7.1.72 (see Figure 10; cf. Figure 8). Although both rules occur in the section headed by *A.* 6.4.1 अङ्गस्य and therefore refer to stems followed by affixes, which are morphological elements, some of the terms used in these rules refer to these elements in phonetic terms. The terms झल् and अच् in the compound झलचः in *A.* 7.1.72 characterize stems subject to augmentation with नुम् most generally solely in phonetic terms. The terms उगित् and अच् in the compound उगिदचां in *A.* 7.1.70 characterize such stems more specifically in morphological terms. The term उगित् refers to stems formed with affixes marked with particular markers, and the term अच् refers to a particular verbal root.[3] Given the characterization of the stem provided by the phonetic and morphological terms झलचः in *A.* 7.1.72

[3]The root is listed in *Mādhavīya Dhātuvṛtti* 595 (Shastri 1983: 221) with a

and उगिदचां in *A.* 7.1.70, the term नपुंसकस्य adds an additional restriction in the latter rule in semantic terms by reference to gender. If the latter rule did not have the term नपुंसकस्य, the scope of the former rule would be entirely included within the scope of the latter, since nominative stem-forming affixes marked with उ, ऋ, or ऌ all end in non-nasal stops or spirants. The scope of the term उगित्, as well as the root अन्च्, in the former rule is included within the scope of the term झल् in the latter rule. (The root अन्च् restricts the augment नुम् to just this root in non-neuter forms. *A.* 7.1.71 allows it in the root युज् too when not in a compound.) Within the overlapping domain of the two rules, the added semantic term नपुंसकस्य in *A.* 7.1.72 constitutes an addition to a situation of domains already described in phonetic and morphological terms that resolves the conflict. Within the shared domain described in phonetic and morphological terms, नपुंसक states a semantic restriction higher on the specificity hierarchy so that *A.* 7.1.72 has the narrower domain. The rule with the narrower domain applies.

Sometimes where two rules occur in the same section it is the preceding rule that is desired to take precedence. For example (see Figure 11), *A.* 7.1.73 इको ऽचि विभक्तौ (see Figure 5) and *A.* 7.1.92 सख्युरसंबुद्धौ (सर्वनामस्थाने 86, णित् 90, अङ्गस्य 6.4.1) come into conflict, and it is *A.* 7.1.73 that is desired to take precedence. *A.* 7.1.92 provides that a termination termed सर्वनामस्थान following the stem सखि is marked with ण् except in the vocative singular. The domain of *A.* 7.1.73 is neuter stems (नपुंसकस्य) ending in इ, उ, or ऋ (इकः) followed by vowel-initial nominal terminations (अचि विभक्तौ). The domain of *A.* 7.1.92 is the stem सखि (सख्युः) followed by a nominal termination termed सर्वनामस्थान other than the vocative singular (असंबुद्धौ). The domains of the two rules overlap when सखि occurs in the neuter plural as in the compound अतिसखि in the phrase अतिसखीनि ब्राह्मणकुलानि (MBh. 3.275.26–276.1). To derive the desired forms, the augment नुम् provided by *A.* 7.1.73 must occur; not vṛddhi conditioned by marking with ण् brought about by *A.* 7.1.92. Now the topicality principle formulated in section VI would erroneously give *A.* 7.1.92 precedence over *A.* 7.1.73. The topic set by *A.* 7.1.72 is apparently narrowed by the term इक् in *A.* 7.1.73, to a neuter stem that ends in a vowel of the pratyāhāra इक्, namely, इ, उ, ऋ, or ऌ. The term सख्युः in *A.* 7.1.92 limits the topic to a particular stem. Even though *A.* 7.1.92 applies to the stem सखि in the masculine and feminine as well, the broader scope of the term सखि does not change the topic. The topicality principle does not permit earlier terms with narrower reference to limit the scope of the terms introduced later. It does not permit the term

penultimate nasal and marker उ, i.e. अन्चु; however, Sāyaṇa cites Maitreya's citation that some read the root अच्: 'अचु इत्येके' इति मैत्रेयः. Kṣīrasvāmī's reading of a root अन्चि marked with इ is not accepted by others.

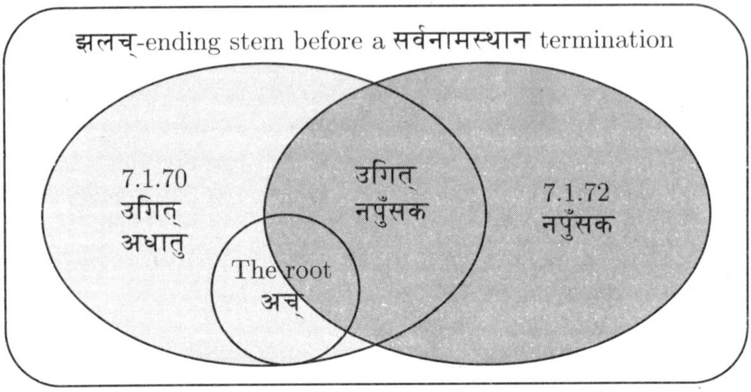

Figure 10: Solution to Example 5

(Cf. Figure 8.) The two rules occur within the section headed by *A.* 6.4.1 अङ्गस्य; hence they refer to morphological elements, namely stems. Yet, the term झलच् in *A.* 7.1.72 नपुंसकस्य झलचः specifies the universe in which the augment नुम् occurs in phonetic terms: a nominal stem ending in a non-nasal stop or vowel. The augment नुम् does not occur under any other conditions. Within this universe, the term सर्वनामस्थान in 7.1.70 उगिदचां सर्वनामस्थाने ऽधातोः recurs in 7.1.72; thereby it limits both rules to contexts in which a nominal termination so termed follows the stem. For consideration of the scope of these two rules, the term may be taken as part of the specification of the universe. The term उगित् in 7.1.70 limits the scope of the rule to stems marked with उ, ऋ, or ऌ or formed by the provision of affixes so marked. The root अच् is so marked. While the term अधातु in 7.1.70 limits the domain of the rule to stems that are not verbal roots, the term अच् in 7.1.70 excepts the root from the exclusion. All stems marked with उ, ऋ, or ऌ end in non-nasal stops, i.e. by sounds in the pratyāhāra झल् so that 7.1.70 falls entirely within the domain of 7.1.72 devoid of the term नपुंसक. The term नपुंसक in 7.1.72 stipulates a limitation that specifies the domain of 7.1.72. The gender term must be understood to be higher on the specificity scale to override the term उगित् in the shared domain of neuter stems marked with उ, ऋ, or ऌ.

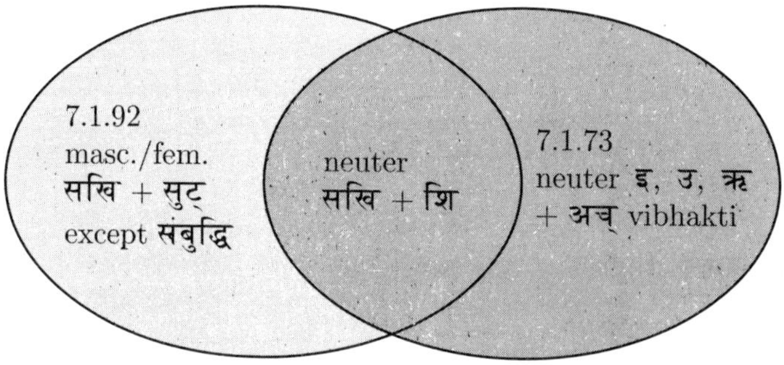

Figure 11: Example 6

7.1.73 इको ऽचि विभक्तौ (नपुंसकस्य 72, नुम् 58). Followed by a vowel-initial nominal termination, the last vowel of a neuter stem ending in a vowel in the pratyāhāra इक् receives the augment न् (नुम्). 7.1.92 सख्युरसंबुद्धौ (सर्वनामस्थाने 86, णित् 90, अङ्गस्य 6.4.1). A nominal termination termed सर्वनामस्थान following the stem सखि is marked with ण् except in the vocative singular. 7.1.73 domain: नपुंसक 'neuter' इ, उ, ऋ stems + अच् vibhakti. 7.1.92 domain: सखि in the masculine and feminine + a सर्वनामस्थान ending, i.e. a termination in the pratyāhāra सुट् (सु, औ, जस्, अम्, औट्), except vocative singular; सखि in the neuter + a सर्वनामस्थान ending, i.e. शि. 7.1.73 exclusive domain: (neuter इ, उ, and ऋ stems other than सखि) + अच् vibhakti. 7.1.92 exclusive domain: सखि in the masculine and feminine + a termination in the pratyāhāra सुट्, except vocative singular. Shared domain: neuter सखि + शि.

नपुंसक to limit the term सखि. Hence the principle would force *A*. 7.1.92 to take precedence over *A*. 7.1.73 undesirably. To produce the correct form, *A*. 7.1.73 must take precedence.

The specificity principle produces the correct results, as it does in the case of the conflict between *A*. 7.1.73 and *A*. 7.3.111 (see Figure 5, Example 4). There, the fact that the term नपुंसकस्य, which recurs from *A*. 7.1.72, is a semantic qualifier rather than a phonetic one makes *A*. 7.1.73 more specific than *A*. 7.3.111. Within the overlapping domain, one considers scope of the phonetic terms describing that domain first, then the morphological ones, then the semantic ones; more general qualifiers before more specific ones. Both rules concern morphological elements, namely stems with following affixes, not merely phonetic elements. Yet some of the terms used refer to items in phonetic terms. The terms इक् in *A*. 7.1.73 and घि in *A*. 7.3.111 refer to stems that terminate in certain vowels. The term घि specifies a narrower domain than the scope of the term इक्, since all stems termed घि

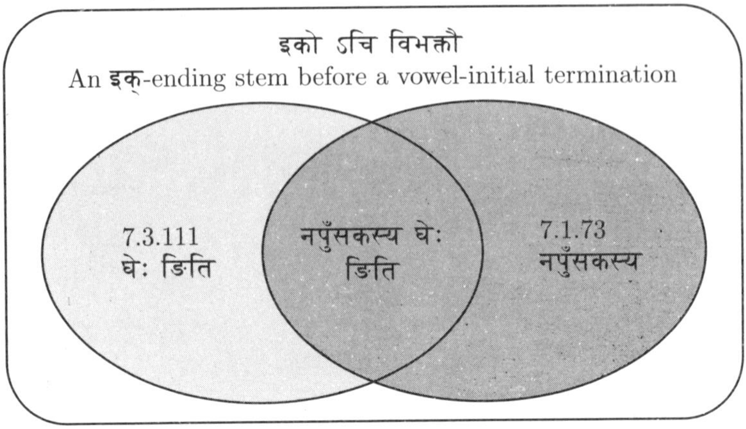

Figure 12: Specificity solution to Example 4

(Cf. Figure 5.) The two rules 7.1.73 इको ऽचि विभक्तौ (नपुंसकस्य 72, नुम् 58) and 7.3.111 घेर्ङिति (गुणः 108) occur within the section headed by *A.* 6.4.1 अङ्गस्य; hence they refer to morphological elements, namely stems. Yet, the terms इकः अचि विभक्तौ in 7.1.73 specify the universe in which the two rules apply in phonetic terms: a nominal stem ending in a vowel other than अ followed by a vowel-initial nominal termination. Neither rule applies under any other conditions. Within this universe, the terms घेः ङिति in 7.3.111 limit the scope of the rule to stems termed घि followed by nominal terminations marked with ङ्. Hence the domain of 7.3.111 falls entirely within the domain of 7.1.73 devoid of the term नपुंसक. The term नपुंसक, which recurs in 7.1.73 from 7.1.72, stipulates a limitation that specifies the domain of 7.1.73. The gender term must be understood to be higher on the specificity scale to override the term घि in the shared domain of neuter stems ending in इ or उ so that 7.1.73 takes precedence over 7.3.111.

end in the vowels इ and उ which are included within the pratyāhāra इक्. The terms ङिति in *A.* 7.3.111 and विभक्ति in *A.* 7.1.73 are morphological terms. The term ङिति specifies a narrower domain than, and is wholly included within, the domain specified by अच् विभक्ति, since all four nominal terminations marked with ङ् are vowel-initial. Now the term नपुंसक 'neuter' in *A.* 7.1.73, a semantic term, carves out a subdomain within the domain specified by the phonetic term घि in *A.* 7.3.111. Hence *A.* 7.1.73 describes the more specific domain and is the exception that takes precedence in the overlapping domain, as shown in Figure 12.

Similarly, in the case of conflict between *A.* 7.1.73 इको ऽचि विभक्तौ and *A.* 7.1.92 सख्युरसंबुद्धौ (see Figure 11, Example 6), the morphological term

नपुंसक 'neuter' in *A.* 7.1.73 must be understood to carve out a subdomain within the domain specified by other terms. The two rules occur within the section headed by *A.* 6.4.1 अङ्गस्य; hence the rule refers to morphological elements: inflectional terminations after stems. Nevertheless, इकः अचि in *A.* 7.1.73 specifies the domain in phonetic terms: a nominal stem ending in a vowel in the pratyāhāra इक् before an affix beginning with a vowel. The morphological terms सख्युः असंबुद्धौ in *A.* 7.1.92 with सर्वनामस्थाने read in from *A.* 7.1.86 specify the domain of the stem सखि followed by a nominal termination termed सर्वनामस्थान other than the vocative singular (असंबुद्धौ). The common domain specified by these terms is the nominal stem सखि followed by vowel-initial terminations termed सर्वनामस्थान, i.e. the dual and plural of the first triplet, and the dual of the second triplet in the masculine and feminine, and the plural of the first two triplets in the neuter. The morphological term नपुंसक in *A.* 7.1.73 now specifies a subdomain within that common domain consisting of the stem सखि in the neuter followed by शि, the neuter nominative, vocative, accusative plural termination. In order for *A.* 7.1.92 to take precedence over *A.* 7.1.73, the term नपुंसक in the *A.* 7.1.73 must limit the domain already specified by the other terms; it must be considered a more specific qualifier than morphological terms such as अङ्ग 'stem' and विभक्ति 'affix', even more specific than terms for particular stems such as सखि, as shown in Figure 13.

In order to account for proper rule precedence in the preceding examples the specificity hierarchy must explicitly rank semantic qualifiers such as number and gender as more specific than morphological qualifiers. The specificity ranking that places semantics at the top of the scale more specific than morphological qualifiers correctly resolves rule conflicts in a number of other cases besides between *A.* 7.1.73 and *A.* 7.3.111, and between *A.* 7.1.73 and *A.* 7.1.92 where it is desired that the preceding rule take precedence. For example, it correctly gives priority to the preceding rule in the conflict between *A.* 7.1.73 and *A.* 7.1.97 विभाषा तृतीयादिष्वचि and between *A.* 7.1.73 and *A.* 7.3.119 अच्च घेः (which are not dealt with in the present paper). The resolution of these conflicts by virtue of ranking gender at the top of the specificity hierarchy agrees with the resolution specified by Kātyāyana in vārttika 10 under *A.* 7.1.95–96: गुणवृद्ध्यौत्त्वतृज्वद्भावेभ्यो नुम्पूर्वविप्रतिषिद्धम् (MBh. 3.295.23–296.5).

VIII Yena nāprāpte

Three principles of determining domain specificity have been articulated in order to determine rule precedence in overlapping domains. In section VI, the topicality principle was introduced according to which terms in earlier rules declare the topic of the section that terms in later rules specify; later

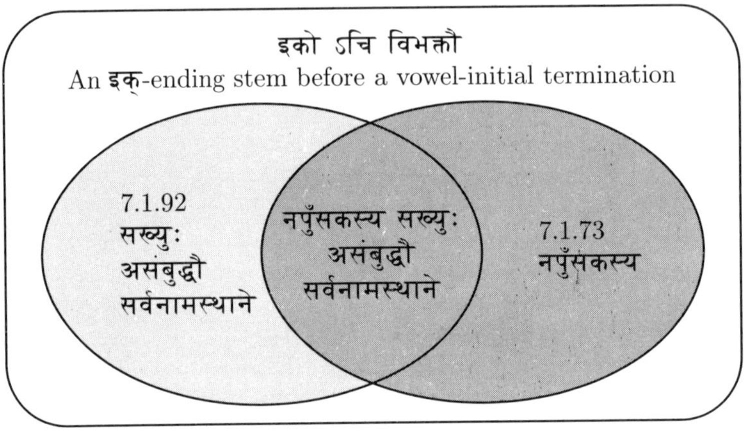

Figure 13: Specificity solution to Example 6

(Cf. Figure 11.) The two rules 7.1.73 इको ऽचि विभक्तौ (नपुंसकस्य 72, नुम् 58) and 7.1.92 सख्युरसंबुद्धौ (सर्वनामस्थाने 86, णित् 90) occur within the section headed by 6.4.1 अङ्गस्य, and 7.1.73 includes the term विभक्तौ; hence the two rules refer to morphological elements, namely a stem followed by a nominal termination. Yet, the terms इकः अचि in 7.1.73 specify the universe in which the two rules apply in phonetic terms so that the rules apply to a nominal stem ending in a vowel other than अ followed by a vowel-initial nominal termination. Neither rule applies under any other conditions. Within this universe, the terms सख्युः असंबुद्धौ in 7.1.92, and सर्वनामस्थाने which recurs in it, limit the scope of the rule to the stem सखि followed by nominal terminations termed सर्वनामस्थान other than the vocative singular. Hence the domain of 7.1.92 falls entirely within the domain of 7.1.73 devoid of the term नपुंसकस्य. The term नपुंसक, which recurs in 7.1.73 from 7.1.72, stipulates a limitation that specifies the domain of 7.1.73. The gender term must be understood to be higher on the specificity scale to override the terms सख्युः असंबुद्धौ सर्वनामस्थाने in the shared domain of the stem सखि followed by the neuter nominative/vocative/accusative plural nominal termination शि so that 7.1.73 takes precedence over 7.1.92.

rules therefore constitute exceptions to earlier rules in the same section. Later in section VI, the principle was introduced according to which rules in which terms that describe the shared domain more narrowly take precedence. This principle operates regardless of the order of the conflicting rules. Then in section VII, the specificity ranking was introduced, whereby semantic qualifiers such as gender are more specific than morphological qualifiers, which are more specific than phonological qualifiers, which are more specific than simple phonetics. None of these three principles succeeds by itself to resolve all of the cases of rule conflict in overlapping domains.

The specificity ranking described in section VII does not resolve rule conflict correctly in all circumstances. The specificity ranking that places gender at the top of the scale more specific than morphological qualifiers fails to resolve rule conflict correctly between *A*. 7.1.54 ह्रस्वनद्यापो नुट् (आमि 52) and *A*. 7.1.73 (see Figure 14). The earlier rule must take precedence even though the latter rule includes the term नपुंसक. *A*. 7.1.54 provides that the initial augment न् (नुट्) is attached to the plural sixth triplet nominal termination आम् after stems ending in a short vowel (ह्रस्व), after feminine stems ending in the long vowels ई and ऊ termed नदी (which they are optionally before आम् by *A*. 1.4.5 वामि), and after stems ending in the feminine affix आप्. *A*. 7.1.73 इको ऽचि विभक्तौ (नपुंसकस्य 72, नुम् 58) provides that the last vowel of a neuter stem ending in a vowel in the pratyāhāra इक् receives the augment न् (नुम्) when followed by a vowel-initial nominal termination. Both rules occur in the section headed by *A*. 6.4.1 अङ्गस्य, so they apply to morphological elements, namely to stems and affixes. Yet some of the terms that describe these elements are phonetic. The term इक् in *A*. 7.1.73 is a more specific phonetic term than ह्रस्व in *A*. 7.1.54. Conversely the morphological reference to the specific termination आम् that recurs in *A*. 7.1.54 is more specific than the reference to a nominal termination (विभक्ति) in phonetic terms as beginning with a vowel (अच्) in *A*. 7.1.73. Without consideration of the gender term नपुंसक in *A*. 7.1.73, the specification of the particular morphological termination आम् would carve out the more specific domain making *A*. 7.1.54 an exception to *A*. 7.1.73 by virtue of the specificity hierarchy. However, if gender ranks higher in the specificity hierarchy than morphological references as determined in section VII, then *A*. 7.1.73 would incorrectly take precedence. In this case one must consider that the stem is the topic. After neuter stems in इ, उ, ऋ, the specific morphological reference to the nominal termination आम् specifies a narrower domain than the phonetic term अच् that refers to any vowel-initial nominal termination. Similarly designating particular stems as the topic and allowing the specific reference to the termination to determine the more specific domain is required to obtain correct results in determining rule precedence between *A*. 7.1.54 and *A*. 7.1.97 विभाषा तृतीयादिष्वचि (तृज्वत् क्रोष्टुः 95), and between

A. 7.1.54 and *A.* 7.2.100 अचि र ऋतः (विभक्तौ 84).[4] Otherwise criteria are lacking to give preference to specificity of the termination over specificity of the stem.

The specificity hierarchy similarly does not correctly resolve rule conflict between *A.* 6.1.89 एत्येधत्यूठ्सु (आत् 87, वृद्धिः एचि 88) and *A.* 6.1.95 ओमाङोश्च (आत् 87, पररूपम् 94). *A.* 6.1.89 provides that the sequence of a preceding short or long अ and the following ए belonging to the roots इ or एध्, as well as ऊठ् (a replacement for व् provided by *A.* 6.4.19–20), is replaced by the single vr̥ddhi sound corresponding to the latter. *A.* 6.1.95 provides that the sequence of a preceding short or long अ and an ए or ओ of the following word ओम् or preverb आ (the latter combined with a vowel इ or उ to yield ए or ओ) is replaced by the latter form alone. Both rules specify short or long अ as the preceding phonetic context. The following context in the domain of the former rule is one of the roots इ or एध्, or the replacement ऊठ्. The following context in the domain of the latter rule is the word ओम् or the preverb आ. The shared domain is where a short or long अ is followed by the preverb आ combined with the initial vowel इ in a form of the root इ. Both rules specify the overlapping domain specifically by mentioning a particular morphological form. The former rule mentions the root इ; the latter rule mentions the preverb आ. The specificity hierarchy described in section VII does not provide criteria to determine rule precedence. Given प्र + एतः (< प्र + [आ + इतः]), one can equally well argue that the specific mention of आ by *A.* 6.1.95 is an exception to प्र + forms of the root इ provided by *A.* 6.1.89 as one can argue that the specific mention of the root इ by *A.* 6.1.89 is an exception to प्र + आ combined with a following इ or उ provided by *A.* 6.1.95.

It does not appear to be possible to settle the question of rule precedence considering just the two rules in question *A.* 6.1.89 and *A.* 6.1.95 ओमाङोश्च. One must consider the relationships of the rules with other rules in related contexts. Vāmana, in the *Kāśikā* under *A.* 6.1.89, states that in the context where the roots इ and एध् follow a short or long vowel अ, the rule is an exception to *A.* 6.1.94 एङि पररूपम् (एत्येधत्योः तु एङि पररूपापवादः). The latter rule provides that the sequence of a short or long अ followed by any vowel ए or ओ is replaced by the single replacement consisting of the following vowel alone. The mention of the particular roots इ and एध् in *A.* 6.1.89 clearly specifies a subset of the domain specified by the phonetic term एङ्. Now if *A.* 6.1.89 had not been stated, there would be no reason to state *A.* 6.1.95 because *A.* 6.1.94 would already achieve the desired result. It is therefore only because *A.* 6.1.89 would undesireably obtain that *A.* 6.1.95 is stated. Therefore *A.* 6.1.95 is the exception to *A.* 6.1.89 and not vice versa.

[4] not dealt with in the present paper; see MBh. 3.276.6–12.

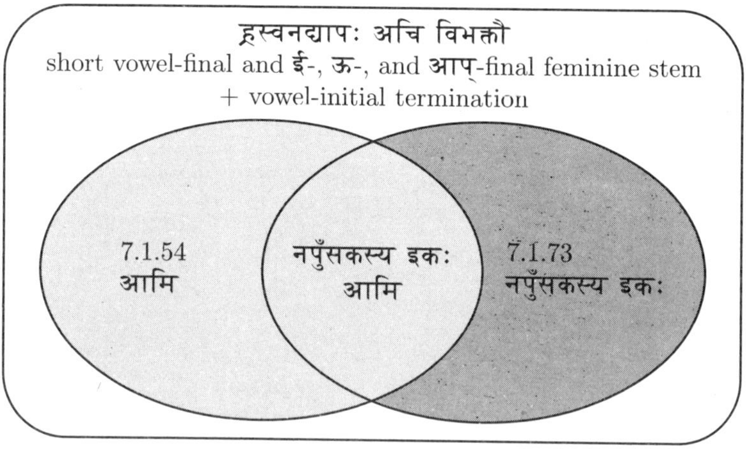

Figure 14: Example 7

(Cf. Figure 11.) The two rules 7.1.54 ह्रस्वनद्यापो नुट् (आमि 52) and 7.1.73 इको ऽचि विभक्तौ (नपुंसकस्य 72, नुम् 58) occur within the section headed by 6.4.1 अङ्गस्य; hence they refer to morphological elements, namely stems. The terms ह्रस्वनद्यापः in 7.1.54 and अचि विभक्तौ in 7.1.73 specify the universe in which the two rules apply in a mixture of phonetic and morphological terms: stems ending in a short vowel (ह्रस्व), feminine stems ending in the long vowels ई and ऊ termed नदी, and stems ending in the feminine affix आप् followed by a vowel-initial nominal termination. Neither rule applies under any other conditions. Within this universe, the phonetic term इक् in 7.1.73 limits the scope of this rule to a nominal stem ending in a vowel other than अ, and the morphological term आमि in 7.1.54 limits the scope of that rule to stems followed by the nominal termination आम्. The additional term नपुंसक, which recurs in 7.1.73 from 7.1.72, determines the scope of that rule. The shared domain of the terms besides the term नपुंसक is a nominal stem ending in a vowel other than अ followed by the nominal termination आम्. Within this shared domain, the term नपुंसक stipulates an additional limitation. If the gender term is understood to be higher on the specificity scale than a particular nominal termination, 7.1.73 would erroneously take precedence over 7.1.45. The reverse is the case: 7.1.54 takes precedence over 7.1.73.

7.1.54 domain: stems ending in a short vowel, feminine affix नदी ई/ऊ, feminine आ + आम् (ह्रस्वनद्यापः आमि). 7.1.73 domain: neuter stems ending in इ, उ, ऋ followed by a vowel-initial nominal termination (नपुंसकस्य इकः अचि विभक्तौ). 7.1.54 exclusive domain: non-neuter stems, neuter अ-final stems + आम्. 7.1.73 exclusive domain: neuter stems in इ, उ, ऋ + vowel-initial terminations other than आम्. Shared domain: neuter stems in इ, उ, ऋ + आम् (नपुंसकस्य इकः आमि).

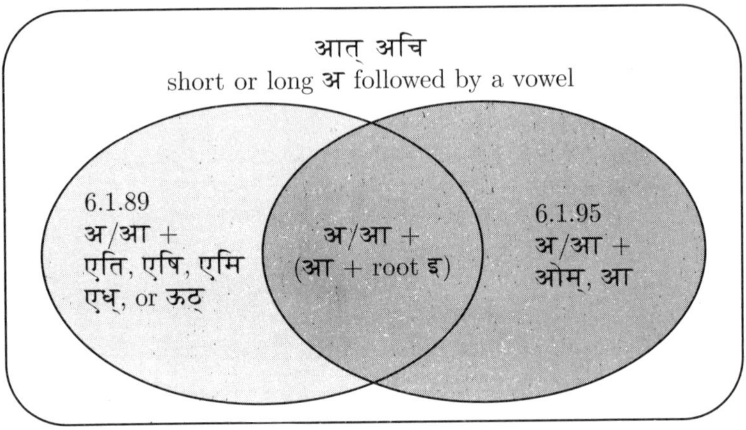

Figure 15: Example 8

(Cf. Figure 11.) The two rules 6.1.89 एत्येधत्यूठ्सु (आत् 87, वृद्धिः एचि 88) and 6.1.95 ओमाङोश्च (आत् 87, पररूपम् 94) occur within the section headed by *A.* 6.1.72 संहितायाम् and *A.* 6.1.84 एकः पूर्वपरयोः: In continuous speech, a single replacement occurs in place of the sequence of a preceding and subsequent sound. The universe in which the two rules apply is specified by the phonetic terms आत्, which recurs in both rules from 6.1.87, and अचि stated in 6.1.77, which is superseded and further specified by terms in each rule: a vowel of the class अ followed by a vowel. Within this universe, the morphological terms एति, एधति, and ऊठ् in 6.1.89 limit the scope of the rule to contexts in which the subsequent sound is the initial vowel of the root इ, the root एध्, or the replacement ऊठ्. The morphological terms ओम् and आङ् in 6.1.95 limit the scope of the rule to contexts in which the subsequent sound is the initial vowel of the word ओम्, or the word आ marked with ङ्. The shared domain of the terms is where the guṇa vowel ए resulting from the sandhi of the preverb आ with the initial इ of a form of the verbal root इ follows a vowel of the class अ. Both the root इ specified in 6.1.89 and the word आ specified in 6.1.95 are morphological terms. The specificity hierarchy does not provide grounds on which to determine rule precedence.

6.1.89 domain: अ/आ + roots इ or एध्, or replacement ऊठ्. 6.1.95 domain: अ/आ + word ओम्, or preverb आ. 6.1.89 exclusive domain: अ/आ + एति, एषि, एमि, root एध्, or replacement ऊठ्. 6.1.95 exclusive domain: अ/आ + word ओम्, or preverb आ combined with a vowel other than of the root इ. Shared domain: अ/आ + (आ + root इ).

Vāmana explains why *A.* 6.1.95 blocks *A.* 6.1.89 by citing the principle that an operation provided (by rule 1) where another would obtain (by rule 2) blocks the other operation (provided by rule 2). He states in the *Kāśikā* under *A.* 6.1.89, "But the latter form (पर-रूप) provided by *A.* 6.1.95 is not blocked because of the principle that an operation provided where another would obtain blocks the other." ('ओमाङोश्च' इत्येतत्तु पररूपं न बाध्यते, 'येन नाप्राप्ते यो विधिरारभ्यते स तस्य बाधको भवति' इति). As stated, the principle appears to take only the two rules in question into account. But considering just the two rules does not provide grounds for a determination. In their shared domain, each of the two rules is provided where the other would obtain. However, the principle includes a double negative: the term नाप्राप्ते, literally 'not un-obtained'. The principle requires not just that the blocked rule would obtain, but that if it didn't obtain the rule in question would not have to be stated. This requires considering not just rule 1 and rule 2 but also the more general rule or rules to which rule 2 is an exception. In the overlapping domain, if *A.* 6.1.95 were not stated, *A.* 6.1.89 would still have to be stated in order to block *A.* 6.1.94; the operation it provides would not obtain otherwise. But if *A.* 6.1.89 were not stated, *A.* 6.1.95 would not have to be stated, since the operation it provides would already be obtained by *A.* 6.1.94. Therefore, *A.* 6.1.95 blocks *A.* 6.1.89 and not vice versa.

Insisting on the significance of the double negative in the term नाप्राप्ते in the येन नाप्राप्ते principle solves the problem of rule precedence in the case of *A.* 6.1.89 and 95 in Example 15. However, the principle in this stronger form is inapplicable to rule precedence in cases such as *A.* 7.1.54 and *A.* 7.1.73 in Example 14. The operations provided by each of these rules would not obtain by any more general rule in the absence of the other.

IX Conclusion

Pāṇini's *Aṣṭādhyāyī* presents a complex system of interrelated rules. While it is clear that rules that apply to included domains take precedence over the rules that apply to the domain in which they are included, some of the rules have overlapping domains. Four different principles were resorted to in the present paper to attempt to determine rule precedence: the topicality principle, the principle that narrowness of the scope of terms referring to the shared domain determines rule precedence, the specificity hierarchy principle, and the strong form of the येन नाप्राप्ते principle. While these principles appear to solve all of the cases considered, none of them by itself solved all of the cases. Determining which rule has precedence in the shared domains is not reducible to a single principle. Moreover, the scopes of these four principles overlap. The criteria for deciding which principle should have priority in their overlapping domain is as much of a problem as deciding which rule should apply to the shared domain of two rules. It is not clear that these principles are implementable without detailed knowledge of the rules and their intended outcomes. Nor is it clear that there may not be additional principles required for unconsidered cases of the conflict of rules with overlapping domains. It is possible that a different principle altogether provides the correct ordering in some cases. For example, in order to solve cases of conflict such as in Example 3, there may be a principle that rules that apply to affixes take precedence over rules that add augments.

A thorough consideration of the topic of rule precedence requires examination of all cases of conflict. While all cases mentioned in commentaries may be collected and brought under consideration, commentators themselves may not have noticed all such cases. A full examination of the problem will probably require the assistance of computational modeling of Pāṇini's grammar. A broad spectrum of conflicting rules could then be discovered and various possible solutions could then be tested. The author of the present paper is working to develop such a computational model, as are other colleagues in the Sanskrit Computational Linguistics Consortium.

References and abbreviations

Cardona, George

1970 Some principles of Pāṇini's grammar. *Journal of Indian Philosophy* 1: 40–74.

1976 *Pāṇini: A Survey of Research.* The Hague; Paris: Mouton. [Indian edition, Delhi: Motilal Banarsidass, 1980.]

1997 *Pāṇini, his Work and its Traditions.* Volume I: *Background and Introduction.* 2nd ed. Delhi: Motilal Banarsidass.

Kiparsky, Paul

1991 On Pāṇinian studies: a reply to Cardona. *Journal of Indian Philosophy* 19.4: 331–367.

MBh. *Mahābhāṣya* (Edited by F. Kielhorn, 3. vols. Revised by K. V. Abhyankar, 3rd ed. 1962, 1965, 1972). (references: volume, page, line)

Scharf, Peter

2009 *Mādhavīya Dhātuvr̥tti* Canonical Index. Providence: The Sanskrit Library, 2009. http://sanskritlibrary.org/

Shastri, Dwarikadas

1983 The *Mādhavīya Dhātuvr̥tti: A Treatise on Sanskrit Roots Based on the Dhātupāṭha of Pāṇiniby Sāyaṇācārya; With a Foreword by Raghunath Sharma.* Prachya Bharati Series 1. 1st. ed. Kamachha, Varanasi: Prachya Bharati Prakashan.

Vibhakti in Pāṇini

Ram Karan Sharma

Introduction

Pāṇini inherited from predecessors like Sphoṭāyana the terms *prathamā*, *dvitīyā*, *tṛtīyā*, *caturthī*, *pañcamī*, *ṣaṣṭhī*, and *saptamī*, which refer to seven triads (*trika*) of nominal endings,[1] and uses these in rules such as 2.3.46, 2, 18, 13, 28, 50, and 36: *prātipadikārthaliṅgaparimāṇavacanamātre prathamā*, *karmaṇi dvitīyā*, *kartṛkaraṇayos tṛtīyā*, *caturthī sampradāne*, *apādāne pañcamī*, *ṣaṣṭhī śeṣe*, *saptamy adhikaraṇe ca*. The respective endings of each such group are called *ekavacana*, *dvivacana*, *bahuvacana*, as are verbal endings of sets *tip tas jhi* and so forth.[2] Both nominal and verbal endings are also called *vibhakti*.[3]

I will consider here several aspects of the use of this term.

1. *Vibhakti* as a technical term

While explaining the phrase *sapta hastāso asya* in the famous Ṛk mantra *catvāri śṛṅgā trayo asya pādā* . . . ,[4] Patañjali says that the seven hands are the seven vibhaktis.[5] Kaiyaṭa too first comments that Patañjali means the seven sets of nominal endings: *sapta vibhaktayaḥ supa ity arthaḥ* (Pradīpa I.1.31a). But he then goes on to say further: *kecit tu tiṅām aparigraha-prasaṅgāt saha śeṣeṇa sapta kārakāṇi vibhaktiśabdābhidheyānīti vyācakṣate*

[1]See, for example, Kāśikā 2.3.2: *dvitīyādayaḥ śabdāḥ pūrvācāryaiḥ supāṃ trikeṣu smaryante | tair evātra vyavahāraḥ*, Siddhāntakaumudī on 1.4.104 (I.93): *tatra su au jas ityādīnāṃ saptānāṃ trikāṇāṃ prathamādayaḥ saptamyantāḥ prācāṃ saṃjñās tābhir ihāpi vyavahāraḥ*. Cf. Bālamanoramā thereon.

[2]1.4.102–103: *tāny ekavacanadvivacanabahuvacanāny ekaśaḥ, supaḥ*. *tāni* here refers to verb endings; by 1.4.101 (*tiṅas trīṇi trīṇi prathamamadhyamottamāḥ*), the triads in the two groups *tip tas jhi*, *sip thas tha*, *mip vas mas* and *ta ātām jha*, *thās āthām dhvam*, *iṭ vahi mahiṅ* are respectively called *prathama*, *madhyama* and *uttama*.

[3]1.4.104: *vibhaktiś ca* |

[4]Ṛgveda 4.58.3: *c̱atvāri̱ śṛṅgā̱ trayò asya̱ pādā̱ dve śī̱rṣe sa̱pta hasà̄so asya* | *tridhà̄ ba̱ddho vṛ̀ṣa̱bho ròravīti ma̱ho de̱vo martyā̐m ā vìveśa* ||

[5]Mahābhāṣya I.1.30b: *sapta hastāso asyeti sapta vibhaktayaḥ* |

('However, since otherwise verbal endings would not be included, some explain that what is denoted by the term *vibhakti* is seven kārakas along with the residual relation'). Nāgeśa (Uddyota I.1.31b) clarifies the position further: *śeṣaḥ ṣaṣṭhyarthaḥ tatsahitakārakābhidhāyakatvena suptiṅor ubhayor api saṅgraha iti bhāvaḥ* ('This is what [Kaiyaṭa] intends: the meaning of the sixth triplet of nominal endings is a residual relation; since [*vibhakti*] denotes kārakas along with this, there is thus an inclusion of both nominal and verbal endings'). Thus, some schools interpreted Patañjali's *sapta vibhaktayaḥ* as six kārakas—viz. apādāna, sampradāna, karaṇa, adhikaraṇa, karman, kartṛ[6]—together with the meaning of the sixth vibhakti, as accounted for in 2.3.50: *ṣaṣṭhī śeṣe*, in order to allow the coverage of both *sup* and *tiṅ* under the term *vibhakti*. So 1.4.104 read with 101 and 103[7] widens the scope of the inherited term *vibhakti* so as to include both conjugational (tiṅ) and declensional (sup) affixes. Moreover, by using *ca* in the definitional sūtra 1.4.104, Pāṇini blocks the jurisdictional limitation of 1.4.1: *ā kaḍārād ekā saṃjñā* and so paves the way for multiple saṃjñās concerned—viz. *vibhakti*; *ekavacana, dvivacana, bahuvacana*; and *prathama, madhyama, uttama*—simultaneously.

2. *Vibhakti* as a jurisdictional term

Thus as a technical term *vibhakti* covers both tiṅ and sup affixes. Besides, as a jurisdictional term,[8] it includes all secondary derivative affixes beginning with 5.3.2 and ending with 5.3.26. The Nyāsa and Padamañjarī question the very rationale behind adopting the same saṃjñā applicable to sup and tiṅ for specified secondary derivative affixes as well.[9] But they conclude with a

[6]See, for example, 1.4.14: *dhruvam apāye 'padānam*, 32: *karmaṇā yam abhipraiti sa sampradānam*, 42: *sādhakatamaṃ karaṇam*, 45: *ādhāro 'dhikaraṇam*, 49: *kartur īpsitatamaṃ karma*, 54: *svatantraḥ kartā* |

[7]See notes 2–3. Why ignore the intermediary 1.4.102?

[8]According to 5.3.1: *prāg diśo vibhaktiḥ*, the saṃjñā *vibhakti* applies up to 5.3.26.

[9]The preliminary argument presented in both commentaries concerns the status of the term *vibhakti*. This is made a saṃjñā for both sup and tiṅ by 1.4.104 (see **Introduction** and note 3) and saṃjñās serve to signify their saṃjñins. Therefore, in 5.3.2 *vibhakti* should refer to sup and tiṅ endings. 5.3.2 would then let secondary derivative affixes be called *sup* and so forth. Nyāsa on 5.3.1: *nanu ca vibhaktiśabdaḥ suptiṅāṃ saṃjñā* | *saṃjñā ca pradeśavākyeṣūccāritā saṃjñinaṃ pratyāyayatīti suptiṅām eva saṃjñātvaṃ prāpnoti na vibhaktiśabdasya svābhidheye guṇībhūtasya* | ('Now, the word *vibhakti* is a saṃjñā for sup and tiṅ, and a saṃjñā in rules denotes its saṃjñin. Therefore, the result is that sup and tiṅ only are saṃjñā, not the word *vibhakti*, which is subordinate to what it denotes'). Padamañjarī on 5.3.1: *nanu vibhaktiśabdaḥ pūrvam eva suptiṅāṃ saṃjñātvena*

reconciliatory tone,[10] and Haradatta mentions the interpretation according to which the sūtra 5.3.1 is treated just like *ādṛgamahanajanaḥ kikinau liṭ ca* (3.2.171), that treats the relevant kṛt affixes as "liṭ-like" (*liḍvat*) in forms like *papiḥ, dadiḥ* in order to allow reduplication of verbs concerned. According to this view, the rule 5.3.1 is to be interpreted as under: 'all secondary derivative affixes beginning with 5.3.2 and ending with 26 are to be treated vibhakti-like (*vibhaktivat*).'[11] The more generally accepted interpretation, however, is that 5.3.1 introduces the saṃjñā *vibhakti*, which will apply to affixes introduced in rules up to 5.3.26.[12]

3. *Vibhakti* represented in the sūtras

The term *vibhakti* occurs at least ten times in the sūtras.[13] For example: *taddhitaś cāsarvavibhaktiḥ* (1.1.38) determines the indeclinability of such secondary derivative forms as *nagarataḥ* 'from the city'; *ekavibhakti cāpūrvanipāte* (1.2.44) facilitates the operation of *gostriyor upasarjanasya* (1.2.48) by designating *kauśāmbī* (a place name), for example, as upasarjana —but not preposed in a compound—in forms like *niṣkauśāmbiḥ* 'someone who came out of Kauśāmbī'; *sarūpāṇām ekaśeṣa ekavibhaktau* (1.2.64) paves the way for the expression of multiple meanings by a single word;[14] *avyayaṃ vibhakti . . . vacaneṣu* (2.1.6) provides the formation of an avyayībhāva compound like *adhihari* (= *harau*) 'in Hari'.

The sūtra *na vibhaktau tusmāḥ* (1.3.4) represents the most significant objective of this designatory rule. To quote Katre: '(the t.t. [= technical term] IT 2) does not (ná) denote (final 3) dental stops (tU 1.1.69) and the phonemes [s] and [m] in vibhákti (1.4.104) endings.' Katre continues, 'While 3 is specifically a general rule, the exception given here restricts the scope of that general rule: thus in [°-āt replacement of ṄasI 7.1.12] after

---

viniyuktaḥ saṃjñā ca pradeśeṣu saṃjñinaṃ pratyāyayati na svarūpam | ataḥ suptiṅām eva saṃjñātvaṃ yuktaṃ na vibhaktiśabdasya |

[10]For example, the Nyāsa notes that if sup and tiṅ endings were made saṃjñās by 5.3.1, then giving the saṃjñā *vibhakti* to sup and tiṅ would have no purpose: *naiṣa doṣaḥ | evaṃ sati suptiṅāṃ saṃjñāvidhānam anarthakaṃ syāt |*

[11]Padamañjarī 5.3.1: *apara āha yathā kikinau liṭ ceti liḍvadbhāvo vidhīyate tathātrāpi vibhaktivadbhāvo vidhīyate iti |*

[12]For example, Kāśikā 5.3.1: *dikśabdebhyaḥ saptamīpañcamīprathamābhya iti vakṣyati | prāg etasmād diksaṃśabdanād yān ita ūrdvham anukramiṣyāmo vibhaktisaṃjñās te veditavyāḥ* ('(Pāṇini) will state *dikśabdebhyaḥ saptamīpañcamīprathamābhyaḥ . . . .* The (affixes) which we will cover from here on up to the stating of the word *dik* are to be recognized as having the saṃjñā *vibhakti*').

[13]Vide 1.1.38; 2.44, 64; 3.4; 2.1.6; 5.3.1; 6.1.168; 3.132; 7.1.73; 8.4.11.

[14]Mahābhāṣya 1.2.64 (I.2.99–100): *iṣyate caikenāpy anekasyābhidhānaṃ syād iti |*

stems ending in short [°-a-] [t] is not an IT marker; similarly in the case of Jas, Ṅas, am, ām, [s, m] are not IT-s, as in the case of verbal endings °tas, °-thas, °ātām, °āthām, dhvam (3.4.78). Since [tU, s, m] are not markers when occurring at the end of a vibhákti affix by this rule, they are not subject to the operation of 9 below [replacement by ϕ].'

The sūtra *tyadādīnām aḥ* (7.2.102), in which *vibhaktau* is read from *aṣṭana ā vibhaktau* (84), represents another significant objective of *vibhakti* designations; e.g. *tyau*, *tau*, *dvau*, etc. In deriving these, the final *d* of *tyad*, *tad* 'that' is replaced by *a* before the vibhakti *au*, as is the *i* of *dvi*.[15] Similarly *ūḍidampadādyappumraidyubhyaḥ* (6.1.171), with *vibhaktiḥ* read from *sāv ekācas tṛtīyādir vibhaktiḥ* (168) and *asarvanāmasthānam* from *añceś chandasy asarvanāmasthānam*, provides udātta accent of vibhakti in forms like *praṣṭhauháḥ* (acc. pl.) 'young bulls being trained to the yoke', *ābhyā́m* (instr.-dat.-abl. dual) 'these two', *padbhyā́m* 'feet', *apsú* (loc. pl.) 'water', *puṃsā́* (instr. sg.) 'man', *rāyé* (dat. sg.) 'wealth', *divé* (dat. sg.) 'day'.

4. Questions about jurisdiction

4.1. First question

A question is raised about whether or not the clause *trīṇi trīṇi* from 1.4.101 (see note 2) is to be brought in the definitional sūtra 104 (see note 3).[16] It is pointed out that there are problems both ways. If that clause is brought in, then *aṣṭana ā vibhaktau* (7.2.84) would cease to operate in formations like *aṣṭābhiḥ* because it would be impossible to find all the three members of the vibhakti concerned following *aṣṭan* simultaneously.[17] On the other hand if the clause is not brought in then the word *prathamayoḥ* in *prathamayoḥ pūrvasavarṇaḥ* (6.1.102) would just stand to mean the first two affixes (*su* and *au*) of vibhakti and not the first two triads of vibhaktis, leading to its applicability to nominal singular affix *su* as well.[18] But as usual, Patañjali reconciles the problem by his emphatic assertion that either way there is no problem. Even if the clause *trīṇi trīṇi* is brought in (as part of adhikāra) there should be no problem about the applicability of *aṣṭana ā vibhaktau* in formations like *aṣṭābhiḥ* in as much as it is impossible to get all members of a triad at one point of operation simultaneously. So the fact that the rule *aṣṭana ā vibhaktau* is stated (*vacanāt*) has the capacity to imply that,

---

[15] *tyad-au* → *tya-au* → *tyau* (*vṛddhir eci* [6.1.88]), *tad-au* → *ta-au* → *tau*, *dvi-au* → *dva-au* → *dvau*. The vibhakti in each form (nom.-acc. du.) is either *au* or *auṭ*.

[16] Mahābhāṣya 1.4.104 (I.2.437): *trīṇi trīṇīty anuvartate utāho na* |

[17] Mahābhāṣya I.2.437: *yady anuvartate aṣṭana ā vibhaktāv iti na prāpnoti* | Pradīpa I.2.437: *na prāpnotīti : na hy aṣṭanśabdāt paraṃ yugapat trikam asti* |

[18] Mahābhāṣya I.2.437: *atha nivṛttaṃ prathamayoḥ pūrvasavarṇa ity atra pratyayor eva grahaṇaṃ prāpnoti* |

although *vibhakti* signifies a triad of endings, here it refers to a single ending that follows *aṣṭan*.[19] If, on the other hand, one is satisfied just with *tiṅaḥ* being brought in the definitional sūtra in order to cover supaḥ and tiṅaḥ both under the purview of the term, even then there is no problem. The word *prathamayoḥ* in 6.1.102 has to be read with *aci* understood from *iko yaṇ aci* (6.1.77) and so it will stand to mean affixes beginning with a vowel of the first two vibhaktis.[20]

4.2. Second question

Why designate secondary derivative affixes of 5.3.2–26 as vibhakti or vibhaktivat? Kātyāyana first proposes[21] that the purpose for these affixes being vibhaktis is to prevent their final consonants from being classed as anubandhas, 1.3.4 (*na vibhaktau tusmāḥ*) denying this classification for final dental stops, *s* and *m* in a vibhakti. Patañjali illustrates with *idānīm* 'now', where affixal final *m* of *dānīm* (5.3.18: *dānīṃ ca*) will not be elided.[22] Kātyāyana goes on[23] to recall what was said earlier, in the first vārttika to 1.3.4,[24] namely that IT designation of dental stop class of vibhakti endings should not operate in a taddhita. This avoids any problem with, for example, the operation of *kimo 't* (5.3.12), together with *kvāti* (7.2.105), leading to the formation of *kva* 'where?'. But Patañjali disagrees with Kātyāyana and states[25] that the rule *idamas thamuḥ* (5.3.24) makes it clear that 1.3.4 does not (fully) operate in taddhita and so there is no problem with the operation of 5.3.12 and 7.2.105 leading to the formation of *kva*, etc. So

[19]Mahābhāṣya I.2.437: *astu tāvad anuvṛttam* | *nanu coktam aṣṭana ā vibhaktāv iti na prāpnotīti* | *vacanād bhaviṣyati* | Pradīpa I.2.347: *trikasya yugapatprayogābhāvāt sāmarthyāt samudāyavṛttir vibhaktiśabdo 'vayave vartiṣyata iti bhāvaḥ* |

[20]Mahābhāṣya I.2.437: *athavā punar astu nivṛttam* | *nanu coktaṃ prathamayoḥ pūrvasavarṇa ity atra pratyayayor eva grahaṇaṃ prāpnotīti* | *naiṣa doṣaḥ* | *acīty anuvartate* | *na cājādī prathamau pratyayau staḥ* | I omit arguments that follow.

[21]5.3.1 vārttika 1: *vibhaktitve proyojanam itpratiṣedhaḥ* |

[22]Mahābhāṣya 5.3.1 (IV–V.425): *vibhaktitva itpratiṣedhaḥ prayojanam idānīm* | *na vibhaktau tusmā itītpratiṣedhaḥ siddho bhavati* |

[23]5.3.1 vārttika 2: *tau coktam* |

[24]1.3.4 vārttika 1: *vibhaktau tavargapratiṣedho 'taddhite* 'The negation (of the designation *it*) for a dental stop in a vibhakti (should be stated as applying to a vibhakti) other than a taddhita.'

[25]Mahābhāṣya 1.3.4 (I.2.186): *sa tarhi pratiṣedho vaktavyaḥ* | *na vaktavyaḥ* | *ācāryapravṛttir jñāpayati na vibhaktau taddhite pratiṣedho bhavatīti yad ayam idamas thamur iti makārasyetsaṃjñāparitrāṇārtham ukāram anubandhaṃ karoti* 'Must this negation, then, be stated (thus). It need not be stated. By putting the anubandha *u* in *thamu* (of the rule) *idamas thamuḥ* in order to keep *m* from having the saṃjñā *it*, the teacher (Pāṇini) makes known that the negation (of this designation) does not apply in a vibhakti that is a taddhita.'

the limited application of 1.3.4 (e.g. *idānīm*, *kva*, etc.), *tyadādīnām aḥ* (7.1.102) (e.g. *yadā* 'when', *tadā* 'then'), and *ūḍidampadādyappumraidyubhyaḥ* (6.1.171) (e.g. *itáḥ* 'from here, hence' , *ihá* 'here') leading to the given surface forms in usage seems to be the objective of treating the term *vibhakti* as a jurisdictional saṃjñā.

5. Nature of the taddhita vibhakti

Generally speaking, the vibhakti affixes of taddhita deal with time and place. For example, *idānīm* 'now', *kadā* 'when?', *yatra* 'where', *kutra* 'where?', *abhitaḥ* 'on both sides', *paritaḥ* 'on all sides', *parut* 'last year', *aiṣamaḥ* 'this year', *paredyavi* 'the other day', *adya* 'today', *pūrvedyuḥ* 'yesterday', etc. But there is one sūtra, *itarābhyo 'pi dṛśyante* (5.3.14), read with 5.3.7–13, that, as explained by Patañjali, stands for honorific formations like *tatrabhavān* and *atrabhavān*.[26]

There is one formation dealing with time where only a vibhakti affix remains and the base becomes invisible altogether. The Mahābhāṣya on the sūtra *adhunā* (5.3.17) states as follows: *adhuneti kiṃ nipātyate | idamo 'śbhāvo dhunā ca pratyayaḥ | idamo vā lopo 'dhunā ca pratyayaḥ | asmin kāle adhunā* |[27]

Commenting on this unique formation, where only pratyaya is visible with the entire prakṛti attaining invisibility, Bālamanoramā (I.715) cites the following verse that brings Pāṇini and Advaita Vedānta together:

uditavati parasmin pratyaye śāstrayonau
gatavati vilayaṃ ca prākṛte 'pi prapañce |
sapadi padam udītaṃ kevalaḥ pratyayo yat
tad iyad iti mimīte ko 'dhunā paṇḍito 'pi ||

---

[26]5.3.14 vārttika 1: *bhavadādibhir yoge*, Mahābhāṣya IV–V.430: *bhavadādibhir yoga iti vaktavyam | ke punar bhavadādayaḥ | bhavān dīrghāyur devānāṃpriya āyuṣmān iti | sa bhavān tatra bhavān* ... |

[27]'What is allowed to occur in *adhunā* without being formally stated? The substitution of *aś* [that is, *a*] for *idam* and the affix *dhunā*; or the elision of *idam* and the suffix *dhunā*. *adhunā* = *asmin kāle* ("at this time").' In Guru Prasad Shastri's edition (IV–V.430), *idamo 'śbhāvo dhunā ca pratyayaḥ | idamo vā lopo 'dhunā ca pratyayaḥ* is considered two vārttikas of Kātyāyana, but a note (IV–V.430 n. 1) points out that some consider this to be said by Patañjali; in Kielhorn's edition, the text appears simply as part of the Bhāṣya, not vārttikas.

Bibliography

Aṣṭādhyāyī: See Katre.

Bal Shastri

1987–88 *Mahabhashya of Patanjali, with the commentaries Mahabhashya Pradipodyota of Shree Nagoji Bhatta & Mahabhashya-Pradip by Kaiyat.* Edited by Acharya Shree Guru Prasad Shastri (second edition) revised by Dr. Bal Shastri. Nine volumes in seven parts. Varanasi: Vani Vilas Prakashan. [Title given as on title page of vol. I.2]

Bālamanoramā: See Siddhāntakaumudī.

Kāśikā: See Tripathi and Malaviya.

Katre, Sumitra Mangesh

1987 *Aṣṭādhyāyī of Pāṇini.* Austin: University of Texas Press. Reprinted with corrections, 1989, Delhi: Motilal Banarsidass.

Mahābhāṣya: See Bal Shastri.

Nyāsa: See Tripathi, Jaya Shankar Lal.

Padamañjarī: See Tripathi, Jaya Shankar Lal.

Pradīpa: See Bal Shastri.

Siddhāntakaumudī: *Mahāmahopādhyāya Śrī Bhaṭṭojidīkṣitaviracitā Vaiyākaraṇa-siddhānta-kaumudī Śrīmajjñānendrabhikṣuviracitayā Tattva-bodhinīṭīkayā, Śrīvāsudeva Bhaṭṭa Dīkṣitaviracitayā Bālopa-kāriṇyā Bālamanoramākhyayā vyākhyayā, (Tatpuruṣād ārabhya) Mahāmahopādhyāyaśrīnāgeśabhaṭṭaviracitayā Laghuśabdendu-śekharaṭīkayā ca samanvitā.* Two volumes. Delhi: Bharatiya Book Corporation, 1997.

Tripathi, Jaya Shankar Lal and Sudhakar Malaviya

1984-89 *Kāśikā (A commentary on Pāṇini's Grammar), Vāmana and Jayāditya, with Nyāsa or Kāśikāvivaraṇapañjikā of Jinendra-buddhi, Padmamañjarīī of Haradatta Mishra with Bhāvabodhinī Hindi exposition by and edited by Dr. Jaya Shankar Lal Tripathi and Dr. Sudhakar Malaviya.* Foreword by Professor Bishwanath Bhattacharya, Varanasi. Nine volumes. Varanasi: Tara Printing Works.

Uddyota: See Bal Shastri.

Śabdajyotsnā: A less-known Sanskrit Grammar by Pt. Bhiksharama of Kurukshetra*

Shri Krishan Sharma

Introduction

The learning and teaching of Sanskrit grammar has been a continuous practice flowing down since very early times. Patañjali, in his *Mahābhāṣya*, interprets at least five *ṛcs* as having philosophical and phonetical thoughts inherent in them.[1] So, it is very much clear that grammatical studies had been founded before the period of Saṁhitās. Analysis of *prakṛti* (radical form of a word), *pratyaya* (affix), *dhātu* (root), *upasarga* (preverb) and various components of compound words in the padapāṭha of Vedic *mantras* shows a refined stage of grammatical practice. The term *vyākaraṇa* for science of words (*śabdānuśāsana)* is found used in Brāhmaṇas,[2] Upaniṣads,[3] the *Rāmāyaṇa*,[4] the *Mahābhārata*,[5] etc.

According to Sanskrit works of Pāṇinian school, Brahmā, Bṛhaspati and other sages like Bharadvāja composed their grammars in their peculiar styles.[6] Śākaṭāyana and other scholars like Gārgya presented an interesting

*I express my deep gratitude to Prof. George Cardona for his useful comments and valuable suggestions.

[1]In the Paspaśā (I.3.24–4.27) Patañjali quotes five mantras: *catvāri vāk* (ṚV I.164.45), *catvāri śṛṅgā* (ṚV IV.58.3), *sudevo asi* (ṚV VIII.69.12), *saktum iva* (ṚV X.71.2), and *uta tvaḥ* (ṚV X.71.4). See also *Nirukta* 13.7 (178).

[2]*Gopathabrāhmaṇa* 1.24 (I.12): *oṅkāraṁ pṛcchāmaḥ ko dhātuḥ, kiṁ prātipadikam, kiṁ nāmākhyātam, kiṁ liṅgam, kiṁ vacanam, kā vibhaktiḥ, kaḥ pratyayaḥ, kaḥ svara upasargo nipātaḥ, kiṁ vai vyākaraṇam ...* |

[3]*Muṇḍakopaniṣad* 1.1.5 (16): *tatrāparā ṛgvedo yajurvedaḥ sāmavedo 'tharvavedaḥ śikṣā kalpo vyākaraṇaṁ chando jyotiṣam iti* |

[4]*Rāmāyaṇa*: Kiṣkindhākāṇḍa [Chapter 3, Appendix 1, no. 3] (416): *nūnaṁ vyākaraṇaṁ kṛtsnam anena bahudhā śrutam* |

[5]*Mahābhārata*: Udyogaparvan 43.36: *sarvārthānāṁ vyākaraṇād vaiyākaraṇa ucyate* |

[6]In the Paspaśā (I.5.25–26) Patañjali states: *bṛhaspatir indrāya divyaṁ varṣasahasraṁ pratipadoktānāṁ śabdānāṁ śabdapārāyaṇam provāca nāntaṁ*

ı on the relation of word and root.[7] Pāṇini quotes ten grammari- ne *Aṣṭādhyāyī* as a token of regard. Pt. Yudhishthira Mimansaka (19o. I.68) has claimed that 85 scholars practiced the formulation of Sanskrit grammar before Pāṇini. Max Müller (1968: 126–127) also has presented a list of 64 scholars quoted in pre-Pāṇini ancient literature, which is sufficient to show the active interest taken by ancient scholars in grammatical subjects. After a deep study of previous works, Pāṇini composed his Sanskrit grammar, which stands like a beacon. In the light of this work, all other works were obscure and faintly visible. But the practice of Sanskrit grammar remained in continuous process or tradition and after Pāṇini about 20 works on Sanskrit grammar came to light.[8] In the same way, Pt. Bhiksharama, a prolific and erudite scholar of Sanskrit grammar, composed his Sanskrit grammar named *Śabdajyotsnā* (ŚJ), which can be taken as a new step in the same tradition.

1. Author of *Śabdajyotsnā*

The author of the *Śabdajyotsnā* was born on 25 June 1887 in the family of Pt. Jagannatha Parashara at the village of Bāraṇā near Kurukshetra, the holy land of the *Śrīmadbhagavadgītā*. He was the disciple of Pt. Ramachandra of the village of Hathīrā (Kurukshetra). He had a son and four grandsons. He passed away on 8 August 1975 and on this very day he was to be honored by Department of Languages, Govt. of Haryana for his profound scholarship and noteworthy contribution to Sanskrit literature. Besides the *Śabdajyotsnā*, Pt. Bhiksharama composed numerous Sanskrit kāvyas and stotras: *Neharucarita*, *Gāndhicarita*, *Paṭelacarita*, *Mālavīyacarita*, *Paraśurāmacarita*, *Vyāsapūjopahāra*, *Jātisamālocanā*, *Śuddhisamālocanā*, etc., which are preserved in the form of manuscripts. He was known as a tremendous scholar of astronomy and astrology also. Thus, H. H. Jagadguru Shankaracharya of Kanchikamakotipeetham honored his profound wisdom conferring on him the title *Vedavedāṅgācārya*. He was also designated as *Śikhariṇīsamrāṭ* in an academic meeting at Shimla.

---

jagāma | In his *Laghuśabdenduśekhara* (22) Nāgeśa also says: *yathācāryā ūcuḥ—brahmā bṛhaspataye provāca, bṛhaspatir indrāyendro bharadvājāya bharadvāja ṛṣibhyaḥ* . . . | See also ṚT I.4 (3).

[7] *Nirukta* 1.12 (24): *tatra nāmāny ākhyātajānīti śākaṭāyano nairuktasamayaś ca* | *na sarvāṇīti gārgyo vaiyākaraṇānāṁ caike* |

[8] See Mimansaka 1984: I.77–78.

2. Date of *Śabdajyotsnā*

The colophon of the *Śabdajyotsnā* presents a description regarding the date of completion of this work. The text runs as follows:

> सिते माघे मासे शरमिततिथौ श्रीगुरुदिने
> द्विसाहस्रे चाब्दे नरपतिवरे(सुधी) विक्रमकृते ।
> स्वशिष्याणां बोधो भवतु सपदीत्थं स्मृतियुतो
> बुधो भिक्षारामः कुरुसदनवासी व्यरचयत् ॥

According to this statement, the *Śabdajyotsnā* was completed on Thursday and fifth day of white-half (*śuklapakṣa*) of Māgha (*vasantapañcamī*) in 2000 + 1 = 2001 vikramasaṁvat, which is equivalent to 18 January 1945 A.D. Thus, the *Śabdajyotsnā* can be safely dated to 1942–1945 on the basis of the internal evidence cited above.

3. Purpose of *Śabdajyotsnā*

The *Śabdajyotsnā* was composed for the purpose of teaching Sanskrit grammar to ordinary students in a simple style. In the introductory verses of this work, the author mentions the aim in composing the work. He describes:

> इदानीं ये छात्राः पठननिरता नो श्रमकरा
> न तेषां सा बुद्धिः कठिनविषये या झटिति हि ।
> प्रबोधे साफल्यम् भजति विदुषाम् मानविषयम्
> इयं ज्योत्स्ना तेभ्यो भवतु विमलादर्शसदृशी ॥[9]
>
> "At present, the students of this generation do not want to put effort in studies. They do not succeed in having a quick understanding of a hard subject (like grammar), which is worthy of adoration by scholars. So, I have written this book, *Śabdajyotsnā*, in a simple style especially for such students. May this *Śabdajyotsnā* be to them like a spotless mirror."

Our author expresses his deep gratitude to Lord Śiva and grammarians like Pāṇini, Kātyāyana, Patañjali, the authors of the *Kāśikā* and Kaumudīs and the commentators of these works. He makes obeisance to them in the following way:

> महेशं पाणिनिं चैव कात्यायनपतञ्जली ।
> काशिकाकौमुदीकर्तॄन् व्याख्यातॄंश्च नतोऽस्म्यहम् ॥[10]

[9]Introduction 5.
[10]Introduction 2.

4. Structure of *Śabdajyotsnā*

The sūtras of the *Śabdajyotsnā* are composed in a subject-wise style (according to prakaraṇa) on the pattern of prakriyā works. We have no complete edition of this grammar. Only sañjñā- and sandhi-prakaraṇas of this work were published on 24 May 1958. The rest of the text is still in the form of manuscripts as written by the author himself on paper in the Devanāgarī script. The samāsaprakaraṇa and some portion of taddhitaprakaraṇa have been lost. The mss. of the *Śabdajyotsnā* have been procured from the house of the author.

The work has 39 sūtras in sañjñāprakaraṇa, 81 sūtras in sandhiprakaraṇa, 140 sūtras in ṣaḍliṅgas, 2 sūtras in avyayaprakaraṇa, 63 sūtras in strīpratyayaprakaraṇa, 33 sūtras in kārakas, 638 sūtras in samāsa- and taddhitaprakaraṇas, 266 sūtras in 10 gaṇas and 170 sūtras in prakriyās and 144 sūtras in kṛdantaprakaraṇa. Discussions on accentual system and other Vedic rules are not available. However, the author's treatment of *leṭ*-lakāra (subjunctive mood) in the tiṅantaprakaraṇa suggests that the author must have dealt with the Vedic language or Vedic Sanskrit. In the Hindi translation of the introductory verses of this work (ms. B., one of available four manuscripts) the author himself says that he has written a separate chapter for the rules pertaining to Vedic language. Unfortunately, this chapter is missing from the available manuscripts of this grammar.

5. Peculiarities of *Śabdajyotsnā*

The *Śabdajyotsnā*, as said above, was composed with a view to teaching Sanskrit grammar to an ordinary student in a simple style. The author adopts pratyāhāra, anuvṛtti, anubandha, etc. in his work to impart the abridgment on the pattern of *Aṣṭādhyāyī* and other works like Prātiśākhyas. For this purpose, the author tries his best to simplify the tough process of Sanskrit grammar. Some peculiarities of the work are presented in the following sections.

5.1. Brevity in sūtras

The sūtras of the *Śabdajyotsnā* are quite briefer than those of Pāṇini. For example, *iko yaṇ aci* (A 6.1.77) and *eco 'yavāyāvaḥ* (A 6.1.78) are formulated in a single sūtra: *icām yaṇayavāyāvo 'ci* (ŚJ 42).[11] Similarly, the sūtra of the *Śabdajyotsnā*: *jhalāṁ jaś jhaśyante ca* (ŚJ 44) performs the operations of two sūtras of Pāṇini: *jhalāṁ jaś jhaśi* (A 8.4.53) and *jhalāṁ*

[11]In this connection it is interesting to note that Nāgeśa makes the following statement in his *Laghuśabdenduśekhara* on A 6.1.78 (260): *ico 'ci yaṇayavāyāvaḥ, avāvau yi pratyaye iti sūtrayitum ucitam ity āhuḥ* |

jaśo 'nte (A 8.2.39); and ŚJ sūtra *sargād ṛti vri subdhau vā* (ŚJ 56) carries out the purpose of *upasargād ṛti dhātau* (A 6.1.91) and *vā supy āpiśalcḥ* (A 6.1.92). ŚJ sūtra *stoḥ ścuṣṭubhyāṁ ścuṣṭū* (ŚJ 74) works for *stoḥ ścunā ścuḥ* (A 8.4.40) and *ṣṭunā ṣṭuḥ* (A 8.4.41). Some more examples are listed below:

Aṣṭādhyāyī	*ŚJ*
akaḥ savarṇe dīrghaḥ (A 6.1.101)	*ako 'ki dī* (41)
ṅamo hrasvād aci ṅamuṇ nityam (A 8.3.32)	*hrād ṅamo 'ci* (93)
etattadoḥ sulopo 'kor anañsamāse hali (A 6.1.132)	*saiṣād hali* (119)
tasmāc chaso naḥ puṁsi (A 6.1.103)	*so naḥ puṁsi* (126)

5.2. Conciseness of sañjñās

To make his work concise, the author uses rather short sañjñās in an abbreviated style. For example:

Aṣṭādhyāyī	*ŚJ*	*Aṣṭādhyāyī*	*ŚJ*
dhātu	*dhu*	*samāsa*	*sa*
pratyaya	*tya*	*taddhita*	*ta*
vibhakti	*kti*	*kāraka*	*ka*
guṇa	*gu*	*visarga*	*vi*
vṛddhi	*vri*	*padānta*	*da*
hrasva	*hra*	*sambuddhi*	*dhi*
dīrgha	*dī*	*upasarga*	*sarga*
pluta	*plu*	*upadhā*	*dhā*

This style of technical terms seems to have been adopted from Prātiśākhyas and other works like the *Jainendravyākaraṇa*.[12]

[12]Some monosyllabic technical terms found in various works are given below:

A. *Ṛktantra* and *Sāmatantra*:

bha = *stobha*	ṚT 150	ST 235. 377, 393, 398
da = *pada*	ṚT 69, 272	ST 415
gha = *dīrgha*	ṚT 50, 93, 103, 112, 113, 148	ST 63, 171, 368, 412
ghu = *laghu*	ṚT 236, 237	ST 640, 665
sya = *rahasya*	ṚT 277 (*vṛtti*)	ST 369, 403, 417, 639, 757

5.3. New sañjñās

Besides the popular sañjñās found in the Pāṇinian grammar, the author employs some new sañjñās in the *Śabdajyotsnā*. The terms *lopa* and *lopaś* are two different sañjñās in the *Śabdajyotsnā* which are defined as *adarśanaṁ lopaḥ* (ŚJ 2) and *varṇavirodho lopaś* (ŚJ 3), respectively. Most probably *lopaś* was borrowed from the Sārasvata grammar.[13] Here *lopaś* is used to block the application of *guṇa, vṛddhi*, etc. which is governed by *purvatrāsiddham* (A 8.2.1) in the Pāṇinian system. In another case, the *Śabdajyotsnā* has the sañjñā *ḍhi* (ŚJ 162: *yū strīliṅge ḍhiḥ*) instead of *nadī* of the Pāṇinian grammar (A 1.4.3: *yū stryākhyau nadī*).

The *Śabdajyotsnā* ignores the sañjñās *sārvadhātuka* and *ārdhadhātuka* employed by ancient grammarians like Āpiśali and Pāṇini in their works. The *Śabdajyotsnā* uses the sigla (*pratyāhāras*) *lac* and *lik* for this purpose, In fact, the *Śabdajyotsnā* presents the list of lakāras (L-suffixes) in the following manner: *laṭ laṅ loṭ liṅc liṭ liṅ luṭ lṛṭ lṛṅ luṅk leṭ*. The *Śabdajyotsnā* provides the two pratyāhāras by taking the first letters of *laṭ* and *liṭ* with the last consonants *c* and *k* attached with *liṅc* and *luṅk* respectively. In this way, *lac* covers *laṭ, laṅ, loṭ* and *liṅ* (*vidhi*) (sārvadhātukalakāras) and *lik* indicates *liṭ, liṅ* (*āśis*), *luṭ, lṛṭ, lṛṅ* and *luṅ* (ārdhadhātukalakāras). So there is no need of terms like *sārvadhātuka* and *ārdhadhātuka*.

5.4. Word formation (*śabdasādhutva*)

Word formation (*rūpasiddhi*), according to the *Śabdajyotsnā*, is very simple and concise.

To take, as an example, *san* + *śambhuḥ*. Pāṇini provides in *śi tuk* (A 8.3.31) that a pada ending with *n* optionally takes the final augment *tuk* (= *t*) before *ś*. After *t* and *n* are respectively replaced by *c* and *ñ* by *stoḥ ścunā ścuḥ* (A 8.4.40), *ś* is optionally replaced by *ch* by *śaś cho 'ṭi* (A 8.4.63).

ṭhya = *kaṇṭhya*	ṚT 147	ST 409
ti = *gati*	ṚT 29, 110	ST 150

B. *Śuklayajuḥprātiśākhya*
jit (1.50), *mut* (1.52), *dhi* (1.53)

C. Gaṇapāṭha of Pāṇini:
ase = *asamāse* utsādigaṇa, A 4.1.86 (gaṇasūtra: *baṣkayāse*)
gargādigaṇa, A 4.1.105 (gaṇasūtra: *vājāse*)

D. *Jainendravyākaraṇa*
dī = *dīrgha* (1.1.11)
dhu = *dhātu* (1.2.1)
sa = *samāsa* (1.3.2)
tya = *pratyaya* (2.1.1)

[13]In the *Sārasvatavyākaraṇa* the term *lopaś* occurs in the following sūtras: sañjñāprakaraṇa, sūtra 11; svarasandhi, sūtra 13; visargasandhi, sūtras 8, 18.

san + *śambhuḥ* > *san-t-śambhuḥ* > *san-c-śambhuḥ* > *sañ-c-śambhuḥ* > *sañcchambhuḥ*

But the *Śabdajyotsnā* adds the augment *c* directly by the rule *śi cak* (ŚJ 91) and hence an extra exercise for the palatalization of *t* is not required. This rule was borrowed from Ācārya Malayagiri's *Śabdānuśāsana*, which states the rule *śi cak* (sūtra 21) in the fifth sandhi.

According to Pāṇini, the process of the formation of *sakhā* (nom. sg. masc. of *sakhi* 'friend') is lengthy since it needs six or seven sūtras, as shown below.

sakhi + *su* (= *s*)

Here by *anaṅ sau* (A 7.1.93) the final *i* of *sakhi* is replaced by *anaṅ* (= *an*) as per the guidelines set by the rule *ṅic ca* (A 1.1.53). So we have

sakh-an-s.

Then the apṛkta element *s* (-*s*) is deleted by *halṅyābbhyo dīrghāt sutisy apṛktaṁ hal* (A 6.1.68).

sakh-an

Then the penultimate (*upadhā*) *a* is lengthened by *sarvanāmasthāne cāsambuddhau* (A 6.4.8)

sakh-ān

The final *n* is deleted by *nalopaḥ prātipadikāntasya* (A 8.2.7). Thus we arrive at

sakhā.

In the system of the *Śabdajyotsnā*, on the other hand, *ḍā* (= *ā*) substitutes for *su* by *sakhyṛvarṇośanaspurudaṁśahehobhyaḥ sor ḍā* (ŚJ 154). Because of the *ḍit* nature of *ḍā*, the elision of the ṭi element *i* of *sakhi* takes place, so that we arrive at *sakhā*.

In the kṛdantaprakaraṇa, the *Śabdajyotsnā* states the rule *ḍvitaḥ ktrimap* (ŚJ 164) in order to account for the formation of a kṛdanta such as *paktrima* 'cooked, baked'. This rule provides that after a verb with the marker *ḍu* the kṛt affix *ktrimap* (= *trima*) occurs. For example,

$\sqrt{}$*ḍupacaṣ* = *pac*
pac + *ktrimap* (= *trima*)
paktrima[14]

[14]Here *c* is replaced by *k* by *kutva* (A 8.2.30: *coḥ kuḥ*; ŚJ 220: *ṛtvij dadhṛṣ . . . spṛś cūnāṁ kuḥ*).

According to Pāṇini, the kṛt affix *ktri* (= *tri*) is introduced after the verb *pac* by *ḍvitaḥ ktriḥ* (A 3.3.88) and then the taddhita affix *map* (= *ma*) is introduced after the kṛdanta *paktri* by *trer mam nityam* (A 4.4.20).

In the kārakaprakaraṇa, the *Śabdajyotsnā* states the rule *anuktakartṛkaraṇahetuviśeṣaṇabhedakeṣu trī* (ŚJ 334). The occurrence of the instrumental case ending in *akṣṇā kāṇaḥ* 'blind in one eye', which is explained by *yenāṅgavikāraḥ* (A 2.3.20) in the Pāṇinian grammar, is accounted for by this rule. According to the author of the *Śabdajyotsnā*, one-eyed-ness can be considered to be caused by an eye (*akṣi*): *akṣihetukaṁ kāṇatvam.*

In order to account for the taddhitānta *yaujanika* 'one who covers a distance of one yojana', Pāṇini states the rule *yojanaṁ gacchati* (A 5.1.74). In the vārttika *krośaśatayojanaśatayor upasaṅkhyānam*, however, Kātyāyana suggests that additional provision has to be made to account for *krauśaśatika* (*krośaśataṁ gacchati*) and *yaujanaśatika* (*yojanaśataṁ gacchati*). But the *Śabdajyotsnā* states in the taddhitāntaprakaraṇa a simple rule, *abhigamanaṁ karoti* (ŚJ 831), which invites considering another vārttika on A 5.1.74: *tato 'bhigamanam arhatīti ca vaktavyam* and which also covers all these instances.

5.5. Some demerits

The author of the *Śabdajyotsnā* formulated the rules of Sanskrit grammar by means of studying the works on the subject composed by sage Pāṇini and other scholars like Kātyāyana and Patañjali. He summarized the formulas established by them in a lucid style. The *Śabdajyotsnā* certainly has the virtue of being a clear and concise exposition of Sanskrit grammatical rules. But this grammar has some weak points too. For one thing, the *Śabdajyotsnā* cannot stand alone as an independent treatise, since it needs the support from the dhātupāṭha, gaṇapāṭha, paribhāṣās (metarules) and other relevant sources well established in the Pāṇinian school.

There are also some irregularities in the formation of sūtras. The author presents the rule *ṭitkidāv ādyantau* (ŚJ 24) in the sañjñāprakaraṇa and again formulates the sūtra *ādyantau ṭakitau* (ŚJ 88) in the sandhiprakaraṇa. Likewise, in the sannantaprakaraṇa the author formulates two sūtras for the affix *san* (= *sa*): *āśaṅkāsvecchayoḥ san* (ŚJ 1) and *āśaṅkārthe san pratyayaḥ* (ŚJ 11). The latter sūtra can be subsumed in the former.

In some cases the author does not seem to follow his own rules. For example, in spite of assigning the term *dī* to a dīrgha vowel in the rule *dvimātro dī dīrghaḥ* (ŚJ 7), he uses the term *dīrgha* instead of *dī* while formulating the sūtra *parau vrajeḥ ṣo dānte dīrghaś ca* (ŚJ 224). Also the following sūtras do not have the uniformity in the use of the technical term *sa* (= *samāsa*):

i. *samāsasya saḥ* (ŚJ 29)
ii. *eko 'same 'ci hro vāse 'siti* (ŚJ 67)[15]
iii. *samarthe padaikyaṁ saḥ* (ŚJ 344)
iv. *ārhād ... asamāse niṣkādeḥ* (ŚJ 818)

Due to merger of several sūtras of the *Aṣṭādhyāyī* in a single sūtra, many sūtras of the *Śabdajyotsnā* have become lengthy, abstruse and as a consequence they are not easy to remember in a sequence. For example, the following sūtras may be referred to:

i. *eṇyā ḍhañ drugopayaso yat mānārthe vayaḥ phale luk ca* (ŚJ 766). This sūtra corresponds to five sūtras of Pāṇini (A 4.3.159–163).
ii. *pratijanādeḥ khañ bhaktāṇ ṇaḥ pariṣadaḥ ṇyaḥ kathādeṣ ṭhak* (ŚJ 804). This is the group of four sūtras of Pāṇini (A 4.4.99–102).
iii. *sarvapuruṣābhyāṁ ṇaḍhañau puruśādvadhavikārasamūhatenakṛteśu māṇavacarakābhyaṁ khañ* (ŚJ 814). This sūtra covers two sūtras of Pāṇini (A 5.1.10–11) and the vārttika on A 5.1.10.
iv. *sryato jas ṅe ṅasi ām ṅīnāṁ śī smai smāt sāṁ sminaḥ* (ŚJ 139). This sūtra works for four sūtras of Pāṇini (A 7.1.14, 15, 17 and 7.1.52).

Conclusion

In spite of these minor defects, the work deserves recognition in academic circles. The author of the *Śabdajyotsnā* aimed at and indeed succeeded in fully exposing the rules of Sanskrit grammar in lucid and clear diction. The work, a pioneering attempt of its kind, may very well be considered as a significant contribution to the tradition of Sanskrit grammar. It is supposed to be a simpler and smaller version of the *Siddhāntakaumudī* of Bhaṭṭojidīkṣita. The book, for sure, will stimulate greater interest in the principles of ancient Sanskrit grammar amongst modern grammarians and students equally.

References and abbreviations

A: Pāṇini's *Aṣṭādhyāyī*. See Katre.

Abhyankar, Kashinath Vasudev

1962–72 *The Vyākaraṇa-mahābhāṣya of Patañjali, edited by F. Kielhorn, third edition, revised and furnished with additional readings, references and select critical notes by K. V. Abhyankar.* 3 vols (1: 1962; 2: 1965; 3: 1972). Pune: Bhandarkar Oriental Research Institute.

[15] *vāse* ← *vā ase* (= *asamāse*).

Bhiksharama

1958 *Śabdajyotsnā*. Kurukshetra: Kurukshetra University.

De, Sushil Kumar

1940 *Mahābhārata: Udyogaparvan; Being the Fifth Book of the Mahābhārata, the Great Epic of India*. Poona: Bhandarkar Oriental Research Institute.

Dikshita, A. M. Ramanath

1961 *Sāmatantra: A Prātiśākhya of the Sāmaveda; Critically Edited with an Introduction and Appendices*. Varanasi: Vedic Research Committee, Banaras Hindu University.

Doshi, Bechardas J.

1967 *Ācārya Malayagiri's Śabdānuśāsana*. Ahmedabad: Lalbhai Dalpatbhai, Bharatiya Sanskriti Vidyamandir.

Gopathabrāhmaṇa. See Mitra.

Griffith, R. T. H.

1888 *Śuklayajuḥprātiśākhya: Kātyāyana's Prātiśākhya of the White Yajurveda with Commentary of Uvaṭa*. Benares Sanskrit Series 8, 10, 18, 21, 31. Benares: Messrs. Braj. B. Dass & Co.

Jainendravyākaraṇa. See Tripathi.

Katre, Sumitra Mangesh

1989 *Aṣṭādhyāyī of Pāṇini*. Delhi: Motilal Banarsidass.

Laghuśabdenduśekhara. See Shastri, Guruprasad.

Mahābhārata. See De.

Mahābhāṣya. See Abhyankar.

Mankand, D. R.

1965 *The Vālmīki-Rāmāyaṇa: The Kiṣkindhākāṇḍa; the Fourth Book of the Vālmīki-Rāmāyaṇa, the National Epic of India*. Baroda: Oriental Institute.

Mitra, Rajendra Lal

1972 *Gopatha Brāhmaṇa of Atharva-Veda; with Elaborate Introduction*. Delhi: Indological Book House.

Mimansaka, Yudhishthira

1984 *Saṁskṛta Vyākaraṇa Śāstra kā Itihāsa*. Part 1. 4th ed. Bahalgarh: Ram Lal Kapoor Trust.

Müller, F. Max

1968 *A History of Ancient Sanskrit Literature*. Varanasi: Chowkhamba Sanskrit Series Office.

Muṇḍakopaniṣad. See Shastri, J. L.

Nirukta. See Rajavade.

Rajavade, V. K.

1940 *Yāska's Nirukta*. Government Oriental Series, class A, no.7. Poona: Bhandarkar Oriental Research Institute.

Rāmāyaṇa. See Mankand.

ṚT: *Ṛktantra*. See Suryakant.

ṚV: *Ṛgveda*. See Sonattake.

Sastry, P. V. Naganatha
1974–1983 *Śrī Bhaṭṭoji Dīkṣita's Vaiyākaraṇasiddhāntakaumudī.* Vol. I (1974); Vol. II (1983). Delhi: Motilal Banarsidass.

Sārasvatavyākaraṇa. See Śāstrī.

Śabdānuśāsana (Malayagiri). See Doshi.

Śāstrī, Nava Kishora
1985 *Sārasvata-Vyākaraṇam of Anubhūtisvarūpāchārya: with Two Commentaries.* 2 vols (I: 3rd ed., 1985; II: 2nd ed., 1971). Varanasi: Chaukhamba Sanskrit Sansthan/Series Office.

Shastri, Guruprasad
1936 *Laghushabdendushekhara of M. M. Nagesh Bhatt with Seven Commentaries.* Benares City: Bhargava Pustakalaya.

Shastri, J. L.
1980 *Upaniṣatsaṁgrahaḥ; Containing 188 Upaniṣads.* Delhi: Motilal Banarsidass.

ŚJ: *Śabdajyotsnā.* See Bhiksharama.

Śuklayajuḥprātiśākhya. See Griffith.

Sonattake, N. S.
1933–46 *Ṛg-Veda Saṁhitā; with Commentary of Sāyaṇa.* Part I (1933); Part II (1936); Part III (1941); Part IV (1946). Poona: Vaidika Samshodhana Mandala.

ST: *Sāmatantra.* See Dikshita.

Suryakant
1970 *Ṛktantra: A Prātiśākhya of the Sāmaveda.* Delhi: Meharchand Lacchamandass.

Tripathi, Shambhu Nath
1956 *Jainendravyākaraṇam by Pūjyapāda Devanandī with Jainendra-mahāvṛtti of Shri Abhayanandī.* Kashi: Bhāratīya Jñānapīṭha.

पाणिनेरष्टाध्याय्या अधिकारसूत्राणां गङ्गोत्री

कालिन्दी शुक्ला

०. पाणिनिकृताष्टाध्यायी मानवमस्तिष्कस्यानुपमा कृतिरिति मन्यन्ते विद्वांसः। पाणिनिः स्वग्रन्थे लाघवायानेका युक्तीः प्रयुक्तवान्। स सूत्रशैल्या शास्त्रमरचयत्। शास्त्रेऽस्मिन् षड्विधानि सूत्राणि सन्ति। तेषु षड्विधेषु सूत्रेष्वधिकारसूत्राणां विभावनां पाणिनिः कुतः प्राप्तवानित्यस्य शोधपत्रस्य प्रतिपाद्यो विषयः।

१. पाणिनेरपि पूर्वं वेदानां विविधाभिः शाखाभिः संबद्धानां पार्षदानामर्थात्प्रातिशाख्यानां[1] परम्परा प्रचलितासीत्। वेदानां यथावज्ज्ञानार्थं संक्रमणार्थं च तेषामध्ययनविधेर्वर्णोत्पत्तेः पदप्रकाराणां छन्दसश्च संप्रतिपत्तिरनिर्वार्या[2]। एतद्विषयकाणि शास्त्राणि वेदाङ्गानि भवन्ति। प्रातिशाख्येषु वेदानां शाखाविशेषानधिकृत्य एते विषया एकत्रीकृत्य विचारिताः। प्रातिशाख्यग्रन्था वैदिकीमेव वाचं वर्णयन्ति। किंतु स्वातन्त्र्येण षड्वेदाङ्गरूपेण संग्रथितेषु शिक्षाकल्पच्छन्दोव्याकरणादिग्रन्थेषु भाषाया अपि वर्णनमस्ति। तेन प्रतिभाति यत्प्रातिशाख्यग्रन्थेभ्यः क्रमशः शिक्षाकल्पच्छन्दोव्याकरणवेदाङ्गानां स्वातन्त्र्येण विकासोऽभूत्। अतः प्रातिशाख्यग्रन्था वेदाङ्गानां मूलाधाराः स्युर् इतीमं तर्कमुररीकृत्य विचारणायाः प्रवर्तनं नानुचितं भवेत्।

परम्परया पाणिनेरष्टाध्यायी व्याकरणाख्यवेदाङ्गत्वेन स्वीक्रियते। प्रातिशाख्यानां साम्प्रतमुपलभ्यमानाः पाठा अनेकेभ्यः प्रक्षेपेभ्यः परिवर्तनेभ्यश्चानन्तरमाकारिताः सन्ति[3]। तेन कारणेन पाणिनिप्रातिशाख्ययोः पौर्वापर्यस्य निर्णयो दुष्करो विवादग्रस्तश्च[4]। डो. सूर्यकान्तमहाभागेनान्तराणि बाह्यानि च प्रमाणानि प्रस्तुत्यैतत् तर्कितं यदृक्तन्त्रस्य प्राचीनावृत्तिरन्येषां प्राचीनानां प्रातिशाख्यानां समकालिकैवास्ति[5]। ऋक्तन्त्रस्य शाकटायनकृता द्वितीयावृत्तिरप्यन्येषां प्रातिशाख्यानां समकालिका सती

[1]स्वचरणपर्षद्येव यैः प्रतिशाखानियतमेव प्रगृह्यक्रमसंहितास्वरलक्षणमुच्यते तानीमानि प्रातिशाख्यानि॥ मुकुन्दशर्मकृतटिप्पणी ४ (निरुक्तम् ४६)।

[2]वर्णोत्पत्तेः संप्रतिपत्तावुच्चारणस्थानप्रयत्नप्रकाराणामुदात्तानुदात्तस्वरितप्रचितानां संप्रतिपत्तिरन्तर्भूता। पदप्रकाराणां च संप्रतिपत्तौ लोपागमवर्णविकारप्रकृतिभावादीनां संप्रतिपत्तिरन्तर्भूता।

[3]Cardona 1980: 273: "...the text of the prātiśākhyas as we have them now contains accretions to older core texts."

[4]Cardona 1980: 273: "The relative chronology of Pāṇini and the prātiśākhyas is a vexed question which has not yet been answered satisfactorily."

[5]Surya Kant 1939: 67: "Thus, Ṛktantram, in its original form, is not later than other Prātiśākhyas."

पाणिनेः पूर्वकालिकेति[6]। इत्थं सर्वेषामपि प्रातिशाख्यग्रन्थानामारम्भकालिकी परम्परा पाणिनेः पूर्ववर्तिनीति स्वीकर्तव्यम्[7]। पाणिनिरेतेभ्यः पूर्ववर्तिभ्यः प्रातिशाख्येभ्यः प्रेरणां प्राप्याष्टाध्यायीमरचयत्। प्रातिशाख्येष्वृग्वेदप्रातिशाख्यं प्राचीनतममस्तीति विज्ञा मन्यन्ते। वाजसनेयिप्रातिशाख्यम् ऋग्वेदप्रातिशाख्यं च पाणिनेः पूर्वं विरचितमित्यनेकेषां विदुषां मतम्[8]।

२. इदानीं विचार्यते प्रातिशाख्यव्याकरणयोर्मध्ये कियत्पर्यन्तमुपकार्योपकारकभावो वर्तत इति। व्याकरणमहाभाष्ये पतञ्जलिर्भणत्युत्सर्गापवादन्यायमनुसृत्य पाणिनिना सूत्राणि विरचितानीति। तस्मादुत्सर्गापवादन्यायस्य प्रथममुपयोजनं कुत्र दृश्यत इत्यन्वेष्टव्यम्।

ऋग्वेदप्रातिशाख्यस्य प्रथमे पटले शौनकेन **न्यायैर्मिश्रानपवादान्प्रतीयात्** (ऋ.प्रा. १.५३) इत्युक्तम्। अत्र न्याया नामोत्सर्गाः। उत्सर्गाश्च महाविषयविधयो यैरनुलोमान्वक्षरसन्धयो विधीयन्ते। अपवादा नामाल्पविषयविधयो यैः सामवशाः सन्धयो विधीयन्ते। सन्धिविषयेऽपवादविषयं मुक्त्वोत्सर्गाः प्रवर्तन्ते। एवं प्रातिशाख्यकारेणोत्सर्गापवादयोर्व्यवस्था प्रतिपादिता। ततश्च **सर्वशास्त्रार्थं प्रतिकण्ठमुक्तम्** (ऋ.प्रा.१.५४) इत्यनेन सूत्रेण प्रातिशाख्यकारेण निपातनस्य व्यवस्था प्रतिपादिता। शास्त्रस्य सकलान् विषयान् सामान्यरूपेण प्रस्तुत्य तेषामपवादरूपेण प्रतिकण्ठमर्थान्निपातनानां विधानं कृतम्[9]। तद्यथा।

> नू इ॒त्था ते॑ (ऋ.सं.१.१३२.४a)

इति। अस्य पदपाठः।

> नू। इ॒त्था। ते॒।

[6]Surya Kant 1939: 68: "In its second stage, i.e. as the work of Śākaṭāyana, it is not later than other Prātiśākhyas. Śākaṭāyana is quoted by RPr. VPr., and CA. In its third stage, the work may be later than Pāṇini and even Kātyāyana."

[7]Surya Kant 1939: 68, note 1: "And this is exactly what Westergaard concluded about other Prātiśākhyas.... Burnell agrees with it. Cp. RT, p. LVI. But Burnell rightly adds that all the Prātiśākhyas, in their original form, existed before Pāṇini."

[8]Cardona 1980: 356, note 428: "... but Liebich (1916b: 38, 45–46) thought the Ṛk-Prātiśākhya and the Vājasaneyi-Prātiśākhya were the oldest. Siddheshwar Verma (1929: 21) treated the Ṛk-Prātiśākhya as the most ancient, but Thieme (1958: 41) claimed that the Vājasaneyi-Prātiśākhya is the oldest. My own view is that the Ṛk-Prātiśākhya is probably the most ancient in its present form, since it shows less influence of Pāṇinian methodology than the others."

[9]सर्वशास्त्रार्थम् उत्सर्गत्वेन पुरस्कृत्य तस्यैवापवादत्वेन प्रतिकण्ठमुक्तं जानीयात्॥ उवटभाष्यम् (ऋग्वेदप्रातिशाख्यम् १.५४)।

इति। अत्रेपरस्योकारस्य **समानाक्षरमन्तःस्थां स्वामकण्ठ्यं स्वरोदयम्** (ऋ.प्रा.२.२१) इत्यनेन सूत्रेण क्षैप्रसन्धिः प्राप्नोति।

किंतु

> **नू इत्था ते सानो अव्ये वा अस्मे वासौ वेद्यस्याम्।**
> **धिष्ण्येमे नू अन्यत्रा चित् पादादौ नू इन्द्रोत्यर्वाक्॥** (ऋ.प्रा.२.७०)

इत्यनेन नु इत्यत्रोकारस्य निपातनेन दीर्घभावः। अत्र संहितायां दीर्घभावह्रस्वभावादीनामनेकेषां शास्त्रीयाणां कार्याणां प्रदर्शनं प्रातिशाख्यकार उत्सर्गापवादनिपातनविधिना करोति। तमनुसृत्य पाणिनिः स्वस्य शास्त्रमप्युत्सर्गापवादनिपातनरीत्या प्रणयति।

३. अष्टाध्याय्यां षड्विधानि सूत्राणि वर्तन्ते। तत्र विधिनियमसूत्राणां विभावना पूर्वमीमांसायां यानि विधिनियमपरिसंख्यावचनानि सन्ति तैः साम्यं भजते। परिभाषासूत्राणां तु विभावना प्रातिशाख्यग्रन्थेभ्य उद्धृता स्यादिति प्रतिभाति। ऋग्वेदप्रातिशाख्ये पादज्ञानविषयकहेतूनां बलाबलभावं विशदीकर्तुं **विशेषसंनिपाते तु पूर्वं पूर्वं परं परम्** (ऋ.प्रा.१७.२६) इति सूत्रं वर्तते। अनेन सूत्रेण पूर्वसूत्रोक्तानां हेतूनां बलाबलं सूचितम्। एतस्मात्प्रातिशाख्यसूत्राद्बलाबलस्य विभावनामुद्धृत्य पाणिनिनाष्टाध्याय्यां **विप्रतिषेधे परं कार्यम्** (१.४.२) इति सूत्रं समावेशितम्। एतादृशानि सूत्रार्थनिर्णयोपकारकाणि परिभाषासूत्राणि प्रातिशाख्येषु दृश्यन्ते। तथाहि। ऋग्वेदप्रातिशाख्ये (१.५६) **असावमुमिति तदभावमुक्तं यथान्तरम्** इति सूत्रं वर्तते। वाजसनेयिप्रातिशाख्ये **तस्मिन्निति निर्दिष्टे पूर्वस्य** (१.१३४), **तस्मादित्युत्तरस्यादेः** (१.१३५), **षष्ठीस्थाने योगः** (१.३६), **तेनेत्यागमः** (१.१३७) इति सूत्रचतुष्टयं परिभाषात्वेन दृश्यते। अष्टाध्याय्यां **तस्मिन्निति निर्दिष्टे पूर्वस्य** (१.१.६६), **तस्मादित्युत्तरस्य** (१.१.६७), **षष्ठी स्थानेयोगा** (१.१.४९) इति त्रीणि परिभाषासूत्राणि सन्ति। अत्र प्रातिशाख्यस्थानां परिभाषासूत्राणां पाणिनिकृतानां परिभाषासूत्राणां च साम्यं सुस्पष्टं निभाल्यते।

४. अष्टाध्याय्यां विधिसूत्राणां प्रणयनेऽपि प्रातिशाख्यानां प्रेरकत्वमनुमातुं शक्यम्। तद्यथा। पाणिनेः षत्वविधायकेषु सूत्रेष्वृग्वेदप्रातिशाख्यस्य नतिपटलस्य प्रभावो दृश्यते। यानि मूर्धन्यादेशविधायीनि सूत्राणि पाणिनेरष्टाध्याय्यां पठ्यन्ते तानि सर्वाण्यृग्वेदप्रातिशाख्ये पूर्वं प्रस्तुतान्यासन्। ऋग्वेदप्रातिशाख्ये (१) **अन्तःपादं नाम्युपधः सकारः षकारमप्यूष्मपरैर्यथोक्तम्। अन्यैरेकारात्** (५.१) इत्यधिकृत्य (२) **युग्मान्तस्थादन्तमूलीयपूर्वैरन्तःपदं नम्यतेऽन्तःपदस्थैः** (५.२०) (३) **सेति चास्य परिपन्नोपधा चेत्** (५.२५) इति सूत्राणां यत्कथनमस्ति तदनुसृत्याष्टाध्याय्याम् **अपदान्तस्य मूर्धन्यः** (८.३.५५), **सहेः साडः सः** (८.३.५६), **इण्कोः** (८.३.५७),

नुम्विसर्जनीयशर्व्यवायेऽपि (८.३.५८) इति सूत्राणि दृश्यन्ते।

ऋक्तन्त्रेऽपि कतिपयानि सूत्राणि सन्ति यैर्महासाम्यम् अष्टाध्यायीस्थानां सूत्राणां सपद्येव प्रतीयते। ऋक्तन्त्रे (१) **स सं करोतौ** (१८९) इति वर्तते। **संपरिभ्यां करोतौ भूषणे** (६.१.१३७) इत्यष्टाध्याय्याम्। (२) **उपप्रती हिंसायाम्** (१९७) इत्यृक्तन्त्रे। **हिंसायां प्रतेश्च** (६.१.१४१) इति पाणिनिः कथयति। (३) **कुस्तुम्बुरु जातिः** (१९९) इत्यृक्तन्त्रकारो भणति। **कुस्तुम्बुरूणि जातिः** (६.१.१४३) इत्यष्टाध्याय्यामुपदिष्टम्। (४) **अपरस्परं सातत्ये** (२०१) इत्यृक्तन्त्रे पठितम्। **अपरस्पराः क्रियासातत्ये** (६.१.१४४) इति पाणिनिर्वक्ति। एतादृशान्यन्यान्यपि बहूनि सूत्राणि सन्ति[10] यैः साम्यमष्टाध्यायीस्थसूत्राणां सुस्पष्टम्।

५. संज्ञाकरणेनैव लोकव्यवहारः सुगमो भवति[11]। तस्मात् कारणात् पाणिनेः पूर्वाचार्याः संज्ञाकरणप्रयुक्तिं शास्त्र उपयुक्तवन्तः।ताननुसृत्य पाणिनिरपि लाघवार्थं सारल्यार्थं च संज्ञासूत्राणि प्रणयति। वाजसनेयिप्रातिशाख्ये सिम्जित्मुज्ञाव्यादिसंज्ञाः प्रयुक्ताः। ऋग्वेदप्रातिशाख्येऽपि नामिन्नतिप्रगृह्यादयः संज्ञाः प्रयुक्ता दृश्यन्ते। तेनैव प्रकारेणाष्टाध्याय्यां संज्ञासूत्राणां प्रणयने पाणिनिः पूर्वाचार्याणामाधमर्ण्यं स्वीकरोतीति वक्तुं पार्यते।

६. एतत् तुलनात्मकमध्ययनं पुरस्कृत्येदं निवेदयितुमिच्छामि यन्निखिलेऽपि वैदिकवाङ्मये प्रातिशाख्यग्रन्थेषु प्रथमतया सूत्रशैली प्रादुर्भूता। ततश्च सूत्राणां प्रवृत्तिविषये संजातं वैविध्यं ज्ञापयितुं संज्ञापरिभाषाविधिनियमादिसूत्राणां संकल्पना समुद्भूता। यदि प्रातिशाख्येषु वर्तमानानां विधिपरिभाषादिसूत्राणां प्रतिबिम्बं पाणिनेरष्टाध्याय्यां वर्तत इति प्रतीयते तर्हि पाणिनेरधिकारसूत्राणामपि बीजं प्राक्तने काले प्रातिशाख्येषु संभाव्यते। विषयेऽस्मिन्नृग्वेदप्रातिशाख्यं सूक्ष्मेक्षिकया परीक्ष्यतेऽधस्तात्।

७. ऋग्वेदप्रातिशाख्यस्यान्तिमेषु त्रिषु पटलेषु विस्तरेण छन्दसां चर्चा वर्तते[12]। तत्र छन्दसां सप्त भेदाः प्रतिपादिताः। तद्यथा। गायत्री, उष्णिक्, अनुष्टुप्, त्रिष्टुप्, बृहती, पङ्क्तिः, जगती चेति। ऋग्वेदसर्वानुक्रमण्यामप्यृग्वेदे प्रयुक्तानां छन्दसामवान्तरभेदैरुल्लेखो वर्तते, पदपङ्क्तिः, यवमध्याः, वर्धमानाश्चेत्यादिः। अन्यच्च चत्वार एव प्राकृताः पादाः। सर्वेषां छन्दसां रचनैतैश्चतुर्भिः प्राकृतैः पादैर्भवति।

---

[10]

ऋक्तन्त्रम्	अष्टाध्यायी
मित्र ऋषौ (२१९)	मित्रौ चर्षे (६.३.१३०)
तः (१८९)	तः (६.१.१३५)
पर्यन्तम् (२११)	पर्यन्तम् (६.१.१७७)

[11]अणीयस्त्वाच्च शब्देन संज्ञाकरणं व्यवहारार्थं लोके॥ निरुक्तम् १.२।

[12]एवं कृप्तप्रमाणानां छन्दसामुपदिश्यते॥ ऋग्वेदप्रातिशाख्यम् १७.१।

इमे प्राकृताः पादाश्छन्दसां मूलाधारः[13]। गायत्रपादोऽष्टाक्षरो भवति। वैराजपादो दशाक्षरो भवति। त्रैष्टुभपाद एकादशाक्षरः। जागतपादश्च द्वादशाक्षरो भवति[14]। सर्वाणि छन्दांसि चतुर्विधैः पादै रच्यन्ते। किंतु कस्यामृचि कः प्राकृतः पादो घटकतत्त्वरूपेण वर्तत इत्येतस्य निर्णय ऋग्वेदप्रातिशाख्यस्य **प्रायोऽर्थो वृत्तमित्येते पादज्ञानस्य हेतवः** (१७.२५) इतीदं सूत्रं मार्गदर्शकं भवति। अस्मिन् सूत्रे प्राय इत्यत्र भाष्यकारस्य एतद्व्याख्यानमस्ति। **त्रिष्टुभः प्रायः गोर्न पर्व वि रद** (१.६१.१२) इति प्रकृत्या दशाक्षरो व्यूहेनैकादशाक्षरः क्रियत इति। तेन ज्ञायते यत् प्रायःपदेन सूक्तस्यारम्भेऽनुक्रमण्यादिग्रन्थेषु वा छन्दसो य आधिकारिको निर्देशो वर्तते तस्य सूचनं भवति। निरुक्ताख्ये वेदाङ्गेऽपि प्रायःशब्दोऽधिकारार्थे प्रयुक्तो वर्तते[15]। इत्थमृग्वेदप्रातिशाख्ये प्रायःशब्दोऽधिकारसूचक एव। तेनैकैकस्य सूक्तस्य प्रारम्भे निर्दिष्ट ऋषिदेवताछन्दसामुल्लेख आधिकारिको भवति। तद्यथा। ऋग्वेदस्य प्रथममण्डलान्तर्गतस्यैकषष्टितमसूक्तस्यारम्भे त्रिष्टुप्छन्दसः प्रायिकत्वं निर्दिष्टम्। तेन सर्वास्वृक्षु न्यूनाधिकाक्षरासु सतीष्वपि त्रिष्टुप्छन्द एव विराजत इति स्वीकरणीयं त्रिष्टुप्छन्दोऽनुसारं च मन्त्रगानं कर्तव्यम्। एतद् एकेनोदाहरणेन स्पष्टीक्रियते।

> अस्मा इदु प्र भरा तूतुजानो वृत्राय वज्रमीशानः कियेधाः।
> गोर्न पर्व वि रदा तिरश्चेष्यन्नर्णांस्यपां चरध्यै॥ ऋ.सं.१.६१.१२॥

मन्त्रेऽस्मिन् पूर्वार्धे द्वाविंशतिरक्षराणि सन्ति। अतस्तत्र त्रैष्टुभपादौ सम्यग्रूपेण दृश्येते। किंतूत्तरार्धे केवलमष्टादशाक्षराणि गण्यन्ते। अर्थात् चतुर्णामक्षराणां न्यूनता लक्ष्यते। अतोऽत्र व्यूहस्यावश्यकतास्ति[16]। किंतु व्यूहेनापि दशैवाक्षराणि द्वयोः पादयोः सिध्यन्ति। अर्थात् त्रैष्टुभपादस्य कृतेऽपेक्षितान्येकादशाक्षराणि न भवन्ति। एतादृश्यां परिस्थित्यां प्रायिकत्वेनैवार्थादधिकारत्वेन त्रिष्टुप्छन्दसः स्वीकृतिः कर्तव्या। तदनुसारं च त्रिष्टुप्छन्दस्यस्य मन्त्रस्य गानं विधेयमिति निश्चीयते।

८. अत्र प्राय इति शब्दस्य कोऽर्थः स्यादिति विचार्यते। शब्देऽस्मिन् प्रोपसर्गपूर्वकादयधातोरसुन्प्रत्ययमुत्पाद्य प्रायस् इति शब्दो निष्पाद्यते। अतोऽस्य प्राय इति शब्दस्य प्रकृतमयनम् (= गमनम्) अथवा प्रकृष्टमयनम् (= गमनम्) इत्यर्थः स्वीक्रियते[17]। अस्मिन्नेवार्थे प्राय इति शब्दस्य प्रयोग ऋग्वेदस्यैकस्मिन् मन्त्रेऽपि

[13]एतैश्छन्दांसि वर्तन्ते सर्वाण्यन्यैरतोऽल्पशः। एतद्विकारा एवान्ये सर्वे तु प्राकृताः समाः॥ ऋग्वेदप्रातिशाख्यम् १७.४०।

[14]पादौ गायत्रवैराजावष्टाक्षरदशाक्षरौ। एकादशिद्वादशिनौ विद्यात् त्रैष्टुभजागतौ॥ ऋग्वेदप्रातिशाख्यम् १७.३८।

[15]प्रायोदेवता वा (निरुक्तम् ७.४)। अत्र सा स्यादित्यनुषज्यते। प्राय इति ह्यधिकार उच्यते। अथवा प्रायः कल्प्या देवता यस्यां सा तथाभूता सा ऋक् (स मन्त्रः) स्यात्। अयमर्थः यद्देवताधिकारेऽध्ययनपाठानुक्रमे यो मन्त्रोऽनाविष्कृतदेवतालिङ्गो भवति स तद्देवत एव। तद्यथा—अग्न्यधिकारे वर्तमाने आग्नेय एव मन्त्रो भवति। इन्द्राधिकारे चैन्द्र एवेति॥ मुकुन्दशर्मकृतटिप्पणी (निरुक्तम् ३४९)।

[16]व्यूहेदेकाक्षरीभावान्पादेषूनेषु संपदे॥ ऋग्वेदप्रातिशाख्यम् १७.२२।

[17]शब्दकल्पद्रुमः। तृतीयो भागः। (पृ. ३१९)

दृश्यते। तद्यथा।

> न म इन्द्रेण सख्यं वि योषदस्मभ्यमस्य दक्षिणा दुहीत।
> उप ज्येष्ठे वरूथे गभस्तौ प्रायेप्राये जिगीवांसः स्याम॥ ऋ.सं.२.१८.८॥

अत्र प्राय इति शब्दस्य व्याख्याने सायणो लिखति **यद्वा प्राये प्राये प्रकर्षेण ईयते गम्यते योद्धृभिरिति**। अर्थात् यदा प्रकृष्टं पौनःपुन्येन वा गमनं भवति तदा तत्र प्राय इति शब्दः प्रयुज्यते। ऋग्वेदे प्रत्येकसूक्तस्य प्रारम्भ ऋषिदेवताछन्दसां य आधिकारिको विधिर्वर्तते। तस्यापि प्रकृष्टमयनम् (= प्रत्येकमृचि) गमनं भवति। तेनैव कारणेन प्रकृष्टगमनलक्षणवानधिकारः परम्परायां (प्रातिशाख्य एवं निरुक्ते) प्रायःसंज्ञया उक्तो भवति। पाणिनेरष्टाध्याय्यामप्यधिकारोऽधिकारलक्षणसूत्रानुगामिषु सूत्रेषु प्रकृष्टतया पौनःपुन्येन वाविर्भवति। अतोऽधिकारस्य संकल्पना पाणिनिना ऋग्वेदप्रातिशाख्ये प्रायःसंज्ञया निर्दिष्टादधिकाराद् गृहीता स्यादिति प्रतीयते।

तैत्तिरीयप्रातिशाख्येऽनुक्रमण्यादिग्रन्थेषु चाथ इति शब्दोऽधिकारार्थे प्रयुज्यते। भगवता पाणिनिना **स्वरितेनाधिकारः** (१.१.११) इति सूत्रं प्रणीय स्वरितत्वयुक्तं शब्दस्वरूपमधिकृतं वेदितव्यमिति निर्दिष्टम्। सूत्रमिदमधिकारसूत्रस्येत्थंभूतत्वं निवेदयति। एवं च स्वरितरूपेण चिह्नेनानुवृत्तेरवधिः प्रदर्श्यते। किंतु तस्य प्रवर्तना कथं कर्तव्येति न निवेद्यते। ऋग्वेदप्रातिशाख्येऽधिकारवाचिन्या प्राय इति संज्ञया यत् प्रकृतमयनं पौनःपुन्येन गमनं वेत्यर्थोऽवबोध्यते तस्मात् प्रेरणां लब्ध्वा भगवता पाणिनिनाधिकारसूत्रस्य संकल्पना स्वकीयायामष्टाध्याय्यां प्रकटीकृतेति मन्ये॥

॥ सन्दर्भग्रन्थाः॥

अष्टाध्यायी॥ पदच्छेदवृत्तिवार्तिकटिप्पणीसहिता। परिष्कर्ता—म.म. पण्डितराज डो. श्री. गोपालशास्त्री दर्शन केसरी। चौखम्बा सुरभारती ग्रन्थमाला १९। वाराणसी। चौखम्बा सुरभारती प्रकाशन। १९९७॥

ऋक्तन्त्रम्॥ सामप्रातिशाख्यम् ऋक्तन्त्रविवृतिसामवेदसर्वानुक्रमणीभ्यामुपेतम्। संपादकः—सूर्यकान्त। लवपुरि। १९३९। पुनर्मुद्रणम्। दिल्ली। मेहरचन्द लछमनदास। १९७०॥

ऋग्वेदः॥ पादपाठसहिता सायणाचार्यकृतभाष्यसंबलिता, सैव हिन्दीभाषामन्त्रानुवादसमन्विता। भाग (१–९)। अनुवादकः—पण्डित रामगोविन्द त्रिवेदी। वाराणसी। चौखम्बा विद्याभवन। २००७॥

ऋग्वेदप्रातिशाख्यम्॥ संपादकः—डो. वीरेन्द्रकुमार वर्मा। वाराणसी। काशी हिन्दु विश्वविद्यालय। १९७०॥

ऋ.प्रा. = ऋग्वेदप्रातिशाख्यम्॥

ऋ.सं = ऋग्वेदसंहिता॥

काशिका॥ सटिप्पणप्रकाशहिन्दीव्याख्योपेता। व्याख्यानकारः—श्री नारायणमिश्र। वाराणसी। चौखम्भा संस्कृत संस्थान। २००५॥

तैत्तिरीयप्रातिशाख्यम्॥ व्याख्याकारः—पं. सुशीलकुमार पाठकः। सम्पादकः—जमुना पाठकः। चौखम्भा संस्कृत सीरीज १२६। वाराणसी। चौखम्भा संस्कृत संस्थान। २००७॥

निरुक्तम्॥ (कश्यपप्रजापतिकृतनिघण्टुभाष्यरूपम्)। श्रीमद्भगवद्दुर्गाचार्यकृत-ऋज्वर्थाख्यव्याख्यानुसारिण्या पण्डितश्रीमुकुनशर्मणा कृतया निरुक्तविवृत्त्या समुपेतं तेनैव च टिप्पण्यादिभिः परिष्कृतं संशोधितं च। व्रजजीवन प्राच्यभारती ग्रन्थमाला ४१। पुनर्मुद्रितसंस्करण। दिल्ली। पाणिनी। २००२॥

वाजसनेयिप्रातिशाख्यम्॥ संपादकः—डो. वीरेन्द्रकुमार वर्मा। वाराणसी। काशी हिन्दु विश्वविद्यालय। पुनर्मुद्रित संस्करण। व्रजजीवन प्राच्यभारती ग्रन्थमाला १९। दिल्ली। चौखम्भा संस्कृत प्रतिष्ठान। १९८७॥

शब्दकल्पद्रुमः॥ ले.स्यार-राजा राधाकान्तदेव बहाद्दूरेण विरचितः। वाराणसी। चौखम्बा संस्कृत सीरीझ् ओफिस्। १९६१॥

Cardona, George
1980 *Pāṇini: A Survey of Research.* 1976. First Indian reprint, Delhi: Motilal Banarsidass.

Surya Kant 1939. उपरि ऋक्तन्त्रं द्रष्टव्यम्।

On *eke pracakṣate* ('some say') in *VP* 3.9.1*

Jaehyung Yi

Introduction

The third kāṇḍa of the *Vākyapadīya* of Bhartṛhari, consisting of fourteen samuddeśas, deals with word meanings abstracted from a sentence meaning (*apoddhārapadārtha*). Bhartṛhari begins most of the samuddeśas by expressing his own views on the word meanings. For example, in the first two kārikās of the Jātisamuddeśa (*VP* 3.1.1–2), which serve as an introduction to the whole third kāṇḍa, he says that only a generic property (*jāti*) or an individual substance (*dravya*) is the meaning of words abstracted from sentences, and that the meaning of words, whether it is a generic property or an individual substance, is described as eternal;[1] in the first kārikā of the Dravyasamuddeśa (*VP* 3.2.1), he asserts that the substance posited as a word meaning is identical with what is referred to by terms such as *ātman* 'self'.[2] This is more conspicuous in the Diksamuddeśa and the following two samuddeśas. In the Diksamuddeśa, he states in the first kārikā (*VP* 3.6.1) that direction (*diś*), what brings an action to accomplishment (*sādhana*), an action (*kriyā*), and time (*kāla*) are powers (*śakti*);[3] and, in the following two kārikās (*VP* 3.6.2–3), he gives his own definition of direction.[4] In the first kārikās of the Sādhanasamuddeśa (*VP* 3.7.1) and the Kriyāsamuddeśa

*My special thanks are due to Professor George Cardona for reading the entire text in its original form and making a number of helpful suggestions.

[1] *VP* 3.1.1–2: *dvidhā kaiścit padaṃ bhinnaṃ caturdhā pañcadhāpi vā / apoddhṛtyaiva vākyebhyaḥ prakṛtipratyayādivat // padārthānām apoddhāre jātir vā dravyam eva vā / padārthau sarvaśabdānāṃ nityāv evopavarṇitau //* In *VP* 3.1.2 Bhartṛhari alludes to the views maintained by Vājapyāyana and Vyāḍi: according to the former, a nominal signifies only a generic property (*ākṛti, jāti*); according to the latter, a nominal signifies only an individual substance (*dravya, vyakti*).

[2] *VP* 3.2.1: *ātmā vastu svabhāvaś ca śarīraṃ tattvam ity api / dravyam ity asya paryāyās tac ca nityam iti smṛtam //*

[3] *VP* 3.6.1: *dik sādhanaṃ kriyā kāla iti vastvabhidhāyinaḥ / śaktirūpe padārthānām atyantam anavasthitāḥ //*

[4] *VP* 3.6.2–3: *vyatirekasya yo hetur avadhipratipādyayoḥ / ṛjv ity evaṃ yato 'nyena vinā buddhiḥ pravartate // karmaṇo jātibhedānām abhivyaktir yadāśrayā /*

(*VP* 3.8.1), which follow the Diksamuddeśa, he expounds his own views on what brings an action to accomplishment and an action, respectively.[5]

Interestingly, however, Bhartṛhari begins the Kālasamuddeśa, which is meant for discussing time (*kāla*), by stating the following kārikā which introduces the view of 'some theorists' (*eke*) on time:

> *VP* 3.9.1: *vyāpāravyatirekeṇa kālam eke pracakṣate / nityam ekaṃ vibhu dravyaṃ parimāṇaṃ kriyāvatām //*
>
> "Of time, some say (*eke pracakṣate*): it exists independently of an activity (*vyāpāravyatirekeṇa*); it is eternal (*nitya*); it is single (*eka*); it is all-pervasive (*vibhu*); it is a substance (*dravya*); it is the measure (*parimāṇa*) for things that have actions (*kriyāvat*)."

Helārāja seems to explain that the word *eke* 'some' in this kārikā refers to Vaiśeṣikas. On the basis of this interpretation of Helārāja's, it has so far been generally accepted that, by the kārikā in question, Bhartṛhari intends to introduce the Vaiśeṣika view of time. For example, Sharma (1972: 13) in his synopsis of the Kālasamuddeśa regards the view presented in *VP*3.9.1 as that of Vaiśeṣikas. Iyer (1974: 36) offers the same interpretation, too. Houben (1995: 119) accepts their interpretation, saying the following:

> "Next, in the Kāla-samuddeśa, the Vaiśeṣika-view receives again full attention, as is clear from the first kārikā, which defines it as 'one permanent all-pervasive substance'."

A close look at the Kālasamuddeśa, however, reveals that Bhartṛhari uses the expression *eke pracakṣate* with the conscious intention of viewing time from one of the two points of view from which he considers it in the *Vākyapadīya*. The aim of this paper is thus to show that Bhartṛhari holds that time is twofold: time as a power (*śakti*) and time as a substance (*dravya*) and that in *VP* 3.9.1 he describes the latter kind of time, setting forth his own view of time.

1. *Prakāśa* on *VP* 3.9.1

As a beginning, let us consider the *Prakāśa* on *VP* 3.9.1. Helārāja introduces the kārikā by saying the following:

---

sā svair upādhibhir bhinnā śaktir dig iti kathyate //

[5] *VP* 3.7.1: *svāśraye samavetānāṃ tadvad evāśrayāntare / kriyāṇām abhiniṣpattau sāmarthyaṃ sādhanaṃ viduḥ // VP* 3.8.1: *yāvat siddham asiddhaṃ vā sādhyatvenābhidhīyate / āśritakramarūpatvāt tat kriyeti pratīyate //*

> *Prakāśa* on *VP* 3.9.1: *kriyānantaraṃ kāla uddiṣṭaḥ / sa hi kriyāyāḥ paricchedakaḥ / tatra darśanāntaralakṣitaṃ tāvat tatsvarūpam āha /*
>
> "[In *VP* 3.6.1] time (*kāla*) has been mentioned immediately after action (*kriyā*).[6] For it [i.e., time] is a delimitor of an action. To begin with, [Bhartṛhari] states its essential nature which is defined in another philosophical system (*darśanāntara*)."

It is important to note that Helārāja says, for the purpose of explaining the sequence of the Kriyāsamuddeśa and the Kālasamuddeśa, that time serves as a delimitor of an action. This point will cast light on an intricate problem connected with the present kārikā.

What Helārāja states under the kārikā is as follows:

> *Prakāśa* on *VP* 3.9.1: *parāparādipratyayaliṅgo vyāpaka eko 'mūrto 'ta evākṛtakatvān nityaḥ kālaḥ kriyāvyatirikto janmādikriyādvāreṇa bhāvaparicchedako vaiśeṣikair āmnātaḥ / sa vistaratas tata evāvagantavyaḥ //*
>
> "Time is something known through inference from the cognitions of priority, posteriority and such, omnipresent, single, and incorporeal. For this very reason, time is not something produced but something eternal. And time, being eternal, exists independently of an action; it delimits things (*bhāvaparicchedа*) through actions such as birth. The tradition handed down by Vaiśeṣikas declares that time is of such a nature. The details about time [as conceived of by the Vaiśeṣikas] should be learned just from them."

It is clearly shown here that Helārāja takes the word *eke* as referring to Vaiśeṣikas. According to him, the definition of time by a different philosophical system, namely the Vaiśeṣika, is presented in the kārikā in question.[7]

Now the *Vaiśeṣikasūtra* characterizes time as follows:[8]

---

[6]See note 3 and §4.

[7]*VP* 3.9.1, together with *VP* 3.9.76, is quoted by Bhaṭṭotpala, a contemporary of Helārāja, in his *Vivṛti* on Varāhamihira's *Bṛhatsaṃhitā* 1.7. Bhaṭṭotpala takes these two kārikās as stating the definition of time provided by some Paurāṇikas according to whom time is the cause of cosmic creation and destruction. *VP* 3.9.1 is also cited by Kamalaśīla in his *Tattvasaṃgrahapañjikā* on Śāntarakṣita's *Tattvasaṃgraha* 2300–01. Kamalaśīla says that the kārikā states Kālavādins' view of time, explaining how Bhāṭṭa Mīmāṃsakas, who accept the Kālavādins' view of time according to which time is single, eternal and all-pervasive, account for the division of time.

[8]For the details of the Vaiśeṣika view of time, see Faddegon 1969: 208–21; Halbfass 1992: 205–28.

(1) Time is a single (*tattva* 'unity') and eternal substance;[9]
(2) Time is existent separately from an action.[10]

In addition, the *Praśastapādabhāṣya* describes time as follows:

(3) Time has the properties of having contact with all corporeal entities (*sarvagatatva*),[11] of being of ultimate dimension (*paramamahattva*),[12] and of being a common locus of all corporeal entities (*sarvasaṃyogisamānadeśatva*);[13]
(4) Time is incorporeal (*amūrta*);[14]
(5) Time is a regulative cause (*nimittakāraṇa*) for everything that has an origin (*sarvotpattimat*).[15]

---

[9] *VS* 2.2.7: *dravyatvanityatve vāyunā vyākhyāte //* *VS* 2.2.8 states that the unity of time is explained by the analogy of being (*bhāva*). Being is, according to *VS* 1.2.18, single because of the uniformity of its mark, i.e., the cognition 'is' (*sat*), and because of the absence of any mark of differentiation. *VS* 2.2.8: *tattvaṃ bhāvena //*; *VS* 1.2.18: *salliṅgāviśeṣād viśeṣaliṅgābhāvāc caiko bhāva iti //* Candrānanda, who cites *VS* 1.2.18 at the beginning of his *Vṛtti* on *VS* 2.2.8, paraphrases *tattva* with *ekatva*. *VSV* on *VS* 2.2.8: *yathā salliṅgāviśeṣāt viśeṣaliṅgābhāvāc caiko bhāvas tathā kālaliṅgāviśeṣād viśeṣaliṅgābhāvāc caikaḥ kālaḥ / kālasyaikatve .../*

[10] *VSV* on *VS* 2.2.10: *yadi kriyāvyatiriktaḥ syān nityaḥ kāla evaṃ nityeṣv apy ākāśādiṣu kālaliṅgāni pratibhāseran / anityeṣv eva tu bhavanti / tasmād abhinirvartyamāneṣv evāvadhiḥ kālaḥ / tasmāt kriyaiva kāla iti / naitat, vastunirvṛttyuttarakālabhāvitvāt kālaliṅgāny anityeṣu bhavanti, na tu kriyāyāḥ kālatvāt /* *NK* 66: *na tu prārambhādikriyaiva kālo vilakṣaṇabuddhivedyatvād iti /*

[11] Śrīdhara says that *sarva* of *sarvagatatvam* refers to corporeal entities, which are referred to by *mūrta* in *mūrtatva* of the immediately preceding passage (*PBh* 21: *kṣitijalajyotiranilamanasāṃ kriyāvattvamūrtatvaparatvāparatvavegavattvāni*). He also explains that by *sarvagatatvam* Praśastapāda intends to say that space and so on have contact with all corporeal entities. *NK* 22: *sarvaśabdenātra prakṛtāpekṣayānantaroktāni mūrtadravyāṇi parāmṛśyante / sarvagatatvaṃ sarvair mūrtaiḥ saha saṃyoga ākāśādīnām .../*

[12] What is intended by the expression 'time has the property of being of ultimate dimention (*paramamahattva*)' is that time is not limited by having any particular dimension. *NK* 22: *paramamahattvam iyattānavachinnaparimāṇayogitvam /*

[13] *PBh* 22: *ākāśakāladigātmanāṃ sarvagatatvaṃ paramamahattvaṃ sarvasaṃyogisamānadeśatvaṃ ca //* According to Śrīdhara, *sarvasaṃyogisamānadeśatva* means that space, time, direction (*diś*), and *ātman* are a common locus of all corporeal entities which have contact with them. *NK* 22: *sarvasaṃyogisamānadeśatvaṃ sarveṣāṃ sarvasamyogināṃ mūrtadravyāṇāṃ ākāśaḥ samāno deśa eka ādhāra ity arthaḥ / evaṃ digādiṣv api vyākhyeyam /*

[14] *PBh* 308: *ākāśakāladigātmanāṃ saty api dravyabhāve niṣkriyatvaṃ sāmānyādivad amūrtatvāt /*

[15] *PBh* 25: *dikkālayoḥ pañcaguṇavattvaṃ sarvotpattimatāṃ nimittakāraṇatvaṃ*

Thus we can say that the characterization of time given by the Vaiśeṣikas accords with that given by Helārāja. Helārāja therefore seems to be justified in taking the word *eke* to refer to the Vaiśeṣikas.

2. Analysis of the Kālasamuddeśa

2.1. In order to understand the significance of *VP* 3.9.1, it will be useful to take a general survey of the Kālasamuddeśa at this point. This samuddeśa consists of 114 kārikās. Unlike Sharma (1972: 13–17) and Aklujkar/Potter (1990: 169–71), I will lay stress on making clear the interrelationship among the kārikās.

I. 3.9.1–79
Establishment of time as an essential factor of verbal activities (*vyavahāra*)
   (a) 3.9.1
   Definition of time by *eke*
   (b) 3.9.2
   Time differentiates one action from another.
   (c) 3.9.3–5
   Time, which is eternal (*nitya*) and all-pervasive (*vibhu*), is the cause of coming into being (*janman*), being in a state (*sthiti*), and perishing (*vināśa*): preventing (*pratibandha*) and permitting (*abhyanujñā*) functions of time.[16]
   (d) 3.9.6–8
   Time, which is a substance (*dravya*), is differentiated by an action, which is the property (*dharma*) of the former.
   (e) 3.9.9–26
   Amplification of (c)
   (f) 3.9.27–28
   Time is a single (*eka*) entity that is the measure (*parimāṇa*) of different actions.
   (g) 3.9.29–78
   Amplification of (b) and (d)
      i. 3.9.29–47
      Illustration for the mutual differentiation of time and actions

ca / When a certain entity arises at a specific time, time is said to be the cause of the arising of the entity. That time delimits an entity which has an action means that the entity arises at a specific time. *NK* 25: *idam eva ca deśasya kālasya ca nimittatvaṃ yad ekatra kāryotpattir anyatrānutpattir iti* //

[16]According to Helārāja, time prevents the powers of entities serving as what brings an action to accomplishment from taking effect and permits them to take effect. *Prakāśa* on *VP* 3.9.30: *kasyāścit kriyāyāḥ sādhanaśaktīnāṃ vyāpāravighāte pratibandhaḥ / tadviparyayo 'bhyanujñā* /

ii. 3.9.48–62
Different views on three time divisions: the past (*bhūta*), present (*vartamāna*), future (*bhaviṣyat*)
 A. 3.9.48–52
 The time divisions are the three powers (*śakti*) of time.
 B. 3.9.53–56
 Triguṇa theory and three time divisions
 C. 3.9.57
 Definition of time by *kecit*: time is the mental unification (*buddhyanusaṃhāra*) of component instants (*kalā*).
 D. 3.9.58
 Bhartṛhari's view of time: time, external or mental, is essential in verbal actitivities.
 E. 3.9.59–61
 Pariṇāma theory and three time divisions
 F. 3.9.62
 Different views of time obtain only in the realm of nescience (*avidyā*).

iii. 3.9.63–75
The mutual differentiation of time and actions is a mere conceptualization.

iv. 3.9.76
Definition of time by *kālavid* ('those who are familiar with time'): time is the movements of celestial bodies.

v. 3.9.77–78
An action, which delimits another action, is called 'time'.

(h) 3.9.79
Indirect connection of a substance with time through the action of the substance

II. 3.9.80–114
Grammatical discussions on time
 (a) 3.9.80–90
 MBh on *A* 3.2.123 *vartamāne laṭ*
 (b) 3.9.91–92
 A 3.3.139 *liṅnimitte lṛṅ kriyātipattau* and *A* 3.3.140 *bhūte ca*
 (c) 3.9.93–101
 MBh on *A* 3.4.1 *dhātusambandhe pratyayāḥ*
 (d) 3.9.102
 A 3.3.131 *vartamānasāmīpye vartamānavad vā*
 (e) 3.9.103–105
 A 3.3.132 *āśaṃsāyāṃ bhūtavac ca*
 (f) 3.9.106–114
 MBh on *A* 3.3.133 *kṣipravacane lṛṭ*

2.2. What is immediately apparent in the analysis is as follows: The Kālasamuddeśa consists of two sections, the first of which (I: *VP* 3.9.1–79) discusses various aspects of time as an essential factor for verbal activities and the second of which (II: *VP* 3.9.80–114) deals with grammatical discussions concerning tense, which relates the meaning of a verb to time in the past, present, or future.[17] For our purpose, it is sufficient to consider section I.

Section I is also further divided into two parts: one ((a)) in which the view of time held by *eke* is presented and the other ((b)–(h)) in which this view is amplified. What Bhartṛhari argues in part (b)–(h) is the following. First, time differentiates an action from another ((b)). Time is a differentiator of an action because it is a measure of the action. Secondly, time, which is eternal and all-pervasive, delimits an action through functioning as the cause of an action ((c)), so that a certain thing is said to arise at a specific time. Thirdly, time in turn, as a substance, is differentiated by an action which is its property ((d)), in consequence of which one may have concepts such as the time of coming into being (*utpattikāla*), the time of remaining in a state (*sthitikāla*), and the time of perishing (*vināśakāla*). To be a substance is to be what is to be differentiated.[18] Fourthly, time is a single entity which is the measure of different actions ((f)). Accordingly one may have concepts such as 'quick' (*kṣipra*) movement and 'slow' (*cira*) movement. Lastly, time is indirectly connected with a substance through an action which abides in the substance. Thus in the usage *bhūto ghaṭaḥ* 'the pot is past', since the act of being, which is denoted by the verb *bhū* is referred to past time, an agent with respect to this act, the pot, is also said to be referred to past time ((h)).

It is clear that the second part (I-(b)–(h)), devoted to discussing various aspects of the time which is considered to be an essential factor for verbal activities, is intended to describe in detail the characteristics of time which are mentioned in the first kārikā. See the following:

(1) *kriyāvatparimāṇa*: Time is the measure of things that have actions. (*VP* 3.9.3) [I-(c)]

(2) *vyāpāravyatireka*: Time has as its property an action which is distinct from it. (*VP* 3.9.6) [I-(d)]

(3) *dravya*: Time is a substance. (*VP* 3.9.7) [I-(d)]

(4) *nitya*: Time is eternal. (*VP* 3.9.10) [I-(e)]

(5) *vibhu*: Time is all-pervasive. (*VP* 3.9.14) [I-(e)]

(6) *eka*: Time is single. (*VP* 3.9.27) [I-(f)]

[17] For a full account of grammatical discussions concerning tense, see Cardona 1991.

[18] On Bhartṛhari's concept of substance (*dravya*), see §5.

Relevant kārikās run as follows:

> (c) *kriyāvatparimāṇa VP* 3.9.3: *utpattau ca sthitau caiva vināśe cāpi tadvatām / nimittaṃ kālam evāhur vibhaktenātmanā sthitaṁ //*
>
> "They consider that time, established as divided (*vibhakta*), is the cause of coming into being (*utpatti*), being in a state (*sthiti*), and perishing (*vināśa*) of things which go through these states."[19]
>
> (d) *vyāpāravyatireka VP* 3.9.6: *tasyātmā bahudhā bhinno bhedair dharmāntarāśrayaiḥ / na hi bhinnam abhinnaṃ vā vastu kiṃcana vidyate //*
>
> "[Time] itself is differentiated in many ways on the basis of the divisions which reside in properties [i.e., actions] different from it. No entity is something identical or different in itself."[20].
>
> (d) *dravya VP* 3.9.7: *naiko na cāpy aneko 'sti na śuklo nāpi cāsitaḥ / dravyātmā sa tu saṃsargād evaṃrūpaḥ prakāśate //*.
>
> "A substance is neither one nor many, neither white nor black in itself. The substance appears in such a manner on the basis of its relation [with properties different from it]."[21]
>
> (e) *nitya VP* 3.9.10: *janmābhivyaktiniyamāḥ prayogopanibandhanāḥ / nityādhīnasthititvāc ca sthitir niyamapūrvikā //*
>
> " The limitations on [things] coming into being or being manifested [at particular moments] are dependent on [something's]

[19]The point made here is the same as the Vaiśeṣika view of time (5). See §1. According to Helārāja, when functioning as the cause of the arising of an entity, time is said to delimit the entity in such a way that this entity comes into being just at a particular time. *Prakāśa* on *VP* 3.9.3: *janmasthitivinaśaḥ samastakriyākalāpāntarbhāvanahetava iti taddvāreṇa janmādimatāṃ padārthānāṃ nimittakāraṇaṃ kālam āhuḥ / tadapekṣo hi padārthānām udayādir avatiṣṭhate pravibhaktaśarīraḥ / tathā hi / kecid vasante prasūyante, apare śaradi, prāvṛṣy anya ityādi vācyam / evaṃ sthitivināśayor api /*

[20]According to Helārāja, Bhatṛhari means an action (*kriyā*) by the term *dharma* 'property'. *Prakāśa* on *VP* 3.9.6: *dharmāntarāṇi vakṣyamāṇāni saṃsargīṇi kriyārūpāṇi /* Vaiśeṣikas also state that time, which is single and eternal, is differentiated by various actions. *VS* 2.2.9: *kāryaviśeṣeṇa nānātvam //* In his *Vṛtti* on the sūtra, Candrānanda notes that *kārya* refers to an action (*kriyā*). *VSV* on *VS* 2.2.9: *kāryaṃ kriyā, . . . /*

[21]In this kārikā Bhartṛhari intends to apply his definition of *dravya* 'substance' to time. See §5.

causing [these];[22] [things] remaining in states is also [necessarily] subject to limitation, [which, one concludes,] is because this is dependent on a permanent [entity, namely time] ."

(e) *vibhu VP*3.9.14: *jalayantrabhramāveśasadṛśībhiḥ pravṛttibhiḥ / sa kalāḥ kalayan sarvāḥ kālākhyāṃ labhate vibhuḥ //*

"Through activities similar to the motion imparted by the turning of the water-wheel, time, being all-pervasive, sets into play (*kalayati*) all the fragments (*kalā*) [of the universe]; thus, time is called *kāla*."

(f) *eka VP* 3.9.27: *kriyayor apavargiṇyor nānārthasamavetayoḥ/ saṃbandhinā vinaikena paricchedaḥ kathaṃ bhavet //*

"Of two actions which are brought to completion [after beginning] and which inhere in different entities, how could one make delimitation [such that one is slow and the other is quick] without their being related to a single entity [i.e., time]?"

Thus we see that the six characteristics of time given in *VP* 3.9.1 are elaborately explained by subsequent kārikās.

2.3. It is important to note that in (g) two definitions of time are mentioned: one by *kecit* 'some' and the other by a kālavid. In the former definition, time is held to be not an external entity but a mental unification (*buddhyanusaṃhāra*).[23] In this connection *VP* 3.9.58 ((g)–ii–D) is to be noted. In the kārikā Bhartṛhari states that time, be it external or mental, is an essential factor for verbal activities, implying that

[22]In *VP* 3.9.9 Bhartṛhari says that time functions as the cause which sets powers into activity (*śaktīnāṃ saṃprayogasya hetuḥ*). According to Helārāja, the powers are those which are attributed to entities serving as what bring an action to accomplishment (*sādhana*). *Prakāśa* on *VP* 3.9.9: *vasantādikāle sādhanaśaktīnāṃ pravṛttidarśanāt tāsāṃ prayojako hetur nimittakāraṇaṃ kāla unnīyate /*

[23]*VP* 3.9.57: *kalābhiḥ pṛthagarthābhiḥ pravibhaktaṃ svabhāvataḥ / kecid buddhyanusaṃhāralakṣaṇaṃ taṃ pracakṣate //* ("Of time some say (*kecit pracakṣate*): time, which is in essence divided into parts with separate purposes, is characterized by mental unification.") The view of time presented here closely parallels the Yoga school's. According to this school, time divisions such as an hour and a day, which brings about verbal expression such as 'an hour' and 'a day', have an unreal status since they are simply the moments mentally unified by the mental activity of gathering together; a moment alone is a real entity. *YSBh* on *YS* 3.52: *kṣaṇatatkramayor nāsti vastusamāhāra iti buddhisamāhāro muhūrtāhorātrādayaḥ / sa khalv ayaṃ kālo vastuśūnyo buddhinirmāṇaḥ śabdajñānānupātī laukikānāṃ vyutthitadarśanānāṃ vastusvarūpa ivāvabhāsate/ kṣaṇas tu vastupatitaḥ kramāvalambī, .../*

in *VP* 3.9.1 time is defined on the assumption that it is an external entity.[24] In the latter definition, time is considered to be not an entity existing independently of an action but the movements of heavenly bodies (*ādityagrahanakṣatraparispanda*) themselves.[25] Thus we find three different definitions of time in the Kālasamuddeśa: the first that is attributed to the Vaiśeṣika; the second to 'some' (probably the followers of Yoga); the third to kālavids (astronomers).

2.4. As shown above, section I consists of the part in which the definition of time by *eke* is given and the part in which the amplification of this definition is made. I have pointed out in §1 that Helārāja takes the word *eke* to refer to Vaiśeṣikas. Does this mean that in the Kālasamuddeśa Bhartṛhari devotes himself largely to expounding the Vaiśeṣika view of time? It is unlikely that he does not advance his own view of time there. To be sure, Helārāja states that the view of time presented in *VP* 3.9.1 is what is traditionally accepted in the Vaiśeṣika system (*vaiśeṣikair āmnātaḥ*). But this does not necessarily mean that the view is proper to the Vaiśeṣika system.

Rather, it is reasonable to think that the view put forward by Bhartṛhari can be shared by this system, which can easily account for the fact that the characteristics of time mentioned in *VP* 3.9.1 are described in detail in subsequent kārikās.

---

[24] *VP* 3.9.58: *jñānānugataśaktiṃ vā bāhyaṃ vā satyataḥ sthitam / kālātmānam anāśritya vyavahartuṃ na śakyate //* ("One cannot have a verbal activity without resorting to time itself, whether it be something whose power is what accompanies a cognition or what externally exists in reality.") According to Helārāja, what is meant by the term *jñānānugata* is a mental image (*buddhyākāra*). *Prakāśa* on *VP* 3.9.58: *jñāne buddhāv anugatās tadākārās śaktayaś cirakṣipravartamānādibhedarūpā yasyāsau* . . . / This mental image is a power in that it brings about verbal expressions. Thus, according to Helārāja, Bhartṛhari intends to say by using the term *jñānānugataśakti* that time has a mental existence. Helārāja paraphrases the term *jñānānugataśakti* as *buddhyanusaṃhāramātrasvabhāva* '[time which] is in essence mere mental unification'. *Prakāśa* on *VP* 3.9.58: *yasyāsav evaṃvidho buddhyanusaṃhāramātrasvabhāvo vāstu kālo* . . . /

[25] *VP* 3.9.76: *ādityagrahanakṣatraparispandam athāpare / bhinnam āvṛttibhedena kālaṃ kālavido vidhuḥ //* ("Other knowers of time (*kālavid*) declare that time consists in the movements of the sun, planets, and stars which are distinguished from one another by the recurrence [of the rising and setting of heavenly bodies at particular moments].") In the kālavid's view, the movement of heavenly bodies such as the sun is time. It is reasonable to assume that the view of time entertained by the kālavid is closely related to that of astronomers or astrologers.

3. Time as a power (*śakti*)

Let us now suppose that Bhartṛhari sets forth his view of time, which is acceptable to the Vaiśeṣika system, in the first kārikā of the Kālasamuddeśa. There still occurs a question: Why does he use the expression *eke pracakṣate* in presenting his view? In order to answer this question, we must note that Bhartṛhari views time as a power (*śakti*) in the Brahmakāṇḍa.

In *VP* 1.3 and the *Vṛtti* thereupon, Bhartṛhari says the following:

> *VP* 1.3: *adhyāhitakalāṃ yasya kālaśaktim upāśritāḥ / janmādayo vikārāḥ ṣaḍ bhāvabhedasya yonayaḥ //*
>
> *Vṛtti* on *VP* 1.3: *kālākhyena hi svātantryeṇa sarvāḥ paratantrā janmavatyaḥ śaktayaḥ samāviṣṭāḥ kālaśaktivṛttim anupatanti /*
>
> "Depending on whose [i.e., Brahman's] time-power on which parts are superimposed, six modifications (*vikāra*),[26] which are coming into being and so forth, take place. The six modifications are the sources (*yoni*) of specific actions (*bhāvabheda*)."
>
> "By virtue of the power of functioning independently (*svātantrya*), called time, effective things (*śakti*),[27] which are those whose activities depend on factors other than time and hence are causally conditioned (*janmavat*), come into play (*samāviṣṭa*); consequently, they are what follow the activities of the time power."

The important point to note here is that Bhartṛhari declares that time is a power (*śakti*). The time power, depending on which six modifications of action (*bhāva*) take place, is attributed to Śabdabrahman. Vṛṣabha, in his *Paddhati*, glosses the term *bhāva* with the term *dhātvartha* 'a meaning denoted by a verb' and explains that a specific action such as cooking (*pāka*) is meant by the term *bhāvabheda*.[28] This shows that the time power conceived of by Bhartṛhari is the one which brings about specific actions that are to be denoted by verbs. This amounts to saying that the time power is an essential factor for verbal activities.[29]

[26]The six modes of modifications of action (*bhāva*), according to Yāska, are coming into being (*janman*), being in a state (*sthiti*), undergoing change (*vipariṇāma*), growing (*vṛddhi*), diminishing (*apakṣaya*), and perishing (*vināśa*). *Nirukta* 1.2: *ṣaḍ bhāvavikārā bhavantīti vārṣyāyaṇir jāyate 'sti vipariṇamate vardhate 'pakṣīyate vinaśyatīti /*

[27]Vṛṣbha, in his *Paddhati*, glosses the term *śakti* with *padārtha* 'thing, entity'. *Paddhati* on *Vṛtti* to *VP* 1.3: *śaktayaḥ iti / padārthāḥ /*

[28]*Paddhati* on *VP* 1.3: *bhāvabhedasya iti / bhāvaḥ sattvaṃ dhātvarthaḥ, tasya bhedaḥ pacādikriyāḥ tāsām /*

[29]It is interesting to note that in *VP* 1.3 Bhartṛhari describes time as that upon

In the *Vṛtti* this power is said to be the power of functioning independently (*svātantrya*). According to Vṛṣabha, the term *svātantrya* here means *kartṛśakti* 'the power of functioning as agent'.[30] An agent (*kartṛ*), in Pāṇinīyas' view, is a participant in an act (*kāraka*) which sets other participants such as object (*karman*), instrument (*karaṇa*) and locus (*adhikaraṇa*) into play (*pravartaka*).[31] The power Bhartṛhari calls *svātantrya* is, therefore, the power which sets things in the universe into play. In Bhartṛhari's view, not to mention, the things in the universe are simply those which enter the universe of discourse.[32]

In *VP* 3.9.14 also Bhartṛhari touches on time as such a power.[33] Under the kārikā Helārāja states:

> *Prakāśa* on *VP* 3.9.14: *anenaitat sūcayati / viśvātmaika eva parabrahmābhidhānaḥ satyo bhāvaḥ / sa eva nānāvidhakāryakāritayānantaśaktitvena vyavahriyate / tathā ca kramikāṃś cakrabhramavat parāvartamānān bhāvān prakāśayan kālayati bhūtānīti kāla ity ucyate / sa vibhuḥ svatantraḥ / ata eva svātantryaśaktiḥ kāla iti vākyapadīye siddhāntitam / adhyāhitakalāṃ yasya kālaśaktim upāśritāḥ ity atra /*
>
> " Hereby [Bhartṛhari] indicates the following: The essence of the universe is the one and only real entity called Parabrahman. This very entity is spoken of as having an infinite number of powers because of bringing about multiple results. This being the case, the entity is called *kāla* 'time', since it sets [all] things in the universe (*bhūta*) into play (*kālayati*), manifesting the entities which occur in a sequence and which rotate like a wheel. The entity is all-pervasive and hence something independent (*svatantra*) [with respect to all things in the universe]. For this very reason it is established in *VP* 1.3 of the *Vākyapadīya* that time is the power of functioning independently (*svātantryaśakti*)."

---

which parts are superimposed. Time cannot bring about specific actions insofar as it remains single. In order to function as an essential factor for verbal activities, time should be divided. As we will see in §5, Bhartṛhari makes this point in *VP* 3.9.3.

[30] *Paddhati* on *Vṛtti* to *VP* 1.3: *svātantryaṃ kartṛśaktiḥ /*

[31] For a full account of the Pāṇinīyas' view of an agent, see Ogawa 2006.

[32] In Bhartṛhari's view, one absolute reality, or Śabdabrahman, appears (*prakāśate*) as manifold (*bahurūpaḥ*) in order to be conveyed by words (*śabdavācyatve*). *VP* 3.3.87: *tasmāc chaktivibhāgena nityaḥ sadasadātmakaḥ / eko 'rthaḥ śabdavācyatve bahurūpaḥ prakāśate //* The universe is nothing other than this manifold appearance of the one absolute reality.

[33] See §2.2.

According to Helārāja, time (*kāla*) is what sets all things in the universe into play (*kālayati* = *pravartayati*),[34] so that it has the characteristic of being an agent, or that of functioning independently. This is exactly what Bhartṛhari says in *VP* 1.3. It is to be noted that, in Bhartṛhari's view, in reality there does not exist time-power separately from Brahman since the power is a mere assumption and hence unreal.[35]

4. Power as it really is and power as it is spoken of

It has been shown that time has the nature of being a power. In this connection it is highly important to note that in Bhartṛhari's view a power is something that has the status of being absolutely dependent (*paratantra*) and hence to be sharply distinguished from a substance (*dravya*), which has the status of being independent (*svatantra*).

Besides time, according to Bhartṛhari, there are abstracted meanings (*apoddhārārtha*) that consist in being a power: they are direction (*diś*), what brings an action to accomplishment (*sādhana*), an action (*kriyā*), and a relation (*sambandha*).

To begin with, let us note the following kārikā:

> *VP* 3.6.1: *dik sādhanaṃ kriyā kāla iti vastvabhidhāyinaḥ / śakti-rūpe padārthānām atyantam anavasthitāḥ //*
>
> "The terms *diś* 'direction', *sādhana* 'what brings an action to accomplishment', *kriyā* 'action', and *kāla* 'time' denote substances (*vastu*). They absolutely do not refer to the power aspect of the entities in question."

According to Bhartṛhari, the nominals *diś*, *sādhana*, *kriyā*, and *kāla* do not refer to direction and so on as powers. For nominals denote substances. In his view, an entity which is a power cannot be referred to as power on account of its dependent nature; therefore, the entity must be substantialized, or treated like a substance, so as to be verbalized.[36]

---

[34] *Prakāśa* ad *VP* 3.9.14: ... *parāvartamānasya kālasya punaḥ punar vasantādi-bhāvenāvṛttayaḥ tābhir ayaṃ vibhuḥ vyāpako nityo 'pi vikalpayati vikṣipati kalāḥ bhāvaparyāyāḥ samutsṛjati svakāraṇebhyaḥ pravartayatīti ... /*

[35] In his *Vṛtti* Bhartṛhari says that the powers of Śabdabrahman are defined neither as identical with it (*tattva*) nor as different from it (*anyatva*) and neither as existent (*sattva*) nor as non-existent (*asattva*). *Vṛtti* on *VP* 1.4: *ekasya hi brahmaṇas tattvānyatvābhyāṃ sattvāsattvābhyāṃ cāniruktāvirodhiśakty-upagrāhyasya ... /* According to Vṛṣabha, the powers of such a character are what is not real but conceptualized. *Paddhati* on *Vṛtti* to *VP* 1.1: *śaktīnāṃ ca svarūpatve tattvānyatvavicāraṇā / yujyate kalpitānāṃ tu yuktānvayavivartatā //*

[36] For a full account of this theme, see Ogawa 2009.

Concerning a relation, it is interesting to note the following *Vṛtti* on *VP* 2.441,[37] since Bhartṛhari there uses expressions similar to *eke pracakṣate* in order to distinguish the way in which a relation is spoken of (*śabdārtha*) and that in which it really is (*vastvartha*).

> *Vṛtti* on *VP* 2.441: (a) ... *tatra bhedadarśanam āśritya kaiścid ucyate pratipadārthaṃ tasyātmā vyavasthita iti /*
>
> (b) *kecid āhuḥ / nityaṃ*[38] *paropakārarūpatvād iha vyavasthita iti vyavahāra evāyaṃ tatra nāsti / na hy asau śaktimadrūpeṇa*[39] *kadācid avatiṣṭhate / śaktirūpa evāsau kāryaprasavasūcita iti /*
>
> "(a) In regard to this relation (*tatra*), some say, on the basis of the experience of the division of speech into components (*bhedadarśana*), that the essence of the relation is established as residing in each word meaning[, namely that the meanings of words in a sentence are related to one another].
>
> (b) [Similarly, on the basis of such experience,] others say the following. Of the relation, one does not have the very verbal expression '[The relation] is established as residing here' (*iha vyavasthitaḥ*), since [a relation] is what always renders service to others (*paropakārarūpa*). Indeed, such a relation is never established as a power-holder (*śaktimat*). The relation, which is essentially a power (*śakti*), is indicated by the arising of an effect."

It is important to note that with reference to a relation as a sentence meaning two views are dealt with here.

> (1) *bhedadarśanam āśritya kaiścid ucyate pratipadārthaṃ tasyātmā vyavasthita iti /*
>
> (2) *kecid āhuḥ / nityaṃ paropakārarūpatvād iha vyavasthita iti vyavahāra evāyaṃ tatra nāsti /*

The point made by Bhartṛhari here is clear. A relation, which always renders service to others and hence has the status of being absolutely dependent, is a power, so that of the relation, one cannot have verbal expressions such as 'It is established as residing here' (*iha vyavasthitaḥ*), for such an expression can be made only of a power-holder (*śaktimat*), namely, a substance. However,

[37] On the text and translation of the *Vṛtti* on *VP* 2.441, see Ogawa forthcoming. The text in question given by Ogawa is based on Prof. Ashok Aklujkar's unpublished critical edition of the *Vṛtti*.

[38] Iyer: *nitye*.

[39] Iyer: *śaktipakṣeṇa*.

when one speaks of a relation by using a particular nominal term such as *abhisambandha*, one can have verbal expressions as such. On this occasion, a relation is signified by such a nominal term after it is substantialized.

What Bhartṛhari states in the above-cited *Vṛtti* accords with what he states in the Sambandhasamuddeśa.

> *VP* 3.3.1: *jñānaṃ prayoktur bāhyo 'rthaḥ svarūpaṃ ca pratīyate / śabdair uccaritais teṣāṃ sambandhaḥ samavasthitaḥ //*
>
> *VP* 3.3.5: *upakārāt sa yatrāsti dharmas tatrānugamyate / śaktīnām api sā śaktir guṇānām apy asau guṇaḥ //*
>
> "The cognition of the speaker, the external thing meant and the own form [of the word] are understood through words which are uttered. The relation of these (namely, the cognition, external thing meant and own form) [with the words which are uttered] is well-established."
>
> "Where this [relation] is, because some service is rendered [from one thing to another, or: from signifier to signified and vice versa], there one arrives at a property (viz. dependence) [but not at the relation itself]. It is even a capacity (i.e. something dependent) of capacities [which are themselves dependent upon the entity which possesses the capacity]; it is even a quality (i.e. something dependent) of qualities [which are themselves dependent upon the entity which possesses the quality] [so it is extremely dependent]."[40]

We may introduce *VP* 3.3.1 and 3.3.5 by saying *kaiścid ucyate* and *kecid āhuḥ*, respectively. It is clear that Bhartṛhari distinguishes two levels of relation: the relation as it is spoken of and the relation as it really is.

5. Time as a substance

It is to be recalled that Bhartṛhari characterizes time as a substance in *VP* 3.9.1. We must say that in the *Vākyapadīya* Bhartṛhari approaches time from different angles, viewing it differently, as a power and as a substance. This may imply, therefore, that Bhartṛhari uses the expression *eke pracakṣate* in *VP* 3.9.1 in order to show this distinction.

Now let us consider why Bhartṛhari defines time as a substance in *VP* 3.9.1. In my opinion this point cannot be emphasized too strongly.

---

[40]Translation by Houben 1995: 145, 170. The term *dharma* 'property' in *VP* 3.3.5 refers to the property of being absolutely dependent (*atyantaparatantratva*) mentioned in *VP* 3.3.4: *nābhidhānaṃ svadharmeṇa sambandhasyāsti vācakam / atyantaparatantratvād rūpaṃ nāsyāpadiśyate //*

Bhartṛhari says that there are two kinds of substance (*dravya*): in Helārāja's terminology, *pāramārthika-dravya* 'ultimate substance' and *sāṃvyavahārika-dravya* 'conventional substance'.[41] The former corresponds to Brahman and the latter is what can be referred to by demonstratives such as 'this' or 'that'. It is the latter type of substance that Bhartṛhari means by the term *dravya* in *VP* 3.9.1. The following kārikā which defines the conventional substance is to be considered.

> *VP* 3.4.3: *vastūpalakṣaṇaṃ yatra sarvanāma prayujyate / dravyam ity ucyate so 'rtho bhedyatvena vivakṣitaḥ //*
>
> "An object, with reference to which a demonstrative pronoun referring to a thing is used[42] and which is intended to be conveyed as something to be differentiated [by a quality], is called substance."[43]

What is important here is to note that the substance is what is intended to be conveyed as something to be differentiated by a quality (*guṇa*).

In the Vaiśeṣika system a substance is defined as having actions and qualities and serving as an inherential cause.[44] Bhartṛhari also accepts that a substance is what bears actions and qualities. But, for Bhartṛhari, what is treated as a substance is posited in dependence on a speaker's intention. Of two entities which are related to each other, if one entity is intended to be conveyed as something to be differentiated (*bhedya*) by the other, the former is treated as a substance and the latter as a quality (*guṇa*). Thus, in Bhartṛhari's view, even something conceived as an action or quality in the Vaiśeṣika system can be regarded as a substance, if they are intended to be conveyed as what is to be differentiated. For example, in the utterance *paṭasya rūpam* 'the color of the cloth', the color which is related to the cloth is differentiated from the one which is related to other things, so that the color in question, though being a quality in the Vaiśeṣika system, is treated as a substance and the cloth in question, though being a substance in the

---

[41] *Prakāśa* on *VP* 3.4.3: *dravyaṃ ca dvividham, pāramārthikaṃ sāṃvyavahārikaṃ ca /* Bhartṛhari discusses these two kinds of substance in the Dravyasamuddeśa (*pāramārthikaṃ dravyam*) and in the Bhūyodravyasamuddeśa (*sāṃvyavahārikaṃ dravyam*), respectively.

[42] Just as Bhartṛhari has two concepts of *dravya*, so also does he have two concepts of *vastu*. The terms *dravya* and *vastu* are synonymous with each other, so that the term *vastu* refers not only to the ultimate reality (see *VP* 3.2.1) but also to what can be denoted by a nominal. The term *vastu* mentioned in this kārikā and *VP* 3.9.6 refers to the latter.

[43] Kobayashi 2009: 484.

[44] *VS* 1.1.14: *kriyāvad guṇavat samavāyikāraṇam iti dravyalakṣaṇam //*

same system, is treated as a quality.[45]

As shown in §2, in *VP* 3.9.6 Bhartṛhari states that time, which is a single entity, is differentiated in many ways on the basis of different actions which are properties (*dharma*) that are different from and related to time. Thus time claims to be a substance in that it is something to be differentiated.

However, we have to note here what is said in *VP* 3.9.2.

> *VP* 3.9.2: *diṣṭiprasthasuvarṇādi mūrtibhedāya kalpate / kriyābhedāya kālas tu saṃkhyā sarvasya bhedikā //*
>
> "The length measure *diṣṭi*, the capacity measure *prastha*, the weight measure *suvarṇa* and the like serve to differentiate one corporeal thing from another. Time serves to differentiate one action from another. Number serves as a differentiator for everything."

In the kārikā Bhartṛhari states that time differentiates an action from another (*bhedāya kalpate*), namely that time is a differentiator (*bhedaka*) of an action.

Bhartṛhari, however, defines time as a single entity. As a single entity, how can time serve as a differentiator of an action? *VP* 3.9.3, which has already been quoted in §2.2, affords a clue for solving this problem.

A certain flower puts forth its buds in spring and another in fall. According to *VP* 3.9.3, such a situation can be explained in terms of time: time divisions such as spring and fall serve as the cause of the birth of the buds. Helārāja explicitly addresses this point as follows:

> *Prakāśa* on *VP* 3.9.3: *upādhibhedāc ca bhidyamānaḥ kālaḥ saṃsargiṣu bhedāyālam //*
>
> "Time, when differentiated according to different delimiting factors, make a difference among things that are related to it (*saṃsargin*)."

The delimiting factor of time is an action, which in turn, related to time, is differentiated by time.[46] Thus time does not become a qualifier of an action until the former is qualified by the latter.

---

[45] *Prakāśa* on *VP* 3.11.7: *tathā ca dravyavad guṇo 'pi paṭasya rūpam iti svātantryeṇābhidhīyamānaḥ saṃsargisaṃkhyādikṛtopakāra evābhidhīyate /*

[46] In this case time can be taken as a quality (*guṇa*) of the action. For Bhartṛhari whatever is related to a certain entity (*saṃsargin*) and carries out the activity of differentiating the entity (*bhedaka*) is treated as a quality. *VP* 3.5.1: *saṃsargi bhedakaṃ yad yat savyāpāraṃ pratīyate / guṇatvaṃ paratantratvāt tasya śāstra udāhṛtam //*

All this shows that time must be a substance so that it has divisions and that with time divisions one can have expressions which denote actions referred to a specific time.

Conclusion

We have seen that in his *Vākyapadīya* Bhartṛhari deals with time in two different ways: as a power and as a substance. Time as a power, attributed to Śabdabrahman, underlies verbal expressions whose core meaning is an action which is denoted by a verb and which is referred to a specific time. Bhartṛhari discusses this type of time in the Brahmakāṇḍa. Time as a substance, on the other hand, is what is referred to by words such as *bhūta* 'past', *vartamāna* 'present', *bhaviṣyat* 'future', and *saṃvatsara* 'year'. He discusses this type of time in the Kālasamuddeśa.

What is important is that he defines time as a substance in *VP* 3.9.1. Time as a substance, being a single entity, is what is to be differentiated by an action which in turn is what is to be differentiated by time. Time as a substance has divisions so that such words as *bhūta* may be meaningful.

In *VP* 3.9.1 Bhartṛhari uses the expression *eke pracakṣate*. This is for the purpose of showing that in the Kālasamuddeśa he deals with time on the assumption of time divisions. *VP* 3.9.1 is the kārikā in which he advances his own view of a 'conventional' time.

References and abbreviations

Āranya, Swāmi H.

1963 *Yoga Philosophy of Patañjali*. Calcutta: University of Calcutta Press.

Aklujkar, Ashok, and Karl H. Potter

1990 Bhartṛhari. In *Encyclopedia of Indian Philosophy, vol. V: The Philosophy of the Grammarians*, edited by Harold G. Coward and K. Kunjunni Raja, 121–74. Princeton: Princeton University Press. [We understand that Potter wrote the post-Sādhanasamuddeśa summary.]

Bṛhatsaṃhitā: Varāhamihira's *Bṛhatsaṃhitā*. See Pāṇḍeya 2002.

Cardona, George

1991 A path still taken: some early Indian arguments concerning time. *Journal of the American Oriental Society* 111 (3): 445–64.

Dvivedin, V. Prasad

1984 *Praśastapāda Bhāṣya with Commentary Nyāyakandali of Śrīdhara*. 2nd ed. Sri Garib Dass Oriental Series 13. Delhi: Sri Satguru Publications.

Faddegon, B.

1969 *The Vaiśeṣika-system, Described with the Help of the Oldest Texts.* Wiesbaden: Dr. Martin Sändig oHC.

Halbfass, Wilhelm

1992 *On Being and What There Is: Classical Vaiśeṣika and the History of Indian Ontology.* New York: State University of New York Press. Reprinted, 1993, Delhi: Sri Satguru Publications.

Jambuvijaya

1961 *Vaiśeṣikasūtra of Kaṇāda with the Commentary of Candrānanda.* Gaekward's Oriental Series 136. Baroda: Oriental Institute.

Kobayashi, Yoshie

2009 All words denote the universal (jāti): Bhartṛhari's approach. In *Bhartṛhari: Language, Thought and Reality (Proceedings of the International Seminar, Delhi, December 12–14, 2003)*, edited by Mithilesh Chaturvedi, 483–97. Delhi: Motilal Banarsidass.

Krishnamacharya, E.

1926 *Tattvasaṃgraha of Śāntarakṣita with the Commentary of Kamalaśīla Vol. II.* Gaekward's Oriental Series 31. Baroda: Oriental Institute.

Nirukta: Yāska's *Nirukta*. See Sarup 1967.

NK: Śrīdhara's *Nyāyakandalī*. See Dvivedin 1984.

Ogawa, Hideyo

2006 Being an agent . *The Annals of the Research Project Center for the Comparative Study of Logic* 4: 93–99.

2009 On Bhartṛhari's notion of 'power' (śakti). In *Bhartṛhari: Language, Thought and Reality (Proceedings of the International Seminar, Delhi, December 12–14, 2003)*, edited by Mithilesh Chaturvedi, 225–252. Delhi: Motilal Banarsidass.

forthcoming Patañjali's view of a sentence meaning and its acceptance by Bhartṛhari. In Johannes Bronkhorst Festshcrift.

Paddhati: Vṛṣabha's *Paddhati*. See Iyer 1966.

Pāṇḍeya, Nāgendra

2002 *Bṛhatsaṃhitā by Śrīvarāhamihirācārya with the Commentary of Bhaṭṭotpala and Hindi Commentary by Ācārya Nāgendra Pāṇḍeya.* Gaṅganāthajhā-Granthamālā 20. Varanasi: Sampurnanand Sanskrit University.

PBh: Praśastapāda's *Praśastapādabhāṣya*. See Dvivedin 1984.

Prakāśa: Helārāja's *Prakīrṇaprakāśa*. See Iyer 1963, 1973.

Raghunātha Śarmā

1979 *Vākyapadīyam, Part III , Vol. II (Bhūyodravya, Guṇa, Dik, Sādhana, Kriyā, Kāla, Puruṣa, Saṃkhyā, Upagraha and Liṅga Samuddeśa) with the Commentary Prakāśa by Helārāja and Ambākartrī by Pt. Raghunātha Śarmā.* Sarasvatībhavana-Granthamālā 91. Varanasi: Sampurnanand Sanskrit University.

Rau, Wilhelm
1977 *Bhartṛharis Vākyapadīya. Die Mūlakārikās nach den Handschriften herausgegeben und mit einem Pāda-Index versehen.* Abhandlungen für die Kunde des Morgenlandes 42, 4. Wiesbaden: Franz Steiner Verlag.
2002 *Bhartṛharis Vākyapadīya. Versuch einer vollständigen deutschen Übersetzung nach der kritischen Edition der Mūla-Kārikās, herausgegeben von Oskar von Hinüber.* Abhandlungen der Akademie der Wissenschaften und der Literatur 8. Stuttgart: Franz Steiner Verlag.

Sarup, Lakshman
1927 *The Nighaṇṭu and the Nirukta.* Lahore: University of the Panjab. Reprinted, 1967, Delhi: Motilal Banarsidass.

Sharma, Peri S.
1972 *The Kālasamuddeśa of Bhartṛhari's Vākyapadīya.* Delhi: Motilal Banarsidass.

Subramania Iyer, K. A.
1963 *Vākyapadīya of Bahrtṛhari with the Commentary of Helārāja, Kāṇḍa III, Part I.* Deccan College Monograph Series 21. Poona: Deccan College.
1966 *Vākyapadīya of Bhartṛhari with the Commentaries Vṛtti and the Paddhati of Vṛṣabhadeva, Kāṇḍa I.* Deccan College Monograph Series 32. Poona: Deccan College.
1973 *Vākyapadīya of Bahrtṛhari with the Prakīrṇaprakāśa of Helārāja, Kāṇḍa III, Part II.* Poona: Deccan College.
1974 *The Vākyapadīya of Bahrtṛhari, chapter III, part ii: English Translation with Exegetical Notes.* Delhi: Motilal Banarsidass.
1983 *The Vākyapadīya of Bhartṛhari (An Ancient Treatise on the Philosophy of Sanskrit Grammar), Containing the Ṭīkā of Puṇyarāja and the Ancient Vṛtti, Kāṇḍa II, with a foreword by Ashok Aklujkar.* Delhi: Motilal Banarsidass.

TS: Śāntarakṣita's *Tattvasaṃgraha*. See Krishnamacharya 1926.
TSP: Kamalaśīla's *Tattvasaṃgrahapañjikā*. See Krishnamacharya 1926.
Vivṛti: Bhaṭṭotpala's *Vivṛti*. See Paṇḍeya 2002.
VP: Bhartṛhari's *Vākyapadīya*. See Rau 1977.
Vṛtti: *Vākyapadīya Vṛtti*. See Iyer 1966, 1983.
VS: Kaṇāda's *Vaiśeṣikasūtra*. See Jambuvijaya 1961.
VSV: Candrānanda's *Vaiśeṣikasūtravṛtti*. See Jambuvijaya 1961.
YS: Patañjali's *Yogasūtra*. See Āranya 1963.
YSBh: Vyāsa's *Yogabhāṣya*. See Āranya 1963.

Pāṇini's *suṭ* Insertion Rules and the Reconstruction of the Root *skṛ-*

BORIS A. ZAKHARYIN

1. The stems *saṁskṛta-* 'Sanskrit', *saṁskṛti-* 'culture' (originally 'preparation, formation') and *saṁskāra-* 'purificatory rite' for many centuries have been serving as bases for important cultural terms of the Indian civilization. They are usually explained as nominal derivatives from the verbal base *saṁskṛ-* 'to unite, accumulate, prepare, elaborate, adorn, polish, refine'; the latter in its turn has been interpreted in the Aṣṭādhyāyī and in works by Pāṇini's followers as a combination of the prefix *sam-* '(al)together', the inserted element *-su**ṭ**-*[1] and the root *kṛ-* 'to do/make'.[2]

The treatment provided by linguists of Classical India has been readily accepted and later on continuously repeated by many linguists in their dictionaries and works on Sanskrit.[3] In recent time scholars have been making efforts to analyze the base *saṁskṛ-* and the derivatives from it, but still a lot of problems remain unsolved. An attempt to cope with at least some of them will be undertaken in this paper.

2. As is well known, the standard model for generating Sanskrit imperfect forms is: 'necessary prefix(es) + augment *á-* + corresponding present stem + secondary personal endings'; e.g., from *sam-pat-* 'to fly together' the form *sam-á-pat-a-n* (impf. act. 3rd pl.) '(they) flew together' may be derived. The standard formula for perfect is: 'prefix(es) + (usually reduplicated) perfect stem + perfect personal endings'; e.g., from the non-prefixed perfect stem *cakar-* (< *kṛ-*) the perf. act. 3rd sg. form will be *cakār-a* 'did', but from the prefixed perfect stem *sam-babhūv-* 'to come into being/be possible' (< *sam-* + *bhū-* 'to be/become') it will be *saṁ-babhūv-a* 'came into being, became possible'.

[1] A letter typed in bold in a Sanskrit term is used to mark *anubandha*(s) and to separate the latter from the meaningful portion.

[2] See *A* 6.1.137.

[3] See, for example, Renou 1957: 309; Macdonell 1954: 72; Monier-Williams 1951: 1120; Kochergina 1978: 671.

Contrary to standard derivation rules, we find in the Taittirīyasaṁhitā (6.2.3.1) the form *sámaskurvata* (impf. mid. 3rd pl.) '(they) prepared (ritually)' which morphologically must be treated only as 'prefix *sám-* + augment *-a-* + present stem *skuru-* (< **skr̥-*) + secondary ending *-ata*'. The main problem then is with the potential root **skr̥-* with unknown meaning, unfixed in dictionaries and grammars. It seems that the same root is present in the form *saṁcaskāra* (perf. act. 3rd sg.) 'made', which we find in Yāska's Nirukta: *...yo 'nanvite 'rthe saṁcaskāra ... sa tena garhyaḥ* "...the person who made such a derivation in spite of the meaning being irrelevant ...should be blamed" (Sarup 1998: 1.14, 15).

The following questions arise. What is the morphological status of the element *-s-* in the participial form *saṁskr̥ta-* 'elaborated' (> 'Sanskrit') and in other nominal derivatives of the same type? Is *saṁs-* a phonetic variant of the prefix *sam-* or some other, separate, prefix? Is *-s-* which follows *saṁ-* a component of the hypothetical root **skr̥-*, its initial consonant?

In efforts to find necessary answers we shall first of all observe the corresponding rules in Pāṇini's Aṣṭādhyāyī and comments by early Pāṇinīyas on some of them.

3.1. In adhyāyas 6–8 of his treatise Pāṇini analyzes morphonemic changes happening at boundaries between stems and affixes. To the 6th adhyāya belongs *A* 6.1.72, which, functioning as the heading rule (*adhikāra*), controls the subsequent sūtras (till 6.1.157).[4] *A* 6.1.72 *saṁhitāyām* means: "[When the two language elements occur] in an uninterrupted utterance (*saṁhitā*), [the sandhi changes take place]." Further on we find sūtra *A* 6.1.135 coming under the domain of *A* 6.1.72 and serving as another heading itself (Subrahmanyam 1999: 77). *A* 6.1.135 *suṭ kāt pūrvaḥ* means: "[In continuous utterance the increment] *-s-* (= ***suṭ***) [is to be inserted] before (*pūrvaḥ*) *k-*."

Thus, by *A* 6.1.135 Pāṇini states that this and the subsequent sūtras refer primarily to forms (to *signifiers*, not to *the signified*). Later on, in *A* 6.1.136 and in *A* 6.1.140–142, he formulates a set of grammatical and lexicosemantic restrictions on ***suṭ*** insertion. When generalized, those restrictions may be stated as follows: (1) not only the root *kr̥-* is involved; other verbal roots or nominals of different types having *k-* as initial consonant may also participate in the described sandhi processes; (2) only stems that originate from the combinations of a limited set of prefixes with the restricted sets of roots, and nominal stems that have particular meanings and imply specified grammatical usage are allowed to participate in the formulated processes.

The conditions which are formulated by Pāṇini on inserting ***suṭ*** before the initial *k-* of particular verbs combined with certain prefixes have evidently been found not fully satisfactory by his followers, as forms like *sámaskurvata*

[4]See Subrahmanyam 1999: 77.

or *saṁcaskāra* (see above) still remained unexplained by *A* 6.1.135. This is why Kātyāyana, when commenting on *A* 6.1.135, stated (in vārttikas 5 and 6): *aḍvyavāya upasaṅkhyānam, abhyāsavyavāye ca* "The act of adding [of the increment *-s-* happens even] if the interposition (*vyavāya*) [of the augment] *-áṭ-* or of the syllable of reduplication (*abhyāsa*) [takes place]." Commentators of later times, for example, the authors of the Kāśikā, transformed these vārttikas by Kātyāyana (as they were presented in Patañjali's Mahābhāṣya[5]) into a new rule of the sūtrapāṭha and placed it straight after *A* 6.1.135. Nevertheless, later Pāṇinīyas remained aware of the additional character of *A* 6.1.136—e.g., Bhaṭṭoji Dīkṣita immediately after citing the new sūtra added: ... *ity uktam* "... thus [it] has been said,"[6] and the Bālamanoramā, elucidating the meaning of this phrase, remarked: *vārttikam iti śeṣaḥ* "the remaining portion [is presented by] vārttika." This information was also known to specialists in vyākaraṇa of the nineteenth–twentieth centuries.[7]

The newly incorporated sūtra *A* *6.1.136 *aḍabhyāsavyavāye 'pi* means: "[The increment *-s-* must be inserted] before [the stem-initial consonant *k-*] even in case there is [between them] an interposition (*vyavāya*) by the syllable of reduplication (*abhyāsa*) [of perfect tense or] by [the imperfect, aorist or conditional augment] *-áṭ-*." In accordance with this additional rule the above-cited forms of imperfect (= ***laṅ***) middle, like *sámaskurvata* '(they) prepared (ritually)', attested in the Taittirīyasaṁhitā, or forms of perfect (= ***liṭ***) active, like Yāska's *saṁcaskāra* 'made', might be produced and considered grammatically correct; the same applies also to aorist (= ***luṅ***) forms of the type *sámaskārṣīt* '(he) prepared' (from *sam-* + *kr̥-* + ***luṅ***), etc.

3.2. Having formulated the *-s-* insertion rule on the level of morphonemes (*A* 6.1.135) and the grammatical rule dealing with verbal forms (*A* 6.1.136), Pāṇini and Pāṇinīyas[8] turn to stating the lexico-semantic and co-occurrence restrictions valid for certain types of prefixes that can combine with a limited set of verbal stems and nominals implying certain special meanings. Thus,

---

[5]See Bhāṣya on *A* 6.1.135 (III.93.13).

[6]Siddhāntakaumudī 2553 (*A* 6.1.135).

[7]Kielhorn already pointed out (1887: 184) that *A* 6.1.136 does not belong to Pāṇini and is composed on the basis of two vārttikas by Kātyāyana. This has also been noted by Śrīnārāyaṇa Miśra in his comments on the Kāśikā's treatment of *A* 6.1.136 (Kāśikā 2000: II.164). Cardona (1997: 650, 711) marks *A* 6.1.136 with an asterisk in order to show that the rule originating from the appropriate vārttikas was not a part of Pāṇini's sūtrapāṭha.

[8]It should be reminded here that *A* 6.1.136 does not belong to Pāṇini himself, but was interpolated by later commentators.

sūtras *A* 6.1.137–139 deal with the insertion of ***suṭ*** after the prefixes *sam-*, *pari-* and *upa-* before the stem-variants *kar-o-/kar-/kār-* of the verbal root *kr̥-* that usually signifies 'to do/make' but on these special occasions implies 'listed' (that is, restricted) meanings.

Rule *A* 6.1.137 *saṁparyupebhyaḥ karotau bhūṣaṇe*[9] means: "[The increment ***suṭ*** is to be inserted] after [the prefixes] *sam-*, *pari-*, *upa-* [and] before [derivatives from the root *kr̥-*, which is presented here by a citation form of pres. 3rd sg.] *karoti*, under the condition [that the prefixed stem implies the particular meaning of] 'adorning/decorating' (*bhūṣaṇa*)." Correspondingly, we would have forms like pres. act. 3rd sg. *saṁskaroti* 'adorns/decorates', imperf. act. 3rd sg. *samáskarot* '(he/she) adorned/decorated', perf. act. 3rd sg. *saṁcaskāra* 'adorned/decorated' (see above) and also the past participle base *saṁskr̥ta-* 'decorated' (> 'Sanskrit').

In their desire to follow Pāṇini's prescriptions with absolute thoroughness the authors of the Kāśikā, the treatise that came to light after more than a millennium of years after Pāṇini's passing away, derive some nominals with *-s-* doubled: e.g., *saṁsskarttā* (nom. ag.) 'one who decorates', *saṁsskartum* (inf.) 'to decorate', *saṁsskartavyam* (p. n.) 'to be decorated' (Kāśikā 1952: 495)—thus, assuming the division of the base into the modified prefix *saṁs-* and stem *kar-*.[10] The derivatives with *upa-* or *prati-* (plus ***suṭ***, plus stem *kar-*), suggested by the Kāśikā, do not imply *-ss-*; e.g., *upaskarttā* (nom. ag.) 'one who adorns/decorates', *pariṣkartum* (inf.) 'to adorn/decorate

[9]There existed an earlier version of *A* 6.1.137 where only the prefixes *sam-* and *pari-* combining with *kr̥-* (with a particular meaning) were mentioned. The earlier text of *A* 6.1.137—*samparibhyām karotau bhūṣaṇe* —was known to Patañjali, and the prefix *upa-* was incorporated into this sūtra later by the authors of the Kāśikā. See details in (Cardona 1997: 341–346). For our analysis here we prefer the later version suggested by the Kāśikā.

[10]Kāśikā on *A* 6.1.137 goes: *sam pari upa ity etebhyo bhūṣaṇe 'rthe karotau parataḥ* ***suṭ*** *kāt pūrvo bhavati | saṁsskarttā | saṁsskartum | saṁsskartavyam | atra saṁpuṁkānāṁ satvam iti samo makārasya sakāraḥ pūrvasya cākārasyānunāsikaḥ |* "After [prefixes] *sum-*, *pari-*, *upa-* [and] before [forms, derived from the root *kr̥-*, which is presented here by a citation form] *karoti*, under the condition [that the resulting base implies the meaning of] 'adorning/decorating', before [the morphoneme] /*k*/ ***suṭ*** is to be [inserted]. [E.g.,] *saṁsskarttā*, *saṁsskartum*, *saṁsskartavyam*. Here [we follow the first vārttika by Kātyāyana on *A* 8.3.12:] *saṁpuṁkānāṁ satvam*, [which means]: '[For the finals of the items] *sam-*, *pum-*, *kān-* [the morphoneme] /*s*/ [is] always [ordained and not visarga /*ḥ*/]." Thus, the Kāśikā, strictly following Pāṇini and Kātyāyana, suggests rather an artificial explanation for doubled *-ss-* in forms like *saṁsskarttā*, etc., which is based on the sandhi-rules for consonants. A different treatment of *saṁsskar-* seems also possible, however, if we admit in the corresponding forms the preservation of the rudimental root *skr̥-*: *saṁs-* + *skar-*, etc.

fully', etc.[11]

The combinations of the same prefixes with forms derived from *kr̥*-, when the specific meaning of 'a group/assemblage' (*samavāya*) is implied by co-occurring components, are also possible. In such cases ***suṭ*** is inserted following *A* 6.1.138 *samavāye ca* "Also, when [the meaning of] 'a group/assemblage' [is evident, the increment -*s*- is to be inserted after enlisted prefixes]." Correspondingly, there may be produced forms like *saṁskr̥ta*- or *pariṣkr̥ta*-, or *upaskr̥ta*- on the line of semantics belonging to the described domain.

The particle *ca* in *A* 6.1.138 has exclusively metalingual value: it demonstrates that *A* 6.1.138 is a continuation (*anuvr̥tti*) of the previous rule *A* 6.1.137. Thus, according to *A* 6.1.137–138, the prefixed bases from *kr̥*- (including *sam*- + *kr̥*-) may imply two sets of meanings: 'decoration' (*bhūṣaṇa*) and 'assemblage' (*samavāya*). For example, semantically the participial form *saṁskr̥tam* (n.) may be twofold: (a) it may mean 'the Sanskrit language' (with understandable transitions of the kind 'decorated/adorned' > 'elaborated' > 'Sanskrit'); (b) it may also mean 'the act of assembling'.[12]

The noun *samavāya*- implies at least two distinct meanings: (1) 'a group, assembly'; (2) a particular relation of 'container-contained' type. While translating the term into English as 'collection, assemblage, putting together', Katre (1989: 490, 691) takes into account only the first set of semantic implications, thus repeating the treatment that has been suggested by the Kāśikā.[13] For the first time the stem *samavāya*- is mentioned in *A* 4.4.43 where Pāṇini, explaining one of the usages of the taddhita suffix -*ṭhak*- (that is, of the derivational suffix -*ika*-), states: *samavāyān samavaiti* '(he) becomes a frequenter of communities'. Katre illustrates this sūtra by *sāmavāyika*- 'frequenter (of communities)', thus borrowing the sample from a group of synonyms, supplied by the Kāśikā.[14]

Pāṇini then adds two more sūtras in order to elucidate *A* 4.4.43. *A* 4.4.44, which is an exception to the previous one, states: *pariṣadaḥ ṇyaḥ* "[If the analyzed pada contains the nominal stem] *pariṣad*- 'assembly/society', [the suffix] -*ṇya*- [is to be used];" thus, *pariṣad*- + -*ṇya*- > *pāriṣad-ya*- 'assemblyman, councillor'. The other sūtra *A* 4.4.45, which optionally blocks *A*

[11]See the explanation for -*s*- > -*ṣ*- in *A* 8.3.70.

[12]Of the meaning of participial formations like *saṃskr̥tam*, *pariṣkr̥tam* or *upaskr̥tam* (each one of neuter gender) the Kāśikā (952: 495) gives the following explanation: *samuditam ity arthaḥ* | *tatra naḥ samuditam* | "The meaning [of these formations is] 'the act of assembling' as in *tatra naḥ samuditam* 'There [is] where the act of our assembling [happens]'."

[13]In its comments on *A* 6.1.138 the Kāśikā glosses (1952: 351) *samavāyaḥ* with *samudāyaḥ* 'collection, aggregate'.

[14]Besides *sāmavāyika*-, the Kāśikā gives three other synonyms with the same meaning of 'frequenter (of communities)': *sāmājika*-, *sāmūhika*-, *sānniveśika*-.

4.4.43, says: *senāyā vā* "[After pada, represented by the nominal stem] *senā-* 'army', [the suffix *-ṇya-* may be used] optionally"—thus, for 'soldier' both secondary stems (*sain-ika-* as well as *sain-ya-*) are possible. All the three sūtras (*A* 4.4.43–45) operate in the same semantic domain, and accordingly *samavāya-* signifies a group or assemblage in general, while *pariṣad-* and *senā-* imply reference to particular groups.[15]

Having described in *A* 6.1.137–8 the semantic restrictions on derivatives from *sam-kr̥-*, Pāṇini shifts to analyzing the base *upa-kr̥-*, formed as congregation of the prefix *upa-* 'near, nearby' with *kr̥-*. According to *A* 6.1.139, the derivatives from *upa-kr̥-* are characterized by obligatory insertion of *-s-*: *upāt pratiyatnavaikr̥tavākyādhyāhāreṣu* "[In contexts formulated above, the increment *-s-* is to be inserted in forms derived from the base *upa-kr̥-*] after [the prefix] *upa-* [and before derivatives from *kr̥-*, if the meanings] 'making an effort' (*pratiyatna*), 'transforming' (*vaikr̥ta*) or 'filling in the elements formerly omitted in the utterance' (*vākyādhyāhāra*) [are to be expressed]."

In its comments on *A* 6.1.139, the Kāśikā (1952: 50), when treating derivatives from *upa-kr̥-*, does not mention the existence of any correlations between the grammatical (voice-bound) and the semantic features of forms. Thus, members of pairs like *upa-s-karoti* (act.) and *upa-s-kurute* (mid.), on one hand, and *upa-karoti* (act.) and *upa-kurute* (mid.), on the other, assumingly have identical meanings. For derivatives from *upa-kr̥-* devoid of ***suṭ*** the Kāśikā suggests the meaning of 'serving' (*sevana*) and illustrates it by samples *gaṇakān upakurute* '(he) serves astrologists' and *mahāmātrān upakurute* '(he) serves persons of high rank'. For forms from

[15]The other block of meanings associated with *samavāya* is the one of a particular relation (*sambandha*) implying a mutually dependent and logically inseparable (*ayutasiddhānām*) existence of relata which also are coordinated as locus and something residing in this locus, so that the relation of this type produces the cognition of X being in Y (*ihapratyayahetu*). I am indebted to Professor Cardona for the above-stated clarifications concerning the meaning 'relation' of the term *samavāya-*. Affiliations with this very meaning are present in Vaiśeṣika philosophical texts where *samavāya-* is a widely used term signifying 'constant and intimate union, inseparable concomitance' (Monier-Williams 1951: 157) or even 'inherence'. See Lysenko 1998. And it is this relation that has drawn attention of Bhartr̥hari who studied contrasts existing between 'contact' or 'connection' (*saṁyoga*) and 'relation' (*samavāya*) (Iyer 1994: kaṇḍa III, pt. I, 3.1.17–18): while the meaning of the former term is based on the idea of distinct 'differentiation of objects' (*bhinnavastvāśraya*), the meaning of the latter implies 'standing away from the perception of (any) differentiation' (*bhedasya grahaṇaṁ vinivartate*). It may also be noted in passing that the semantic opposition *saṁyoga-samavāya* is grammatically paralleled in Sanskrit by the opposed syntactic constructions with the meanings of 'organic-nonorganic possession' (Zakharyin 2000: 254–263; Zakharyin 2003: 193–206).

upa-kr̥- with inserted *suṭ* the Kāśikā implies the meaning of 'transforming (the existing quality)' (*pratiyatna*); this is illustrated by samples: *kāṇḍaṁ guḍasyopaskurute* 'the cane transforms the (quality of) treacle' and *edhodakasyopaskurute* '(someone) gives a new quality to the firewood and water', that is, 'prepares the firewood and water (for cooking)'.

The latter sample is also supplied by the Kāśikā to illustrate *A* 2.3.53 *kr̥ñaḥ pratiyatne* "[In forms from] *kr̥-*, if [the latter implies the meaning of] 'transforming'." By this rule Pāṇini explains that if the meaning of 'transforming (the existing quality' (*pratiyatna*) is implied, the case-number endings of the 6th triplet (that is, of the genitive case) may be used with nominals derived from *kr̥-* and associated with the verb's patient (*karman*). The Kāśikā also adds (1952: 119) that the 6th triplet is used on a par (*śeṣa ity eva*) with the 2nd one (that is, of the Accusative case); thus, *edhodakam upaskurute*, being also correct, has the same meaning '(someone) gives a new quality to the firewood and water' = '(someone) prepares them for cooking'.[16] These comments by the Kāśikā show distinctly that the specific meaning of 'transforming' is associated not with the functional roles (*kāraka*) or case-number markers, but with the verbal root itself.

According to Varadarāja, in derivatives from the base *sam-kr̥-* the sememes 'decorating' and 'congregating' may intermingle in the declension of one and the same word-form: e.g., the form *saṁskaroti* (pres. 3rd sg.) Varadarāja glosses as *alaṁkaroti* 'decorates', but the form *saṁskurvanti* (pres. 3rd pl.) he explains as *saṁdhībhavanti* '(they) congregate' (Ballantyne 1995: 248; Zakharyin 2007: 290–293).

The same base *sam-kr̥-* and derivatives from it may also imply the meaning of 'cooking/preparing (something eatable)'. The derivate meaning 'prepared (in something)' is met for the first time in *A* 4.2.16; the latter is a continuation (*anuvr̥tti*) of the heading rule *A* 4.1.83, by which Pāṇini informs us that the conditions for usage of the derivative suffix *-áṇ-* (belonging to the taddhita subclass of affixes) are to be discussed in *A* 4.1.83–4.4.2. *A* 4.2.16 is: *saṁskr̥taṁ bhakṣāḥ* "[Here a derivate meaning] 'prepared', [refers to] eatables, [prepared in a certain vessel]." In its comments on *Á* 4.2.16 the Kāśikā defines precisely the functional value of *-áṇ-*: in contexts where nominal word-forms signifying 'eatables' (*bhakṣāḥ*) co-occur with forms from the base *saṁskr̥-*, the affix *-áṇ-* is used as a substitute of the 7th triplet of endings (that is, of the locative case inflections). The Kāśikā also notes (1952: 291; 1.367, 1.438) that in the contexts examined the implied manner of preparing food is not an ordinary, but a special one—such that through transformation of the ingredients purifies the final product and heightens

[16] Bhaṭṭoji Dīkṣita gives two other interpretations for the samples supplied by the Kāśikā: 'the wood gives a new quality to the water' and '(he) prepares the wood and water for sacrifice'. See Vasu 1975: I.367.

its quality: *sata utkarṣādhānaṁ saṁskāraḥ* "the purification (*saṁskāra*) [consists in] heightening the quality of substances [used in the process of preparing food]."[17] Having stated this, the Kāśikā provides the illustrations: *bhrāṣṭrā apūpāḥ* 'cakes of flour prepared in a frying pan (*bhrāṣṭra*)' or *kālaśāḥ* '[eatables] prepared in a pot (*kalaśa*)', or *kaumbhāḥ* '[eatables] prepared in a cooking vessel (*kumbha*)'.

While proceeding with their comments on *A* 4.2.16, the authors of the Kāśikā (1952: 291) ask: '*bhakṣā iti kim?* "Why [only with forms signifying] 'eatables' [*saṁskr̥ta* implies this meaning 'prepared in']?" To this the following brief answer is given: *puṣpapuṭe saṁskr̥to mālāguṇaḥ* "The string [is] applied through the garland of flowers [placed] in a bowl." By the latter sample the Kāśikā stresses the fact that the form *saṁskr̥taḥ* ('applied, connected') in contexts like this does not imply any idea of 'cooking/preparing', but is used to express the meaning of '(temporary) congregation'.

The Kāśikā also clarifies the referent of *bhakṣāḥ* to a certain extent, pointing out that it is *kharaviśadam abhyavahāryaṃ bhakṣam* 'a food consisting of hard white grains'. The interpretation has been approved by Varadarāja, and Ballantyne in his translation of the Laghusiddhāntakaumudī renders the word (rather freely) as 'granular food', adding 'as barley, etc.' (Ballantyne 1995: 364).[18] In general, Ballantyne's rendering seems to be appropriate in connection with the meaning of *sam-kr̥-* 'to cook/prepare (eatables)'; the other meanings of the base—namely, *alaṁ-kr̥-* 'to decorate/adorn', *sam-ava-i-* 'to be/become integral', *saṁdhī-bhū-* 'to congregate/get congregated'[19]—also should not be forgotten.

3.3. We have in detail observed sūtras *A* 6.1.137–139. The next three rules (*A* 6.1.140–142) deal with insertion of ***suṭ*** after the prefixes *upa-*, *prati-*, *apa-* which are conjoined with the root *kr̥̄-* when forming derivates. Normally signifying 'to spread/scatter' *kr̥̄-* in these contexts implies the special meanings of 'splitting' (*lavana*), 'hurting/violating' (*hiṁsā*) and 'scraping (the ground)' (*ālekhana*). The Kāśikā (1952: 496) and later Katre (1989: 692) illustrate the corresponding occurrences by pairs of utterances where one member has a form with ***suṭ*** and the opposed one is devoid of it: *upa-s-kīr-ṇa-* 'hurt/injured/violated' ↔ *upa-kīr-ṇa-* 'bestrewed'; *apa-s-kir-a-te bhakṣyārthī kukkuṭaḥ* 'the rooster scratches the earth in search of food' ↔ *apa-kir-a-ti devadattaḥ* 'Devadatta scatters', etc.

---

[17]The analyses of the latter passage from the Kāśikā has been earlier suggested by Cardona (1997: 558), and his treatment is fully accepted here.

[18]In Monier-Williams 1951: 742 only explanations like 'food', 'drinking' or 'eating' are supplied for *bhakṣa-* .

[19]See in this connection *A* 6.1.137–138 above and also Varadarāja's commentary on *A* 6.1.138 (Zakharyin 2007: 290–291).

3.4. Pāṇini strictly follows his principle of grammatical description: grammar treats what is general and particular (*sāmānyaviśeṣaval lakṣaṇam*), and this explains ordering of sūtras: *A* 6.1.137–139 concern *kr̥*- used in particular meanings, after them follow *A* 6.1.140–142 dealing with *kr̥̄*- used in particular meanings, *suṭ* applies to forms with these bases in general. Afterwards come the remaining rules *A* 6.1.143–157 that concern bases in nominal derivates occurring as parts of compounds, but not the bases in general.

3.5. In *A* 6.1.143–156 Pāṇini provides formal and semantics-bound restrictions on *suṭ* in different sets of forms that do not necessarily have /*k*/ as initial of the second pada (in accordance with *A* 6.1.135[20]). The analysis starts with -*s*- insertion before pada with initial /*t*/, and *A* 6.1.143 states: *kustumburūṇi jātiḥ* "[The word] *kustumburu* 'coriander' [with *suṭ* before /*t*/ is used if the meaning of] genus (*jāti*) [is to be expressed]." The Kāśikā suggests the following explanation: *dhānyakam* | *tatphalāny api kustumburūṇi* | "[The plant meant is] Coriander Sativum;[21] and also its seeds are called *kustumburūṇi*." Thus, the word-form *kustumburūṇi* (with *suṭ*) is opposed to *kutumburūṇi* (without *suṭ*). The comments for the latter, suggested by the Kāśikā, are the following: *kutsitāni tumburūṇi kutumburūṇi* | *tumburuśabdenātra tindukīphalāny ucyante* | "The vile seeds (*tumburūṇi*) [are also called] *kutumburūṇi*; by the word *tumburu* here are meant the seeds of Diospyros embriopteris (*tindukī*)."[22] Thus, a semantic opposition implied is: *ku-s-tumburu*- '(useful) seeds of Coriander Sativum' ↔ *ku-tumburu*- '(vile) seeds of Diospyros embriopteris'.

Further on, in *A* 6.1.144–146, Pāṇini suggests rules for inserting -*s*- before /*p*/ under certain semantic restrictions. Thus, *A* 6.1.144 runs: *aparasparāḥ*

[20]As has been clarified by Professor Cardona (personal communication), *A* 6.1.135, being a heading rule, does not presuppose that all the other rules, controlled by it, should have to involve -*k*- if contradiction is to be avoided. According to Cardona, the heading *A* 6.1.135 may functionally be compared to *A* 4.1.82: *samarthānām prathamād vā* "[Affixes introduced by subsequent rules] follow the first of the padas (*prathamād*) [and occur] optionally (*vā*), [if the padas in question are] semantically and syntactically related to each other (*samarthānām*)." *A* 4.1.82, thus, does not demand that all the sūtras involved have to deal with related padas (Cardona 1988: 80). In the same way, not all the sūtras that come into the domain of *A* 6.1.135 should necessarily have only /*k*/ as the initial segment of the second pada, other initial consonants may also allow insertion of -*s*- before them, in case the semantic restrictions are formulated.

[21]In Monier-Williams 1951: 509 the word for Coriander Sativum is spelled differently from the one in the Kāśikā, i.e., *dhanyākaḥ*.

[22]In Monier-Williams 1951: 417 the word for Diospyros embriopteris is spelled *tinduki*.

kriyāsātatye "[***suṭ*** is inserted before /*p*/ of the second pada, when the resultant expression] *aparasparāḥ* [denotes] continuity of action (*kriyāsātatya*)." *A* 6.1.145 is: *goṣpadaṃ sevitāsevitapramāṇeṣu* "[***suṭ*** is inserted before /*p*/ of the second pada, when the resultant expression] *goṣpada-* [signifies a locality, which is] frequented (*sevita*) or not frequented (*asevita*), or [signifies] a measure (*pramāṇa*)." *A* 6.1.146 runs: *āspadaṃ pratiṣṭhāyām* "[***suṭ*** is inserted before /*p*/ of the second pada, when the resultant expression] *āspadam* [denotes] a fixed place (*pratiṣṭhā*)." Commentators illustrate *A* 6.1.144–146 by contrasting forms with and without *-s-*: *a-para-s-par-āḥ* (*gacchanti*) '[they go] one after another (without a break[23])' ↔ *a-para-par-āḥ* (*gacchanti*) '[these and other traders go] simultaneously'; *go-ṣ-pada-m* '[place] frequented by cows' ↔ *go-pada-m* 'impression of a cow's hoof in soil'; *ā-s-pada-m* (n.) 'seat/abode' ↔ *ā-pada-m* (adv.) 'up to the foot', where *āpada-* is an avyayībhāva compound.

A 6.1.147 is dedicated to a unique case of *-s-* insertion before the initial /*c*/ of the nominal derivative from the root *car-* 'to move/go': *āścaryam anitye* "[***suṭ*** is inserted before /*c*/ into the expression] *āścaryam* [with the purpose of denoting] something unusual (*anitya*)." According to commentators, the resulting adjective *āścarya-* 'astonishing' contrasts with the gerundive *ācarya-* (Kāśikā 1952: 496; Katre 1989: 693).

In *A* 6.1.148–150 Pāṇini describes the conditions of ***suṭ*** insertion in a small set of derivatives from the root *kr̥̄-*, which preserves its original meaning 'to scatter'; *-s-* may appear after the prefixes *ava-*, *apa-*, *vi-* and before the initial /*k*/ of a following pada in a compound. Thus, *A* 6.1.148 states: *varcaske 'vaskaraḥ* "[In order to denote] excrement, ordure (*varcaska*) [the derivate] *avaskara-* [with *-s-* inserted is to be used]." *A* 6.1.149 runs: *apaskaro rathāṅgam* "[The expression] *apaskara-* [with ***suṭ*** inserted is used to signify] part of a chariot (*rathāṅga*)." Commentators illustrate *A* 6.1.148 and *A* 6.1.149 by contrasting pairs: *ava-s-kar-a-* 'excrement' ↔ *ava-kar-a-* 'dust'; *apa-s-kar-a-* 'part of a chariot' ↔ *apa-kar-a-* 'scattering, throwing' (Kāśikā 1952: 497).

In Katre's edition of the Aṣṭādhyāyī, *A* 6.1.150 is presented as *viṣkiraḥ śakunir vā*. But to Patañjali the sūtra is known in the form *viṣkiraḥ śakunau vā*, and to this form of sūtra Kātyāyana supplies a vārttika: *viṣkiraḥ śakunau vikiro vā*, demonstrating by this that *vā* refers to a form with ***suṭ*** and has no connection with the word *śakunau*. Much later the Kāśikā suggests another variant of *A* 6.1.150: *viṣkiraḥ śakunir vikiro vā* "[The derivates] *viṣkira-* [with inserted *-s-* or] *vikira-* [into which *-s-* before /*k*/ may optionally be inserted] [to denote] a bird (*śakuni*). In commenting on this Katre remarks that *vikira-* also has the general sense of 'scattering'. Thus partial con-

[23]The meaning 'without a break' (*avicchedena*) is supplied by the Kāśikā's comment on *aparasparāḥ* (Kāśikā 1952: 496).

trast: *viṣkira-*/*vikira-* 'domestic fowl' ↔ *vikira-* 'scattering/throwing down' is implied (Kāśikā 1952: 497, Katre 1989: 694).

After these sūtras Pāṇini shifts to problems of *-s-* insertion in Vedic and formulates rule *A* 6.1.151 *hrasvāt candrottarapade mantre* "In [the language of Vedic *mantras* [*-s-* is to be inserted] before [the nominal stem] *candra* [functioning] as a second part of the compound (*uttarapade*) [and] after a short vowel (*hrasvāt*) [which comes as final segment of a prior member of the same compound]." Katre (1989: 694) illustrates this by *su-ś-candra-* 'very brilliant' and by the proper name *hari-ś-candra-* the literal meaning of which is 'brilliant as Hari'. He also remarks in passing that in post-Vedic Sanskrit both the forms described are used without *-s-* and function as ordinary proper names: *su-candra-* and *hari-candra-*.

In *A* 6.1.152 Pāṇini describes *suṭ* insertion between the prefix *prati-* 'against/near to' and the nominal stem *kaśa-*, a derivate from the root *kaś-* 'to go/move', 'to strike/hurt': *pratiṣkaśaś ca kaśeḥ* "[Also *-s-* is to be inserted before /*k*/] of *kaśa-* [when the prefix] *prati* [co-occurs with *kaśa-* in one pada]." The Kāśikā (1952: 497) and Katre (1989: 695) show that derivatives from the base *prati-kaśa-* may contrast in accordance with the presence or absence of *suṭ* and the semantic differences: *pratiṣkaśa-* 'messenger/spy' ↔ *pratikaśa-* 'a horse not obeying the whip'.

In sūtras *A* 6.1.153 and *A* 6.1.155 Pāṇini again turns to the analysis of two pairs of the proper names which are used in Vedic and demand *suṭ* insertion. They are either names of the seers[24] or town-names. Thus, *A* 6.1.153 runs: *praskaṇvahariścandrāvṛṣī* "[*suṭ* is to be inserted before /*k*/ and /*c*/ of the corresponding padas in order to denote names of] two [Vedic] seers: *praskaṇva* and *hariścandra*." The commentators explain: besides *praskaṇva-* there also exists *prakaṇva-* signifying the name of the country (*deśa*). In addition they clarify the difference between the personal names *hariścandra* and *haricandra*: the bearer of the first of the names may be only a Vedic seer, while the second name belongs to an ordinary Brāhmaṇa boy (Kāśikā 1952: 497; Katre 1989: 695).

A 6.1.155 states: *kāstīrājastunde nagare* "[*suṭ* is to be inserted before /*t*/ of the second pada to denote the names of] cities *kāstīra-* [and] *ajastunda-*." When providing its comments on *A* 6.1.155, the Kāśikā notes (1952: 498) that the two expressions with *suṭ* serving as names of the towns are opposed to the other pair of expressions (without *suṭ*): *kāstīra* (town-name) ↔ *kātīra* 'small shore'; *ajastunda* (town-name) ↔ *ajatunda* 'protruding belly of a ram'. In connection with *kātīra* the Kāśikā clarifies (1952: 568) that the constituent *kā-* 'small' is in accordance with *A* 6.3.105:

[24]Katre explains (1989: 695) the second mentioning of the proper name which has already been discussed in *A* 6.1.151 as serving "the purpose of showing its occurrence outside the domain of Mantra also."

īṣadarthe "[Before a final member of a tatpuruṣa compound the element *kā́-* substitutes the element *kú-*] if the meaning 'a little' (*īṣad-*) [is to be expressed]."

A 6.1.154 runs: *maskaramaskariṇau veṇuparivrājakayoḥ* "[***suṭ*** is to be inserted before /*k*/ of the second pada to denote] a bamboo cane (*maskara-*) [and] a Brāhmaṇa mendicant carrying a bamboo cane (*maskarin-*)." There exists (found in Dhātupāṭha only) the root *mask-*/*maṣk-* 'to go/move' which probably (but not with certainty) might form the base for both the derivates (Monier-Williams 1951: 794). In its comments on *A* 6.1.154 the Kāśikā suggests (1952: 497–498) opposing pairs: *maskaraḥ* 'cane' ↔ *makaraḥ* 'crocodile', *maskarī* 'monk' ↔ *makarī* 'ocean'. The expression *makara* is glossed by it as *grāha* 'beast of pray' and *makarī-* as *samudra* 'ocean' (that is, 'having sea monsters in it'). It is also important that *makara-* is characterized by the Kaśikā (1952: 498.8) as an 'underived nominal base' (*avyutpannam prātipadikam*), and hence that its contrast with *mascara-* is not evident.

In *A* 6.1.156 Pāṇini describes the insertion of *-s-* before /*k*/ in the name of a tree: *kāraskaro vr̥kṣaḥ* "[Before /*k*/ of the second pada ***suṭ*** is to be inserted so that the expression] *kāraskara-* [might denote a certain] tree." According to Katre (1989: 695), there exists an opposition: *kāraskara-* '(a certain) tree' ↔ *kārakara-* 'a work-doer'. But the stem *kāraskara-* also has variants: *kāraskāra* and *kāraskr̥ta* (Monier-Williams 1951: 275). This may be considered as additional evidence that not *kr̥-* 'to do/make' but the proto-Indo-Aryan root **skr̥-* has served as the base for generating all these allomorphs.

3.6. *A* 6.1.157, which concludes the section, says: *pāraskaraprabhr̥tīni ca sañjñāyām* "In [an open list of specimens] beginning with *pāraskara-* [***suṭ*** should be inserted before the initial consonant of the posterior member of a nominal compound in order] to form names." In connection with *pāraskara-prabhr̥ti-* the Kāśikā clarifies that the expression belongs to an ākr̥tigaṇa, that is, to an open list (*gaṇa*) of specimens (*ākr̥ti*) sharing features with other terms accounted for and destined to illustrate the corresponding grammatical rule; the list mentioned in the sūtra starts with the term *pāraskara-* which the Kāśikā explains as the name of the country (*pāraskaro deśaḥ*). In addition to *pāraskara-* the commentators also mention *vanaspati-* '(large) tree' (etymologically, 'lord (*pati*) of the forest (*vana*)') and *rathaspā* (*nadī*) '(the river) protecting (*pā-*) the chariot (*ratha-*)' (Kāśikā 1952: 168; Katre 1989: 696). Historically *-s-* in *vanaspati-* is not an increment, but rather a residual genitive singular ending (compare **van-a-s* equivalent to later *van-a-sya*), but to the synchronic description of the language, relevant for Pāṇini and Pāṇinīyas, this is of no import.

3.7. It may be ascertained that in the whole section of the Aṣṭādhyāyī dedicated to *suṭ* insertion (*A* 6.1.135–157) the description is based primarily on formal grounds and only for a portion of data problems of semantic changes (in roots and bases) are taken into consideration. The functional differences between groups of the analyzed lexemes are not accounted at all: in sūtras *A* 6.1.136–142, which come immediately after the adhikāra-sūtra *A* 6.1.135, the description is concentrated on verbal forms, but in *A* 6.1.143 the noun *kustumburu-* is treated; then, in *A* 6.1.144, the adverb *apara-s-para-* is analyzed, while sūtras *A* 6.1.145–156 are again dedicated to nominals of different types. Most often the rules deal with common nouns of Sanskrit, but *A* 6.1.151 is dedicated to two proper names in Vedic, one of which is analyzed again in *A* 6.1.153, and this time it is associated with Sanskrit. Some sūtras operate with the unique proper names of human beings, but others deal with names of plants (*A* 6.1.143), birds (*A* 6.1.150) and towns (*A* 6.1.155), etc. Thus, the selection of specimens presented in almost all the sūtras of the section is not fully determined either by semantics or by functional criteria—the homogeneity of data reposes exclusively on one formal feature which share all the analyzed signifiers: on the element *-s-* that may be inserted before surd consonants /*k*/, /*t*/, /*c*/, /*p*/.

3.8. Turning now to Pāṇini's more narrow and more concrete analysis of the derivatives from *sam-kr̥-*, we may arrive at the following conclusions:

(1) In order to explain the appearance of the increment *-s-* between the prefix *sam-* (and a few other prefixes) and a verbal root with initial /*k*/, Pāṇini formulates a special morphonological rule (*A* 6.1.135).

(2) The applicability of *A* 6.1.135 to *sam-kr̥-* is determined by a considerable number of grammatical and lexico-semantic limitations on the base.

(3) Contrary to present tense forms like *saṁskaroti* (< *saṃ-* + *karoti*) 'decorates', the imperfect forms of the type *sámaskurvata* '(they) prepared (ritually)', deviating from the standard rules of generating verbal forms, cannot be explained on the basis of *A* 6.1.135 only. The inevitability of amendments has forced Pāṇinīyas to introduce *A* 6.1.136 intended exclusively for explaining occurrences of the described type.

(4) Besides their non-standard structural properties, forms derived from the base *sam-kr̥-* imply also a rather wide dispersion of meanings—this may be viewed as an additional evidence for the potential historical mergence of the two initially separate roots into one unit.

4.1. One of the possible ways for solving problems produced by forms like *sámaskurvata* may be the assumption that in course of the evolution of Ancient Indo-Aryan (AIA) the initially different verbal roots *kr̥-* and **skr̥-* have later got merged. Conjectures concerning this assumed merging have been hazarded by Whitney who already in 1879 remarked (1969: 400 [§1087.d]): "the root *kr̥- make* sometimes assumes (or retains from a more original condition) an initial *s* after the prefixes *sam-*, *pari-*, *nis-* and *upa-* ...." Probably taking Whitney's remark into account Mayrhofer in his Etymological Dictionary has transcribed the corresponding participial stem as '*sam-skr̥ta-*' (Mayrhofer 1976: 680), where from the root **skr̥-* (of uncertain meaning) may be easily reconstructed.

Formal grounds for this reconstruction may be supported by some data from Proto-Indo-European (PIE): the sibilant **s* of the latter, being the initial member of a consonant cluster, has been preserved in a set of forms in many later Indo-European dialects, including AIA: e.g., Vedic *sphā́yate* 'ripens', Lithuanian *spéti* 'to ripen', Latin *spatium* 'scope', Old English *spōwan* 'prosper', etc. But in the other set of contextually identical forms this initial PIE **s* is represented by AIA 'zero'. Compare, e.g., Latin *speciō* '(I) am looking at', Old High German *spehōn* 'to look at', English *spy* (originally 'one who looks at') ↔ AIA *páśyati* 'sees/looks', Avestan *paśna-* 'gaze', etc. In word-middle position the original PIE **-s-* of the root has been retained in AIA: e.g., Vedic perfect *paspaśé* 'sees', aorist *áspaṣṭa* 'has seen', etc. This preserved word-middle **-s-* might even cause the appearance of analogous forms with the initial *s-* in AIA (Gamkrelidze and Ivanov 1984: 119), like, e.g., *spáś-* 'a spy', *spāśáyate* (middle voice present from causative stem) 'clarifies/observes', etc. The same alternations of *s-/ϕ-* we find in forms derived from AIA root *kr̥̄-* (< PIE **skr̥̄-*) 'to scatter': e.g., *kiráti* (pres. act. 3rd sg.) 'pours out/scatters', but *apa-skar-a-* 'an excrement' (< 'something that has been scattered out').

According to Gamkrelidze and Ivanov (1984: 121), both the PIE reconstructed sibilants (**s* and **ś*) might be used before velar stops, particularly, before **k°*; thus, not only the well-attested root **k°er-/*k°ər-/*k°r̥-* 'to do/make' (> AIA *kr̥-*) but also the hypothetical **sk°er-/*sk°ər-/*sk°r̥-* (> AIA *skr̥-*) might exist; in addition, PIE **s* and **ś* in the initial position of lexical morphemes "may be interpreted as the most ancient prefixes though their morphological function remains obscure."[25] This 'obscurity', presumed already for PIE, must have eventually become greater, and inconsistencies in ***suṭ*** insertion rules for AIA that have been noticed in the Aṣṭādhyāyī are actually the result of it. Gamkrelidze and Ivanov note also (1984: 121) that AIA forms with initial zero (*ϕ-*) corresponding to structures with *ś-* or *s-* in other Indo-European dialects, cannot be explained on the basis of the traditional concept of '*s*-mobile', as the latter notion is more or less applicable only to a few isolated cases where no regularity in presence or

[25] My translation from Russian.

absence of the initial *s-* is determinable—a number of typical occurrences are provided by the authors. In case of AIA the list of expressions demanding *s*-mobile notion for their interpretation may be constituted by nominals derived in accordance with Pāṇini's rules *A* 6.1.143–157 and organized (by later Pāṇinīyas) into pairs with formally contrasting members.

As for meanings, associated with the reconstructed PIE root **sk^{o}er-/*sk^{o}ər̥-/*sk^{o}r̥-*, which probably resulted in AIA *skr̥-*, the situation is far from certainty. On the level of formal correspondences the nearest to PIE **sk^{o}r̥-* seems to be **sker-* 'to cut/crush/grind'—compare Russian (dial.) *skorodá* 'harrow', Lithuanian *skardýti* 'to dig (the earth)/grind', Old Prussian *skurdis* 'mattock', Old English *sceort* 'short', etc. (Vasmer 1996: 652). The other line of filiations of the meaning of the same PIE root might, probably, be illustrated by the set that includes Ancient Scandinavian *skrá* 'the dried up skin or fur', Old High German *screnkan* and Old English *screncan* 'to deceive', English *shrink* and *shrinkage*, etc. (Vasmer 1996: 652, 659–660). Still, the differences in form between PIE roots **sker-* and **sk^{o}er-* are quite evident; besides, the original set of the sememes that may be reconstructed for PIE **sker-* does not really help to grasp the meaning of AIA *skr̥-*.

4.2. To achieve this aim it seems important to rely not only on Pāṇini's rules and Pāṇinīyas' interpretations analyzed above, but also to take into consideration the concrete meanings of the corresponding derivates through studying different contexts of their usage in culturally significant texts. A great amount of work necessary for this has been fulfilled by Cardona who turned to the analysis of literary sources, and namely to treatises created by early religious authors and to ancient works of art (Cardona 1997: 557–564). Cardona's attention has primarily been drawn to meanings of the word *saṁskāra-*, the derivative of AIA *kr̥-* or *skr̥-*. Having analyzed numerous stylistically different contexts, Cardona managed to extricate the most basic meanings of the term and came to the following general conclusions:

1) in connection with the process of cooking *saṁskāra-* means 'imparting a higher quality to the prepared edibles';
2) it also means 'enhancing one's body', for ritual as well as for secular purposes;
3) it means 'a purificatory rite' (an upanayana ceremony, a vessel purifying rite, etc.);
4) applied to speech, it means either 'a purification of speech through segregation of the correct forms from corrupt ones' or 'an explanation how to produce ideal speech forms described in grammars'. It is on the basis of these latter meanings the use of *saṁskr̥ta-* as a term signifying 'pure, correct speech' has become firmly established in post-Pāṇini India.

4.3. Taking into account the facts analyzed above and the data supplied by Cardona in connection with *saṁskāra-*, it might be assumed that the original basic meaning of the reconstructed AIA *skr̥*-(< PIE **sk^{o}r̥-*) was 'to transform', probably with implied connotations like 'to elevate', 'to change the quality of something for the better/form well' (from which have later developed such meanings as 'to purify/perfect' and 'to embellish/adorn'). As for the stem *saṁ-kr̥-*, its prototypical meanings seem to have been 'to congregate/join together/compose/get united/be put together'.

Because of the similarities of forms the stems *saṁ-skr̥-* and *saṁ-kr̥-* must have become merged already at the pre-AIA or at early AIA period of language history—with all the corresponding consequences on the line of meanings. It is highly probable that the starting point for merging was the sphere of consuming ritual edibles in course of different rites: the final product of the process of transforming the initial raw substances into some integral eatable mass was to be ritually pure. And becoming ritually pure actually meant changing the ingredients for the better and heightening the quality of the things prepared.

In its turn the sphere of ritual has always served in Indian culture as a kind of a canonical model for different phenomena of worldly life, and thus, the ideas of 'purification' and of 'purity' have got adjusted to everyday cooking of ordinary meals. 'Pure' then implied notions like 'perfected' and consequently 'decorated, adorned'.

All those characteristics of material substances have in later times become also associated with social and cultural phenomena, such as, for example, speech and its elements. This was the necessary prerequisite for appearance of such terms as *śabdasaṁskāra* 'speech purification' (aimed, according to Bhartr̥hari, at attaining felicity), *saṁskr̥tam* 'the Sanskrit language' and *saṁskr̥ti-* 'culture' and for employment of the stem *saṁskr̥-* in texts by grammarians as near synonyms to stems *anuśiṣ-* 'to teach' and *vyutpad-* 'to explain' (Cardona 1988: 652, 654).

5. In spite of the early merging of AIA roots *skr̥-* and *kr̥-* and of the stems *saṁ-skr̥-* and *saṁ-kr̥-*, traces of their former separate functions have got preserved in Indo-Aryan even at later phases of language evolution. The historical merging of the roots was the real cause for the above-mentioned difficulties in treatment of certain Sanskrit forms with *suṭ* provided by ancient grammarians. Due to his linguistic intuition, Pāṇini was the first to fix the unusual phenomena in the Aṣṭādhyāyī and to give them treatment appropriate to his system of views.

At present it is not possible to reconstruct with positive results the AIA root **skr̥̄-* as opposed to *kr̥̄-* 'to throw/scatter/cover with', because too little data on the usage of the derivatives with inserted *-s-* from *kr̥̄-* is available.

The Kāśikā, while illustrating rules *A* 6.1.140–142 that deal with forms produced from *kr̥̄-*, mentions either a few nominals (like *upaskīrṇa-* 'injured' ↔ *upakīrṇa-* 'bestrewed', etc.) or exclusively present tense forms (like *apaskirate* 'scratches' ↔ *apakirati* 'scatters', etc.). As no information concerning the functioning of the hypothetic root **skr̥̄-* in forms of imperfect, perfect or aorist tenses is available, the reliable grounds for the restoration of this root are absent. The described contrasts of verbal word-forms like *apa-s-kirate* ↔ *apa-kirati*, etc. are then to be treated as the effects of the comparatively late analogous processes. With even greater reasons this might be also assumed for pairs of the derived nominals (those with inserted *-s-* and their counterparts without *-s-*), elucidated by the grammarians' comments on Pāṇini's rules *A* 6.1.143–157.

References and abbreviations

A: Aṣṭādhyāyī. See Katre.

Bālamanoramā: See Giridhara Śarmā Caturveda and Parameśvarānanda Śarmā Bhāskara.

Ballantyne, James R.
1995 *The Laghukaumudī: A Sanskrit Grammar by Varadarāja.* Reprint, Delhi: Motilal Banarsidass.

Bhāṣya: Mahābhāṣya. See Madhusūdana Prasāda Mishra.

Cardona, George
1988 *Pāṇini: His Work and Its Traditions; Volume One: Background and Introduction.* Delhi: Motilal Banarsidass.
1997 *Pāṇini: His Work and Its Traditions; Volume One: Background and Introduction.* 2nd ed. Delhi: Motilal Banarsidass.

Gamkrelidze, Tamaz V., and Viacheslav V. Ivanov
1984 *Indoevropejskij jazyk i indoevropejtsy* (Indo-European and the Indo-Europeans, part I). Tbilisi: Tbilisi University.

Giridhara Śarmā Caturveda and Parameśvarānanda Śarmā Bhāskara
1958–61 *Śrībhaṭṭojīdīkṣitaviracitā vaiyākaraṇasiddhāntakaumudī śrīmadvāsudevadīkṣita-praṇītayā bālamanoramākhyavyākhyayā śrīmajjñānendrasarasvatīviracitayā tattvabodhinyākhyavyākhyayā ca sanāthitā.* 4 vols. Varanasi: Motilal Banarsidass.

Kāśikāvr̥tti: See Śobhita Miśra and Śrīnārāyaṇa Miśra.

Katre, Sumitra M.
1989 *Aṣṭādhyāyī of Pāṇini.* Delhi: Motilal Banarsidass.

Kielhorn, Lorenz Franz
1887 Notes on the Mahābhāṣya; 6. the text of Pāṇini's sūtras, as given in the Kāśika-vritti, compared with the text as known to Kātyāyana and Patañjali. *Indian Antiquary* 16: 178–84 (= *Kleine Schriften* [1969]: 226–32).

Kochergina, Vera. A.

1978 *Sanskritsko-russkij slovar* (Sanskrit-Russian Dictionary). Moscow: Russkij jazyk.

Lysenko Victoria. G.

1998 "Diskretnoe i kontinual'noe v istorii indijskoj mysli: lingvistićeskaja tradicija i vajśeṣika (The discretion and continuance in the history of Indian thought: the linguistic tradition and Vaiśeśika)." Ph.D. diss. Moscow: Institut filosofii RAN.

Macdonell, Arthur A.

1954 *A Practical Sanskrit Dictionary.* Reprint, Oxford: Oxford University Press.

Madhusūdana Prasāda Mishra

1967 *Vyākaraṇa-mahābhāṣya of Maharṣi-Patañjali with the 'Pradīpa' Sanskrit Commentary by Kaiyaṭa Upādhyāya Edited with the 'Prakāśa' Hindi Commentary by Ācārya Madhusūdana Prasāda Mishra.* Varanasi: Chowkhamba Sanskrit Sansthan.

Mayrhofer, Manfred

1976 *Kurzgefasstes etymologisches Wörterbuch des Altindischen.* Band III. Heidelberg: Carl Winter.

Monier-Williams, M. A.

1951 *A Sanskrit-English Dictionary.* Reprint, Oxford: Oxford University Press.

Renou, Louis

1957 *Terminologie grammaticale du Sanskrit.* Paris: Champion.

Sarup, Lakshman

1998 *The Nighaṇṭu and the Nirukta.* Reprint, Delhi: Motilal Banarsidass.

Ṣiddhāntakaumudī: See Vasu.

Śobhita Miśra

1952 *The Kāśikā-vṛtti of Vāmana and Jayāditya on Pāṇini's Grammatical Rules, with a Preface by Brahmadatta Jijñāsu.* 2 parts. The Kashi Sanskrit Series 37. Benares: Chowkhamba Sanskrit Sansthan.

Śrīnārāyaṇa Miśra

2000 *Pāṇinīyavyākaraṇasūtravṛtti Kāśikā of Pt. Vāmana and Jayāditya; edited with the 'Prakāśa' Hindi Commentary and Introduction by Śrī Nārāyaṇa Miśra; Preface by Pt. Brahmadatta Jijñāsu.* 8th ed. 2 parts. The Kashi Sanskrit Series 37. Benares: Chowkhamba Sanskrit Sansthan.

Subrahmanyam, P. S.

1999 *Pāṇinian Linguistics.* Tokyo: Institute for the study of Languages and Cultures of Asia and Africa, Tokyo University of Foreign Studies.

Subramania Iyer, K. A.
1994 *Vākyapadīya of Bahrtr̥hari with the Commentary of Helārāja, Kāṇḍa III, Part 1.* Deccan College Monograph Series 21. 1963. Poona: Deccan College.

Vasmer, Max
1996 *Etimologicheskij slovar' russkogo jazyka* (Russian edition of Vasmer's 'Russisches Etymologisches Wörterbuch', Heidelberg, 1950–58), vol. III. St. Petersburgh: Azbuka.

Vasu, Śrīśa Chandra
1975 *The Siddhānta Kaumudī of Bhaṭṭoji Dīkṣita.* 2 vols. 1906. Delhi: Motilal Banarsidass.

Whitney, William Dwight
1969 *Sanskrit Grammar.* 2nd Indian edition. Delhi: Motilal Banarsidass.

Zakharyin, Boris A.
2000 Kategoriya 'samavāya' u paninistov i ejo mesto v obśćem i indijskom jazykoznanii (The Pāṇinīya's category 'samavāya' and its place in general and Indian linguistics). *Istoriya filosofii* 7: 254–264.
2003 "The Semantic Category 'Relationship' (*sambandha*) of Pāṇinīyas and some of the corresponding syntactic phenomena in Old and New Indo-Aryan." *Indologica Taurinensia* 26: 193–206.
2007 *Sanskritskaya grammatika Varadaraji* (The Sanskrit Grammar by Varadarāja). Moscow: Moscow University.